Arab Human Development Report 2009

Challenges to Human Security in the Arab Countries

United Nations
Development
Programme

Regional Bureau
for Arab States

Available through:
United Nations Publications
2 UN Plaza
DC2 - Room 853
New York, NY 10017
USA

Telephone: 212 963 8302 and 800 253 9646 (From the United States)
Email: publications@un.org
Web: https://unp.un.org/
Web: www.undp.org/rbas and www.arab-hdr.org

Cover is printed on 350 GSM coated-one-side paper that is chlorine-
free and meets the Sustainable Forest Initiative guidelines.
Text pages are printed on 100 GSM uncoated white opaque, woodfree
paper. Both cover and text papers are printed with vegetable-
based inks and produced by means of environmentally-compatible
technology.

Cover Design: Rima Rifai
Layout and Production: Alarm SARL, Beirut, Lebanon
Printed at: Karaky Printing Press, Kraitem, Beirut, Lebanon

ISBN: 978-92-1-126211-7

Sales #: E.08.III.B.3

Printed in the Republic of Lebanon

Foreword by the Administrator, UNDP

Since its inaugural edition in 2002, the Arab Human Development Reports have stimulated debate and brought attention to the opportunities and challenges for enhancing human development in the Arab region.

Part of the reason for that impact stems from the fact that the Reports' central thesis—that reform is necessary and that sustainable change can only come from within— has the authority of having been written *about* the region by a team of independent Arab scholars, policy analysts, and practitioners *from* the region.

The path breaking first Arab Human Development Report (AHDR) presented three development "deficits" which stunt human development in the region, related to the acquisition of knowledge, political freedoms, and women's rights. This year's Arab Human Development Report 2009: Challenges to Human Security in the Arab Countries examines human development through a human security lens.

The Report calls on policymakers and other stakeholders to move away from a traditional, state-centric conception of security to one which concentrates also on the security of individuals, their protection and their empowerment. It argues for governments and other partners to prioritize the "liberation of human beings from those intense, extensive, prolonged, and comprehensive threats to which their lives and freedom are vulnerable". In so doing, it draws attention to a multitude of threats which cut across different aspects of human development in the region, highlighting the need for an integrated approach to advancing development, security, good governance and human rights.

In 1994 the United Nations General Assembly affirmed that the Human Development Report is "not an official document of the United Nations". This regional report was prepared in this tradition of independence, which since 1990 has brought critical development issues to the fore at the global, regional, and national levels worldwide.

As has been noted in the forewords to previous AHDRs, they "are, deliberately, not formal UN or UNDP documents and do not reflect the official views of either organization. Rather they have been intended to stimulate and inform a dynamic, new, public discourse across the Arab world and beyond" and "some of the views expressed by the authors are not shared by UNDP or the UN."

By providing a platform for debate which reflects the way in which a number of the most pressing development challenges are seen by some of those who live them day-in and day-out, this Report can play an important role in framing the development agenda in the region for years to come. UNDP hopes that governments, civil society, international and regional bodies, and the global development community, will find this fifth AHDR useful as a tool for motivating an open and serious discussion about human development issues in the Arab world.

Helen Clark
Administrator, UNDP

Foreword by the Regional Director, UNDP Regional Bureau for Arab States

The present *Report* is offered as a contribution to the debate on development underway in the Arab region. Entitled the *Arab Human Development Report 2009: Challenges to Human Security in the Arab Countries*, it is a continuation of the well-known *Arab Human Development Report* (AHDR) series that, since 2002, has brought together eminent scholars and advisers from the Arab region to conduct frank, realistic analyses of development challenges in the region. The first AHDR identified gaps in knowledge, freedom, and women's empowerment as the three critical deficits, and the three follow-up reports analyzed each in depth and in turn. Their research and analysis resonated in Arab countries and around the world, providing a platform for policy dialogue and debate, and re-focusing the development agenda firmly on people's well-being. The present *Report* is intended to sharpen this focus with a new and independent look at the region through the lens of human security.

While the AHDR since 2002 has taken up a variety of development topics, the unifying theme is that of human development. Human development is a way of looking at development that is about much more than the rise and fall of national incomes. It is about creating an environment in which people can develop their full potential and lead productive, creative lives in accord with their needs and interests. It is about understanding that people are the real wealth of nations, and that investing in their human development is the surest way to achieve sustainable, stable economic growth.

The starting point for the present *Report* is that, since the publication of the first volume in the series, the region's human development fault lines have grown more complex, and in some cases deepened. While there has been some improvement in quality of life in some countries, there are still too many people in the Arab region living insecure lives, too many people living under persistent pressures that inhibit them from realizing their potential as human beings, and too many traumatic events cutting lives short. In some Arab countries, more than half of the population lives in hunger and want, with no means to look after their families or safeguard their own quality of life. Recent fluctuations in global food prices as well as the current global economic crisis have sent even more people into poverty and malnutrition. Health systems leave many beyond their reach. Water scarcity looms as an existential threat on the horizon. And armed conflicts take their grim toll in the destruction of human lives.

In analyzing these and other threats to human security in the Arab countries, the scope of the *Report* is broad. But there is a common thread tying the analysis together. The AHDR 2009 argues that the trend in the region has been to focus more on the security of the state than on the security of the people. While this adherence to the traditional conception of security has in many cases ensured the continuity of the state, it has also led to missed opportunities to ensure the security of the human person, and has left the bond between state and citizen less strong than it might otherwise be. And it has hampered the region's embrace of diversity, curtailing opportunities to welcome population groups of differing origins and inclinations into the national project. The result is an all-too-common sense of limited opportunities and personal insecurity, witnessed in the world's highest levels of unemployment, deep and contentious patterns of exclusion, and, ultimately, strong calls from within for reform. Indeed, the pursuit of state security without attention to human security has brought on suboptimal outcomes for the state and citizen alike. And in the long run, the government that pursues state security without investing in human security is the government that achieves neither.

The *Report* argues that the inverse is also true: that indeed human security and state security are two sides of the same coin. Ensuring human security leads not only to more opportunities for human development, but also enables states to benefit sustainably from the environment, to earn legitimacy in the eyes of the governed, to benefit from diversity, to fortify economies against global vicissitudes, to reach a higher level of food security, to imbue societies with health, and, last but not least, to be able to address sources of conflicts, and possibly avert them. Approaching human security in this way, the present report was able to use the concept as a lens through which to view a broad range of dimensions affecting people's lives: environmental security, the state's performance in guaranteeing human security, the human security of vulnerable groups, economic security, nutrition and food security, health and human security, and the human security impact of conflict and occupation.

While the primary responsibility to provide for human security lies with the Arab state, the *Report* also argues that the policies of international powers have not been helpful. Foreign interventions and occupations have had devastating impacts on human security in the region in the immediate sense, while also damaging long-term prospects by making it difficult for the voice of reform to be heard above the din.

Like its predecessors in the AHDR series, the present *Report* is an independent work authored by experts deeply rooted in the Arab region and its development dynamics. Like all UNDP Human Development Reports, it is neither a UN consensus document, nor an articulation of UNDP policy, nor an official publication of any government. In a region full of agendas, this is a document that caters to none. Instead, it is a self-critical look in the

mirror, captured in text and disseminated to a broad audience in order to stimulate informed, constructive debate. Not everyone will agree with all of its messages, but the thorough reader will find the *Report's* analysis quite balanced, with messages offered in a constructive spirit to enrich the thinking of all actors interested in promoting the human security of the people of the Arab region.

The AHDR 2009 is the fruit of a two-year research process drawing on the efforts of many dedicated people. I congratulate and thank all who took part in its preparation. A core team of researchers and authors contributed the bulk of the analysis. I am very grateful to them for their tireless commitment and inquisitive spirit. A distinguished Advisory Board made up of Arab scholars and former senior-level policy makers provided strategic and thematic advice. I am thankful for their wise counsel and their devotion to fair analysis. The *Report* also benefitted from the views of over 100 young people from all over the region, who taught us about human security from their own perspective. I appreciate their engagement, and I am hopeful for their future. I am also indebted to Kemal Derviş, former Administrator of UNDP, for his encouragement of this exercise and the guidance he provided. I take this opportunity to welcome the new Administrator of UNDP, Helen Clark, and to thank her for supporting the publication of this report. And I owe a particular note of appreciation to my colleagues in the Regional Programme Division of the UNDP Regional Bureau for Arab States, for their wholehearted support and substantial undertaking. May these tremendous efforts be rewarded with a stimulating debate in the interest of human security and human development for all the people of the Arab countries.

Amat Al Alim Alsoswa
Assistant Secretary-General and Assistant Administrator, Regional Director, Regional Bureau for Arab States, United Nations Development Programme

Report Team

* Salim Nasr: Distinguished sociologist, policy analyst and author, whose intellectual influence on the reform of Arab governance extended well beyond his native Lebanon, and whose prized collaboration with the Report Team was sustained through a long and courageous fight against illness.

Acronyms
and abbreviations

AFED	Arab Forum for Environment and Development
AFESD	Arab Fund for Economic and Social Development
AHDR	Arab Human Development Report
AI	Amnesty International
ALO	Arab Labour Organization
AMF	Arab Monetary Fund
AOAD	Arab Organization for Agricultural Development
AOHR	Arab Organization for Human Rights
BWC	Biological and Toxin Weapons Convention
CEDAW	Convention on the Elimination of All Forms of Discrimination against Women
CHS	Commission on Human Security of the United Nations
CIS	Commonwealth of Independent States
DALY	Disability-Adjusted Life Years
DESA	Department of Economic and Social Affairs
DOTS	Directly Observed Treatment Short courses (method of detection and treatment of tuberculosis)
DPA	Darfur Peace Agreement
ESCWA	Economic and Social Commission for Western Asia of the United Nations
FAO	Food and Agriculture Organization of the United Nations
FGM	Female genital mutilation
GCC	Gulf Cooperation Council
GDI	Gender-related development index
GDP	Gross domestic product
GEM	Gender empowerment measure
HCV	Hepatitis C virus
HDI	Human development index
HDR	Human Development Report
HIC	High income countries
HIV/AIDS	Human Immunodeficiency Virus/Acquired Immune Deficiency Syndrome
HPI-1	Human poverty index (for developing countries)
HRW	Human Rights Watch
IBC	Iraq Body Count
ICC	International Chamber of Commerce
ICRC	International Committee of the Red Cross
ICU	Islamic Courts Union
IDP	Internally Displaced Persons
IFHS	Iraq Family Health Survey
IHR	International Health Regulations
ILO	International Labour Organization
IMB	International Maritime Bureau
IMF	International Monetary Fund
IUCN	International Union for Conservation of Nature
IWM	Integrated Water Management
JAER	Joint Arab Economic Report
JEM	Justice and Equality Movement of Sudan
KUNA	Kuwait News Agency
LAS	League of Arab States
LDC	Least developed countries
LIC	Low income countries

MDG	Millennium Development Goals
MENA	Middle East and North Africa
MIC	Middle income countries
MMR	Maternal mortality ratio
MNF	Multinational Forces of Iraq
NGO	Non-governmental organization
NISS	National Intelligence and Security Services of Sudan
OAPEC	Organization of Arab Petroleum Exporting Countries
OCHA	Office for the Coordination of Humanitarian Affairs of the United Nations
ODA	Official Development Assistance
OECD	Organization for Economic Co-operation and Development
OPEC	Organization of the Petroleum Exporting Countries
OPT	Occupied Palestinian Territory
PA	Palestinian Authority
PCBS	Palestinian Central Bureau of Statistics
PLO	Palestinian Liberation Organization
PPP	Purchasing power parity
R&D	Research and development
SAF	Sudan Armed Forces
SARS	Severe Acute Respiratory Syndrome
SEDAC	Socioeconomic Data and Applications Centre
SIPRI	Stockholm International Peace Research Institute
SPLA	Sudan's People's Liberation Army
TDS	Total dissolved solids
TFG	Transitional Federal Government of Somalia
TFR	Total fertility rate
TPES	Total primary energy supply
UAE	United Arab Emirates
UN	United Nations
UNAIDS	Joint United Nations Programme on HIV/AIDS
UNAMI	United Nations Assistance Mission for Iraq
UNCCD	United Nations Convention to Combat Desertification
UNDP	United Nations Development Programme
UNDP-POGAR	Programme on Governance in the Arab Region
UNEP	United Nations Environment Programme
UNESCO	United Nations Educational, Scientific and Cultural Organization
UNFPA	United Nations Population Fund
UNHCR	Office of the United Nations High Commissioner for Refugees
UNICEF	United Nations Children's Fund
UNIFEM	United Nations Development Fund for Women
UNODC	United Nations Office on Drugs and Crime
UNRWA	United Nations Relief and Works Agency
UNSC	United Nations Security Council
WFP	World Food Programme
WHO	World Health Organization
WMO	World Meteorological Organization

Contents

Chapter 3   The Arab State and human security – performance and prospects   53

Chapter 4   The personal insecurity of vulnerable groups   79

Chapter 8 Occupation, military intervention and human insecurity 165

Chapter 9 Concluding reflections 189

Boxes

Figures

Tables

The report in brief

This is the fifth volume in the series of Arab Human Development Reports sponsored by the United Nations Development Programme (UNDP) and independently authored by intellectuals and scholars from Arab countries.

Like its predecessors, this Report provides eminent Arab thinkers a platform from which to articulate a comprehensive analysis of their own contemporary milieu. It is not a conventional report produced by the United Nations. Rather, it is an independent publication that gives a voice to a representative group of Arab intellectuals whose sober and self-critical appraisals might not otherwise be heard in the particular circumstances of the region. The views of the authors are supplemented by an opinion poll conducted in four Arab countries—Kuwait, Lebanon, Morocco and the Occupied Palestinian Territory—that represent a range of political and cultural contexts for the Report's analyses. A special Youth Forum convened for the Report also provides insights from young Arabs.

This Report is an independent publication

Inspired by UNDP's 1994 global Human Development Report on human security, the present study takes up that subject as it concerns the Arab countries.[1] Its starting point is that, seven years after the publication of the first Arab Human Development Report, the region's fault lines as traced in that analysis may have deepened.[2] The question thus arises: why have obstacles to human development in the region proved so stubborn?

This new Report proposes that the answers lie in the fragility of the region's political, social, economic and environmental structures, in its lack of people-centred development policies and in its vulnerability to outside intervention. Together, these characteristics undermine human security—the kind of material and moral foundation that secures lives, livelihoods and an acceptable quality of life for the majority. Human security is a prerequisite for human development, and its widespread absence in Arab countries has held back their progress.

Human insecurity at the global and regional levels

Widespread absence of human security in Arab countries has held back their progress

The world order that followed the end of the Cold War has proved to be tumultuous. External and internal challenges to the integrity of states have multiplied. From without, environmental pollution, international terrorism, large population movements, a melting global financial system and the rise of other cross-border threats such as pandemics, the drug trade and human trafficking have all laid siege to traditional notions of security. Within countries, spreading poverty, unemployment, civil wars, sectarian and ethnic conflicts and authoritarian repression have exposed the limits of many states in guaranteeing their citizens' rights and freedoms. While preserving the integrity of states remains the highest consideration of national security, a newer concern with protecting the lives of the people who reside in them has overtaken that preoccupation. The concept of human security, which complements that of national security, brings this change in perspective into focus.

In the Arab region, human insecurity—pervasive, often intense and with consequences affecting large numbers of people—inhibits human development. It is revealed in the impacts of military occupation and armed conflict in Iraq, Sudan, Somalia and Occupied Palestinian Territory. It is found in countries that enjoy relative stability where the authoritarian state, buttressed by flawed constitutions and unjust laws, often denies citizens their rights. Human insecurity is heightened by swift climatic changes, which threaten the livelihoods, income and access to food and water of millions of Arabs in future. It is reflected in the economic vulnerability of one-fifth of the people in some Arab states, and more than half in others, whose lives are impoverished and cut short by hunger and want. Human insecurity is palpable and present in the alienation of the region's rising cohort of unemployed youth and in the predicaments of its subordinated women, and dispossessed refugees.

The concept

Human security is the "rearguard of human development". Whereas human development is concerned with expanding the individual's capabilities and opportunities, human security focuses on enabling peoples to contain or avert threats to their lives, livelihoods and human dignity. The two concepts look at the human condition from different ends of a continuum, summarized by Amartya Sen as "expansion with equity" (human development) and "downturn with security" (human security). The intellectual frameworks they provide are co-extensive and mutually reinforcing. Moreover, human security is related to human rights inasmuch as respect for people's basic rights creates conditions favourable to human security.

Beginning with these insights, the Report adopts the comprehensive categorization of threats to human security originally posited by UNDP and defines human security as *"the liberation of human beings from those intense, extensive, prolonged, and comprehensive threats to which their lives and freedom are vulnerable"*. Its chapters focus on:

- Pressures on environmental resources
- The performance of the state in guaranteeing or undermining human security
- The personal insecurity of vulnerable groups
- Economic vulnerability, poverty and unemployment
- Food security and nutrition
- Health and human security
- The systemic insecurity of occupation and foreign military intervention

Human security can be measured on both an objective and subjective level, and in quantitative and qualitative terms. The Report takes the view that no single composite index of human security would be valid, reliable or sufficiently sensitive to varying levels of human security and to different circumstances in the region. Rather, it affirms the relevance of discrete quantitative indicators and opinion surveys at the level of the region, its sub-regions and country groups.

Seven dimensions of threat

1. People and their insecure environment

The Arab region faces growing challenges to the security of its population from environmental stresses. Potential conflicts originating in competition for dwindling natural resources may heavily strain relations among communities, populations and states, Arab or non-Arab. These challenges will result from population and demographic pressures, the overexploitation of land, water shortages, desertification, pollution, and climate change.

Population pressures: according to UN estimates, the Arab countries will be home to some 395 million people by 2015 (compared to about 317 million in 2007, and 150 million in 1980). In a region where water and arable land are shrinking, population growth at these rates while

Human security focuses on enabling peoples to contain or avert threats to their lives, livelihoods and human dignity

The region faces growing challenges to the security of its population from environmental stresses

falling, will still put intense pressures on the carrying capacity of Arab countries' lands and further threaten environmental sustainability.

Urban growth poses particular challenges. An accelerating drift to cities and towns is straining already-overstretched infrastructure and creating overcrowded, unhealthy and insecure living conditions in many Arab centres. In 1970, 38 per cent of the Arab population was urban. By 2005 this had grown to 55 per cent, and it is likely to surpass 60 per cent by 2020.

Demographic pressures: the most evident and challenging aspect of the region's demographic profile is its 'youth bulge'. Young people are the fastest growing segment of Arab countries' populations. Some 60 per cent of the population is under 25 years old, making this one of the most youthful regions in the world, with a median age of 22 years compared to a global average of 28.

Water scarcity: Total available surface water resources in the Arab countries are estimated at 277 billion cubic meters per year[3], only 43 per cent of which originates within the Arab countries. Surface water resources shared with neighbouring countries outside the region account for approximately 57 per cent of its total water requirements. Years of effort have yielded the establishment of formal agreements (such as the Nile Basin Initiative) on the management of shared water resources. However, most are partial, ineffective and inequitable in terms of the full spectrum of riparian rights. At the regional and interregional levels, cooperation on water usage and management is heavily affected by prevailing political tensions and ongoing conflicts.

Stressed groundwater systems are often the only source of fresh water in the region, yet reserves in renewable aquifers are being withdrawn faster than they can be replenished. Transboundary conflicts, poor distribution and heavy use, especially of ground resources, characterize water use in much of the Arab countries. This leads to a lack of clean water for much of the population and the waste of significant amounts in the agriculture, industry and tourism sectors.

Desertification is a peril in the region. It is formally defined under the United Nations Convention to Combat Desertification (UNCCD) as "land degradation in arid, semi-arid, and dry sub-humid areas resulting from various factors, including climatic variations and human activities." A UN Environment Programme study estimates that desert has swallowed up more than two-thirds of total land area of the region (9.76 million square kilometres of desert, or 68.4 per cent of the total land area). The highest ratio of desert to total land area is in the Arabian Peninsula (nine-tenths or 89.6 per cent). This is followed by North Africa (over three-fourths of the land or 77.7 per cent), the Nile Valley and the Horn of Africa (less than a half or 44.5 per cent) and the Mashreq (35.6 per cent). Ongoing desertification threatens about 2.87 million square kilometres or a fifth of the total area of the Arab countries.

Water pollution in Arab countries has grown into a serious challenge. It is mainly attributed to the increasing use of chemical fertilizers, pesticides, and horticultural and veterinary medical treatments whose long-lasting traces find their way into the water. The lack of access to sufficient clean water threatens human security in many ways. It can lead to the spread of disease among children, such as dysentery, and affect school attendance and academic achievement. It deprives women of long hours of the day which they could devote to personal and income-generating activities rather than fetching water for their families. In addition, water scarcity and pollution threaten agricultural and food production and precipitate domestic rivalries over scarce water resources.

On the other hand, levels of ***air pollution*** in Arab countries, in general, are among the lowest in the world. In 2004, carbon dioxide emissions did not exceed 1,348.4 metric tons, compared to 12,162.9 metric tons in middle-income countries and 13,318.6 metric tons in the OECD countries. However, Arab countries have relatively low carbon dioxide emission rates mainly because most have not progressed very far with industrialisation.

Stressed groundwater systems are often the only source of fresh water in the region

Desert has swallowed up more than two-thirds of total land area of the region

Even so, carbon dioxide emissions in North Africa and the Middle East are increasing at a faster rate than any other region in the world, except for South Asia (driven by India) and East Asia (driven by China). From 1990 to 2004 the average annual rate of growth was 4.5 per cent, which means that carbon dioxide emissions had nearly doubled over that period.

Climate change: the Arab region is one of those least responsible for the direct creation of the greenhouse effect. According to the global Human Development Report (HDR) 2008 and world development indices for 2007, the region's share of carbon dioxide emissions, which contribute to this phenomenon, was no more than 4.7 per cent—lower than any other region except Sub-Saharan Africa. However, the region is also the nearest to becoming a direct victim of climate change, which will affect it in the following ways: a) water shortages; b) reduced agricultural production; c) large population transfers to foreign countries (environmental refugees); d) lower levels of economic activity; e) threats to national security.

Global warming: according to the UNDP Global Human Development Report 2007/2008, Egypt, Lebanon, Sudan, and the countries of North Africa could be those in the region most affected by climate change.[4] An increase in the Earth's temperature by three or four degrees would raise the sea level by approximately one metre, creating 6 million refugees in Egypt, with 4,500 square kilometres of agricultural land in the Delta flooded. Even if the sea level rises by only one-half metre, it could create two million refugees and cause more than $35 billion in economic losses. In the Kordofan region of Sudan, an increase in temperature of 1,5 degrees centigrade between 2030 and 2060 would reduce average rainfall by 5 per cent, leading to a general drop in agricultural production and a decrease in the production of maize by 70 per cent of current levels. An increase of 1.2 degrees centigrade by 2020 would reduce available water in Lebanon by 15 per cent and in some areas of Morocco by over 10 per cent.

2. The State and its insecure people

In terms of levels of human security among citizens, is the Arab State part of the solution or problem? To answer that question, the Report compares the performance of the Arab states with the norms associated with good governance. It analyzes whether the former win the acceptance of their citizens, uphold and guarantee their rights to life and freedom and protect them from aggression. Its analysis is based on four criteria: 1) the acceptability of the state to its own citizens; 2) state compliance with international charters pertaining to human rights; 3) how the state utilizes its monopoly of the means of force and coercion; 4) how far institutional checks and balances prevent abuses of power. The Report concludes that large and frequent shortfalls in these areas often combine to turn the state into a threat to human security, instead of its chief support.

Identity, diversity and citizenship
States are artificial creations. The borders of many Arab states reflect this fact, often enclosing diverse ethnic, religious and linguistic groups that were incorporated as minorities in the post-colonial era. Few Arab states saw a smooth transition towards inclusion in their post-independence phases. Rather, a strong nationalistic trend developed with the objective of masking the diversity of the population and subduing its cultural, linguistic and religious heterogeneity under command structures. The majority of states failed to introduce democratic governance and institutions of representation that ensure inclusion, the equal distribution of wealth among various groups, and respect for cultural diversity.

One result of this is that identity-based groups in some Arab countries have sought to free themselves from the captivity of the nation-state in whose shadow they live. This rejection of the legitimacy of the kind of state which the modern Arab countries inherited and perpetuated has been accompanied by conflicts that threaten human security and to which some states have responded by imposing authoritarian controls.

Large and frequent shortfalls can turn the state into a threat to human security

Most states failed to introduce institutions of representation

In western political history, the normative concept that has contributed most to the management of ethnic, cultural and linguistic diversity is that of citizenship. Arab states are undergoing a similar political evolution rather slowly and, consequently, few sustain a level of civic consciousness that makes it possible for citizens themselves to resolve their differences peacefully without state action.

Observation confirms that, in the Arab countries, ethnic, religious, sectarian, and linguistic differences can be associated with persistent group struggles, especially in countries where the population is not homogenous. In countries such as Somalia, Sudan, Lebanon, and Iraq, ethnic, religious and tribal loyalties have become the axis along which communities have been mobilized to press for inclusion or separation. This mobilization has been destructive and destabilizing, undercutting both human security and the integrity of states. Tragically, these conflicts have engendered the largest volume of human casualties in the Arab countries.

The Report argues that identity, *per se*, is not necessarily the cause of a conflict or even the main source of tension between different groups in the region. Clashes that appear on the surface to stem from identity in fact often originate in skewed access to political power or wealth, in a lack of channels for representative political participation, and in the suppression of cultural and linguistic diversity. Most commonly, such conflicts start with the exploitation by political leaders, for their own ideological ends, of loyalty ties among groups who share feelings of exclusion, deprivation and discrimination.

Adherence to international charters
Most Arab states have acceded to the major international charters pertaining to human rights which stipulate both the right to life and the right to freedom. Accession and ratification entail an obligation on the concerned Arab states to bring national legislation and practices in line with these conventions, an obligation that is however more honoured in the breach than the observance. At the regional level, the norms on human rights adopted by states and reflected in the *Arab Charter on Human Rights* (2004) are inconsistent with international standards. Indeed, the death penalty, which more than half the countries of the world have abolished and which the United Nations condemns, is applied liberally in several Arab countries, which do not limit it to the most serious crimes or exclude its imposition in cases of political crime.

Constitutional failings
State constitutions do not adhere in several key respects to the international norms implicit in the charters to which Arab countries have acceded. This gravely compromises levels of human security in the countries concerned. Many Arab countries' constitutions adopt ideological or doctrinal formulas that empty stipulations of general rights and freedoms of any content and which allow individual rights to be violated in the name of the official ideology or faith. Others deal ambiguously with freedom of opinion and of expression, tending to restrict rather than to permit. Arab countries' constitutions also routinely delegate the definition of rights to state regulation. In doing so, they allow freedoms and individual rights to be violated at the point when the latter are translated into ordinary law. While Arab laws and constitutions generally do not mandate discrimination between citizens on the basis of language, religion, doctrine, or confession, discrimination against women is quite evident on the law books of several states.

Legal restrictions
Across the Arab region, six countries continue to prohibit the formation of political parties. In many other cases, varying degrees of repression and restrictions on the establishment and functioning of political parties, particularly opposition parties, effectively amount to their prohibition. With one exception, all Arab countries support the right to form civil associations. However, most legal systems and regulations governing and regulating the civil society sector involve a wide and escalating array of restrictive measures that hinder the exercise of that right. Civil society groups face restrictions on their formation and ability to operate. The groups themselves, or their boards, can be summarily dissolved by the state. And their affiliations and sources of funding are subject to tight controls.

Ethnic, religious, sectarian, and linguistic differences can be associated with persistent group struggles

Many Arab countries allow freedoms and individual rights to be violated

National security measures

Many Arab states have undergone extraordinarily long periods of martial law or emergency rule, transforming interim measures into a permanent way of conducting political life. Declarations of emergency are often simply a pretext to suspend basic rights and exempt rulers from any constitutional limitations, however weak. Post-9-11, most Arab countries passed anti-terror laws based on a wide and unspecific definition of "terrorism". These moves have given government security agencies sweeping powers which, although effective in some contexts, can form a threat to basic freedoms in others. Such laws allow undefined periods of pre-trial detention and multiply instances where the death penalty may be applied. They also curb freedom of expression and increase police powers of search, eavesdropping and arrest. In some cases, these laws increase the use of military courts. In general, these laws have failed to find the required balance between the security of society and that of the individual.

State-sponsored violations of citizens' rights to life and freedom are committed through the practices of torture and illegal detention. Between 2006 and 2008, the Arab Organization for Human Rights (AOHR) found examples of the official practice of torture in eight Arab states. In the same period, the AOHR reported on the more widespread practice of illegal detention in eleven countries of the region.

Obstructions of justice

Independent judiciaries form a major part of any state system of checks and balances. Threats to judicial independence in the Arab states come not from constitutions, which generally uphold the principle, but from the executive branch. All Arab justice systems suffer in one form or another from blows to their independence that stem from executive domination of both the legislative and judicial branches. In addition, judicial independence is being undermined by the spread of state security courts and military courts, which represent a negation of the principles of natural justice and detract from guarantees of a fair trial. The result is a considerable gap between constitutional texts and actual legal practice in protecting the personal security of the Arab citizen. Judges in some Arab countries have struggled in order to give some substance to judicial independence, but their efforts are undertaken in a very challenging environment.

State-enforced security

Human security is reinforced when the state is the sole wielder of the instruments of coercion and uses them to carry out its commitment to respect people's rights, those of citizens and non-citizens alike. When other groups gain control of instruments of force, the outcomes seldom favour security for citizens. The state authorities in some Arab countries have proved unable to impose security while confronting armed groups and others have suffered from the armed violence in which some of their citizens, or those of other Arab states, have been caught.

On the other hand, while many Arabs live under various 'un-freedoms' which effectively deny them voice and representation, and while the threat of state-initiated violence against them is ever-present, the region offers a degree of protection from crime not found in other developing regions. Barring the cases of foreign occupation and civil war, a relatively low incidence of conventional violent crime remains the norm for the Arab countries. Statistics from 2002 indicate that, at that time, the region had the lowest police-recorded homicide and assault rate, not only among all regions of the South, but also in both the developing and developed worlds.

Executive branches and security and armed forces that are not subject to public oversight present grave potential threats to human security. All Arab heads of state wield absolute authority, answering to none. They maintain their hold on power by leaving the state's security apparatus an extremely wide margin for manoeuvre, at the expense of citizens' freedoms and fundamental rights. Arab security agencies operate with impunity because they are instrumental to the head of state and account to him alone. Their powers are buttressed by executive interference with the independence of the judiciary, by the dominance (in most states) of an unchanging ruling party over the legislature, and by the muzzling of the media.

Going by the preceding criteria, the relationship between the state and human

Anti-terror laws have given government security agencies sweeping powers

Many Arabs live under various 'un-freedoms'

security in the region is not straight-forward. While the state is expected to guarantee human security, it has been, in several Arab countries, a source of threat undermining both international charters and national constitutional provisions. The Report holds up the nature and extent of state failures behind the crisis in Darfur, which provide an archetypal illustration of how state performance impacts human security. Establishing the rule of law and good governance in the Arab countries remains a precondition for the foundation of the legitimate state and the protection of human security.

Calls for state reform

Recent state-sponsored reform initiatives aimed at enhancing citizens' rights have been welcomed yet found to be ineffec-tual in changing the dictated nature of the Arab social contract or the structural basis of power in the region. The path to reform in the region has been laid out most clearly by its increasingly active and vocal civil society. The latter's demands focus on:

- Respect for the right to self-determina-tion of all people.
- Adherence to the principles of human rights, and rejection of all prevarication based on cultural particularism and the manipulation of national sentiment.
- Public tolerance of different religions and schools of thought.
- Sound parliamentary systems.
- The incorporation in Arab constitu-tions of guarantees of political, intel-lectual, and party political pluralism, with political parties based on the principle of citizenship

Specific calls by citizens for change include: an end to martial law; the aboli-tion of emergency laws and courts; a halt to the practice of torture; the reform of Arab countries' legislations that is incompatible with freedom of thought and expression; and the full establishment and practice of the rule of law.

3. The vulnerability of those lost from sight

The personal security of citizens in Arab countries is compromised by legal loop-holes, overseen and regulated by coercive institutions and based on the forfeiture of freedoms. But for some groups of people beyond mainstream society—abused and subordinated women, the victims of human trafficking, child soldiers, refugees and internally displaced persons—no per-sonal security exists at all.

Violence against women

Many Arab women are still bound by patriarchal patterns of kinship, legalised discrimination, social subordination and ingrained male dominance. Because women find themselves in a lowly posi-tion in relation to decision-making within the family, their situation continuously exposes them to forms of family and institutionalised violence. Arab women, like many of their peers in other regions, sustain both direct and indirect violence. In the first category, they suffer forms of physical assault, from beating to rape and murder. In the second, they are victims of cultural and social practices that cause material harm to women, such as female genital mutilation (FGM) and child mar-riage. Although some states have banned the practice of FGM, it continues to be widespread in many countries because traditional beliefs favour it. Influential fig-ures aligned with conservative political or social forces also speak out in its defence.

Arab countries have yet to adopt laws prohibiting child marriage before the age of majority, namely, eighteen years of age. Yet studies indicate that early marriage and teenage pregnancies threaten the health of mothers and children, and increase female vulnerability to violence. Early marriages often lead to divorce, family breakdown and poor child-rearing. They commonly encourage early childbearing and high fertility, which carry marked health risks for very young mothers and their infants. Although early marriage is on the decline in the Arab countries, the numbers of teenage girls who are married remains significant in some countries. Based on the most recent available data in the period 1987-2006, UNICEF estimates that the proportions of women aged 20-24 that were married by the age of 18 were 45 per cent in Somalia, 37 per cent in Yemen and Mauritania, 30 per cent in Comoros, and 27 per cent in Sudan. These proportions were 10 per cent in Tunisia, 5 per cent in Djibouti, and 2 per cent in Algeria.

The relationship between the state and human security in the region is not straightforward

No personal security exists for some groups of people beyond mainstream society

It is difficult to gauge the prevalence of violence against women in Arab societies. The subject is taboo in a male-oriented culture of denial. Much of this violence is inflicted unseen in the home, on wives, sisters and mothers. The under-reporting of offences is widespread. Marriage laws contribute to the problem since most of them confirm a husband's custodial rights over a wife. The consecration of male supremacy within the family culminates in Personal Status laws since, under these laws, most women in Arab countries do not have the right to ask for divorce or to oppose polygamy. Steps to reform personal status laws have been taken, especially in the Maghreb countries, and more are required.

So-called 'honour crimes' are the most notorious form of violence against women in several Arab societies. Here too, under-reporting makes the prevalence of such crimes difficult to establish, but the practice is known to continue. The punishment for women can be as severe as death, especially if the prohibited act results in pregnancy. In some Arab countries the law stands on the side of those who perpetrate such crimes by reducing penalties.

Rape is considered to be a more common form of violence against women than incidents reported to the police, or covered by the press, may suggest. In Arab countries, where laws on rape are either equivocal or actively biased against women, and where family and society join to deny occurrences, preserve the image of virginity and downplay the crime, few cases come before the courts. Thus, one of the most violent, intrusive and traumatic threats to women's personal safety continues while society averts its eyes.

War-time assaults on women take place in a context of lawlessness, displacement and armed clashes such as those in Iraq, Sudan (Darfur) and Somalia where gender roles are polarized. In these theatres of conflict, men often compensate for their own insecurities and loss of dominance through intensified aggression against women. In June 2008, the UN Security Council unanimously adopted Resolution 1820 demanding the "immediate and complete cessation by all parties to armed conflict of all acts of sexual violence against civilians". The resolution noted that women and girls are particularly targeted by the use of sexual violence as "a tactic of war".

Human trafficking

Human trafficking is a multi-billion dollar transnational industry that is spreading across the Arab countries. In the region, this underground business has certain clear traits. One is that the Arab states play various roles and sometimes multiple roles. They can be destinations for the trade, they may act as a transit point for such commerce, or they may be a source of persons being trafficked. As destinations, they receive trafficked persons from various regions of the world: Southeast Asia, South Asia, Eastern Europe, Asia Minor, Central Asia and Sub-Saharan Africa.

For men, the trade entails forced labour under dehumanizing conditions and without respect for labour rights. For women, it usually means domestic service often indistinguishable from slavery, or sexual exploitation; and, for children, it leads to employment as beggars, itinerant vendors or camel jockeys, or to sexual abuse. For all victims, bondage through trafficking spells a life of permanent abject insecurity.

Children are easy prey to practices ruinous to their security. Not only do such practices impair their liberty, they expose them to extreme harm, ranging from psychological stunting and physical injury, to death. The cruellest of such practices is the recruitment of children for war. Two different forms of children's involvement in military activities are found in the Arab countries. The first is that in Sudan and Somalia, where the recruitment of child soldiers is widely reported. The second is that in the region's other conflict zones— the Occupied Palestinian Territory and Iraq—where children, voluntarily or under coercion, play support roles, while suffering disproportionately under the armed conflicts in these areas.

The plight of refugees and internally displaced persons

The Arab countries are the site of both the world's longest-standing refugee question, that of the Palestinians, and its latest such problem, in Darfur. Propelled to flee by conditions of grave insecurity—at a minimum, loss of work and income, and at worst loss of life at the hands of occupying armies or rival militias—refugees continue to live with the insecurities associated with their status. They are at the mercy of conditions in camps or political and economic events in their host countries, which could suddenly turn against them. The refugee experience may never end, for a person may die a refugee and pass this status on to a second generation.

While statistics on refugees are often difficult to verify, it is estimated that the Arab countries contain approximately 7.5 million refugees, in the form of those registered by the UN High Commission for Refugees (UNHCR) and the UN Relief and Works Agency (UNRWA), for the year 2008. This share represents 46.8 per cent of the 16 million global refugees registered under UNHCR and UNRWA for 2008. The largest number of these refugees, mostly Palestinians and Iraqis, is found in Jordan, Syria, and the Occupied Palestinian Territory.

Internally displaced persons (IDPs) in the region are more widespread geographically than refugees, whom they outnumber at an estimated total of about 9.8 million. Most are to be found in six Arab states—Sudan, Iraq, Somalia, Lebanon, Syria and Yemen—with Sudan alone accounting for up to 5.8 million. IDPs share many of the insecurities of refugees: loss of livelihoods, status, families, roots and, sometimes, life itself.

The Report concludes that what the state and society do not see, they cannot protect. Alleviating the insecurity of the region's most vulnerable groups starts with recognition of the fact and extent of the injustices they suffer, and of the political, social and developmental roots of their exclusion.

4. Volatile growth, high unemployment and persisting poverty

The fabled oil wealth of the Arab countries presents a misleading picture of their economic situation, one that masks the structural weaknesses of many Arab economies and the resulting insecurity of countries and citizens alike. The Report discusses economic security in terms of the dimensions originally identified by UNDP's 1994 Human Development Report on human security: real per capita

income levels and their growth patterns; employment options; poverty; and social protection. It underlines the erratic course of oil-led growth in the Arab countries, the fragility of the economic model associated with it, and changing trends in intraregional spillovers from oil producing countries. It also identifies policy gaps that have consequences for the economic security of millions of people: acute unemployment and persisting income poverty.

Economic vulnerability

One clear sign of the vulnerability of Arab economic growth is its high volatility. Tied to capricious oil markets, the region's economic security has been—and remains—hostage to exogenous trends. Rocky ups-and-downs in the Arab countries, from high growth in the 1970s to economic stagnation through the 1980s and back to extraordinary growth in the early 2000s, directly reflect the turbulent cycles of the oil market. Steep drops in oil income during the 1980s had major impacts on oil producing countries (Saudi Arabia, for example, saw its GDP halved between 1981 and 1987 in current prices). A number of other countries experienced negative economic growth, of which the hardest hit was Kuwait, where GDP declined by around 18 per cent in 1981 and 1982. The shocks were transmitted to non-oil Arab economies whose receipts from remittances fell away. Jordan and Yemen both had negative growth in some years.

For nearly two and half decades after 1980, the region witnessed hardly any economic growth. World Bank data show that real GDP per capita in the Arab countries grew by a mere 6.4 per cent over the entire 24 year period from 1980 to 2004 (i.e. by less than 0.5 per cent annually).

Oil-led growth has created weak structural foundations in Arab economies. Many Arab countries are turning into increasingly import oriented and service-based economies. The types of services found in most Arab countries fall at the low end of the value adding chain, contribute little to local knowledge development and lock countries into inferior positions in global markets. This trend has grown at the expense of Arab agriculture, manufacturing and industrial production. The structural fragility of Arab economies as

Alleviating the insecurity of vulnerable groups starts with recognizing the injustices they suffer

The fabled oil wealth of the Arab countries presents a misleading picture of their economic situation

a result of oil-led growth is reflected in a conspicuous decline in the share of non-oil productive sectors (agriculture and manufacturing) to GDP in all Arab countries except the high-income countries. Overall, the Arab countries were less industrialized in 2007 than in 1970, almost four decades previously.

In the region's most recent episode of prosperity, fluctuation in growth rates has abated somewhat across all country groups. While this development is comforting, it offers no grounds for complacency, since the current plunge in oil prices is bound to undo growth prospects and once again cause volatility.

Arab oil producing countries have opted to put much of their latest windfall into foreign investments, external reserves and oil stabilization funds, and to pay down debts. They have also embarked on major domestic investments in real estate, construction, oil refining, transport and communication and social services. This approach clearly differs from patterns of the past, which emphasized imports and consumption. Some Arab oil exporting countries have also been in a position to direct large streams of revenue towards their military and security forces.

However, their new patterns of investment also expose Gulf Cooperation Council (GCC) countries more widely than in the past to global economic downturns, the latest of which poses severe challenges to their capital-intensive growth model. New external shocks for the Arab countries are associated with the current global recession. All of the major oil producers have substantial holdings in the US and elsewhere abroad, and are not able to decouple their economies from the spreading international crisis. The knock-on effects on the rest of the Arab countries of a protracted slow-down in investment financing and remittances from GCC countries would be considerable.

In fact, other Arab countries may have gained less from the short-lived third boom than they did from the first two. Although oil wealth still crosses borders, and while several rich countries switched a number of foreign investments to regional markets in the aftermath of 9-11, intraregional flows are becoming less copious and are having less impact than in the past. First, population increases in non-oil countries

offset much of these flows. Second, worker remittances from the oil states have been hit by the practice of 'job nationalization'; and third, non-oil countries are incurring higher energy costs through rising oil import bills and expensive fuel subsidies.

The spectre of unemployment

Unemployment is a major source of economic insecurity in most Arab countries. Data from the Arab Labour Organization (ALO) show that in 2005 the overall average unemployment rate for the Arab countries was about 14.4 per cent of the labour force compared to 6.3 per cent for the world at large. The weighted average growth rate in unemployment in the Arab countries (using the number of unemployed in 2005) was about 1.8 per cent annually. While national unemployment rates vary considerably, ranging from about 2 per cent in Qatar and Kuwait to about 22 per cent in Mauritania, youth unemployment is a serious challenge common to many Arab countries.

These trends in unemployment, coupled with population growth rates, indicate that Arab countries will need about 51 million new jobs by 2020. Most of those jobs will be essential to absorb young entrants to the labour force who will otherwise face an empty future. ALO estimates for the year 2005/6 show that youth unemployment rates in the region vary from a high of about 46 per cent in Algeria to a low of 6.3 per cent in the United Arab Emirates. With the exception of the latter, high income Arab countries suffer from double digit youth unemployment rates. Relatively high youth unemployment rates are also recorded for the middle and low income Arab countries. Overall, the unemployment rate among the young in the Arab countries is nearly double that in the world at large.

Unemployment also often wears a female face. Unemployment rates for Arab women are higher than those for Arab men, and among the highest in the world. This reflects more than the failure of Arab economies to generate sufficient jobs; it points as well to entrenched social biases against women.

Three primary factors account for the region's slumping employment trends: first, the contraction under structural reforms of the large public sector, which employs more than a third of the workforce; second,

Overall, the Arab countries were less industrialized in 2007 than in 1970

Arab countries will need about 51 million new jobs by 2020

the limited size, hobbled performance and weak job-generating capacity of the private sector, which has not taken up the slack; and third, the quality and type of education generally provided, which does not stress technical or vocational skills in demand.

Arab policies will have to focus on revamping education to close skills gaps, respond to labour market signals and stimulate knowledge-based capabilities matching opportunities in the global, as well as regional economy. National savings will need to be converted efficiently into sizeable investments for expanding health, housing and labour markets in order to cater for the needs of this young workforce and provide it with the facilities to increase productivity. A special effort is required to remove entrenched social barriers to women's entrance to high-productivity jobs. In many of these policy shifts, private-public partnerships offer the best option for mobilizing resources, transferring skills and creating new jobs.

The backlog of poverty

The Report considers economic insecurity associated with poverty from two perspectives: income poverty (defined in terms of people's enjoyment of goods and services, represented in real per capita consumption expenditure); and human poverty (defined by income as well as by other valued dimensions of life, such as education, health, and political freedom). Its analysis of income poverty, in turn, takes into account both the international poverty line at two-dollars-a-day and national poverty lines.

Arab countries are generally regarded as having a relatively low incidence of income poverty. In 2005, about 20.3 per cent of the Arab population was living below the two-dollars-a-day international poverty line. This estimate is based on seven Arab middle and low income groups, whose population represents about 63 per cent of the total population of the Arab countries not in conflict. Using the international line indicates that, in 2005, about 34.6 million Arabs were living in extreme poverty.

However, the two-dollars-a-day threshold may not be the most illuminating metric for looking at poverty in the Arab countries. Applying the upper national poverty line shows that the overall poverty rate ranges from a low of 28.6 – 30 per cent in Lebanon and Syria to a high of 59.5 per cent in Yemen, with that for Egypt being about 41 per cent. Extrapolating from a sample of countries representing 65 per cent of the region's population, the Report projects that the overall headcount poverty ratio at the upper poverty line is 39.9% and that the estimated number of Arabs living in poverty could be as high as 65 million.

Extreme poverty is especially acute in the low-income Arab countries, where some 36.2 per cent of the population are living in extreme poverty. Expectably, income poverty, and the insecurity associated with it, is more widespread among rural populations.

Another lens for the analysis of impoverishment is human poverty, which refers to the deprivation of capabilities and opportunities, and can be measured through the Human Poverty Index (HPI), a composite index built on three components: a) longevity, b) knowledge and c) standard of living. Applying that index, low income Arab countries exhibit the highest incidence of human poverty in the region, with an average HPI of 35 per cent compared to a 12 per cent average in high income countries. This metric shows that insecurity undercuts health, education and standards of living, all of which puts in question the effectiveness of the state in providing, and ensuring access to the basic necessities of life. In particular, human poverty affects children's attendance at elementary school and their levels of continuation at post-elementary stages. Low school completion rates perpetuate the insecurity of the poor.

Arab countries scoring an HPI of 30 per cent or more include three low income countries and a lower middle income country: Sudan (with an HPI of 34.3 per cent), Yemen (36.6 per cent), Mauritania (35.9 per cent), and Morocco (31.8 per cent). In almost all of these countries, significant insecurity (i.e. a value of more than 30 per cent) is recorded for the education component, represented by the adult illiteracy rate. In addition, in Mauritania, Sudan and Yemen insecurity from lack of access to safe water and child nutrition is also significant.

Despite moderate levels of income inequality, in most Arab countries social

The Report projects that the estimated numbers of Arabs living in poverty could be as high as 65 million

Extreme poverty is especially acute in the low-income Arab countries

exclusion has increased over the past two decades. In addition, there is evidence to suggest that the inequality in wealth has worsened significantly more than the deterioration in income. In many Arab countries, for example, land and asset concentration is conspicuous and provokes a sense of exclusion among other groups, even if absolute poverty has not increased.

The patterns of economic insecurity illustrated in the Report are the result of several policy gaps. First, the increased structural fragility of Arab economies is an evident consequence of continuing to rely on volatile, oil-led growth. Economic growth itself has been, for the most part, erratic and low. Correspondingly, the performance of productive sectors (and manufacturing in particular) has been weak and uncompetitive. Second, this growth model has negatively impacted the labour market, and Arab countries now suffer the highest unemployment rates in the world. Third, overall poverty, defined as the share of the population under the national upper poverty line, is significantly higher than the underestimate yielded by using the international poverty line of two dollars a day. Hence, poverty in the Arab countries is a more conspicuous phenomenon than commonly assumed.

5. Hunger, malnutrition and food insecurity

Despite its ample resources, and low incidence of hunger relative to other regions, the Arab countries are seeing hunger and malnutrition among their people rise. Although prevalence rates and absolute numbers in individual countries vary quite markedly, *the region, as a whole, is falling behind in achieving the hunger-reduction target of the Millennium Development Goals (MDGs)*. In addition, the backlog from hunger and malnutrition in the past continues.

According to Food and Agriculture Organization (FAO) figures, among developing country regions, the Arab countries have a low ratio of undernourished people to the total population. It is only surpassed in this regard by transition countries in Eastern Europe and the former Soviet Union. *Yet it is one of two world regions—the other being sub-Saharan Africa—where the*

number of undernourished has risen since the beginning of the 1990s—from about 19.8 million in 1990-1992 to 25.5 million in 2002-2004.

Considerable disparities exist among individual Arab countries in their fight against hunger. The countries that have made the greatest progress towards lowering the prevalence of undernourishment between 1990 and 2004 are Djibouti, Kuwait and Mauritania. Sudan has also made strides, but still experiences serious hunger prevalence. Saudi Arabia, Egypt, Lebanon, Jordan, Morocco and Yemen, on the other hand, recorded increases in both the absolute numbers and prevalence of undernourishment, while Syria and Algeria achieved very small reductions in prevalence but none in numbers.

The direct causes of hunger in the region are related to insufficient daily nutritional intake, which is attributable to limited supplies of different foods and the resulting imbalance in diets. Food availability, in turn, is connected with the forces of supply—which is contingent upon such factors as agricultural production, access to global markets, the growth of food industries, and the size of foreign aid—and demand, which is connected, in particular, to per capita income levels. In terms of local food production, some Arab countries have the lowest cereal yields in the world and, moreover, between 1990 and 2005, production in 7 countries declined. The Report illustrates that Arab countries are altogether more self-sufficient in food commodities that are favoured by the rich (meats, fish and vegetables) than in those likely to be consumed by the poor (cereals, fats and sugar).

In a seeming paradox, while malnutrition is on the rise in both absolute and relative terms in some Arab countries, obesity is also an increasing health risk in the region. In fact, the two are linked by their common origins in poor diet. Obesity and overweight are more common among women than men in Arab countries, contrary to the situation in the US, for example, where these problems are more prevalent among men. In the region, obesity is generally attributed to over-consumption of high-fat foods combined with little physical activity, which may partly explain its prevalence among Arab women, who are often prevented by

Inequality in wealth has worsened significantly more than the deterioration in income

Patterns of economic insecurity are the result of several policy gaps

custom from pursuing sports and other physical exercise. Obesity contributes to such non-contagious chronic illnesses as diabetes, high blood pressure, coronary arterial diseases, degenerative joint diseases, psychological illnesses, and some types of cancer. Such ailments are steadily increasing in Arab countries.

The main indirect causes of hunger in the region are poverty, foreign occupation and domestic conflict and economic policies for dealing with globalization. The Report shows that, while poverty and malnutrition often co-exist in Arab countries, poverty is not necessarily associated with undernourishment when the consumption pattern of the poor tends towards inexpensive but nutrient-rich foods, and when such foods are readily accessible under targeted government programmes. Conversely, when conditions of conflict disrupt food supplies, as in Iraq, the Occupied Palestinian Territory, Somalia and Sudan, a high degree of malnutrition and food insecurity follows.

Food accessibility is strongly influenced by government economic policies and openness to world markets. Subsidising food commodities to make them more affordable to the public is one such policy; lifting subsidies is another. Most Arab governments have adopted food supply policies as part of a social contract based on state provision of essential needs in exchange for the people's loyalty. But since the 1980s, economic and market deregulation policies adopted by governments have rendered domestic food prices vulnerable to fluctuations in international prices.

Arab countries as much as any others, have recently suffered from spiralling food prices traceable to various causes. Among these are the climate changes that have affected production in grain exporting countries, the extensive depletion of grain stocks, and the rising consumption of meat and dairy products in emerging economies, especially in China. Another major cause is the growing demand in the US and Europe for biofuels derived from grain, in response to the rising costs of oil and transportation. The Report contrasts how Arab economic policies have fared in coping with these pressures with the relative successes of countries such as Brazil and Mexico, which have simultaneously

followed liberal economic policies and ensured a minimum level of food for the poor.

The Report discusses the feasibility of achieving food sovereignty and food security in Arab countries. It concludes that food security needs to be pursued, not in terms of absolute sovereignty in food production, a goal impractical in light of regional water scarcities, but rather in terms of sufficiency for all members of society in essential commodities. In this context, the region's low self sufficiency rate in staple foods is one of its most serious development gaps.

6. Health security challenges

Health is both a vital goal of human security that is influenced by non-health factors, and an instrumental capability that significantly impacts other aspects of human security. In the last 40 years, Arab countries have made striking progress in forestalling death and extending life, as evidenced by falling infant mortality rates and rising life expectancy. Yet health is by no means assured for all citizens of Arab countries, with women suffering the most from neglect and gender biased traditions. Health systems are often shackled by bureaucratic inefficiency, poor professional capabilities and underfunding; and health risks from new infectious diseases are on the rise.

General status
Despite improvements in health across the region,

- The health status of Arabs, in general, is lower than that enjoyed by citizens of industrialized countries.
- While life expectancy increased and child mortality declined between 2000 and 2005, other health indicators stagnated.
- Disparities are apparent between countries and within countries
- Health data are insufficient, incomplete and often unreliable, making it difficult to frame effective health policies or reach those in need
- Harmful health practices, deeply rooted in culture, continue to lower health levels, especially among women

The region's low self sufficiency rate in staple foods is one of its most serious development gaps

Health is by no means assured for all citizens of Arab countries

Limits of health systems

Health care systems in the region are let down by:

- A narrow biomedical model based on hospital and curative care, and focused on the treatment of diseases
- The absence of inter-sectoral linkages that would help to bring vital indirect health determinants into the equation. Arab health systems do not recognize the role of such factors as the quality and coverage of education, women's empowerment, and social and economic justice. Neither do they evince the mindset required to address key factors such as gender, social class, identity and ethnicity, all of which have obvious effects on health and human security
- Disparities in health care provision and financing
- Profitable high technology hospitals that provide expensive state-of-the-art treatment for only a small minority of wealthy citizens
- Over-stretched public health services, frequently low in quality

Health financing

Health system financing is challenged by:

- The rising costs of health care
- Inadequate government expenditure on health in low and middle income countries
- Inefficient systems in the high income countries where ample funding does not translate into health gains
- Increasing out-of pocket expenditures on health that burden individuals and families
- A general lack of social health insurance and employer-provided benefits

Emerging health threats

HIV/AIDS represents a stubborn, proximate and misunderstood danger in the region. In 2007, more than 31,600 adults and children died from AIDS in the Arab countries (80 per cent of which are in Sudan). Between 2001 and 2007, there were 90,500 estimated new cases of HIV infections in the Arab countries, 50,000 of which in Sudan alone.

According to WHO and UNAIDS estimates, the number of those living with HIV in Arab countries was 435,000 in 2007, 73.5 per cent of which were in Sudan. A significant observation about Sudan concerns the relatively high percentage of HIV-positive women. Compared to a world average of 48 per cent in 2007, 53 per cent of adults living with HIV in Sudan were women. This percentage stood at 30.4 in the other Arab countries, for the same year, which is comparable to the situation in Western Europe. It is estimated that about 80 per cent of female infections in the region occur within the bonds of marriage where the subservient position and weak negotiating capacity of many women leave them exposed to their husbands' high risk behaviours.

The destructive power of the disease lies not solely in the power of the virus which causes it, but also in the social stigma that comes with it. Those living with the virus are often deprived of their livelihoods and, with their families, denied access to social opportunities in a climate of shame.

While malaria has been almost eliminated in the majority of Arab countries, it remains highly endemic in the Arab LDCs where on average 3,313 cases per 100,000 were reported in 2005. Djibouti, Somalia, Sudan and Yemen accounted for 98 per cent of notified cases in the region; Sudan alone bore about 76 per cent of the regional burden. Achievement of the MDG target of halting and beginning to reverse malaria in the sub-region, and in the region as a whole, is therefore heavily dependent on progress in Somalia, Sudan and Yemen.

7. Occupation and military intervention

Many of the threats to human security discussed in the Report coalesce in situations of occupation, conflict and military intervention. In Iraq, the Occupied Palestinian Territory and Somalia, people's basic rights to self-determination and peace have been forcibly annulled. They face threats to their lives, freedom, livelihoods, education, nutrition, health and physical environment from outside forces whose presence wreaks institutional, structural and material violence on them every day.

The Report assesses in detail the damage to human security that ensues from such travesties of human rights, focusing on the impacts of the US intervention in Iraq, Israel's continuing hold on Occupied

HIV/AIDS represents a stubborn, proximate and misunderstood danger

Many of the threats to human security coalesce in situations of occupation, conflict and military intervention

Palestinian Territory, including its recent campaign against Gaza, and on the special circumstances of the beleaguered people of Somalia.

Military intervention and occupation not only contravene international law and abrogate the rights of peoples in the affected countries. They spark both resistance and a cycle of violence and counter-violence that engulfs occupied and occupier alike. Occupation and military intervention undercut human security in other Arab and neighbouring countries in several ways. First, they displace peoples across borders, creating humanitarian challenges for affected states and seeding tensions in them. Second, as a *cause célèbre* of extremist groups that resort to violence, they strengthen the militant appeal of those who perpetuate the cycle of destruction in the region and whose acts provoke a backlash against citizens' rights and freedoms. Finally, as a threat to sovereignty, occupation and military intervention allow Arab governments to cite national security as a pretext for halting or postponing democratization and for prolonging oppressive rule. Occupation and military intervention are thus responsible for creating conditions of systemic insecurity in the region.

The Report observes that the fact that occupation and intervention have plagued the region so long indicates its vulnerability to the policies of external parties. Prospects for settling major conflicts in the affected countries are very largely governed by the will of non-Arab parties. This throws into strong relief the responsibility of the UN as the sole impartial guarantor of human and national security in occupied countries, a role however which the world body has been kept from playing effectively by the powers that have marginalized it.

Seven building blocks of Arab human security

The Report's analysis illustrates that the concept of human security provides a framework for re-centring the Arab social contract on those vital yet neglected priorities that most affect the wellbeing of citizens of Arab countries. While the state of human security is not uniform throughout the Arab countries, no country can claim to be free from fear or free from want, and many are affected by spillovers from insecurity in neighbouring countries. The Report's individual chapters outline various policy orientations that the state, civil society, individual citizens and international actors could adopt within their respective spheres of action, suggesting specific steps that can be taken to reduce threats across all dimensions of the concept. In doing so, the Report underlines the central importance of:

1. The preservation and enhancement of the land, water, air and ecology that sustain the Arab peoples' very existence under rising national, regional and global environmental, population and demographic pressures;

2. The guarantees of essential rights, freedoms and opportunities without discrimination, that only a well governed, accountable and responsive state ruled by just laws can provide; and the diffusion of identity conflicts rooted in competition for power and wealth that becomes possible when such a state wins the trust of all citizens;

3. The recognition by the state and society of the abuse and injustice that vulnerable women, children and refugees across the region encounter each day, and the resolve to change their legal, economic, social and personal conditions for the better;

4. The will to address the weak structural underpinnings of the Arab oil economy, reduce income poverty and move towards knowledge-based, equitable and diversified economies that will create the jobs and protect the livelihoods on which coming generations will depend in the post-oil era;

5. Ending persisting hunger and malnutrition in all sub-regions, but especially the poorest, which continue to erode human capabilities, cut short millions of lives and set back human development. The economics of food security in the global economy may call for a new realism in defining food security less in terms of absolute food sovereignty and more in terms of sufficiency

Occupation and military intervention spark a cycle of violence and counter-violence that engulfs occupied and occupier alike

The concept of human security provides a framework for re-centring the Arab social contract on vital yet neglected priorities

*Occupation
and military
intervention
undermine the
fragile progress
of political reform
in the region*

for all members of society in essential commodities.

6. The promotion of health for all as a human right, a prerequisite for human security and an instrumental enabler across the gamut of human functioning. The significant progress that Arab countries have made in this field is being undercut by policy and institutional failures that produce disparities in access, affordability and quality, and by the growing health threats from serious diseases such as malaria, tuberculosis and HIV/AIDS.

7. Policy recognition abroad that long-standing human rights violations against the Arab peoples and the continuing violation of Arab sovereignty and lives by regional and global powers through occupation and military intervention are self-defeating and unacceptable to the international and regional public. Such violations have inflicted enormous damage through the disproportionate use of force and a total disregard for civilian lives, as highlighted in Israel's recent campaign on Gaza. These violations have caused untold human suffering and chaos, stained the image of the powers implicated in them and undermined the fragile progress of political reform in the region by bolstering extremist forces and driving moderate voices out of the public arena.

Endnotes

1   UNDP 1994.
2   UNDP 2002.
3   UNDP/AHDR calculations based on FAO's AQUASTAT database.
4   UNDP 2007.

Applying the concept of human security in the Arab countries

*Human insecurity
is the result
of pervasive,
recurrent or
intense threats that
produce complex
ripple effects*

In this first chapter, we define human security as "the liberation of human beings from those intense, extensive, prolonged, and comprehensive threats to which their lives and freedom are vulnerable". The definition rests on the classic analysis of human security advanced in the 1994 global Human Development Report sponsored by UNDP, and takes into account present-day circumstances in the Arab countries.

Chapter 1 contextualises this definition. It begins by recounting why the concept of human security has been chosen to launch a new series of Arab Human Development Reports. It next discusses the evolution and scope of the concept at the global level, its relationship to similar concepts, such as human development and human rights, and the metrics used to illustrate its dimensions. The chapter then outlines a move towards Arab views of human security anchored in Arab thinking on the subject and in the realities of the region. In doing so, it sets out the methodology of the report and its approach to measurement in the Arab context. The chapter concludes by introducing a poll of citizens from four Arab countries and the views of a group of young Arabs, which reflect their understanding and assessment of human security in their respective countries.

Why human security?

*Widespread
human insecurity
relentlessly
undermines human
development*

Human insecurity is the result of pervasive, recurrent or intense threats that produce complex ripple effects touching large numbers of people. In the Arab countries, widespread human insecurity relentlessly undermines human development. It is brought on by the depletion of natural resources under pressure, by high population growth rates and by rapid climate change, which could threaten the livelihoods, income, food and shelter of millions of Arabs. It is ingrained in the predicament of one-fifth of the people in some Arab countries, and of more than half in others, whose lives are impoverished and cut short by hunger and want. It reverberates in the military occupation and armed conflicts witnessed in Iraq, Sudan, Somalia and the Occupied Palestinian Territory. Human insecurity rears its head even in Arab countries that enjoy relative stability where the latter's security forces hold wide sway in curtailing or violating citizens' rights. And it is aggravated by the contrast between the lives of citizens hollowed out by scarcity and those of their neighbours, whether in their own countries or countries next door, whose ills often stem from excess.

This portrayal is no exaggeration: the people of Darfur, Iraqis, Palestinians and Somalis go in fear for their lives each day, with the spectre of random violence and destruction all around them. Such fears also permeate more fortunate Arab societies which, although free from armed conflicts or occupying forces, suffer under the dead hand of authoritarian power. In many Arab countries, the ordinary person enters a police station at his or her peril, knowing he or she is liable to be hauled away on the merest suspicion of crime or public agitation. Dissenting citizens risk being thrown in prison for exercising their civic duty to speak out against state repression. Gripped by dread of actual or potential harm from fellow Arabs and foreign powers alike, torn by conflicts and hobbled by unjust laws, too many Arabs live out an existential nightmare of insecurity that numbs hope, shrivels initiative and drains the public sphere of the motivation for co-operative and peaceful change.

Few subjects, therefore, are more appropriate than human security as the starting point for the present series of reports, which seeks to reappraise the state of Arab human development in the first decade of a new millennium.

Firstly, the concept shifts attention from questions of state security—which are generally overemphasized in the political discourse of the region and sometimes sought at the expense of citizens' security—to that of human security, without which state security has little value. This understanding of the concept, then, views human security as a condition for the achievement of state security. Citizens liberated from fear and need are far more likely to acknowledge the political, economic, and social legitimacy of a responsible and responsive state that protects their interests. Such citizens will be motivated to work together in confronting any external or internal dangers they may face; and they will be fortified against the temptation to ally themselves with foreign powers against the interests of the state.

Secondly, human security, when viewed correctly, helps to re-balance the preoccupation with terror, and the so-called war on it, which have come to dominate international and regional politics. That preoccupation, which has spread in the post-9-11 environment, has turned policy attention back to issues of national security, state enforcement and military solutions. The manner in which this so-called war has been prosecuted has created a backlash in the region that has worsened the security and rights of individual citizens. Indeed, in Iraq and other countries, it has wrought destruction, caused loss of life among Arab and foreign nationals and infringed human rights on a scale that, according to the campaign's many critics, have left the world more divided and less secure than ever.

Thirdly, the subject provides a framework for analysing and addressing critical hazards to which the region, at the time of writing, is increasingly vulnerable. These manifest themselves not only in direct threats to life in cases such as Iraq, Sudan, Somalia, and the Occupied Palestinian Territory, but also in the indirect threats posed by hunger, poverty and environmental stresses. The latter include the drastic consequences of external and regional competition for Arab oil, rising pressure on scarce water resources from fast-growing populations, and the impacts of repeated droughts, encroaching deserts and deteriorating climate conditions.

The concept at the global level

In the volatile world order that has followed the end of the cold war, external and internal challenges to the integrity of states have multiplied. From without, environmental pollution, international terrorism, large population movements, a melting global financial system and other cross-border threats such as pandemics, the drug trade and human trafficking have all laid siege to traditional notions of security. Within countries, spreading poverty, unemployment, civil wars, sectarian and ethnic conflicts and state repression have sharply underlined the weak or negative role of many states in securing their citizens' lives and livelihoods. Not surprisingly, attention has shifted away from safeguarding the integrity of states to protecting the lives of the citizens who reside in them. The concept of human security emerges from this shift.

The concept shifts attention from questions of state security to that of human security

Unlike human development, human security has no widely accepted definition. Although the term has entered humanitarian, diplomatic and developmental discourse in the last twenty years, the scope of the concept behind it varies from one context to another. This is to be expected. The number of threats that could potentially befall people is almost limitless. What is, and what is not considered a threat to human security depends upon the definition adopted.

However, while definitions of human security vary in scope, their common centrepiece is the individual, and not the state. The direction of this paradigm shift is summarized below:

The differences between state security and human security may be summarized as follows:

- The source of threat to state security is generally a military one, whereas the sources of threat to human security are varied; they include the environment, the economy, and even the state itself.
- The actors who threaten the security of the state tend to be located outside the state concerned. Hence, they are generally other states or opposition organizations based in other states.
- The object of threat in the case of state security is the state itself, including its cohesiveness, its powers, and its territory, whereas the object of threat in the case of human security is individuals' lives, freedom, or both.

Studies pertaining to state security generally assume that the 'default mode' in human life and among state entities is one of struggle and conflict, whereas studies of individual human security assume that, given the common interests human beings share, they gravitate naturally toward mutual cooperation.

The primary entry points for studies related to national security are found in political science, whereas studies pertaining to human security use a variety of entry points that draw not only on political science, but also on areas such as sociology, economics, psychology, public health, and environmental science.

In the absence of a universally adopted definition of human security, various attempts have been made at the international level to identify the scope of the concept. In the main, two interpretive

Table 1-1	State security versus human security		
Form of Security	**Referent**	**Object of Protection**	**Potential Threats**
Traditional security	The state	The integrity and safety of the state	Inter-state war and foreign intervention Nuclear proliferation Civil disorder
Human security	The individual	The safety and freedom of the individual	Poverty Disease Environmental depletion Human rights violations Conflicts, violence and repression

Source: The Report team.

schools have emerged into which most current definitions fit. These are the narrow and broad conceptions of human security. Thus, one can compare such definitions along a spectrum.

The narrow end of the spectrum, while focused on the individual, is limited to violent threats such as those posed by land-mines, the spread of small arms and grievous human rights abuses. The normative movements which gave rise to the Convention on the Prohibition of the Use, Stockpiling, Production and Transfer of Anti-Personnel Mines and on Their Destruction, the International Criminal Court and international campaigns to halt the spread of firearms, drug trafficking and violence against women are examples of policy actions taken in a narrow human security perspective. This approach continues to influence international initiatives in peace-building and conflict prevention, as well as interventions under the still-controversial rubric of the Responsibility to Protect.

The broad end incorporates a long list of possible threats, from traditional security threats such as war to developmental threats in the areas of health, poverty and the environment. The categorization adopted by UNDP in its milestone 1994 Human Development Report (HDR) is a pioneering example of this approach. The latter report posited seven dimensions of human security:

- Economic security threatened by poverty;
- Food security threatened by hunger and famine;
- Health security threatened by injury and disease;

Sources of threat to human security are varied and include the environment, the economy, and even the state itself

The object of threat in the case of human security is individuals' lives, freedom, or both

- Environmental security threatened by pollution, environmental degradation and resource depletion;
- Personal security threatened by crime and violence;
- Political security threatened by political repression;
- Community security threatened by social, ethnic or sectarian conflict.

The hallmarks of the UNDP categorization are its breadth compared to the traditional understanding of security; its incorporation of human freedom, as well as human life, as a core value; the interrelated causes and effects that it identifies among the dimensions of human security; and its focus on the individual. Importantly, the UNDP approach recognises the individual's relationship to the state as another possible threat to human security. The 1994 HDR, and the debate it prompted, underwrite the UN's commitment to a world order "free from fear and free from want", as advanced in the Millennium Report of the UN Secretary-General,[1] which in turn led to the establishment of the Commission on Human Security (CHS) in 2001.

The CHS defined human security as the protection of the "vital core of all human lives in ways that enhance human freedoms and human fulfilment". It also set threshold criteria that, once crossed, elevate an issue to the status of a human security threat. In the Commission's original definition, the "vital core of the individual" is that which affords a minimum level of survival. However, the

CHS subsequently extended its definition beyond issues of survival. Its revised definition transcends enabling people simply to withstand threats. Rather, it encompasses defending people's basic human rights, livelihoods and human dignity from preventable reversals and empowering them to overcome or avoid further threats through individual and collective action. Human security, by this definition, is not merely about survival; it is about re-launching people at risk on a safer course, supported by the political, economic, social and cultural building blocks for a better life.[2]

Relationship to other concepts

In this fuller view, human security can be seen as the "rearguard" of human development. Whereas human development is concerned with expanding the individual's capabilities and opportunities, human security is concerned with enabling peoples to contain or avert threats to their lives, livelihoods and natural dignity. Human development, by its nature, is open-ended. It can expand to various levels of aspiration in different settings with different potentials. But in conditions of critical hazard, all people absolutely must enjoy a minimum level of security to protect their lives and livelihoods and move forward from there. Human security more narrowly prioritizes the rights, capabilities and preventive actions required in such life-threatening situations. The two look at the human condition from different ends of a continuum, summarized by Amartya Sen as "expansion with equity" (human development) and "downturn with security" (human security).[3] The two concepts are therefore complementary, meeting and overlapping along a line running from human desperation to human aspirations, as illustrated in (simplified) figure 1-1.

On the one hand, human security is a basic requirement for the achievement of human development, since the range of choices available to people can only expand if they are in a position to guarantee their survival and their liberty. On the other, raising people's educational levels, improving their health conditions, increasing their basic incomes and assuring their basic freedoms serves to consolidate their

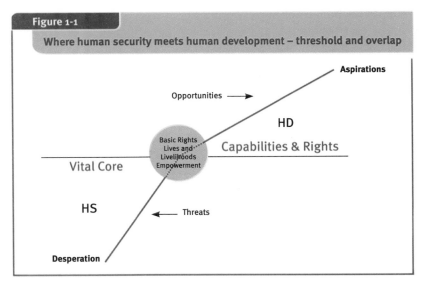

Figure 1-1

Where human security meets human development – threshold and overlap

Box 1-1   MOHAMED EL-BARADEI* – Human security and the quest for peace

The current security picture is paradoxical. As a writer in the *Financial Times* aptly put it, "The world has rarely been more peaceful or felt so insecure."

According to a recent report on human security, there has been a sharp decline since the early 1990s in civil wars and other forms of armed conflict. The number of refugees has also gone down, and human rights abuses have decreased. These statistics indicate that the world is becoming more peaceful.

Yet at the same time, the collective sense of insecurity is higher than at any time before, because the forces that drive insecurity remain persistent and pervasive. These drivers of insecurity fit into four categories:

First, poverty, and poverty-related insecurities, for the billions who lack access to reliable food supplies, safe drinking water, adequate health care, and modern energy supplies. This is the rawest form of insecurity—a reality for 40 per cent of our fellow human beings, who live on the edge of survival on less than two dollars per day.

A second category is the lack of good governance—not infrequently linked to poverty—which ranges from corruption to severely repressive regimes whose hallmark is egregious human rights abuses. Democracy recently has made remarkable strides, particularly in Eastern Europe and Latin America. But many tyrants remain, in the Middle East and other regions.

A third driver of insecurity is the sense of injustice that results from the imbalance between the 'haves' and 'have-nots'—the sharp contrasts in wealth and power that we see between the North and the South. This sense of injustice is magnified by the perception that the sanctity of human life is not equally valued—that society grieves the loss of life in the developed world far more than it grieves the greater loss of life in places like Darfur or Iraq...

Fourth is the artificial polarization along religious or ethnic lines. This is a centuries-old phenomenon, but it continues to flare up recently, leading some to worry about a 'clash of civilizations' between Muslims and the West. In my view, it is an utter mistake to think that these tensions arise from clashing religious values. But for people who suffer gross inequities— many of them in the Muslim world—it is easy to be convinced that their suffering is due to religious or ethnic prejudice, instead of the real causes that have existed throughout history, warring people and nations, fighting over power and resources. This conviction can make them more likely to seek refuge in distorted views of religion or ethnicity in order to channel their rage and redress their grievances.

The human security picture would not be complete without factoring in the impact of globalization. Modern society is interdependent as never before. This interdependence is a double-edged sword; it provides opportunities to address these problems more effectively, but can also accentuate them...

Against this backdrop, it should be apparent why conventional concepts of security—rooted in the protection of national borders and old concepts of sovereignty—are no longer adequate. Most of the drivers of insecurity I have mentioned are without borders. If a new extremist group emerges in the Middle East, it makes me worry. If a new civil war breaks out in an African state, I will be disturbed. Not only because we are all members of the same human family—but also because of the probability that each of these developments will affect me sooner or later.

In other words, the modern age demands that we think in terms of *human security*—a concept of security that is people-centred and without borders. A concept that acknowledges the inherent linkages between economic and social development, respect for human rights, and peace.

* Director General of the International Atomic Energy Agency (IAEA)

Source: El-Baradei 2006.

human development, which, in turn, leads to greater human security. Thus, human security and human development are mutually reinforcing.

Some thinkers have also broadened the concept of human security to cover all aspects of human rights. Yet human security is not coterminous with the concept of human rights. Rather, it would be more accurate to think of it as the *outcome* of a set of conditions, one of which is respect for all human rights—whether civil, political, economic, social, or cultural, or individual or collective. When such rights are respected, a significant degree of human security is achieved as well. However, this may not be entirely sufficient, since respect for these rights does not, for example, protect people from climate change or natural disasters, the effects of which can deprive millions of people of shelter and employment. Indeed, such disasters can cause thousands to lose their lives, as happened during the tsunami that struck some South Asian countries in 2004. Moreover, some of these rights, such as the right to form associations, may not be necessary for the achievement of human security as defined in this report. It follows that respect for a number of fundamental human rights, particularly civil rights, as well as some economic and social rights such as the right to employment, nutrition and medical care, is a necessary but insufficient condition for the achievement of human security.

Human security and human development are mutually reinforcing

Towards Arab views of human security

Few Arabic studies deal directly with the concept of human security

How do Arab writings on human security, few as these may be, engage with human security? How might we define the concept in the Arab context? What major threats in the region should it refer to? Do the dimensions proposed in the 1994 global Human Development Report include all those that are most significant and illuminating for our countries?

Arab writings on the subject

Few Arabic studies deal directly with the concept of human security. However, warnings against various human threats, including non-military threats, recur in the Arab written heritage and in the popular culture of some Arab countries. These traditional references at best approximate some of the dimensions of the modern concept but do not attain its comprehensive and multidimensional stature nor did

---

Box 1-2   **AZIZ AL AZMEH* – Arabs and human security**

The narrowing, as opposed to the broadening, of the concept of human security, is not unconnected to two other closely related notions that have left their mark on the concepts and theories of contemporary political science. Concepts associated with this phase, which are manifested in the programmes of local and international non-governmental organizations, tend, in one respect, to shift concern away from the state and the national entity while placing greater emphasis on ethnic, religious, and local groups. At the same time, such concepts tend to lend greater importance to the individual than to the group, be it national or sub-national.

When I say that these notions are closed related, what I mean by this is that they result from the discourse of democracy and pluralism, which is linked in turn to the application of market-related freedom to the realm of political freedom.

Notions such as human security are undoubtedly a result of globalization in its current phase, and the shift of attention away from the state and the national community is justified by obstacles on the path to the structural reform of Arab state systems. However, if we take this trend to its logical conclusion without any consideration for the overall national interest or even for the pan-Arab interest, we will find ourselves careening headlong into an unforeseen abyss. We will capitulate unthinkingly to exquisite but empty words and phrases instead of considering possibilities that fit with the ever-changing reality of the Arab world.

This said, it may be permissible to speak of "human security in the Arab world" if one adheres to two principles, one negative and one positive. The negative principle requires great caution in wresting their objective and subjective character from ethnic, religious, and local groups that form part of the framework of the Arab state, a state which is called upon to construct the foundations of citizenship and not those of provincialism, sectarianism, clan-ism or tribalism. This is because individual human security and such national component groups are, politically speaking, inseparable, regardless of one's perspective on human development.

The positive principle entails covering all elements that might go to make up human security as a comprehensive concept capable of providing direction for human development in a way that transcends 'security'—which is overly general—to give the notion cohesion and specificity.

Such a comprehensive framework for addressing the security of Arab citizens is certainly needed, for the latter are confronted with a multiplicity of threats. Their economic survival is at risk (as a result of the failure and disunity of economic structures following the atrophy of the concept of comprehensive economic and social development adopted during the 1950s, 1960s and 1970s). Their personal safety is often jeopardized (owing to—in addition to physical, spiritual, familial, and societal violence—the tyranny of security apparatuses or attempts by ruling powers to terrorize societies into being virtuous and God-fearing). Their national and pan-Arab identity is disintegrating (under sectarian conflicts, wars, foreign occupation, and obstacles on the path to political reform). Their cultural and educational security has waned (which requires that we restore the concept of cultural development rather than adopting the prevailing view of our societies, which see themselves as communities founded on civilized manners, social conservatism, and cultural purity). Their social security has collapsed (resulting from the erosion of social security systems and growing negligence on the part of legal and judicial systems), and their environmental security is under great pressure, which is linked in turn to the world economy.

If we wish to combine these elements, highlight the points of intersection among them, and transform them into a comprehensive concept capable of guiding and lending cohesion to 'human development,' we must enrich the concept of human security by placing it within the framework of Arab community movements. We must bring it down to earth from abstraction and fuzziness, keeping clearly before our eyes that our fundamental purpose in concerning ourselves with human security is to achieve human and national development.

* Syrian national and Professor, Arab and Islamic Historical Studies, at the Central European University in Budapest, Hungary.

---

they enter the mainstream culture. On the other hand, we find that the term 'human security' has made its way into the works of contemporary Arab authors, both those who write in foreign languages and those who write in their native Arabic.

Writings in Arabic on the concept of human security have appeared in the context of academic research at Western universities, speeches or writings addressed to the Western public, or Arab conferences focusing on the issue. The most significant axes that have engaged Arab authors are the relationship between human security and state security, the scope of human security, the areas included within human security, and the relationships among these concerns.

Most contemporary Arab writers express the belief in an unbreakable bond between individual human security and national security on the one hand and human security and external military threats on the other. Other writers believe that the authoritarian state is the source of the greatest threats to human security in the region (Abdul Monem Al-Mashat, in Arabic, background paper for the report). However, such writers do not maintain that the achievement of human security rules out state security. Rather, they hold that the achievement of individual human security will have the effect of transforming the authoritarian state into one that respects the rule of law. This shift may require, among other things, the reform of existing security apparatuses or possibly even the establishment of new security institutions.[4]

There are disparate views among Arab writers concerning the scope of the concept of human security. Some hold that the individual is the focal point and goal of human security. One representative of this view is Mohamed El Baradei, who states that "... the modern age demands that we think in terms of human security—a concept of security that is people-centred and without borders. A concept that acknowledges the inherent linkages between economic and social development, respect for human rights, and peace".[5] Others likewise affirm that human security is personal security and, as such, revolves around the individual—his or her rights, well-being, freedoms and dignity,[6] and that state security and human

security are complementary concepts, in the sense that the former should be seen as one of the means to achieve the latter.[7] On this view, the concept of human security is bound intimately to human rights in general and, more specifically, to women's rights, in which connection it draws authority from international covenants and agreements.

Arab writers disagree over the areas of life encompassed by the concept of human security. Some have greatly expanded its scope, rejecting its restriction to military dimensions. Others, by contrast, have narrowed the concept. Representatives of the first trend include Korany and al-Mashat. Korany, for example, holds that human security is linked to liberation from fear and respect for human dignity.[8] Al-Mashat maintains that the broader concept of human security depends on the achievement of material prosperity, and of balance or harmony in society. On this basis, he divides states into three types, namely, (1) safe states, in which civil society is dominant, (2) unsafe states, which are ruled by the military, and (3) states that lie somewhere between the first two. Other Arab writers either narrow the concept of human security to a single dimension, such as freedom from want, or they approach it by looking at specific social groups (such as the poor), gender groups (such as women), or age groups (such as children). In all such cases, however, they affirm the mutual interdependence and complementarity among the various areas encompassed by human security, namely, the economic, the social, the political, the domestic, and the international (Abdul Monem Al-Mashat, in Arabic, background paper for the report).

Human security as defined in this report

Drawing on UNDP's broad approach and the concerns of Arab thinkers, this report defines human security as *the liberation of human beings from those intense, extensive, prolonged, and comprehensive threats to which their lives and freedom are vulnerable*. In this definition, freedom is a central value for the individual since, in the Arab context, it is frequently threatened from within and without, by powers at home

The term 'human security' has made its way into the works of contemporary Arab authors

There are disparate views among Arab writers concerning the scope of the concept of human security

and abroad. The definition also encompasses a well defined range of human concerns. It includes employment opportunities, income adequate to meet basic needs, nutrition, health care, peaceful relations among different identity groups, the state's fulfilment of its basic duty to protect its citizens from internal and external aggression, and the individual's safety from personal threats.

The degree of seriousness of these threats is determined by four factors: (1) intensity, (2) extent, (3) temporal duration, and (4) comprehensiveness. The *intensity* of a threat is manifested when it affects people's ability to survive and when it deprives people of the minimum level of liberty consistent with basic human freedoms. The *extent* of a threat varies depending on whether it affects a larger or smaller number of people. Similarly, the *seriousness* of a threat increases when it lasts for a longer period of time. Lastly, the more *comprehensive* the range of areas of human activity affected by a given threat, the more serious it will be. Hunger and poverty, for example, affect an individual's health, the manner in which he or she relates to the environment, his or her political participation, and individual productivity.

In focusing on the security of individual Arab citizens, the report does not overlook the threats to the Arab world as a whole or to the individual states therein. The distinction between state security and individual human security does not mean that one is necessarily at odds with the other or that the achievement of one rules out the achievement of the other. In fact, state security is necessary for individual human security. If a state should fall under foreign occupation and lose its autonomy or territorial integrity, this will have a negative impact on individual human security. Military occupation does not generally take place peacefully, and the measures taken by occupation authorities to ensure their soldiers' safety involve, in most cases, restricting the freedoms of the citizenry of the occupied country. Indeed, they may involve wanton disregard for recognized standards for fair trials.

At the same time, state security may at times be achieved at the expense of the individual security of its citizens and those residing in its territories. This occurs when state authorities seek to arrive at what they imagine to be 'absolute security' by resorting to extraordinary measures parading as 'law and order' and by restricting the freedoms of those they suspect of threatening national security. The continuation of such strictures on citizens' freedoms may in fact end up threatening the security of the state itself when some of its citizens might join forces with a foreign power with its own designs on their territory, and when such citizens succeed, with the help of such foreign powers, in toppling their government. In so doing, they open the door for their country to fall under foreign occupation and internal fragmentation.

In fact, it is evident that the individual can only be secure in a strong, accountable and well-governed state. After all, the process of protecting people from unemployment, poverty, hunger, and deteriorating health conditions can only succeed within a state that can manage its economy, institutions and infrastructure in a way that guarantees its citizens suitable employment, adequate incomes, and appropriate levels of nutrition and health. Such 'good governance' also ensures that relations among the country's varied ethnic and cultural groups will be peaceful and tension-free. This kind of state fulfils its responsibility to preserve security and order and is successful in maintaining its political autonomy and territorial integrity. There can be no doubt that a state's success in carrying out all these functions accountably is the basis of its ability to acquire legitimacy and to win and maintain its citizens' support. In other words, such a state will be all the stronger for protecting its citizens' individual security and welfare.

Mapping relevant threats

Any identification of threats to Arab human security needs to reflect the status of the region as a highly diverse area which, through most periods of its history, has been the object of conflict among the world's superpowers. It is also a region that has trailed the world on leading measures of good governance, democracy and social cohesion. Consequently, while this report engages with the internationally recognized dimensions of human security

The distinction between state security and individual human security does not mean that one is necessarily at odds with the other

The individual can only be secure in a strong, accountable and well-governed state

as identified in the 1994 global Human Development Report, it also invokes specific threats to human security in the Arab countries. These include dimensions such as foreign occupation, foreign and regional military interventions, violence that springs from mobilization along primordial identities, and oppressive state practices that undermine human security.

In keeping with its status as a regional report, the present study approaches these threats to human security in Arab countries as follows:

Its primary focus is on those proximate areas of threat where the Arab countries can largely take the initiative themselves. These comprise threats to people that stem from damage to the natural resource base; that originate with, or undermine the state, including group conflicts arising from competition for power and resources; and that disproportionately affect vulnerable groups. Proximate threats also cover dangers posed by economic vulnerability, unemployment, lack of social protection and other economic conditions; and by inadequate levels of nutrition and health. Such threats fall chiefly within the scope of response of the Arab countries themselves, albeit some have important global intersections and implications for the international community. The focus of most chapters lies in these areas. A final chapter, however, considers a major source of threats to human security—the foreign occupation of Arab lands—where, self-evidently, responsibility for change directly involves the powers in question. Any Arab discussion of this topic must, in the end, be addressed to those parties with whom the initiative remains. The report therefore ends with this important subject.

Thus, the sequence of topics the report addresses is:
- Pressures on environmental and natural resources
- The state and human security: performance and prospects
- The insecurity of vulnerable groups
- Economic vulnerability, poverty and unemployment
- Food security and nutrition
- Health and human security
- Occupation and foreign military intervention

In starting its analysis with pressures on natural resources, the report acknowledges that environmental management has become a serious challenge in the region. Countries such as Somalia and Sudan have suffered in recent years from massive killer droughts. Climate change may threaten the survival, employment and income prospects of millions of Arabs. Population growth rates remain among the highest in the world. A deteriorating environment has eroded the health conditions of millions in Egypt, for example, in recent decades. Moreover, the question also includes the geostrategic importance of the region—and of its oil wealth specifically—which have long exposed some Arab states to external influence and intervention. Another precious resource—water—is increasingly behind intense struggles that may inflict a large toll on peoples and communities. For all these reasons, the dwindling of the region's natural resource base is becoming a source of human insecurity, a trend which warrants renewed policy attention.

Indeed, features of the resource base peculiar to the region, and the patterns of development to which these have led, have cast their shadow over economic conditions. The marked division between rich and poor Arab states reflects a lopsided endowment in natural wealth. Economic conditions, in their turn, impact human security with respect to the availability of employment opportunities and the ease or difficulty of obtaining food and health services; similarly, they also influence relations between various cultural groups such as farmers and pastoralists in Darfur.

Measuring levels of human security

Can human security be measured? There have been numerous attempts to answer this question. Acknowledging the complexity of the issue, those concerned[9] have concluded that there are two essential approaches to dealing with measurement. The first is termed the objective approach, since it attempts to construct quantitative indicators of the various dimensions of human security in a number of different countries, and, at times, throughout the world. The most salient example of this approach is found in the metrics produced by the Human Security Centre Committee in Uppsala, Sweden, which were published

The report focuses on proximate areas of threat where the Arab countries can largely take the initiative themselves

A major source of threat to human security is the foreign occupation of Arab lands

in 2005 under the title, 'The Human Security Audit'. This, in turn, formed part of a larger report issued by the Human Security Centre at the University of British Columbia in Canada under the title, "War and Peace in the 21st Century," the second part of which treats the topic of measuring human security.[10] The objective approach is also illustrated by a study that appeared in the magazine, Foreign Policy, issued by the Carnegie Endowment for International Peace, which identifies and ranks what are termed 'failed states'.[11] Although this study does not concern itself directly with the assessment of human security, many of the indicators are relevant to the subject.

No single study based on people's perceptions, or what might be termed the subjective approach to measuring human security, has been made on an international scale. However, many of the questions used in the most well-known studies of values and

---

Box 1-3 | **THE HUMAN SECURITY SURVEY – Overall findings**

To explore the various dimensions of the concept of human security as understood by Arab citizens, the participants were asked to consider up to 21 potential threats to human security, and choose whether or not they thought each one was indeed a threat in their context. Reponses across the four surveys varied extensively. Environmental pollutants were considered the most serious threat by Kuwaitis, whereas Lebanese participants felt that assaults on persons and private property were the leading threats, followed by hunger. By contrast the overwhelming majority of Palestinians regarded foreign occupation as the greatest threat to their safety, while Moroccans thought that poverty and unemployment caused the greatest insecurity.

Where the survey explored in greater depth, Lebanese and Palestinians agreed in their assessment of the seriousness of specific threats, such as the government's relative inability to protect citizens' lives, water shortages, slow legal procedures, and the difficulty of exercising basic rights. They also focused on tense relations among rival groups, corruption, disintegration of the family, and foreign occupation, though without rating these in the same order of importance:

Principal perceived threats to human security (%)

Threats	Kuwait	Lebanon	Morocco	OPT
Environmental pollutants	91.2	77.8	74.9	..
Water shortages	73.5	80.5	76.9	82.3
Deterioration of agricultural land	..	..	..	78.4
Occupation and foreign influence	..	85.1	..	96.2
Governmental failure to protect citizens	..	87	..	86.9
Arbitrariness of government	..	80.1	..	..
Lack of social protection	..	73.4	..	71
Poor health services	..	80.9	72.3	73.4
Poor educational services	..	..	..	..
The spread of corruption	..	86.3	..	89.4
Slow legal procedures and difficulty in obtaining rights	..	73.2	..	73.7
Weak solidarity among members of society	..	70.2	..	..
Tense relations among different groups	..	80.8	..	83.7
Religious extremism	..	79.9	..	..
Disintegration of the family	..	74.7	..	75.2
Lack of access to basic services	..	81.1	..	75.4
Epidemics and communicable diseases	..	86.2	70	75.6
Unemployment	..	86.5	81.2	91
Poverty	..	86.4	86	90.6
Hunger	..	88.7	75.9	85.4
Assaults on persons and private property	..	89.1	..	80.4

.. = not available

attitudes throughout the world are closely linked with human security. Such studies include the Pew Global Attitudes Project[12] and the World Values Survey undertaken by the University of Michigan.[13]

Despite differences of approach, these international attempts at measurement show that levels of human security in Arab countries have deteriorated in recent years, albeit in varying degrees. However, most of these attempts were either not related to human security directly, did not cover all Arab states, contained value judgments of questionable validity or are now out-of-date since they were conducted before recent major developments in the Arab countries. It may thus be necessary to take a different approach to gauging levels of human security in the region at the present time.

Is it possible to arrive at a general composite indicator of human security? Whereas the Human Development Index (HDI), which is built on basic, universal and quantifiable variables, constitutes a robust and viable composite indicator for that concept, a universally satisfactory human security index remains out of reach. Statistical research on this subject shows how complex and difficult it would be to arrive at such an index.

Firstly, there is no universally accepted definition of human security. Narrow approaches centre on thresholds of survival and major harm (death, extreme violence, life-threatening injury, etc). Broad approaches include a wide range of development and human rights indicators.

Secondly, human security relates to material and moral dimensions, and is context-specific. It is best illustrated by both qualitative indicators that denote perceptions of risk as well as quantitative indicators of objective threats. Combining these two types in one index is highly problematic and open to criticisms of subjectivity.

Thirdly, the value of any indicator lies in its ability to direct public policy makers and civil society organizations to priority areas. The kind of general indicator that assigns each country an arithmetical average would do nothing to reveal the areas that require intervention, since the arithmetical average would conceal the very conditions that call for such intervention.

Finally, a composite indicator in this field presents real problems of comparability and weighting. It would be difficult,

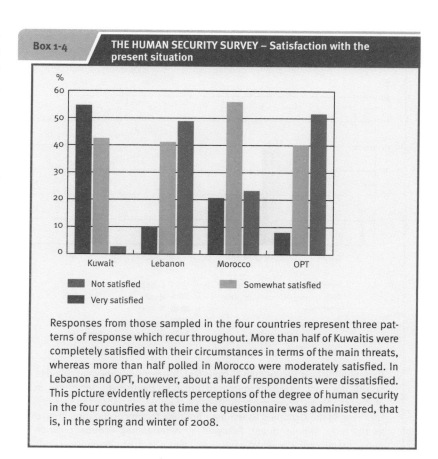

Box 1-4 **THE HUMAN SECURITY SURVEY – Satisfaction with the present situation**

Responses from those sampled in the four countries represent three patterns of response which recur throughout. More than half of Kuwaitis were completely satisfied with their circumstances in terms of the main threats, whereas more than half polled in Morocco were moderately satisfied. In Lebanon and OPT, however, about a half of respondents were dissatisfied. This picture evidently reflects perceptions of the degree of human security in the four countries at the time the questionnaire was administered, that is, in the spring and winter of 2008.

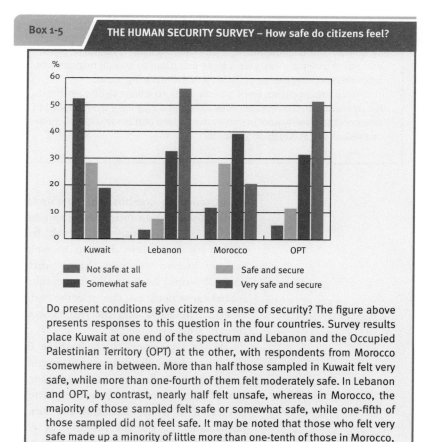

Box 1-5 **THE HUMAN SECURITY SURVEY – How safe do citizens feel?**

Do present conditions give citizens a sense of security? The figure above presents responses to this question in the four countries. Survey results place Kuwait at one end of the spectrum and Lebanon and the Occupied Palestinian Territory (OPT) at the other, with respondents from Morocco somewhere in between. More than half those sampled in Kuwait felt very safe, while more than one-fourth of them felt moderately safe. In Lebanon and OPT, by contrast, nearly half felt unsafe, whereas in Morocco, the majority of those sampled felt safe or somewhat safe, while one-fifth of those sampled did not feel safe. It may be noted that those who felt very safe made up a minority of little more than one-tenth of those in Morocco, and barely 5 per cent in OPT and Lebanon.

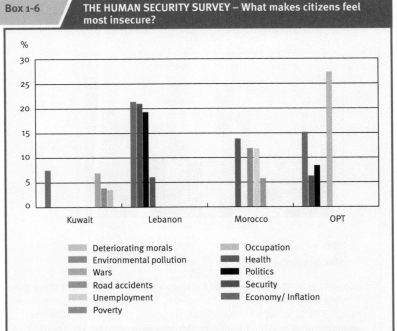

Deteriorating morals
Environmental pollution
Wars
Road accidents
Unemployment
Poverty

Occupation
Health
Politics
Security
Economy/ Inflation

To determine how secure Arab citizens feel, the respondents were asked to specify the most important sources of threat, for themselves personally. In all four countries, economic conditions were viewed as a threat to security. However, in the Occupied Palestinian Territory, foreign occupation ranked as the most serious threat, followed by deteriorating economic conditions, deteriorating political conditions, and a lack of personal security. In Lebanon, concern over the economy took first place, followed by a lack of personal security and deteriorating political conditions. In Morocco, by contrast, the sources of threat were less directly linked to political conditions. Instead, health conditions came first in importance, followed by poverty and unemployment, then traffic accidents. Economic threats and war or external threats were given first place by Kuwaiti respondents, followed by environmental pollution and deteriorating morals.

Poor nutrition did not figure directly among the most significant threats felt by citizens in the four countries although it may have been implied in references to poverty and unemployment, given that these latter phenomena reduce the ability to obtain food.

Polling Arab views on human security

In order to supplement its quantitative assessments, the team investigated Arab citizens' personal views on human security by means of a questionnaire, designed and distributed with the help of opinion-polling organisations in four Arab states that represent a range of political and cultural contexts for human security. These were (1) Morocco, considered to have gone farther than any other Arab state along the path of political emancipation, (2) Lebanon, which combines political emancipation with sharp sectarian divisions that have erupted more than once into civil war, (3) Kuwait, which reflects a distinctive culture, and whose citizens enjoy one of the highest levels of affluence in the Arab countries, and (4) the Occupied Palestinian Territory, which still languishes under Israeli occupation.

In each of the four countries, the questionnaire was administered to a sample of one thousand individuals who had been randomly selected in such a way as to represent a variety of age groups and educational and economic levels while also providing a representative cross-section in terms of gender, ethnicity, and geographical location. The questions revolved around the perception of security, the sources of threat to such security, the relative seriousness and importance of these threats, respondents' opinions of state efforts to confront these threats, and what more they believed should be done to confront them.

The questionnaire addressed eight aspects[14] of human security: the concept; environmental security; security in its political and global dimensions; security in society (relations among groups); economic security; nutritional security; health security; and personal safety.

How young Arabs see human security—the youth forums

The report team organized three discussion forums[15] with young Arabs between the ages of eighteen and twenty-five, all of whom had track records as civil society activists.

These young people made important contributions to the discussions, reference

The Report team investigated Arab citizens' personal views on human security

for instance, to combine the threats that result from deteriorating environmental conditions with those that result from civil wars. If it were decided to weight various human security threats differently, it would be virtually impossible to reach agreement on the specific values to attach to each, and the results would remain arbitrary.

It was for reasons such as these that the report team discontinued attempts to construct a single composite indicator of human security in Arab countries. Instead, it elected to assess discretely the various dimensions of human security as they apply to individual Arab countries in order to capture important differences among the Arab states.

to which will be made throughout the chapters of the present report. The most important included how they conceptualized human security and how they prioritized threats to human security in the region. The majority of the participants from both the Arab East and the Arab West agreed that the concept of human security is a comprehensive one with multiple dimensions, including the political, the economic, the environmental, and the physical, and that it differs from one context to another. Contributions reflected a high level of awareness of the complexity of the concept and the interdependence among its various components. As such, participants were able to draw connections among the various levels and dimensions of human security.

Similarly, the young people demonstrated awareness of the distinctions between the concept's subjective and objective dimensions. As they saw it, the concept of human security involves a dual notion which is related to a balanced relationship between moral and material dimensions. The points of contrast among participants' perspectives on the concept revolved around the question of whether it encompasses the individual, the state, or the external environment, with some holding that the concept of human security is a personal concept that relates to the individual's right to exercise civil rights, to obtain shelter and food, and to have access to such things in a democratic setting.

Expressing the modern outlook of many young Arabs, some participants believed that human security in the Arab countries should mean being able to choose between different options and having the opportunity to contribute to society, without being subjected to social or political pressures. Another team expressed the view that human security has to do with the state, that is, with the latter guaranteeing and respecting the rights of individuals by providing educational and employment opportunities and by ensuring the security of those who take part in political activities. Others thought of human security in terms of a global model that concerns not just Arab countries, but human beings wherever they happen to be. The main feature of this global model is that it guarantees

human freedom within a framework of responsibility.

Some believed that the subjective aspect of human security is more important than its objective dimensions while others argued the opposite case. Still another group thought that the moral and material dimensions of human security are inseparable, pointing, for example, to the link between human dignity, awareness of one's rights, and a sense of freedom on the one hand, and sound legal systems and stable economic conditions on the other. This group also observed that an individual's psychological security affects his or her social, cultural, and intellectual security, and is itself affected by whether or not basic needs are being met. Similarly, security was linked with other values such as those of freedom, dignity, and peace, and the effect these have on education, health and the economy. A consensus emerged that human beings should be able to live in a threat-free environment which provides them with dignity, a suitable standard of living, and freedom.

Most participants had difficulty prioritizing threats to human security. In all three forums, they took the view that all dimensions of life involve potential sources of threat to human security in the Arab countries, and that all dimensions of human security are interlinked and interdependent.

Conclusion

As this chapter emphasizes, the concept of human security has particular relevance to Arab countries at this juncture. Yet valuable as the concept is, it is not free from ambiguities, notably as it relates to considerations of state security, a fact that can open it to appropriation for questionable ends. The concept can—and has—been used as another means to license foreign interference, including military intervention, in the affairs of sovereign states, as the cases of Iraq and, to some extent, Somalia illustrate. The so-called war on terror has at times provided spurious justification for such interference. In a review of national human development reports and the human security framework, two international scholars have discussed how the principles of human

The Report team organized three discussion forums with young Arabs

The concept of human security has particular relevance to Arab countries at this juncture

security can be distorted when the concept is hijacked to serve vested interests. They conclude:

"In the post-9/11 security environment, this concept has effectively been turned on its head... Whereas the goal of human security has been the empowerment of people and communities, the same cannot be said for initiatives undertaken in the name of human security in the post-9/11 world."[16]

A concept should not be judged by its abuse but by the positive contribution it can make to the public and private good. This Report believes that human security offers a strong framework for addressing threats to human development by promoting freedom from fear and freedom from want.[17] Thus, this Report agrees with Jolly and Ray that when "the human security of people in other countries is largely ignored, this approach to human security must be judged as seriously unbalanced and far from the basic concept. Human security properly conceived is not a zero-sum calculation—the attainment of security by one party cannot come at the expense of the security of another party."[18]

In light of the understanding of the concept of human security discussed in this chapter, this Report does not aim merely to list the various types of threats to which Arabs are vulnerable. Rather, the objective

is to examine the roots of these threats and to suggest strategies for coping with them. Moreover, there is no predisposition in its analysis either against or for Arab governments; rather, this Report addresses itself openly to both governments and enlightened Arab public opinion. Given the supreme importance of this subject to the well being of the Arab peoples, it hopes its analysis and findings will be taken up, discussed and applied by policy makers and civil society alike.

The chapters that follow set out the challenges that confront human security in the Arab countries within their historical context, recognizing them to be the outcome of specific conditions that prevail in the region at the present time. However, there is no reason to believe that such conditions are permanent or inevitable. On the contrary, they can undoubtedly change if the relevant Arab players summon the resolve to envision and test their scope of influence within their particular circumstances and those that prevail regionally and internationally. This Report draws encouragement from the experiences of other peoples of the world, particularly in those developing countries that have faced situations similar to those that challenge the Arab countries in the opening decade of the 21st Century.

Endnotes

1   Annan 2000.
2   Commission on Human Security 2003 (in Arabic).
3   Commission on Human Security 2003 (in Arabic).
4   Korany 2005a, 2005b.
5   El-Baradei 2006.
6   Abdel Samad 2004.
7   Abdel Samad and Zeidan 2007.
8   Korany 2005a, 2005b.
9   Bajpai 2000.
10   Bajpai 2000.
11   Foreign Policy Magazine 2008.
12   The Pew Global Project Attitudes 2007.
13   Inglehart et al 2008.
14   See Annex III.
15   The first forum, held in Cairo on 15-16 December, 2007, brought together thirty young men and women from Djibouti, Egypt, the Sudan, and Somalia. The second, held in Amman on 11-12 January, 2008, involved thirty-one young men and women from Bahrain, Iraq, Jordan, Lebanon, the Occupied Palestinian Territory, Saudi Arabia, Syria, the United Arab Emirates, and Yemen. The third forum, held in Cairo on 8-9 February, 2008, brought together a number of young men from Algeria, Libya, Mauritania, Morocco, and Tunisia. Participants were chosen by the UNDP office in Beirut and the report team to provide a balanced representation in terms of gender, nationality, major capitals, regional cities, and professional backgrounds, with an age range of eighteen to twenty-five years. The discussions held by these young people revolved around the same five major questions addressed by the country survey.
16   Jolly and Basu Ray 2006.
17   In this context, the authors recall US President Franklin Delano Roosevelt's 1941 Congressional Address in which he articulated his Four Freedoms: freedom of speech and of religion and freedom from want and from fear. This celebrated formulation influenced both the UN Charter and the Universal Declaration of Human Rights; in fact, the second pair of freedoms anticipated the human security approach.
18   Jolly and Basu Ray 2006.

Chapter 2

The environment, resource pressures and human security in the Arab countries

The relationship between resource pressures, environmental sustainability and human security is a matter of utmost importance

In this chapter, the authors illustrate that the relationship between resource pressures, environmental sustainability and human security in the Arab countries is a matter of utmost importance. Oil, the resource most commonly associated with the region, has generated untold riches and power for some yet disempowered many more and left entire societies vulnerable to geopolitics. Despite this source of wealth, the region will increasingly face tremendous challenges to the security of its population, in terms of physical survival and access to jobs, income, food and health services. Potential conflicts originating in competition for dwindling natural resources may heavily strain relations among communities, populations and states, Arab or non-Arab. These challenges will result from population and demographic pressures, the overexploitation of land, water shortages, desertification, pollution and climate change. Such threats may appear less formidable than those examined in other chapters yet their effects are often irrevocable, more damaging and more extensive. Thus, they constitute an appropriate starting point in the report's analysis.

A mixed endowment

The natural environment of the Arab countries is both a blessing and a curse

The natural environment of the Arab countries is both a blessing and a curse. It is a blessing because the region's location and natural endowments enabled it to play a leading role in past civilisations: enabled the three religions that arose there to spread throughout the world; and enabled the Arab peoples to establish contact with, learn from, and enrich other civilisations. This environment also includes some of the world's largest known oil reserves whose exploitation has facilitated an extraordinary transfer of wealth to certain Arab societies, especially the Gulf States, that has affected every aspect of material, social and cultural life. However, while this environment still offers theoretically extensive prospects for Arab human development, should Arabs interact with it more prudently, it is also in some respects a curse. This same environment suffers critical water deficits and is largely arid. It is subject to population pressures, the over-exploitation of resources and rapid urbanization, which contribute to its degradation.

The most significant challenges

The following review treats the most important environmental threats in the Arab countries. It considers population and demographic pressures as a major cross-cutting issue present in each area of threat. These threats include, water shortages, desertification, pollution, and climate change. A key aspect to these environmental threats is the dynamic, interactive relationship among them. Water shortages, for example, contribute to desertification, while climate change may lead to floods in some areas and to worsened water shortages, drought and desertification in others. Similarly, air pollution is an underlying cause of climate change.

Environmental threats include water shortages, desertification, pollution and climate change

Population pressures and demographic trends

For most of the latter half of the 20th century, the Arab countries had one of the highest population growth rates in the world.[1] From 1975-1980, the total fertility rate (TFR) of the region was 6.5, meaning that the average Arab woman living to the end of her childbearing years would give birth to six or seven children. This rate declined to 3.6 in 2000-2005, a rate that is still higher than the population replacement rate of 2.1. Such a high TFR has contributed to a high population growth rate, although declining from 3.2 per cent per year for 1970-1975 to 2.1 per cent per year for 2000-2005. For the period 2005-

---

Box 2-1   **MOSTAFA KAMAL TOLBA* – Core environmental challenges in the region**

We have entered the 21st century facing most of the high-priority environmental challenges that confronted us in the latter half of the twentieth century, with only differences of intensity and priority. These include: water shortages and deteriorating water quality, land constraints, desertification, the environmental effect of increasing energy production and consumption, the pollution of coastal areas, forest loss, unwise consumption of natural resources, deteriorating urban environments, and the spread of pollution resulting from dangerous solid and liquid wastes.

A new problem which has emerged is the lack of rigour in the use of modern economic tools such as environment-based and natural wealth-based economics and accounting. To this we must add the acute negative effects of global environmental problems, foremost among them climate change and global warming.

Water scarcity, a problem exacerbated by the spread of water pollution, remains one of the most significant challenges to the Arab countries. It calls for concentrated effort in the absence of ideal methods for regulating the use of surface, ground and river water, increasing the economic return yielded per unit of water used, and overcoming the problem of decentralized responsibility for the implementation of water and land management policies. Because this responsibility is divided among a large number of institutions and ministries, it is essential to establish an autonomous institutional entity with sole responsibility for water resource management. Only such an institution can achieve the ideal balance between supply and demand on a sound socio-economic basis. In addition, serious work needs to be done to localize water desalinisation technology in the region, particularly for the local production of reverse osmosis membranes, and to develop means of using solar energy in the desalinisation process.

Still another challenge for us is a shortage of land resources, in that 54.8 per cent of the region's total area is considered 'empty'. Pastureland makes up 26.8 per cent, arable land 14.5 per cent, forests approximately 3.9 per cent, and cultivated land approximately 29 per cent of all arable land, or approximately 4.2 per cent of the Arab region's total land area. The Arab countries' forests, more than 80 per cent of which are located in Sudan, Algeria, and Morocco, cover approximately 3.9 per cent of its total land area. These forests are being subjected to increasing pressures, and are being lost at an annual rate of 1.59 per cent. At the same time, economic activity is increasing in coastal areas in the region, particularly urban and industrial expansion. Consequently, seacoast areas in Arab states, which are inhabited by 40 to 50 per cent of their populations, are being threatened by pollution from petroleum and heavy elements.

In terms of climate change, the Arab region's share of greenhouse gas emissions is still negligible, although per capita emissions are rising, especially in crowded cities. Inevitably, however, Arab states will suffer numerous negative consequences resulting from climate change.

These environmental issues can only be confronted through scientific research and serious technological development. Moreover, no one Arab state alone can undertake these tasks single-handedly. A serious beginning thus needs to be made on creating networks of specialized research centres in these critical areas for the purpose of distributing roles and sharing expertise in order to develop a menu of alternative solutions from which decision makers in the various Arab states may choose.

* Former Executive Director of the United Nations Environment Programme (UNEP).

2010, the population of the Arab region is projected to grow by 2.0 per cent per year, and, over 2010-2015, the projection is 1.9 per cent per year. This is nearly double the world average for these periods, 1.2 per cent and 1.1 per cent, respectively.[2] Taking into account existing population momentum, the UN estimates that the Arab countries will be home to some 385 million people by 2015 (compared to about 331 million in 2007, and 172 million in 1980).[3] In a region where water and arable land are increasingly very scarce, population growth at these rates will still put intense pressures on the carrying capacity of Arab lands and further threaten environmental sustainability.

With more mouths to feed, countries that have come to depend on food imports as a result of water shortages and

UN estimates indicate the Arab countries will be home to some 385 million people by 2015

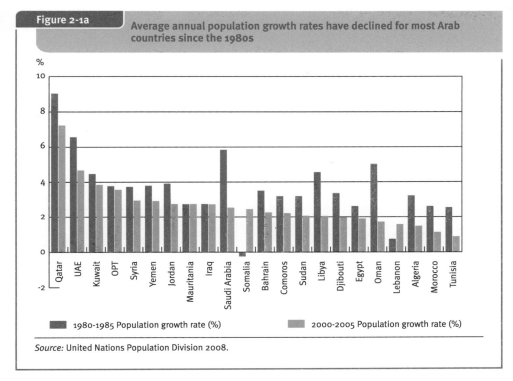

Figure 2-1a Average annual population growth rates have declined for most Arab countries since the 1980s

■ 1980-1985 Population growth rate (%)   ■ 2000-2005 Population growth rate (%)

Source: United Nations Population Division 2008.

Population growth at these rates will still put intense pressure on the carrying capacity of Arab lands

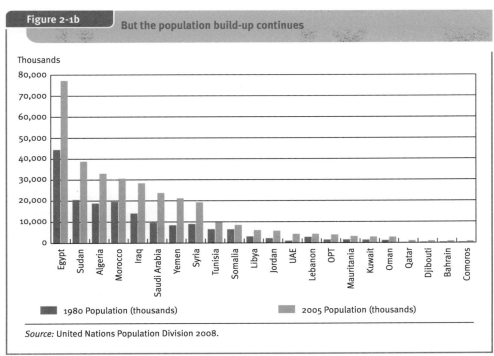

Figure 2-1b But the population build-up continues

■ 1980 Population (thousands)   ■ 2005 Population (thousands)

Source: United Nations Population Division 2008.

spreading urbanization will find their trade balances and economic growth options increasingly affected. The growth of Arab cities and towns poses particular challenges. Accelerating urban drift in the region is straining already-overstretched infrastructure and creating overcrowded, unhealthy and insecure living conditions in many cities. In 1970, 38 per cent of the Arab population was urban. By 2005 this had grown to 55 per cent, and it is likely to surpass 60 per cent by 2020.[4]

The most evident and challenging aspect of the region's demographic profile is its 'youth bulge'. Young people are the fastest growing segment of Arab populations. Some 60 per cent of the population is under 25 years, making this one of the most youthful regions in the world, with a median age of 22 years compared to a global average of 28.[5] Young people consume resources and require large investments before they become economically productive. They also represent

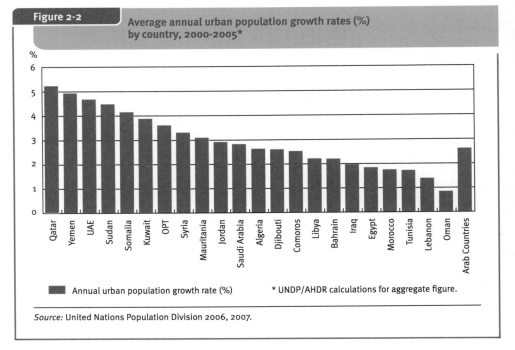

Figure 2-2 — Average annual urban population growth rates (%) by country, 2000-2005*

■ Annual urban population growth rate (%)   * UNDP/AHDR calculations for aggregate figure.

Source: United Nations Population Division 2006, 2007.

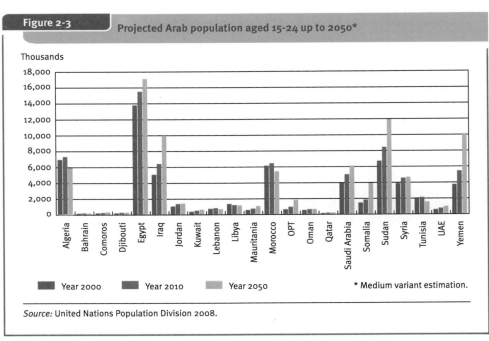

Figure 2-3 — Projected Arab population aged 15-24 up to 2050*

■ Year 2000   ■ Year 2010   ■ Year 2050   * Medium variant estimation.

Source: United Nations Population Division 2008.

coming generations with the right to an environmental inheritance that has not been overdrawn or mismanaged by their predecessors.

Water scarcity

Arab countries suffer from a scarcity of water resources because most of them are in arid or semi-arid regions. The situation is becoming more severe owing to the continual increase in withdrawal under pressure of demographic and economic growth. Permanent rivers are the main source of surface water in the Arab countries, followed by springs, riverbeds, and seasonal rivers.

Total available water in the Arab countries is estimated at 300 billion cubic meters per year.[6] Total available surface water resources in the Arab countries are estimated at 277 billion cubic meters per year,[7] only 43 per cent of which originates within the Arab countries, the rest elsewhere. External surface water resources shared with neighbouring countries outside the region account for approximately 57 per cent of the total available surface water in the region.

The major international rivers in the region are shared between countries lying both within and beyond the region, and include the following: the Tigris and the Euphrates, both shared by Iraq, Syria and Turkey; the Orontes (or Assi), shared by Lebanon, Syria and Turkey; the Jordan (including the Yarmouk), shared by Jordan, OPT, Israel and Syria; and the Nile, with nine riparian parties of which only Sudan and Egypt are Arab countries. Years of effort have yielded the establishment of formal agreements (such as the Nile Basin Initiative) on the management of shared water resources. However, most are partial, ineffective and inequitable in terms of the full spectrum of riparian rights. At the regional and interregional levels, cooperation on water usage and management is heavily affected by prevailing political tensions and ongoing conflicts. Tensions have emerged on sharing resources as the needs of the riparian countries are increasing.[8]

Underground water reserves in the Arab countries are estimated at 7,734 billion cubic metres, while the amount of water being fed into these reserves is estimated

at no more than 42 billion cubic metres annually over the various regions; that available for use is no more than 35 billion cubic metres annually. The greatest and most abundant renewable reserve in the Arab countries is in North and East Africa (Algeria, Egypt, Libya, Morocco, Somalia, Sudan, and Tunisia).[9]

Aquifers are groundwater systems that are often the only source of fresh water, particularly in regions with arid and semi-arid climatic conditions (as in some Arab countries), and represent a vital guarantee of both national and regional water security. At the regional level, some cross-national groundwater aquifers are renewable, including the aquifers underlying the border areas between Syria and Turkey; Israel and Lebanon; Jordan and Syria; Iraq and Syria; and Israel and the West Bank. Others are non-renewable aquifers containing fossil water, including the Nubian sandstone aquifer underlying Chad, Egypt and Libya; the basalt aquifer underlying Jordan and Saudi Arabia; and that underlying the Arabian Peninsula shared by Iraq, Jordan and Syria. Additional deep non-renewable aquifers underlie Iraq, Kuwait and Saudi Arabia; Jordan and Iraq; and Iraq and Syria. Although the water in some of these aquifers is partially sufficient to meet freshwater demand, the quality varies greatly owing to the level of salinity in the shallow renewable aquifers, and in the case of deep non-renewable aquifers, due to the variation in amounts of total dissolved solids (TDS).

Water scarcity is becoming more severe

Tensions have emerged on sharing resources as the needs of the riparian countries are increasing

As water becomes scarce relative to demand, transboundary competition for shared rivers and other water resources will grow. Without institutional mechanisms to respond to these transboundary problems, competition has the potential to lead to disruptive conflicts. The spectre of growing competition for water between states has generated a sometimes polarized public debate. Some predict a future of "water wars" as states assert rival claims to water. Others point out that there have been no wars over water since an event some 4,000 years ago in what is now southern Iraq—and that countries have usually responded to transboundary water competition through cooperation rather than conflict. From this more optimistic perspective, rising competition is seen as a catalyst for deeper cooperation in the future... water has the potential to fuel wider conflicts but also to act as a bridge for cooperation.

Source: UNDP 2006b.

| Figure 2-4 | Arab internal freshwater resources are often below scarcity levels and the world average, 2005 |

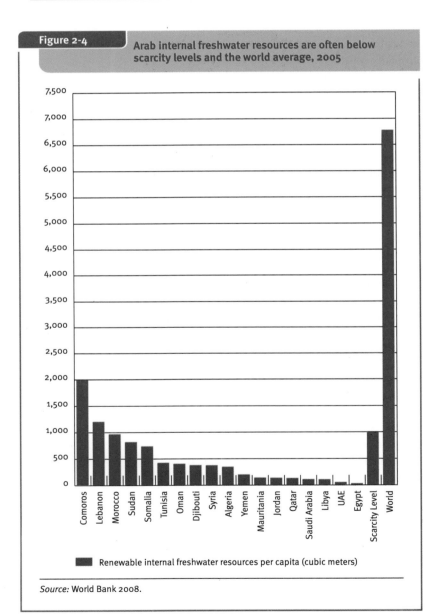

Renewable internal freshwater resources per capita (cubic meters)

Source: World Bank 2008.

On the transboundary level, any disruption of the aquifer in any of these countries can have a damaging impact on the groundwater resources in the adjacent countries in terms of quantity and/or quality of water. These transboundary implications may not be immediately apparent, but may nevertheless be very hard to reverse. Over-pumping from groundwater reserves is often carried out to meet the demands of population growth, agricultural development and industrial needs. This harms the future viability and productivity of the aquifers and, in coastal areas, may result in the intrusion of seawater into the aquifer as a consequence of the formation of large cones of depression. Poor distribution and heavy demand, especially of ground resources, characterize water use in the Arab countries. This leads to a lack of clean water for much of the population and the waste of significant amounts in the agriculture, industry and tourism sectors.[10]

Many sources refer to the dimensions of the water crisis in the region. The Joint Arab Economic Report (JAER) [11] of 2001 confirmed that the region had actually entered a stage of water poverty that, at the time, was the worst in the world based on available per capita renewable water resources. The report estimated these resources at 265 billion cubic metres, or approximately 1,000 cubic metres per capita. The worldwide per capita share was seven times that. The report stated that an increasing population's demand for water would reduce per capita share to 460 cubic metres by 2025, lower than the extreme water poverty level according to international classifications. What is even more worrying is that these rates would be accurate if these amounts of water were usable. However, much of the water is located far from areas of consumption, making container and transportation costs economically impractical either for drinking or for agricultural and industrial uses.

The global HDR 2006 confirms this, pointing to the ballooning of the water problem in Arab countries with the reduction of average water availability by more than one-fourth.[12] That report agrees with the JAER that per capita share in the Arab countries will drop by almost 500 cubic metres, while more than 90 per cent of

Figure 2-5

Use of withdrawn water in Arab countries (%) by sector, 1999-2006*

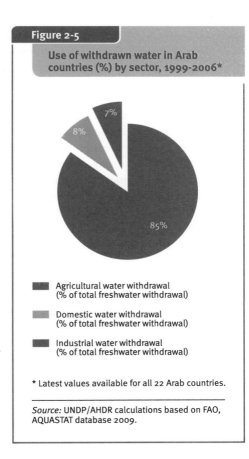

- ■ Agricultural water withdrawal (% of total freshwater withdrawal)
- ■ Domestic water withdrawal (% of total freshwater withdrawal)
- ■ Industrial water withdrawal (% of total freshwater withdrawal)

* Latest values available for all 22 Arab countries.

Source: UNDP/AHDR calculations based on FAO, AQUASTAT database 2009.

Table 2-1	Levels of water stress in thirteen Arab countries, 2006		
Critical water stress (More than 10,000 persons per million cubic metres)	**Serious water stress** (Between 5,000 and 10,000 persons per million cubic metres)	**Significant water stress** (Between 2,500 and 5,000 persons per million cubic metres)	**Slight water stress** (Less than 2,500 persons per million cubic metres)
Kuwait	Bahrain	Jordan	Egypt
UAE	Iraq	Saudi Arabia	Lebanon
	Occupied Palestinian Territory		Oman
	Qatar		Syria
	Yemen		

Source: UN-ESCWA 2007.

Alleviating water scarcity

Arab governments have certainly exerted great efforts to supply drinking water and water for economic uses to their citizens. As a result of such efforts, coverage of water needs of the Arab people increased from 83 per cent in 1990 to 85 per cent in 2004, bearing in mind that this population increased from 180.1 million to 231.8 million during the same period.[16] Although there is no magical cure for the increasingly grave problem of water scarcity in the Arab countries, studies give some broad outlines of the steps that can be taken to minimise the potential threat. These include:[17]

1. Optimization of water allocation among the three domains (agricultural, industrial, domestic).
2. Implementation of an optimal water productivity strategy that leads to the import of water through virtual water.[18]
3. Holistic and integrated approaches to water resources supply and demand planning and management.
4. Capacity building and technical upgrading of all stakeholders.
5. Awareness-raising at all levels, from end-users to decision-makers.
6. Issuing and implementing sustainable water policies based on the above points and on current and prospective water data and research.
7. Development of water resources management models that can simulate different solution scenarios to select the optimal approach.

the population will be in countries suffering from a water shortage. The same report stated that while the water deficit lessened relatively quickly from 1990 to 2004 in other parts of the world, the rate of reduction was the slowest in the Arab countries. In the foreseeable future, much of the population of the region will suffer from water stress, obtaining less than 1,700 cubic metres of water annually, while many others will experience a water shortage, receiving less than 1,000 cubic metres annually.[13]

A report from the UN Economic and Social Commission for Western Asia (UN-ESCWA)[14] applies the question of water stress to that national level in the Arab states.[15] It distinguishes between four levels of water stress as gauged by the ratio of population to renewable freshwater— slight, significant, serious and critical. As shown in Table 2.1, the study shows that four countries are facing "slight" water stress, two are facing "significant" water stress, five are facing "serious" water stress, and two – Kuwait and the UAE – are facing "critical" water stress.

Much of the population of the region will suffer from water stress, and many others will experience a water shortage

Steps can be taken to minimise the potential threats

The creeping desert

Across the various geological epochs, the climate of the Arab countries has fluctuated between dry and humid eras, the former leading to the creation of the Great Sahara in North Africa and the Empty Quarter in the Arabian Peninsula. The humid periods having ended some millennia ago, the region has long been prey to a dry climate conducive to desertification. This climate is characterised by repeated protracted or short periods of drought, declining precipitation rates, irregular rainfall and torrential rains, high temperatures, frequent heat waves and protracted daily and annual highs; and harsh winds consisting mainly of continental over maritime prevailing winds. Such variations, both ancient and modern, contributed to fragile ecosystems in arid and semi-arid areas which are characterised by sparse

Desertification is a peril in the region

vegetation and a prevalence of shallow, undeveloped topsoil structurally vulnerable to wind and water erosion.[19] Table 2.2 shows the annual precipitation per capita across the region.

Desertification is a peril in the region. It is formally defined as "land degradation in arid, semi-arid, and dry sub-humid areas resulting from various factors, including climatic variations and human activities."[21] This definition is the basis of the United Nations Convention to Combat Desertification (UNCCD). Environmentalists distinguish between two degrees of desertification: land that had once been under cultivation or vegetation but is now completely desertified; and land under cultivation or vegetation on which soil degradation will result in desertification unless preventive action is taken.

A joint LAS-UNEP study[22] estimates that the highest ratio of desert to total land area is in the Arabian Peninsula (nine-tenths or 89.6 per cent). This is followed by North Africa (over three-fourths of the land or 77.7 per cent), the Nile Valley and the Horn of Africa (less than a half or 44.5 per cent) and the Mashreq (35.6 per cent).

Ongoing desertification threatens about 2.87 million square kilometres or a fifth of the total area of the Arab countries. Here the ratios proceed in the opposite direction to the preceding figures, with 48.6 per cent of the land area in the Mashreq facing the peril, 28.6 per cent in the Nile Valley and the Horn of Africa, 16.5 per cent in North Africa, and 9 per cent in the Arabian Peninsula.[23] The amounts of desertified land or land threatened by desertification vary greatly from one country to another within these regions. In North Africa, for example, they are the greatest in Libya and the least in Tunisia; in the Nile Valley-Horn of Africa region, they are the greatest in Egypt and Djibouti and the least in Somalia; and in the Mashreq they are the greatest in Jordan and the least in Syria. In the Arabian Peninsula, Bahrain, Kuwait, Qatar, and the U.A.E. are the most affected countries and together form the most desertified area in the Arab region, in contrast with Syria, which is the least desertified.

The most apparent impacts of desertification are aridity due to the depletion of groundwater or subterranean water

Table 2-2 Precipitation in the Arab countries, long term annual average[20]	
Country	**Precipitation in cubic meters per capita**
Mauritania	31,099.60
Sudan	27,678.10
Somalia	21,322.30
Libya	16,311.60
Oman	10,446.40
Algeria	6,341.60
Djibouti	6,230.80
Saudi Arabia	5,355.00
Morocco	4,918.60
Yemen	4,064.40
Tunisia	3,554.50
Comoros	3,259.40
Syria	2,406.30
Jordan	1,793.00
Lebanon	1,701.50
United Arab Emirates	1,536.80
Qatar	987.4
Kuwait	830.9
Egypt	693
Bahrain	79.8

Source: UNDP/AHDR calculations based on UNSD 2007.

Note: Precipitation refers to the total volume of atmospheric wet deposition (rain, snow, hail, dew, etc.) falling on the territory of the country over one year, in millions of cubic metres.

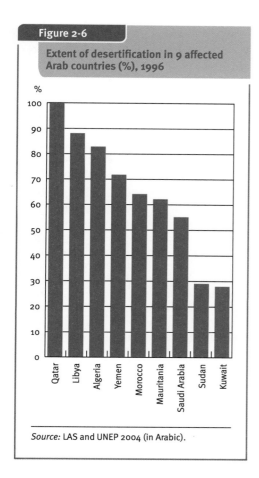

Figure 2-6

Extent of desertification in 9 affected Arab countries (%), 1996

Source: LAS and UNEP 2004 (in Arabic).

Changing social systems: Large portions of the population of the Arab countries, particularly in arid and semi-arid areas, once engaged in nomadic or semi-nomadic pastoral or crop-gathering lifestyles. However from the 19th century in some countries and the mid-20th century in others, these populations gradually became sedentary. The transition from one lifestyle to the other in many cases brought with it overgrazing, tree-felling, and unregulated use of the soil in both rain-fed and irrigated agriculture, together contributing to despoliation of vegetation and soil degradation and erosion.

Changes in the mode of agricultural production: As traditional modes of production failed to meet the needs of the growing population, modern agricultural tools and technologies were increasingly brought into play. Many of these technologies, particularly in ploughing, are inappropriate to arid and semi-arid lands as they cause soil to decompose and disintegrate, rendering it vulnerable to erosion.

Box 2.5 illustrates how some of these trends have contributed to desertification in Algeria, (Ali Ghazi, in French, background paper for the report). In addition, the UNEP study summarizes the impact of human activities on desertification in the region as follows: [25]

Desertification results from harmful activities undertaken by humans

resources, shrinking forest areas and their further degradation through felling, cattle-raising, burning, and the loss of soil fertility and composition in arid lands.

The Arab countries' large proportion of desert land is due in large part to the arid natural endowment of the region, but is not solely the product of natural causes. It can also result from harmful activities undertaken by humans who, for the most part, are unaware of the detrimental impact of their activities on the natural environment. A study by the Arab Organization for Agricultural Development has attributed the causes of desertification in the Arab countries to the following developments:[24]

Demographic explosion: The enormous growth in population, its mounting needs, its increasing use of modern technologies and methods in cultivation, and the overexploitation of the earth's various resources have greatly weakened the rejuvenating capacities of the region's ecosystems, distorted the environmental equilibrium, and propelled it towards degradation.

Box 2-4   West of Sudan: economic and social costs of desertification

In the western provinces of Darfur and Kordofan, competition over pastureland erupted into tribal warfare on a scale that led to international intervention. Among the foremost factors aggravating the fighting in this region were scarcity of rainfall, the population explosion, and changes in the prevailing social system from nomadic shepherding or crop gathering to sedentary agriculture. These factors augmented rates of soil degradation and desertification. In addition, cropland was expanded at the expense of natural pasturage while modern tools and equipment were employed in ploughing, transportation, and other agricultural processes, resulting in the decomposition, disintegration and erosion of the soil structure. To this list should be added the destruction of the natural vegetation through the felling of trees and uprooting of shrubs for fuel and manufacturing, wasteful over-irrigation, and the unsustainable use of land in both rain-fed and irrigated agriculture. All these factors, individually or combined, are conducive to desertifying forces such as water or wind erosion, the exposure of the subsoil rock strata and the salinisation or over-saturation of the soil.

Source: Dia El-Din El-Quosy, in Arabic, background paper for the report.

Box 2-5 | **Desertification in Algeria**

About 44 per cent, or more than 9 million hectares, of cultivated land in Algeria is now at risk of primary or secondary degree desertification. This threat is primarily attributed to the transition from traditional modes of animal husbandry and agriculture to modern systems. For example, in the past, severe drought waves would kill off large numbers of livestock, thereby alleviating pressure on available pasturage. While it is true that land reclamation operations were introduced to offset the effects of the transition, these were restricted to the lower altitudes where the soil was deeper and more humid.

For centuries, land management had been subject to long established social regulations that enabled generation after generation of rural societies to know the entitlements bequeathed to them. However the inherited system of land management that had been in harmony with nature quickly fell under the pressures of social, political, and economic change in Algeria, the roots of which are to be found in:

- The rapid growth of the population from around 11 million in the 1960's (10,800,000 in year 1960) to around 33 million in the first years of the third millennium (32,854,000 in year 2005). This tripling of the population, despite the decline in annual growth rate from 3.2 per cent to 2.3 per cent, has generated enormous pressures on the environment. Simultaneously, increased rates of urbanisation have increased the demand for meat, which, in turn, has driven an expansion in the area of land cultivated to meet this demand.

- The use of inappropriate agricultural methods and machinery. In particular, the disk ploughs used in land reclamation, while appearing efficient, render vast tracts of land easy prey to wind erosion because of the way they break up the top soil.

- The impossibility of alleviating the pressures on pastureland. While the increases in flocks owing to advances in veterinary medicine may have come to the temporary aid of herdsmen, these increases have also come at the expense of the regeneration of the pasturage. This development also coincides with the emergence of a class of large, mainly urban-based livestock farmers whose wealth enables them to overcome water shortages, and deal with the need to move herds from one place to another. The large livestock farmers, who were drawn to this activity because it is lucrative, are displacing the poor shepherds and farmers who do not possess the wherewithal to care for their flocks or fields.

As a result of such conditions, Algeria is losing some 7,000 hectares a year to desertification. If urgent remedial action is not taken, the rate of loss could double or triple.

Source: Ali Ghazi, in French, background paper for the report.

- Degradation and desertification of pastureland.
- Deterioration of forests.
- Degradation of the soil due to land mismanagement.
- Attrition of subterranean aquifers.
- Water shortages and waste of water.
- Incursion of saline water.
- Pollution of the soil.
- Inappropriate irrigation systems.

Confronting the deserts

In spite of the challenging natural endowment of the region and the complicating factors of human impact, continued desertification is not inevitable. Equipped with information on its specific causes in each Arab climatic ecological region, Arab governments and societies can adopt the appropriate policies to halt it. Based on background papers carried out for this Report, the following sets of policy objectives can provide orientation to combat desertification in the three major zones of the region:

In countries that depend on *both irrigation and rainfall* for agriculture, policies should aim to:
- Strengthen infrastructure through the construction of dams, reservoirs, canals, drainage systems, and road and electricity networks.
- Halt overgrazing in pastoral areas and tree felling in forested areas.
- Reduce the use of non-biodegradable pesticides, such as DDT, to the lowest possible levels.
- Promote the use of conventional and non-conventional means to prevent sand dune encroachment.
- Install precipitation gauges throughout the country and abroad and import and set up early warning systems to enable people to prepare for and take the appropriate precautions against high floods.
- Designate permanent and inviolable boundaries for the waterbeds of the major river courses and prohibit the

Continued desertification is not inevitable

use of the floodplains within these boundaries during all flooding seasons, low, medium, and high.

- Engage civil society organisations in the design and execution of anti-desertification projects and in the recruitment of volunteers to help government agencies in emergencies.
- Train and build the capacities of those involved in combating desertification and also raise the capacities of the general public in this domain, drawing and building on indigenous knowledge and expertise.

In countries dependent *solely on irrigation* for agriculture, policies should aim to:

- Curb the effects of sand-carrying winds through windbreaks made of trees or solid materials and stabilise sand dunes by means of sand fences using plant materials, petrochemical sprays, or rubber blocks.
- Halt urban encroachment onto agricultural land by allocating desert land for the construction of public and private edifices, especially in towns and cities that back onto the desert.
- Promote agricultural drainage projects. Attention should extend beyond the implementation of such projects to continual monitoring and maintenance.
- Develop new water resources in order to keep up with the exponential growth of the population and its demands on clean water for domestic and public purposes and to meet the needs of industry, domestic navigation, tourism, electricity generation, and environmental preservation. In particular, attention should be devoted to collective Nile Valley projects to minimize water losses in the Upper Nile and to develop subterranean water resources, rain harvesting technologies, and water desalinisation research and technology.
- Take precautions against the anticipated effects of the rising sea level on the land and subterranean water reservoirs in the Delta. Scenarios should be drawn up to anticipate all possibilities so that the country is not forced to contend with this phenomenon unprepared.

(Dia El-Din El-Quosy, in Arabic, background paper for the report.)

Countries dependent on *rain-fed agriculture* should endeavour to:

- Adopt a strict and sustained land management policy that comprises diverse plans for soil usage.
- Intensify efforts aimed at combating desertification, especially in the depressions behind dams and in the plains areas.
- Stimulate agricultural extension services addressing, specifically, such concerns as crop rotation and the use of appropriate farming technologies. Care should be taken to attune these services to the social and cultural conditions of the farmers.
- Draw up long-range plans well in advance of the construction of dams and reservoirs so as to enable the relevant agencies to take the appropriate measures to protect the steep basins behind these dams and reservoirs five to ten years before their construction.
- Record the types of existing plants with an eye to identifying and protecting them, and eventually to diversifying them or selecting strains with particular characteristics for reproduction.
- Identify the areas most vulnerable to desertification so that they can be prioritised in anti-desertification programmes.
- Promote continued forestry research aimed at sustaining existing forests and woodlands and using their products rationally.
- Intensify reforestation efforts, particularly those taking place within the framework of national reforestation plans.
- Promote all appropriate means to support and protect forests and woodlands.

(Ali Ghazi, in French, background paper for the report.)

Pollution: no grounds for complacency

With the Arab region's quickly increasing population and pressured, fragile environment, pollution is increasingly becoming a concern of policy makers and civil society. Pollution is not only a nuisance, but is also a considerable threat to human security when it contributes to the deterioration of the air, water and soil upon which people depend. While pollution is recognized by all to be a threat in the region, to date

Pollution is increasingly becoming a concern of policy makers and civil society

Pollution is a considerable threat to human security

detailed data on its levels and trends are not yet available. The statistics that do exist are limited to conditions at the national level, in spite of the fact that levels of pollution vary greatly between urban and rural areas and from one city to the next.

Pollution threatens the water, air, and soil of the Arab region. As the report team was unable to obtain data on the latter for this Report, this section focuses on pollution of the former two: water and air.

Water pollution

Water pollution is now a serious challenge in the region. In the Arab countries, water pollution is primarily attributed to increased use of chemical fertilisers, pesticides, and horticultural and veterinary medical treatments that leave long-lasting traces that eventually find their way into the water. The influx of domestic and industrial wastewater has also considerably raised levels of water pollution.

In several parts of the Arab region, water pollution is manifested in low levels of access to clean water, a resource already constrained by general water scarcity, as analyzed above. The lack of access to sufficient clean water in particular threatens human security in many ways. It can lead to the spread of disease among children, such as dysentery, and affect their regular attendance at school and academic achievement. It deprives women, for example, of long hours of the day which they could devote to personal and income-generating activities rather than fetching water for their families. In addition, water scarcity and pollution threaten agricultural and food production and precipitate domestic rivalries over scarce water resources, as in the ancestral dispute between farmers and herders in Darfur. Water shortages can also cause tensions between neighbouring countries.

Access to clean water for domestic or economic purposes reflects power relationships. In general, the poor do not get clean water and the rich consume enormous amounts and have no problem obtaining the quantities they want. Unsurprisingly, the parts of a country that have the most difficult access to water are the rural areas and the poorer quarters of the city.[26]

The World Bank's World Development Indicators provide water pollution data for 15 Arab Countries, showing, as in Table 2.3, that Egypt, Algeria, Tunisia, Morocco and Iraq are among the largest polluters in the Arab region, in terms of daily emissions of organic water pollutants. However the data also shows that these rates pale in

Box 2-6 | **MDG goal 7, target 10 - halve, by 2015, the proportion of people without sustainable access to safe drinking water**

Distressingly, on Target 10, the Arab countries are off track. The proportion of the population in the region using improved drinking water sources rose slightly between 1990 and 2004 from 83 per cent to 85 per cent. It increased from 65 to 68 per cent in Arab LDCs. However, this sub-regional average does not include Somalia where only 29 per cent of the population had access to safe water in 2004. In the other three sub-regions, it reached 86 per cent in the Maghreb, 94 per cent in the GCC countries, and 86 per cent in the Mashreq.

Proportion of population with access to improved drinking water sources in urban and rural areas, 1990 and 2004 (%)

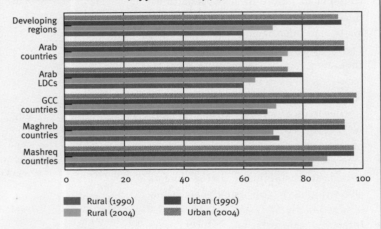

Rural (1990) Urban (1990)
Rural (2004) Urban (2004)

Source: UN-ESCWA 2007.

This slight improvement indicates that significant efforts are still required to achieve the target, which continues to elude the Arab region as a whole.

Arab countries will miss the 2015 target for access to safe drinking water by 27 years

Source: UNDP 2006.

Source: UN-ESCWA 2007a.

comparison to the daily rates of countries such as the United States, which showed in 2003 an absolute rate of pollution more than 10 times that of the highest Arab polluter, and the Russian Federation, which in that same year "out-polluted" the highest Arab polluter by a factor of nearly 7.5.

Nevertheless, these absolute comparisons offer no basis for complacency, as the per-worker ratio of pollution is relatively higher in Arab countries than in industrialised ones. Of the Arab countries, Tunisia succeeded in reducing this rate reaching levels comparable with the United States of America—from 0.18 kg per worker in 1990 to 0.14 kg per worker in 2003. Yemen and Syria also succeeded in reducing these rates respectively from 0.27 and 0.22 kg per worker daily in 1990 to 0.23 and 0.20 kg per worker in 2003.[27] Consequently, while the low rates of water pollution in some Arab countries indeed reflect efforts made by their governments, such countries must remain vigilant lest their plans for industrialisation eventually drive water pollution rates up to levels being experienced by developed countries and the newly industrialised countries of East and South Asia. In Egypt, for example, organic substances dumped in water fall into the following categories: food and drink (about 50 per cent), textiles (17.7 per cent), primary minerals (10.8 per cent), plus lower ratios of chemicals, paper, stones, glass and wood.[28]

Also connected to water pollution is the region's uneven and cumulatively lagging progress in providing its people with access to sanitation services. Based on the most recent data, Figure 2.7 shows that in some Arab LDCs (Comoros, Mauritania and Sudan), over 60 per cent of the population has no access to improved sanitation services. It also shows that, at the regional level, approximately 30 per cent of the population goes without such access. Not only does poor access to sanitation services infringe on the health and dignity of human beings, but it is also a factor contributing to water pollution, with widespread consequences for human security. According to the Human Development Report 2006, in Egypt, to name just one example, high levels of pollution from raw sewage in the Nile Delta region "undermines the potential health benefits of near universal access to water."

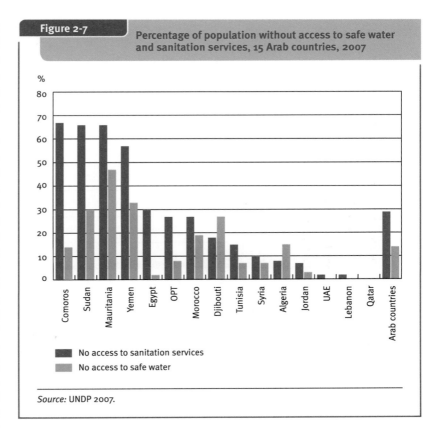

Figure 2-7 — Percentage of population without access to safe water and sanitation services, 15 Arab countries, 2007

■ No access to sanitation services
▨ No access to safe water

Source: UNDP 2007.

Table 2-3	Water pollution levels from organic pollutants in 15 Arab countries and 2 industrialised countries, 1990-2003 (in descending order based on 1990 pollution levels)			
Country	Emissions of organic water pollutants (metric tons daily) in 1990	Emissions of organic water pollutants (metric tons daily) in 2003	Emissions of organic water pollutants (kilograms per worker daily) in 1990	Emissions of organic water pollutants (kilograms per worker daily) in 2003
Egypt	211.5	186 .1	0.2	0.2
Algeria	107	...	0.25	..
Tunisia	44.6	55.8	0.18	0.14
Morocco	41.7	72.1	0.14	0.16
Iraq	26.7	...	0.19	..
Syria	21.7	15.1	0.22	0.2
Saudi Arabia	18.5	..	0.15	..
Kuwait	9.1	11.9	0.16	0.17
Jordan	8.3	23.5	0.19	0.18
Yemen	6.9	15.4	0.27	0.23
UAE	5.6	..	0.14	..
Oman	0.4	5.8	0.11	0.17
Sudan	..	38.6	..	0.29
Lebanon	..	14.9	..	0.19
Libya	..	..	..	..
United States	2565.2	1805.2	0.15	0.13
Russian Federation	1991.3	1388.1	0.13	0.18

Source: World Bank 2007.

Figure 2-8

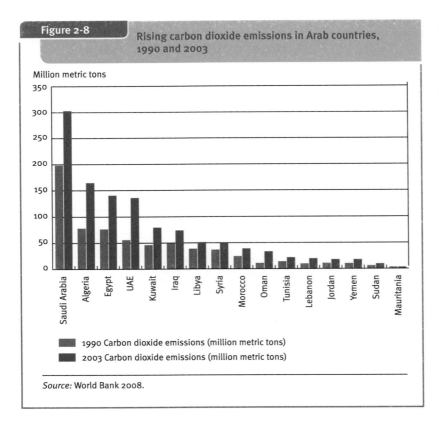

Figure 2-8 — Rising carbon dioxide emissions in Arab countries, 1990 and 2003

Source: World Bank 2008.

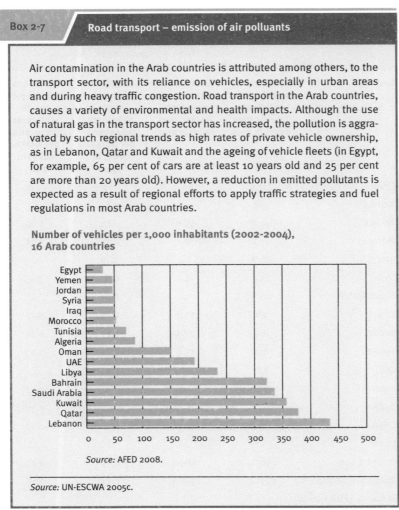

Box 2-7 — Road transport – emission of air polluants

Air contamination in the Arab countries is attributed among others, to the transport sector, with its reliance on vehicles, especially in urban areas and during heavy traffic congestion. Road transport in the Arab countries, causes a variety of environmental and health impacts. Although the use of natural gas in the transport sector has increased, the pollution is aggravated by such regional trends as high rates of private vehicle ownership, as in Lebanon, Qatar and Kuwait and the ageing of vehicle fleets (in Egypt, for example, 65 per cent of cars are at least 10 years old and 25 per cent are more than 20 years old). However, a reduction in emitted pollutants is expected as a result of regional efforts to apply traffic strategies and fuel regulations in most Arab countries.

Number of vehicles per 1,000 inhabitants (2002-2004), 16 Arab countries

Source: AFED 2008.

Source: UN-ESCWA 2005c.

Air pollution

Although Arab countries are among the world's largest producers of petroleum-based energy sources, the levels of air pollution in Arab countries, in general, are among the lowest in the world. In 2003, carbon dioxide emissions did not exceed 1,012.5 metric tons in the Middle East and North Africa region, compared to 10,753.5 million metric tons in middle-income countries and 12,738.4 million metric tons in high-income nations. The only countries with lower carbon dioxide emission rates that year were sub-Saharan African countries, with an average of 531.9 million metric tons.[29]

Nevertheless, what offsets this seemingly optimistic portrait is that Arab countries have such relatively low carbon dioxide emission rates mainly because most have not progressed very far in industrialisation. Even so, carbon dioxide emissions in North Africa and the Middle East are increasing at one of the fastest rates in the world. From 1990 to 2003 this rate was 4.5 per cent per year, which means that carbon dioxide emissions had nearly doubled by the end of that period. The only region in the world to surpass the Arab countries on that score was South Asia, at a rate of 4.9 per cent per year. It should also be borne in mind that carbon dioxide emissions vary between Arab countries, with the highest, in general, found in the oil producing and exporting countries, particularly those of the Gulf, as well as the countries with the largest economies. The top three are Saudi Arabia, Algeria and Egypt. Furthermore, carbon dioxide emissions rates vary considerably within Arab countries, the most marked contrast being between rural areas and major urban centres. The same observations apply to methane and nitrogen oxide emissions.[30]

Efforts at the global level to decrease or at least stabilize air pollutant emissions have had some success since the introduction of stricter environmental regulations and enforcement policies, beginning in the 1970s. However, in the Arab region, socio-economic development, population growth, water scarcity and the growth of the oil industry have led to increased use of heavy fuels to meet development needs including power generation, cement production, oil refining and desalination of water.

Apart from meeting development needs, transport is another major factor in air pollution in the region. Air traffic is increasing in the Arab countries, which is considered a major air transit route. The fleets that operate exclusively within it do not all meet mandatory aircraft engine certification standards, and therefore do not all abide by the international environmental protection standards governing aircraft emissions and the improvement of air traffic management systems.[31] The growth of private vehicles has also made a significant impact, as illustrated in Box 2.7.

Climate change – the global threat

The climate system is an interactive, interwoven system composed of the atmosphere and the surface of the Earth, of ice and snow, of oceans and other water surfaces, and of living creatures. Climate change is the alteration in the overall climate of the Earth or specific regions over time. The term is applied to recent man-made climate changes. Industrial production, especially cement production, burning of fuels, air-borne particles, and human use of land and animals are the most significant man-made causes of climate change.

International concern with the problem of climate change became widespread when the "ozone hole" first attracted attention in 1974. The First World Climate Conference was held in 1979, with the World Meteorological Organization (WMO), the United Nations Environmental Programme, the World Health Organization (WHO), the Food and Agriculture Organization, and UNESCO participating. These international organizations reviewed research results that pointed to a clear increase in the amount of greenhouse gases.

Focusing on this subject, the WMO monitored gas emissions between 1974 and 1982 and measured their actual effects on the ozone layer. This layer, 15 or 20 km thick in the upper atmosphere, prevents ultraviolet light, considered harmful to humans, animals, and plants, from reaching the Earth.

The U.N. Intergovernmental Panel on Climate Change has said that the Earth's temperature has already risen by about 0.75 degrees Celsius since before the Industrial Revolution. It has estimated that by 2050, the Earth's temperature will have increased by two degrees centigrade, compared with the beginning of the Industrial Revolution. As a result of the increased temperature, worldwide rainfall patterns will be altered causing a drop in global food production. From another angle, increased temperature will increase the rate of snow thaw, raising the sea level and submerging entire islands in the Pacific and Indian Oceans as well as all areas that lie below sea level.

These changes could affect human security in general as follows:

- Increasing numbers of heat waves and a gradual rise in the Earth's temperature
- Extremes in rainfall trends, with rainy regions experiencing more rain and dry and arid areas becoming drier
- Increased tropical hurricane activity in the North Atlantic region and increased ocean temperature in tropical regions
- Higher sea level because of warmer water and thawing of ice and snow cover
- Higher sea water levels of carbonic acid, endangering many marine organisms because of the harmful effect on the calcification necessary for their protection
- Effects on food production. If the rise in temperature is moderate, there could be greater agricultural production in some areas; however, if the rise in temperature continues, production could be threatened in other regions, particularly Africa, which will see more occurrences of famine
- Decreased biodiversity and depletion of forested areas; 20 per cent could disappear according to some reports
- Significant health-related effects. The WHO has estimated that climate change caused 2.4 per cent of the world's cases of diarrhoea and 6 per cent of malaria in certain middle-income countries in 2000. Even though the rise in temperature might have positive effects in cold regions by reducing cold-related deaths, the overall health-related effect would be negative because of food shortages, diarrhoea, malaria, and floods.

Industrial production and human use of land and animals are the most significant man-made causes of climate change

Climate change – the threats to the Arab countries

Along with other regions, the Arab countries will be greatly affected by climate change in the coming decades. Certain countries in the region share directly or indirectly in the activities that lead to climate change. The region is a major producer and source of oil, one of the types of fuel that raises the temperature of the atmosphere. In fact, it is more reliant on oil as a fuel source than any other region of the world, using oil for 54.2 per cent and natural gas for 40.2 per cent of its fuel needs. While it is true that reliance on oil dropped in most Arab countries in 2005 compared with 1990 (Kuwait, Libya, Qatar, and Sudan being exceptions), reliance on oil is still high in comparison with the rest of the world.

Nonetheless, the region is one of those least responsible for the direct creation of the greenhouse effect. According to the global Human Development Report (HDR) 2007/2008 and World Development Indicators for 2007, the region's share of

The region is one of those least responsible for the direct creation of the greenhouse effect

carbon dioxide emissions, which contribute to this phenomenon, was no more than 4.7 per cent, which is lower than any other region except Sub-Saharan Africa. Furthermore, its share of methane and nitrogen oxide emissions, which also contribute to heat retention, was the lowest of any region in the world because of its relatively low level of industrial development.

The region is also the nearest to becoming a direct victim of climate change, which affects it in the following ways:

- Water shortages
- Reduced agricultural production
- Large population transfers to foreign countries (environmental refugees)
- Lower levels of economic activities
- Threats to national security

The next section explains the dimensions of climate change in the Arab countries.

According to the Stern Report, temperature rises of between two and three degrees will have the following consequences affecting the region:

Spreading drought, reduced water levels in rivers, stunted agricultural production,

Table 2-4	Climate change future scenarios – water and agriculture		
Scenario	**Type of change**	**Effects on human security**	**Affected area**
WATER	2 °C rise in Earth temperature	1 to 1.6 billion people affected by water shortages	Africa, the Middle East, Southern Europe, parts of South and Central America
	3 °C rise in Earth temperature	Increased water stress for additional 155 to 600 million people	North Africa
	Climate change	Repeated risk of drought known in recent years, with economic and political effects	Mauritania, Sudan and Somalia
	Climate change	Reduced average rainfall	Egypt, Jordan, Lebanon, and OPT
	Rising sea levels	Risk of flooding and threats to coastal cities	Gulf coast of Arabian peninsula
	Climate change	50% decline in renewable water availability	Syria
	1.2 °C rise in Earth temperature	Decreased water availability by 15%	Lebanon
	1 °C rise in Earth temperature	Reduced water runoff in Ouergha watershed by 10%	Morocco
	Climate change	Greater water shortages	Yemen
	Climate change	Reduced water flow by 40-60%	Nile river
	3 °C rise in Earth temperature	Increased risks of coastal surges and flooding	Cairo
AGRICULTURE	2-3 °C temperature rise in tropical regions	A drop by 25-35 % in crop production (with weak carbon enrichment) and by 20-15% (with strong carbon enrichment)	Africa and West Africa (Arab countries included)
	3 °C rise in Earth temperature	Reduced agricultural productivity and unsustainable crops	North Africa
	1.5 °C rise in Earth temperature	70% drop in yields of Sorghum	Sudan (Northern Kordofan)
	Climate change	Flooding of 4,500 km² of farmland and displacement of 6 million people	Lower Egypt

Source: UNDP 2006; Stern 2006.

and incursion by sea water will force large numbers of people to emigrate, turning millions of people, particularly in the Nile River Delta and coastal areas in the Arab Gulf, into "environmental refugees."

These developments could affect not only human security among communities, but national and regional security as well. Such severe changes may also affect political stability and increase domestic tension. Sudan has experienced internal conflicts in Darfur, for example, between pastoralists and farmers over access to water sources. Tension has also increased between Mauritania and Senegal with the disappearance of the river from flood plains, and Palestinian farmers suffer because Israeli settlers monopolize most ground water sources.

The 2007/2008 Human Development Report[32] indicates that Egypt, Lebanon, Sudan, and the countries of North Africa could be the areas in the region most affected by climate change. Global warming caused by an increase in the Earth's temperature by three or four degrees would raise sea level by approximately one metre, creating 6 million refugees in Egypt, with 4,500 square kilometres of agricultural land in the Delta flooded. Even if sea level rises by only one-half metre, it could create two million refugees and cause more than $35 billion in economic losses. In addition, the ability to generate hydroelectric power would be affected, and flood precautions would leave millions of people unprotected. In the Kordofan region of Sudan, an increase in temperature of one and one-half degrees between 2030 and 2060 would reduce average rainfall by 5 per cent, leading to a general drop in agricultural production and a decrease in the production of maize by 70 per cent of current levels. An increase of 1.2 degrees centigrade would reduce available water in Lebanon by 15 per cent as a result of the change in rainfall patterns and evaporation. If the Earth's temperature rises by one degree centigrade, it would reduce available water by 10 per cent in some areas of Morocco by 2020.

The international community has become more aware of the effects of these changes, formed committees, and ratified many agreements, like the Kyoto Protocol and the Climate Change Agreement, to which the Arab countries are bound.

Yet efforts in the Arab countries to confront the effects of these changes do not match the gravity of the threat. There is no single Arab institution concerned with the effect of climate change on the region. The only example of a collective effort is the earmarking by Kuwait, Qatar, Saudi Arabia, and the United Arab Emirates of $750 million for a new fund, established at the conclusion of the 18 November 2007 OPEC meeting, to counter the effects of climate change on these countries. Saudi Arabia contributed $300 million, with the other three countries giving $150 million each. The fund is intended to increase the use of environmentally friendly, more efficient technology to protect the local, regional, and global environment. It supports the development of technologies to remove and sequester carbon, as well as to facilitate the transfer of environmental technologies from advanced countries to all OPEC and other developing countries.

Such efforts would be a welcome change, and would hopefully break new paths in this region that has not yet accorded sufficient attention to environmental concerns. Protection of the environment ranks low on the agendas of Arab governments. The Environmental Sustainability Index, which covers 146 countries (16 Arab countries), and classifies countries according to their plans for natural resources, low population density, and successful management of the environment and development ranks several Arab countries at the bottom. For 2005 Iraq ranked near the bottom at 143, Sudan 140, Kuwait 138, Yemen 137, Saudi Arabia 136, Lebanon 129, Libya 125, Mauritania 124, Syria 118, Egypt 115 and the U.A.E. at 110. The highest-ranking Arab countries were Tunisia at 55, Oman at 83 and Jordan at 84. Finland, Norway, Uruguay, Sweden, and Iceland are at the top of the Index.[33]

Conclusion

This chapter has attempted to clarify the implications for human security of the region's particular resource endowments and the threats posed by their mismanagement, over-exploitation, neglect or degradation. It has also touched on the risks and opportunities associated with

Protection of the environment ranks low on the agendas of Arab governments

its population growth patterns and youthful demographic profile. The potential dangers of environmental shocks in the near future will be far graver in their consequences than the toll of armed violence in Arab countries, whether the source of conflict is foreign occupation or internal strife. Victims of the drought that struck East Africa several years ago were estimated in the hundreds of thousands. Similarly, the conflict in Darfur, which is connected, in part, to drought and the fight over scarce sources of water and pastureland, has affected 4.27 million people in need of assistance of which, 2.5 million are internally displaced.[34]

The very controversy over the number of victims of disputes whose roots can be traced to local environmental properties raises a deeper issue, namely the difficulty of determining accurately the effects of environmental degradation on human security conditions. The effect of the environment on human security is not in most cases direct, but mediated by such variables as the degree of wisdom brought to bear on interactions with the environment or the extent to which disputes that have their origin in environmental conditions are politically exploited. In addition, environmental degradation is a cumulative process in that a certain effect triggers others. Consequently, the impact of environmental change on human security varies from one country to another in accordance with these intermediate variables and the nature and extent of the cumulative chain reaction.

Nevertheless, environmental deterioration resulting from climate change, water scarcity, desertification, losses in biodiversity and deforestation is certain to produce a range of effects. These include:

1. Shrinkage in arable land area and, hence, a declining ability to produce food and agricultural raw materials.
2. The spread of unemployment and poverty in the countryside as a consequence, in particular, of the shrinkage in arable land and the decline in the quality of soil caused by drought and desertification.
3. Decline in the levels of public health as a result of the predicted rise in temperatures and failure to curb water, air, and soil pollution.
4. Rising tensions within agrarian societies and between farmers and shepherds owing to rivalries over the control of water resources.
5. Rising conflicts between countries within a single river basin.

Naturally, it is impossible to confront all these challenges at the national and regional levels alone. Environmental issues are inherently global in nature and attempts to address them should thus be global as well. The Arab countries have kept pace with the global concern for environmental affairs and have ratified most environment-related conventions. Moreover, the brunt of the responsibility for some of these issues, particularly climate change, should be borne by the industrialized powers that contribute most to them.

At the regional level, it is essential for Arab countries to work together to confront the challenges posed by environmental degradation, especially the threats of water shortage, desertification, and pollution. Arab countries should move quickly to establish an Arab agency to coordinate specialised networks for environmental issues, collecting available information from Arab regional organisations, harnessing expertise and formulating the alternatives needed to tackle these issues.

At the country level, Arab governments have many means available to them to ensure the participation of influential social forces and the business community above all, in environmental protection efforts. Such means include the taxation system, incentives to use environmentally friendly technology, drives to use non-polluting renewable energy sources (solar power), policies that encourage economic uses of energy sources, campaigns for the use of mass transport over private automobiles, and the implementation of tough measures to combat desertification and deforestation.

Of course, no measure can successfully combat environmental degradation if it is not founded upon a thorough and accurate base of information and a precise understanding of changing environmental conditions. Therefore, the existing agencies in charge of protecting the environment must be fully supported, equipped and empowered to enable them to undertake the necessary studies and data collection. In countries where such agencies do not exist, they should be created.

Environmental shocks in the near future will be far graver in their consequences than the toll of armed violence in Arab countries

Arab countries should move quickly to establish an Arab agency to coordinate specialised networks for environmental issues

Endnotes

1 UN-ESCWA 2008.
2 UN-Department of Economic and Social Affairs (DESA) 2007a.
3 UN-Department of Economic and Social Affairs (DESA) 2007a.
4 UN-Department of Economic and Social Affairs (DESA) 2007b.
5 UNFPA 2009.
6 UNDP/AHDR calculations based on FAO AQUASTAT database 2008.
7 UNDP/AHDR calculations based on FAO AQUASTAT database 2008.
8 AOAD 2003 (in Arabic).
9 AOAD 2003 (in Arabic).
10 AOAD 2003 (in Arabic).
11 AMF, AFESD, LAS and OAPEC 2001 (in Arabic).
12 UNDP 2006a.
13 UNDP 2006b.
14 UN-ESCWA 2007b.
15 UN-ESCWA member countries are Bahrain, Egypt, Iraq, Jordan, Kuwait, Lebanon, Oman, OPT, Qatar, Saudi Arabia, Syria, UAE and Yemen.
16 UNDP 2006b.
17 AFED 2008b.
18 The water used in the production process of an agricultural or industrial product is called the virtual water contained in the product. For additional information on virtual water see box 6-5 in Chapter 6 of the Report.
19 AFED 2008b.
20 Long term annual average is the arithmetic average over at least 20 years
21 United Nations, Convention to Combat Desertification 1994a.
22 LAS and UNEP 2004 (in Arabic).
23 LAS and UNEP 2004 (in Arabic).
24 AOAD 2003 (in Arabic).
25 LAS and UNEP 2004 (in Arabic).
26 UNDP 2006b.
27 World Bank 2007b.
28 World Bank 2007b.
29 World Bank 2007b.
30 World Bank 2007b.
31 AFED 2008b.
32 UNDP 2007.
33 SEDAC 2005.
34 UN Special Rapporteur on the situation of human rights in the Sudan, 2008k.

Chapter 3

The Arab State and human security—performance and prospects

The state, in its normative role, wins the acceptance of its citizens and upholds their rights to life and freedom. It protects them from aggression and lays down rules that guarantee them the exercise of their essential freedoms. The state that fulfils this role is a "legitimate state". It adheres to the rule of law, which serves the public interest, not that of a particular group. The state which departs from these rules becomes a source of risk to life and freedom. Instead of guaranteeing human security, the state itself turns into a major threat to it.

It is fair to say that, across key dimensions of performance, the record of Arab states has been mixed, with negative impacts on human security. While most Arab states have embraced international treaties and adorned their constitutions with clauses that enjoin respect for life, human rights, justice, equality before the law, and the right to a fair trial, their performance shows a wide gap between theory and practice. Factors such as weak institutional curbs on state power; a fragile and fragmented civil society; dysfunctional elected assemblies, both national and local; and disproportionately powerful security apparatuses often combine to turn the state into a menace to human security, rather than its chief supporter.

Introduction

Across key dimensions of performance, the record of Arab states has been mixed

This chapter measures the performance of Arab states against four criteria:
1. The acceptability of the state to its own citizens
2. State compliance with legal charters pertaining to human rights
3. How the state manages its monopoly over the use of force and coercion
4. Whether institutional checks and balances prevent abuses of power

Part II of this chapter considers the prospects and limitations of Arab political, legal and institutional reform in response to this performance. It examines how the reform process has been generated by the triangulation of three poles of initiative: governments, societal groups, and external powers.

Part I:
STATE PERFORMANCE IN GUARANTEEING HUMAN SECURITY

1. The acceptability of the state to its own citizens

States are artificial creations. Their borders do not represent naturally ordained living spaces for homogenous ethnic, linguistic, and religious groups. Britain, France and Spain, to mention just three states older than the Arab states, all include diverse populations. Their rise as states coincided with the development of inclusive institutions, democracy, popular participation and respect for cultural diversity. Their political and institutional development has enabled these states to counter-balance separatist tendencies, but provides no guarantee that such tendencies will remain dormant. At different times, most established states have faced challenges from groups seeking either to maximise their local autonomy or to secede from central authority altogether. This challenge, with its well-known consequences for stability, peace and security within the borders of a state, seems to be especially acute in some Arab countries.

The consolidation of the Arab state did not take into consideration the extent of kinship and ethnic ties among the human groups that formed the administrative units of countries which subsequently went on to become states.[1] Their borders often appear contrived, enclosing diverse ethnic, religious and linguistic groups that were incorporated as minorities in the post-colonial era. The homogenising project of the Arab state has never been a smooth transition towards inclusion. Rather, a strong nationalistic trend developed with the objective of masking the diversity of the population and subduing its cultural, linguistic and religious heterogeneity under command structures. Most Arab states failed to introduce democratic governance and institutions of representation that ensure inclusion, the equal distribution of wealth among various groups, or respect for cultural diversity.

Such failures of political and economic governance have led identity-based groups in some Arab countries to try to free themselves from the captivity of the nation-state in whose shadow they live. This rejection of the legitimacy of the kind of state which the contemporary Arab countries inherited and perpetuated has been accompanied by conflicts that threaten human security and to which some states have responded by imposing authoritarian controls. However, the suppression of channels through which public grievances can be heard has only further reduced the acceptability of these states to many groups within their territory. The resulting political vacuum is being filled by militant political and religious groups, a number of them with strong track records in providing social services as well as high levels of credibility with the public—sometimes even higher than that of the government they oppose.

Identity and diversity

Collective and individual identities are normal components of social life, whether they are part of a conflict or not. Indeed, any person may have multiple identities. A Moroccan may be Arab or Amazight, Muslim or Jew, African or Mediterranean, and part of the human family all at once. A Sudanese may be Arab or African, Muslim or Christian, and a member of the human family. A Lebanese, while being in all cases Arab, may also be Maronite, Shia, Sunni, or Druze, and, again, also a member of the human family. A person's perception of his or her nested identities is in fact one of the factors which strengthens the bonds between people, and helps support human security. The more identities a person has, the greater will be his or her comfort zone when moving between the various communities of membership, even though one of these will likely form the person's primary identity.

Some political scientists argue that it is not these *inherited* or ascribed traits that count the most in defining a particular group but rather its *constructed* bases, such as its ideology, political affiliations or intellectual viewpoint, which are achieved through interaction among its members and between them and their social setting.

The homogenizing project of the Arab state has never been a smooth transition towards inclusion

Collective and individual identities are normal components of social life

The point to underline is that identity is not a fixed property of the individual or group, but rather a fluid choice among several options. This choice, which can vary depending on circumstances, expresses the *volition* of the individual or the group, and not a *predetermined disposition*. How we choose to see ourselves among the several "selves" we can be, whether inherited or constructed, decides our identity and response in a given situation.

In Western political history, the normative concept that has contributed most to the management of ethnic, cultural and

Identity is not a fixed property of the individual or group, but rather a fluid choice

---

BAHIYA AL-HARIRI* – The powerful and just State: conditions for human security in Lebanon

The Arab Human Development Reports have renewed Arab intellectual vitality by casting light on many of the problems (differing from one country to another) that we are living through in the Arab world and on the issues and subjects the Reports have tackled, including freedom, the knowledge society, and women.

Each subject addressed has formed an entry point to many further or related issues, but the key focus has always been the human being in the Arab world. If we were to put on record one absolutely characteristic positive feature of these reports, it would be the adoption of Arab specificity in the development field, where the UN and its publications in the field of human rights and its social, economic, health-related, and environmental corollaries have previously talked in comprehensive fashion on the human being in general. We have been able, through the means of these Arab reports, to lay the foundations for an Arab debate over the challenges of an Arab renaissance, and come to realise the importance of dealing with Arab specificity. However, we have come to find, when we wish to approach these subjects, that there is a specificity within each Arab region over and above the general Arab specificity.

Taking one's point of departure for the definition of human security from Lebanon—this country whose citizens have for more than three decades lived through a range of experiences that have had a profound effect on its human infrastructure and on the human conscience of both the individual and society—compels one to approach the issue of human security in a new way.

During the decades when people in Lebanon were exposed to all forms of threat, there was a total collapse of security in all its traditional and modern senses. These threats ran from the right to life and education to the right to a decent life. All the basic means of subsistence such as water, electricity, freedom of movement, freedom of belief, and freedom of affiliation were targeted, and every individual in all his constituent parts, needs, and aspirations became a target. As a result, the state, the natural guarantor of security in terms of the most basic forms of growth and progress, collapsed. Growth and progress can only be realised on the foundation of stability, which gives rise to security, in all its meanings, and the true essence of which is the capable, just, and nurturing state as the basic framework for human security in all its dimensions and components. Such a state can only exist where individuals are free to form a social contract concerning the framework that guarantees their freedom and stability, and such a state

can only guarantee security and stability through an encompassing environment of security and stability.

Lebanon, which tried to achieve security for individuals, society, and the state, was unable to achieve security and stability within its area of operation. Today, this has made the Lebanese confront two memories: a distant memory replete with recollections of the targeting of their human security, and a recent memory filled with recollections of their work and effort to restore their security and stability and rebuild their state. Present reality brings back to mind the targeting of their structure, humanity, freedom, and state.

During the period of renaissance, and since the beginning of the 1990s, we have tried to forget the tragedies lived through by the Lebanese individually and collectively. We have done so by the call to tolerance and reconciliation, by strengthening human security for every individual in Lebanon—and I am certain that every Lebanese man, woman, and child could write a thesis about what their security, humanity, conscience, and freedom were exposed to. However, these Lebanese hoping for rebirth, freedom, stability, and progress have been able to transcend these tragedies. This has been made clear through their capacity to overcome these trials, restart the course of life, and offer a major humanitarian model for restoring life, building the state, achieving rebirth, and restarting political, economic, and social life. This Lebanese paradigm can be an Arab example of the people's will for rebirth and development and for making a major leap over our stumbling reality. This requires that we begin from an axiom that forms, in my opinion, the first item on the list of those necessary for an understanding of human security. This is not less than the recognition that Arabs are human beings, with their constituent parts, capacities, and needs, since dealing with our humanity on false preconceptions as to what it is, what it has, and what it needs is the greatest violation of humanity, while the renewal of a preconceived picture of what it must be is to condemn this humanity and its capabilities in advance.

This phenomenon may be the prime cause for extremism, fanaticism, and rejection of this image. We must learn a lesson from our experiences of those who claimed to work for the progress and development of our societies while in the background acting to reaffirm their underdevelopment and weakness, such as the mandatory rule and tutelage which formed the former colonial understanding and which are currently emerging in new forms from the same foundations and with the same unjust view of our people and societies.

*Minister of Education in the Lebanese government, 2008.

linguistic diversity is that of citizenship. The evolution of this concept has been part and parcel of the rise of democracy and democratic governance linked to the emergence of the modern European state. A seminal discussion of citizenship in the European tradition is T.H Marshall's essay collection, "*Class, Citizenship and Social Development*", which considered the European experience as the gradual expansion of citizenship rights, from civil, to political, and to social rights.[2] Citizens are rights-bearing persons conceived as equals under the laws of the state, to which they have common obligations, and citizenship is the active or passive participation of individuals in the common identity that these universal rights and obligations confer. Whatever other identities the individual or group may possess, that of citizenship provides the common denominator shared with all other individuals in the society.

Even in mature democracies, the concept of citizenship is still a work-in-progress, evolving in its most enlightened forms to accommodate the complexities of minority rights in multi-ethnic and multi-cultural societies. This evolution represents a balance, which is also potentially a tension, between the rights of the majority and those of minorities whose claims on the state would otherwise not be treated equally. However, the point here is that the Arab states have hardly perfected their transition to good governance, let alone to true democracy, or the further refinement of democracy that respect for minority rights represents. Thus, the first step to managing diversity, which several Arab countries have begun to take, is to adopt and apply the concept of citizenship under the law and in practice.

A key development in the evolution of citizenship is the understanding that it entails not only a 'vertical' relationship to the state, but also 'horizontal' relations between citizens. To be a citizen is necessarily to be a co-citizen, with the responsibilities, interactions and accommodations that go with 'civil behaviour'.[3] Inculcating this advanced view of citizenship is one of the primary functions of education; it is not to be confused with instilling crude or narrow notions of patriotism, but concerns instead the transmission of civic values of cooperation, co-existence and good neighbourliness. Where citizens share a high level of civic consciousness, peaceful conflict resolution is often possible locally, without state action.

Contemporary events in Arab countries show that the degree to which identity issues surface in internal conflicts váries, and there is no single pattern to the form these issues take. For example, in some cases, the crux of the conflict may centre on identity, but the disagreement may be over *national* identity (is the nation Arab or Muslim, or does another identity take precedence over both of these?). Thus, the conflicting parties may not necessarily belong to separate racial or cultural loyalty groups, and their conflict may not revolve around power relations between those groups. Rather, the contention is among divergent political visions of the political entity to which they belong. An example is the debate over identity in several Arab countries between the State and some Islamic groups. This debate is largely about the imposition of a specific political identity on these states, and not about the inherited identities of the adversarial parties, who do not necessarily come from different racial or ethnic groups.

On the other hand, empirical observation confirms that, in the Arab countries, ethnic, religious, sectarian, and linguistic differences can be associated with persistent group struggles, especially in countries where the population is not homogenous. In countries such as Iraq, Lebanon, Somalia, and Sudan, ethnic, religious and tribal loyalties have become the axis along which communities have been mobilized to press for inclusion or separation. This mobilisation has had destructive and destabilizing effects that undercut both human security and the integrity of states. Tragically, these conflicts have engendered the largest volume of human casualties in the Arab countries, a number exceeding those resulting from foreign occupation.

Our report takes the view that identity, *per se*, is not necessarily the cause of a conflict or even the main source of tension between different groups. Clashes that may appear on the surface to stem from identity in fact often originate in skewed access to political power or wealth, in a lack of channels for representative political participation, and in the suppression of cultural and linguistic diversity. Most commonly, such conflicts start with the

The first step to managing diversity is to adopt and apply the concept of citizenship under the law and in practice

Identity, per se, is not necessarily the cause of a conflict or even the main source of tension between different groups

exploitation by political leaders, for their own ideological ends, of primordial ties among groups who share feelings of exclusion, deprivation and discrimination. Such exploitation, which puts the bonds among group members above the interests of the society, becomes possible when states fail to extend and ensure full rights of citizenship to all. By this standard, the practices of many Arab states are wanting.

2. Compliance with international and regional conventions and constitutional frameworks

International and regional conventions

Most Arab states have acceded to the principal international charters pertaining to human rights. Accession and ratification entail an obligation on the concerned Arab states to bring national legislation and practices in line with these conventions, however, as noted by the *Arab Human Development Report 2004, Towards Freedom in the Arab World,* Arab states seem content to ratify certain international human rights treaties, but do not go so far as to recognize the role of international mechanisms in making human rights effective.

As for regional instruments, by mid-May 2009, ten Arab countries had ratified the Arab Charter on Human Rights, which had come into effect in 2008 (Algeria, Bahrain, Jordan, Libya, Occupied Palestinian Territory, Qatar, Saudi Arabia, Syria, the UAE and Yemen).[4] This, again, does not mean that the states that have acceded necessarily demonstrate greater respect for these rights than those that have not. However, accession and subsequent ratification of these conventions is a formal indication of the acceptance of a degree of accountability in the eyes of the world.[5]

Apart from the question of how many states have ratified the Arab Charter on Human Rights, there is also an issue with respect to whether the instrument is consistent with international standards. One of its shortcomings is with respect to the death penalty. In its revised version, as adopted by the League of Arab States in 2004, the Charter mentions the right to life (Article 5) and the right to freedom (Article 14), but it nevertheless allows for their curtailment,

provided that such curtailment is in accordance with the law. Specifically, it is unique among regional and international treaties addressing the death penalty in that its ban on the juvenile death penalty is not absolute (Articles 6-7). It may be noted that the death penalty, which more than half the countries of the world have abolished and which the United Nations condemns, is applied liberally in several Arab countries, which do not limit it to the most serious crimes or exclude its imposition in cases of political crime.

Arab constitutions and legal frameworks

The ratification of international charters and conventions does not necessarily mean that their provisions will be translated into state constitutions and laws. And even

Identity conflicts start with the exploitation by political leaders of primordial ties

Box 3-2	Arab Satellite Broadcasting Charter

At a time when voices within the Arab world are asking for freedom of opinion and expression, as well as freedom of the press and the media, and when an open cyberspace—the main recourse of independent and private media channels for the free exchange of ideas and information—is available, Arab governments agreed in early 2008 to suppress this breathing space. Their instrument is called *"The Charter of Principles for Regulating Radio and Television Satellite Broadcasting and Reception"*, which in reality aims to muzzle voices and diminish the margin of freedom available, despite what might appear to be some positive goals. The Charter was issued by subterfuge in the form of a declaration and not a treaty, to avoid presenting it to Arab parliaments for discussion and approval, and because Qatar and Lebanon had reservations on the text, which would not have applied had the document been drafted as an Arab treaty that required unanimity.

The Charter was approved by Arab Ministers of Information on February 13, 2008, and contains many restrictive provisions covering all forms of audio-visual programming on satellite channels in the arts, politics, literature and entertainment. Its provisions are stiffened by penalties for any infractions. The Charter stipulates that the authorities in every Arab country must approve the institution of a satellite broadcasting station as well as the re-broadcasting of material produced by other stations. However, it does not define clear standards for giving such approval, which leaves the granting of licenses to the will and whim of governments. In effect, it represents a kind of pre-censorship on the information content that needs to be licensed. These provisions directly contradict Article 32 of the Arab Charter on Human Rights which guarantees the right to information and freedom of expression and which was adopted by the Council of Ministers of the League of Arab States in 2004. They also violate article 19 of the International Covenant on Civil and Political Rights ratified by many governments in the region.

Source: AOHR 2008 (in Arabic).

when they are, as the AHDR 2004 pointed out, all too often, what Arab constitutions grant, Arab laws curtail. And what those laws render legal, actual practice often contravenes.

The content of rights, the scope of freedoms, and the protection inscribed in each Arab constitution vary according to the ruling political philosophy of the state (Mohamed Nour Farahat, in Arabic, background paper for the report). These constitutions range in their defence of citizens' rights from terse summary to detailed exposition. While they are unanimous on the need to maintain the sanctity of the home and freedom of expression in all its forms, some fail to defend other rights at all, or they deal with them ambiguously.

Constitutions of Arab countries frequently adopt ideological or doctrinal formulas that empty stipulations of general rights and freedoms of any meaningful content, and that allow individual rights to be violated in the name of the official ideology or faith. An example is the Syrian constitution which in its preamble presents socialism and Arab nationalism as the only path for national struggle and proclaims the pioneering role of the Socialist Arab Baath Party. Article 38 of this constitution subordinates freedom of expression to the ideology of state and society by making it conditional upon "safeguarding the soundness of the domestic and nationalist structure and strengthening the socialist system."

Other Arab constitutions deal ambiguously with freedom of opinion and of expression, tending to restrict rather than to permit. For example Article 39 of the Saudi Basic Law stipulates, "Mass media, publishing facilities, and other means of expression . . . shall play their part in educating the masses and boosting national unity. All that may give rise to mischief and discord, or may compromise the security of the State and its public image, or may offend against man's dignity and rights, shall be banned. Relevant regulations shall explain how this is to be done."

Many Arab constitutions delegate the definition of rights to state regulation. In doing so, they open the door to restrain freedoms and to encroach, by means of legal provisions, on individual rights at the point when the latter are translated into ordinary law. In Iraq, according to the new constitution, all existing laws, including those developed under Saddam Hussein, are considered to continue in effect unless specifically annulled or amended (article 130). As a result, many laws which are highly restrictive remain in effect. Under article 226, it is a crime to insult any public institution or official. It is also a crime, under article 227, to publicly insult a foreign country or an international organization with an office in Iraq.[6]

Arab constitutions step on fundamental rights in other ways as well. The laws and constitutions in the Arab states generally do not mandate discrimination between citizens on the basis of language, religion, doctrine, or confession. However, discrimination against women is quite evident in laws of some countries. The laws of most of the Arab states contain discrimination against women in matters of personal status, criminal sanction, employment, and the nationality of children born to foreign husbands. While in most of the Arab countries women have acquired their political rights, women in Saudi Arabia do not have the right to vote. It should also be noted that most of the Arab states have often entered reservations against certain provisions pertaining to gender equality in the International Covenant on Civil and Political Rights; the International Covenant on Economic, Social, and Cultural Rights; and the 1979 Convention on the Elimination of All Forms of Discrimination against Women, and basing the reservation on the avoidance of conflict with Islamic law. A welcome development is the progressive evolution of laws on personal rights in the three Maghreb states of Algeria, Morocco and Tunisia, which have gone a long way towards achieving gender equality in family law.

Varying positions exist within the Arab countries concerning the right to form and support political parties and the degree to which such parties should be allowed to operate. Across the Arab region, six Arab countries, Kuwait, Libya, Oman, Qatar, Saudi Arabia, and the United Arab Emirates, continue to prohibit in principle the formation of political parties. Bahrain is the only one of the six Gulf states which affords the freedom of formation to 'political organizations'. Most of the other Arab countries continue to practice considerable and varying degrees of restrictions on the establishment and functioning of political parties, particularly opposition parties, whose members may also be subject to repressive actions. However, an increasing margin of political freedom is currently being witnessed in countries such as Lebanon and Morocco.

All Arab countries, with the exception of Libya, support the right to form civil associations. But throughout the region, legal systems and regulations governing and regulating the civil society sector involve a wide and escalating array of restrictive measures that hinder the fulfilment of that right. Civil society organizations in Arab countries face a number of restrictions, hindrances and practices that can be grouped under three main categories. Firstly, restrictions on their formation and ability to operate. Secondly, state authoritarian power to dissolve, suspend or terminate the associations or their boards of directors. And thirdly, tight restrictions on their sources of funding, particularly from abroad and on their affiliations with other international federations and networks. These restrictions vary widely from one country to another and from time to time. But in general, excessive state control and infringement of

Civil society organizations in Arab countries face a number of restrictions

| Box 3-3 | RADWAN ZIYADEH* – The State and human rights in the Arab world |

The relationship of the Arab state to human rights is inherently problematic in that human rights in their legal sense can be conceived of only in confrontation with the state. This is what makes the issue complex: how can the state, as the totality of executive, legislative and judicial institutions accountable for human rights violations, at the same time uphold these rights? Here we find the most important areas of political difference over the question of the state and human rights. The modern state solidified around the subjection of power to a number of legal precepts which serve to defend human rights from the state itself. That is, the prime and most important guarantees of human rights are that the state itself is subject to the law. This is the fundamental condition for talking about any right, because if the state is not subject to the law, there is no basis for talking about a right, whatever it may be.

Thus, improving conditions for human rights in a country is always firmly linked with the development of its legal and judicial organisations and the robustness of its political and democratic institutions.

It follows, too, that discussion of human rights can take place only under a ruling regime that adheres to specific principles based on separation of powers, independence of the judicial system, and a constitution that guarantees general political and constitutional liberties.

The modern Arab state drew its inspiration from the model of modern legitimacy, patriotic or national. But in reality, the exercise of power has not been based on any clear foundation owing to the clash of opposing values and inconsistencies between longings and aspirations. Across the region, in varying degrees, elements of power, appropriation, and upheaval mix with elements derived from Islamic, royal or tribal legitimacy.

It was thus natural that the Arab state should move deliberately to secure both its legitimacy and its regime at one and the same time. It did so by adopting Western patterns of modernisation focused on the structural form of state institutions, rather than on the substance of their role. It was assumed that this focus on outer form was more calculated to guarantee it international recognition and legitimacy than would attention to inner questions of human rights, which grant the state genuine internal legitimacy as the true interpreter of society's aspirations and interests.

Concepts of human rights therefore remained secondary in the modern Arab state compared to its aspirations for progress and growth. While Arab constitutional provisions for human rights and basic freedoms exist, they differ in the level of guarantees provided for these and in the scope allowed for their exercise. In most categories of rights, constitutions generally give the state a role and justification. This is true of civil and political rights, including the individual rights to equality without discrimination, the right to life, liberty and security of the person, freedom of residence and movement, the right to enjoy a nationality and not be deprived of it, the rights to enjoy a private life and private property, equality before the law, the right to seek legal redress, freedom of creed and practice, and the key freedoms of opinion, association and public participation. The state is also present in economic and social rights.

Most Arab constitutions have taken as an example the political, civil, economic, social, and cultural rights guaranteed by the two international covenants proclaimed by the UN General Assembly in 1966. However, all these rights, which are provided for in varying degrees by the Arab constitutions, are abolished by the general states of emergency in force in more than one Arab country. They are also negated by the lack of any legal convention that guarantees respect for the law and its institutions, that is bound together by political and social relationships, and that possesses convincing cultural and behavioural roots.

What constitutions legally decree is, in practice, lost under a mass of legal restrictions and exceptional measures, and through a lack of safeguards for these rights. The situation is the same with respect to international charters and conventions. All too often, it appears that Arab states have endorsed these conventions with the aim of improving their international image but without bringing national laws into line and without ratification having any tangible benefit for the Arab citizen.

*Syrian Human Rights activist and researcher, founder of the Damascus Centre for Human Rights Studies.

In four Arab states—Kuwait, Lebanon, Morocco and the Occupied Palestinian Territory—respondents were asked to characterize their relationship with their states and state institutions. When asked if they trusted various civic organisations, representative assemblies, and local councils, there was a clear difference in their responses. Those who expressed a strong level of trust in state institutions were in the minority in all four countries, the majority having only limited trust in them. The highest level of trust in institutions was in Kuwait, followed by the Occupied Palestinian Territory; the lowest was found in Morocco, followed by Lebanon. This is an arresting finding in that it reflects disappointment with the performance of representative institutions in the two Arab states furthest on the path to granting political freedoms to citizens. Conversely, with the exception of Kuwait, citizens in the other three countries assigned a greater degree of trust to charitable associations. Is the reason for this that state institutions in these countries do not allow the enjoyment of public freedoms? The responses of the four samples to this question are illustrated in the figure below:

To what extent does the state respect your basic rights?

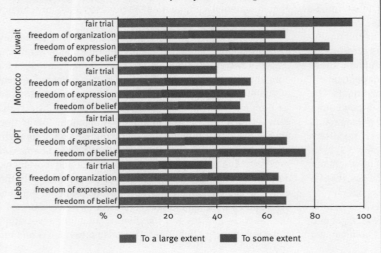

Responses in the four countries reveal similar variations in how people rate the availability of public freedoms in their countries. The percentage of those who thought that the freedoms of belief and expression and the right to a fair trial were available to a large extent was highest in Kuwait. Kuwaitis believed that the right to organise was not prominent in their country, and relatively far less available than the other rights. Lebanese respondents came next after the Kuwaitis in thinking that these particular rights were available to them: a plurality (40 per cent) of them thought that the rights of belief, expression, and organisation were well protected in Lebanon, more so than their counterparts in Morocco and the Occupied Palestinian Territory. With the exception of freedom of belief in the Occupied Palestinian Territory—where 40 percent of the sample thought it available to a large degree, and a smaller proportion (38 per cent) considered it moderately available—few in Morocco and Occupied Palestinian Territory thought that the freedoms of expression and organisation were well protected—barely a quarter of the samples. A very small minority—less than a fifth of the sample in Lebanon and the Occupied Palestinian Territory and hardly a tenth of the sample in Morocco—considered a fair trial to be readily available in their country. The majority thought the opposite was the case.

the state on the functions of civil society organizations remain dominant features of the relationship between the state and civil society in the Arab region.

The most serious threat to the citizen's security in some Arab countries, in the context of fighting terrorism, is providing the state with pretexts to violate individual rights and freedoms without legal recourse. Following September 11, 2001, the UN Security Council adopted resolution 1373 which calls on all states to cooperate in preventing and suppressing terrorist acts and to ratify and implement the relevant international conventions related to combating terrorism. It requires all States to "ensure that terrorist acts are established as serious criminal offences in domestic laws and regulations and that the seriousness of such acts is duly reflected in sentences served". This resolution, which was adopted under Chapter VII of the UN Charter, did not provide a definition of the term "terrorism". In this context, it is important to note that, according to the International Covenant on Civil and Political Rights, even in states of emergency, no derogation is allowed regarding the right to life; the prohibition of torture; the prohibition of holding anybody guilty on account of any act or omission which did not constitute a criminal offence at the time when it was committed; the right to recognition everywhere as a person before the law; and the freedom of thought, conscience and religion.

Nonetheless, most Arab countries have passed anti-terror laws which employ a broad and unspecific definition of "terrorism" and which have given government agencies broad authority to tackle terrorist crimes. Their imprecision and ambiguity form a threat to basic freedoms. Such laws allow undefined periods of pre-trial detention; widen the applicability of the death penalty; curtail freedom of expression; and increase police powers to search properties, tap telephone calls and intercept exchanges of other types of communication. In some cases, these laws increase the use of military courts. In general, counter-terrorism laws in most of the Arab countries have failed to find the required balance between the security of society and the preservation of individual rights and freedoms.

A review of reports by international and regional human rights organisations (the Arab Organisation for Human Rights,

Table 3-1	Arab countries under a declared state of emergency in 2008
State	**Year of declared state of emergency**
OPT	2007
Sudan	2005 (in the Darfur region), extended to the whole country in May 2008
Iraq	2004
Algeria	1992
Egypt	1981
Syria	1963

Source: AOHR 2008 (in Arabic).

Amnesty International, and Human Rights Watch), reveals violations of the obligation to defend human rights by states that have ratified the international conventions and included provisions for the respect of these rights in their constitutions, and equally by states that have not ratified these conventions.

We consider below some indicators of the Arab states' relevant practices, without reproducing, however, the detail in which the *AHDR 2004* dealt with the issue of freedoms in the Arab countries.

States of emergency and human rights

Many Arab states have undergone extraordinarily long periods of martial law or emergency rule, transforming interim measures into a permanent way of conducting political life. A state of emergency grants the government in question the power to suspend the operation of some constitutional and legal provisions pertaining to human rights, and this is in conformity with the International Covenant on Civil and Political Rights. However, a number of these rights—such as the freedom of belief, the prohibition of torture, and non-retrospective application of the law—must continue to be respected. A state of emergency is also assumed to be temporary and imposed only in the face of a danger that threatens the independence of the state, its territorial integrity, or the regular functioning of constitutional institutions. Nevertheless, a number of Arab governments have resorted to declaring long states of emergency without clear reasons

for their continuation. These are often simply a pretext to suspend basic rights and exempt rulers from any constitutional limitations, however weak. According to the Arab Organisation for Human Rights, there were six ongoing states of emergency in the region during 2008.

Violation of the right to life through torture and mistreatment

This violation implicates the state directly insofar as it is generally perpetrated within government facilities and by public employees. In its report for 2008, the Arab Organisation for Human Rights (AOHR) cites examples of the violation of the right to life in eight Arab states.[7] In addition to Iraq and the Occupied Palestinian Territory, these states were Egypt, Jordan, Kuwait, Morocco, Saudi Arabia and Syria. Reports of the UN High Commission for Human Rights indicated that instances of torture took place in Algeria, Bahrain, Morocco and Tunisia. The Commission relied in this respect on the reports of regional and international human rights organisations.[8]

Illegal detention and violations of the right to freedom

Violation of the right to freedom is a more widespread practice in the Arab countries. It takes place in numerous states and the number of its victims reaches thousands in some cases. The prevalence of this practice in some states is connected with the so-called "war on terror." However the victims of this practice in most other states are often members of the political opposition. The AOHR report names eleven states that have restricted citizens' freedoms by extra-judicial detention: Bahrain, Egypt, Jordan, Lebanon, Libya, Mauritania, Saudi Arabia, Sudan, Syria, Tunisia and Yemen. Although no official statistics are available on the number of detainees in these countries, the numbers given in the organisation's report suggest the magnitude of this violation. According to the report, the numbers of detainees sometimes exceed ten thousand. The organisation's report for 2008 indicates that the relevant authorities in a number of Arab states have begun to release some detainees.[9]

Some Arab governments have resorted to declaring long states of emergency without clear reasons for their continuation

Table 3-2	Political prisoners in 5 Arab states, 2005 and 2007	
State	**Number of political prisoners, 2005**	**Number of political prisoners, 2007**
Iraq	26,000 (reduced to 14,000)	24,661
Egypt	10,000	--
Lebanon	--	5,870
OPT	9,000	11,000
Yemen	1,000	--

Source: AOHR 2008 (in Arabic).

Judicial independence – the de facto gap

Threats to judicial independence in the Arab states come not from constitutions, which generally uphold the principle, but from the executive branch. All Arab justice systems suffer in one form or another from blows to their independence that stem from executive domination of both the legislative and judicial branches. The result is a considerable gap between constitutional texts and actual practice. Not only are rulings made and enforced in the name of the heads of state (in all their different designations and nominations), the latter have also been entrusted with the right to preside over the organs of judicial oversight. This is to say nothing of the executive's powers over judicial appointments and promotions, the assignment of judges to extracurricular work, and the inspection and disciplining of judges.

However, in many Arab countries, the most prominent violation of the institutional independence of the judiciary is represented by the spread of extraordinary forms of justice, along with the infringements of the legal protection of individuals' rights, particularly in the criminal domain, that these non-independent forms of justice entail. Forms of extraordinary justice—the most prominent of which are military courts and state security courts—represent a negation of the rule of natural justice and detract from guarantees of a fair trial.

Military justice, whose remit in some Arab states extends to the trial of civilians, particularly for political crimes, is bolstered by ordinary law. The most prominent example of this is Law no. 25/1966 in Egypt, where Article 6 extends the competency of military justice, particularly during a state of emergency, to enable it to consider any offence stipulated in the penal code that may be transferred to it by the president of the republic. What is significant here is that the wide scope of military jurisdiction enjoys the endorsement of Arab constitutions, which make explicit provision for it.

Other forms of extraordinary jurisdiction, such as state security courts, lack guarantees of the right to a fair trial. These courts are found in a number of Arab countries. In Jordan, there are state security courts, created by Law no. 17/1959 and its amendments, which are competent to consider certain crimes, among them crimes against internal and external state security, and narcotics offences. In Syria, legal ordinance 47 of 28 March 1968 included the creation of the Supreme State Security Court. The first article of the ordinance, paragraph (a), stipulates that "these courts carry out their functions on the order of the military governor", while Art. 7, paragraph (a) ordains that "state security courts are not restricted by the procedural rules stipulated in the operative legislations at any stage and procedure of the pursuit, investigation, and trial".

Judges in some Arab countries have struggled in order to give some substance to judicial independence. The Algerian reforms deserve to be noted in this respect, particularly after the legal reform of 2006, which gave elected judges the majority on the Supreme Council of the Judiciary. (Mohamed Nour Farahat, in Arabic, background paper for the report).

3. State monopoly of the use of force and coercion

It is widely accepted that human security is reinforced when the state alone wields the instruments of coercion and uses them to protect and uphold people's rights, those of citizens and non-citizens alike. When other groups gain control of instruments of force, the outcomes seldom favour security for citizens.[10]

A number of Arab states have confronted this problem over the past two decades. In addition to Sudan, Iraq, Lebanon, and Somalia, which were plunged into civil wars where identity slogans were raised, a number of other Arab states have faced the challenge of armed rebellion by a part

Threats to judicial independence in the Arab states come not from constitutions but from the executive branch

of the citizenry. If, in these latter cases, the question of identity arose, it was in relation to the government's political identity more than to any demand for recognition of the rights of the members of a particular group within the nation. The state authorities in some Arab countries have proved unable to impose security while confronting armed groups, particularly during the first half of the 1990s. Some Arab governments have plunged into minor wars against opposing groups in recent years, while other states have suffered from the armed violence in which some of their citizens, or those of other Arab countries, have been caught up.

One of the major questions about human security in the Arab countries is how states should address Islamic political movements. States frequently cite threats from the latter quarter as their justification for clamping down on political and civil rights. Yet the most hopeful prospect of maintaining stability and citizens' security lies in bringing the non-violent groups into the framework of legitimate political activity.[11]

The state's capacity to achieve security in its territory is clearly the outcome of numerous factors that do not depend solely on material and organisational capabilities such as the size of the police and armed forces and the quality of their weapons and training. No state, however large and well armed, can guarantee absolute security on its soil. A state may impose its will briefly through its might; but the state that protects its citizens' rights, and which is seen as legitimate, worthy of trust and open to power-sharing, is much more likely to prevail.

While many of its citizens live under various 'un-freedoms' which effectively deny them voice and representation, and while the threat of state-initiated violence against them is ever-present, the Arab countries, in some cases, offer a degree of protection from crime higher than other developing countries. Barring the cases of foreign occupation and civil war, a relatively low incidence of conventional violent crime remains the norm for Arab countries.

A useful indicator for comparing this situation in the Arab countries with that in other regions, is homicide rates. The data from the United Nations Office on Drugs and Crime (UNODC) illustrates how a number of world regions compare with respect to this indicator.[12]

Going on this data, the Arab countries have the lowest rates of homicide in the world. It should be underlined that these statistics date from 2002, that is, before the invasion of Iraq and the intensification of conflicts in Sudan and in Gaza.

When non-state groups gain control of instruments of force, the outcomes seldom favour security for citizens

The state's capacity to achieve security on its territory does not depend solely on the size of the police and armed forces

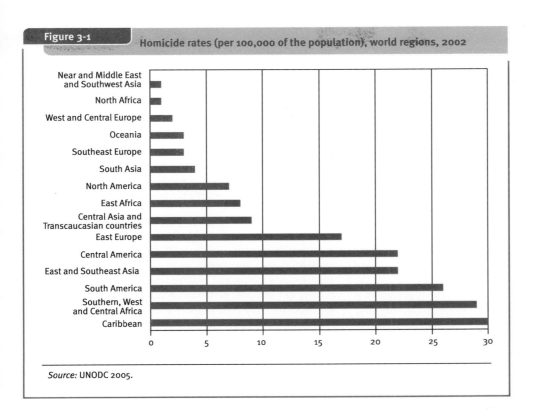

Figure 3-1   Homicide rates (per 100,000 of the population), world regions, 2002

Source: UNODC 2005.

Nevertheless, the Arab countries, indicated in Figure 3-1 by two sub-regions (North Africa and the Near and Middle East/South-West Asia, which also includes Iran, Israel and Turkey), not only has the lowest police-recorded homicide rate of all regions of the South, but also in both the developing and developed worlds.

4. Institutional checks against abuses of power

Security and armed forces that are not subject to public oversight present grave potential threats to human security, as the experience of numerous Arab states attests. Most Arab governments wield absolute authority and maintain their hold on power by leaving the state's security apparatus an extremely wide margin for manoeuvre, at the expense of citizens' freedoms and fundamental rights. The resulting violations have been recorded by local, regional, and international human rights organisations and by the UN agencies that monitor such questions—that is, when Arab governments have allowed them to assemble such reports.[13]

Arab security agencies operate with impunity because they are instrumental to the head of state and account to him alone. Their enormous powers are buttressed by executive interference with the independence of the judiciary, by the dominance (in most states) of an unchanging ruling party over the legislature, and by the muzzling of the media. In these circumstances, judicial or popular oversight of these agencies is a forlorn notion.

True, this lack of oversight varies in degree from state to state: Egyptian civil judges for example have acquitted many of those accused by the security bodies of terrorist offences and Egyptian members of parliament have requested information from the Interior Ministry on the number and conditions of those detained. Local and regional human rights organisations have also criticised the state of freedoms in many Arab states. The Moroccan government offered an apology to the Moroccan people for state-led human rights violations during the last three decades of the 20th century, and King Mohamed VI dismissed the interior minister whose name was linked with these practices. Human rights education is even taught in some police academies in

---

Box 3-5   Executive control versus reform in the security sector

As in many genuine democracies, virtually all Arab heads of state are constitutionally defined as the supreme commander of national armed forces. But the key difference in the Arab region is the lack of any parliamentary checks and balances by which to hold the executive ultimately accountable.

Arab parliaments have little or no effective control over the security sector. Indeed, far more common in the Arab region is for parliaments to treat defence and security matters as taboo. The legislature most often lacks the constitutional mandate to question the executive over these matters or to require submission of even the most general defence budgets (let alone details of expenditure and procurement). Even those few that are constitutionally authorized to oversee budgets—in Egypt, Lebanon, Kuwait, Morocco, and Yemen—prefer not to exercise their authority. In Arab countries that lack a legislature altogether, there are even fewer public safeguards and the executive has absolute leeway in setting policies, operational plans, and budgets.

The executive branch has proven effective in deflecting or pre-empting parliamentary scrutiny even where this is nominally allowed. Kuwait offers an impressive but solitary case of parliamentary oversight. The ministers of defence and interior answer to the National Assembly, and the Interior and Defence Affairs Committee of the Parliament also questions ministers and top security officials including heads of intelligence, and, since 2002, has published an annual human rights report.

The exclusive, non-accountable control of executive branches over the security sector has had problematic consequences for the latter's capacity, and led to a lack of proper budgeting, fiscal controls and transparency. Furthermore, despite the absence of effective parliamentary challenges, executive branches in a number of Arab countries have taken security matters further out of public debate and scrutiny by establishing national security councils that are accountable only to heads of state.

The proliferation of security organizations has naturally been accompanied by a significant inflation in personnel numbers, poor functional differentiation between the various services, duplication of roles, structural disinclination to inter-service coordination, and bloated payrolls. These factors are leading to ineffective performance and financial inefficiency, which severely debilitate capacity in the security sector across the region.

Source: Sayigh 2007.

the Arab countries, and the authorities in some of these countries allow the organisation of training sessions for police officers around these topics.[14] However all of this amounts to no more than a chink in the wall of immunity around the security forces of almost all Arab states.

Measuring the performance of the Arab states on the preceding scorecard confirms that the relationship between the state and human security is not straightforward. While the state is expected to guarantee human security, it has been, in several Arab countries, a source of threat undermining both international charters and national constitutional clauses. Establishing the rule of law and good governance in the Arab countries remains a precondition for the foundation of the legitimate state, which is ultimately in charge of protecting human life and freedoms and limiting all forms of unchecked coercion and discrimination. Until that development is completed, citizens will continue to suffer from the levels of exclusion and political insecurity to which Figure 3-2 points:

The crisis in Darfur: a tragic lesson in state failure

Without doubt, the ongoing conflict in Darfur is among the most serious conflicts in the Arab region at the time of writing. The magnitude of this humanitarian crisis, to which both the past policies of the Sudanese government and its present approach to handling events have contributed, provides an archetypal illustration of the state's role in aggravating human insecurity. Although the Sudanese state threatens citizens' security in other regions of the country as well, its role in Darfur is an extreme example of failure under all the norms of state conduct adopted in this chapter.

In its report to the Secretary General issued in January 2005, the UN Commission of Inquiry on Darfur noted that government forces and allied militia had committed widespread and consistent war crimes and crimes against humanity including murder, torture, mass rape, summary executions and arbitrary detentions.[15] The Commission found that, technically, the term 'genocide' did not apply in the legal sense, since genocidal intent appeared to be missing. However, it confirmed

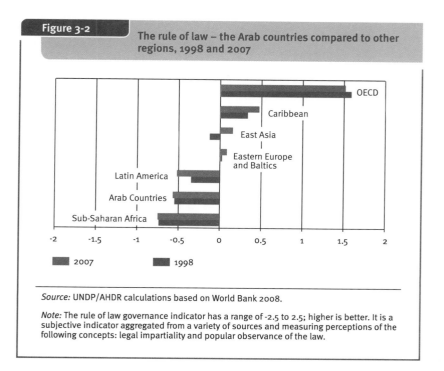

Figure 3-2

The rule of law – the Arab countries compared to other regions, 1998 and 2007

■ 2007   ■ 1998

Source: UNDP/AHDR calculations based on World Bank 2008.

Note: The rule of law governance indicator has a range of -2.5 to 2.5; higher is better. It is a subjective indicator aggregated from a variety of sources and measuring perceptions of the following concepts: legal impartiality and popular observance of the law.

that massive violations of human rights and humanitarian law, "which may be no less serious or heinous than genocide",[16] were continuing. The Commission also found that the Janjaweed militia operated alongside Government armed forces or with their ground and air support.

The situation in Darfur continues to be characterized by widespread and systemic violations of human rights and international humanitarian law. Fighting involving Government of Sudan forces, signatories and non-signatories to the 2006 Darfur Peace Agreement (DPA), and other armed groups has resulted in civilian casualties; widespread destruction of civilian property, including homes and markets; loss of livelihoods; and mass displacement of affected communities. In addition, increasing insecurity negatively impacts on the humanitarian space and the security of the civilian population. Violence and sexual abuse of women and children by state, non-state, and private actors such as criminal groups and bandits also continue almost unabated throughout Darfur. A culture of impunity is prevalent: the State fails to investigate, punish and prosecute perpetrators of human rights violations.[17]

Despite some action taken by the Government to prevent and protect the civilian population against attacks, the civilian population in Darfur is reported to remain exposed to a host of threats.

Arab security agencies operate with impunity

The situation in Darfur continues to be characterized by systemic violations of human rights

According to UN sources,[18] as of July 2008, there were 4.27 million affected people in need of assistance, of which 2.5 million are internally displaced. An additional 250,000 Darfurians have sought refuge in Chad. The upheavals affecting thousands continue. 150,000 people were displaced in the first four months of 2008 and 780,000 since the signing of the DPA in 2006.[19]

Failure to win the acceptance of all citizens

While the Darfur conflict is often characterized as a clash between "Arab" and "non-Arab" African people, it is rather the ways in which both the rebel movements and primarily the Sudanese Government have manipulated ethnic tensions that have served to polarize much of Darfur's population along ethnic lines. These tensions create shifting alliances among the government, Arab and non-Arab tribes, and rebel groups, as well as internecine conflicts among competing Arab groups and among rebel factions.

In its report "Darfur 2007: Chaos by Design", Human Rights Watch (HRW) referred to the Government's stoking of chaos and, in some areas, its exploitation of inter-communal tensions as an effort to "divide and rule" and to maintain military and political dominance over Darfur.[20] HRW indicated that state institutions have failed to provide protection to Darfur's beleaguered population, serving rather as the agents of repressive policies and practices.

Failure to protect the Darfuris' right to life and security

In its resolution 9/17 issued on 18 September 2008, the UN Human Rights Council stressed the "primary responsibility of the Government of the Sudan to protect all its citizens, including all vulnerable groups".[21] However, despite some action taken by the Government, the people of Darfur were reported to remain largely unprotected. Not only has the state in Sudan failed in its primary responsibility for guaranteeing the life and safety of its citizens in Darfur, but government air and ground forces have repeatedly conducted indiscriminate attacks in areas of rebel activity, causing numerous civilian deaths and injuries.[22]

Lack of civilian protection: UN sources indicate that from January to July 2008 there were indiscriminate Government aerial bombardments of civilian towns specifically in West and North Darfur.[23] The attacks led to killings; widespread looting and destruction of civilian property, including hundreds of houses; the theft and killing of large numbers of livestock; as well as the displacement of thousands of people. In the Northern corridor of West Darfur, the Government embarked on a major military campaign using armed militias and Sudan Armed Forces (SAF) ground troops, supported by SAF air assets, to regain control of areas that were seized by the armed group, Justice and Equality Movement (JEM). In its campaign, the Government failed to discriminate between civilians and combatants belonging to armed groups. In April and May 2008, in North Darfur, ten civilian villages including cultivated land were subjected to aerial bombardments in violation of the principle of distinction.

Weak police response:[24] The Government of Sudan's systematic failure to address these abuses is reflected in its reluctance to ensure that Darfur's regular police have even minimal capabilities. The state has failed to invest in its own police force, which is too weak to disarm the Janjaweed, let alone protect people from rape and robbery and other crimes. Some police officers themselves commit such abuses with impunity. Thus, the militia forces that subject Darfur to violence remain strong, active, and unchallenged. Some former militiamen have been incorporated into civil defence forces, such as the Central Reserve Police, whose duty is to protect displaced persons and other civilians.

Failure to comply with international charters on human rights

In its resolution 9/17 issued on 18 September 2008, the UN Human Rights Council expressed its "deep concern at the serious violations of human rights law and international humanitarian law in Darfur".[25]

Summary executions, arbitrary detention, disappearances, torture: According to UN sources, the Government's security apparatus continued to commit human rights violations including arbitrary arrests, arbitrary detention, torture and ill-treatment of detainees.[26] Individuals targeted included community leaders and people perceived to have ties with rebel movements. Violations of the right to a fair trial are endemic. Individuals are often arrested and kept incommunicado for prolonged periods of time by the National Intelligence and Security Services (NISS), frequently in unofficial detention centres known as "ghost houses". Detainees are often held without being charged, thus not allowing them to legally challenge their detention.[27]

For example, according to UN sources, the attack on 10 May 2008 by the Justice and Equality Movement (JEM) on Omdurman, Khartoum, was followed by hundreds of arrests in Khartoum by the NISS, mainly targeting Darfuris.[28] The Government responded to the events of 10 May by making numerous arrests. According to police figures, in the Khartoum area 481 people were detained and then released again in the immediate aftermath of the attack. It was also reported that several hundred civilians were arbitrarily arrested and detained without charge, in addition to combatants and some 90 alleged child combatants. At the end of July, two and a half months after the attacks, some 500 were feared to still be in NISS detention, their whereabouts unknown. Other sources report even higher figures of detainees remaining in custody in connection with the attack. Those held reportedly include human rights activists, journalists, family members of the accused, and women. As the United Nations still does not have access to places of detention in Khartoum, the exact number of detainees is impossible to verify. However, most appear to be of Darfurian origin and there is credible evidence that many were arrested on grounds of their ethnicity.[29]

As of 20 August 2008, 50 alleged members of the JEM had been sentenced to death by Special Counter-Terrorism Courts set up by the Ministry of Justice in the aftermath of the 10 May 2008 attack. The judicial process in these courts failed to satisfy international fair trial standards. Most of the accused were allowed access to lawyers only after their trials had begun, and

in some cases the accused persons alleged that they had been forced to confess under torture and other ill-treatment.[30]

State abuse of its monopoly of the use of force and coercion

The continued failure of the Sudanese state to protect the civilian population from the fighting, distinguish between combatants and civilians, and use proportionate force during clashes and military operations has exacerbated the spread of violence.[31]

Disproportionate use of force: There are several reports of air attacks by Government forces, leading to extensive civilian casualties. These include attacks on civilians in Saraf Jidad, Sirba, Silea and Abu Suruj in West Darfur in January and February 2008 and the bombing of a number of villages in North Darfur, such as the air attacks on Helif village on 29 April or on Ein Bissar and Shegeg Karo villages on 4 May 2008.[32] In May alone such air strikes reportedly caused the death of 19 civilians and injury of another 30, including women and young children. Information suggests that the bombing of these villages was indiscriminate, and the impact on civilian communities was disproportionate to any military advantage likely to be gained as a result of the strikes.[33]

State retaliation to 10 May Justice and Equality Movement attack on Omdurman: On 10 May 2008 armed members of the Darfurian Justice and Equality Movement (JEM) launched an attack on Khartoum. The United Nations Secretary-General condemned the attack and expressed concern over its possible effect on civilian lives and property.[34] The fighting that took place in the Omdurman district of Khartoum entailed violations of international human rights and humanitarian law reportedly committed by both sides.

The Government's response in the weeks after the attack entailed serious violations of civil and political rights.[35] There were reports of grave violations by combatants on both sides, including the targeted killings of civilians, indiscriminate fire, the disproportionate use of force and the execution of wounded or captured enemy combatants.[36] The Government launched

Violations of the right to fair trial are endemic

Individuals are often arrested and kept incommunicado in what are known as "ghost houses"

several airstrikes and bombing raids against villages suspected of harbouring JEM fighters, which caused heavy civilian casualties.

Such imprecise bombings of populated areas violate the prohibition under international humanitarian law of attacks that do not discriminate between military targets and civilians. Persons knowingly or recklessly conducting or ordering such attacks are considered to have committed war crimes.[37]

Failure to operate within institutional checks and balances

Lack of accountability for human rights violations: One of the major obstacles to improving the human rights situation in Darfur remains the widespread absence of justice and accountability for violations and the impunity this promotes. This is manifest in the lack of follow-up to incidents in which no investigations are carried out to identify the perpetrators and bring them to justice, as was the case with the 12 May 2008 Central Reserve Police attack on Tawilla. According to UN sources, no legal action was taken against the perpetrators, including those in command, and no compensation provided to the victims.[38] The prevalence and negative effects of impunity are only-too-apparent in the many incidents of sexual and gender-based violence in Darfur and in other grave violations which are prohibited by international law.[39]

Enshrining legal immunities for state agents in law: Legal immunities for armed state agents continued to be enshrined in Sudanese law. The new Police Act touches on immunity of police personnel in its Article 45: "1) No criminal procedures shall be taken against any Policeman, who committed any act which is deemed to be an offence, during or because of executing his official duties and he may not be tried except by a permission issued by the Minister of Interior or whoever authorizes. 2) The State shall bear the payment of the compensation or the blood money for any police man in case he committed an act which is considered a crime during or because of his official duty. 3) Any Policeman who faces any legal procedures, which require placing him under legal custody, shall be confined to the police barracks, pending the decision on procedures; and the regulations, shall specify the placing him to confinement." The Government has confirmed that the Act gives police personnel procedural immunity which shall be lifted automatically at the request of the aggrieved persons. It also provides for accountability procedures in cases of transgressions.[40]

Insufficiency of state reforms: Despite some Government steps to reform laws, the human rights situation on the ground remains grim, with many interlocutors reporting an overall deterioration in the country.[41] Human rights violations and breaches of humanitarian law continue to be committed by all parties. It is essential that impartial, transparent and comprehensive inquiries be held to investigate allegations, identify perpetrators and hold them accountable. The Special Rapporteur on the situation of human rights in the Sudan reiterated her request that the Government of National Unity make the reports of investigative committees public in order to combat impunity and promote the rule of law.[42]

Sadly, justice in Darfur is undermined by a lack of resources and political will. In the first quarter of 2006 there was one prosecutor for the whole of West Darfur, and for extended periods of time the area had no more than two or three prosecutors. In July 2007, more prosecutors reportedly arrived. However, most of them are based in large towns, remote from detainees and complainants in distant villages and towns, who remain in need of a fair, accessible and functional justice system.[43]

One of the major obstacles to improving the human rights situation in Darfur remains the widespread absence of justice and accountability

Despite some Government steps to reform laws, the human rights situation on the ground remains grim

Part II:
THE PATH TOWARDS REFORM

Given the limitations discussed in Part I which compromise the Arab states' ability to underwrite human security, it is important to consider the prospects for a transformation to the rule of law in these countries. Reforming the state's governing apparatus in order to provide guarantees against discriminatory practices and human security violations is the first step on this long road.

The last decade witnessed several attempts by Arab governments to address the question of reform. At the same time, the role of political movements and civil society increased noticeably. And, in the aftermath of 9/11, some Arab countries came under external pressure from Western powers to embark on political reform. All three actors have played different roles in pursuing reform efforts in the Arab countries.

The Arab Youth Forums held in conjunction with this Report produced a damaging indictment of the region's political shortcomings, faulting the general environment on multiple counts. Analysing the Arab countries' insecurities, participants singled out the exclusion of civil society from decision making, the absence of political freedoms, the politicisation of Islam, the absence of good governance, terrorism, the lack of peaceful rotation of power, the suppression of pluralism, obstacles young people face in attaining public office, the oppression of minorities, and stifling bureaucracy and wide corruption in governments. Many remarked that the forms of democracy found in the Arab countries were little more than make-believe and pageantry; however, several observed that the region cannot import democracy from abroad but has to encourage its evolution within Arab culture.

Young people from the Mashreq pointed to the weakness of political opposition groups, which, they said, simply act out an empty role. This criticism was echoed by some participants from the Maghreb. There was general agreement that some of the greatest threats to Arab human security come from authoritarian regimes; restrictions on core freedoms; and deficits

in institutionalisation, transparency and accountability. The Lebanese participants concurred with their peers in the Maghreb states that foreign meddling deepens internal political differences in the region. The Egyptian and Sudanese participants cited detention without charge and torture, particularly of students and members of opposition groups, as growing threats.

1. The drive for reform from governments

A spate of political reforms initiated by leaders has cascaded across the Arab countries in recent years. They include for example the establishment of representative assemblies in United Arab Emirates, Oman, and Qatar; the return of an elected parliament in Bahrain; the holding of multi-candidate presidential elections in Egypt in 2005; and the organisation of partial local elections in Saudi Arabia in 2006 (limited to men only). Reform initiatives also included the adoption of a code of personal status law in Algeria and Morocco, and the creation of the Justice and Reconciliation Commission in Morocco.

The motivation for such reforms is widely debated. To some, it appears that governments are bowing to necessity: mounting popular unrest and agitation have pressured them to make changes to reduce the likelihood of civil disturbance. Others believe that "advice" from foreign strategic allies to make concessions to popular demands, in the wake of the 1991 Gulf War or the 2003 invasion of Iraq, largely account for these developments. Whatever their origins, these reforms, despite their significance, have not changed the structural basis of power in the Arab states, where the executive branch still dominates, unchecked by any form of accountability. Certainly, the value of the reforms introduced by the governments has been diminished by constitutional or legislative amendments that curtail citizens' rights in other areas, in particular the right to organise and to participate in free and fair elections.

A spate of political reforms initiated by leaders has cascaded across the Arab countries in recent years

The motivation for such reforms is widely debated

Along with a new constitution in Iraq came the extension of the state of emergency that permits the suspension of constitutional provisions relating to freedoms. In Egypt, amendment of Article 76 of the constitution on presidential elections so as to allow multiple candidates was followed by a law that limited the right to stand as a candidate to the leaderships of parties existing when the law came into force. The state of emergency was extended for another two years or until the issuance of an anti-terror law, when the extension came up for review in May 2008. This was followed by the agreement to constitutional amendments making it permissible to transfer civilians to military courts and ban any party formed on a religious or class basis, as well as any political activity on a religious basis.

In the same fashion, in Algeria, on the heels of agreement on the Charter for Peace and National Reconciliation, which addressed the effects of the violent confrontations of the 1990s, came the extension of the period of the presidency by two years, the removal of the limit on the number of times the president could stand for election, and the continuation of the ban on the Islamic Salvation Front. There was a similar move in Tunisia which amended its constitution to increase the maximum allowable age of the president, and to remove limits on the number of presidential terms. The Islamic-oriented Renaissance Party remained outside the frame of legally recognised parties.

Qatar, Saudi Arabia, Sudan and the United Arab Emirates (UAE) took the same pattern: the first proclaimed a constitution calling for the election of a State Council and then temporarily removed citizenship from around six thousand citizens who became stateless on the pretext that there was no proof they belonged to the nation; the Sudanese government proclaimed a new constitution after the ratification of the Naivasha agreement, and subsequently introduced a law that gave it wide power to recognise or dissolve political associations; Saudi Arabia allowed the formation of a human rights organisation, but restricted elections to some cities and only to local councils; the government of the UAE reformulated the ground rules of the National Unity Council, half of whose members would be elected from only two thousand citizens chosen by the seven Emirati rulers by means of an indirect election.[44]

Journalists and academics often speculate that there are multiple wings within the Arab states' ruling elites. Some go to great lengths to describe these wings—the one characterized as hard-line, the other as reformist—and to link the adoption of reforms with what they see as the rising influence of the reformist wing. It is true that members of ruling elites, and even their various institutions, do not always and in all circumstances agree on all details of general policy. However, it is by no means clear that such differences revolve around the transition to greater democracy. Rather, the most important dividing lines within the ruling elites of Arab states—that is, those which are visible to people outside them—seem to reflect generational differences, institutional power-bases, and ideological affiliations.

Ideological divisions within the Arab countries' political elite are also a hindrance to reform. The most important of these separates the Islamic movements, wedded to restructuring the political system in their respective countries according to their conception of Islamic law, from most members of the ruling elite, who may show respect for the principles of this law, but who are open to other sources of guidance in developing the political system. This division is clear in the states which permit the Islamic movements to be politically active, even if not necessarily through recognised parties. While Islamic movements in the opposition demand more political freedom, the key difference between them and the ruling elites is over how to adopt Islamic laws and how each side understands the rulings of these laws.

2. Demands for reform: societal groups

Could transformation come about as a result of political mobilisation by societal groups that see their interests and those of the state converging around the rule of law? In the Arab countries there are four forces that could have a role in that respect—political opposition groups (with the Islamic movements to the fore), civil society organisations, business people and, lastly, citizens, when they are allowed to

The most important dividing lines within the ruling elites reflect generational differences

participate through the ballot box. What are the prospects for change originating in these quarters?

Political opposition forces and the Islamic movements

In most Arab states that evince some form of multi-party system, such as Algeria, Egypt, Jordan, Tunisia, and Yemen, or in those where the political system accommodated political pluralism since independence, such as Lebanon and Morocco, the Islamic movement represents one of the main strands of political opposition. Moreover, the Islamic movements have been part of the main governing group in Iraq since the fall of Saddam Hussein, in Sudan since the coup of August 1989, and in the Occupied Palestinian Territory following the election of 2006. Some Opposition Islamic movements support demands for the right to form political parties and to organise, freedom of thought, fair elections, and limits on the power of the executive.

Arab governments have followed different policies to deal with the Islamic movements. These include adopting some of their demands and allowing them the right to organise and participate politically alongside other political parties, as is the case in Iraq, Jordan, Lebanon, the Occupied Palestinian Territory, Yemen, and, to a certain extent, Morocco. Non-party Islamic associations are also present in Bahrain and Kuwait. However, Egypt and Tunisia have banned the Islamic movements outright, and the Algerian government has banned the main strand of this movement. Nevertheless, the Egyptian government allows individuals belonging to the Muslim Brotherhood to take part in elections as independents. In all cases where Arab governments make concessions to political pluralism, they nonetheless take precautions against a possible victory of Islamic movements in parliamentary elections and use methods both legal (using their majority in representative assemblies), and administrative, to prevent them from coming to power.

Despite the Islamic movements' positioning on the political stage, transition to democracy is not their strategic demand. It is, rather, their path to power, which will then enable them to implement their strategic goal of rebuilding Arab societies on their vision of Islam. Without commenting on the intentions of their leaderships, doubts about them are common among some groups in the Arab countries and abroad. The chief concern is that these movements would rescind the very freedoms they need in order to come to power once they have gained it. Freedom of belief, opinion and expression and a range of personal freedoms have, at different times, been singled out by some Islamic opposition leaders as inconsistent with what they conceive of as true Islam. The manifestos of some of these movements, such as the programme of the Muslim Brotherhood in Egypt, have not dispelled such doubts.[45] On the other hand, given the Islamic movements' popular standing, it is not conceivable to continue denying the avenue of legally recognised parties to those groups that reject violent methods.

Civil society organizations

Civil society movements are active in several Arab states where they have developed a political identity and have begun to make their views felt. While stiff resistance to calls from civil society organizations (CSOs) for transparency and greater freedom of expression in Tunisia and Syria has blocked their activities in those countries, movements in Egypt and Lebanon have attained more far-reaching influence. In Egypt the *Kifaya* movement's tactics inspired citizens to use mass protest to press their demands on the government. This was reflected in the unprecedented wave of mass protests involving a spectrum of social classes and groups which followed, particularly in 2007 and 2008.

Arab governments respond differently to pressures from rights-based CSOs. Some ban their activities altogether; others tolerate them while making it as difficult as possible for them to operate by tying them up in red tape, interposing obstacles to their registration and scrutinizing their finances, especially from foreign sources.

Most organisations live with these restrictions and try to work around them. For most, the main avenues open for promoting democratic development in the Arab countries are analysis and advocacy efforts such as producing position statements on freedom

Arab governments have followed different policies to deal with the Islamic movements

It is not conceivable to continue denying the avenue of legally recognised parties to those groups that reject violent methods

issues, consciousness-raising through reports monitoring the state of human rights in their countries, and training sessions and conferences on human rights questions. Some organizations also make use of the law when opportunities materialize to stop violations through the courts.

Arab CSOs play a significant role in spreading awareness of human rights issues by expanding the agenda and by demonstrating public concern for that agenda through their intervention. Their public image is however often tarred by Arab governments, which characterize them as agents of foreign powers dependent on foreign funding. They frequently encounter government-imposed restrictions, obstacles and harassment, and hence have limited membership. The general reluctance of political parties to work with them considerably hampers their efforts to propel Arab societies towards the rule of law.

Business people

The private sector does not generally play an independent political role in the Arab countries, although it has begun to emerge in the political life of the region's growing market economies. So far, business people have not gone further than becoming junior partners to the state bureaucracy. The main reason why they are not greater driving forces lies in the particular economic weight of the Arab states—which exceeds that found in other developing regions. The ratio of the states' consumption to GDP and of their revenues to GDP is greater than that of counterparts among other regions of the South. This gives Arab states a control over economic life unmatched in most developing countries. This control relies for the most part on oil, most of whose extraction revenues go to the government, and which is the main source of direct or indirect income for the oil-exporting Arab states. A number of other Arab states such as Algeria, Egypt, Libya, and Sudan preserve a large public sector, whose role is still influential in the economy despite their moves to transfer state-owned assets to the private sector and foreign companies.

The fact that the ratio of government revenues to GDP for the states of the Middle East and North Africa (MENA) is higher by a significant degree than in other countries of the South in general may serve to clarify these observations. In 2005 this ratio reached 25.6 per cent in the MENA states, while in low-income countries it was 13.0 per cent; ten years previously (1995) the average for the former states was

Arab CSOs play a significant role in spreading awareness of human rights issues

The general reluctance of political parties to work with CSOs considerably hampers their efforts

---

Box 3-6   The Second Declaration of Independence: towards an initiative for political reform in the Arab world

Many Arab Civil Society organizations took the Arab Summit in Tunis in May 2004 as an occasion to reinforce their calls "outside the tent" during a conference they convened in Beirut in March 2004. Fifty-two organizations from thirteen Arab countries attended the conference. The initiative for the meeting came from the Cairo Institute for Human Rights Studies, Human Rights Watch, and the Palestinian Human Rights Organization. The conference issued a document called the Second Declaration of Independence, which summarized civil society demands for political change, while rejecting suggestions for reform from abroad, underlining that these reflected foreign, not Arab interests. The Declaration set out principles of political reform in the Arab region. It called for:

- Respecting the right to self-determination of all people.
- Adhering to the principles of human rights, and rejecting all interpretations based on cultural particularism and the manipulation of nationalism.
- Rejecting the fragmentation of human rights and the prioritization of certain categories of rights over others.
- The tolerance of different religions and schools of thought.
- Establishing sound parliamentary systems.
- Incorporating guarantees in Arab constitutions for political and intellectual pluralism.
- Rejecting violence in political life.
- Opposing the state of emergency other than in the event of war or natural disaster.

Source: Cairo Institute for Human Rights Studies 2004.

26.1 per cent, it stood at 13.3 per cent for low-income developing countries, and for the middle-income developing nations it was 17.2 per cent.[46] According to the Joint Arab Economic Report (2006), this ratio in 2005 reached its peak in the OPEC-member Arab states, at 68.04 per cent in Libya; 48.62 per cent in Saudi Arabia; around 40 per cent or slightly less in Algeria, Oman, Qatar, and Kuwait; and between one-third and less than one-fifth in the other Arab states. The lowest rate was in Sudan where it reached 17.84 per cent. The explanation for the rise in this ratio is that oil, most of the revenues from which go to the state, represents 71 per cent of total government income in the Arab states.[47]

This political economy translates into government domination of the private sector in most Arab states. The government remains the major partner, either because it has its own roots in the private sector, as is the case in the Gulf states, or because banks owned by the state are the source for capital accumulation in large private-sector companies, or because government contracts are the source of profits for companies which carry out the projects.[48] In contrast with the private sector's role in supporting democratic transition in some Latin American and South Asian states, notably South Korea, the upper echelons of the private sector in the Arab states, with limited exceptions, are partners of growing influence in government. Even where the Arab governments are in transition to a degree of political plurality, business people tend to support the ruling party or family. Thus the kind of liberal political parties known in the West which enjoy an influential social base among business people, or within a progressive middle class, are missing from the political opposition. As a result, Arab entrepreneurs have not been prominent in the political reform process. Perhaps they have been content with the political influence and economic space they have obtained through the move to market policies in the Arab states.

The role of Arab citizens

As individual citizens, few Arabs feel they have any power to change current conditions in their country through political participation. This seems clear from the

decline in levels of political participation in some of the most stable Arab states. The rise in levels of participation in other states is linked to the successful mobilisation of voters along sectarian or tribal lines which have no relation to general political issues, as in Kuwait and Yemen, or because of the novelty of contested elections as in Iraq, and in Mauritania after the temporary abandonment of military rule in May 2007. Lastly, the rise in levels of participation in states such as Tunisia or Yemen has not necessarily led to advances in the political reform process in those cases.

Popular demand for democratic transformation and citizens' participation is a nascent and fragile development in the Arab countries. These goals have not been high on the list of demands by the majority of protest movements over the last three decades. Historically, among the most important waves of public demonstrations in Arab cities were those against the economic measures of some Arab

Arab entrepreneurs have not been prominent in the political reform process

Table 3-3	Electoral turnout in eighteen Arab states between 2003 and 2008		
State	**Parliamentary**	**Presidential**	**Local**
Algeria	35.5% (2007)	59.3% (2004)	--
Bahrain	72% and 73.6% (two rounds in 2006)	--	61% (2006)
Djibouti	72.6% (2008)	78.9% (2005)	--
Egypt	31.2% (2007) 28.1% (2005)	23% (2005)	--
Iraq	79.6% (2005)	--	--
Jordan	54% (2007)	--	56% (2007)
Kuwait	59.4% (2008)	--	Less than 50% (2005)
Lebanon	46.4% (2005)	--	--
Mauritania	73.4% and 69.4% (two rounds in 2006) 98.2% and 97.9% (two rounds in 2007)	70.1% and 67.5% (two rounds in 2007)	73.4 and 69.4% (two rounds in 2006)
Morocco	37% (2007)	--	54% (2003)
Oman	62.7% (2007)	--	--
OPT	77.6% (2006)	66.5% (2005)	--
Qatar	--	--	30% (2007)
Saudi Arabia	--	--	70% (2005)
Sudan	--	86% (2000)	--
Syria	56% (2007)	95.8% (2007)	49.5% and 37.8% (2007)
Tunisia	91.4% (2004)	91.5% (2004)	82.7% (2005)
Yemen	75.9% (2003)	65.1% (2006)	65% (2006)

Source: UNDP/RBAS 2008; IPU 2008; Egypt SIS 2008 et al. (See Statistical references).

governments in response to International Monetary Fund prescriptions, as in Egypt during January 1977, Morocco in 1981 and 1984, Tunisia in 1985, Algeria in 1988, and Jordan in 1989. In some cases, such as Algeria and Jordan, these protests led to the introduction of significant political reforms that were not sustained in some cases. These reforms, however, were equivalent to compensation given to citizens for allowing the same economic policies subsequently, albeit more gradually, to proceed. The absence of democracy as the core and chief demand of organised opposition movements, of mass demonstrations and of voters in general, has long lulled Arab governments into believing that no significant internal pressure for democratic evolution exists and that it therefore requires no serious attention.[49]

3. External pressures

With limited, and sometimes faltering, prospects for a transition to the rule of law through its internal dynamics, the region remains vulnerable to external pressures for political transformation. Repeated calls have been made by Western powers with strategic interests in the Middle East to respect human rights, mobilize civil society and accelerate political reform.

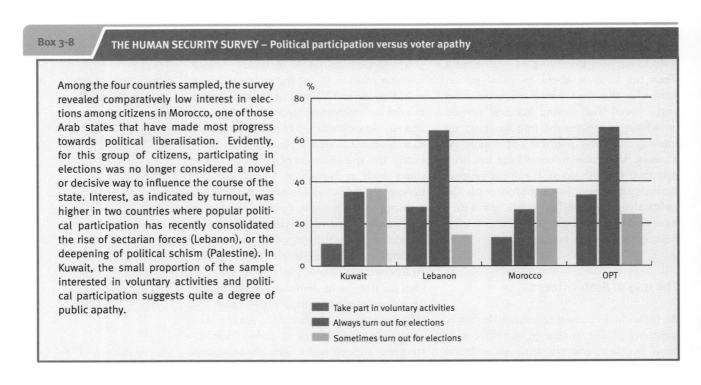

| Box 3-8 | THE HUMAN SECURITY SURVEY – Political participation versus voter apathy |

Among the four countries sampled, the survey revealed comparatively low interest in elections among citizens in Morocco, one of those Arab states that have made most progress towards political liberalisation. Evidently, for this group of citizens, participating in elections was no longer considered a novel or decisive way to influence the course of the state. Interest, as indicated by turnout, was higher in two countries where popular political participation has recently consolidated the rise of sectarian forces (Lebanon), or the deepening of political schism (Palestine). In Kuwait, the small proportion of the sample interested in voluntary activities and political participation suggests quite a degree of public apathy.

■ Take part in voluntary activities
■ Always turn out for elections
▨ Sometimes turn out for elections

The most significant initiatives of this kind have occurred in the context of the 1995 Barcelona Process and the G8's Broader Middle East and North Africa initiative of July 2004. To these may be added moves by the former US administration, such as the Middle East Partnership Initiative, as well as policy statements by the former American president calling for democratic transformation in the Arab states.

US policy discourse on reform in the Arab countries in the last few years has not been consistent. In 2004 it strongly advocated for specific democratic changes in "the Greater Middle East". Subsequently, US policy favoured more guarded policy statements as it found it necessary to strengthen alliances with undemocratic but cooperative Arab governments in the so-called "war on terror". After 2006, US diplomatic efforts focused on other priorities. The target of such diplomacy was not mainly political reform in the Middle East, as had predominantly been the case in 2004 and 2005. Rather, the goals were to overcome Arab reservations about a proposed conference on peace in the Middle East that would bring Arab, Israeli and Palestinian leaders together in the United States; to secure Arab help in stabilizing the Iraqi government; and to gain Arab support for international efforts to make the Iranian government abandon its uranium enrichment programme.

The electoral victories for some Islamic movements in elections in recent years

The region remains vulnerable to external pressures for political transformation

---

Box 3-9   **AZMI BISHARA* – Human rights and citizenship: the first building block of a nation**

Citizenship is the flip-side of sovereignty. There is no complete sovereignty, in the modern meaning of the term, without an equivalent and meaningful citizenship. A secure society guarantees its people stable citizenship, does not treat the latter as a gift to be given and taken away, protects its people from arbitrary and tyrannical authority, provides for their health and education and protects them in old age. Creating such a society forms one of the most important elements of nation-building.

This is particularly true in the case of developing countries, with their weak institutions and emaciated public spheres, which are still deeply caught up in the process of self-realization. Many of these states have succumbed to the belief that creating an army in uniform, a centralised government, a nationalized education system, a "unified" official history, and a national airline is what it takes to build a nation.

The challenge of forming a secure society become more acute under conditions of sectarian and ethnic pluralism which can turn all politics into identity politics and a horizontal conflict among religious, cultural, or "ethnic" groups. It is not only meaningful citizenship, i.e., that which goes beyond the formalistic, that prevents national unity from collapsing. The more components are added to citizenship rights, the larger the meaning of citizenship becomes. Its diversity can be a society's strength.

The best that may be asserted at the Arab level is that the political and civil rights of citizenship are incomplete. This empties citizenship of its content. Indeed, in a number of Arab cases, citizenship means very little.

Indeed, in states lacking a broad middle class, where growth and privatisation in some cases and corruption in others, are accompanied by widespread impoverishment, a human rights discourse on civil and political rights without a corresponding debate over social rights is meaningless.

The right to work, the right to medical treatment, the right to education, and the right to appropriate housing are examples of social rights. They can only be guaranteed by institutions maintained by the state and financed by a national economy from a tax base. The exception, of course, is the rentier state which uses handouts to buy public acceptance with minimal representation. These issues are linked and mutually interrelated components.

Where a broad middle class is either non-existent, eroding or in atrophy, as is the case in most Arab states, and thus cannot claim its social rights, the latter's absence can polarize the nation.

Members of the privileged class receive medical care in the best hospitals at home or abroad and are educated in private schools. The poor are unable to visit a doctor or obtain treatment or ensure a decent life for their children or themselves in old age. They depend on mass public education the quality of which has dropped through neglect and under-investment. These stark and ever-expanding divisions in meeting needs and providing the basics and fundamentals of a decent life find expression in cultural and religious and even linguistic divides: for example, the orientation of private education for the privileged towards the English language versus the domination of conservative religion over the official education system in Arabic. In both cases, over time, common citizenship loses its meaning; the ruling power stays afloat by extolling national unity against parties and pluralism or against other states or external and internal enemies, or against various conspiracies.

Shared social guarantees and the institutions that back them up, financed by public revenue in the public interest, not only make the difference between misery and a decent life; they are also among the most important components of nation-building in our times.

*Former National Democratic Party member of the Israeli Knesset, and Palestinian political writer.

reduced, unsurprisingly, the enthusiasm of external parties for reforms that bring to power groups considered unfriendly to their interests. In 2007, President Bush acknowledged the difficulty of a shift to democracy that, in his words, allowed the enemies of democracy the chance to regroup and wage a campaign against the recently created democracies in the region, especially in Iraq and Lebanon.

But whatever motives drove the adoption of democratic reform as the first article of new policies towards the "Greater Middle East", its relegation has confirmed the worst fears of Arab reformers. Their conclusion is that, from the perspective of outside powers, democracy in the region only matters to the extent that it achieves their own security and other goals. Where it does not, security and those other goals take precedence, and reform may find itself friend-less.

Mirroring this trend, on the regional level, talk of reform no longer dominates the communiqués of the Arab summits. Here, one might compare the resolutions of the 2004 Tunis Meeting titled the "Development and Modernization Summit", with those issued later in other Arab summits. The former discussed civil society, women's rights, and human rights as major issues, in addition to ratifying the Arab Charter on Human Rights. The other summits, however, adopted an apologetic and defensive stance, stressing the importance of Arab security, the dangers threatening that security, and the importance of maintaining the Arab identity.

Conclusion

This chapter examined the role of the Arab states in guaranteeing human security as defined in this report. It assessed the performance of Arab states against four criteria and concluded that there is a human security deficit in state provisions despite the constitutional commitments of Arab states and the international charters signed by most of them.

The civil state—that is, one which is ruled by laws that respect civil and political rights—is the best safeguard of human security. This chapter underlines that a wide gap exists between the expectations of Arab citizens for the protection of their

A wide gap exists between the expectations of Arab citizens and what they are given on the ground

Reform from within remains the first and best hope for meaningful security in Arab countries

rights and freedoms, and what they are given on the ground, even if the distance between hopes and reality is not the same in all Arab states.

The chapter suggested that ethnic, sectarian, tribal and religious diversity does not in itself constitute a threat to human security. However, it is evident that, in the Arab countries, the politicization of identities leads to polarization, violence and armed conflict. Active tolerance of diversity is the only certain means of alleviating the potential eruption of conflicts along communal lines. The responsibility for containing volatile situations lies within the Arab states, which need to manage their own diversity through policies of inclusion and social equity. Peaceful co-existence in multi-ethnic and multi-sectarian societies rests on evolved forms of citizenship. The catastrophic consequences of failing to pursue this path have become only too apparent in the collapse of entire states.

The chapter, furthermore, discussed the limitations of factors contributing to the reform process. Reforms introduced by Arab governments are mostly driven by the concern to maintain control over the population rather than to enhance human security. The state still privileges its own security at the expense of that of society. Society itself, especially its economic elites, civil society and opposition groups, is weak and lacks a clear reform agenda. For its part, the international community has adopted damagingly intrusive policies and initiatives that have set back Arab reform, first through aggression and then through equivocation. The overall result is that the Arab states still lag behind other developing countries in adopting serious measures for enhancing the human security of their citizens.

Reform from within remains its first and best hope for meaningful security in Arab countries, starting with the essential rights of the people. This reform cannot be imposed from outside; neither can democratic models be imported wholesale. Arab countries need to adapt different institutional forms suited to the context of each of them—as long as these forms respect human rights in full, protect freedoms, guarantee popular participation and ensure both majority rule and minority rights. All social groups should be allowed to organize and compete in the public space as long as they respect the right to differ, and neither resort to violence nor abort the democratic process.

In all this, the relationship between Arab reformers and their international supporters has to be conducted in a spirit of partnership, not one of spineless dependence or crude interference. In the Arab countries and abroad, it has to be recognized that, on both sides, regressive public forces, vested interests, and misperceptions fed by prejudice could put sizable obstacles in the way of building the 21st century Arab civil state on foundations of tolerance, peace and security.

Endnotes

1   Clapham 1985.
2   Marshall 1977.
3   Van Hensbroek 2007.
4   KUNA 2009 (in Arabic).
5   UNDP 2007.
6   UNDP and Article 19 Global Campaign for Free Expression 2007.
7   AOHR 2008 (in Arabic).
8   Human Rights Council. Working Group of the Universal Periodic Review. First Session. Geneva 7-18 April 2008. Summary prepared by the UN High Commission on Human Rights according to paragraph 15(c) of the annex to Human Rights Council decision 1/5. This summary was issued on the four Arab states of Bahrain, Algeria, Tunisia, and Morocco. See p.4 of each of these reports. The periodicity of the review for the first cycle being four years, information reflected in these reports mostly relates to events after 1 January 2004.
9   AOHR 2008 (in Arabic).
10 Wolfe 1977; and Bienen 1978.
11 Hafez 2003; Bayat 2005; The Emirates Centre for Strategic Studies and Research 2004.
12 UNODC 2005.
13 See the reports of the UN Human Rights Council on Algeria, Bahrain, Morocco, and Tunisia. Summary prepared by the UN High Commission on Human Rights according to paragraph 15(c) of the annex to Human Rights Council decision 1/5. Human Rights Council. Bahrain Report pp.4-5, Tunisia Report pp. 2-3, Algeria Report p.6, and Morocco Report p.4.
14 Kawakibi 2004 (in Arabic).
15 UN 2005.
16 UN 2005.
17 UN Special Rapporteur on the situation of human rights in the Sudan, 2008l.
18 UN Special Rapporteur on the situation of human rights in the Sudan, 2008k.
19 UN Special Rapporteur on the situation of human rights in the Sudan, 2008k.
20 HRW 2007.
21 UN Human Rights Council 2008h.
22 HRW 2007.
23 UN Special Rapporteur on the situation of human rights in Darfur, 2007d.
24 HRW 2007.
25 UN Human Rights Council, 2008h.
26 UN Report to the Secretary General, 2008e.
27 UN Report to the Secretary General, 2008e.
28 UN Special Rapporteur on the situation of human rights in the Sudan, 2008l.
29 UN Special Rapporteur on the situation of human rights in the Sudan, 2008l.
30 UN Report to the Secretary General, 2008e.
31 UN Special Rapporteur on the situation of human rights in the Sudan, 2008l.
32 UN 2007c.
33 UN Special Rapporteur on the situation of human rights in the Sudan, 2008l.
34 OHCHR 2008.
35 UN Report of the Secretary-General, 2008b.
36 UN Report of the Secretary-General, 2008b.
37 HRW 2007.
38 UN Special Rapporteur on the situation of human rights in the Sudan, 2008l.
39 UN Special Rapporteur on the situation of human rights in the Sudan, 2008l.
40 UN Special Rapporteur on the situation of human rights in the Sudan, 2008k.
41 The Government provided information on criminal cases of violence against women in South and North Darfur, involving accused who are members of the regular forces (armed forces and police). These efforts to combat impunity through investigation, prosecution of perpetrators and compensation must continue.

42 UN Special Rapporteur on the situation of human rights in the Sudan, 2008l.
43 UN Special Rapporteur on the situation of human rights in the Sudan, 2008l.
44 AOHR 2008 (in Arabic).
45 Brown, Hamzawy and Ottaway 2006.
46 World Bank 2007b.
47 AMF, LAS, AFESD and OAPEC 2006 (in Arabic).
48 Heydemann 2004.
49 Bayat 2003.

Chapter 4

The personal insecurity of vulnerable groups

The previous chapter assessed the performance of the Arab state in providing human security to citizens. That performance was found, on the whole, to be unsatisfactory. In many countries, the framework of state-provided security is compromised by legal loopholes, overseen and regulated by coercive institutions, and based on the citizen's forfeiture of personal freedoms in exchange for a limited form of personal and social security. In most cases, the citizen's personal safety is bounded by strict rules of a game that exclude him or her from effective voice and participation.

This chapter considers the situation of people from or in the Arab countries who have no personal security at all. These groups—abused and coerced women, victims of human trafficking, child soldiers, internally displaced persons and refugees—are acutely vulnerable to threats arising from discrimination, exploitation or displacement. Such groups merit a particular focus because their situations lie beyond society's field of vision. Often hidden from the public eye, they are victimized in their own families and societies or abused as little more than slaves or left uprooted in places where their lives have taken them. They have little power to defend their own rights and few champions to defend those rights for them. Their insecurity lies beyond the pale of mainstream society, which offers them virtually no personal protection.

Violence against women: impunity and insecurity

Violence against women is a worldwide phenomenon, and not one limited to the Arab countries

It has been estimated that, around the world, one in three women, will be raped, beaten, forced into sex or otherwise assaulted in her lifetime.[1] Indeed, violence against women is a worldwide phenomenon, and not one limited to the Arab countries. However, as the *Arab Human Development Report 2005, Towards the Rise of Woman in the Arab World (AHDR 2005)* illustrated, in societies where women are still bound by patriarchal patterns of kinship, legalised discrimination, social subordination and ingrained male dominance, women are continuously exposed to forms of family and institutionalised violence. Indeed, in some Arab countries the penalties for assaults against women, even lethal assaults, are reduced if it can be established that the perpetrator committed a so-called "crime of honour."

In the Arab countries, women find themselves in a subservient position within the family and receive little protection from the legal system against violations inflicted by male family members. Arab women encounter violence throughout the different phases of their lives: in girlhood, violence can come in the form of physical, sexual and psychological abuse; female genital mutilation; child marriage; and child prostitution and pornography; in adolescence and adulthood, such violations can expand to include sexual abuse and rape, forced prostitution and pornography, trafficking in women, marital rape, and partner violence and homicide.[2]

Violence directed against women takes many forms. The UN General Assembly's *"Declaration on the Elimination of Violence against Women"*,[3] defined its focus as "any act of gender-based violence that results in, or is likely to result in, physical, sexual or psychological harm or suffering to women, including threats of such acts, coercion or arbitrary deprivation of liberty, whether occurring in public or in private life."

Arab women encounter violence throughout the different phases of their lives

Female genital mutilation

Some have distinguished between what they term direct and indirect violence against women. They list in the first category all forms of physical assault, from beating to rape and murder. This category also includes other practices that

---

Recorded cases of violence against women, although grave and widespread, do not reflect the real situation in the Arab region but, rather, reveal only the noticed and reported cases. There are many cases that go undetected by studies on the subject. In addition, some forms of violence pass unnoticed and cannot be reported. Examples of these are insults, verbal violence, and cases of violence which women are very often embarrassed to report.

Some analysts classify violence against women into *direct* and *indirect* violence. Direct violence includes all forms of physical abuse. Examples of these are battering, rape, killing, and other practices that cause physical harm to women. Sexual abuse, which ranges from sexual harassment to rape and desertion, falls under this category. Although cases of sexual violence against women in the Arab region have increased, they are shrouded in secrecy because casting light on them will tarnish the image of the female victim and her family.

Indirect violence refers to how prevailing social and cultural institutions—including values, customs, and laws—actively discriminate against women. Verbal violence can be included among forms of indirect violence as it results from such discrimination, which permits men to exercise violence against women.

Verbal violence is often directed against young girls who, by custom and tradition, are punished and cautioned against behaviour that puts their chastity at risk. Divorced women are even more exposed to this kind of violence, as families find their liberty potentially threatening and seek to curb it. Married women sometimes suffer verbal violence in cases where the marital relationship is unbalanced, or where the husband takes out his frustrations and problems on those weaker than him (his wife, daughter, sister).

Other analysts expand the scope of violence to encompass *social* violence. Examples of social violence include restraining women's integration into the community and preventing them from exercising their social role or denying a wife her social and personal rights in order to indulge her husband's intellectual and emotional propensities. This, of course, adversely affects the woman's self-esteem, emotional growth, psychological health, liberty and social integration.

A female faces this kind of social violence when the family seeks to curb, coerce or subdue her by preventing her from leaving the house without permission, compelling her to marry against her wishes, and rejecting her opinion in matters affecting her own life and fate.

Arbitrary divorce is another form of social violence against women. For example, a husband may divorce his wife without her knowing of that divorce, or for reasons not permitted under Islamic Shari'a.

Health violence is yet another form of violence suffered by many women. Forcing a woman to live in unsuitable conditions, denying her adequate health care and ignoring her reproductive health needs by failing to regulate pregnancy periods and limit the number of births can destroy her health and shorten her life. In the Arab and Islamic culture, people tend to have many children. The consequences of this for women may not constitute intentional violence but rather illustrate how cultural and social heritage can be harmful to them. What counts here is whether the desire to have many children is shared by a husband and his wife and whether a woman's physical health is not impaired.

Finally, *economic violence* is another form of violence commonly practiced against Arab women. Examples range from depriving a woman of an inheritance to taking control of her economic resources. Husbands sometimes force their working wives to forfeit their incomes under the pretext of making ends meet and supporting the family. In this guise, a woman's assets and income are sometimes appropriated unjustifiably.

Source: Maryam Sultan Lootah, in Arabic, background paper for the report.

---

cause material harm to women, such as female genital mutilation (FGM), which inflicts excruciating pain, gives rise to lasting physical and psychological damage, and can cause premature death through bleeding, infection and neural shock.

FGM is an illegitimate operation which seldom receives mention in medical textbooks. Moreover, it is classified as a crime under international law.[4] Specifically, the performance of this operation entails at least three types of crime: (1) causing physical harm; (2) violation of a woman's honour; and (3) the unauthorized practice of medicine. However, legal systems' stances on this practice have ranged from that of permission to that of prohibition, and in fact, some states continue to allow it. Moreover, the legal prohibition of this practice may have no real impact on life on the ground because traditional beliefs favour it. Influential figures aligned with conservative political or social forces also speak out in its defence.

It may be noted that, in the mid-2008, Egypt issued amendments to the Law on the Child,[5] banning and penalizing FGM, hence closing a previous legal loophole, which permitted health professionals and others to undertake the practice. However, while most Arab countries where FGM is practiced profess to be keen to adopt laws banning it, their slow progress means that the harmful practice continues, abetted by poverty, low levels of health awareness and sex education, pervasive legal discrimination against women and a lack of persuasive enlightened religious discourse.

Indirect violence covers a whole gamut of social and cultural practices, conventions, and laws that discriminate on the basis of gender. Some women's advocates extend the concept to include what they term social violence, one aspect of which restricts women's involvement in society and public life, while a second aspect deprives married women of the right to exercise their social and personal rights and to compel them to cater to their husbands' emotional demands. Such violence is detrimental to the status of women. It impairs their emotional growth and their psychological well-being by depriving them of their freedom to live a normal life and interact with society. A woman may encounter such social violence when her family or a family member prohibits her from leaving the house, or forbids her an opinion on matters crucial to her well-being and future. Some include under social violence arbitrary divorce—where a husband divorces her wife without her knowledge or for reasons not justified under law (Maryam Sultan Lootah, in Arabic, background paper for the report).

Table 4-1	Estimated prevalence of female genital mutilation (FGM), 6 Arab countries	
Country	Year	Estimated prevalence of FGM in girls and women 15-49 years (%)
Somalia	2005	97.9
Egypt	2005	95.8
Djibouti	2006	93.1
Sudan (northern)	2000	90
Mauritania	2001	71.3
Yemen	1997	22.6

Source: WHO 2008.

FGM is an illegitimate operation which seldom receives mention in medical textbooks

Child marriage

In many parts of the Arab world, girls are married off at a young age, often to men who are much older. Early marriage and teenage pregnancies threaten the health of mothers and children, and increase female vulnerability to violence. Moreover, early marriages often lead to divorce, family

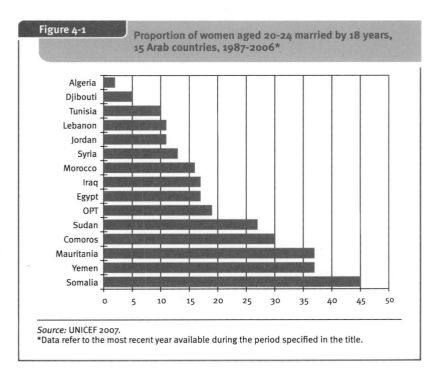

| Figure 4-1 | Proportion of women aged 20-24 married by 18 years, 15 Arab countries, 1987-2006* |

Source: UNICEF 2007.
*Data refer to the most recent year available during the period specified in the title.

breakdown and poor child-rearing and commonly encourage early childbearing and high fertility, which carry marked health risks for very young mothers and their infants. Adolescent brides are less likely to know about contraception and sexually transmitted diseases, and are more prone to being bullied by abusive partners. For these reasons, more often than not, child and teenage brides embark on marriages fraught with personal insecurity.

Although early marriage is on the decline in the Arab countries, the numbers of teenage girls who are married remains significant in some countries. As shown in figure 4-1, UNICEF estimates the proportions of women aged 20-24 that were married by the age of 18 at 45 per cent in Somalia, 37 per cent in Yemen and Mauritania, 30 per cent in Comoros, and 27 per cent in Sudan.

Physical violence

It is difficult to gauge the prevalence of physical violence against women in Arab societies. The subject is taboo in a male-oriented culture of denial. Much of this violence is inflicted unseen in the home, on wives, sisters and mothers. Victims are unlikely to report abuse by family members. Authorities, the police and the public are disinclined to look into domestic matters, especially those concerning women. This applies especially in poorer communities where such treatment is considered the natural fate of women. Hence the under-reporting of offences is widespread since women know that complaints lead nowhere, or that complaining itself brings shame. A disturbing finding from a survey of women conducted for the 2008 Iraq National Human Development Report is that many married women accept their partners' violence against them as justified, having internalised centuries-old traditions about the superior rights of men.

Marriage laws

Laws in several Arab countries provide numerous articles and provisions under family law that effectively confirm men's custodial rights over women in marriage. The standpoint implicit in such provisions is that the personal safety and welfare of a woman, as an inferior being, can only be assured by a man. Thus laws ostensibly intended to secure women's safety in marriage in fact discriminate against them and tie them to their husbands' whims.

Women are subjugated as the result of the consecration of male supremacy within the family as enshrined in Personal Status Laws. In most Arab countries, under prevailing Personal Status Laws, women do not have the right to ask for divorce or to oppose polygamy. Divorce is normally considered a male right and not a solution to specific marital problems, even

---

Box 4-2 — **In Yemen, a child bride sues for justice**

Early in 2008, a newly-wed bride, Nojood Ali, took a taxi to the West Court of Sana'a, Yemen and requested a divorce from the husband she was forced into marrying. Her husband, who was about three times her age, used to rape and beat her almost every day and the bride decided that she had had enough.

While tragic, the bride's story would have gone unnoticed had it not been for her age; Nojood Ali was only nine years old.

After hearing about Nojood's case by chance, Shaza Nasser—one of Yemen's foremost lawyers and human rights advocates—decided to represent her free of charge. A week later, and in a historic ruling, the 'marriage' was annulled.

Nojood's tale of suffering and rebellion caused a public stir. Many saw her as a victim of patriarchy in all its oppressiveness and brutality, but for others, she was a source of inspiration. Following in her footsteps, victims of child marriage have begun speaking out and demanding justice, while activists and government officials in Yemen have called for measures to end the practice. In the wake of Nojood's case, a group of Yemeni lawmakers has lobbied to increase the legal age of marriage from 15 to 18.

Source: Verna 2008; Kawthar 2008.

Table 4-2 — **Estimated prevalence of assaults on women (physical violence), 7 Arab countries**

Country	Percentage of women assaulted	Source	Year of study
Algeria	31.4%	UNHRC	2008
Egypt	35% (of married women)	UN-ESCWA	2007
Iraq	22.7% (South/Center)	WHO	2006/7
	10.9% (Kurdistan)		
Lebanon	35%	UNFPA	2002
OPT	32%	UNICEF	2000
Syria	21.8%	UNIFEM	2005
Yemen	50% (of married women)	UNFPA	2003

Source: UN-ESCWA 2007; UNFPA and Yemeni High Council for Women 2007; UN 2008; UNIFEM 2005; UNFPA 2005; WHO 2007; UNICEF 2000. (See statistical references).

when women are officially given that right. Nonetheless, recent years have seen some advances, reflected in progressive laws or amendments in certain Arab countries. Such developments include the adoption of the Khul' (divorce initiated by the wife) Law in Egypt (2000), as well as amendments to the Family Law in Morocco (2002) and Algeria (2005), which have adopted certain laws similar to some of the Family Laws applied in Tunisia, and which uphold the woman's right to give herself in marriage, and dispense with the requirement of a guardian's consent. Other progressive legal steps in these two countries restrict polygamy more tightly, grant women the right to register their objection to polygamy in their prenuptial agreements; and provide for divorce through the courts, or by mutual consent between spouses, and recognize that a woman at 21 becomes her own guardian.

Discrimination against women is evident in personal status laws

Box 4-3   **Arab women's legal rights under Personal Status Laws**

If we look at how different rules of law are applied to equal legal positions, the Arab personal status laws that cover both Muslims and non-Muslims appear as an example of legalized gender discrimination. This is mostly because the personal status rules are basically derived from religious interpretations and individual opinions that go back deep into remote history. At that time, the culture of discrimination was entrenched and these interpretations and opinions were surrounded with an aura of sacredness and absoluteness while well-established and absolute religious beliefs were largely mixed with the relative historical realities of the communities.

The personal status rules for Muslims, derived totally from Islamic jurisprudence, reserve the right of divorce to man alone upon his sole will. A husband may, also upon his sole will, revoke divorce in certain cases. In contrast, a wife may divorce her husband only by court judgment and for specific reasons. Examples of these reasons are damage caused to wife; a husband's absence, desertion, or failure to support his wife; and the husband's imprisonment. According to these rules, only a husband is under a duty to maintain the family regardless of his wife's wealth. In return, a wife has to obey her husband. Thus, a husband provides maintenance in exchange for constraints on his wife. Further, a husband has a well-established right to exercise polygamy.

It is only within the framework of preserving these absolute fundamentals that attempts are made to introduce reform and eliminate some of the manifestations of discrimination in a number of Arab family laws. These reforms merely attempt to soften certain discriminatory practices. Examples of these attempts are prohibiting enforcement of *ta'a* court judgments (binding a wife to obey her husband by force); requiring a husband and the marriage registrar to notify the husband's first wife when the husband intends to marry another woman; restricting the right of a husband to marry more than one wife only to cases where there is an acceptable excuse and on condition that a husband will be fair among his wives; and giving a wife the right to divorce if her husband marries another woman. Another example is the case of *khol'* (giving a wife the right to divorce herself without suffering damage if she renounces her financial rights). Thus, both spouses are given the right to terminate the marriage contract. Further,

a husband incurs an obligation to consult his divorcee, in case he decides to return to her, and to register this return. In addition, a wife is given the right to introduce conditions in the marriage contract insofar as these conditions are not inconsistent with any of the well-established principles of the Shari'a law. A wife is also given the right to keep custody of her children until the end of their custody period if this is in their interest. Further, a wife is given the right to continue to stay in the marriage house insofar as she has child custody.

The personal status rules for non-Muslims are derived from their doctrinal and denominational laws. In general, these rules narrow, if not prohibit, the right of a wife to divorce herself. For example, an Orthodox wife may divorce herself only for limited reasons and by a court judgment. In contrast, a Catholic wife may not under any circumstances divorce herself. Only separation between a husband and a wife is permitted. With regard to the rights of the husband and the wife during marriage, the husband invariably has the upper hand over the wife.

In terms of legal regulation, while most Arab states have uniform personal status laws for Muslims, some states do not. Examples of these states are Egypt, Lebanon, Qatar and Bahrain. Hence, it is very important to develop a clear and disciplined code of personal status rules, whose aim should be to achieve legal clarity. It is only when this code is developed that the attempts to eliminate discrimination against woman will succeed.

In short, discrimination against women is evident in the Arab states' personal status laws. However, in a number of states such as Egypt, legislative amendments have been introduced to ease the impact of that discrimination. But these attempts have not risen up to the level of the progressive amendments that have been introduced into the Arab Maghreb's legislation, such as the Tunisian laws, the Moroccan code and, to a lesser degree, the Algerian laws. The lesson derived from the Arab Maghreb's legislation is that it is possible to develop Arab laws that would preserve the religious fundamentals while adopting interpretations that achieve greater equality between men and women and thus eliminate the historical injustice against women in family relations.

Source: Mohamed Nour Farahat, in Arabic, Background paper for AHDR 2005.

Convention on the Elimination of All Forms of Discrimination against Women

Some countries have demonstrated real progress in amending personal status laws

Increasing Arab women's personal security will require substantial changes to laws governing marriage, divorce, violence against women and women's personal status. Although countries such as Morocco, Tunisia and Algeria have demonstrated real progress in amending personal status laws, many others lag far behind.

Most Arab states have signed and ratified the Convention on the Elimination of All Forms of Discrimination against Women (CEDAW) and are thus obligated by its provisions, reservations excepted. Yet the devil hides in the details. The reservations entered by many Arab states, which often cite clashes with *shari'a*, are numerous, significant and often demur over Article 2, which enshrines the principle of equality between men and women. As the AHDR 2005 noted, objections to that principle effectively cancel out the ratifications of states and "put in doubt the will to abide by the provisions of CEDAW". The credibility of Arab states, and any real progress towards implementing its provisions, thus begins with the reconsideration and removal of these reservations.

Table 4-3	Convention on the Elimination of All Forms of Discrimination against Women (CEDAW) – overview of Arab countries' ratifications, 2009		
Countries	**Date of ratification[a]**	**Reservations on articles[b]**	**Ratification of Optional Protocol**
Algeria	22-May-96	2, 9, 15, 16, 29	
Bahrain	18-Jun-02	2, 9, 15, 16, 29	
Comoros	31-Oct-94	No reservations	
Djibouti	2-Dec-98	No reservations	
Egypt	18-Sep-81	2, 9, 16, 29	
Iraq	13-Aug-86	2, 9, 16, 29	
Jordan	1-Jul-92	9, 15, 16	
Kuwait	2-Sep-94	9, 16, 29	
Lebanon	21-Apr-97	9, 16, 29	
Libya[c]	16-May-89	2, 16	18-Jun-04
Mauritania[c]	10-May-01	General reservation	
Morocco	21-Jun-93	No reservations	
Oman[c]	7-Feb-06	9, 15, 16, 29	
OPT			
Qatar			
Saudi Arabia[c]	7-Sep-00	9, 29	
Somalia			
Sudan			
Syria	28-Mar-03	2, 9, 15, 16, 29	
Tunisia[c]	20-Sep-85	9, 15, 16, 29	
UAE	6-Oct-04	2, 9, 15, 16, 29	
Yemen[d]	30-May-84	29	

Source: UN Division for the Advancement of Women 2009.

Note: a/ Ratification includes ratification, accession or succession.
b/ Reservations of Arab countries are mainly related to the conflict between national legislation and shari'a on articles 2, 9, 15, 16 and 29, which respectively stipulate the following:
Article 2 stipulates equality before the law and prohibits discrimination against women in national constitutions and legislation.
Article 9 pertains to nationality rights.
Article 15 regards women's equality with men in their legal capacity in civil matters.
Article 16 relates to marriage and family relations.
Article 29 pertains to arbitration between States Parties and the referral of disputes over the interpretation or application of the Convention to the International Court of Justice.
c/ Declaration denotes that the State is not committed to the implementation of any articles of CEDAW whose provisions do not comply with the provisions of Islamic shari'a.
d/ On 22 May 1990 the Yemen Arab Republic and the People's Democratic Republic of Yemen merged into the Republic of Yemen. In respect of treaties concluded prior to their union, Yemen is considered a party as from the date when one of the former States first became a party to those treaties. In terms of CEDAW, the People's Democratic Republic of Yemen ratified the Convention on 30 May 1984.

Box 4-4	Morocco withdraws its reservations on CEDAW

On December 11, 2008, Morocco nullified its reservations to the Convention on the Elimination of All Forms of Discrimination Against Women (CEDAW). The country had acceded to the Convention on 21 June 1993, but with reservations on three sections that were incompatible with Islamic Shari'a law. One of Morocco's reservations concerned Article 16 regarding spousal equality on entry into, and dissolution of marriage, because Islamic Shari'a "confers the right of divorce on a woman only by decision of a Shari'a judge." These reservations were considered to be no longer necessary after Parliament passed the reformed Family Code (the Moudawana) in 2004, which increased women's rights overall. In particular, Book Two, Title Four of the Code is about rights and responsibilities in divorce.

Source: International Knowledge Network of Women in Politics 2008; Stop Violence against Women 2008.

Honour crimes

'Honour crimes' are the most notorious form of violence against women in several Arab societies. Such crimes single out women for engaging in what their families regard as immoral behaviour, which could entail anything from extra-marital sex to merely mixing with men from outside the family circle. The punishment for women can be as severe as death, especially if the prohibited act results in pregnancy. And in some countries, the law stands on the side of those who perpetrate such crimes by providing for reduced penalties in cases where "honour" is a motive.

The battles over Articles 98 and 340 of the Jordanian penal code are a case in point. Article 98 mandates the reduction of the penalty against a person who commits a crime when in a state of extreme fury over an unlawful or dangerous act committed by the victim. Article 340, in paragraph 1, used to exempt a man from all punishment for killing, wounding, or maiming his wife or a female relative or the partner in the act of adultery. In 2001, after a long legislative battle, Article 340 was amended. The continuance of Article 98, which judges still resort to, effectively invalidates the amendment to Article 340.

In Lebanon, two studies on murders of women in the country issued in 2007[6] and 2008[7] on behalf of the Council on Violence against Women and the NGO, *Kafa*, show that article 562 of the Lebanese Penal Code allows for the application of reduced penalties for crimes intended to "preserve honour". This provision has softened penalties for different forms of homicide targeting women, and has made committing crimes against them easier. One study shows that out of 66 deliberate murders of women, 26 per cent were motivated by honour, yet 55 per cent of the sentences

'Honour crimes' are the most notorious form of violence against women

The punishment for women can be as severe as death

| Box 4-5 | THE HUMAN SECURITY SURVEY – How would you deal with a "wayward" female? |

The report's Human Security Survey asked respondents in Lebanon, Occupied Palestine and Morocco how a male family member would react if a female member committed an act he regarded as a violation of custom or tradition. Respondents in Kuwait were not asked the question. In the Occupied Palestinian Territory, the majority were inclined to investigate the matter and to offer advice. The same applied, to a lesser extent, in Lebanon. In Morocco, opinion was spread more evenly over the three categories of response (advice, financial penalty, physical violence). The Palestinian respondents were given the opportunity to choose multiple answers. Over 60 per cent approved of stopping the woman's financial allowance or confining her to the house, and 40 per cent favoured beating her. More than 40 per cent of the Moroccan respondents approved of physical beating. On the other hand, the numbers of those willing to let the matter drop, at one end of the scale, or to kill the woman, at the other, were low.

Response to a female family member who violates custom and tradition

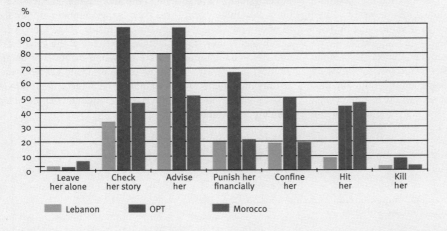

Table 4-4	Reported honour killings, 5 Arab countries		
Country	**Reported honour killings**	**Source**	**Period studied**
Egypt	52	UN Division for the Advancement of Women/UNODC	Year 1995
Iraq (Erbil and Sulaimaniya)	34	UNAMI	Apr-June 2007
Jordan	25-30	UN-ESCWA	Year 2007
OPT	12	Save the Children	Year 2005
Lebanon	12	Save the Children	Year 1998

Sources: UN-ESCWA 2007; Save the Children 2007; UNAMI 2007; UN Division for the Advancement of Women and UNODC 2005. (See Statistical references).

Laws on rape are either equivocal or actively biased against women

showed the perpetrators leniency, ranging from finding them innocent to imposing prison sentences of just 14-15 years. By contrast, the usual penalty for first-degree homicide in Lebanon is either life in prison or death. A previous study in 1999, based on records of the Lebanese authorities between 1995 and 1998, has shown that the number of honour killings in Lebanon was around 12 crimes a year.[8]

There are no reliable figures on the prevalence of honour crimes in the Arab

countries from sources in the region. However, it is possible to form some impression from the limited estimates available from international sources which, however, are based on reported cases only.

Rape and society

Rapes are seldom reported to the police in Arab countries, or covered by the press. The general perception is that sexual assaults on women are few and far between. In countries the world over, rape victims who let their cases go to trial face painful questioning, public exposure and the risk of being stigmatized. In Arab countries, where laws on rape are either equivocal or actively biased against women, and where family and society join to deny occurrences, preserve female virginity and downplay the crime in order to safeguard honour and reputation, few cases come before the courts. Thus, one of the most violent, intrusive and traumatic threats to women's personal safety continues while society averts its eyes. Where cases do surface, it is a courageous Arab woman

Box 4-6	Gang rape

In recent years, there has been an increased and explicit recognition of some forms of violence against women as gang rape. Below are a selection of reported cases of gang rape in two Arab countries, (Algeria and Saudi Arabia) which were communicated to the UN Special Rapporteur on violence against women.

Algeria: The incident took place in Hassi Messoud (Southern Algeria) on the night of 13 to 14 July 2001. Several hundred men violently attacked a group of 39 women living on their own. The men physically and sexually abused almost all the women and ransacked their rooms. Several women were raped or gang raped. Subsequently 30 suspected perpetrators were prosecuted in the tribunal of Ouargla, which eventually sentenced 20 men to prison terms of six months to three years. Not a single perpetrator was convicted of rape. The Supreme Court quashed the judgement and ordered a retrial. In 2005, the tribunal of Biskra condemned the majority of indicted perpetrators to long prison sentences and ordered them to pay compensation to the victims.

Saudi Arabia: On 22 March 2007, a 19-year-old woman from al-Qatif met with a male companion. Shortly after, the two were kidnapped at knifepoint by a gang of seven men. The companion was attacked by the gang, but was then released. The woman was then raped by the gang. Four members of the gang were at the time sentenced by the Qatif General Court to prison terms ranging from one to five years, with floggings of up to 1000 lashes. The sentences were increased on 15 November 2007. Three other gang members reportedly turned themselves in before the conclusion of the trial. In an extraordinary inversion of justice, the *victim* of the gang rape and her male companion were convicted in 2006 of being alone in private with a member of the opposite sex who was not an immediate family member. The Special Rapporteur acknowledges that the victim was subsequently pardoned by the King in December 2007.

Source: UN Special Rapporteur on violence against women 2008n.

indeed who sues for her rights in the face of entrenched prejudice.

The UN Special Rapporteur on violence against women noted that, although Governments are asked to promote research, collect data and compile statistics concerning violence against women and encourage studies of its causes and consequences, there is still an alarming lack of such data in relation to women and girls.[9]

In the 2006, 2007 and 2008 reports, the UN Special Rapporteur has documented several cases of rape in different Arab countries namely in Bahrain, Iraq, Libya, Saudi Arabia, and Sudan. The Special Rapporteur also emphasized that the omission of a particular country or territory should not be interpreted as indicating that there is no problem of violence against women in that country or territory.[10]

Human trafficking

Human trafficking is a multi-billion dollar transnational industry that operates almost entirely underground. Its victims are the men, women and children who are abducted, coerced or enticed into various degrading forms of servitude for the gain of traffickers. For men, the trade entails forced labour under dehumanising conditions and without respect for labour rights. For women, it usually means domestic service often indistinguishable from slavery, sexual exploitation and work

Human trafficking is a multi-billion dollar transnational industry that operates almost entirely underground

Table 4-5	Incidence of reporting trafficking in persons according to the UN Office on Drugs and Crime (UNODC) citation index (alphabetical order)[11]				
Countries	Country of origin	Country of transit	Country of destination	Profile of victims	Purpose of trade
Algeria	Medium	Low	Very low	Women and children	Sexual exploitation
Bahrain	NR	Very low	Medium	Women and children (girls and boys)	Forced labour and sexual exploitation
Egypt	Very low	Medium	Low	Women	Sexual exploitation
Djibouti	Low	NR	Very low	Women and girls	Sexual exploitation
Iraq	Low	NR	Low	Women and children (girls and boys)	Forced labour and sexual exploitation
Jordan	Low	Very low	NR	Women	Sexual exploitation
Kuwait	NR	NR	Medium	Women and children (girls and boys)	Forced labour and sexual exploitation
Lebanon	Low	Very low	Medium	Women and children (girls and boys)	Forced labour and sexual exploitation
Libya	NR	NR	Low	Women	NR
Morocco	High	Low	Very low	Women and girls	Sexual exploitation and forced labour
Oman	NR	NR	Low	Children (girls and boys)	Forced labour and sexual exploitation
Qatar	NR	NR	Medium	Women and children (girls and boys)	Forced labor and sexual exploitation
Saudi Arabia	NR	Very low	High	Women and children (girls and boys)	Forced labor and sexual exploitation
Somalia	Low	NR	NR	Women, children (boys and girls), men	Forced labor and sexual exploitation
Sudan	Low	NR	Very low	Women, men and children (mainly boys)	Sexual exploitation and forced labour
Syria	Very low	NR	Medium	Women	Sexual exploitation
Tunisia	Low	NR	NR	Women and children	Sexual exploitation
UAE	NR	NR	High	Women, children (girls and boys), men	Sexual exploitation and forced labour
Yemen	Very low	NR	Low	Women and children	Forced labour and sexual exploitation

Source: UNODC 2006.

*NR: Not reported.

in nightclubs; and, for children, it leads to forced employment as, for example, beggars, itinerant vendors, or camel jockeys, or to sexual exploitation, including child pornography. For some children, tragically, it begins with their conscription into armed combat, sometimes in official armies and at other times in the militias which fight them.

Little accurate information is available on human trafficking. Most of this criminal enterprise is hidden behind legitimate activities, with cross-border trails that are hard to track. In countries where the central authorities have collapsed, smuggling is carried out in the open. In most other countries, human trafficking rings frequently conceal themselves as employment agencies. Behind this front they practice the most atrocious forms of exploitation, deceiving people into believing that they are mere middlemen working to connect their "clients" to a labour market or prospective employer. In fact, these agencies keep their victims dangling with false promises the fraudulence of which is only discovered when the vision of paradise in destinations such as Europe or the Gulf is punctured in the face of the dubious and often dangerous channels for the journey to their destination, or when the victims discover that the jobs marked for them bear no relationship to the type, legality or terms of service of the employment originally promised.[12]

Trafficking in persons in the Arab countries has certain clear traits. One is that countries play various roles and sometimes multiple roles. They can be destinations for the trade, as is the case with all the Gulf countries and, to a certain degree, Jordan and Lebanon. They may act as a transit point for such commerce, as in the cases of Algeria, Egypt, Jordan, Lebanon and Morocco. Or they may be a source of persons being trafficked, as from Algeria, Jordan, Morocco, Somalia, Sudan and Tunisia.

However, Arab countries are not the only sources of victims of human trafficking in the region. The Arab countries have become a major destination for trade in persons coming from many regions around the world: Southeast Asia, Eastern Europe and Asia Minor and Central Asia. The end-points of this traffic are, primarily, the Gulf countries and countries, such as Egypt, Jordan, and Lebanon. Sub-Saharan countries are another point of origin of such traffic. Countless numbers of persons from that region make their way to North African countries, notably Libya, Morocco, and Tunisia, with the aim of crossing into Europe. Many fail in their attempts to do so, and are left stranded until their hoped-for opportunity arrives. Meanwhile, they eke out a living in menial jobs, if they are lucky, or turn to begging, itinerate vending or prostitution. In addition to these trans-border dynamics, the source-to-destination cycle of human trafficking may sometimes be confined to one country, as occurs in Djibouti, Mauritania, Somalia, and Sudan, and, to a lesser extent, Egypt and Tunisia.

The minimum harm that can come to the victims of such commerce is that they end up as domestic servants. Many who have fallen into the clutches of this trade, however, have met far worse fates, having been driven into conditions akin to slavery and forced to work as servants or as a source of pleasure for the warring militias in Somalia and Sudan. In other cases, if they do not end up as household slaves in the Gulf or Mali or Mauritania, for example, they might be exported to militias in neighbouring countries, such as the Lord's Resistance Army in Uganda, which has recruited children and captive women from southern Sudan.

Traffickers use different techniques to intimidate and enslave victims. Some simply lock their charges up. Other less obvious techniques include:

- Debt bondage and other financial strings to keep victims in a state of dependence, including holding back wages "for safekeeping"
- Quarantine from the public: limiting and monitoring victims' contact with outsiders
- Isolation from their families, kinsfolk and religious communities
- Confiscation of passports, visas and/or identification documents
- The use or threat of violence toward victims and/or their families
- The threat of humiliation by exposing victims' circumstances to their families
- Telling victims they will be imprisoned or deported for immigration violations if they contact authorities

The Arab countries have become a major destination for trade in persons

Traffickers use different techniques to intimidate and enslave victims

Women and children in theatres of conflict

Rape as a weapon of war

Arenas of war and conflict extend the continuum of violence to which women are exposed in peacetime, but with heightened and distinct forms of vulnerability. The World Health Organization classifies these vulnerabilities as including random acts of sexual assault by both enemy and "friendly" forces and mass rape as a deliberate strategy of ethnic cleansing and domination.[13] Around the world, armed conflicts have compelled women into military sexual slavery, forced prostitution, forced "marriages" and forced pregnancies. These conflicts are scenes of multiple rapes and gang rape. During wars, women are sometimes forced to offer sex for survival, or in exchange for food, shelter, or "protection". Young unaccompanied girls, elderly women, single female heads of household and women in search of fuel wood and water are especially exposed to such attacks. Rape victims suffer profound and lasting physical and psychological trauma. For many, the transmission of HIV-AIDS from their violators is effectively a death sentence. Ethnic conflicts are notorious scenes of such mass violations, among the most abominated examples of which in recent times have been the Democratic Republic of Congo, Rwanda, Uganda, and Yugoslavia, and, in the Arab countries, Darfur.

War-time assaults on women take place in a context of lawlessness, displacement and armed clashes in which gender roles are polarized. In these theatres, men often compensate for their own insecurities and loss of dominance through intensified aggression against women. Encouraged by their military commanders, in a climate of "guts and glory", invading troops may use

For many women, the transmission of HIV-AIDS from their violators is effectively a death sentence

---

Box 4-7   **Screams in the desert – the women of Darfur**

Five years into the armed conflict in Sudan's Darfur region, women and girls living in displaced persons camps, towns, and rural areas remain extremely vulnerable to sexual violence. Assaults on women continue to occur throughout the region, both in the context of attacks on civilians, and during periods of relative calm. Those responsible are usually men from the government security forces, militias, rebel groups, and former rebel groups, who target women and girls predominantly (but not exclusively) from Fur, Zaghawa, Masalit, Berti, Tunjur, and other non-Arab ethnicities.

Survivors of sexual violence in Darfur have no meaningful access to redress. They fear the consequences of reporting their cases to the authorities and lack the resources needed to prosecute their attackers. Police are physically present only in principal towns and government outposts, and they lack the basic tools and political will for responding to sexual violence crimes and conducting investigations. Police frequently fail to register complaints or conduct proper investigations. While some police seem genuinely committed to service, many exhibit an antagonistic and dismissive attitude toward women and girls. These difficulties are exacerbated by the reluctance to investigate crimes committed by soldiers or militia, who often gain effective immunity under laws that protect them from civilian prosecution.

The Sudanese government has said it is committed to combating sexual violence in Darfur. In November 2005 it launched a National Action Plan on Combating Violence against Women and in December 2005 the Ministry of Justice created a special Unit to Combat Violence against Women and Children to oversee the National Action Plan and coordinate activities. The governors of the three Darfur states have each established state-level committees—composed of a cross-section of local authorities—to address violence against women.

But these measures have so far failed to address root causes of sexual violence, prevent pervasive and persistent incidents of sexual violence throughout Darfur, or reverse the climate of impunity that perpetuates it. The government has not yet made serious efforts to deter or stop soldiers or militia forces from committing sexual violence. Neither has it held those who do accountable. Finally, it has done too little to address debilitating weaknesses in the police and justice sectors. Women and girls continue to be brutally beaten and raped. Social stigma and obstacles to justice continue to discourage women and girls from seeking redress, while members of the armed forces remain shielded from prosecution.

From 2004 on, the African Union peacekeeping mission, known as AMIS, made efforts to protect women and girls victimized by sexual violence. But a lack of resources and various logistical and security challenges undermined these efforts. On January 1, 2008, an expanded United Nations-African Union mission (UNAMID) took over the mandate of the African Union mission and has been tasked to ensure security for humanitarian agencies, protect civilian populations and monitor peace agreements.

Source: HRW 2008c.

---

rape as a weapon of war to subjugate and humiliate their targets.

In June 2008, the UN Security Council unanimously adopted Resolution 1820[14] in which it demanded the "immediate and complete cessation by all parties to armed conflict of all acts of sexual violence against civilians". The resolution noted that women and girls are particularly targeted by the use of sexual violence, in some cases as "a tactic of war to humiliate, dominate, instill fear in, disperse and/or forcibly relocate civilian members of a community or ethnic group".

Child rape during armed conflict

In conflict situations, rape and sexual violence against children continue to be systematic and widespread. Children in and around refugee camps and internally displaced persons' settlements are especially vulnerable.

In Somalia, according to the 2008 report of the Secretary-General on children and armed conflict,[15] reported cases of rape and other sexual assaults carried out against children increased from 115 in 2006 to 128 during the period from 16 March 2007 to 15 March 2008. Of the rape cases of children reported by child protection monitors, only a minority are alleged to have been carried out by parties to the conflict. Nonetheless, the continued fighting has rendered women

and children more vulnerable to sexual violence because of displacement, destitution, the breakdown of the rule of law and the re-emergence of armed groups and freelance militias—all a result of the ongoing conflict. There are reports of victims as young as 3 months old. Most at risk are women and girls living in open and unprotected settlements for internally displaced persons, particularly those who belong to a minority clan in the area where they are living.

In the Raf and Raho and Tuur Jalle settlements for internally displaced persons (IDPs) in Bosaso there were 31 cases of rape against children reported in one month alone. In the Bulo Mingis settlement in Bosaso 25 rapes of children were reported in October 2007. In the first week of November 2007, three girls, aged 7, 12 and 18 years, were raped in the settlement. During 2007, forty children were raped and 12 children experienced attempted rape in five settlements for internally displaced persons in Somaliland, including Hargeisa and Sheikh-Nur. Internally displaced persons in most settlements reported that the perpetrators were fellow IDPs, people from the host community and the police. Though most of the reported rapes were carried out by civilians, there are several reports of sexual assaults by parties to the conflict, including militia members and Transitional Federal Government and Ethiopian troops. In particular, roadblocks set up and controlled by militias or gangs are locations where many incidents of sexual violence have reportedly occurred. In May 2007, militia members stopped a minibus at a checkpoint and raped eight women and five girls. There have also been several cases of girls raped while fleeing Mogadishu. In the first half of 2007, there were four such verified cases of girls attacked by men dressed in Transitional Federal Government uniforms.

These rapes and other sexual assaults are often carried out with impunity. Traditional and community justice mechanisms frequently ignore the victim and negotiate with members of the perpetrator's clan, proposing a financial settlement (ranging from camels to such sums as $800) with the family of the victim by the perpetrator or his clan, or marriage of the victim to the perpetrator. Meanwhile, the victim is considered dishonoured.

In conflict situations, rape and sexual violence against children continue to be systematic and widespread

There are reports of victims as young as 3 months old

Box 4-8   The case of Abeer

The Al-Mahmudiyah killings took place on March 12, 2006 in a family house in a small village, south of Baghdad, Iraq.

Five United States soldiers with the 502nd Infantry Regiment, gang-raped and murdered a 14-year old Iraqi girl named Abeer, after shooting dead her mother, Fakhriyah, 34; her father, Qasim, 45; and her sister, Hadeel, aged 5.

In sworn testimony given under plea bargain, one of the soldiers stated that the soldiers noticed Abeer, at a checkpoint. They stalked her after one or more of them expressed his intention to rape her. On March 12, 2006, they burst into Abeer's home, locked her mother, father, and five-year-old sister in another room and then killed them. The soldiers then took turns raping Abeer. Finally, they murdered her.

Between November 2006 and August 2007, martial courts gave sentences ranging between 90-110 years in prison to the perpetrators.

Source: BBC News 2007a, 2007b, 2008.

According to the 2007 report of the Secretary-General on children and armed conflict in Sudan,[16] rape is widespread in Darfur, and used as a weapon of war. It is clear that the problem extends far beyond the 62 cases that have been confirmed. Generally, perpetrators are armed men, often in uniform, targeting internally displaced persons or village women and girls on their way to and from livelihood activities. In many incidents, victims identified perpetrators as elements of Sudanese Armed Forces, the central reserve police and the Janjaweed. Unidentified armed men have allegedly committed rape in a number of other incidents. Increasingly, the trend in Darfur seems to indicate that younger girls are being specifically targeted for rape. There were also five boys among 62 confirmed reports of rape during the year. Also, in Southern Sudan and the three areas, there were six confirmed cases of rape reported during the period from 16 July 2006 to 30 June 2007, with responsibility attributed to members of armed forces or groups.

On 15 April 2007, two girls, ages 10 and 12, from Northern Darfur, returning home from working on a farm, were approached by two armed soldiers dressed in green khaki uniforms. One soldier pushed the 12-year-old girl to the ground and raped her while the other continued beating the 10-year-old. Upon seeing a group of internally displaced persons approaching, the soldiers reportedly quickly escaped southward in the direction of the Sudan Alliance Forces military camp in nearby Umm Dereisa. Two Sudan Liberation Army (Minawi) soldiers raped a 12-year-old girl at Taradona in Northern Darfur on 15 October 2006. She was brutally attacked and beaten. The allegation was confirmed and attributed to Sudan Liberation Army (Minawi). In September 2006, it was confirmed that four Sudan Alliance Forces soldiers raped a girl 16 years of age in Eastern Jebel Marra. The attack was carried out in the presence of the girl's six-month-old son, who was born as a result of an earlier rape. These rape cases reflect the daily atrocities to which girls are subjected, many of which occur when girls are fetching water, collecting firewood or performing other such domestic chores.

In Darfur, investigation and prosecution of the crime of rape is very rare and the justice system is very weak. Many cases go unreported owing to the stigma attached to the survivor. During the reporting period, there were three cases recorded that involved two central reserve police officers and one Sudan Alliance Forces soldier who were prosecuted for the alleged rape of children as young as 13 years of age.

Marching children to war

Children are easy prey to practices ruinous to their security. Not only do such practices impair their liberty, but they also expose them to extreme harm, ranging from psychological stunting and physical injury to death. The cruellest of such practices is the recruitment of children for war, which generally takes three forms: firstly, their recruitment into active combat, a phenomenon known as child soldiering; secondly, their use in 'support' activities such as carrying equipment, spying and surveillance, transmitting messages, and the performance of sexual services; and, thirdly, their use as human shields or to disseminate propaganda.

Internal strife or foreign occupation in developing countries furnishes the conditions that facilitate the exploitation of children in these ways. Such conditions include the breakdown of public security, political instability, disruption in the work of educational institutions, the break-up of families, poverty, rampant unemployment, and the displacement of populations and their flight abroad. Such circumstances render it difficult to distinguish between children who "volunteer" to serve in battle as a source of income and those who are pressed into this service which is so detrimental to their intellectual, psychological, and physical growth.

Nevertheless, it is possible to distinguish between two different types of cases of children's involvement in military activities in the Arab countries. The first is that of Sudan and Somalia, where the recruitment of child soldiers is widely reported. The second is that of the other conflict zones, in Iraq, Lebanon, and the Occupied Palestinian Territory, in which

Many cases go unreported owing to the stigma attached to the survivor

Children are easy prey

children, voluntarily or under coercion, play support roles, while suffering under the armed conflicts in these areas.[17]

Only a small number of Arab countries have committed themselves before the international community to prohibit the recruitment of children into military activities. Thirteen Arab countries have ratified the Optional Protocol to the Convention on the Rights of the Child pertaining to the participation of children in armed conflict. These are Bahrain, Egypt, Iraq, Jordan, Kuwait, Libya, Morocco, Oman, Qatar, Sudan, Syria, Tunisia and Yemen. Three other countries (Djibouti, Lebanon, and Somalia) have signed the protocol but have not ratified it. The protocol reaffirms the states' commitment to protecting children from involvement in armed conflict and calls for the demobilization of all children under the age of 18.[18] Even if the recruitment of child combatants is restricted to conflict zones in the Arab countries, all Arab governments must clearly commit themselves to fighting the phenomenon. This applies all the more to those governments that ratified the protocol, which need to take all measures necessary to put their obligations into effect.

According to the Global Report on Child Soldiers produced by the 'Coalition to Stop the Use of Child Soldiers', there were an estimated 17,000 children in government forces, allied militias and opposition armed groups in the north, east, and south of Sudan in March 2004. Between 2,500 and 5,000 children served in the armed opposition group, the Sudan's People's Liberation Army (SPLA), in the south. Although the SPLA claimed to have demobilised over 16,000 children between 2001 and 2004, the report maintains that the army continues to recruit child soldiers. In addition, the Ugandan rebel Lord's Resistance Army has held some 6,000 children as hostages in southern Sudan. The humanitarian crisis in Darfur has also had alarming consequences for children. As this crisis unfolded, there were increasing reports of children being abducted and pressed into service with the armed forces and warring militias. Children below the age of 14 were reported to have been seen serving in the government forces and police in Darfur, as well as in the ranks of the pro-government militias known as the Janjaweed. There is corroborated evidence that the Sudanese armed forces, the Justice and Equality Movement (al-Salam Faction), the four factions of the Sudan Liberation Army, the Popular Defence Forces, the Janjaweed and the central police reserves all recruit child soldiers.

While the use of children in military activities in Sudan has not ceased, there have been signs of some improvement in the south and east and in Darfur. Firstly, some warring parties in these areas have undertaken pledges to UNICEF to demobilise child soldiers and to permit international organisations to inspect their camps in order to ensure that these parties are fulfilling their commitments. Secondly, governing authorities have agreed to criminalise these activities and to allocate funds to the re-assimilation of children into normal life. The National Unity Government in Khartoum and the government of South Sudan pledged themselves to these obligations following the visit of the UN Special Envoy on Sudan to the country in January 2007. In Darfur, in June 2007, the Minni Minnawi faction of the Sudan Liberation Army signed an action plan with UNICEF to end the recruitment and the use of children in combat, in accordance with which SLA/Minnawi pledged to demobilise the children serving its ranks. Nevertheless the Global Report notes that, as of June 2007, this faction had so far undertaken no concrete action to meet its obligations. It further concludes that all parties to the conflicts in Sudan were guilty of killing, maiming, and abducting children and committing rape and other sexual violence against them during the period covered by the report, which went up to August 2007.[19]

In Somalia, all warring factions including the interim government engage in the recruitment of child soldiers. The practice has become extremely widespread since the collapse of the central government and under conditions of the proliferation of militias and the massive flight and internal displacement of persons. The UN Special Representative for Somalia estimated that about 200,000 Somali children, or about 5 per cent of all children in the country, have carried arms or otherwise taken part in militia activities at one point in their lives.[20] There have been numerous reports of boys aged 14 or 15 participating in militia

Only a small number of Arab countries have committed to prohibit the recruitment of children into military activities

Governing authorities have agreed to criminalise these activities

attacks, and many youths have joined the criminal gangs known as the moryaan (parasites).[21] Among the many groups that recruit children into combat are the Transitional Federal Government, the Juba Valley Alliance, the Somali Reconciliation and Reconstruction Council, and the Somali Reconciliation and Reconstruction-Mogadishu, and the Rahanwein Resistance Army.

According to the 2007 Report of the Secretary-General on children and armed conflict in Somalia,[22] one of the challenges in addressing the recruitment and use of children in fighting forces is the fact that this is a long-standing practice in Somali culture. Boys over the age of 15 are considered adults and as such it is considered acceptable for them to carry arms. Moreover, given the nomadic and clan-based structure of traditional Somali life, boys have historically been expected to defend family or clan property from a young age. The use of children in conflict is thus particularly pervasive and difficult to challenge.

Furthermore, displacement, abandonment and neglect, orphanhood and destitution have made many children, especially those living and working on the streets, particularly vulnerable to recruitment. Reports indicate that the recruitment of children significantly increased in 2006 owing to the conflict in Mogadishu between the Islamic Courts Union (ICU) and the warlord groups of the Alliance for the Restoration of Peace and Counter-Terrorism, as well as the conflict throughout central and southern Somalia between the ICU and the Transitional Federal Government (TFG). However, the number of children recruited or involved in the hostilities cannot easily be verified as there is no birth registry in Somalia, making it difficult to determine the age of an adolescent or young person involved with an armed group. Beyond the widespread eyewitness reporting of children as young as 11 years of age at checkpoints and in the military vehicles of various parties to the conflict in Mogadishu in 2006, interviews were conducted by UN child protection monitors with 14 boys actively serving in the Union of Islamic Courts and armed groups.

The obvious physical and psychological damage inflicted upon children through their participation in armed conflict leaves its mark on them throughout their lives, if they are fortunate to survive the experience. Deprived of a stable family life, they lose the opportunity for a regular education and the chance to acquire life-sustaining skills. Instead, they become accustomed to using force to resolve disputes or to gain a living. Guns, not books, become their way of life. It is not surprising that many youths have enlisted with organised crime rings or engaged in piracy along the Somali coast. Somali piracy and banditry extend anarchy to the high seas; with rampant unemployment and poverty closing off the avenues to a legitimate livelihood, they have become a high-risk, high-reward source of income for some.

Guns, not books, become children's way of life

The situation of refugees and internally displaced persons

Among regions, the Arab region may be unique in the nature of its refugee situations. It is the site of the world's longest-standing refugee question, that of the Palestinians, as well as its latest such problem, in Darfur. Two types of refugee must be distinguished: those forced to leave their original home but remaining within their own country—these are internally displaced persons (IDPs)—and those forced to leave their country. However, the legal status of refugee, as defined in the 1951 Convention relating to the Status of Refugees, is only accorded to those who, owing to well-founded fears of being persecuted for reasons of race, religion, nationality, membership of a particular social group or political opinion, are outside the country of their nationality and who are unable or unwilling, for fear of persecution, to seek the protection of that country; or those who, not having a nationality and being *outside* the country of their former habitual residence, are unable or, owing to such fear, are unwilling to return to it.

Somali piracy and banditry extend anarchy to the high seas

Refugees

The issue of refugees is connected to human security in three respects—the place of origin, the progress of the experience, and its conclusion. The reasons for becoming a refugee are themselves grave threats to human security—at a minimum, loss of work and source of income, and at the worst threats to life coming from occupying armies or rival militias. The entire refugee experience is fraught with risks—inability to obtain work or income to meet basic needs, exposure to discrimination and oppression, and social exclusion. And the refugee experience may never end, for a person may die a refugee and pass this status on to a second generation.

The entire refugee experience is fraught with risks

There are real difficulties in calculating the number of refugees in the world. However, it is estimated that the Arab countries contain approximately 7.5 million refugees, in the form of those registered by the UN High Commission for Refugees (UNHCR) and the UN Relief and Works Agency (UNRWA), for the year 2008. This share represents 46.8 per cent of the 16 million global refugees registered under UNHCR and UNRWA for the year 2008.[23]

Most refugees remain permanently scarred by humiliation and persecution

The largest number of refugees, mostly Palestinians and Iraqis, is found in Jordan, Syria, and OPT. Jordan and Syria each hosts more than 2 million refugees, and approximately 1.8 million are in the OPT. In terms of their countries of origin, more than half are Palestinians, who in 2007 exceeded 4 million. They are followed by Iraqis at more than 2 millions, Sudanese,

estimated at around 300,000, and Somalis at more than 200,000.

Approximately 4.6 million Palestinian refugees, live in camps divided between three Arab states in addition to the West Bank and Gaza. The largest concentration of them is in Jordan, the next is inside the Palestinian territories, followed by Syria and Lebanon.

Conditions for refugees vary considerably according to how long they have been refugees, the country of asylum, and the assets they possessed or were able to access when they left their original places of domicile. These include educational and skill levels, savings, and friends and acquaintances able to provide assistance. Those living the first stage of being a refugee and who do not possess assets of value encounter common economic threats through the loss of employment, adequate income, housing, and appropriate nutritional and health conditions.

The longer one remains a refugee, the more one adjusts to difficult circumstances. This is particularly the case for the Palestinians inside and outside the Occupied Palestinian Territory. Nevertheless, receiving aid and becoming inured to harsh conditions do not mean an end to suffering. (Sari Hanafi, background paper for the report). Most refugees remain permanently scarred by humiliation and persecution, and continue to feel the loss of their homeland.[24] In some host countries, Palestinian refugee camps have become developed neighbourhoods. In some countries, the Palestinian refugees are eligible to work and receive social services, such as in Syria and Jordan.[25] In contrast, Palestinian refugees in Lebanon face severe difficulties in obtaining work and are denied ownership rights. As a result they live in very straitened circumstances and in poor and overcrowded camps.

Some data is available on the conditions of Iraqi refugees in Jordan. They migrated largely as families and consist of a higher proportion of females than males. The educated represent a high proportion, and 70 per cent are of working age (over fifteen years old). Yet less than 30 per cent actually work, so most live off their savings or remittances from Iraq. Thus the return to Iraq of small numbers in the latter part of 2007 at times reflected more the exhaustion of savings than it showed

Table 4-6	Total UNHCR and UNRWA refugees, by country of origin and residence, 2007			
Refugees originating from	**Residing in****			
Iraq	Syria	Jordan	Iran	Lebanon
	1,500,000	500,000	57,414	50,000
Somalia	Kenya	Ethiopia	Djibouti	Yemen
	192,420	25,843	5,980	110,616
Sudan	Chad	Ethiopia	Egypt	Eritrea
	242,555	35,493	10,499	729
OPT * (UNRWA refugees)	Jordan	OPT	Syria	Lebanon
	1,930,703	1,813,847	456,983	416,608

Source: UNHCR 2008; UNRWA 2008.

Notes: UNHCR refugees include UNHCR-assisted refugees and people in refugee-like situations. UNRWA refugees include registered refugees in official camps.

* Data as of June, 2008. Under a UNRWA operational definition, Palestine refugees are persons whose normal place of residence was Palestine between June 1946 and May 1948, who lost both their homes and means of livelihood as a result of the 1948 Arab-Israeli conflict.

** The number residing in countries that are the main destination countries of the refugees.

relative improvements in the security situation. Refugee agencies indicate that increasing numbers are seeking asylum in advanced industrial nations. (Sari Hanafi, background paper for the report).

A recent survey indicates that a significant number of Iraqis lack the residence permit that Jordan requires for all foreigners. The survey showed as well that there was an important income dimension to possession of permits; while some 80 per cent of the wealthy held these permits, only 22 per cent of poor refugees possessed them. Over one-third (35 per cent) of Iraqis asked said they would like to register with the UNHCR, but the proportions of those actually registered were higher among Christians and the poor —only 15 per cent of wealthier refugees had registered, compared with 50 per cent of poorer ones (Sari Hanafi, background paper for the report).

Another study of Iraqis, in Syria, indicates that they are not living in refugee camps but residing in residential apartments. Some came to Syria on their own under the threat of death or abduction and are waiting for their families, who may or may not join them. Health care depends on income: those who can afford it are able to see a doctor, while the poor depend entirely on primary health centres in cases of emergency and for their health needs. They can also attend Palestinian Red Crescent clinics which are not usually frequented by Syrians. While these clinics may be crowded, they are well run.

Although Syrian educational institutions have opened their doors to Iraqis, one study noted that the number of Iraqi children enrolled in Syrian schools was about 30,000. The study attributed this to children having to work to support their families, neglecting their education. The study indicates that Iraqis who arrive in Syria bring little money with them for fear of being robbed on the way; if they stay in Syria, they depend on remittances from relatives, if these are able to send anything. Otherwise, they are forced to look for work in Syria, which is finding it hard enough to provide full employment to its citizens.[26]

The situation for Sudanese and Somali refugees is undoubtedly much worse. The two countries are poorer and refugees flee

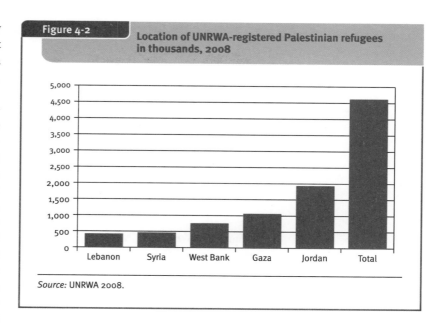

Figure 4-2

Location of UNRWA-registered Palestinian refugees in thousands, 2008

Source: UNRWA 2008.

to equally poor countries, such as Chad and Yemen. Moreover, their predicament is more recent, particularly for those from Darfur and for the victims of the armed conflict between the Islamic Courts Union and their opponents among the Somali warlords and Ethiopian forces. According to the World Food Programme (WFP) 670,000 people fled fighting in Mogadishu in 2007.[27] Conditions in Somalia have deteriorated to the extent of making people take the risk of crossing the sea. Indeed, of these refugees, 30,000 reached Yemen during 2007 by crossing the Gulf of Aden, a voyage which another 1,400 attempted only to die or disappear along the way.[28]

For those that find refuge, whether in Chad, Jordan, Syria, Yemen, survival does not lessen the sense of omnipresent danger. Propelled to flee by conditions of grave insecurity, refugees continue to live with the insecurities associated with their status. They are at the mercy of political and economic events in the host country, which could suddenly turn against them at any time, especially if public opinion links their presence to increases in the cost of living or to competition for jobs and public services. If states like Jordan and Syria treat Iraqi and Palestinian Arab refugees decently, this is not the case regarding the Sudanese and Somalis in their countries of asylum. The reason why people become refugees is that their human security is threatened; the extension of their plight is also such a threat.

Propelled to flee by conditions of grave insecurity, refugees continue to live with insecurities associated with their status

Internally displaced persons

Alongside the refugees are the Internally Displaced Persons (IDPs). Reasons for becoming a refugee or IDP are many, but there are some common factors: both are victims of international and local conflicts; both are victims of occupation and attacks from warring militias.

The total number of internally displaced persons is not less than 9.86 million.[29] A large proportion is found in six Arab states—Sudan, Iraq, Somalia, Lebanon, Syria and Yemen. The greatest number is found in Sudan which the Internal Displacement Monitoring Center[30] has estimated to be between 4.5 million and 5.8 million. Iraq comes second, with around 2.4 million, then Somalia with approximately 1 million.

In Somalia, two years of unconstrained warfare and violent rights abuses have generated an ever-worsening humanitarian crisis. According to the report of the Secretary-General on the situation in Somalia,[31] almost 750,000 people or about two-thirds of the population of Mogadishu are reported to have fled that city between 15 March 2008 and 15 July 2008. This brings the estimated number of people who have streamed out of Mogadishu since the current conflict started to well over 1 million. Some 300,000 of them are living in tents on the outskirts of the capital. Urban dwellers are being forced to make stark choices—pulling their children out of school, forgoing medicines and having only one meal a day—to cope with the lack of food. If the humanitarian situation continues to deteriorate, 3.5 million people could be in need of assistance by the end of 2008. According to a 2008 Human Rights Watch report,[32] across south-central Somalia, 1.1 million Somalis are displaced from their homes. Hundreds of thousands of displaced people are living in squalid camps along the Mogadishu-Afgooye road that have themselves become theaters of brutal fighting. Freelance militias have robbed, murdered, and raped displaced persons on the roads south towards Kenya.

In Sudan, recent clashes in Abyei resulted in approximately 30,000 people being displaced from Abyei town.[33] According to UNHCR,[34] protection remains the most fundamental need of IDPs in Sudan. IDPs settlements lack security, basic services and livelihood opportunities. In Darfur, insecurity remains the major constraint for IDPs, returning refugees and humanitarian workers. Attacks and tribal clashes continue in the villages, causing more displacement. Access to persons of concern is a challenge for humanitarian workers. Furthermore, road attacks targeting NGOs and international organizations are frequent. Helicopters are the only reliable means of transportation, increasing operational costs. In Khartoum, the displaced population has specific needs related to their situation such as documentation, access to land and physical safety. Access to adequate information on areas of origin must also be addressed. The absence of livelihoods and jobs increases the risk of women and children being exploited. UNHCR reports that, with so many humanitarian challenges in the Sudan, addressing IDP needs has not been given priority. The agency further notes that particular attention should be paid to preventing sexual and gender-based violence, of which there are many cases among displaced persons.

Conclusion

Societies can be measured by how they treat the vulnerable in their midst. On that measure, this chapter has tried to illustrate how far Arab countries have to go to understand and address the human predicaments of those who fall below their radar: the women routinely abused and

> *The total number of internally displaced persons in Arab countries is not less than 9.8 million*

Table 4-7	Estimated numbers of internally displaced persons in Arab countries, 2007	
Country	**Number of IDPs**	
	Total (rounded figures, high estimates)	IDPs protected/ assisted by UNHCR
Sudan	5,800,000	1,250,000
Iraq	2,480,000	2,385,865
Somalia	1,000,000	1,000,000
Syria	430,000	-
Lebanon*	390,000	200,000
OPT	115,000	-
Yemen	35,000	-

Source: UNHCR 2008; IDMC 2008.

* UNHCR data for Lebanon refers to 2006.

violated while the public looks the other way; the slaves trafficked underground to service the mills, households and sex spots of the wealthy; the children conscripted to the profession of death; and the displaced who take risk-fraught flight from the region's wars, lack of freedoms and diminished livelihoods.

What the state and society do not see, they cannot protect. It is necessary to begin the search for answers to human insecurity on this scale by acknowledging the existence, extent and sources of such vulnerabilities.

Box 4-9	Breaking the silence surrounding violence against women

The silence surrounding acts of violence against women is one of the most significant obstacles to ending such violations as it makes it difficult to determine facts and consequences. The long-term nature and cost of cultural development programmes, which could help address the problem, are other obstacles. But this phenomenon is starting to be exposed through the reports of national and international human and women's rights organizations and through studies conducted by research centres and women's shelters. Furthermore, the media have lately started to break through the taboos surrounding this subject.

All Arab countries need laws that unequivocally criminalize acts of violence against women. However, changing laws alone will not suffice to change the culture of impunity that perpetuates threats to Arab women's personal security. A profound shift in attitudes is required to combat deep-seated discrimination against women. Beyond the necessary reform of how laws are written, applied and interpreted lie complex questions about culture, tradition and society. In a 21st century environment, Arab states have a profound responsibility to help bring about overdue social and cultural changes to increase women's personal security. A firm stand must be taken against gender biases in all areas of life, beginning with values implanted through the education system and continuing through to discriminatory practices and stereotyping in the workplace, the media and society at large.

Source: The Report team

Endnotes

1   UNICEF and Innocenti Research Center 2000.
2   UN General Assembly Resolution, 1994.
3   UN-Department of Economic and Social Affairs (DESA) 2007a.
4   UNICEF 2009a. "FGM is a fundamental violation of the rights of girls. It is discriminatory and violates the rights to equal opportunities, health, freedom from violence, injury, abuse, torture and cruel or inhuman and degrading treatment, protection from harmful traditional practices, and to make decisions concerning reproduction. These rights are protected in international law."
5   The Arab Republic of Egypt 2008.
6   Hoyek, Sidawi and Abou Mrad 2005.
7   Beydoun 2008.
8   Moghaizel and Abd el Sater 1996 (in Arabic).
9   UN Special Rapporteur on Violence against Women, 2008m.
10 UN Special Rapporteur on Violence against Women, 2006.
11 The index indicates the number of sources reporting an information variable concerning a particular country according to a 5-point scale, from very low to very high, in comparison to all other countries (e.g. information indicating that a specific country or territory is an origin, transit or destination of trafficking in persons).
12 ILO 2008a.
13 WHO 1997.
14 UN Security Council Resolution, 2008g.
15 UN Report of the Secretary-General, 2008a.
16 UN Report of the Secretary-General, 2007b.
17 McManimon 1999.
18 Coalition to Stop the Use of Child Soldiers 2004; 2008.
19 Coalition to Stop the Use of Child Soldiers 2004; 2008.
20 Coalition to Stop the Use of Child Soldiers 2004.
21 Coalition to Stop the Use of Child Soldiers 2008.
22 UN Report of the Secretary-General, 2007a.
23 UNDP/AHDR calculations based on UNHCR 2008; UNRWA 2008.
24 Abu Zayd 2008.
25 According to the United Nations Relief and Works Agency, Palestinian refugees in Jordan are eligible for temporary Jordanian passports, which do not entitle them to full citizenship rights such as the right to vote and employment with the government. [http://www.un.org/unrwa/refugees/jordan.html].
26 Al-Khalidi, Hoffmann and Tanner 2007.
27 WFP 2008a.
28 UN-OCHA 2008b.
29 Internal Displacement Monitoring Centre 2008.
30 Internal Displacement Monitoring Centre 2008.
31 UN Report of the Secretary-General, 2008i.
32 HRW 2008a.
33 UNMIS 2008.
34 UNHCR 2009.

Chapter 5

Challenges to economic security[1]

A major constituent of freedom from want is economic security

The first Arab Human Development Report (AHDR 2002) characterized the Arab world as "richer than it is developed". That description highlighted the disjunction between the region's material wealth and its real levels of human development, which pointed to a backlog of policy failures often overlooked by conventional economic analyses at the time. Yet the fabled oil wealth of the Arab countries is itself misleading in that it masks the structural weaknesses of many Arab economies, and the resulting economic insecurity of states and citizens alike.

This chapter considers patterns of economic vulnerability in the Arab countries. Its point of departure is that "human security means that people can exercise choices safely and freely and that they can be relatively confident that the opportunities they have today are not totally lost tomorrow".[2] As noted in Chapter 1, central to this concept of human security are its two major components: freedom from fear and freedom from want. A major constituent of freedom from want is economic security.

Introduction

Policy gaps have consequences for economic security

This chapter examines economic security in terms of the most important dimensions originally identified by the UNDP Human Development Report 1994 on Human Security: real per capita income levels and their growth patterns; employment options; poverty; and social protection. In doing so, the chapter considers the erratic course of oil-led growth in the Arab countries, the fragility of the economic model associated with it and changing trends in intraregional spillovers from oil producing countries. It also identifies policy gaps that have consequences for economic security in terms of acute unemployment and persisting income poverty. It suggests that comprehensive solutions begin with the adoption and coordinated implementation of sensible long-term integrated social and economic policies, including a revival of industrial policies, and the provision of better functioning social safety nets.

Regional economic vulnerability

The story of Arab economies since the 1970s is largely the story of oil. Producer countries gained most in that narrative, amassing untold wealth, but non-oil Arab countries also benefitted substantially from oil-related services, worker remittances, intraregional investment flows, regional tourism receipts, and aid. While the going was good, oil was good to the region. Yet tied to capricious oil markets,

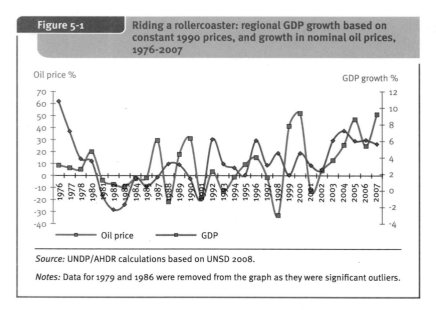

Figure 5-1

Riding a rollercoaster: regional GDP growth based on constant 1990 prices, and growth in nominal oil prices, 1976-2007

Source: UNDP/AHDR calculations based on UNSD 2008.

Notes: Data for 1979 and 1986 were removed from the graph as they were significant outliers.

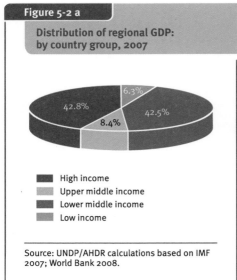

Figure 5-2 a

Distribution of regional GDP: by country group, 2007

- High income
- Upper middle income
- Lower middle income
- Low income

Source: UNDP/AHDR calculations based on IMF 2007; World Bank 2008.

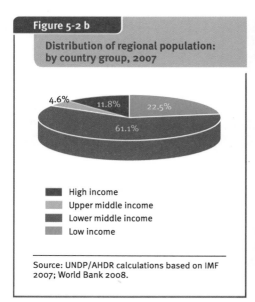

Figure 5-2 b

Distribution of regional population: by country group, 2007

- High income
- Upper middle income
- Lower middle income
- Low income

Source: UNDP/AHDR calculations based on IMF 2007; World Bank 2008.

the region's economic security has been—and remains—hostage to exogenous trends. The first oil boom, which lifted the Arab countries in the late-1970s, also brought them low during the busts of the 1980s and early 1990s, as world oil prices fluctuated sharply.

The analysis that follows adopts the World Bank's classification of Arab countries into income brackets: low, lower middle, upper middle and high income countries.[3] In this classification, the high income Arab countries are Bahrain, Kuwait, Qatar, Saudi Arabia, and the United Arab Emirates; while low income countries include Comoros, Mauritania, Sudan, and Yemen. The rest of the Arab countries belong to the middle income group. The upper middle income group includes Lebanon, Libya, and Oman; the remaining states are low-middle income countries namely, Algeria, Djibouti, Egypt, Jordan, Morocco, Syria, Tunisia.[4]

Oil exports, growth and volatility

Arab GDP growth since the 1970s has been closely tied to the rise in export revenues, dominated by fuel exports. The latter constituted 75, 72.6 and 81.4 per cent of merchandise exports of the high income (HIC), middle income (MIC) and low income (LIC) groups respectively in 2006.[5] The fitful ups-and-downs in the Arab countries, from high growth in the 1970s to economic stagnation through the

1980s and back to extraordinary growth in the early 2000s directly reflects the turbulent cycles of the oil market. This is illustrated both by Figure 5-1, which shows the strong link between movements of the global oil price and the region's GDP growth, and Figure 5.3, which shows the average rate of growth of exports as compared to the average rate of GDP growth for different boom and bust periods.

The steep drops in oil income during the 1980s had major impacts on oil producing countries (Saudi Arabia, for example, saw its GDP at current prices halved between 1981 and 1987). A number of other countries experienced negative economic growth, of which the hardest hit was Kuwait, where GDP at current prices declined by around 18 per cent in 1981 and 1982. The shocks were transmitted to non-oil Arab economies whose receipts from remittances fell away. Jordan and Yemen both had negative growth in some years.

Through all the ups and downs during nearly two and half decades after 1980, the region's per capita economic growth hardly increased at all. Based on World Bank data, real GDP per capita in the Arab countries rose by a mere 6.4 per cent over the entire 24 year period from 1980 to 2004 (i.e. by less than 0.5 per cent annually). Since the 1990s, real per capita growth rates in non-oil as well as oil countries have fluctuated erratically, often turning negative.

The region's per capita economic growth hardly increased at all

---

Box 5-1   **WALID KHADDURI*: Arab oil policy – the fundamentals**

Arab oil revenues fuel extraordinary wealth and rapid infrastructural and other areas of development in the 12 oil-producing states of the region, accounting for almost 90 per cent of their annual public budgets. These revenues also power associated industries, jobs, income and remittances for the citizens of other Arab states. Oil income is thus a major driver in the economic security of the region, and it is essential to understand the fundamentals of the policy that governs this strategic resource.

Arab oil policy is based on the recognition that oil is a vital and strategic commodity for the world economy, and that producer countries have a responsibility to provide it reliably, without interruptions, and at reasonable prices. These strategic premises underwrite the thinking and decision-making process behind the policy. This responsibility requires the investment of tens of billions of dollars annually to expand capacity in order to meet incremental demand. It also extends to substituting for any major shortage in global markets, whether caused by industrial or political developments or natural disasters. The maintenance of spare production capacity for emergencies costs billions because such capacity remains idle most of the time, representing lost income.

Arabs shouldered this responsibility during at least three crises in the last 5 years: when the late 2002-early 2003 oil workers' strike in Venezuela almost halted that country's oil exports; during the 2003 invasion of Iraq, when oil exports ceased for several months; and in the aftermath of the damage wrought by Hurricane Katrina on offshore production platforms in the Gulf of Mexico and on refineries in Texas and Louisiana. Major Arab oil producers all chipped in to help make up for supply shortfalls at these times, preempting major disruptions in the world economy.

The speed and flexibility of producers on these occasions is due to their policy of retaining spare production capacity for emergency use. It is highly costly because it entails leaving readily available oil in the ground, to be used only in emergencies, instead of for financing social projects.

Oil being a global commodity, Arab oil policy requires close cooperation and monitoring with the consuming countries to retain equilibrium in supply and demand. It also entails cooperation with International oil Companies (IOCs), to benefit from their experience and technology. By ensuring global markets sustained supplies under all conditions and by steadily 'greening' the technologies of production, Arab oil policy meets two core objectives : international interest, and the self-interest of the producing countries themselves, particularly of states that have vast reserves and seek to prolong the oil age as long as possible.

Arab oil policy is often obscured by myths and false assumptions. One of these is that the Arab states are behind high oil prices. Yet the price of oil is principally determined by free markets, especially in New York and London, with frequent speculation accounting for the constant rise and fall of prices.

Increasingly, there is also talk about "oil security" amid fears that Arabs will cut oil supplies as a political weapon. This kind of talk is heard globally, but particularly during political campaigns in leading industrial countries. It is used to build the case for sustainable sources of energy, instead of "Arab oil". While there is every reason to mobilize long-term energy alternatives, the "Arab oil insecurity problem" is probably the least rational among them. To place these fears in perspective, recall that the US, for example, consumes around 21 million barrels of oil a day and imports 9-10 million barrels a day, of which only 2.5 million barrels a day are imported from Arab states.

Recently, "peak oil" theorists have argued that current proven oil reserves in the Arab world cannot meet rising global demand, and that prospects of discovering more oil fields in the region are slight. In fact, Arab oil producing countries have allotted more than $100b billion annually to raise capacity and scores of projects are under way to replace what is produced and to bring on new supplies. However, this policy requires coordination with consumer countries that need to be more transparent and forthcoming with their projected demand.

While Arab oil fuels the world economy, it is also the region's most important local industry and the largest contributor to national wealth. The use and distribution of this wealth have been controversial, and it is sometimes considered a mixed blessing. Such reservations have been accentuated by the fact that, in oil producing countries, public budgets lack transparency and the state falls short on good governance. Oil has also led to wars and armed conflicts. Yet in the past half-century (since the region's oil exports began to flow in earnest) oil revenues have lifted social, educational, health and general living standards. Non-oil states of the region continue to benefit through employment opportunities, remittances, investments in infrastructure and economic assistance. Much more could be done to ensure that oil becomes a force for human development in the Arab world, but there is little doubt that it has a major role to play in that respect.

*Former Editor-in-Chief and Executive Editor of the Middle East Economic Survey (MEES).

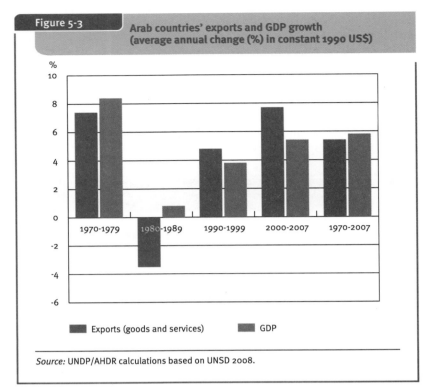

Figure 5-3   Arab countries' exports and GDP growth (average annual change (%) in constant 1990 US$)

Exports (goods and services)   GDP

Source: UNDP/AHDR calculations based on UNSD 2008.

Table 5-1	Volatile real GDP growth per capita in the Arab countries, 1961-2006 (coefficient of variation)		
Income group (number of countries)	Share in total GDP (%)	Coefficient of variation of GDP per capita growth (1961-2000)	Coefficient of variation of GDP per capita growth (2000-2006)
Low income (4)	6.3	4.05	1.25
Lower middle income (6)	42.5	3.12	0.61
Upper middle income (3)	8.4	4.74	1.45
High income (5)	42.8	5.9	1.36
Total (18)	**100**	**4.51**	**1.04**

Source: UNDP/AHDR calculations based on World Bank 2008.

Note: It is a normalized measure of dispersion of a probability distribution. Technically, the coefficient of variation is the ratio of the standard deviation divided by the mean. The coefficient of variation is useful for comparing the degree of variation from one data series to another, even if the means are drastically different from each other.

Table 5-2	Value of petroleum exports of oil-producing countries, 2003 and 2006 (US$ million in current prices)		
Country	2003	2006	Percentage increase between 2003 and 2006
Algeria	16,476	38,342	132.7
Iraq	7,519	27,500	265.7
Kuwait	19,005	53,178	179.8
Libya	13,567	36,950	172.3
Qatar	8,814	24,290	175.5
Saudi Arabia	82,271	188,468	129
UAE	25,153	69,810	177.5

Source: OPEC 2007.

Table[6] 5-1 illustrates this characteristic of the Arab countries by compiling evidence of the volatility of real GDP per capita growth. It reports the coefficient of variation for the Arab income groups based on the World Development Indicators of the World Bank.

Over the long run (1961-2000), real per capita GDP growth was extremely volatile, reflected in the fact that the coefficient of variation for each country group exceeds one. The highest variability is in the high income group, followed by the upper middle income group. The lowest volatility is that recorded for the lower middle income group, followed by the low income group. At the country level, the highest volatility is calculated for Bahrain (with a coefficient of variation of 11.3) while the lowest volatility is calculated for Djibouti (with a coefficient of variation of 0.57).

As Table 5-1 suggests, in the most recent episode of prosperity, this fluctuation in growth rates has abated somewhat across all country groups. While this development is comforting, it offers no grounds for complacency since the current plunge in oil prices is bound to undo growth prospects and once again cause volatility. The general historical pattern is not encouraging. Combining the two interval periods in table 5-1 by using the time periods as weights, it is evident, for instance, that the overall weighted average coefficient of variation for the period 1962-2006 remains very high at 4.05.

Indeed, the data seem to show that Arab countries most recent growth burst may belong to this pattern of high-volatility. In the early 2000s, oil prices reached new highs, putting some Arab economies on the crest of a revenue surge not experienced since the 1970s. According to the World Bank,[7] in 2003–2006, the Middle East and North Africa region averaged economic growth at 6.2 per cent a year, its strongest growth in thirty years. This striking average rate very largely reflects an extraordinary jump in oil revenues. The OPEC basket price of oil averaged between US$24 and US$29 in 2003. Prices climbed to between US$51 and US$66 in 2006. They continued to rise until they peaked at a record high of US$147.2 per barrel in July 2008. Between 2003 and 2006, export revenues in Arab oil-producing countries more than doubled.

But new external shocks for the Arab countries are associated with the current global recession, which began with the 2007 US subprime crisis. The global downturn will impact all Arab countries and could severely disrupt the growth models of the major Arab oil producers. All of the latter have substantial investments in the US, and are not able to decouple their economies from the spreading international crisis. The knock-on effects on the rest of the Arab countries of a protracted slow-down in investment financing and remittances from GCC countries would be considerable. Some analysts forecast that the GCC countries, supported by their general liquidity and the strength of their Sovereign Wealth Funds, may be able to weather the storm by reducing oil production to keep prices from dropping further. But at the time of writing, despite the steep production cut of 2.2 million barrels a day announced by OPEC on December 17, 2008, prices continued to fall. This effectively means that, in the last five months of 2008, crude oil gave up all the gains of the preceding four years.

The structural fragility of Arab economies

Oil-led growth has created weak structural foundations in Arab economies. Many Arab countries are turning into increasingly import oriented and service-based economies. The types of services found in Arab countries fall at the low end of the value adding chain, contribute little to local knowledge development, and lock countries into inferior positions in global markets. This trend, which has been at the expense of Arab agriculture, manufacturing and industrial production, is therefore of concern.

Although the share of services in regional GDP declined quite significantly from over 60 per cent in 1986 to 45 per cent in 2007, this was largely due to the rise in share of the oil sector. By the year 2007, the share of services in GDP still exceeded 50 per cent in all non-oil producing Arab countries and was above 65 per cent in Bahrain, Djibouti, Jordan, Lebanon and Morocco. Furthermore, the sector accounted for over 50 per cent of total employment in most Arab countries. The increasing dominance of the mining (mainly oil) and service sectors at the regional and country group levels is shown in figure 5-4 (A). The figure also shows the trend of a declining share of the agricultural sector. Figure 5-4 (B) depicts a general trend of expanding imports and consumption fueled by the rise in exports (though the share of consumption has declined since the mid 1980s, along with rising exports). Meanwhile the share of investment has been relatively stable since the mid 1970s.

Not surprisingly, most Arab countries have experienced significant deindustrialization over the last four decades (Figure 5-5 A). *In fact, the Arab countries were less industrialized in 2007 than in 1970, almost four decades ago.* This includes MICs with a relatively diversified economic base in the 1960s, such as Algeria, Egypt, Iraq and Syria. True, Jordan, Oman, Tunisia, and UAE have made noticeable progress in industrial development. Nonetheless, in general, the contribution of manufacturing to GDP is anemic, even in Arab countries that have witnessed rapid industrial growth (Figure 5-5 B) and especially when compared to the shares of other developing countries such as the East Asian economies. For the majority of Arab countries, manufactured goods made up less than 11 per cent of total commodity exports in for the year 2006/2007.[8] Moreover, all country groups appear to be converging on the modest regional average, which was below 10 per cent in 2007, from an initially diverse subregional industrial base in 1970 (Figure 5-5 C). Finally, the structural fragility of Arab economies as a result of oil-led growth is highlighted by the conspicuous decline in the share of non-oil productive sectors (agriculture and manufacturing) to GDP in all Arab countries except the HICs. It should be noted that the rapid increase in manufacturing shares in the latter is due, in part, to the very low initial base in the 1970s and the rapid growth in value added by petrochemical industries.

The global downturn will impact all Arab countries

Oil-led growth has created weak structural foundations in Arab economies

Figure 5-4

Structure of GDP, by economic sector (A) and type of expenditure (B), 1970-2007 for the region, HICs, MICs, and LICs, respectively

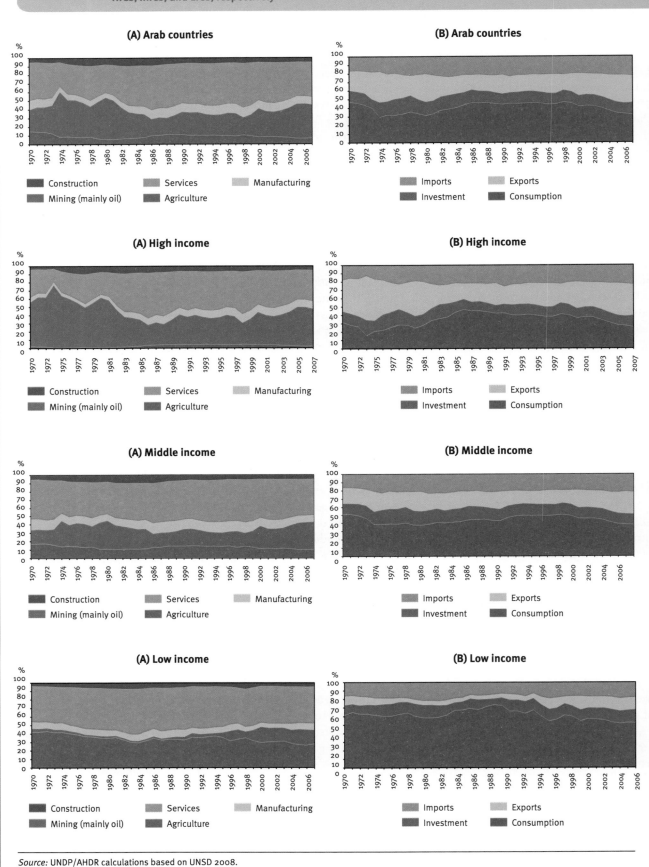

Source: UNDP/AHDR calculations based on UNSD 2008.

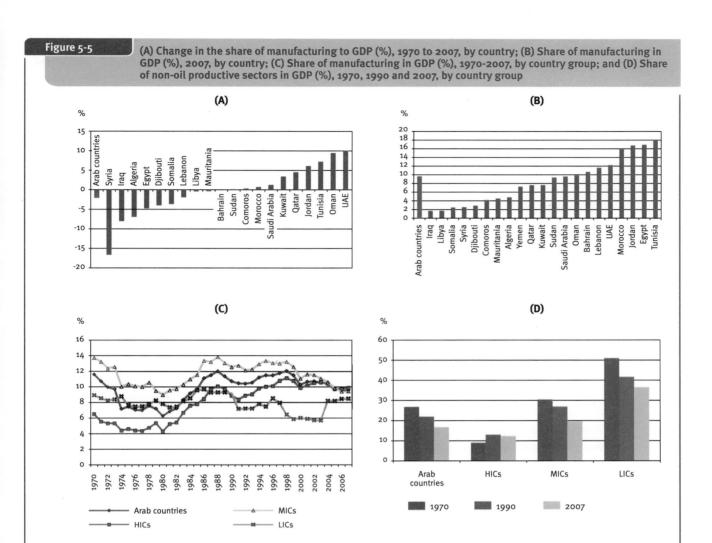

Figure 5-5 (A) Change in the share of manufacturing to GDP (%), 1970 to 2007, by country; (B) Share of manufacturing in GDP (%), 2007, by country; (C) Share of manufacturing in GDP (%), 1970-2007, by country group; and (D) Share of non-oil productive sectors in GDP (%), 1970, 1990 and 2007, by country group

Source: UNDP/AHDR calculations based on UNSD 2008.

New and old policy questions

With turbulence once again buffeting the region, two pressing questions that emerge are: will Arab countries slip into a boom-and-bust cycle, as in the 1970s and 1980s? Will both oil and non-oil Arab countries share the benefits of the recent surge in oil revenues, as in the previous episode? A third question relates to an older challenge: the Arab countries legacy of unemployment and poverty, and whether efforts to overcome a backlog of deficits in these areas will be weakened.

The answers bear directly on the sustainability of the economy of the Arab countries and whether they can contribute to human security in terms of jobs, income and social equity.

From the short-lived third boom to the financial crisis

On the first question, it may be observed that, adopting a common strategy of prudence, Arab oil producing countries have opted to put much of their latest windfall into foreign investments, external reserves and oil stabilization funds, and to pay down debts. They have also embarked on major domestic investments in real estate, construction, oil refining, transport and communication and social services.[9] This approach clearly differs from patterns of the past, which emphasized imports and consumption. International financial institutions have been quick to commend the emerging improvements in the oil producing countries' macroeconomic indicators

With turbulence once again buffeting the region, two pressing questions emerge

Table 5-3	Military expenditure in four Arab countries (millions of dollars in constant 2005 prices)				
Country	1998	2003	2004	2005	2006
Saudi Arabia	20,500	18,944	21,060	25,372	29,032
Algeria	1,801	2,453	2,801	2,925	3,014
UAE	3,036	2,853	2,629	2,559	-
Libya	414	536	699	749	741

Source: SIPRI 2008.

The largest portion of this enormous increase in reserves undoubtedly belongs to the Gulf States

for GDP, trade and foreign direct investment. However, the new pattern also exposes GCC countries more openly than in the past to global economic downturns, the latest of which poses severe challenges to their capital-intensive growth model.

The huge revenues recently earned by these countries have allowed some, such as Algeria and Saudi Arabia, to repay all their foreign debts while simultaneously holding onto substantial foreign currency reserves. According to the IMF's Regional Economic Outlook: Middle East and Central Asia, the boom led to an increase in reserves for Middle Eastern countries from 163.9 billion dollars in 2002 to 198.3 billion the following year, and which then reached 476 billion in 2006 and 591.1 billion in 2007. This data includes Iran and some Arab countries that are not among the large oil exporting states or which depend on oil imports, such as Egypt and Jordan. It also excludes Arab oil exporting countries in Africa. However, the largest portion of this enormous increase in reserves undoubtedly belongs to the Gulf States.

In addition to investing in development and settling their foreign debts, Arab oil exporting countries have been in a position to direct large streams of revenue towards their military and security forces. The Arab country with the highest expenditure on defence and security, according to the Stockholm International Peace Research Institute (SIPRI), is Saudi Arabia, which occupies ninth position internationally in respect of military expenditure, ahead of Australia, Brazil, Canada, India, South Korea, and Spain. Algeria and the UAE follow at a large distance, with the UAE actually decreasing its outlays on arms. The Iraqi government holds fourth position, followed by Libya, whose defence expenditure is half that of Iraq.

With the exception of Saudi Arabia, military expenditure does not represent a

Renewed prosperity has propelled some governments to play an active role in seeking peace

high percentage of GDP in these countries. It is true that Saudi Arabia's percentages have decreased during this period compared to high levels in the late eighties, (15.2 per cent in 1988 and 13.4 per cent in 1989) and again in the late nineties (14.3 per cent in 1998 and 11.4 per cent in 1999). But despite the downward trend in the new millennium, in 2005 Saudi Arabia's military spending remained at 8.2 per cent, much higher than in Algeria, Libya and the UAE. In 2005, defense spending ranged between 2.9 per cent in Algeria and 2 per cent in each of the other two countries. Some observers note that, so long as the Arab countries are subject to armed strikes and military interventions by powers in the region and abroad, Arab governments will continue to justify such expenditures in the name of regional security.

On the other hand, renewed prosperity has also propelled some governments to play an active role in seeking peace in the Arab countries. Saudi Arabia has led the Arab states in suggesting the Arab Peace Initiative, a proposed settlement with Israel based on land for peace. It has also intervened to seek reconciliation between the two factions of the Palestinian resistance and have made active efforts on the Lebanese front. Libya also played a leading part in an attempt to reach a peaceful settlement in the Darfur crisis. Qatar has been active in various initiatives concerning the Lebanese 2008 crisis, the Palestinian situation, and the Darfur crisis.

If none of these diplomatic efforts was particularly effective, the signs of a new regional responsibility in matters of peace and stability are nonetheless encouraging; which leads to the second question about the Arab countries at large. Will the wealthy Arab countries use their new riches to interpret security in terms of human development and to promote such development in their own societies and in the region as a whole? There has not been a complete dearth of valuable initiatives. One might cite the establishment of the King Abdullah University for Science and Technology, which offers Arab graduates, women as well as men, grants to conduct scientific research with state-of-the-art facilities and resources. There is also the Mohammed Bin Rashid Al Maktoum Foundation, with the objective of developing the knowledge and human capabilities of the Arab region, as well as the Arab Open University, financed by the Prince Talal Bin Abdul Aziz. These are important initiatives to promote human development in the region.

The initial signs, however, suggest that non-oil exporting Arab countries may have gained less from the third boom than they did from the first two. Although oil wealth still crosses borders, and while several rich countries switched a number of foreign investments to regional markets in the aftermath of 9-11, intraregional flows are becoming less copious and are having less impact than in the past. First, population increases in non-oil countries offset much of these flows. Second, worker remittances from the oil states have been hit by the practice of 'job nationalization' and of replacing expatriate Arab labour with cheaper Asian alternatives; this latter practice has grown under security-related restrictions on employment in the Gulf that have affected Egyptian, Yemeni and Palestinian workers the most. Third, non-oil countries are incurring higher energy costs through rising oil import bills and expensive fuel subsidies.

Nonetheless, oil is likely to remain a key driver of growth in the Arab countries, albeit through different channels than in the past.

At the time of writing, the global economy is mired in the worst financial crisis since the Great Depression. What first appeared as strains in the United States mortgage and housing market during the summer of 2007 began expanding during 2008 into deeper pressures across the global financial system and led to the collapse of numerous major banking institutions, dramatic drops on stock markets around the world, and a credit freeze. These financial fissures had by early 2009 triggered a full-blown global economic crisis, with most advanced economies already in recession and the outlook for emerging and other developing economies deteriorating rapidly, including those with a recent history of strong economic performance. According to the United Nations World Economic Situation and Prospects, published in January 2009, the baseline scenario is for a 1.0 per cent growth of GDP worldwide in 2009, while the more pessimistic scenario envisages negative

| Box 5-2 | The vulnerability of major oil producing states to the international financial crisis |

A study on the size and likely growth of sovereign wealth funds in the Gulf Cooperation Council countries was released in January 2009 by the Council on Foreign Relations. The authors concluded with the following estimations:

The Gulf's external portfolio assets of GCC sovereign funds and central banks fell from almost $1.3 trillion in 2007 to $1.2 trillion in 2008 as market-to-market losses on equity and alternative asset holdings offset record oil revenues. The swing in fortunes of the smaller Gulf states is more extreme: the foreign assets of the governments of Kuwait, Qatar, and the United Arab Emirates—in the authors' estimation—fell from close to $1 trillion at the end of 2007 to close to $700 billion at the end of 2008.

At all oil prices, the authors expect the Gulf countries to be looking to increase the share of their portfolio held in liquid assets in 2009. Major Gulf states will need to provide more foreign currency liquidity to domestic institutions in order to maintain spending levels.

If oil remains below $50, most countries will end up drawing on their funds to support current levels of spending, with only interest and dividend income contributing to the growth of assets under management.

Source: Setser and Ziemba 2009.

growth globally in that year—for the first time since 1930.

Coming on the heels of the food and energy security crises, the global financial and economic crisis shows strong signs of rolling back recent economic growth (2003-2006). The problem is particularly serious given that many of the countries are not in a position to implement effective counter-cyclical macroeconomic policies. While governments of Arab oil producing countries in the Gulf have responded to the crisis through fiscal stimulus packages, the middle-income and low-income Arab countries will not be able to do so. Moreover, with oil prices having retreated precipitously from their record highs, even the Gulf countries are expected to run deficits in 2009.

Arab leaders have been active in working toward a regional response to the crisis as well. At the January, 2009 *Arab Economic, Developmental and Social Summit*, held in Kuwait, they agreed to work together on consolidating close Arab relations and common goals, especially as pertains to promoting social and economic development, including in the areas of empowerment of youth and women, and in addressing food and water issues. Moreover, the *Kuwait Declaration*, issued on January 20th, called for cooperation to enhance the ability of Arab countries to confront the

The global financial and economic crisis shows strong signs of rolling back recent economic growth

Many of the countries are not in a position to implement effective counter-cyclical macroeconomic policies

repercussions of the international crisis, and to participate in international efforts directed at securing international financial stability.

Patterns of unemployment

Unemployment is a major source of economic insecurity in most Arab countries. Data from the Arab Labour Organization show that in 2005 the overall average unemployment rate for the Arab countries was about 14.4 per cent of the labour force compared to 6.3 per cent for the world at large.[10] While national unemployment rates vary considerably, ranging from about 2 per cent in Qatar and Kuwait to about 22 per cent in Mauritania, as noted subsequently, youth unemployment is a serious challenge common to many Arab countries.

In looking at aggregate unemployment trends in the Arab countries, it is necessary to distinguish the high income group, with the exception of Saudi Arabia, from the other income groups. High income Arab countries in general have not experienced high unemployment rates, owing largely to the nature of their oil economies in spite of their heavy dependence on foreign labour. According to the ALO, the unemployment rate in the latter group ranged from a low of 1.7 per cent of the total labour force in Kuwait, to a high of 3.4 per cent in Bahrain; with rates of 2 per cent for Qatar, and 2.3 per cent for UAE. However, emerging strains in the labour markets in these countries indicate that a serious unemployment problem among their nationals may soon become a major challenge. In contrast to these low unemployment rates, the unemployment rate in Saudi Arabia, estimated as 6.1 per cent in 2005, already constitutes a challenge to economic security.[11]

During the 1980s, the average unemployment rate in non oil-producing Arab countries ranged from a high of 16.5 per cent in Algeria to a low of 4.8 per cent in Syria. Morocco's unemployment rate was second highest (14.2 per cent), followed by

Unemployment is a major source of economic insecurity

---

that of Tunisia (13.6 per cent), that of Egypt (7.6 per cent), and that for Jordan (6.2 per cent). The weighted average unemployment rate for this group of Arab countries during the 1980s was 10.6 per cent. In the 1990s, the average unemployment rate for Algeria remained the highest at 25.3 per cent, followed by that for Morocco (18 per cent). Both Jordan and Tunisia recorded the third highest average unemployment rate of 15.5 per cent, followed by Egypt (9.6 per cent) and Syria (8.1 per cent). The weighted average unemployment rate during this decade was 14.5 per cent. Thus, over the two decades, the unemployment rate increased in all countries under consideration. Preliminary evidence from the ALO indicates that by 2005, the weighted average unemployment rate has risen to 15.5 per cent[12], up one per cent from its average in the 1990s.

The annual rate of growth in unemployment between 1980 and 2002 (the most recent year available) ranged from a high of 6.6 per cent in Jordan to a low of 0.8 per cent in Tunisia. Algeria's unemployment growth rate amounted to 2.8 per cent, followed by that for Syria (2.4 per cent), and Egypt (2.2 per cent). The weighted average growth rate in unemployment in the Arab countries (using the number of unemployed in 2005) was about 1.8 per cent.[13] This trend is disturbing when it is considered that Arab countries need about 51 million new jobs by 2020.[14]

Most of those new jobs will be needed to absorb young entrants to the labour force who will otherwise face an empty future. ALO estimates for the year 2005/2006 show that youth unemployment rates vary from a high of about 46 per cent in Algeria to a low of 6.3 per cent in the UAE (figure 5-6). With the exception of the latter, high income Arab countries suffer from double digit youth unemployment rates: Saudi Arabia (26 per cent); Kuwait (23 per cent); Bahrain (21 per cent); and, Qatar (17 per cent). Relatively high youth unemployment rates are recorded for the middle income Arab countries: Jordan (39 per cent); Libya (27 per cent); Tunisia (27 per cent); Egypt (26 per cent); Lebanon (21 per cent); Oman (20 per cent); Syria (20 per cent); and, Morocco (16 per cent). The low income Arab countries also report relatively high rates: Mauritania (44 per cent), Sudan (41 per cent), Djibouti

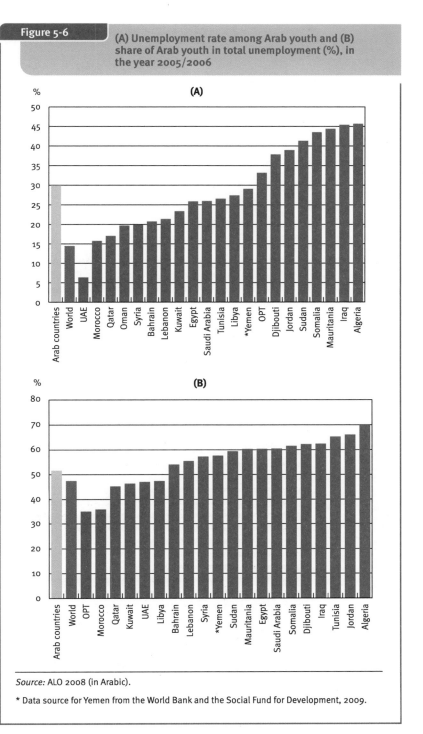

Figure 5-6 — (A) Unemployment rate among Arab youth and (B) share of Arab youth in total unemployment (%), in the year 2005/2006

Source: ALO 2008 (in Arabic).

* Data source for Yemen from the World Bank and the Social Fund for Development, 2009.

(38 per cent), and, Yemen (29 per cent).[15] Overall, in the year 2005/6 the unemployment rate among the young in the Arab countries is nearly double that in the world at large, 30 per cent compared to 14 per cent.

Unemployment in the Arab countries not only affects youth disproportionately; it also often wears a female face. Unemployment rates for young Arab women are higher than those for young Arab men, and among the highest in the

Unemployment in the Arab countries affects youth disproportionately

Box 5-4

1) Is someone in your family unemployed and looking for work?

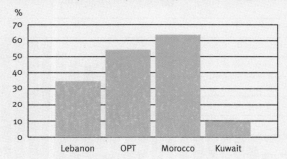

Taking into account the average size of households, answers in the affirmative to the first question suggest unemployment rates ranging between 30-35 per cent in Morocco and the Occupied Palestinian Territory, and 15-20 per cent in Lebanon.

2) Is unemployment worse for particular groups in society?

3) Which groups encounter the worst working conditions when employed?

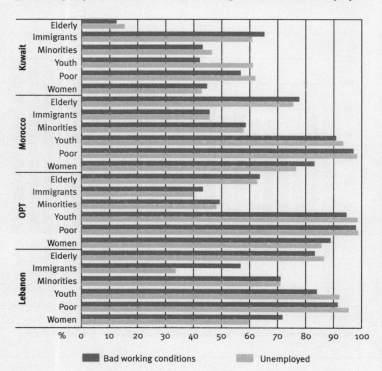

On the second question, concerning labour market discrimination against particular groups, respondents believed that the poor, the young, the elderly and women encounter the steepest hurdles, with youth coming off the worst. Since being poor is at least as much a consequence of unemployment as it is a factor in it, and since the category includes the other groups, the predicament of young people stands out as most acute.

Responses to the third question showed respondents believed that there was a strong correlation between discrimination and poor working conditions in most cases. Answers indicated people in Kuwait thought youth faced the worst conditions, while in Lebanon they thought immigrants fared the worst. Moroccans believed women had to undergo the poorest working conditions.

world. ALO data for the year 2005 shows that the youth unemployment rate for men was 25 per cent of the male labour force compared to 31.2 per cent for women. The female youth unemployment rate varied from a high of about 59 per cent in Jordan (compared to 35 per cent for males) to a low of 5.7 per cent in UAE (compared to a male unemployment rate of 6.4 per cent). There are, however, a few exceptions where the unemployment rate for young women is lower than that for the young men, according to the ALO. These include Bahrain (18 per cent female rate; 28 per cent male rate); Mauritania (41 per cent compared to 49 per cent); Tunisia (20 per cent compared to 29 per cent); and Yemen, where the two sexes fare equally (14 per cent for both).[16]

Signs of discrimination against women in the labour market include the difficulties experienced by young and educated women and the concentration of a high proportion of women in the low-wage agricultural sector, or in jobs without social insurance or benefits. Indeed, the Arab region is the only region in the world where the proportion of women working in agriculture has increased: according to the ILO, between 1997 and 2007, it rose slightly from 31.2 to 32.6 per cent in the Maghreb and from 28.4 to 31 per cent in the Mashreq countries, while employment in industry declined from 19.1 to 15.2 per cent in the Maghreb and from 20.0 to 18.8 per cent in the Mashreq. High unemployment rates for women reflect more than the general failure of Arab economies to generate sufficient jobs. They also indicate entrenched social biases against the employment of women.

Worrisome as the unemployment figures are, they may not fully capture the seriousness of the problem in countries where citizens seize on any means of making a living when they cannot find permanent jobs. For this reason, definitions of unemployment that fit the developed world are of limited relevance to the Arab states, where a few hours' work a week are sufficient to have someone taken off the unemployment register. Thus, in gauging the precariousness of employment in Arab countries, it is instructive to consider, as well, the data, however limited, on the rate and size of employment in the informal sector where workers lack contracts and benefits. The most recent UNDP figures available show that Algeria, Egypt, Morocco and Tunisia have very large informal sectors, comprised between 40 per cent and 50 per cent of the non-agricultural employment. Compared to men, the rate for women is lower in Syria, Algeria, and Tunisia and higher in Egypt and Morocco.

Three primary factors are usually cited in accounting for the Arab countries slumping employment trends: first, the contraction under structural reforms of the large public sector, which employs more than a third of the workforce; second, the limited size, hobbled performance and weak job-generating capacity of the private sector, which has not taken up the slack; and third, the quality and type of education generally provided, which does not stress technical or vocational skills in demand. In this context, job creation, especially for young people, is of paramount importance to the Arab countries, particularly since disguised unemployment adds significantly to the challenge. School-to-work transitions are seldom easy, the result of job shortages and a mismatch between graduate skills and the needs of the labour market. Consequently, some 40 per cent of high school and university graduates between ages 15–25 do not find work on entering the job market, fueling a trend towards high numbers of unemployment even among the educated.

Yet a youth population of the size found in the Arab countries also represents a time-bound window of opportunity for countries—the so-called 'demographic gift'—to move the group into a dynamic, working-age contingent, economically active, healthy, with lower dependency ratios and the capacity to generate income, savings and investment.

But for this to happen, political, economic and social policies must be geared toward mobilizing the potential labour force, a reorientation that is taking place rather slowly. As several studies point out, Arab policies will have to focus on revamping education to close skills gaps, respond to labour market signals and stimulate knowledge-based capabilities matching opportunities in the global, as well as regional economy.[17] National savings will need to be converted efficiently into sizeable investments for expanding

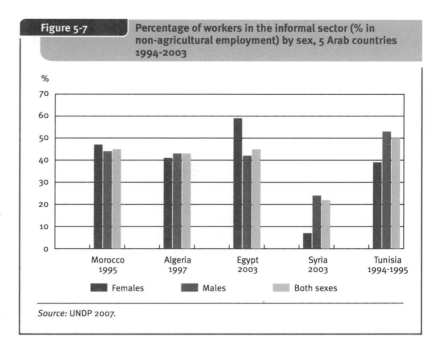

Figure 5-7 Percentage of workers in the informal sector (% in non-agricultural employment) by sex, 5 Arab countries 1994-2003

Source: UNDP 2007.

health, housing and labour markets in order to cater for the needs of this young workforce and provide it with the facilities to increase productivity. A special effort is required to remove entrenched social barriers to women's access to high-productivity jobs. In many of these policy shifts, private-public partnerships offer the best option for mobilizing resources, transferring skills and creating new jobs. Providing the institutional environment for a viable private sector, built on small and medium-size enterprises, as well as independent businesses, is thus a key part of the equation.

The costs of not taking this road could be unbearable pressures on natural and economic resources from a large, unproductive and disaffected contingent. Those costs will be visible in the personal insecurity and alienation of jobless youths that can translate rapidly into protest and in some cases may lead to radicalization, all of which can undermine the security of society at large.

The dynamics of poverty and inequality amid unsettled growth

When considering the relationship between unemployment and poverty in the Arab countries, it is important to be aware that obtaining work does not imply freedom from poverty. While the extent of this disconnect varies from one Arab

Job creation, especially for young people, is of paramount importance

The costs of not taking this road could be unbearable pressures on the Arab countries

country to another, in several cases having a job does not necessarily guarantee being able to meet basic needs. Whatever measures of poverty are used, in every country where data are available, the figures show that the poor outnumber the unemployed by some margin. Even where the unemployed represent a significant portion of those supporting families in poverty, as for example in Jordan (21.5 per cent) and Yemen (24.9 per cent), the majority of economically insecure families in both countries are supported by employed persons (Heba El-Laithy, background paper for the report).

Economic insecurity associated with poverty can be measured from two perspectives: income poverty which describes the welfare of individuals in terms of their incomes (where the welfare of individuals is defined in terms of their enjoyment of goods and services, represented in real per capita consumption expenditure); and human poverty, which looks beyond GDP to a broader definition of well-being (where the welfare of individuals is defined by income as well as by other valued dimensions of life, such as education, health, and political freedom). While income poverty is still the most common measure used by policy-makers worldwide, the use of human poverty and related human development indices provides a fuller prism of the multi-faceted and complex relationship between income and well-being.

Income poverty

The income poverty approach is that most widely adopted in policy making; and the most widely used measure of poverty in this approach is the head-count ratio. The latter is simply the proportion of the total population living below an agreed-upon standard of living, defined as a poverty line. As such, the head-count ratio is a measure of the spread, or incidence, of poverty in a society. It can be interpreted as a fairly obvious measure of economic insecurity. The World Bank has popularized the international poverty lines of one and two US dollars a day per person. Table 5-4 compares the results of applying the two-dollars-a-day measure in the Arab region and other developing regions.

Notwithstanding its diverse income levels, volatile real per capita growth, and high unemployment rates, the Arab region is generally considered to have a relatively low incidence of income poverty. In 2005, about 20.37 per cent of the Arab population was living below the two-dollars-a-day international poverty line. Since this estimate is based on Algeria, Djibouti, Egypt, Jordan, Morocco, Tunisia and Yemen, whose population represents about 63 per cent of the total population of the Arab countries not in conflict, it can be concluded that, in 2005, about 34.6 million Arabs were living under that poverty line in those countries.

The poverty estimates reported above reflect the incidence of poverty according to the international poverty line. We may also consider the proportion of the population under the national poverty line, with its lower threshold (i.e. the lower poverty line). Table 5-5 compares the extreme poverty rate and trend in nine Arab countries based on the lower national poverty line. 1) All poverty estimates selected for this comparison used expenditure as a measure of welfare. Countries such as Sudan, with surveys using non-money metrics, were excluded. 2) All poverty estimates were derived from either World Bank-led or UNDP-led poverty assessments, which used the same methodology consistently. 3) All country reports used were produced by the same consulting team using a common methodology: a) all reports estimated the national poverty line at the cost of food and basic non-food needs; b) all took into account price differences between the country and others; c) all consistently broke down different needs by age; d) all took into account economies of scale.

Table 5-5 shows that, from 2000 to 2005, the rate of extreme poverty for the nine countries in the sample was 18.3 per cent, which is slightly higher than that for the 1990s (17.6 per cent). More significantly, extreme poverty in LICs is more than double that in MICs (36.2 and 15.9 per cent, respectively).

For the purpose of our analysis, we note that applying the two-dollar-a-day international line and the lower national poverty line respectively yields a virtually identical picture of extreme poverty in the region.

However, if this is the picture of extreme poverty in Arab countries at the lower poverty line, it would be reasonable to expect a significantly higher percentage

Table 5-4	Incidence of income poverty – world regions compared, 1981-2005 (percentage living below two dollars a day)								
Region	1981	1984	1987	1990	1993	1996	1999	2002	2005
East Asia and Pacific	92.6	88.5	81.6	79.8	75.8	64.1	61.8	51.9	38.7
Of which China	97.8	92.9	83.7	84.6	78.6	65.1	61.4	51.2	36.3
Eastern Europe and Central Asia	8.3	6.5	5.6	6.9	10.3	11.9	14.3	12	8.9
Latin America and Caribbean	22.5	25.3	23.3	19.7	19.3	21.8	21.4	21.7	16.6
Middle East and North Africa	26.7	23.1	22.7	19.7	19.8	20.2	19	17.6	16.9
South Asia	86.5	84.8	83.9	82.7	79.7	79.9	77.2	77.1	73.9
Of which India	86.6	84.8	83.8	82.6	81.7	79.8	78.4	77.5	75.6
Sub-Saharan Africa	74	75.7	74.2	76.2	76	77.9	77.6	75.6	73
Total	69.2	67.4	64.2	63.2	61.5	58.2	57.1	53.3	47
Arab countries (MENA without Iran)	32	28.52	26.51	22.45	24.42	24.59	23.23	20.8	20.37

Source: Chen and Ravallion 2007.

Note: The Arab countries aggregate includes the following countries: Algeria, Djibouti, Egypt, Jordan, Morocco, Tunisia and Yemen.

Table 5-5	The incidence of (extreme) poverty based on national lower poverty lines (1991-1999 and 1999-2006)							
Country	Survey year	Poverty incidence (%)	Pop. average (1995-2000) in millions	Estimated number of poor (millions)	Survey year	Poverty incidence (%)	Pop. average (2000-2005) in millions	Estimated number of poor (millions)
Lebanon	1997	10	3.6	0.4	2005	7.97	3.9	0.3
Egypt	1999	16.7	63.6	10.6	2005	19.6	69.7	13.7
Jordan	1997	15	4.6	0.7	2002	14.2	5.2	0.7
Syria	1997	14.3	15.6	2.2	2004	11.4	17.7	2.1
Algeria	1995	14.1	29.4	4.1	2000	12.1	31.7	3.8
Morocco	1991	13.1	27.9	3.7	1999	19	29.7	5.6
Tunisia	1995	8.1	9.3	0.8	2000	4.1	9.8	0.4
MICs		14.6	153.9	22.4		15.9	167.6	26.6
Mauritania	1996	50	2.4	1.2	2000	46	2.8	1.3
Yemen	1998	40.1	16.9	6.8	2006	34.8	19.6	6.8
LICs		41.4	19.2	8		36.2	22.4	8.1
Total		17.6	173.1	30.4		18.3	190	34.7

Source: UNDP/AHDR calculations based on World Bank 2007, 2008; UNDP 2005, 2007, 2008. (See Statistical references).

of the population at or below the upper poverty line. Indeed, using that upper line, the overall poverty rate ranges from a low of 28.6 per cent - 30 per cent in Lebanon and Syria to a high of about 59.5 per cent in Yemen with that for Egypt being about 40.9 per cent. Since the countries analyzed in Table 5-6 represent about 65% of the total Arab population, it would be reasonable to extrapolate that the overall headcount poverty ratio at the upper poverty line is 39.9 %. On this measure, it can be estimated that there are 65 million poor Arabs, which is almost double the total implied in Tables 5-4 and 5-5 which measure poverty at the international two-dollars-a-day and lower national poverty lines respectively.

Expectably, income poverty, and the insecurity associated with it, is more widespread among rural populations. The rural population of the 18 Arab countries analyzed in Table 5-7 is approximately 128 million and is distributed among the country groups as shown.

Evidence of poverty prevalence in rural areas is available for six countries from the low and lower middle income groups:

Expectably, income poverty is more widespread among rural populations

Table 5-6	The incidence of poverty at the national upper poverty line, 9 Arab countries, 2000-2006				
	Survey year	Poverty line	Poverty rate	Population (million)	# of the poor (million)
Egypt	2004/5	PPP $2.7 per day	40.93	72.8	29.8
Syria	2003/4	NUPL	30.1	18.3	5.5
Lebanon	2004/5	NUPL	28.6	4	1.1
Jordan	2006	PPP $2.7 per day	11.33	5.5	0.6
Morocco	2000	PPP $2.7 per day	39.65	28.4	11.3
Tunisia	2000	PPP $2.7 per day	23.76	9.56	2.3
MIC			36.52	138.56	50.60
Yemen	2005	PPP $2.43 per day	59.95	21.1	12.6
Djibouti	2002	PPP $2.43 per day	52.6	0.76	0.4
Mauritania	2000	PPP $2.43 per day	53.95	2.5	1.3
LDC			59.10	24.36	14.40
Total			39.90	162.92	65.00

Source: World Bank 2008.

Table 5-7	The rural population in the Arab countries, 2007		
Income group (number of countries)	Rural population (in millions)	Share of rural population in total (%)	Share of income group in rural population (%)
Low income (4)	39.1	61.8	30.1
Lower middle income (6)*	83.2	47.6	64
Upper middle income (3)	2.1	16.9	1.6
High income (5)	5.6	17.6	4.3
Total (18)	130	46.3	100

Source: UNDP/AHDR calculations based on UNDP 2007.

* Egypt dominates the rural population of the lower middle income group, contributing 50 per cent of the total.

Human poverty affects children's attendance at elementary school

Egypt, Jordan, Mauritania, Morocco, Syria and Yemen. This sub-sample accounts for about 64.4 per cent of the Arab countries' rural population. The evidence is compiled, and summarized, in Ali (2008) where poverty estimates are those based on upper national poverty lines. [18] For the respective years of the household budget surveys, the poverty head count ratio ranged from a low of 18.7 per cent for Jordan (2002) to a high of 59 per cent for Mauritania (2004). The remaining countries register a relatively high incidence of rural poverty: 52 per cent in Egypt (2005); 64 per cent in Yemen (2005), 32 per cent in Syria (2004); and 27 per cent in Morocco (2000). Significantly, in all survey periods and in all six countries, the incidence of rural poverty was greater than that of urban poverty.[19]

Human poverty

Human poverty, a term popularized by UNDP to capture the deprivation of capabilities and opportunities, can be measured through the Human Poverty Index (HPI). The HPI, a composite index, is built on three components: a) longevity, b) knowledge and c) standard of living. The first component relates to survival prospects and is measured by the proportion of the population not expected to reach 40 years of age; the second component refers to exclusion from reading and communication, and is measured by the adult illiteracy rate; and the third is a composite value measured by the proportion of the population without access to safe water and the proportion of children under 5 years who are under weight. Countries with an HPI of less than 10 or more than 30 per cent are considered low or high human poverty cases respectively. Values in between these two thresholds denote the incidence of medium human poverty.

The above results correlate closely with those based on income poverty: low income Arab countries exhibit the highest incidence of human poverty, with an average HPI index of 35 per cent. Insecurity, as measured on the HPI, undercuts health, education and standards of living, all of which puts in question the effectiveness of the state in providing, and ensuring access to the basic necessities of life.

In particular, human poverty affects children's attendance at elementary school and their levels of continuation at post-elementary stages. In Egypt, the percentage of poor children in elementary school is 7 per cent lower than that for better-off children, 12 per cent lower at intermediate level, and 24 per cent lower at secondary level. In Morocco, around a quarter of children aged ten to fifteen years have not completed elementary school because of poverty. Many poor children are withdrawn from school to work at an early age to help support their families. In all cases, low school completion rates perpetuate the insecurity of the poor.

Arab countries scoring an HPI of 30 per cent or more include three low income countries and a lower middle income country: Sudan (with an HPI of 34.3 per cent), Yemen (36.6 per cent), Mauritania (35.9 per cent), and Morocco (31.8 per cent). In almost all of these countries, significant insecurity (i.e. a value of more than 30 per cent) is recorded for the education component, represented by the adult illiteracy rate. In addition, in Sudan, Yemen and Mauritania, insecurity from lack of access to safe water and child nutrition is also significant.

Along with falling rates of extreme poverty, insecurity arising from human poverty is also declining over time. Between 1996-1998 and 2005, the region-wide HPI declined by almost one third, from a value of 33 to 22.2 per cent. Figure 5-8 reflects the country achievements behind this regional trend. As shown in Figure 5-8, countries belonging to the high and upper middle income groups achieved the highest rate of decline. Nonetheless, comparing Arab countries with other developing countries shows that the former could have performed better on the HPI, given their levels of GDP and human development. For example, the United Arab Emirates has a Human Development Index (HDI) rank of 31. However, in terms of the HPI, the UAE fares thrice as badly as Hungary, which has an HDI rank of 38. This is true of most other Arab countries except Jordan, Lebanon and Syria. The relatively weaker performance of Arab countries on the HPI compared to other countries with similar HDI is attributable to higher adult illiteracy rates and, to some extent, higher rates of malnutrition among children under 5.

Table 5-8	Incidence of human poverty in 18 Arab countries in 2006				
Income group (number of countries)	Value of HPI (%)	Probability of not surviving to 40 (%)	Adult illiteracy rate (% 15 years and older)	Population without access to safe water (%)	Children under weight for age (%)
Low (4)	35.0	22.8	40.5	31.7	42.1
Lower middle (7)	20.4	7.2	28.9	8.3	6.8
Upper middle (3)	12.0	5.0	11.0	18.0	8.0
High (4)	11.7	5.1	14.7	8.2	13.7
Total (18)	22.3	10.4	29.1	13.9	15.4

Source: UNDP/AHDR calculations based on UNDP 2007.

Note: The HPI values in this chapter are based on UNDP's revised 2009 values.

Income inequality

Information on income inequality in Arab countries is spotty. Out of eleven Arab countries where recent data on the distribution of consumption expenditure are available,[20] there are seven whose Gini coefficient for the year 2000, or more recent years, is known. These are Egypt (0.32 in 2004/05); Jordan (0.359 in 2002); Lebanon (0.360 in 2005); Mauritania (0.391 in 2000); Syria (0.375 in 2004); Tunisia (0.408 in 2000); and Yemen (0.366 in 2005). The simple average Gini coefficient for the seven countries in the sample is 0.365, confirming that the Arab countries exhibit a moderate degree of inequality compared to the world average

Arab countries could have performed better on the Human Poverty Index

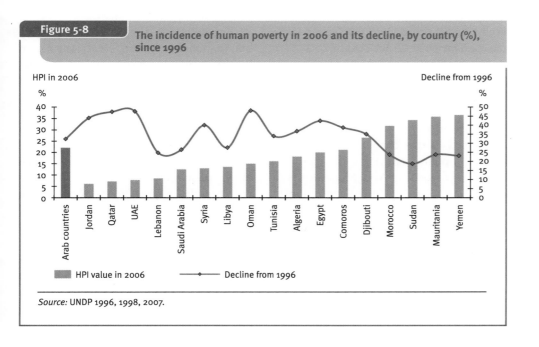

| Figure 5-8 | The incidence of human poverty in 2006 and its decline, by country (%), since 1996 |

Source: UNDP 1996, 1998, 2007.

which also indicates moderate inequality and stands at 0.3757 for the 2000s[21]. This may be seen as the cumulative achievement of social contracts in the Arab countries since independence.

Data limitations make it difficult to analyze changes in income inequality in the Arab countries over time. However, evidence for the last decade indicates that income inequality rose in Morocco, Syria and Yemen and fell in Algeria, Egypt, Jordan and Tunis. The countries experiencing the largest increase in inequality were Syria and Yemen. Algeria experienced the largest decline in inequality, with the Gini falling by 13.7 per cent over the period from 1988 to 1995. Egypt also witnessed a significant reduction in inequality within a span of five years. The other countries experienced relatively small changes in inequality.

Despite moderate levels of income inequality, in most Arab countries social exclusion has increased over the past two decades. In addition, there is evidence to suggest that the inequality in wealth has worsened significantly. In many Arab countries, for example, land and asset concentration is conspicuous and provokes a sense of exclusion among other groups, even if absolute poverty does not increase. Furthermore, the crowding of the poor in slums without sanitation, safe water, recreational facilities, reliable electricity and other services aggravates such exclusion. These trends, combined with high unemployment rates, result in the ominous dynamics of marginalization, visible in the high rates of urban slum dwellers in Arab cities and towns: 42 per cent in 2001.[22]

Policy gaps

The patterns of economic insecurity illustrated in this chapter are the result of several policy gaps. First, the increased structural fragility of Arab economies is an evident consequence of their continuing to rely on volatile, oil-led growth. Economic growth itself has been, for the most part, erratic and low. Correspondingly, the performance of productive sectors (and manufacturing in particular) has been weak and uncompetitive.

Second, this growth model has negatively impacted the labour market, and Arab countries now suffer the highest unemployment rates in the world. Moreover, as AHDR 2004 showed, that model is inappropriate in a globalized world where knowledge, more than capital or labour, accounts for most of the value added in competitive economies. Most Arab countries have not moved fast enough to improve the quality of education, leverage their knowledge assets, stimulate local innovation and shift towards technology-driven models of development. Consequently, they are unable to provide sufficient or satisfying jobs at decent wages for millions of Arabs, most of whom are young.

Third, overall poverty, defined as the share of the population under the national upper poverty line, is significantly higher than the underestimate yielded by using the international poverty line of two dollars a day or lower national poverty lines. Although, this chapter considers the effect of using upper poverty lines for only 9 countries, a reasonable extrapolation from the data is that the overall poverty rate would be in the order of 39.9%. Hence, we conclude that poverty in the Arab countries is a more conspicuous phenomenon than commonly assumed despite these countries' relatively high average per capita expenditure. The explanation is simple: the great majority of the poor are concentrated in countries such as Egypt, Iraq, Mauritania, Morocco, Somalia, Sudan, Syria and Yemen with relatively large populations and lower than average per capita expenditure shares.

Regardless of the choice of poverty line (national or international), the region has made no significant progress on the poverty reduction front in the 2000s if the 1990s are taken as a base period. The Arab LDCs, in particular, still lag far behind, and it is doubtful that any of them will be able to achieve the first Millennium Development Goal by 2015. The absence of pro-poor growth policies and reliance on outmoded approaches to social policy in general largely account for this gap

Finally, the provision and functioning of social safety nets, which are essential for mitigating the impact of economic downturns on vulnerable groups, are uneven across the country groups of the region. A distinction is usually made between informal or traditional, arrangements on the one hand, where relatives or tribe members

Inequality in wealth has worsened significantly

Marginalization is visible in the high rates of urban slum dwellers

Box 5-5 | The importance of integrated social policies

Compared to other developing nations, Arab countries have only recently adopted integrated social policies that treat poverty, inequality and socioeconomic development as interrelated issues. They have belatedly sought to apply the lessons of modern development studies, which favour social policies based on investment and production rather than on redistribution and consumption. This approach does not discount state interventions in social welfare but rather requires a wider role for non-state actors in the formulation and delivery of social policies and services.

Policies:

Multidimensional policies for addressing economic insecurity in the Arab world would simultaneously aim to:

- Push economic growth rates above population growth rates, in order to make a direct and positive impact on income levels. Prioritize financial support for small-scale enterprises, which would significantly improve the economic prospects of the poor.
- Enable all social groups to participate in the development process through equality of opportunity and the just distribution of benefits.
- Target poverty in all social security measures and raise the living conditions of the poor by developing the physical and social infrastructure in their environment.
- Increase access to educational, training and awareness-raising programmes.
- Narrow the gender gap, on all social and economic levels, by equipping women with skills, knowledge, credit and technology so as to enhance their ability to perform productive activities of their choice.

- Strengthen primary health care and expand its coverage.
- Further reduce population growth rates in the Arab countries.
- Make job-intensive economic investments for the poor and provide vocational and in-service programmes to help integrate them in the labour market.
- Increase the funding and reduce the bureaucratic complications of public safety nets and social service provision.

Obstacles:

- Conflicts and occupation in the region, entailing increased military expenditure at the expense of social spending
- The failure of the education system to build adequate professional and scientific capabilities
- Weak social service systems, marred by the absence of appropriate leadership, inefficient administration, unwillingness to empower target groups, inadequate auditing and financial procedures, a thin base of financial and human resources, and a general lack of expertise, skills and commitment among working staff.
- Insufficient funds to replicate successful projects on a wider scale
- Unbalanced distribution of policy attention and financial resources between rural and urban areas
- The limited experience of the civil society with development processes and programme implementation
- Bureaucratic centralization and lack of coordination among government agencies and between them and civil society actors
- Social policies dominated by short-term crisis management rather than an integrated, long-range vision

Source: El-Laithy and Mcauley 2006.

provide social and economic support to one another in times of need; and formal programmes on the other, which are usually run by governments or, more recently, by non-governmental organizations. Formal social safety nets usually provide direct cash or in-kind transfers, subsidies on basic necessities (especially food), and employment in public works projects. A broader definition of social safety nets would include the modern social security and social insurance programmes found in developing countries. Social security "is generally (but not always) associated with a transfer of income to the poor, whereas social insurance is related to earnings and is contributory in nature".[23]

As part of their Arab-Islamic culture, all Arab countries have an interlocking web of traditional social safety nets, but these traditional arrangements are increasingly being undermined by the pressures of modern life.[24] A large number of Arab countries have designed quasi-modern social security and social insurance arrangements, with varying degrees of success, depending on public resources made available by the state.

The high income Arab countries have erected fairly wide and deep formal social safety nets without necessarily crowding out traditional arrangements that preceded the discovery of oil. These arrangements are frequently revised in order to increase efficiency and coverage. Formal safety nets in these countries are similar in scope.[25] they provide special support for widows, the divorced, the sick, the elderly, unmarried and unemployed young women, families of prisoners, and students.

Traditional social safety nets are increasingly being undermined by the pressures of modern life

The main shortcomings of the formal social safety nets in the Arab middle income countries are summarized by Abdel Samad and Zeidan (2008).[26] These include incomplete protection against risks; unequal treatment of individuals; limited coverage of the population; a low level of benefits; relatively costly and inefficient administration; and unsustainable financing.

Not surprisingly, in the low income Arab countries, formal social safety nets are only recent in origin. In Yemen, for example, they were established in 1996, following the implementation of structural adjustment policies. The arrangements included a social welfare fund; a fund to promote agriculture and fisheries production; a fund for social development; a public works project; a poverty alleviation and employment programme; a food security programme; and a special initiative for the southern governorates.

However, whereas social safety nets may be used as an effective means of combating poverty in high and upper middle income countries where the poor constitute a relatively small section of the population, in circumstances of mass poverty, these conventional instruments of anti-poverty policy are inadequate. As argued in UNDP (2006), generalized poverty (i.e. poverty that affects the majority of the population) poses serious new challenges to policy makers as it can affect the behaviour of economic agents and the way in which institutions respond to policy stimuli at the micro level, as well as severely limiting the range and effectiveness of policies available to the government at the macroeconomic level.[27]

Generalized poverty is also usually associated with other broader economic conditions. For example, the majority of the poor population in Arab LDCs live in rural areas surviving on low-productivity, subsistence agriculture and related activities. Levels of human capital are very low and population growth is rapid, which multiplies the number of unskilled

In circumstances of mass poverty, conventional instruments of anti-poverty policy are inadequate

Generalized poverty poses serious new challenges to policy makers

workers. Such economies are often caught in a vicious circle of population growth, environmental degradation and natural resource depletion that ultimately can destabilize the social and political order. In Sudan and Yemen, however, the discovery and production of oil, and the considerable increase in oil revenues, provided a short window of opportunity to break out of this vicious circle. Unfortunately, this opportunity was not fully utilized.

Conclusion

As this chapter illustrates, dependence on oil revenues has left Arab economies exposed to the vagaries of international oil markets and structurally weak. Consequently, for most of the last three decades, economic growth has been highly erratic. It has also been rather low, in per capita terms. Correspondingly, the performance of productive sectors (and manufacturing in particular) has been poor: Arab countries are actually less industrialized today than was the case four decades ago. For oil producers in particular, the current global recession jeopardizes newly adopted patterns of outward investment and trade, as well as domestic development projects, on which hopes for sustained growth were pinned.

Oil-led growth has also negatively impacted the labour market. Some Arab countries now evince the highest unemployment rates (particularly among youth) worldwide, with serious implications for human security. Moreover, although in the Arab region, poverty is not the acute challenge it is in some other developing regions, the Arab LDCs still trail other Arab countries which, as a group, have failed to make significant inroads into poverty since 1990. Together, these trends spell a high degree of economic vulnerability, chronic insecurity in job markets and increasing social exclusion among vulnerable groups.

Endnotes

1   This chapter draws mainly on a special contribution by Ali Abdel-Gadir and Khalid Abu-Ismail, which is based on their study "Development Challenges for the Arab Region: A Human Development Approach", 2009. The study is sponsored by UNDP and the League of Arab States. Contributions to this chapter by Heba El-Laithy and Ahmed Moustafa are also duly acknowledged.

2   UNDP 1994.

3   For 2008, country income groups are defined in terms of Gross National Income (GNI) per capita in 2007 US$ PPP. The average per capita Gross Domestic Product (GDP) for the groups are: low income ($2,152); lower middle income ($5,343); upper middle income ($14,045); and, high income ($27,934).

4   In the absence of reliable economic trends data for Iraq, Somalia and the Occupied Palestinian Territory, those countries are not covered in this chapter. Their special circumstances are however addressed in other chapters.

5   UNDP/AHDR calculations based on UN Comtrade database 2008; World Bank 2008b.

6   Table 5-1 The table reports the coefficient of variation for Arab income groups compiled from available time series reported in the World Development Indicators of the World Bank. Thus, the evidence of volatility is meant to be descriptive and not representative. For the Arab countries the weighted averages for the coefficient of variation is used whereby the weights are 2007 real GDP shares.

7   World Bank 2006.

8   UNCTAD 2008.

9   Islam and Chowdhury 2006.

10   The compilation in this section of unemployment rates in Arab countries are based on the Arab Labour Organization estimates available in the labour statistics tables [www.alolabor.org].

11   Similar results are reported in World Bank report 2007a. Unemployment rates for 2004 were 1.9 per cent for Bahrain, 1.7 per cent for Kuwait, 2.1 per cent for Qatar, and 3 per cent for UAE, while the unemployment rate for Saudi Arabia is reported as 7 per cent of the labor force.

12   ALO (in Arabic) 2008.

13   The time trend coefficient for Algeria is 0.0279 (with a t-value of 7.2 and an R-squared of 0.69), that for Egypt is 0.0223 (with a t-value of 3.9 and an R-squared of 0.4), that for Jordan is 0.0655 (with a t-value of 6.2 and an R-squared of 0.63), that for Morocco is 0.0082 (with a t-value of 1.4 and an R-Squared of 0.08), that for Syria is 0.024 (with a t-value of 6.2; and an R-Squared of 0.52), and that for Tunisia is 0.0082 (with a t-value of 6.3 and an R-Squared of 0.65).

14   For details, see Ali and Abu-Ismail 2009. This figure is much higher than the 34 million jobs estimated by World Bank, 2007. Economic Developments and Prospects, Job Creation in an Era of High Growth, 2007.

15   Similar results are reported in the World Bank report 2007a which reports youth unemployment rates of about 46 per cent in Algeria, 54 per cent in Egypt, 66 per cent in Jordan, 33 per cent in Morocco, and 41 per cent in Tunisia.

16   Similar results are reported in World Bank report 2007a.

17   Rouidi-Fahimi and Kent 2007.

18   Ali 2008.

19   The highest incidence of urban poverty is reported for Yemen (49 per cent of the urban population) followed by Mauritania and Syria (about 29 per cent for each), Egypt (25 per cent), Jordan (13 per cent), and Morocco (12 per cent).

20   Ali and Abu-Ismail 2009.

21   The Gini index, is a number between zero and one that measures the degree of inequality in the distribution of income in a given society. A Gini index of 0 percent represents perfect equality whereas a Gini index of 1 per cent implies perfect inequality.

22   UN-ESCWA 2007a.

23   See, for example, World Bank 2008a.

24   Increasingly, religiously mandated charitable contributions (Zakat and Sadagat) are being institutionalized in the countries of the region.

25   UN-ESCWA 2005b.

26   Abdel Samad and Zeidan 2007; Nasr 2001.

27   UNDP/SURF-AS 2006.

Chapter 6

Hunger, nutrition and human security

Hunger is the most prevalent threat to human security, and one of the gravest. Without sufficient nourishment to furnish the energy for the basic functions of life, no individual can be secure in his or her person or exercise any human capability.

Notwithstanding its ample resources, and low incidence of hunger relative to other regions, the Arab region is seeing hunger and malnutrition among its people rise. Although prevalence rates and absolute numbers in individual countries vary quite markedly, the region, as a whole, is falling behind in achieving Goal One of the MDGs and is not positioned to halve the proportion of its hungry compared to 1990 by the year 2015. In addition, the backlog from hunger and malnutrition in the past continues: in some countries, underweight children shoulder a disproportionately greater share of that burden, and continue to pay a disproportionately greater price among the poor who live on less than two dollars a day.

Hunger is the most prevalent threat to human security, and one of the gravest

The Arab region is falling behind Goal One of the Millennium Development Goals

This chapter first outlines the effects of hunger on human security. It then reviews the status and causes of hunger and its various manifestations in the region, taking into account factors such as food shortages. Lastly, it considers measures for ensuring food sufficiency in Arab countries through regional cooperation and integration and by benefiting from the experiences of other countries in reducing hunger through targeted policies.

How hunger affects human security[1]

At the individual level

Hunger attacks health: it inhibits the physical, mental, and cognitive growth of children, thus reducing the ability to learn, to concentrate, and to attend school regularly. The effects of malnourishment in infancy are irremediable. Even if living conditions improve in later years, children exposed to malnutrition in infancy will continue to bear the marks it has taken on their health (stunted growth, wasting, and mental retardation) and on their lost opportunities for cognitive and income acquisition.

Hunger makes curable childhood diseases lethal: undernourishment and shortages in micronutrients (such as vitamin A, zinc, iodine and iron) weaken children's bodies and impair their immune systems, thereby increasing the risk of death from communicable but ordinarily curable diseases such as dysentery, measles, malaria, and pulmonary infections. Such causes account for three-fourths of infant deaths in most of the Arab countries, for which relevant data are available, and half the infant deaths in the "rich" ones.

Box 6-1 | Falling behind Millennium Development Goal 1. Target 2

Target 2: Halve, between 1990 and 2015, the proportion of people who suffer from hunger

The region's malnutrition rate decreased sluggishly, indicating critical malfunctions in the region's development efforts. The proportion of underweight children under five years of age remained relatively high in 2000 at 12.7 per cent with no noticeable improvement from its 1990 level of 13.2 per cent. This is due to the slow pace of progress in the economic and social determinants of the indicator: modest growth performance of the region as a whole; relatively high female illiteracy rate, particularly in the Arab LDCs; low access of the poor and underprivileged to primary health care services; comprehensive sanctions imposed on Iraq; and conflicts in OPT, Somalia, and Sudan.

The Arab sub-regions and individual countries exhibited wide differences in reducing the proportion of underweight children under-five years of age. In the Mashreq and the Maghreb, the proportion of underweight children declined from 10.8 per cent to 9.1 per cent and from 8.4 per cent to 7.5 per cent between 1990 and 2000, respectively. The Arab LDCs continued to suffer from the highest malnutrition rate in the region, at 27.4 per cent in 2000, down from 37.6 per cent in 1995.

Proportion of population below the minimum level of dietary energy consumption (%)

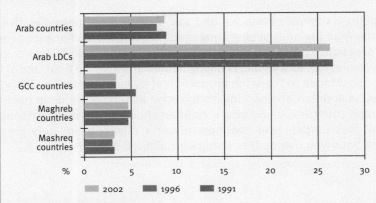

Source: UN-ESCWA 2007

In 1991, food deprivation was a disconcerting threat to overall social welfare in the region and remained so in 2000. Individuals living on less than the minimum level of dietary energy consumption accounted for 8.8 per cent of the Arab population in 1991 and 8.6 per cent in 2002. According to these rates, the number of food-deprived persons rose from approximately 20 million in 1991 to around 23.3 million in 2002. *This implies that the MDG target is unlikely to be met by 2015.*

The negligible change in the region's proportion of food-deprived persons is the result of stagnant rates in the Mashreq, Maghreb and the Arab LDCs. The relatively high levels of food deprivation in the Arab LDCs pulled the regional average significantly above the three other sub-regional averages. In the Maghreb and Mashreq, the proportion of people living below the food deprivation line remained low in 1991 and 2002. The Arab LDCs also did not make any noticeable progress in this area. The number of food-deprived persons amounted to 26.5 per cent of the population in 1991 and 26.3 per cent in 2002. Only the GCC countries showed good progress on this front, though all of it took place in the first five years. Available information shows that the proportion of the food-deprived in the GCC countries dropped from 5.5 per cent in 1991 to 3.4 per cent in 1996, but remained unchanged after that.

Source: UN-ESCWA 2007a.

Hunger makes pregnancy dangerous: in women, it increases the rates of complications during pregnancy and increases the risk of complications and even death during delivery. Undernourishment leads to complications during birth such as haemorrhaging or blood poisoning. Children born to women suffering from hunger are underweight at birth and at a higher risk of death during infancy. Further risks include stunted physical or mental development in childhood, and lower than normal rates of activity and productivity during adolescence. Because of the likelihood that low-weight born females will, themselves, if they live so long, give birth to low-weight children, the cycle of hunger and undernourishment is self-perpetuating.

At the collective level

Hunger debilitates society by increasing rates of disease, mortality and disability: by weakening the human immune system, it weakens the body's ability to fight off communicable diseases such as dysentery, measles, malaria, and acute pulmonary infections. It also increases the likelihood of death from AIDS-related illnesses. Also, by increasing the mortality rate, hunger affects the demographic pyramid, which is reflected in the rise in "Disability-Adjusted Life Years" (DALYs), or the total years lost due to premature death, illness, and incapacitation. In general, of the ten major factors leading to higher DALY rates, six are related to hunger and malnutrition, and include wasting, insufficient protein/energy intake, and lack of iodine, iron, and Vitamin A.

Hunger exacts financial costs and reduces productivity: states incur direct costs for treating the detrimental effects of hunger, such as complications during pregnancy and delivery among women; contagious and frequent paediatric diseases; and communicable diseases such as AIDS and tuberculosis. In addition, economies sustain the indirect costs of lower worker productivity, premature death or disability, absenteeism from the workplace and poor returns on education.

Hunger undermines stability: if hunger grows into a mass problem, it threatens the social and political order. Chronically hungry people are more likely to riot, clash with other groups or migrate to urban centres, straining their infrastructure and causing crime. Petty corruption thrives in a climate where people will do anything for food. When countries have to turn to other countries for help in feeding their hungry, they may open themselves to outside pressures on domestic policies.

In developed nations, as might be expected, undernourishment and lack of nutrients do not figure high on the list of causes of mortality and disability. Nevertheless, ailments connected with nutrition still do. Among these is obesity, which has approached epidemic proportions in some advanced countries, including the United States, where it is the second largest cause of preventable death after tobacco.

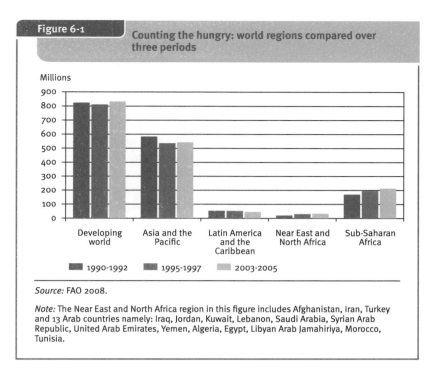

Figure 6-1 — Counting the hungry: world regions compared over three periods

Millions

1990-1992   1995-1997   2003-2005

Source: FAO 2008.

Note: The Near East and North Africa region in this figure includes Afghanistan, Iran, Turkey and 13 Arab countries namely: Iraq, Jordan, Kuwait, Lebanon, Saudi Arabia, Syrian Arab Republic, United Arab Emirates, Yemen, Algeria, Egypt, Libyan Arab Jamahiriya, Morocco, Tunisia.

Hunger and undernourishment in the Arab countries

In 2000, the UN General Assembly adopted the Millennium Development Goals (MDGs), the first of which is that, by 2015, the proportion of people living in poverty and the proportion of people suffering from hunger should be half of that in 1990. How are the Arab countries doing against that target?

According to World Food Programme figures, among developing country regions, the Arab countries have the lowest ratio of undernourished people to the total population. They are only surpassed in this regard by transition countries in Eastern Europe and the former Soviet Union. Yet the Arab region is one of the two world regions in which the number of undernourished has risen since the beginning of the 1990s—from 19.8 million in 1990-1992 to 25.5 million in 2002-2004.[2]

The FAO statistics[3] on undernourishment used here cover fifteen out of the twenty-two Arab countries. Among those excluded are Iraq and Somalia, which are under occupation or armed conflict, and for which it is difficult to obtain accurate data on food and health conditions going back to 1990-92.

The 25.5 million undernourished people in the region represent 10 cent of its total population. This constitutes only

3 per cent of the total undernourished population in the world. The relatively low level in comparison with other regions is due to the relatively high income levels of oil countries, food purchasing power sustained by worker remittances and/or to the food supply policies implemented by some governments.

Among Arab countries, Sudan, which is the scene of internal disputes and under international sanctions, is home to the largest population of hungry (more than 8 million). It is followed closely by Yemen (8 million), a Least Developed Country (LDC) which depends heavily on food imports. It may be noted that even in wealthy countries such as Saudi Arabia, Kuwait, and the UAE there are segments of the population that do not obtain sufficient nourishment.

Viewing the hunger count, not in terms of absolute numbers, but relative to a population, indicates that hunger does not constitute a humanitarian problem in three out of the fifteen Arab countries. Over the period 2002-2004, in Libya, Tunisia, and the UAE, the percentage of undernourished people was less than 2.5 per cent of the population. In marked contrast, Comoros, Yemen and Sudan, at 60 per cent, 38 per cent and 26 per cent respectively, are severely afflicted with food insecurity. In the other countries, the prevalence varies between 2.5 and

The Arab region is one of the two world regions where the number of undernourished has risen since the 1990s

4 per cent, the exceptions being Jordan and Morocco (6 per cent in each), Kuwait (5 per cent) and Mauritania (10 per cent).

National-level figures gloss over the association of hunger with certain groups in these countries. The World Food Programme observes that undernourishment is more prevalent among poverty stricken rural populations, women and children.[4] Although detailed figures are not available for most Arab countries, a study on poverty in Yemen, the Arab country with the second highest prevalence of undernourishment, identifies with greater precision the groups that are most vulnerable to undernourishment. They include large families that own or have access to only small areas of land, whose members are poorly educated and who work in agriculture or are supported by a female. The study reveals that the factor most strongly correlated with undernourishment is education. Whereas predominantly illiterate families account for more than a fifth of the families afflicted by hunger, the figure drops to a little more than a tenth for families with members who have received a university education. Perhaps this phenomenon is due, in general, to the correlation between income and education in Yemen.[5]

There are considerable disparities among individual Arab countries in fighting hunger

Trends since 1990-1992

Figure 6-3 illustrates the progress of Arab countries towards Goal One of the MDGs to halve, between 1990 and 2015, the proportion of people who suffer from hunger. It indicates that, for the region as a whole, there has been no progress towards Target 2 of the Goal. However, the general trend does not reveal the very different situations in individual countries.

The figure reveals considerable disparities among individual Arab countries in their progress in the fight against hunger. The countries that have made the greatest progress towards lowering the prevalence of undernourishment between the two periods are Djibouti, Kuwait and Mauritania (Kuwait's relatively high hunger prevalence in 1990-1992 largely reflected the impact of the First Gulf War). Sudan has also made progress, but still experiences serious hunger prevalence. Egypt, Jordan, Lebanon, Morocco , Saudi Arabia and Yemen, on the other hand, recorded increases in both the absolute numbers and prevalence of undernourishment, while Syria and Algeria achieved very small reductions in the prevalence of undernourishment but no reductions in the numbers of undernourished.

This overall appraisal throws into relief a painful fact: as indicated earlier, the number of undernourished increased by 5.7 million between 1990-1992 and 2002-2004. In other words, the region, as a whole, is moving away from, rather than approaching, Goal One. The picture grows

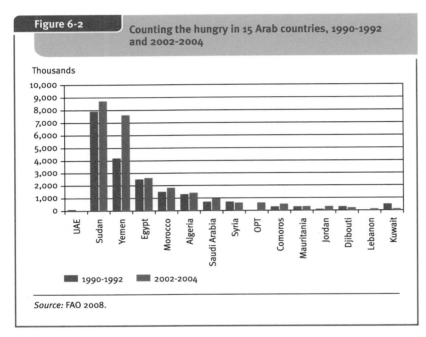

Figure 6-2

Counting the hungry in 15 Arab countries, 1990-1992 and 2002-2004

Source: FAO 2008.

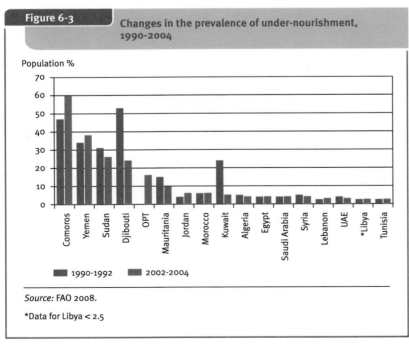

Figure 6-3

Changes in the prevalence of under-nourishment, 1990-2004

Source: FAO 2008.

*Data for Libya < 2.5

bleaker when we reflect on those countries such as Iraq and Somalia for which there is no reliable data: these are countries under occupation or caught in civil strife where deteriorating food supplies, hunger and violence combine to jeopardize human security.

Arab countries, as a whole, must reverse the deteriorating trend they have exhibited since 1990-1992. But to do so they must address the obstacles to the eradication of hunger, which, in turn, entails clearly identifying the fundamental causes and designing and implementing the programmes capable of addressing those causes. In this regard, they need to pay special attention to the more vulnerable sectors of the population such as women, children, and the elderly.

Obesity – a growing problem in Arab countries

Obesity and malnutrition may seem mutually exclusive, but they are commonly linked by their origins in poor diet. As the Director-General of WHO observed in an October 2008 address,[6] curiously enough, televised reports of malnutrition often show undernourished children being tended by overweight adults. This jarring paradox has a simple explanation: the cheap, low-grade and processed foods that starve children of absolutely crucial nutrients also make adults fat. Thus, obesity is not necessarily connected with overeating and, as illustrated in the figure below, it is not just a 'rich' country problem. It can be as widespread in lower income countries such as Egypt, Jordan , Morocco, and Syria as in high income countries such as the Gulf States. It also exists among the poor and the rich alike.

Instructively, obesity and overweight are more common among women than men in Arab countries, contrary to the situation in the US, for example, where these problems are more prevalent among men. In the region, obesity is generally attributed to over-consumption of high-fat foods and/or high sugar products combined with little physical activity, which may partly explain its prevalence among Arab women who are often prevented by custom from pursuing sports and other physical exercise.

Box 6-2   THE HUMAN SECURITY SURVEY – Food access in 4 Arab countries

Respondents were asked if they found it easy or difficult to obtain food, or whether food access was not an issue at all. The lowest number of respondents who found it difficult was in Kuwait and the highest number who found food easily accessible was also in that country. In the other countries, responses differed from those in Kuwait but were similar among the three. In those cases, about 40 per cent of the respondents agreed that food was readily accessible as opposed to between 56 and 59 per cent who thought it difficult to obtain. Those to whom it was apparently not an issue constituted a small minority, just around 3 per cent of the sample. Interestingly, none of the respondents in Kuwait said that obtaining food was not an issue, possibly because they considered easy access the same thing.

Is obtaining food easy, difficult or not an issue at all?

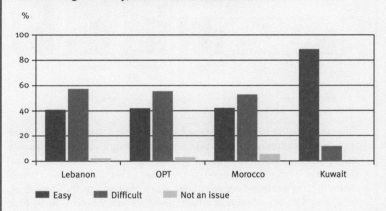

When respondents were asked how easy it had been to obtain food during the six months preceding the survey, a minority of the respondents in Kuwait (20 per cent) and about a third of the respondents in Morocco answered that they had had difficulty obtaining some foodstuffs or that they had been forced to cut down on some kinds during those six months. However, 56 per cent of Palestinians and more than half of the Lebanese polled indicated they had experienced difficulties overall. Their answers undoubtedly reflect the fact that the period in question coincided with the deterioration of conditions in Gaza in the winter of 2008 and the atmosphere of tension in Beirut at that time.

Percentage of respondents who found it difficult to obtain food in the six months preceding the survey

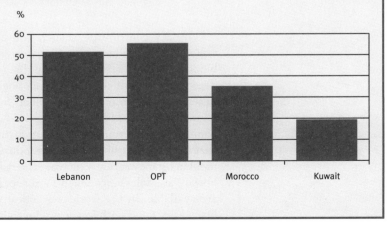

THE HUMAN SECURITY SURVEY – Dietary patterns in 4 Arab countries

Dietary patterns in Kuwait, Lebanon, Morocco and the Occupied Palestinian Territory are similar, with one noticeable difference among the Palestinians. With the exception of vegetables and eggs, they consume other major food types less frequently. They eat more vegetables than the Kuwaitis and more eggs than the Moroccans and Lebanese, while of the four sets of respondents they consume the least amounts of fish and meat, eating the former less than once a week and the latter no more than twice a week. This may be due to the scarcity of fish and to the high cost of meat in the Occupied Palestinian Territory. In general, fish and meat are the least frequently consumed food items among the respondents in three countries, with the Kuwaitis departing from the general pattern in their consumption of fish twice a week and meat four times a week.

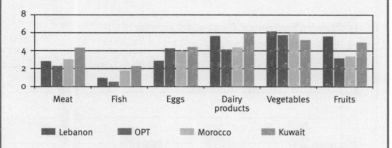

Comparing patterns of food consumption in Gaza and the West Bank reveals salient differences. While in both areas people eat vegetables with about the same frequency—about six times a week—there are significant differences in the consumption of the other types of food. The respondents in Gaza eat less frequently eggs, dairy products, fruits, vegetables, meat and fish, a pattern that reflects levels of nourishment there. Food conditions have deteriorated for most Palestinians, but those in Gaza are particularly affected as a result of Israeli restrictions on the movement of goods and persons and as a result of the blockade.

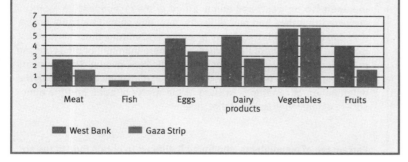

The causes of hunger and malnourishment in Arab countries

Many factors contribute to the problems of undernourishment. Among the direct factors are the lack of means to purchase sufficient food for basic daily requirements and the lack of food supplies. The indirect factors, which are simultaneously causes and consequences, include poverty, ignorance, illness, and gender inequality. Difficult climatic conditions, natural disasters, unsuccessful development policies, political instability, and armed conflict are important factors that contribute indirectly to perpetuating the cycle of poverty, hunger, illness, and suffering. Just as poverty and unemployment are not purely economic phenomena, so too undernourishment and hunger are not necessarily natural or inevitable; indeed, they are most frequently caused by human action, or inaction. The Arab countries most severely affected by undernourishment and hunger are those experiencing conflicts, civil war or foreign occupation while, in other Arab countries, the spread of poverty is associated with high rates of undernourishment. The causes of undernourishment can be summarized in terms of three primary categories: food purchasing power, food availability, and the sustainability of both. The following paragraphs discuss these causes in more detail.

A. Direct causes

Insufficient daily nutritional intake

Every year the FAO appraises each country's per capita food availability using the system of "Food Balance Sheets." These are tabulations of the amounts of foodstuffs produced in a given country within a given year, to which are added the amounts imported or in storage during that period, and from which are subtracted the amounts lost through spoilage during storage or transportation, or fed to livestock, or used for purposes other than human consumption. The result is then divided by the total number of inhabitants in the country. All foodstuffs available for human consumption are also broken down into their caloric value[7], so as to gauge the per capita supplies of nutrient energy.

Undernourishment and hunger are not necessarily natural or inevitable

Obesity contributes to such non-contagious chronic illnesses as diabetes, high blood pressure, coronary arterial diseases, degenerative joint diseases, psychological illnesses, and some types of cancer. Such ailments are steadily increasing in Arab countries. Numerous studies demonstrate that underweight birth and undernourishment in infancy actually increase the risk of obesity at adolescence when food supplies are available. In the workforce, obesity is often associated with lower productivity.

In the appraisal of food supply and dietary patterns in the region according to available data, Arab countries were divided into three categories based on the prevalence of hunger and undernourishment in 2002-2004. The first category consists of those countries in which the prevalence is between 2.5 and 4 per cent of the population, and includes Saudi Arabia, Egypt, Syria, Lebanon, and Algeria. The second, mid-range category, where the prevalence falls between 5 and 19 per cent of the population, includes Morocco, Mauritania, Jordan, and Kuwait. Yemen and Sudan fall into the third category, where the prevalence is 20 per cent or more of the population. The appraisal did not cover Libya, Tunisia, and the UAE, in which hunger and undernourishment do not constitute significant problems. However, we might also add a fourth category, made up of those conflict-plagued countries, Sudan, Somalia, Iraq and Occupied Palestinian Territory, to which we return later.

• **Nutrient energy intake falls below daily requirements**

Figure 6-5 illustrates the per capita caloric intake in Arab countries and compares its levels in 1990-1992 and 2002-2004.

There are evident disparities between the three groups of countries in caloric supply, the latter being lowest in Yemen and Sudan (highest prevalence of hunger) and highest in the countries of the first group (lowest prevalence). All recorded levels of daily per capita caloric intake, which vary from 2,000 (Yemen) to 3,100 (Egypt), show totals higher than the minimal caloric intake needed for the average person to sustain body weight and remain moderately active. The figure thus indicates that the explanation for hunger prevalence in the region lies in disparities *within* individual societies in caloric intake and, hence, that the distribution of available foodstuffs is inequitable.

Looking at changes in the rates of caloric intake between the MDG baseline (1990-1992) and 2002-2004, we note virtually no change in Yemen, Morocco, and Lebanon and a slight increase in the other countries. The sole exception is Kuwait, which registered a considerable 700 per capita caloric increase since 1990-1992.

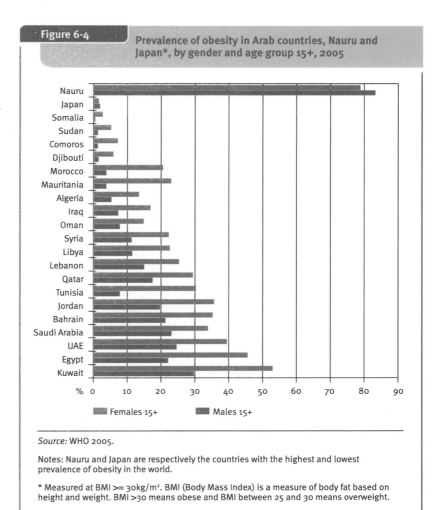

Figure 6-4

Prevalence of obesity in Arab countries, Nauru and Japan*, by gender and age group 15+, 2005

Females 15+   Males 15+

Source: WHO 2005.

Notes: Nauru and Japan are respectively the countries with the highest and lowest prevalence of obesity in the world.

* Measured at BMI >= 30kg/m². BMI (Body Mass Index) is a measure of body fat based on height and weight. BMI >30 means obese and BMI between 25 and 30 means overweight.

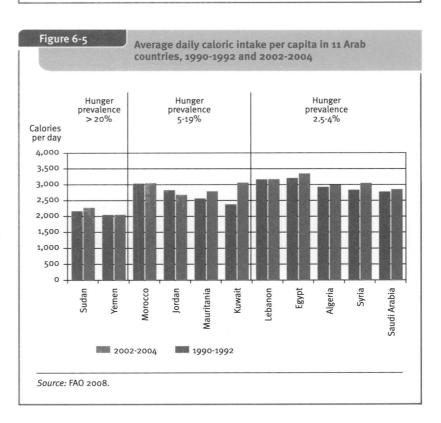

Figure 6-5

Average daily caloric intake per capita in 11 Arab countries, 1990-1992 and 2002-2004

2002-2004   1990-1992

Source: FAO 2008.

• Limited supplies of different foods affect dietary patterns and nutrition

Figure 6-6 depicts the daily per capita intake (measured in grams/person/day) of different types of nutrient sources available in the Arab countries, comparing their levels in 2004 with those in 1990, and contrasting these levels with those in a developed country, Greece.

While the 2002-2004 levels of per capita food availability vary considerably between the three groups of Arab countries, they do not differ markedly among the countries in the same group. Clearly, they are inversely proportional to the prevalence of hunger and malnutrition, with the first group ranking the highest in the quantities of food available to the individual. Thus, for example, the overall quantities range from 2,200 grams per day in Lebanon, in which the prevalence of hunger is 3 per cent of the population, to 1,500 grams per day in Saudi Arabia, in which 4 per cent of the population suffers nutrient deprivation. In the third group, the per capita rates vary from 850 grams per day in Yemen, where hunger afflicts more than a third of the population to 1,150 grams per day in Sudan, where more than a quarter of the population is prey to hunger and undernourishment. The second group recorded levels that fall in between those of the first and third. The recorded rates in all of these countries are considerably lower than the per capita rates in the developed country comparator – Greece.

Examining levels of per capita food availability over the decade between the two assessment periods, we find that they have not changed considerably, with the exception of Kuwait, in which the level nearly doubled from 1990. Lebanon, Jordan, and Yemen, which belong, respectively, to the first, second, and third groups, show minor decreases in the per capita food availability levels, which undoubtedly contributed to the relative increase in the prevalence of hunger these countries have experienced since 1990. In contrast, Algeria, Mauritania and Sudan have recorded small increases in per capita food availability, which, by the same token, helped alleviate the prevalence of hunger

Levels of per capita food availability vary considerably between the three groups of Arab countries

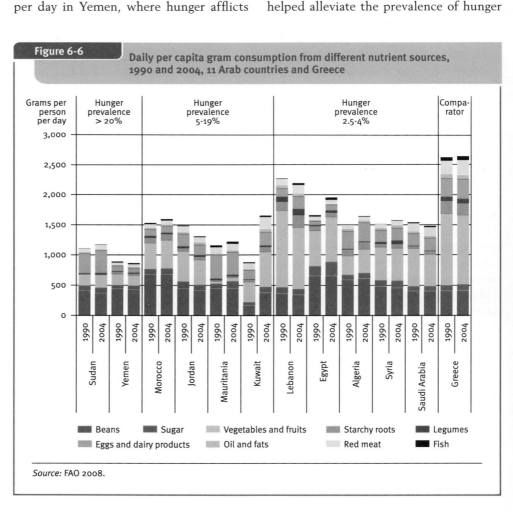

Figure 6-6

Daily per capita gram consumption from different nutrient sources, 1990 and 2004, 11 Arab countries and Greece

Source: FAO 2008.

in these countries, except for Sudan where the deterioration of the situation in Darfur since 2004 aggravated the severity of undernourishment there.

Among types of foodstuffs available in the Arab countries, grains are the most popular form of food; they are an important source of energy, proteins, and vitamin B complex. Wheat is the most widely consumed type of grain in all Arab countries, apart from Sudan in which sorghum prevails. Barley ranks second in the North African countries. In the Mashreq, rice and maize are the second most widely consumed grains, and in the LDCs (Yemen and Sudan), maize and millet. None of these countries has attained self-sufficiency in these grains, which they all import in varying quantities. The highest imports are in wheat, produced in moderate climates and exported primarily by industrial nations, followed by barley and to a lesser extent maize. Grain consumption has declined slightly in all Arab countries over recent years, apart from in Mauritania, Morocco, Egypt, and Saudi Arabia, where the amount of grain consumed has remained stable in terms of quantity but increased in terms of ratio to total caloric intake.

Fruit and vegetables form the second largest dietary component in most Arab countries apart from Mauritania, Sudan, and Yemen, where the per capita intake of these foodstuffs is only between 60 and 200 grams per day. Dairy products and eggs are also major dietary components, especially in the latter three countries. Indeed, in these countries the available quantities of dairy products are equivalent to those in developed nations. The relative abundance of such products in these low income countries is due to the proliferation of dairy farms in recent years.

Meat products form only a small portion of the overall diet in Arab countries, with Lebanon, Kuwait, and Saudi Arabia ranking highest in meat consumption, at between 135 and 190 grams per person per day. Fish and other seafood form only a small fraction of the dietary intake in all the countries.

Dietary patterns in most Arab countries have changed since the 1990-1992 baseline period. While grains still remain the foremost ingredient in the Arab meal, one now finds greater quantities of fruits and vegetables, dairy products and eggs, vegetable oils, sugar, and, to a modest extent, meat and fish. In spite of this trend towards diversity, which largely reflects the preferences of consumers who can afford greater quantities of more expensive foods with higher nutrient values, dietary patterns on the whole, compared to those in developed countries, are still deficient. Particularly lacking are prophylactic foods that are rich in mineral salts and vitamins, such as fruits and vegetables, dairy products and fish.

• **Imbalanced diet**

Undernourishment can arise from insufficient or imbalanced intakes of nutrient energy and/or macro or micro nutrients. A diet deficient in macronutrients, elements that furnish the body with energy (proteins, fats and carbohydrates), causes health problems (wasting, stunting, underweight, drop in body mass). This applies even if the overall caloric intake is sufficient. However, healthy ranges of the proportions of macronutrients to the total caloric requirement are fairly broad: 55-75 per cent carbohydrates, 15-35 per cent fats, and 10-15 per cent proteins.[8]

Figure 6-7 summarises the per capita daily intake of macronutrients in relation to total caloric intake and how these ratios changed over the period from 1990-1992 to 2002-2004. It covers the Arab countries for which data is available, inclusive of those in which hunger does not pose a humanitarian problem.

The ratios of macronutrients in the food available in Arab countries are, on the whole, balanced regardless of the volumes of energy available. Nor have these ratios changed significantly since the baseline period. We also observe that animal foods account for between a third and a fourth of the supplies of proteins and fats, and between 7 and 13 per cent of available nutrient energy supplies in all countries, apart from Mauritania, Sudan, Kuwait, and Lebanon. In these countries, animal foods make up nearly half of the available sources of proteins and fats, and a fifth of the energy; these ratios are equivalent to those recorded in developed countries. However, while animal foods offer abundant sources of high-quality animal protein, they are also causes of high levels of harmful saturated

In spite of this trend towards diversity, dietary patterns are still deficient

Undernourishment can arise from insufficient or imbalanced intake of nutrients

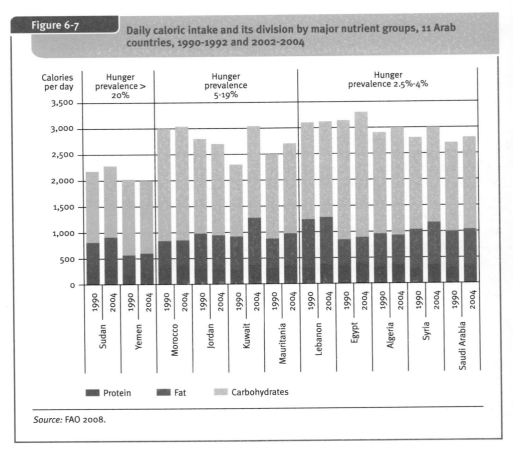

Figure 6-7 Daily caloric intake and its division by major nutrient groups, 11 Arab countries, 1990-1992 and 2002-2004

■ Protein ■ Fat ▨ Carbohydrates

Source: FAO 2008.

triglycerides. These arise particularly from relatively high quantities of dairy products and eggs, combined with low levels of fruit and vegetables (as is the case in Mauritania and Sudan) and relatively high intakes of meat and dairy products and eggs (as in Lebanon and Kuwait).

Yet, as encouraging as these figures may appear, they should be treated with an element of caution. They do not necessarily reflect equality in the distribution of available food among societal groups or indicate the actual intakes or dietary balances of weak and vulnerable groups. The most they offer is a picture of general trends in food availability and intake within groups of countries.

• The relative contributions of food imports and exports to per capita food supplies

How much food is available to a society mirrors developments in its food production sectors and the dynamics of food commodity exchanges with the outside world. In other words, food availability is connected with the forces of supply—which is contingent upon such factors as agricultural production, access to global

markets, the growth of food industries, and the size of foreign aid—and demand, which is connected, in particular, to per capita income levels.

Figure 6-8 shows that some Arab countries have lower cereal yields than the world average and, moreover, that, between 1990 and 2005, production in 7 countries declined.

Figure 6-9 illustrates how far the region moved towards self-sufficiency in major food commodities during the period 1990-2004.

Instructively, as the figure shows, Arab countries are altogether more self-sufficient in food commodities that are favoured by the rich (meats, fish and vegetables) than in those likely to be consumed by the poor (cereals, fats and sugar).

Figure 6-10 illustrates the dependence of Arab countries on aggregate food imports in 2005. In all but one case—Bahrain—this reliance is greater than the world average.

Numerous factors have contributed to the heavy dependence of Arab countries on food imports (Jalila Al-Ati, in Arabic, background paper for the report):

- In Yemen, an LDC, 80 per cent of the population live in rural areas and 50 per cent of the labour force is employed in agriculture. Inadequate water supply and scarce arable land mean agricultural productivity is low, accounting for a small share of GDP (15 per cent), and cannot keep pace with the country's rapid population growth (3.6 per cent annually compared to the 2.6 per cent average in Arab countries as a whole). As a result, the numbers of undernourished people are climbing.

- In Jordan, a middle-income country with a paucity of water and other natural resources, agricultural production accounts for only 2 per cent of GDP and employs only 10 per cent of the labour force. Food imports are, thus, essential to meet its needs. However, the performance of the Jordanian economy is heavily influenced by external factors, especially fluctuations in oil prices and conflicts in the region. Economic decline as a consequence of such factors has contributed to reducing the per capita caloric intake from 2,820 calories per day in 1990-1992 to 2,670 per day in 2002-2004, and thus to increasing the prevalence of undernourishment.

- In Saudi Arabia, a high-income country, agriculture accounts for only 5 per cent of GDP and employs only 7 per cent of the labour force, as a result of which the country is almost entirely dependent on food imports. In spite of the country's economic growth, fuelled by the recent boom in oil prices, no progress has been made towards the elimination of undernourishment. In fact, the number of undernourished in Saudi Arabia has risen since 1990-1992, raising questions about policies of food distribution, social equity and population trends.

On the other hand, in Syria, another middle-income country, 33 per cent of the active population is engaged in the agrarian sector, which contributes a quarter of GDP and occupies a third of the country's land area. Agricultural investment and development in recent years have enabled Syria not only to secure self-sufficiency in the most important foodstuffs but also to improve the performance of its export trade in fruits, vegetables, pulses, grains,

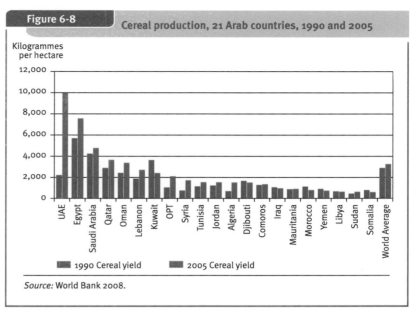

Figure 6-8 — Cereal production, 21 Arab countries, 1990 and 2005

Kilogrammes per hectare

■ 1990 Cereal yield   ■ 2005 Cereal yield

Source: World Bank 2008.

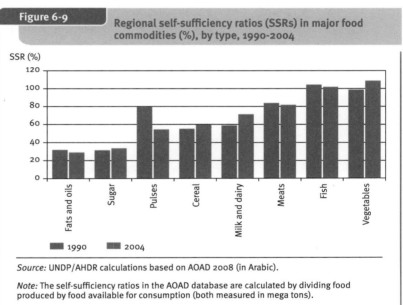

Figure 6-9 — Regional self-sufficiency ratios (SSRs) in major food commodities (%), by type, 1990-2004

SSR (%)

■ 1990   ■ 2004

Source: UNDP/AHDR calculations based on AOAD 2008 (in Arabic).

Note: The self-sufficiency ratios in the AOAD database are calculated by dividing food produced by food available for consumption (both measured in mega tons).

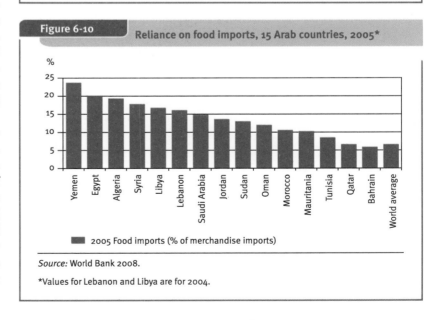

Figure 6-10 — Reliance on food imports, 15 Arab countries, 2005*

%

■ 2005 Food imports (% of merchandise imports)

Source: World Bank 2008.

*Values for Lebanon and Libya are for 2004.

and olive oil. The growth of the agrarian sector contributed to a 200 calorie per day increase in the average available nutrient energy supply since 1990-1992, an increase sufficient to reduce the prevalence of undernourishment from 5 to 4 per cent, although not sufficient to reduce the number of undernourished arising from rapid population growth (3.1 per cent).

The foregoing confirms the findings of various studies that the effect of economic development on reducing hunger depends as much upon the *nature* of economic growth as it does upon its extent and pace. Agricultural development in rural areas has more impact on uprooting hunger and malnourishment than urban industrial development.

In the Arab countries, the dangers of over-dependence on international markets to ensure food needs came home sharply in the spring of 2008 when global food prices skyrocketed. By mid-2008, these prices were 40 per cent higher than at the same time the previous year. The impact of this was felt in virtually all Arab countries, including wealthy Gulf countries such as Saudi Arabia and the UAE. It seems wise, therefore, for Arab governments to attempt to take advantage of their available water and cultivable land in order to move closer to self-sufficiency in food production. This important subject is discussed in the concluding section of this chapter.

B. Indirect causes

Poverty and hunger

Poverty and hunger constitute a vicious cycle. Hunger prolongs poverty because it lowers productivity and poverty prevents people from producing or obtaining the food they need. The poor are not only vulnerable to hunger and an insufficient intake of micronutrients, but also to chronic illnesses linked to diet, habits and situational pressures. The poor and undereducated tend towards behaviour laden with health risks, such as smoking and consuming cheap, fatty, and high-caloric processed and fried foods. They lack health care and health awareness, and are constantly exposed by deprivation to social, physical and mental stress. One review of 144 studies of obesity in developed countries found an inverse relationship between

obesity and socioeconomic status, noting that often the urban poor are forced to settle for "junk food" and do not always understand the fundamentals of a healthy diet.[9] This suggests that obesity and its associated health risks will be higher in countries in which malnourishment increases in tandem with urban development. Confronting this double burden of chronic hunger and the spread of non-contagious diseases demands special food and dietary policies that target vulnerable groups among the urban and rural poor.

Nevertheless, poverty is not necessarily associated with undernourishment when the consumption pattern of the poor tends towards inexpensive but nutrient-rich foods, and when such foods are readily accessible. Where statistics are available for both poverty levels and the levels of undernourishment in a given area, the two indexes do not always overlap. The number of undernourished can exceed the number of poor in certain cases where it is not low income that hampers access to food but other obstacles, such as transport bottlenecks, or political upheavals. The number of undernourished can also fall below the number of poor, as is the case in areas where government policies are in place to provide food for the poor or where the prevalent diets consist of inexpensive foods that meet the body's energy requirements.

Looking at the prevalence of poverty in Arab countries for which there is available data and its correlation to the prevalence of hunger and undernourishment (Figure 6-11) we find that the severest rates of poverty (people living on less than a dollar a day) and deprivation from one or more fundamental services are concentrated in those countries with a high prevalence of undernourishment, which is to say such low-income countries as Mauritania, Sudan, and Yemen.

More than 60 per cent of the inhabitants in Mauritania, about 45 per cent of the inhabitants of Yemen, and about 40 per cent of the inhabitants of Egypt live on less than two dollars a day. It is interesting in this regard to draw a comparison. In Egypt, GDP per capita (calculated by purchasing power parity) is roughly equivalent to that of Morocco ($4,337 and $4,555 respectively in 2005). Yet, the levels of poverty (gauged by the percentage of the population living on less than a dollar

Agricultural development in rural areas has more impact on uprooting hunger than urban industrial development

Poverty and hunger constitute a vicious cycle

a day) and hunger are noticeably lower in Egypt (20 and 4 per cent respectively) than in Morocco (34 and 6 per respectively). The lower figures for Egypt indicate that dietary patterns in Egypt, coupled with the Egyptian government's food subsidy programmes, have contributed to reducing the prevalence of undernourishment.

As figure 6-11 shows, the number of poor in the Arab countries for which data has been provided exceeds the number of undernourished. The prevalence of those living on less than two dollars a day is higher than the prevalence of those suffering hunger in Saudi Arabia, Kuwait, Egypt, Syria, Jordan, Lebanon, Morocco, Algeria, Sudan and Mauritania, whereas the ratios of poverty and hunger are approximately equal in Yemen. World Bank statistics bear out the greater prevalence of poverty over undernourishment in Tunisia as well as elsewhere in the Maghreb and Mashreq, in general. We note, however, that the percentage of sufferers from hunger is higher than the percentage of those who live in extreme poverty, on less than a dollar a day, in Algeria, Jordan and Morocco.

Other useful comparisons may be drawn. Jordan and Lebanon, too, have about the same GDP per capita ($5,530 and $5,584 respectively in 2005) and about the same prevalence of poverty and hunger. However, Saudi Arabia, a high-income country fares no better than Syria, a middle-income country in terms of the prevalence of hunger (4 per cent of the population in each country according to WB data).[10] Again, this demonstrates that having resources, alone, is not sufficient to promote the development of a society or to achieve sustainable economic growth. Any country, even one with relatively limited resources, can rise to the challenge of reducing hunger and poverty. The requirement is that it implements well-considered and designed comprehensive development policies, and that it puts into effect economic and financial structural reforms that guarantee equitable development across all sectors of society, with special attention to the more vulnerable.

Foreign occupation, domestic conflict and hunger

Although reliable and up-to-date information on Arab countries facing occupation

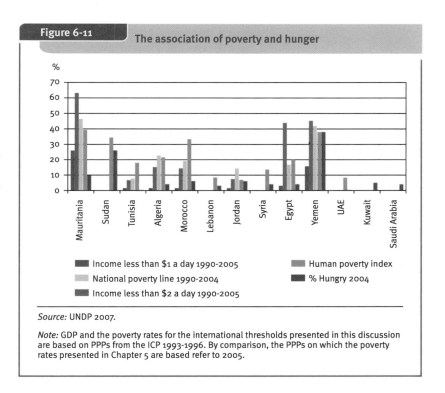

Figure 6-11 **The association of poverty and hunger**

Legend:
- Income less than $1 a day 1990-2005
- National poverty line 1990-2004
- Income less than $2 a day 1990-2005
- Human poverty index
- % Hungry 2004

Source: UNDP 2007.

Note: GDP and the poverty rates for the international thresholds presented in this discussion are based on PPPs from the ICP 1993-1996. By comparison, the PPPs on which the poverty rates presented in Chapter 5 are based refer to 2005.

or civil strife is lacking, thus making comparisons with other Arab countries difficult, World Food Programme figures hint at the magnitude of their problems (Table 6-1).

Countries in these special situations experience declining food conditions for many reasons. Foremost among them is the collapse of those daily patterns of life into which people arranged their work, movements and essential purchases. Such upheavals bring a loss of personal security, with all that that signifies to those who live in conflict zones. They can lead to the death of thousands of farmers and others engaged in the production, transport, or distribution of food. These countries also see, in their rural areas, the recruitment into combat activities of thousands of others who would ordinarily be engaged in producing food; or the flight of yet thousands of others former food growers and distributors to safer areas. Moreover, refugees and displaced persons themselves are often forced into the search for food in their new havens, often meeting with little success and finding themselves without means of subsistence. Compounding these severe disturbances, armed conflicts destroy roads, irrigation systems, electricity grids and other infrastructure, impairing food production and transport, and reducing the ability to respond to

Any country can rise to the challenge of reducing hunger and poverty

floods, droughts and other natural disasters. Under such circumstances, not only does food scarcity drive up prices, but simply guaranteeing the safe transport of food from one area to another becomes fraught with the risk of attack or extortion *en route* by militias or criminal gangs.

Unsurprisingly, these countries have become humanitarian disaster zones the effects of which have spilled over into neighbouring countries, prompting international concern and intervention in response to the sheer number of victims of poverty and hunger these crises have claimed. The following table suggests the extent to which these crises have impaired the ability of the inhabitants of affected areas to obtain essential food requirements.

The FAO lists thirty-six nations as those most at risk from the consequences of the rising prices of food in international markets and, hence, requiring external food assistance. Among them are four Arab countries, three of which are victims of foreign occupation or civil strife or both. Somalia and Iraq are categorised as suffering an "exceptional shortfall in aggregate food production/supplies." Mauritania, facing "a widespread lack of access", is in the second category of severely food insecure countries, Sudan is described as undergoing "severe localised food insecurity".[11]

Food accessibility is strongly influenced by government economic policies and openness to world markets

Economic policies and globalisation

Food accessibility is strongly influenced by government economic policies and openness to world markets. Subsidising food commodities to make them more affordable to the public is one such policy; lifting subsidies is another. Most Arab governments have adopted food supply policies as part of a social contract based on state provision of essential needs in exchange for the people's loyalty. This type of social contract was a major feature of some Arab regimes of the 1960s and 1970s, which patterned their development programmes on the socialist model. It was also a tactic associated with regimes in some Arab oil exporting countries, which used oil revenues to sustain their rule. This helps explain why the number of undernourished in Arab countries is lower than the number of poor who live on less than two dollars a day. Beginning in the late 1970s, the governments of non-oil exporting countries made their first attempts to implement IMF recommendations and shed what they had come to regard as the subsidy burden. They quickly realised how difficult this task would be when their attempts to lift subsidies triggered widespread riots and civil unrest, in Egypt, Morocco and Tunisia, and even in Algeria, an oil exporting country.

Table 6-1	Food relief to conflict zones in the Arab countries, 2000-2008		
Country	**Population affected by food shortages**	**Beneficiaries of WFP food aid**	**Other effects of the crisis**
Somalia	3.5 million people, almost half of the population in Somalia, will require food assistance by December 2008.	Beneficiaries of WFP assistance increased from 700,000 in August 2006 to 1.4 million in May 2008.	In January 2008, rates of acute malnutrition in the Puntland regions of Shabelle, Hiran and Central and Southern Nugal were above the emergency threshold of 15%.
Iraq	In 2005, 39% percent households facing food problems in Iraq	In 2005, over four million people (15.4% of the population) were food insecure in spite of receiving Public Distribution System (PDS) food rations. Without PDS rations, a further 8.3 million people (31.8% of the population) would be food insecure.	In 2005, the prevalence of acute child malnutrition in six governorates (Wassit, Salah Al Din, Najaf, Qadissia, Muthana and ThiQar) was greater than 10% or 'serious'. In Qadissia, at 17%, it was 'critical'.
Sudan	In 2005, 53.8% of IDP households in Darfur were food insecure.	In 2005, the number of monthly beneficiaries of food aid in greater Darfur came to 1,936, 554.	In September 2004, 25.7% of children between 6 to 59 months of age were suffering from severe acute malnutrition rates.
OPT	In 2008, 53% of the population of the Gaza Strip and 21% of that in the West Bank were food insecure.	39.33% of OPT households received food assistance between March and May 2008.	In 2004, stunting was found to affect 9.9% of children under 5 years of age, and was on the rise compared to 1996 and 2000 data.

Source: WFP 2008 (See Statistical references).

Nevertheless, since the 1980s most Arab governments have pressed ahead with economic liberalisation and market deregulation policies. Without passing judgment on such policies, it cannot be denied that, as far as food supply is concerned, they have rendered domestic food prices vulnerable to fluctuations in international prices. Since 2006, Arab food-importing countries, that is, the great majority in the region, have had to contend with soaring food prices in the global market. The FAO and the World Bank have attributed spiralling prices to various causes, among which are the climate changes that have affected production in grain exporting countries, the extensive depletion in grain stocks, and the rising consumption of meat and dairy products in emerging economies, especially in China. Another major cause is the growing demand in the US and Europe for biofuel derived from grain, in response to the rising costs of oil and transportation. This, in conjunction with intensive speculation on grain in international stock markets, has caused the price of wheat to shoot up by 200 per cent and has driven up the prices of food commodities in general by 75 per cent since the beginning of the 21st century.[12] The global food supply crisis this has caused is aggravated in many Arab countries by their governments' mismanagement of food subsidy programmes.

In fact, there is nothing that ordains adherence to the blanket implementation of such policies if they lead to the spread of hunger and undernourishment, as well as to impoverishment and declining

Most Arab countries have had to contend with soaring food prices

---

Box 6-4 **Two initiatives for alleviating poverty – Brazil and Mexico**

Brazil's experience of pro-poor development under President Ignacio Lula da Silva

The government of Brazil has succeeded where all its predecessors, democratic and dictatorial alike, have failed. It has reduced acute social and economic disparity in favour of the poor. In January 2003, the "Lula" government unveiled "Programa Fome Zero"—the Zero Hunger Programme intended to accelerate the improvement of food security for 44 million people. The programme set into motion mechanisms intended to ensure the food and nutritional security of the Brazilian people, enhance their income by increasing basic food supplies, improve means of access to food, and provide urgent relief from hunger though targeted interventions.

In October 2003, as part of the initiative, the government initiated the "Bolsa Familia Programme", which seeks to remedy two problems—lack of education and undernourishment—at once. Under this programme, the government intervenes directly through injections of financial aid to poor families, but on the firm condition that their children attend school regularly and that the family attends primary healthcare facilities. By 2006, the government had brought these services to needy families whose members combined come to about 11.2 million people. From 1990-1992 to 2002-2004, Brazil succeeded in reducing the prevalence of hunger from 12 to 7 per cent and the number of its hungry from 18.5 million to 12.8 million.

In July 2007, the programme was bolstered by the allocation of 2.6 billion Euros for raising living conditions among the poor by supplying Brazil's urban slums—*favelas*—with drinking water, electricity, and sanitation facilities.

Mexico's programme for alleviating poverty and malnourishment

The *Oportunidades* programme launched by Mexico in 1997, under the banner "Progresa," grants cash remittances to poor families on the condition that they ascertain that their children attend school regularly and that family members pay periodic visits to health clinics. This government social assistance programme aims, in the short run, to improve the state of health and education of poor families and, in the long run, to help these families climb above the poverty line through education, which will offer better employment and income prospects to the family members.

Oportunidades targets families that are unable to meet their own basic food, health, and educational needs; these are estimated at five million families or a total of 25 million people. The programme undertakes to provide these basic necessities by means of cash remittances that are given directly to the mothers. The purpose of making the mothers the recipients is two-fold. It bolsters their autonomy and it ensures that the money is actually spent on the family to cover such needs as school expenses, school supplies, food, and periodic health checkups for the whole family.

Educational grants for lower and upper secondary school levels (grades seven to nine and ten to twelve, respectively) are higher for girls than for boys, with the target of narrowing the gender gap in secondary school enrolment. Pregnant women who regularly attend monthly maternity guidance lectures, appear for five prenatal checkups, receive two dental checkups, and take proper care of their teeth are entitled to total coverage of all expenses for delivery and three months' post-natal care, as well as to food supplements for themselves and their infants.

Source: Kenneth 2002.

Source: Braine 2006.

---

productivity. The experiences of some countries, notably Brazil and Mexico in Latin America, demonstrate that it is possible to follow liberal economic policies and, simultaneously, ensure a minimum level of food for the poor.

The effects of undernourishment on human security in Arab countries

Hunger undermines human security at the most basic level of existence. It is detrimental to health, productivity and relations with others. It can constitute a threat to life, and not just by shortening life expectancy from birth. The scramble for bread can erupt into violent clashes and riots, as recent incidents in some Arab countries testify.

At the personal level, acute hunger can be a direct cause of death or a cause of fatal illnesses. An estimated 25,000 people (adults and children) a day die from hunger and related causes around the world.[13] Although no such estimate is available for the Arab countries, the accelerated 200 per cent rise in grain prices since 2001 has made it more and more difficult to obtain bread in most Arab countries, even in oil-rich nations such as Saudi Arabia and the UAE. Since October 2007, Egypt, Morocco and Mauritania have all witnessed public protests over faltering bread supplies and surging prices. Syrians, Lebanese, and Yemenis, too, have found it extremely difficult to obtain bread, a basic component of the Arab diet. In Egypt, in early 2008, brawls in the bread queues in front of bakeries caused a number of deaths and wounded.

Food protests can spill over the borders of a country facing severe food shortages, stirring tensions between neighbouring states or political entities. A salient example was the attempt on the part of Palestinians in Gaza, in January 2008, to storm the Egyptian border in order to overcome the effects of Israel's blockade. Starving Gazans knocked down segments of the barriers at the Egypt-Gaza border, and hundreds of thousands poured into the Sinai in search of food and medicines. The border penetration, which angered the Egyptian authorities, only came to a halt when Egyptian forces succeeded in repairing the barriers. Since then, Egypt has allowed trucks bearing food and medicine to pass through, although the deteriorating situation in Gaza continues.

In the Arab region, the groups especially vulnerable to nutritional deficiencies are children and their mothers, as seen in the prevalence of underweight and stunting among children under five, which stood at 14.6 per cent and 22.2 per cent respectively in 2000-2005 for the Arab region. The prevalence of low-weight births was 12 per cent in the period 2000-2006.[14]

It may be observed that the proportion of underweight children under five, varies sharply among countries: in Yemen it was 45.6 per cent in 2003 and in Lebanon it was 3.3 per cent in 2002.

As Table 6.2 reveals, in spite of the progress most Arab countries have achieved in the fight against undernourishment, children pay a disproportionately greater price for hunger in the past and continue to pay a disproportionately greater price among the poor who live on less than two dollars a day. Many Arab countries continue to show high rates of prevalence of children under five who are underweight or stunted in comparison with the averages in their reference groups. The highest prevalence of these two categories of children is in Arab countries with high concentrations of the poor, namely Yemen, Sudan and Mauritania. At the opposite end of the scale, Jordan has the lowest prevalence of underweight children and Lebanon the lowest prevalence of stunted children. Lebanon and Algeria have the lowest prevalence of low-weight births. Child obesity appears to be a problem of some concern in a few Arab countries, notably Algeria, Egypt and Morocco where the prevalence of overweight children under five is between 13 and 15 per cent. Although malnourishment is not the only cause of these symptoms, it is frequently intertwined with the circumstances of poverty and the consequent increased vulnerability to poor health, dysentery, and contagious diseases.

Distressingly, while the Arab countries have some of the lowest rates in undernourishment among developing countries, some conditions for children in lower middle income countries are worse than in other regions. Compared to children in East Asia and the Pacific, children in the Arab countries suffer from a higher incidence of being underweight, despite the general higher prevalence of under-nourishment in East Asia and the Pacific. Moreover, the rate of low-weight births in the Arab countries is double that of East Asia and the Pacific and low income countries.

Ongoing hunger and malnourishment are reflected in children's educational performance. Hungry children enrol in school late, if they enrol at all, and drop out early, and their performance is poorer than that of well-nourished children even if they can attend school regularly. Poor families without food security can seldom afford to educate their children on whom they frequently depend for domestic chores, supplementary income and family support. Girls are held back most, since their education receives lower priority than that of boys.

Arab food security: some reflections[15]

Food security has been a subject of great national concern around the world since 1974, the year of the global food crisis, which led countries to view it as a component of national security. To many, it seemed that the key to food security lay in self-sufficiency, particularly in grain, and Arab countries took up the call. Many food-importing developing nations succeeded in achieving self-sufficiency

Low-weight birth rates in the Arab countries are double that of East Asia and the Pacific

Hunger and malnourishment are reflected in children's educational performance

Table 6-2	The effects of hunger on children – Arab countries compared with other regions and country groups				
Country	Prevalence of undernourishment (% of population)		Prevalence of children under 5 of less than average weight	Prevalence of children under 5 with stunted growth	Prevalence of low-weight births
	1990-1992	2002-2004	2000-2006	2000-2006	2000-2006
Algeria	5	4	10.2	21.6	6
Egypt	4	4	5.4	23.8	14
Jordan	4	6	3.6	12	12
Kuwait	24	5	..	..	..
Lebanon	2.5	3	3.9*	11*	6
Libya	2.5	2.5	..	..	..
Mauritania	15	10	30.4	39.4	..
Morocco	6	6	9.9	23.1	15
Saudi Arabia	4	4	..	..	..
Somalia	..	..	33*	23.3*	11
Oman	..	..	..	..	8
Sudan	31	26	38.4	47.6	..
Syria	5	4	6.9*	18.8*	9
Tunisia	2.5	2.5	4*	12.3*	7
UAE	4	3	..	..	
OPT		16	4.9*	9.9*	7
Yemen	34	38	45.6*	53.1*	..
North Africa & Middle East	6	7	14.6*	22.2*	12
Lower middle income countries	16	11	10.7	24.8	7
East Asia and the Pacific	17	12	12.9	26.2	6
Developed countries	3	3	..	..	..

Source: World Bank 2007.

*Data refers to the period 2000-2005.(most recent year available)
.. data not available.

after implementing "Green Revolution" programmes that introduced the cultivation of hybrids developed by international research centres.

In the Arab countries, all food-importing countries with the necessary resource capacities adopted self-sufficiency policies in grain and particularly in wheat. One of the countries to have met this goal is Syria. Another is Saudi Arabia, which not only achieved wheat self-sufficiency but also realised a surplus over market demands, albeit at the expense of scarce subterranean water resources.

In spite of changing domestic, regional, and international circumstances, food self-sufficiency remains a chief goal of the agricultural policies of most Arab states. Yet as important as the politics of this goal may be as an expression of national independence, it conflicts, in general, with applying the principle of cost-benefit ratios to the exploitation of natural and financial resources and may therefore lower economic efficiency. In the past, policies of self-sufficiency represented a form of insurance against deficits in food supplies resulting from economic boycotts, shortages in global production, or other causes. Such threats may no longer be pertinent in view of global economic and commercial assimilation. Also, practically speaking, no country can achieve sustainable self-sufficiency in view of the environmental changes that now influence production.

However, even supposing a country could realise overall food self-sufficiency, some sectors of its society could still suffer hunger and undernourishment. This realisation led to a shift in the definition of food security, which moved from the notion of self-sufficiency to the notion of sufficiency for all members of society in essential commodities. The concept of food security thus evolved to rest upon four pillars:
1) Food availability: ensuring sufficient food supply whether from local production or the international market.
2) Food stability: ensuring a stable supply of food throughout the year and from one season to the next.
3) Food accessibility: ensuring that the food is available to the public at affordable prices relative to their income.
4) Food safety.

The four pillars combined mean that all people in the country should be able to obtain their essential nutritional requirements throughout the year with no risk of deprivation, regardless of whether the food is produced locally or imported. Accordingly, the concept of food security can now be summed up in the notion of self-reliance, which is to say that the government should seek to supply its people's food needs from local produce supplemented by imports and that the hard currency needed to purchase such imports must derive from autonomous sources, notably exports in goods and services.

Could Arab countries produce all their food if they wanted? Or are there limitations and, if so, what are they? Are they natural, financial, administrative or human? Otherwise put, would it be possible for the Arab countries to achieve total food self-sufficiency?

The Arab region, taken as a whole, is certainly not short of financial resources. The surpluses it has acquired from oil exports especially since 2002 are more than sufficient to meet the region's development needs and not just in agriculture. What is important, in this regard, is how to move these resources from surplus areas into financial deficit areas that possess the natural potential for development. Clearly a major key here is to improve the investment climate in these areas.

The Arab countries as a whole have no shortage in manpower. Indeed this resource abounds and with high levels of open and masked unemployment there is more than enough available labour to meet the needs of most development projects.

The total area of the Arab countries is 14 million square kilometres, or 10 per cent of the earth's surface area. In 2004, it was estimated that there were 69.6 million hectares of arable land in this region (of which 18.5 million hectares were left fallow) and that the per capita share of this land was 0.23 hectares. The Arab region is well-known for its small ratio of usable land to total land area. At 35 per cent, this ratio is the lowest in the world. Desertification and the deterioration of agricultural land form two of the most important challenges to agricultural production. In general, the contribution of agriculture to the region's economic performance is declining.

No country can achieve sustainable self-sufficiency in view of environmental changes that influence production

The concept of food security can be summed up in the notion of self-reliance

On the other hand, the Arab countries possess vast amounts of livestock and fish. They have some 373 million heads of livestock, mostly in Sudan, a natural but unexploited storehouse of animal wealth. The region has 22.4 thousand kilometres of coastline and 16.6 thousand kilometres of rivers, plus freshwater and semi-freshwater lakes. It produces some 3.8 million tons of fish, mostly in Morocco, Mauritania, Egypt, Yemen, and Oman.

But land resources are not the only limitation on expansion in food production. The first and foremost limitation is water. The region has an estimated 300 billion cubic metres[16] of water, which represents less than 1 per cent of the world's total water resources, noting that the population of the Arab region represents 5% of the world's population. In 2001, the per capita share of water in the Arab countries was 1,000 cubic metres—the worldwide per capita share was seven times that. Between 1996 and 2006, the Arab countries used 71 per cent of their available water compared to a global rate of 6.3 per cent. More than two-thirds of this amount is consumed in agriculture.[17]

More and more Arab countries are sinking below the water poverty level.[18] From three countries in 1955 (Bahrain, Jordan, and Kuwait), the number of countries below the water poverty level came to eleven by 1990 (with the addition of Algeria, the Occupied Palestinian Territory, Qatar, Saudi Arabia, Somalia, Tunisia, the UAE and Yemen). Seven more countries of the region are expected to join them by 2025.

Rendering the problem of available water resources for agriculture even more acute is the exponentially growing demand on water resources for non-agricultural purposes. This is due to population growth, urban development and urban population growth, industrial expansion, growth of the tourist industry and other such factors. These same factors, moreover, have contributed to the mounting levels of water pollution and the deterioration of the quality of water needed for all types of uses. In addition, over-exploitation of subterranean water resources has led to numerous problems in the Gulf countries, Gaza and the West Bank, and elsewhere as a result of the consequent higher salinity levels in aquifers.

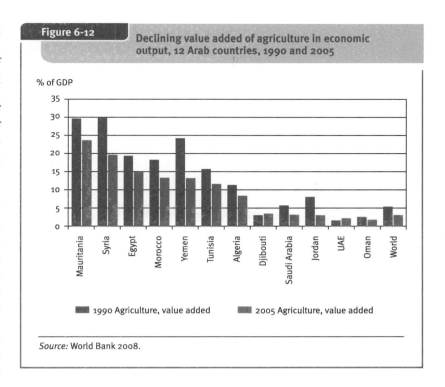

Figure 6-12

Declining value added of agriculture in economic output, 12 Arab countries, 1990 and 2005

% of GDP

■ 1990 Agriculture, value added   ■ 2005 Agriculture, value added

Source: World Bank 2008.

The bottom line here is that, if water resources cannot keep up with the food production needs of the Arab people, Arab countries will necessarily continue to rely on food imports, and this is contingent on their financial resources. In effect, importing food implies importing the water needed to produce it, a fact that has given rise to the concept of "virtual water" (See Box 6-5). The concept is of particular value to the Arab countries. If Arab countries balance their food exports and imports in such a way as to concentrate imports on those goods whose production requires the most water and to concentrate exports on those goods whose production requires the least, they will be able to generate considerable savings in water through trade.

This concept is as applicable to inter-Arab agricultural trade as it is to agricultural trade between Arab and foreign countries. It is estimated that it took 235 billion cubic meters of virtual water—nearly equal to the amount of actual water resources available to the Arab countries—to produce their average volume of food imports from 2001 to 2003. This quantity is almost equal to the amount of water currently allocated to food production, of which 33 per cent was used for plant production while 67 per cent was allocated to the processing of imports of animal, poultry, and fish.

The first and foremost limitation in food production is water

The concept of virtual water is of particular value to the Arab countries

Such studies help point the way forward. Arab countries must raise their water productivity in order to improve their competitiveness. Towards this end, they must study the various economic and commercial aspects involved, with particular attention to international agreements affecting food trade. The importance of this strategy cannot be overstated in view of the Arab countries' increasing dependency on imports for food security.

The concept of virtual water is attracting attention in relation to the analysis of trade flows and increasing water scarcity. Producing goods and services generally requires water. The water used in the production process of an agricultural or industrial product is called the virtual water contained in the product. For instance, to produce 1 kg of wheat we need 1 to 2 m³ of water. Livestock products require even more water: producing 1 kg of cheese requires about 5 m³ of water, and it takes about 16 m³ of water to produce 1 kg of beef.

The concept suggests that, in a reasonably safe, interdependent and prosperous world, a country with limited water resources could rely on imports of agricultural products showing high levels of embedded water (e.g. meat) and apply its own water resources to produce other commodities of lower value in terms of water content (see table). Conversely, a country with abundant water resources could benefit from its comparative natural advantage by exporting products that are high in embedded water.

Virtual water content of selected products, 2003

Product	Litres of water per kilo of crop
Wheat	1,150
Rice	2,656
Maize	450
Potatoes	160
Soybeans	2,300
Beef	15,977
Pork	5,906
Poultry	2,828
Eggs	4,657
Milk	865
Cheese	5,288

Source: UNESCO 2006.

Food trade analysis shows that most trade takes place between countries that show substantial endowments in water resources, indicating that factors other than water drive international food trade. Yet an increasing number of arid countries that face water scarcity (Egypt, Tunisia, etc.) are progressively embracing policies aimed at increasing their imports of staple crops and thus releasing water for more financially productive uses. Such policies usually imply long-term trade agreements between importing and exporting countries and therefore tend to facilitate increased stability in international relations.

Source: UNESCO 2006.

The subject of virtual water is important to Egypt and other Arab countries and merits much closer study and research. Indeed, if the criterion of greatest economic return is brought to bear in prioritising resource allocations, the Arab countries will be much better equipped to develop and steer a regional policy on Integrated Water Management (IWM).

Beyond this key matter, increasing food security in the region requires higher investments in agriculture. The commercial approach, as implemented so far through the lifting of customs barriers in the Greater Arab Free Trade Zone, will not, in itself, suffice to bring about the desired integration in agriculture. If trade is to be effective, agricultural production must be sufficient in quantity and diversity, within the confines of available water resources, and this requires investment.

It has been proposed that Arab governments take steps to stimulate exchanges in production surpluses, such as between Sudanese meat and Moroccan fish. The next stage would require further investment in processing, marketing, and transport. Then at a subsequent stage, resources would be channelled into those investments judged to be most cost-effective. Such an approach would improve people's access to food commodities (through the increase of supply) and, simultaneously, increase their income levels through development. In parallel, Arab countries must create strategic stores, at the country and, if possible, regional levels, so as to be able to offset deficits in supply, whether of locally produced food or imports. Only through such strategic stocks will it be possible to achieve food security and stability for society in the face of fluctuations in climate conditions.

Recent increases in the production of biofuels from plant products (such as grain and sugar) have saddled Arab countries with the soaring costs of importing these goods. In order to alleviate this burden, Arab governments must offer farmers sufficient incentives to expand production horizontally and vertically. The scope for such expansion, in turn, is intrinsically linked to research on new forms of energy, especially renewable energy such as wind and solar power, aimed at increasing the water supply through more cost-effective desalinisation processes.

Conclusion

As unpropitious as the current trend seems to be in many country cases, it is essential for the Arab states to strive to meet Target 2 of Goal One of the MDGs by uprooting hunger, improving nutrition and developing policies for building food security to the extent feasible.

Beating hunger and malnutrition

Addressing this challenge requires intensifying and accelerating a two-pronged strategy for remedying the causes and consequences of poverty, disease, and ignorance. Two major factors must be taken into consideration when planning such a strategy: the need for interventions to improve productivity and income, and urgent steps to furnish direct and immediate food relief to vulnerable groups and the neediest families.

This two-pronged approach would, thus, be translated into far-reaching, low-cost programmes that would focus simultaneously and comprehensively on the following objectives:

- Facilitating the direct and immediate access of needy families to food by putting in place solid food-provision safety nets and remittance programmes. Such programmes and safety nets, it should be stressed, would target the most vulnerable groups in society. Particular attention must be devoted to covering the essential nutritional needs of mothers, infants, and pre-school and school-age children. The interrelated goals here are to end the transmission of the cycle of poverty from one generation to the next, to improve children's physical and mental growth, to enable their regular attendance and better performance at school, and to enhance their opportunities for employment, greater productivity and higher incomes.
- Ensuring that the marginalised and disadvantaged who in rural areas are, for the most part, girls, receive primary education. Education is a human right and should be free, universalised, and compulsory.
- Promoting gender equality in opportunities to access food. All obstacles to equality between men and women

must be eliminated if we are to move forward in human development, the alleviation of poverty and hunger, saving children's lives, and the fight against diseases.

- Accelerating the pace of economic development and, especially, agricultural development. In this regard, it is important to furnish small farmers with the means and know-how to raise production levels in a manner that promotes the consumption of their own produce in their families and local societies. Such means include introducing simple and inexpensive technologies, facilitating access to seed and organic fertilisers, and providing guidance on sound water management practices, such as the use of drip irrigation.

Rapid urban development, the globalisation of food processing industries and the expansion of these into the major markets have had adverse repercussions on most small farmers and itinerant labour in rural areas. Over recent decades, a handful of companies have gained increasing control over world food trade, processing, and sales. Such control may have given rise in some cases to greater consumer choice, lower prices, and higher quality in foods, but it has also created near-monopolistic supply chains in which a few giant food companies and wholesalers have gained growing control over prices, standards, and delivery. Some farmers have managed to merge into the local central markets and reap high profits. However, many small producers are unable to obtain sufficient information, training, and loans to enable them to assimilate into the "globalized" market. They, therefore, find themselves excluded from the processes of both production and consumption.

However, an even more important objective is to work towards integration in food and, especially, grain production in the Arab countries. Efforts towards this end should focus on taking advantage of the large tracts of arable land that are available in the region, notably in Sudan, which has the potential to become the Arab countries' breadbasket, and in Iraq. Arab countries lack neither the financial resources for this project, some of which could be supplied by the oil-exporting states, nor the expertise and manpower. It is possible to envision two such projects.

Beating hunger requires a two-pronged strategy for remedying the causes and consequences of poverty, disease, and ignorance

An important objective is to work towards integration in food and grain production

One project, called for by the Secretary-General of the Council for Arab Economic Unity, is very ambitious, as it would aim to achieve regional integration in the production of all categories of food, from grains and fruits and vegetables to meat and dairy products, by harmonising cultivation and production among Arab countries. A second project, smaller in scope, would focus solely on integration in the production of grain. The two projects are not at all incompatible. Indeed, the less ambitious one may constitute a step towards the more ambitious one. More importantly, the success of either of these two projects would, in itself, stimulate the drive to Arab economic integration which has made no significant progress. Attaining such a goal however demands the requisite political resolve and depends on achieving political stability in countries such as Iraq and Sudan. This, in turn, underscores the degree to which the various dimensions of human security in the Arab countries are intertwined, whether they relate to food availability or achieving peace and stability by ending foreign occupation and intervention and resolving identity conflicts in the region.

Achieving food security

Food insecurity in the Arab countries has partly resulted from declining per capita productivity in agriculture and the widening gap within and between agriculture and other sectors of the economy. The responsibility is shared by: (a) Inadequate investment in the often capital-starved agriculture sectors that still contribute a sizable per cent of national income (particularly in LDCs); and (b) the widespread use of labour-displacing technology that has been facilitated by trade liberalization, combined with the limited labour-absorption capacity of other formal sectors.

There is an intricate nexus between agriculture, rural development, food security and self-sufficiency. It is thus essential to address the linkages between the microeconomics of farm units and the dynamics of household well-being, a relationship which points to broader redistributive (political economy) policy considerations such as: (1) secure access to productive land and credit; (2) targeted price support benefits for the identified rural poor and disadvantaged geographical areas; (3) changing gender roles, which require that women who make up an ever increasing share of agricultural producers are provided with access to land, appropriate tools, extension services, credit, etc; (4) efficient water resource management; (5) incentives to the private sector to invest in agricultural production and marketing and to adopt projects that promote integration between agriculture and industry; and (6) new agricultural research on local plant varieties and on renewable energy, including solar energy.

As this chapter notes, if current trends continue, the Arab countries, despite the varying performances of its constituent countries and sub-regions, will probably not meet Goal One of the MDGs. Winning the fight against hunger, therefore, requires intensive and imaginative efforts in all Arab countries, but most especially in those that are least developed, as well as concerted regional cooperation.

Endnotes

1   This section is largely based on Jalila El-Ati, in Arabic, background paper for the report.
2   UNDP/AHDR calculations based on World Bank, World Development Indicators, 2007.
3   FAO 2006.
4   WFP 2008b.
5   Kabbani and Wehelie 2004.
6   Chan 2008.
7   Daily caloric intake equals total caloric value obtained from all foodstuff divided by the number of inhabitants and the number of days.
8   FAO 1999.
9   Sobal and Stunkard 1989.
10 World Bank 2008b.
11 FAO 2009.
12 World Bank 2008 (in Arabic).
13 FAO 2006.
14 World Bank 2007b.
15 This discussion draws on the contribution of Ahmad Goweily, Secretary-General of the Council for Arab Economic Unity.
16 UNDP/AHDR calculations based on FAO, Food Security Statistics (FAOSTAT) database, 2008.
17 See Chapter 2 for more details.
18 According to UNDP 2006b, the personal water poverty threshold is set at 50 litres a day.

Chapter 7

Approaching health through human security – a road not taken

Health is widely recognized as a cornerstone of human development because it underpins the gamut of human functioning. But health is also essential to human security, since survival and protection from illness are at the core of any concept of people's wellbeing. Good health enables human choice, freedom, and progress. Poor health—illness, injury, and disability—undermines those essential human capabilities and can trigger potentially catastrophic reversals for individuals, communities and economies. In turn, health is interdependent with other components of human security—political, economic, environmental and nutritional—and is therefore best addressed holistically.

Health is essential to human security

In the last 40 years, Arab countries have made striking progress in forestalling death and extending life, as evidenced by rising life expectancy and falling infant mortality rates. Yet health is by no means assured for all citizens in Arab countries, with women suffering the most from neglect and gender biased traditions. Health systems are often shackled by bureaucratic inefficiency, poor professional capabilities and underfunding; and health risks from new infectious diseases are on the rise. Despite the ample resources available in the Arab region, the past 5 years have seen all its major health indicators stagnate. Moreover, compelling international ideas and approaches in health and human security, which have been adapted in some other regions, have not yet taken hold in most Arab countries.

Health in international public policy

This opening section reviews trends in the international discourse on health and security that provide an important perspective on approaches to health in the Arab countries at this time, as discussed subsequently.

Health is by no means assured for all citizens in Arab countries

Health and human security

Following the end of the Cold War, and with the rise of globalisation, the once-separate realms of security and development began to converge. Public health soon became a key area of overlap. In this context, two types of discourse on health and security, each with distinct motivations and targets, set their sights on international public policy.

The first type may be termed developmental and is represented by the work of the United Nations, its development funds and programmes, international and regional commissions and the World

Health Organization (WHO). Through the 1990s, in an age of fast travel and frequent movement of peoples and goods, the recognition that health hazards in one country could quickly spill across others began to influence international development policy. This recognition received impetus from the catastrophic transborder impacts of emerging diseases such as HIV/AIDS, and of re-emerging ones such as cholera, tuberculosis and resistant strains of malaria. A culminating point was the publication of the 1994 Human Development Report (HDR), which gave a new developmental focus to emerging health challenges by positing 'health security' as a component of human security.[1]

Essentially, the HDR 1994 advocated for the view that health was an individual human right and a public good that should be accessible to all. It was a duty of the state, and in its own interest, to protect this basic right, which represented both an ethical imperative and a condition of its own survival. However, the sources and impacts of contemporary health challenges were too complex and wide to be addressed solely by states. Rather, health security was a transnational, multidimensional and people-centered phenomenon that tied other development areas and actors together.

The Report noted that the main threats to health for most people in the world had become fast-spreading communicable diseases and pandemics, and death and illness linked to poverty, unsafe environments and the displacement of peoples. Securing people's health rested not only on traditional medical services and health care but also on other factors such as political, economic, nutritional and environmental security, all of which were vulnerable to abrupt reversals or downturns that could disrupt people's daily lives. Protecting people from these kinds of risks therefore necessitated proactive responses by multiple state and non-state entities, and by individuals and their communities. Because contemporary health threats did not recognize borders, they also required global-local partnerships to help prevent or manage outbreaks of complex diseases and their spillovers.

In 2003, the Commission on Human Security (CHS) released a follow-up report, *Human Security Now*,[2] which broadened and updated the 1994 HDR's analysis. The Commission's work confirmed that those health threats most relevant to human security were a) global infectious diseases, including pandemics such as HIV/AIDS and Severe Acute Respiratory Syndrome (SARS); b) health crises caused by armed conflicts and humanitarian emergencies; and c) health problems arising from poverty that could destabilize families, communities and even entire states. A human security approach to these threats, all of which carried heavy local and global consequences, depended on two fundamentals: protection and empowerment. Ensuring these fundamentals however transcended traditional approaches based on horizontal relations among governments and called, additionally, for vertical programmes and monitoring systems associating non-state actors.

In effect, the UNDP-CHS discourse re-situated the objectives of both national security and public health within a comprehensive, developmental and people-centered framework that broadened the definition and interdependence of both.

Health and strategic security

The second type of international discourse is much narrower, and may be termed strategic. It originates during this same period in the concerns of Western military and diplomatic establishments over biological weapons and the deliberate use of disease in warfare. Such concerns were renewed by the 1995 sarin gas attack in the Tokyo subway and spread to the general public after the anthrax scare in the United States following the attacks of 9/11, 2001. The aim of this discourse is to "securitize" international health surveillance as protection against possible biological warfare and so-called "bioterrorism". The major actors, mainly in the West, are associated with efforts to bring biological weapons control into the realm of global public health and to strengthen the Biological and Toxin Weapons Convention (BWC) with a verification protocol.

The two types of discourse have quite different objectives, constituencies and lobbies yet share a common view of health and security as convergent transnational issues. Thus, the two have come to intersect

Health security is a transnational, multidimensional and people-centered phenomenon that ties development areas and actors together

This strategic discourse aims to "securitize" international health surveillance as protection against biological warfare

at certain points, tipping the international health agenda in one or the other direction at different times. Experts agree that the result of this intersection has generally been to broaden policy discourse on public health security—albeit with reservations from developing countries, including from some in the Arab region—to cover threats from both infectious diseases and biological weapons.[3]

Some analysts note that, as a side-effect, the considerable pressure exerted by the counter-bioterrorism lobby for a strategic interpretation of public health security may have spurred efforts to strengthen intergovernmental health policies. The latter are embodied chiefly in the International Health Regulations (IHR) promulgated and monitored by the WHO.[4] In place during the first 30 years of WHO operations, these Regulations originally required member states to report outbreaks from a list of six diseases, later reduced in 1981 to three—cholera, malaria and yellow fever. Wide criticism of this small and increasingly irrelevant list in light of new threats ranging from HIV/AIDS and the Ebola virus to avian influenza, together with poor reporting compliance by numerous countries, eventually led WHO to issue new and considerably strengthened IHRs in 2005, which went into force in 2007.

The new Regulations now require a state party to notify WHO of "all events which may constitute a public health emergency of international concern" (article 6.1). These events include any unexpected or unusual public health event regardless of its origin or source (article 7). They also require state parties, as far as is practicable, to inform WHO of public health risks identified outside their territories that may cause disease to spread, as manifested by exported or imported human cases, contaminated goods or vectors that may carry infection (article 9.2).[5]

The requirement to report on "all events which may constitute a public health emergency of international concern" provides new latitude to cover a wide range of threats. However, the fact that reporting still rests on information volunteered by states has left some sceptics unconvinced that the new IHRs speak to the kind of security regime entailed by concepts of global governance.[6] On the other hand, the perceptions of some developing countries, including some Arab states, that these Regulations are laced with the national security concerns of the West, and that data shared may not serve their own interests, risks hampering the effective operation of a stronger disease surveillance and prevention system.

Health security in the Arab context

The 2002 Cairo Consultation on Health and Security,[7] co-sponsored by WHO, UNFPA and UNAIDS, attempted to adapt the international discourse on human security originally promoted by UNDP and the CHS to the regional level. The three-day discussion acknowledged the comprehensive scope and interdependencies of health and human security, agreed that health spanned disciplines, sectors and agencies and reaffirmed that good health was a basic human right. Yet in the end the meeting defined health security somewhat narrowly as "relative liberation from illnesses and infection." Most health experts find this definition inadequate whether assessed in terms of the recognized dimensions of health, which are more comprehensive, or in terms of positive security dimensions (what should happen) rather than merely negative ones (what should not happen).

The failure in the Arab context to give wide practical effect to a holistic view of health and human security reflects the limited internalisation of these concepts in the Arab countries. A number of factors may account for this:

First: the Arab reform movement has not embraced human security as a paradigm for change and reform or as a basis for action programmes, which are dominated in general by a socio-economic frame of reference. In the health field, this difference in perspective translates into a more limited focus on expanding health services, clinical facilities and other supply-driven aspects of traditional health care, which continue to be emphasized by both governments and civil society.

Second: as a result, in the absence of an alternative paradigm, approaches to security are restricted to the concept of state security for addressing domestic and

There has been limited internalisation of these concepts in the Arab countries

The Arab reform movement has not embraced human security as a paradigm for change and reform

international dangers. There are very few discussions concerning the non-political and non-state aspects of security; naturally, the same applies to health security and other components of human security. For example, there is virtually no public debate for the major effects of armed conflict in weakening health systems, or for the diversion of resources away from people's basic health to meet urgent health needs related to the conflict in question.

Third: relatively low priority is given to the subject of health itself in budgets and programmes pertaining to development in the Arab countries. Rather, public health is treated as secondary compared to issues such as basic needs, job creation, and economic growth. This makes it impossible for health agencies to deal with the current or potential health challenges that face the region's inhabitants. The multi-sectoral alliances and funding options that a health and human security approach can deliver have rarely been tapped.

Fourth: health receives very little attention in general public discourse. There is, therefore, a glaring inconsistency between the seriousness of certain health problems in the Arab countries on the one hand, and the absence of the subject from discussions engaged in by Arab states on the other.[8] When discussions of health issues do take place, they tend to dwell on matters relating to health services, techniques and technologies. When it comes to public health security, there is little understanding that it consists of a set of effective and multidisciplinary activities required to reduce the incidence of acute public health situations that threaten the health of citizens.

Fifth: Arab civil society is generally weakened by political restrictions and exclusion, and does not often participate in matters relating to health. Hence, non-state actors have had very little effect on health systems and health policy development. Instead, the highly influential Arab medical establishment holds sway over the health field. This "expert" dominance within the existing professional hierarchy is further entrenched by non-democratic health system institutions patterned on Arab political institutions. The resulting dearth of public participation poses an obstacle in the face of health- and security-related initiatives.

These factors, together with the weak, and sometimes contested, linkages between discourse on the international and regional levels, have led to the current situation where the Arab health community appears to have either resisted or ignored a human security approach to health in practice.

Public health is treated as secondary

Vital recording systems are not available

The health situation in the Arab countries

The present report draws health and health system indicators largely from data published by United Nations agencies. However, the accuracy of such data is subject to question in some cases. On some occasions UN agencies, non-governmental organizations (NGOs) and civil society organizations conduct independent statistical studies. For the most part, however, governments themselves are the source of information. In most Arab states, vital recording systems are not available, and when they are, they are seldom reliable. Often, "national" data are not based on national survey studies, nor do they represent all groups in the society. Consequently, generalizations based on such data are of limited value. It

---

Box 7-1	Terms in the discourse

Health security
Relative freedom from disease and infection; 2002 Cairo Consultation on Health & Human Security; *Protection against illness, disability and avoidable death*; Commission on Human Security, 2003.

Public health security
A set of effective and multidisciplinary activities required to reduce the incidence of acute public health situations that threaten the health of citizens; this Report.

Global public health security
The activities required, both proactive and reactive, to minimize vulnerability to acute public health events that endanger the collective health of populations living across geographical regions and international boundaries; WHO, 2007.

Health and human security
A human security approach to health entails treating health '*not just the absence of disease, but as a state of complete physical, mental and social well-being*'; Commission on Human Security, 2003.

is, moreover, not customary for states to release data which would reveal internal inconsistencies, which puts the usefulness of the data in question, particularly when examining social equity and justice.

Nonetheless, it may be acknowledged from the outset that the Arab countries have seen great improvements in health over the past several decades, albeit starting with a backlog to overcome. Indeed, between the 1960s and the start of the new millennium, the Arab countries made greater progress in forestalling death and extending life than most developing regions. This can be observed through the 23-year increase in life expectancy and the reduction in infant mortality rates from 152 to 39 per thousand births.

Even so, while aggregate indicators are positive, challenges remain and Arab countries can achieve better health coverage for their citizens in keeping with the wealth available in the countries. A particular continuing challenge is to resolve the noticeable disparities among different Arab states and the injustices to be found within them. In passing, it needs to be recalled that past successes do not rest solely on the sizeable investments made in the quantitative expansion of health systems. They also stem from the major socioeconomic developments that followed the 1970s oil boom, which helped to raise health conditions.[9]

Health indicators[10]

Average life expectancy at birth in most Arab countries is about seventy years. Nevertheless, one can observe major disparities in this respect between one sub-region and another. In Djibouti, Iraq, Somalia, and Sudan, for example, average life expectancy is no more than sixty years, whereas in Bahrain, Kuwait, Oman, Qatar, and the United Arab Emirates it exceeds seventy-four years. As in other regions of the world, average life expectancy for women exceeds that for men; except for Qatar and Somalia with a gender gap of 1 and 2 years respectively, the gender difference in life expectancy in the region is between 3 to 5 years.

Disparities among sub-regions are evident on other indicators. For example, the maternal mortality ratio (MMR) ranges from 4 deaths per 100,000 live births in Kuwait to more than 400 per 100,000 births in Djibouti, Mauritania, Somalia Sudan, and Yemen. Infant mortality rates range from fewer than 8 per 1,000 live births in the United Arab Emirates to more than 76 per 1,000 live births in Yemen and Mauritania and eighty-eight in Djibouti.

Progress towards MDG 5, target 6, which aims to reduce by three quarters the maternal mortality ratio by 2015, varies across the region owing to the socioeconomic differences between the

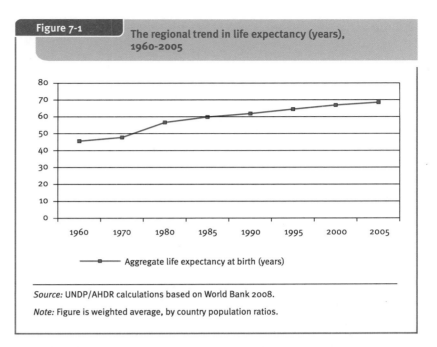

Figure 7-1 The regional trend in life expectancy (years), 1960-2005

Aggregate life expectancy at birth (years)

Source: UNDP/AHDR calculations based on World Bank 2008.

Note: Figure is weighted average, by country population ratios.

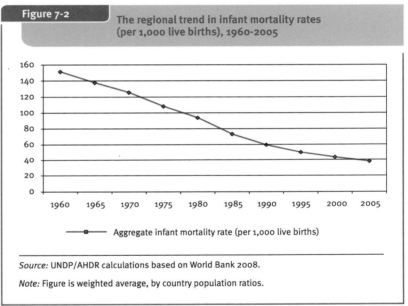

Figure 7-2 The regional trend in infant mortality rates (per 1,000 live births), 1960-2005

Aggregate infant mortality rate (per 1,000 live births)

Source: UNDP/AHDR calculations based on World Bank 2008.

Note: Figure is weighted average, by country population ratios.

The Arab countries made greater progress in forestalling death and extending life than most developing regions

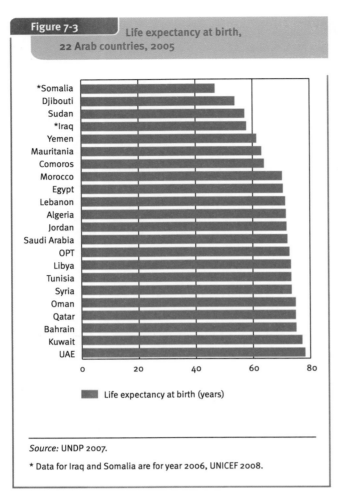

Figure 7-3 Life expectancy at birth, 22 Arab countries, 2005

Life expectancy at birth (years)

Source: UNDP 2007.

* Data for Iraq and Somalia are for year 2006, UNICEF 2008.

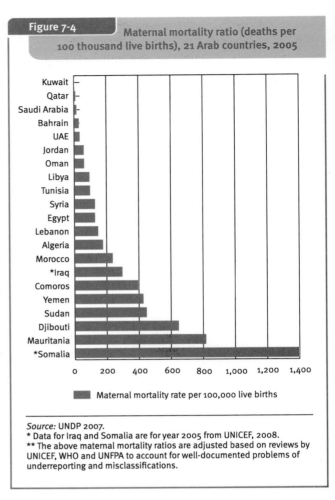

Figure 7-4 Maternal mortality ratio (deaths per 100 thousand live births), 21 Arab countries, 2005

Maternal mortality rate per 100,000 live births

Source: UNDP 2007.
* Data for Iraq and Somalia are for year 2005 from UNICEF, 2008.
** The above maternal mortality ratios are adjusted based on reviews by UNICEF, WHO and UNFPA to account for well-documented problems of underreporting and misclassifications.

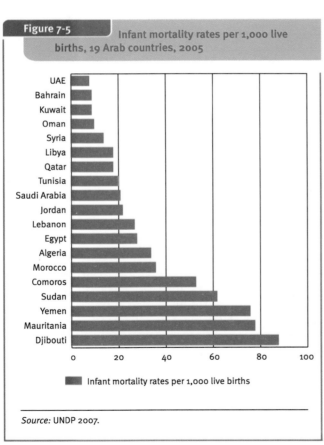

Figure 7-5 Infant mortality rates per 1,000 live births, 19 Arab countries, 2005

Infant mortality rates per 1,000 live births

Source: UNDP 2007.

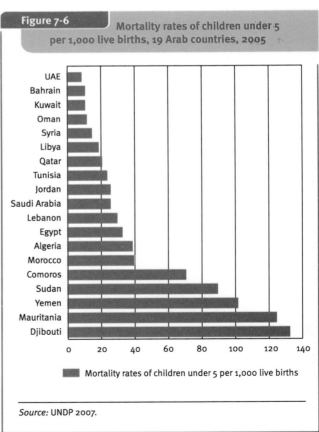

Figure 7-6 Mortality rates of children under 5 per 1,000 live births, 19 Arab countries, 2005

Mortality rates of children under 5 per 1,000 live births

Source: UNDP 2007.

sub-regions. Accordingly, while the region as a whole is on track, this is not the case for all of the four sub-regions. In 2000, the MMR was lowest in the GCC countries at about 17 per 100,000 live births, mostly since 98.2 per cent of births in the GCC are supervised by skilled birth attendants. On the other hand, while the MMR in the Arab LDCs dropped by 37.9 per cent to 637.6 per 100,000 live births in 2000, it remains significantly above the developing world average of 450 per 100,000 live births. The average MMR in the Arab LDCs was the highest in the Arab countries; only 44.8 per cent of newborns were delivered by skilled birth attendants in 2000, up by 22 percentage points from 1990. The trends in maternal mortality and births attended by skilled personnel in the Arab LDCs overall are largely influenced by the respective trends in Sudan, which accounts for almost 50 per cent of live births in the sub-region. Slightly less than half of these births are not attended by skilled personnel, and the MMR in Sudan was 509 per 100,000 live births in 2000.

Similarly, mortality rates for under-five children range from less than 20 per 1,000 births in most Gulf States to more than 100 per 1,000 in Djibouti, Mauritania and Yemen. Disparities between rural and urban areas are wide, with the higher rates being found in rural areas.

One noteworthy trend is the spread of under-nutrition in poor states and war-torn countries, a reflection of growing food scarcities. In Somalia, the prevalence of underweight in children under five is 26 per cent and in Sudan and Yemen it stands at more than 40 per cent (most recent data available in the 1996–2005 period). In addition, the incidence of under-nutrition among children in some wealthy states is a further source of concern; for example, the incidence of moderate and severe under-nutrition among children under five comes to 14 per cent in the United Arab Emirates and 10 per cent in Kuwait, which suggests that, despite the ample financial resources of some states, not all of the expected health benefits have accrued.[11]

WHO statistics indicate that the most important factors accounting for disparity in health levels within Arab countries are income level, place of residence (urban or rural), and mother's educational level.

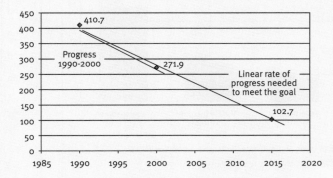

Box 7-2 — Arab States on track for improving maternal health and achieving Millennium Development Goal 5

Target 6: Reduce by three quarters, between 1990 and 2015, the maternal mortality ratio

Maternal mortality ratio, Arab region (per 100,000 live births)

Source: UN-ESCWA, The Millennium Development Goals in the Arab Region 2007: A Youth Lens, an Overview, 2007.

The maternal mortality ratio (MMR) in the Arab countries fell to about 272 per 100,000 live births in 2000, a decrease of almost 34 per cent from its 1990 level. Assuming that the rate of progress achieved between 1990 and 2000 can be maintained, the Arab countries as a whole will meet the goal of reducing the MMR by three quarters by 2015. The considerable decline in maternal mortality is linked to the significant increase in births attended by skilled health personnel. In fact, this ratio rose by over 16 percentage points over the decade. In addition, the reduction in adolescent pregnancy—associated with high risks—has contributed to the overall decline in maternal mortality. Indeed, adolescents aged 15-19 are twice as likely to die during childbirth as are women in their twenties, and those under 15 are five times as likely.

Source: UN-ESCWA 2007a.

Among the most important indicators of the impact of such factors are the likelihood that children will survive beyond age five, the incidence of dwarfism, the chances of childbirth being attended by skilled health professionals, and the availability of vaccinations against measles during the first year of life. The most influential factors in the six Arab states for which such data were available—Egypt, Jordan, Morocco, Sudan, Tunisia, and Yemen—were the level of income and the mother's educational level. In other words, going by some of these WHO indicators, Arab children in families with higher income levels or having mothers with higher educational levels enjoy health care and health levels that are three to four times better than in the cases of children in low-income families and with less-educated mothers.[12]

Disparities between rural and urban areas are wide

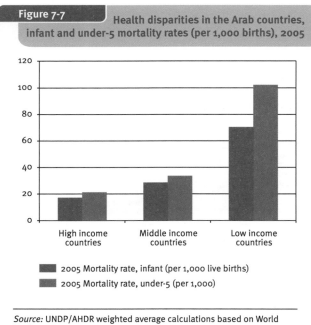

■ 2005 Mortality rate, infant (per 1,000 live births)
■ 2005 Mortality rate, under-5 (per 1,000)

Source: UNDP/AHDR weighted average calculations based on World Bank 2008.

Note: Categorization based on GDP per capita, PPP (current international $) with the following thresholds: Low income $1,100 - $2,200, Middle income $3,600 - $11,000, and High income $20,000 - $44,000.
Low income countries include : Comoros, Djibouti, Mauritania, Somalia, Sudan, Yemen.
Middle income countries include: Algeria, Egypt, Jordan, Lebanon, Libya, Morocco, OPT, Syria, Tunisia.
High income countries include: Bahrain, Kuwait, Oman, Qatar, Saudi Arabia, United Arab Emirates.

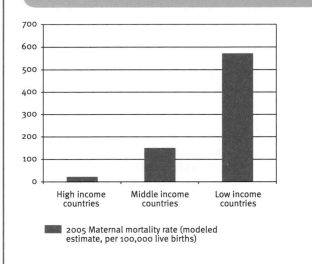

■ 2005 Maternal mortality rate (modeled estimate, per 100,000 live births)

Source: UNDP/AHDR weighted average calculations based on World Bank 2008.

Note: Categorization based on GDP per capita, PPP (current international $) with the following thresholds: Low income $1,100 - $2,200, Middle income $3,600 - $11,000, and High income $20,000 - $44,000.
Low income countries include : Comoros, Djibouti, Mauritania, Somalia, Sudan, Yemen.
Middle income countries include: Algeria, Egypt, Jordan, Lebanon, Libya, Morocco, OPT, Syria, Tunisia.
High income countries include: Bahrain, Kuwait, Oman, Qatar, Saudi Arabia, United Arab Emirates.

Box 7-3   **More efforts required to combat malaria and tuberculosis**

MDG 6 Target 8: Have halted by 2015, and begun to reverse, the incidence of malaria and other major diseases.

While malaria has been almost eliminated in the majority of Arab countries, it remains highly endemic in the Arab LDCs, where on average 3,313 cases per 100,000 were reported in 2005. Djibouti, Somalia, Sudan and Yemen accounted for 98 per cent of notified cases in the region; Sudan alone bore about 76 per cent of the regional burden. Achievement of the MDG target in the sub-region, and in the region as a whole, is therefore heavily dependent on progress in Somalia, Sudan, and Yemen. Furthermore, malaria notification in these countries understates the actual number of cases as surveillance is weak and, in some areas, nonexistent. Lack of adequate health care and laboratory facilities and adverse security conditions are some of the factors hindering progress in survey efforts.

Tuberculosis remains a significant public health problem, and probably the leading cause of communicable disease deaths in adults in the Arab region. It is estimated that in 2005, 240,000 people developed tuberculosis and 43,000 died from it. The Arab LDCs are the countries affected the

most, accounting for almost 56 per cent of all new tuberculosis cases in the region.

An estimated 41 per cent of tuberculosis patients do not have access to quality health care.

Tuberculosis prevalence rate (per 100,000)

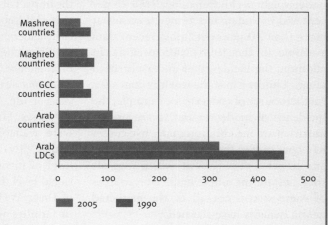

■ 2005   ■ 1990

Source: UN-ESCWA 2007.

Source: UN-ESCWA 2007a.

At the intra-regional level, on all major health indicators, as national income rises, health levels improve, leading to evident differences among Arab countries.

Changes since 2002

The comparison of health indicators for Arab countries for the years 2003 and 2007 shows that life expectancy increased and child mortality declined. Other health indicators remained static.

- Marked disparities continue between the low-income Arab countries and the medium-income and high-income ones.
- With the exception of a small number of indicators, on average, the performance of medium-income states resembles the performance of high-income states.
- The national and regional data which are available give an inadequate picture of the disparities and inequalities that exist within states. This underscores the importance to policymakers, academics and health practitioners of those national human development reports produced in the Arab countries that consider sub-national variations.

Principal health problems

The effects of violence and communicable diseases continue to be the primary causes of death in war-torn or impoverished countries such as Somalia, Sudan, and Yemen. However, most countries in the Arab region are passing through a phase of epidemic transition with the occurrence of an acute increase in non-communicable diseases, injuries related to traffic accidents, and other types of injuries. The dangers posed by non-communicable diseases such as those caused by smoking, diabetes and hypertension increase with the adoption of modern lifestyles.

Figure 7-9 shows that Arab countries with high mortality rates among both children and adults such as Comoros, Djibouti, Mauritania, and Somalia suffer from a heavy burden of communicable diseases[13] in comparison with countries in the region with low mortality rates among children and adults.

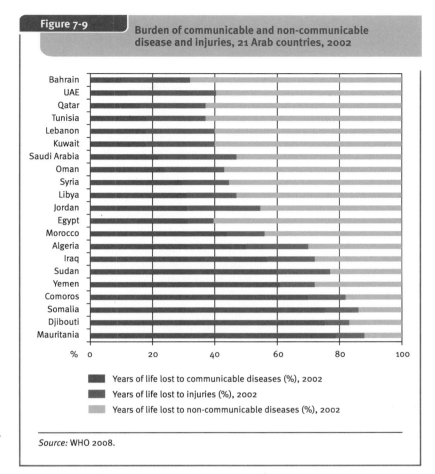

Figure 7-9 | Burden of communicable and non-communicable disease and injuries, 21 Arab countries, 2002

Years of life lost to communicable diseases (%), 2002
Years of life lost to injuries (%), 2002
Years of life lost to non-communicable diseases (%), 2002

Source: WHO 2008.

Box 7-4 | The Hepatitis C virus in Egypt

Hepatitis is a general term meaning inflammation of the liver and can be caused by several mechanisms, including infectious agents. Hepatitis C is caused by infection with the hepatitis C virus (HCV). The virus infects liver cells and can cause severe inflammation of the liver with long-term complications. Of those exposed to HCV, about 40 per cent recover fully, but the remainder, whether they have symptoms or not, become chronic carriers and may develop liver cancer. Hepatitis C virus is usually spread by sharing infected needles with a carrier, from receiving infected blood, and from accidental exposure to infected blood. It is estimated that about 3 per cent of the world's population have HCV. There are about 4 million carriers in Europe alone.

Egypt has a very high prevalence of HCV and a high morbidity and mortality from chronic liver disease. Approximately 20 per cent of Egyptian blood donors are anti-HCV positive. Egypt has higher rates of HCV than neighbouring countries as well as other countries in the world with comparable socioeconomic conditions and hygienic standards for invasive medical, dental, or paramedical procedures.

Source: WHO 2002.

Health in areas of conflict

Good public
health has a
positive impact
on development,
economic growth
and security

The general effects of violent conflict on human security and public health[14] are a matter of common knowledge. War undermines public health systems, and may lead to the sudden appearance of communicable diseases and diseases linked with malnutrition. Wars are also linked with the onset and exacerbation of various non-communicable diseases, including those that affect the blood vessels and increase the risk of strokes (for example, artery-related diseases in Lebanon increased during the civil war there).[15] They are moreover associated with acute mental health problems such as those observed and recorded in Iraq[16] and the Occupied Palestinian Territory, as discussed further in chapter eight of this report.

Factors that interact with health security

As both the discourse on human security and events themselves suggest, health is profoundly affected by non-health factors. These include deteriorating environmental conditions, foreign occupation, identity-related conflicts, poverty, and unemployment, whose impacts are discussed in other chapters. The question that arises here is: Does the opposite also hold true? Does health have a significant impact on aspects of human security which are not health-related? Given the central and interdependent place assigned to health among components of human security, it is to be expected that improved health should strengthen human security in practice, while at the same time being influenced by its other components. Both relationships may be illustrated as follows:

People's health
behaviour is
critically influenced
by their health-
related knowledge

First: health and income

The rise in the adult mortality rate, particularly in early deaths among breadwinners, can have direct and devastating effects on the family, such as impoverishment and the loss of food security. Such a loss can also have indirect effects on the family by driving groups that sink below the poverty level into contact with segments of society that live by violence, and which

stand ready to exploit their weakness. A rise in the incidence of disease may have the same effects when illness depresses families' income levels.[17] Such effects become particularly obvious in the case of catastrophic health expenses.[18] It is an established fact that when worker productivity is lowered by illness and disability, the effects weaken economic performance, raise health costs for employers and the state and reduce GDP. Conversely, good public health has a positive impact on development and economic growth and, as a further consequence, on security. This, indeed, is the primary driver behind the "investment in health" movement in development circles.[19]

Second: knowledge, beliefs, attitudes and behaviours relating to health

People's health behaviour is critically influenced by their health-related knowledge and their attitude towards health and risks. People's behaviour, in its turn, is one of the principal determinants of mortality rates as well as the incidence of disease and disability and their resultant social and economic outcomes. This, in turn, establishes a significant link between behaviour and human security.

Smoking is a particularly telling example of this link. The Arab countries are marked by a high percentage of cigarette smokers; in fact, it has one of the highest smoking rates in the world.[20] And although this may apply primarily to smoking rates among men, we find that in some countries such as Lebanon, for example, smoking rates among women are high as well. In addition to cigarettes, many Arab countries suffer from an epidemic of water-pipe smoking. As is well known, smoking contributes in a major way to an increase in mortality rates, the incidence of disease, and dependence on health care services. Consequently, smoking can place an additional economic burden on the family and deplete resources on the social level in general. The negative impact of smoking on development and the economy has become apparent in many developing countries,[21] and the same is expected to happen in Arab countries as well. Seen from this perspective, smoking in the

Arab countries is a threat not only to health but, in addition, to human security and development.

Public attitudes, influenced by tradition, also account for the silence generally surrounding HIV/AIDS in Arab countries, a silence that by inhibiting the spread of knowledge about the disease, contributes to its advance. The final section of this chapter examines this subject as part of a special focus on HIV/AIDS and human security.

Third: cultural practices that impact women's health[22]

As suggested above, public health is affected not only by economic conditions, social and political stability and the efficiency and quality of health systems; it is also shaped by the sum total of the prevailing beliefs and values in society, which influence both citizens' attitudes to health and the extent to which they take advantage of modern medical and health facilities and procedures. Certain common beliefs and practices greatly impact women's health security. These are society's entrenched preference for male offspring, which has multiple effects, and the harmful practice of female genital mutilation (FGM). (Chapter 4 cited the latter practice for its grave impacts on women's personal security; this section focuses on its health effects).

Boys before girls

Among poorer Arab families especially, the arrival of a new baby boy is customarily greeted with rejoicing. If the new-born is a girl, the occasion may often be lamented by the family at large, and the mother may find herself the object of her kinsfolk's and neighbours' pity. This reception, which tells the female infant as she enters on life that she is unwelcome, signifies attitudes that may lead to severe parental neglect in early childhood and beyond.

A cultural preference with far-reaching consequences for women's health is the pervasive view that a boy's education is more important than a girl's. The most evident result of this bias is that, in a region where one out of every three people is illiterate, two-thirds of those so deprived are female. In 2005, an estimated 40 per cent of Arab women could not read or write. Illiteracy undercuts women's health because it effectively blinds women to the fundamental principles of health, hygiene, nutrition and diet, all of which gravely compromises their own wellbeing and that of their families. Moreover, illiteracy and low levels of knowledge perpetuate customs and traditions that are harmful to health and may even be fatal. These include, for example, child bearing at too early or too advanced an age, which poses serious dangers to a woman's health and to that of her children, who risk being born with congenital abnormaities.

Public health is affected by the prevailing beliefs and values in society

Tradition before women's health

As noted in chapter 4, female genital mutilation, the removal or disfigurement of the external female sexual organ, is still too commonly inflicted upon women of reproductive age in the Arab countries. UNFPA estimates rates among this population group at: Djibouti (about 93 per cent), Egypt (95.8 per cent), Mauritania (71.3 per cent), Somalia (about 98 per cent), Sudan (90 per cent) and Yemen (22.6 per cent).[23] FGM is usually carried out between the ages of eight and ten, although some girls undergo it at a later age, especially prior to marriage. The practice originates in misinformed or misleading views about religious teachings, in folklore about promoting female chastity

Certain common beliefs and practices greatly impact women's health security

Box 7-5	A woman's first entrance

"Notwithstanding her condition, whether as a peasant in Algeria, a doctor in Cairo, or a secretary in Beirut, a student in Baghdad, a worker in Syria, the Arab woman shares with her sisters a common fate: a life of renunciation, of captivity, during which she will have to atone for her sin of having been born a woman in a hyper-male society where the ever-present feminine remains synonymous with shame and threat.

To begin with, her birth is already perceived as an occasion for mourning rather than for festivities. She is received in an atmosphere of barely suppressed disappointment. They hoped for a boy. Her coming will bring opprobrium on her mother, a shock to her father: 'Men beget men,' we always say in our culture; 'She has given birth to a girl, he has produced a boy,' they proclaim... What happens on the day when the baby girl leaves her mother's womb is only a foretaste. It is the beginning of a life to be endured as a 'blameful condition' which will be continuously punctuated by steady and heavy repression and intolerance."

Source: Salman 2003.

and in male-centred cultural notions about the requirements for a 'good' marriage. In all cases, the practice is highly injurious to women's health.

Girls are often forced to undergo the operation without anaesthesia; moreover, it is usually performed by unqualified individuals, including midwives, hair-dressers, and barbers with licenses to perform circumcisions, using unsterilized instruments in unsanitary environments. Of the numerous potential health complications, some are immediate and others are long-term.

Psychological damage: The damage suffered by the young girl from the extreme cruelty of the process leaves lifelong mental scars.[24] Neural complications can lead to potentially fatal nervous shock.

Haemorrhagic shock: Such shock results from damage to tissues and blood vessels which results from the ignorance of basic anatomy of those performing the operation. Fatalities among young girls undergoing FGM are considered common, although documented cases are rare since parents and those performing the operation seldom report incidents for fear of the law. In some cases, the haemorrhaging is less severe and is dealt with by treating wounds with crude traditional compounds. Such substances, however, are unsanitary, as are the instruments and hands of those who perform the operation.

Infections: Consequently, young girls are frequently exposed to the tetanus microbe, the HIV virus, and hepatitis B or C. These infections may affect the urinary tract and kidneys, which sometimes leads to cysts, further infections and even renal failure. The uterus and fallopian tubes may also become infected, which can result in the inability to conceive. The slow-healing wound caused by FGM leaves a sensitive legacy of acute physical and psychological complications that crop up later in life, disfiguring marital relations, pregnancy and childbirth.

Fourth: health systems management

Numerous recent studies have cast light on the achievements and challenges that face health systems in the Arab countries.[25] In the WHO 2000 report on health systems,[26] Arab states ranked low based on standards of good health results, responsiveness to consumers' needs, and equitable funding. There are, in addition, significant and historically based organizational differences among Arab health systems, a fact which makes comparisons among them difficult. Nevertheless, several observations might be made on Arab health systems as a whole,[27] the study of which would be helpful given their importance for human security.

1. Narrow conceptions

To most people, the term 'health system' refers simply to the system of health care. Seen from the perspective of human security, however, this definition is insufficient. If we were to adopt a more comprehensive definition of the term 'health system' which included all activities that directly affect health, such as ensuring appropriate nutrition, sufficient basic foodstuffs and access to clean water for citizens, these matters would assume greater importance in health policy formulation. This in turn would produce positive returns in the area of human security. Unfortunately, however, the politics of health in the Arab countries do not accommodate this comprehensive view, nor is it posed for discussion by the public. Instead, the norm is that the arrangements for, and distribution of commodities directly relevant to health, as well as basic matters of nutrition, food and access to safe water, are referred, in an uncoordinated way, to actors not concerned with health, such as ministries of agriculture.

2. Services are inequitable, often inferior and sometimes technology driven

Over the past several decades Arab states have made huge cumulative investments in the health sector, principally in health care services. Yet despite these investments, health care continues to suffer from chronic problems. The following are a number of important observations in this connection:

- Certain basic health care services (which include, for example, free infant health care) continue to be unavailable to many. This is particularly true of marginalized groups in both urban and rural areas.
- Hospitals consume huge amounts of resources in the Arab countries, and

health ministries in the Arab countries spend more than half their budgets on treatment services which depend upon hospitals. In fact, some government and private hospitals in Arab countries have achieved international status. However, there are serious disparities among their performance levels: urban areas enjoy greater support in this connection than do rural areas, and there is no coordination between the public and private sectors.

- A number of Arab governments have attempted to improve the basic health care services offered to the public. However, these attempts are incomplete in most Arab countries and are subordinated to the existing care health system and third-rate hospitals.
- Public sector health care is widely criticised for its low quality and inefficiency, its unresponsiveness to patients' needs, and the frequent referral of patients to the private sector.

The WHO Regional Office has warned of the dangerous effects of such a situation,[28] identifying areas of inadequacy in the evaluation of actual needs, in adherence to suitable approaches for contracting and purchase, in appropriate installations, in preventive maintenance, in wise use of resources, and in emphasis on quality. The medical equipment and supplies market in the Arab countries is viewed as a profitable one[29] which calls for more profit-based investments. This is important for the health care sector, because it is a recognized fact that the availability of high technology may increase demand. However, the costs of high technology, in addition to the costs of health care, could deplete important resources in the economies of low-income and medium-income Arab countries.

Numerous Arab countries have constructed regional centres to attract patients who wish to obtain high-technology medical services. In view of the fact that the relatively wealthy, even in poor countries, are those most likely to cross national borders in search of health care, 'medical tourism' depletes precious hard currency (dollars) in home countries. For example, in Yemen about 29 per cent of total health expenditure—from private pockets and public funds—is used for treatment abroad. Approximately two out of every three Yemeni Rials spent for health care

are paid by families and households as out-of-pocket payment in cases of illness.[30] This in turn places pressure on governments to construct high-tech centres which, for the most part, are built at the expense of health and preventive services.

3. Funding for health is generally inadequate

Most of the Arab countries have health expenditures ranging between 2.4 and 6 per cent of their GDP. This percentage is higher in Lebanon and Jordan (12 and 10 per cent respectively), while it is lowest in Qatar and Somalia (2.4 and 2.6 per cent respectively). Actual spending on health, which ranges from $25 per capita (in PPP terms) all the way to $871 per capita, reflects clear intra-regional disparities. Current arrangements for health care funding also have a major impact on human security. For, with the exception of the wealthy Arab Gulf states, relatively paltry amounts are directed to the health sector in most Arab states. In many low- and medium-income states—where private expenditures on health come to between 20-72 per cent of total health expenditures—governments spend very

'Medical tourism' depletes precious hard currency

Relatively paltry amounts are directed to the health sector

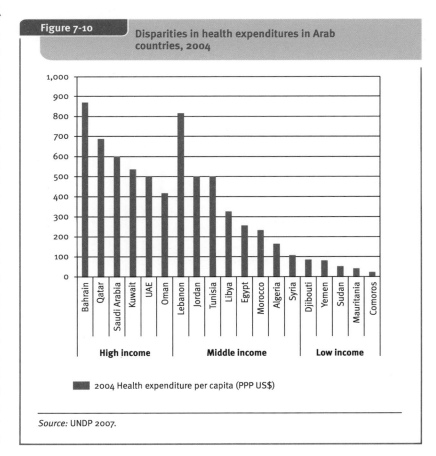

Figure 7-10 **Disparities in health expenditures in Arab countries, 2004**

2004 Health expenditure per capita (PPP US$)

Source: UNDP 2007.

little on health. A distinguished exception is the case of Djibouti and Lebanon, where public spending on health, as a percentage of total government expenditure, exceeds the world average. In terms of absolute levels of funding, oil-rich countries invest vast sums, which however do not translate into equitable health coverage for all their peoples.

Health costs are rising

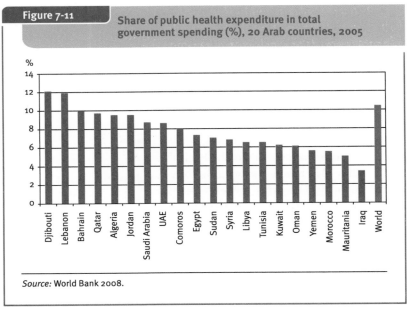

| Figure 7-11 | Share of public health expenditure in total government spending (%), 20 Arab countries, 2005 |

Source: World Bank 2008.

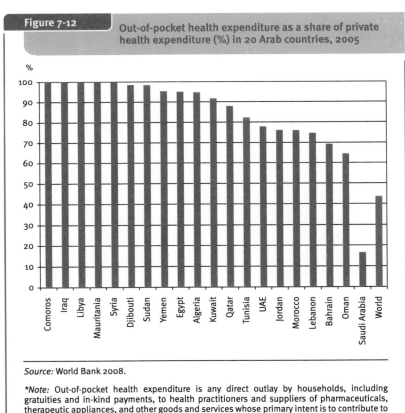

| Figure 7-12 | Out-of-pocket health expenditure as a share of private health expenditure (%) in 20 Arab countries, 2005 |

Source: World Bank 2008.

*Note: Out-of-pocket health expenditure is any direct outlay by households, including gratuities and in-kind payments, to health practitioners and suppliers of pharmaceuticals, therapeutic appliances, and other goods and services whose primary intent is to contribute to the restoration or enhancement of health status of individuals or population groups. It is part of private health expenditure.

Private sector expenditures on health do not take up the slack in total spending. Employee health insurance programmes, the principle vehicle for the private funding of health services in advanced nations, provide only meagre benefits, a fact which leaves significant health-related expenses to be borne by Arab citizens and their families.[31] As illustrated in Figure 7-12, in 19 out of 20 Arab countries studied, out-of-pocket health expenditures are very high by comparison with those in other regions of the world. This has a major impact on low-income families, since a serious or costly illness suffered by the family's breadwinner can plunge the family into poverty. Even families in medium-income states are vulnerable because their purchasing power is limited. Health costs are rising with the widespread adoption of market policies in this sector, which do not take into account income levels among different groups.

4. Public health systems are under-resourced and perform below expectations

Health systems in Arab countries are sometimes flawed by poor public health capabilities. Several features point to this: the weak performance of many public health institutions, the unsuitability of the current structure for raising public awareness of health issues, the dearth of specialized professionals in public health, and the relatively slight weight of public health in decision making on the governmental level. This situation is reflected, in turn, in negative popular perceptions of the performance of the public health sector. The poor capabilities of the public health sector render it ill-equipped to handle the range of functions required to provide public health security.

5. The chain of command in health systems is often obstructive

The chain of command in Arab health system institutions consists of an inefficient, bureaucratic hierarchy with political objectives that are often at odds with public health. Senior officials with influence and interests outside the hospital or clinic will have influence within it as well. The management of these institutions is often driven by unresponsive, uninformed and sometimes obsolete guidelines, standards, and reporting systems. Incentives in such systems work against innovation, risk taking, and improved efficiency. Moreover, their top-down systems of control may prevent health institutions from adapting to, and moving towards the popular participation and empowerment needed to achieve human security goals.

6. Key health determinants are blind spots in the system

Current Arab health systems do not place sufficient emphasis on the important indirect determinants of health recognized by human development practitioners, such as the quality and coverage of education, women's empowerment, and social and economic justice. Neither do they evince the mindset required to address key factors such as gender, social class, identity and ethnicity, all of which have obvious effects on human security.

7. Health professionals and support personnel are unequally distributed

With the exception of the most impoverished Arab countries such as Somalia, Sudan, and Yemen (where there are fewer than fifty physicians per 100,000 members of the population), most Arab countries have acceptable numbers of doctors relative to the sizes of their populations, although most of the doctors in the Arab Gulf countries are expatriates. Nevertheless, doctors are not distributed equitably within their countries, as most of them are concentrated in urban areas. The numbers of public health practitioners, dentists, nurses, and medical assistants are however woefully inadequate and their distribution among urban versus rural areas and between hospitals and basic centres is highly inequitable. Arab countries suffers a high rate of 'brain drain,' particularly among health professionals within the region, either from low-income and medium-income states to high-income, oil-rich Gulf States, or to countries in North America and Western Europe.

A health threat that concerns all – HIV/AIDS[32]

According to the WHO, HIV prevalence in the Arab region is lower than that for many other diseases, including malaria, liver failure, and respiratory diseases. The number of those in the Arab countries living with tuberculosis, for example, is 400 times greater than those living with HIV/AIDS.[33] Indeed, the incidence of HIV in the Arab countries may be the lowest among developing country regions. Nevertheless, all fires start with a spark, and there is no reason to be complacent about this destructive virus whose advance can only be reversed through much greater public awareness, and through scientific methods of prevention. There are, moreover, other good reasons for taking seriously the nature of the illness and the particular features of its emergence in the Arab countries.

A stubborn, proximate and misunderstood danger

AIDS, the acquired immunodeficiency syndrome, is a fatal disease caused by HIV, the human immunodeficiency virus. HIV destroys the body's ability to fight off infection and disease, which can ultimately lead to death. Currently, antiretroviral drugs are available that slow down replication of the virus and can greatly enhance quality of life, but they do not eliminate infection. By the end of 2006, the cumulative number of people infected with the HIV virus since its discovery in 1981 came to approximately 65 million, and AIDS-related deaths around the world had reached a total of approximately

Doctors are not distributed equitably within the Arab countries

Arab countries suffer a high rate of 'brain drain' among health professionals

---

- Surveillance and analysis of the health situation
- Drawing up and enforcing health regulations
- Monitoring, controlling and studying dangers and sources of harm that impact public health
- Evaluating access to necessary health services and ensuring such access in practice
- Improving health and public awareness of health issues
- Developing and training specialized health personnel
- Encouraging community participation and empowering citizens to obtain health services
- Guaranteeing the quality of health services
- Establishing policies and building institutional skills in planning, managing and coordinating the health sector
- Conducting research to find creative solutions to public health problems, and implementing such initiatives
- Minimizing the health-related impacts of emergencies and disasters

Source: The Report team.

---

32 million—more than any other disease in the history of humankind.[34]

The danger is not far from Arab countries. According to UNAIDS, more than 31,600 adults and children died from AIDS in 2007, in the Arab countries (80 per cent of which deaths occurred in Sudan). One needs to note, as well, the relative rise in the number of new infections. Between 2001 and 2007, there were 90,500 estimated new cases of HIV infections in the Arab countries of which 50,000 in Sudan alone.

The destructive power of HIV lies not solely in its potency as a virus, but also with the social stigma that comes with it. Those living with the virus are sometimes deprived of their fundamental human rights: they may be dismissed from their jobs and denied training and promotion, their children may be deprived of valuable opportunities, doctors may refuse to treat them, and they may be slandered and mistreated.

Moreover, people living with HIV may not be aware of their state until long after infection has occurred. In such cases, the virus can remains in the body undetected for a long time. Those who suspect that they have been infected often do not seek the necessary tests out of shame or fear of being stigmatized or discriminated against. Those who know their condition may yet refrain from informing those closest to them, including their partners, which exposes the latter to infection as well.

Those living with the HIV virus are sometimes deprived of their fundamental human rights

In this culture of secrecy, HIV continues to spread. Meanwhile, few programmes are designed or carried out to reach key populations at risk including intravenous drug users, sex workers or men who have sex with men. When it is appreciated that the risk factors are also linked with poverty, displacement, refugee status, permanent or temporary migration, and women's rights, it becomes clear that HIV/AIDS is a serious and broad-based challenge to human security. Facing the threat is only possible through a multi-sector, multi-tiered development policy which addresses the underlying roots of the virus's spread and which, as such, goes beyond simple health awareness in the traditional sense.

Reappraising the numbers

According to WHO and UNAIDS estimates,[35] in 2007, the number of those living with HIV in Arab countries was 435,000, 73.5 per cent of whom were in Sudan. An important observation in this context is that the estimated numbers of those living with HIV/AIDS in the Maghreb (particularly Algeria, Morocco, and Tunisia) are far higher than those in the Mashreq (which includes Egypt, Jordan, and Syria). This may be related to the fact that voluntary testing and counselling centres and other surveillance methods are far greater in the Maghreb and altogether more effective than their counterparts in the Mashreq, which may thus underestimate numbers in the latter subregion.

For example, UNAIDS estimated that in 2007 the number of people living with HIV/AIDS in Bahrain, Jordan, and Kuwait was less than 1,000 in each. These relatively low rates stand in contrast to the estimated numbers of infected people in 2007 in Djibouti (16,000), Morocco (21,000), Algeria (21,000) and Somalia (24,000). In the case of Sudan, the estimated number is altogether higher and reaches 320,000.

Epidemiologists classify epidemics either as 'generalized' (having affected more than 1 per cent of the total population), and 'intensified' (having affected more than 5 per cent in some groups of the population and in certain areas). In

Table 7-1	Estimated number of people living with HIV, 12 Arab countries, 2007	
State	**Estimate 2007**	**[low–high estimate]**
Jordan	<1,000	[<2,000]
Bahrain	<1,000	[<2,000]
Kuwait	<1,000	[<2,000]
Lebanon	3,000	[1,700-7,200]
Tunisia	3,700	[2,700-5,400]
Egypt	9,200	[7,200-13,000]
Mauritania	14,000	[8,300-26,000]
Djibouti	16,000	[12,000-19,000]
Morocco	21,000	[15,000-31,000]
Algeria	21,000	[11,000-43,000]
Somalia	24,000	[13,000-45,000]
Sudan	320,000	[220,000-440,000]

Source: UNAIDS and WHO 2008.

2007, Arab countries in which the epidemic has reached the 'generalized' phase are the Sudan (1.4 per cent) and Djibouti (3.1 per cent).[36] Most of the epidemics are concentrated among particular at-risk populations, including sex workers and their clients, drug injectors, men who have sex with men,[37] prisoners, and girls who marry before the age of 18 years, particularly those who marry men who are much older than themselves.[38]

A significant observation about Sudan concerns the relatively high percentage of HIV-positive women. Compared to a world average of 48 per cent in 2007, 53 per cent of adults living with HIV in Sudan were women. This percentage stood at 30.4 in the other Arab countries, for the same year,[39] which is comparable to the situation in Western Europe. There are indications that as much as 80 per cent of female infections in Arab countries occur within the bonds of marriage. For example, in Saudi Arabia, research indicated that most women infected with HIV were married and had acquired the virus from their husbands.[40]

A rising rate of female infections may reflect Arab women's weak negotiating power in domestic contexts. For reasons at once economic, cultural, and social, women are unable to demand that their husbands be tested for HIV/AIDS or use a condom when they suspect that they have been exposed to HIV. This is the main point of intersection between the role of regressive attitudes and beliefs in promoting practices harmful to women's health in general, as discussed earlier, and their specific impact on women's vulnerability to HIV/AIDS.

Another striking fact is that the percentage of HIV-positive persons in the Arab countries receiving either triple combination therapy or antiretroviral drugs is very low—indeed, the Arab region is the one world region that takes the least advantage of these medical advances. In 2006, only 5 per cent of those needing treatment in the Arab countries had access to such treatment, as compared with 75 per cent in Latin America. Even in Sub-Saharan Africa, a lower-income region than the Arab region and one with an HIV-positive population of approximately 25 million, we find that 23 per cent of those who need treatment obtain it.[41] What makes this

Table 7-2	Comparative rates of access to HIV/AIDS treatment in low and middle-income countries, December 2003 – June 2006
Countries	**Percentage with access**
All	24 %
Latin America/Caribbean	75 %
Sub-Saharan Africa	23 %
East/South-East Asia	16 %
Europe/Central Asia	13 %
North Africa/Middle East	5 %

Source: UNAIDS and WHO 2006.

situation extraordinary is that HIV/AIDS treatment is now available free of charge in most Arab countries.

Means of HIV transmission in Arab countries

In the Arab region, HIV/AIDS is mainly transmitted through unprotected sexual intercourse with a member of the opposite sex. Indeed, this means of transmission accounts for 67 per cent of known cases in the Arab region, ranging from 90 per cent in Saudi Arabia, to 83 per cent in Morocco to 64 per cent in Egypt.[42] In this context, it is worth noting again that a significant number of women who contract HIV are exposed to it within the context of marital relations. The second most common means of transmission is through the utilization by drug users of contaminated injecting equipment. At the regional level, this accounts for 6 per cent of all known transmissions.[43] In contrast, known cases in which the virus is transmitted via unprotected sexual contact between two men do not constitute a high percentage in any Arab country; however UNAIDS/WHO suggest that this factor may be under-estimated. HIV transmission from mother to child represents the next most frequent cause of infection. In terms of HIV transmission through contaminated blood or medical instruments, while this mode accounted for an average of 12 per cent of all cases in 2000, the rate fell to 3 per cent in 2005.[44] The low rate of infection via this particular mode of transmission may reflect growing mastery of sterilization methods—which are comparatively easy to adopt for the HIV virus—as well as more careful examination of blood stocks and blood derivative.

A rising rate of female infections may reflect Arab women's weak negotiating power in domestic contexts

The Arab region is the one world region that takes the least advantage of HIV-related medical advances

The way forward: health as a prerequisite for human security

As this chapter illustrates, health is characterized by a number of unique features which make it an ideal entry point for the discussion and treatment of topics relating to human security. Health is fundamental for the achievement of social stability and economic growth. It is a key requirement for the achievement of human and national security—as the nation-wide impact of HIV/AIDS in some countries makes clear—because health cuts across many other components of human security. Accordingly, effective health intervention requires cooperation among a variety of specializations, sectors, partners and agencies. Moreover, because health has internationally recognized value, it may help in building broad alliances that go beyond national, cultural, and ethnic boundaries. Such alliances can, in their turn, create opportunities to reinforce the broader scope of human security.

Health system priorities in the Arab countries

It is generally recognized that preventing security problems is far more effective and less costly than dealing with them after they land. Moreover, given the importance of prevention in health-related interventions, it may represent an ideal point of departure for discussions of human security. Prevention may offer health policy makers and professionals the optimal way to introduce and conduct approaches to higher health levels among more citizens in the Arab countries. In the areas of both health and human security, people are the fundamental beneficiaries and agents of change. Hence, the most effective health programmes are those which invest individuals and societies with a sense of ownership. The same proposition applies to human security interventions, which confirms the importance of health as a prerequisite of human security.

Moreover, the emphasis on health as a human right is among the most important and central priorities for intervention in the areas of health and security. The constitutions of numerous Arab countries explicitly provide for the right to health. It is time to activate this right by focusing on the social, economic, and cultural determinants of health, and to reform health systems by placing special importance on disparities in access, affordability and quality among citizens. Emphasis should also be placed on priorities consistent with areas specified by WHO/EMRO as summarized below:

- Developing health ministries' administrative capacities
- Allocating equitable and appropriate health system funding
- Providing balanced human health resources
- Enabling all people to obtain basic health services
- Increasing ways of providing, obtaining and using data
- Identifying reasonably priced interventions which target central health problems
- Developing health reinforcement programmes
- Supporting societal initiatives
- Protecting and preserving health in times of emergency and disaster
- Analyzing non-health factors influencing health determinants such as globalization, poverty, gender, and the environment, and applying the lessons

Most health system reforms thus far have focused on the technical aspects of reform, policy making, service delivery, and national health considerations. Customarily, health reform proposals affirm that their aim is to improve the balance between cost, effectiveness, and equity. In reality, however, health professionals in the Arab countries have noted that the first two factors (cost and effectiveness) have received more attention than the third factor (equity). Moreover, the writers of this report believe that equity and equality are the areas in which health interventions need to be made if their aim is to reinforce human security. Those who gain most from such an approach are underprivileged groups such as the poor and those who support them, particularly young children and the elderly, as well as vulnerable and excluded social groups, such as refugees, migrant workers, those with specialized needs, minorities, and women.

There is much to be gained from broadening public health alliances to include

Preventing health problems is more effective and less costly than dealing with them after they land

Equity and equality are the areas in which health interventions need to be made if their aim is to reinforce human security

civil society organizations and members of the public who receive services. It would also repay countries to adopt decision-making systems in which health workers themselves take part, and to give priority to public health while strengthening cooperation and complementarity in the areas of medical service provision both between the Arab state and medical institutions, and among such institutions themselves.

Participation should also be a byword in efforts to combat cultural practices damaging to women's health. Solidarity and cooperation among government institutions, civil society organizations, clerics, the media, and women's organizations offer a way for Arab countries to begin lifting the crushing backlog of ignorance, folklore and gender bias responsible for such anachronisms. Education at all levels has an instrumental role in spreading awareness of the seriousness of these practices, while the authority of the state and the letter of the law must be summoned to ban practices harmful to women's and young children's health and to punish those who encourage or engage in them.

Similarly, national strategies for addressing HIV/AIDS have to look beyond its health-related aspects alone. The disease has a cultural, social, and economic context.

Many past attitudes towards HIV/AIDS will have to be abandoned. Failing to give the challenge the priority it demands, denying its existence and muffling public discussion about it, attributing its prevalence to foreigners alone, and exploiting public fears to further increase the suffering of victims through discriminatory practices, have all worsened the situation in Arab countries. The new norm should start by interpreting the challenge as a growing threat to individual and collective human security in the Arab countries. It should enjoin public compassion and knowledge, supported by a strong public education drive. It should enshrine voluntary testing, counselling and free treatment for those living with HIV/AIDS as a top priority.

THE HUMAN SECURITY SURVEY – Popular perceptions and awareness of HIV/AIDS

How great a threat is HIV/AIDS in the country?

The only country where the majority of survey respondents thought HIV/AIDS is a serious threat (about 60 per cent) was Morocco. In the OPT, by contrast, a similar percentage believed that HIV/AIDS poses no threat whatsoever. With the exception of Morocco, about 20 per cent of respondents in the other countries acknowledged that HIV/AIDS is a major threat. Half of those surveyed in Lebanon considered that the disease is a threat under control, while the Kuwaitis were evenly divided among those who thought it posed no threat at all and those who believed it to be under control.

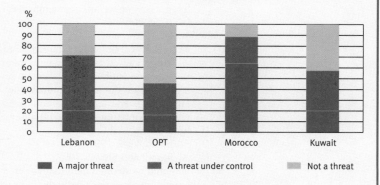

How many modes of transmission does HIV/AIDS have?

Interestingly, while most Palestinians believe that the virus poses no threat, they are the most knowledgeable about how it is transmitted. Half of the Palestinians surveyed were able to identify correctly five modes of transmission; 35 per cent were able to identify four. By contrast, the percentage of those familiar with five modes of transmission was 44 per cent in Morocco, 27 per cent in Lebanon, and 25 per cent in Kuwait. The percentage of those who could name four means of transmission was highest in Kuwait, followed by Lebanon. An empirical observation to be drawn from this admittedly small sample is that the link between public knowledge about how HIV/AIDS is transmitted and low rates of infection is real.

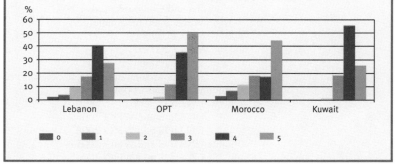

Endnotes

1 UNDP 1994.
2 Commission on Human Security 2003 (in Arabic).
3 Fidler 2003.
4 Kelle 2007.
5 WHO 2005 (in Arabic).
6 Kelle 2007.
7 Gutlove 2002.
8 Fu'ad and Jabbour 2004 (in Arabic).
9 Tabutin and Schoumaker 2005.
10 Unless indicated otherwise, the data cited in this part are from the UNDP Human Development Report 2007/2008. Some figures may differ from those cited in other sources, such as the World Health Organization/Eastern Mediterranean Regional Office (WHO/EMRO) report. These differences, however, are not significant.
11 UNICEF 2007.
12 WHO 2007.
13 According to the World Health Organization, communicable diseases or infectious diseases are those caused by pathogenic micro-organisms, such as bacteria, viruses, parasites or fungi; the diseases can be spread, directly or indirectly, from one person to another. Zoonotic diseases are infectious diseases of animals that can cause disease when to transmitted humans. Cholera, Hepatitis B and C, Malaria and Tuberculosis are examples of communicable diseases. [http://www.who.int/topics/infectious_diseases/en/].
14 Iqbal 2006.
15 Sibai and Alam 1991.
16 Al-Jawadi and Shatha 2007.
17 It should be stressed here that the effects of such a situation are important not only in the case of a male breadwinner's early death or illness but, in addition, in the cases of women who, though they may not necessarily be economically active, nevertheless provide priceless services for their families which serve to reinforce their security and well-being.
18 Catastrophic health expenses are defined as those which equal or exceed 40 percent of the family's available income.
19 This movement has been criticized by members of civil society and health activists for promoting the view that health is a commodity rather than a human right.
20 WHO 2003.
21 WHO 2005a.
22 Lafteya ElSabae, in Arabic, background paper for the report.
23 WHO 2008a.
24 WHO 2008a.
25 WHO 2004.
26 Abdullatif 2006.
27 Jha and Chaloupka (eds.) 2000.
28 WHO 2000 (in Arabic).
29 WHO 2006b.
30 WHO 2005b.
31 WHO 2005b.
32 Khadija Moalla, in Arabic, background paper for the report.
33 World Bank 2008b.
34 UNAIDS 2006.
35 UNAIDS and WHO 2008.
36 UNAIDS and WHO 2008.
37 UNAIDS and WHO 2005a.
38 UNAIDS and WHO 2006b.
39 UNAIDS and WHO 2008.
40 UNAIDS and WHO 2005a.
41 UNAIDS and WHO 2006c.
42 WHO 2008b.
43 WHO 2008b.
44 UNAIDS and WHO 2005b.

Chapter 8

Occupation, military intervention and human insecurity

Occupation and military intervention expose human security to violence on three levels— institutional, structural, and material

Occupation and military intervention expose human security to violence on three levels—institutional, structural, and material.[1] In institutional terms, they violate international law, which prohibits the use of force in international relations except in self-defence; they abrogate the laws of the occupied country; and they interfere in the establishment of government in a manner that serves the occupier rather than the occupied. Structurally, they introduce new conditions for the distribution of wealth and power, which cause more divisions among the population. In material terms, occupation and military intervention are imposed by force, which leads to resistance by force, and to heavy casualties among occupied and occupier alike. They also freeze economic activity, livelihoods and essential freedoms. Through their exponential effects, occupation and military intervention contravene basic human rights, create systemic human insecurity and set back human development. This is the lesson of history and it applies to all occupations and military interventions, whether in the Arab region or abroad.

Occupation and military intervention have compound costs and effects

At the time of writing, there are three cases of occupation and military intervention in the Arab region: the Occupied Palestinian Territory (the West Bank and Gaza strip since June 1967), Iraq (since April 2003), and Somalia (since December 2006). This chapter examines the origins of occupation and military intervention in these different cases and their compound costs and impacts. It starts by noting that the general impacts extend beyond the institutional, structural and material violence inflicted in those three cases. Occupation and military intervention undercut human security in neighbouring and other Arab countries in several ways. First, they displace peoples across borders, creating humanitarian challenges for neighbouring states and seeding tensions among them. Second, as a *cause célèbre* of extremist

groups that resort to violence, they feed the militant appeal of those who continue the cycle of violence in the region and whose acts provoke a backlash against citizens' rights and freedoms. Finally, as a threat to sovereignty, they allow Arab governments to cite national security as a pretext for halting or postponing democratization and for perpetuating authoritarian rule.

Origins and rationales

Occupied Palestinian Territory: In June 1967, Israel occupied territories in Egypt (Sinai)[2] and Syria (Golan Heights),[3] as well as the West Bank and Gaza that had been respectively under Jordanian and Egyptian rule since 1948. Successive Israeli governments have claimed that they are ready to evacuate portions of these lands in exchange for peace and arrangements guaranteeing Israeli security. According to Israel, the wording of the UN Security Council resolution 242 (1967) entitles it to retain portions of these territories, as it refers to "withdrawal of Israeli armed forces from territories" occupied in June 1967 and not "*the*" occupied territories, despite the resolution's emphasis on the "inadmissibility of the acquisition of territory by war". Israel expanded its occupation by constructing settlements on these lands to house settlers. In its resolutions 446 and 452 (July 1979), the UN Security Council determined that the policies of Israel in establishing settlements have no legal validity and called upon the Government and people of Israel to cease, on an urgent basis, the establishment, construction and planning of these settlements.

Iraq: The United States led a military campaign against Iraq on the 20th of March, 2003. The former regime of Saddam Hussein came to an end on the 9th of April 2003, with the capture of Baghdad, the capital of Iraq. Various explanations have been given for this military campaign, chiefly that the former US administration was driven to it in order to rid Iraq of weapons of mass destruction; and that the Saddam Hussein regime supported and harboured anti-US terrorist organisations, such as al-Qaeda, which called for pre-emptive action.[4] These justifications were not substantiated by information from US intelligence agencies themselves before the war, and were not proved afterwards.[5]

In May 2003, the UN Security Council (UNSC), in its Resolution 1483, considered the United States and the United Kingdom as "occupying powers" together with all the "authorities, responsibilities, and obligations under international law". In June 2004, in UNSC resolution 1546, the presence of the American and coalition forces was considered to be at the request of the government of Iraq. The period between 2004 and 2006 saw elections leading to a central government free from the despotic character of the previous regime. It was also marked by US-led efforts to establish law and order and to launch reconstruction. However, these important developments were not sufficient to overcome the rising tide of public resentment of the military presence in its midst. In November 2008, the United States and Iraq signed an agreement[6] by which the American forces will depart from Iraq by 31st December 2011. In his statement on the 27th of February 2009,[7] the US President announced that by August 31, 2010, the "combat mission in Iraq will end".

Somalia: The country has come under two forms of military intervention since the fall of the Siad Barre government in 1991. The declared reason for the first intervention by US forces in 1992 was the rescue of hundreds of thousands of famine-stricken Somalis, victims of the outbreak of war between two camps in the United Somali Congress. American forces departed the following year, after their original mission of guaranteeing the delivery of emergency food relief evolved into a military mission to restore order that brought them into a violent confrontation with the forces of Mohamed Farah Aidid (Salah Al-Nasrawi, background paper for the report).

The second military intervention in Somalia occurred in December 2006 when Ethiopian forces intervened to defend the Transitional Federal Government (TFG) against the forces of the Islamic Courts Union (ICU). The latter had succeeded in extending its control over portions of Somalia, especially in the south, and over the capital, Mogadishu. Ethiopian forces claimed to have entered the country in response to an appeal by the TFG, stating that their presence was a temporary measure to deter ICU's threats to Ethiopia's national security.[8] In addition, two militant movements opposed to the Ethiopian government are operating from inside Somalia and receive support from Eritrea. Shortly after Ethiopia's entrance into Somalia, the African Union sent a peacekeeping force pursuant to UNSC resolution 1744, in February 2007. In December 2008, Ethiopia declared that it would withdraw its forces from Somalia, after having "undertaken numerous activities in the interest of the peace and stability of Somalia".[9]

In all three cases, occupation and military intervention violate international law, the authoritative frame of reference for regulating relations between nations

UN Security Council resolutions 446 and 425 determined that the policies of Israel in establishing settlements have no legal validity

Occupation and military intervention violate international law

and peoples. International law prohibits the occupation of others' land by force or recourse to military force against another nation for purposes other than self-defence.[10] A further common feature of military intervention in these countries is that it has deepened existing class, group, sectarian or tribal divisions, aggravating tensions that have erupted into conflicts-within conflicts.

The compound impacts of military intervention on human security

I. Threats to life

A. Iraq

In Iraq, threats to life are associated with widespread insecurity. The immediate causes of the decline in public security following the US-led invasion are to be found in the military intervention *per se*. This intervention polarized the country. Among the general public, especially in central and southern Iraq, the restrictions brought about by the military invasion were widely resented. In addition, the short-sighted decrees of the first provisional governor of Iraq, which dissolved the army and police force, abolished the Baath Party, banned its members from government and dismantled key government agencies, effectively swept away the very institutions that might have safeguarded public security under such conditions. These decisions also assured the enmity of those who lost their jobs and incomes as a result.

In this environment, the country witnessed fierce fighting in which many forces took part for different motives, and which claimed enormous casualties. In conditions of increasing chaos, the US-led multinational coalition (the number of the American forces varied between 250,000 troops in 2003 and 143,000 troops in September 2008[11] and the number of UK troops varied between 18,000 troops in May 2003 and 4,100 troops in May 2008)[12] was unable to discharge its obligations to ensure the security of Iraqi citizens, many of whom disbelieved in the legitimacy, authority and mission of the foreign forces in their midst. Other parties caught in this conflict were the private security companies, brought in to offset the lack of

sufficient US forces and to perform vital security and support functions. Figures on the numbers of private security contractors in the country have often been conflicting. In mid-2006, the US Federal Accounting Bureau estimated that 181 of these firms had been operating in Iraq, with a total of 48,000 personnel.[13]

The Iraqi militias represent a third party to the chaos in the country. Among these are several armed groups formed by Baathists, Sunni Islamic movements, and al-Qaeda members who infiltrated Iraq with the pretext of resisting the US military presence. A significant development has been the creation of the so-called Sahwa (Awakening) Councils which the US forces persuaded many Sunni tribal chiefs to establish in 2007 in order to fight al-Qaeda members active in Iraq. There are also Shiite militias foremost among which are the Badr Brigade of the Supreme Council for the Islamic Revolution and Muqtada al-Sadr's Mahdi Army. In addition, there are the Kurdish Peshmerga forces, which perform security missions in Kurdistan. Some estimates put the number of such militias at thirty five[14] and others at seventy four,[15] although there are no reliable sources on this. The spread of weapons and power to these militias, each a potential fiefdom of its own, raises questions about their integration into any unified state in the future.

Military intervention has deepened existing class, group, sectarian or tribal divisions.

Iraq witnessed fierce fighting in which many forces took part and which claimed enormous casualties

The proliferation of militias has been encouraged by two major factors: the security and political vacuum in the country, and the ethnically based selection processes of the foreign forces, which have driven forces fighting over power and wealth in Iraq to bolster their autonomy in order to obtain what they consider their rightful share of both. Moreover, not only have the militias taken control of public life, they have also seized sources of national wealth, such as petroleum, which they smuggle out in order to finance their activities.

This lawless situation has had two especially damaging consequences. The first is the deepening of sectarian entrenchment as people clamour for protection from hostile sects, and the consequent rise in levels of violence. The second is the disappearance from public life of that broad segment of Iraqis whose capacity for political organisation and peaceful action in support of the idea of a whole nation has been paralyzed by violence and terrorism (Salah Al-Nasrawi, in Arabic, background paper for the report). Indeed, in the absence of a general consensus over how to handle the military invasion, the concept of resistance itself has become distorted and tangled. It often reflects confusion between a national stance that prioritises the struggle to regain independence, and the narrow defence of the particular interests of national groups.

The victims of violence have been as diverse as the forms of violence inflicted on them. The greatest numbers are found among the Iraqi people, of all faiths, creeds

The greatest numbers of victims are found among the Iraqi people, of all faiths, creeds and ethnicities

Mortalities soared after the invasion

and ethnicities, who have borne the brunt of the situation. But the casualties include foreign civilians working in Iraq, whether for the UN, or for Arab and other foreign embassies, or for private organizations. They also include prominent political and security officials in the Iraqi government. The most vulnerable sectors of the local population have been the small religious minorities, notably Chaldeans, Assyrian Christians, Yazidis, and Sabaeans. These communities have been the victims of frequent attacks by car and suicide bombers aimed at forcing them out of the country (Salah Al-Nasrawi, in Arabic, background paper for the report). After several years of the US-led invasion, the evidence of sectarian polarization is everywhere today in Iraq, with sects barricaded in their neighbourhoods against attack from others and with one sect's members denying or disguising their identities when obliged to pass through another's enclave.

Estimates of mortalities among Iraqis from March 2003 to June 2006 vary considerably. While Iraq Body Count[16] (IBC), which gathers its information from the daily press, lists 47,668 violent deaths in the country since the beginning of the invasion, a field study[17] conducted by Burnham et al. that relied on 1,849 families divided into forty-seven sample segments arrived at a figure of 601,027 deaths due to violence. The Iraq Family Health Survey (IFHS),[18] a larger and more recent national household survey by the Iraqi government and the World Health Organization (WHO) that took a sample of 9,345 families between 2006 and 2007, placed the number of violent deaths at 151,000. Figures 8-1, 8-2 and 8-3 illustrate the diverse reckonings of the three surveys.

Whatever source is consulted, it is evident that mortalities, whether caused by deteriorating health conditions or violence, soared after the invasion. Based on IFHS results, the mortality rate, in general, nearly doubled from 3.17 per 1,000 inhabitants before the invasion to 6.01 per 1,000 afterwards. The number of violent deaths increased ten times, climbing from 0.1 per 1,000 to 1.09 per 1,000 after the invasion. Kurdistan is the only province to experience a decline in the mortality rate, which dropped slightly from 3.7 per 1,000 to 3.68 per 1,000 after the invasion. Also,

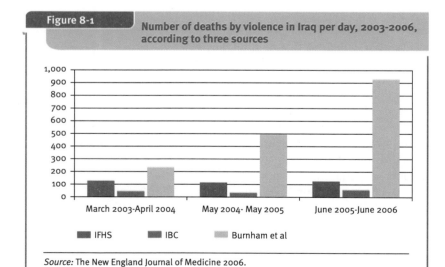

Figure 8-1

Number of deaths by violence in Iraq per day, 2003-2006, according to three sources

■ IFHS   ■ IBC   ▨ Burnham et al

Source: The New England Journal of Medicine 2006.

deaths by violence—around 0.07 per 1,000 after the invasion—have been less common there than in other Iraqi provinces. The reason for Kurdistan's unique situation is fairly clear: it has been effectively autonomous from the central government in Baghdad since being declared a no-flight zone for Iraqi aircraft more than eleven years before the invasion.

In the case of foreign forces, since the start of the campaign in March 2003, a total of 4,212 US soldiers had died by 3 January 2009,[19] and a total of 178 British Armed Forces personnel or Ministry of Defence civilians had died by 12 December 2008.[20] Among the Iraqi security forces the death rate was considerably higher. According to a US Congress report, the estimate of total Iraqi Security Forces and Police deaths, between June 2003 and November 2006 was 5,736,[21] whereas the total US forces killed in the same period came to 2,196.[22]

From February 2007, however, the situation gradually began to improve for both Iraqi civilians and troops. According to the icasualties.org website, civilian casualties declined from 1,598 in August 2007 to less than 1,000 in September and October that year, and to less than 500 per month after that.[23] In February 2008, the civilian toll was 443. Among Iraqi forces, in August 2007, the number of war victims dropped to less than 100 from 232 the previous month. Apart from October 2007, the monthly rate has remained lower than 100 since then. In February 2008, the toll among Iraqi forces was eighty. US forces experienced a similar decline in fatalities, to less than 100 between July and September 2007, and to fewer than fifty since October that year. By March 2008, the total US death toll in Iraq had reached 4,000.[24]

In all events, the toll of violence in Iraq began to fall after September 2007. The most important factors contributing to this development were a) the raising of US military strength by 30,000 troops (the 'surge'); b) General Petraeus's strategy of relying on Iraqi tribes to hunt down non-Iraqi Al-Qaeda fighters; c) the increase in, and proper training of Iraqi security forces; and d) the truce declared by Muqtada Sadr's Mahdi Army, halting, at least at the time of writing, its assaults on both US forces and the Badr Brigade.

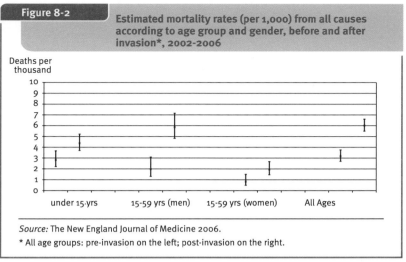

Figure 8-2

Estimated mortality rates (per 1,000) from all causes according to age group and gender, before and after invasion*, 2002-2006

Source: The New England Journal of Medicine 2006.
* All age groups: pre-invasion on the left; post-invasion on the right.

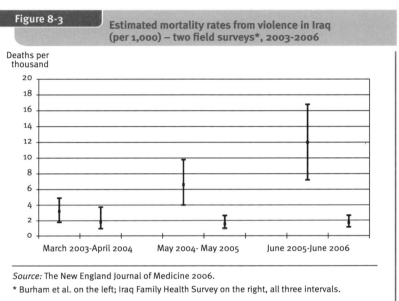

Figure 8-3

Estimated mortality rates from violence in Iraq (per 1,000) – two field surveys*, 2003-2006

Source: The New England Journal of Medicine 2006.
* Burham et al. on the left; Iraq Family Health Survey on the right, all three intervals.

Box 8-2   **The ever-changing body count in Iraq**

In 2007, a leading UK polling group produced a survey indicating that more than one million Iraqis have died as a result of the conflict in their country since the U.S.-led invasion in 2003. The survey, conducted by Opinion Research Business (ORB) with 2,414 adults in face-to-face interviews, found that 20 per cent of people had had at least one death in their household attributable to the conflict, rather than to natural causes. The last complete census in Iraq conducted in 1997 found 4.05 million households in the country, a figure ORB used to calculate that approximately 1.03 million people had died as a result of the war.

The margin of error in the survey, conducted in August and September 2007, was 1.7 per cent, giving a range of deaths of 946,258 to 1.12 million. ORB originally found that 1.2 million people had died, but decided to conduct more research in rural areas to make the survey as comprehensive as possible. It subsequently came up with the revised figure. The research covered 15 of Iraq's 18 provinces. Those not covered included two of Iraq's more volatile regions—Kerbala and Anbar—and the northern province of Arbil, where local authorities refused them a permit to work.

Source: Human Security Report Project 2008.

Box 8-3 | The campaign against Gaza

From the start of the Israeli military operation in the Gaza Strip on 27 December 2008 to the cease fire, implemented unilaterally by Israel on 18 January 2009, and later the same day by Hamas and other Palestinian factions, 1,314 Palestinians had been killed of whom 412 were children and 110 were women. Many more had been injured, according to the Palestinian Ministry of Health. The number of those injured stood at 5,300, of whom 1,855 were children and 795 were women. Israeli operations caused extensive damage to homes and public infrastructure, and seriously jeopardized water, sanitation and medical services. UN schools sheltering displaced persons were hit, humanitarian workers were killed and ambulances struck, and the sick and wounded were left trapped and unassisted. By 15 January 2009, up to 90,000 people had been displaced from their homes.

Alarming number of children killed and injured: As of 15 January, almost 32 per cent of all fatalities (346) were children. Approximately 1,709 children were wounded, some with multiple injuries. From 3 January to 14 January, the number of child fatalities increased by more than 340 per cent. There are almost 800,000 children in Gaza, comprising 56 per cent of Gaza's population in an area with one of the highest population densities in the world.

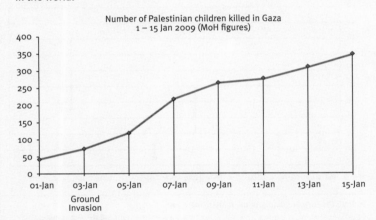

Number of Palestinian children killed in Gaza
1 – 15 Jan 2009 (MoH figures)

Source: UN-OCHA 2009.

MoH = Ministry of Health

Rapid increase of internal displacement: The rise in the number of Palestinians seeking shelter at UNRWA facilities sharply accelerated after the Israeli ground operation began on 3 January. On 8 January, there were approximately 16,000 Palestinians staying at UNRWA facilities. By 14 January, 41 UNRWA facilities were providing shelter for 37,937 displaced persons. Although the total number of displaced Palestinians remains unknown, Al Mezan Centre for Human Rights has estimated 80,000 – 90,000 people displaced, including up to 50,000 children.

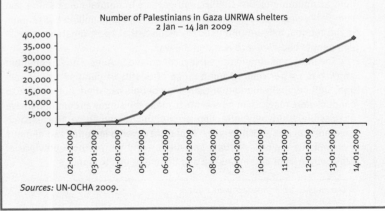

Number of Palestinians in Gaza UNRWA shelters
2 Jan – 14 Jan 2009

Sources: UN-OCHA 2009.

In addition, fortifications surrounding the now mono-sectarian quarters have helped to keep out other fighting forces and to ward off sectarian assaults. It remains to be seen how the security situation will evolve with the gradual withdrawal of the US forces from Iraq and the rise of unfettered and armed militias.

B. The Occupied Palestinian Territory

Fundamental human rights are frequently violated in the Occupied Palestinian Territory, and such violations have intensified since the outbreak of the Al-Aqsa intifada on 29 September, 2000. Most threats to Palestinian human security come from Israeli forces. However, recently, another source of threat to Palestinian human security has emerged, originating within the Palestinian resistance itself. In the absence of a horizon for a political settlement with Israel, differences between the Palestinian organisations notably Fatah and Hamas have widened, culminating in the collapse of the national unity government which had brought together the two chief factions in the Palestinian national authority. The collapse occurred in the wake of armed clashes between these two camps, resulting in Hamas's takeover of Gaza in June 2007. President Mahmoud Abbas subsequently formed a parallel government in Ramallah and, since then, each camp has claimed the sole right to represent the Palestinian people.

At the time this report was finalized in December 2008, the truce between Israel and Hamas had ended. Provoked by Hamas rocket attacks, Israel launched a counteroffensive against Gaza, which had already been under siege since Hamas took over the strip in June 2007. This campaign, which caused an international outcry over its use of disproportionate force, resulted in a significant number of civilian casualties (notably children and women) among a population that had already been impoverished by the siege.[25] A cease-fire was implemented unilaterally by Israel on 18 January 2009, and later the same day by Hamas and other Palestinian factions.

Numerous sources document Israeli violations of Palestinian rights to life and freedom. This section relies on data from the Israeli human rights organisation, B'Tselem, whose figures on these violations are higher than those provided by both Palestinian human rights agencies and the Palestinian authorities themselves. B'Tselem furnishes the following information on the numbers of Palestinians and Israelis who died from violence in the West Bank, Gaza and Israel:

Figure 8-4 shows the breakdown by nationality of victim and assailant of a total of 5,970 deaths by violence in the OPT and Israel between 2000 and 2008: there were 4,908 fatalities among Palestinians and 1,062 fatalities among Israelis. B'Tselem also details the incidents that led to fatalities, the majority of which were among Palestinian civilians, as shown in Table 8-1.

Internal strife between clashing Palestinian factions also brought about a considerable number of Palestinian deaths. Yet, the 594 victims of these conflicts represent barely 6 per cent of the total of those killed by Israelis.[26] The purpose of this observation is not to belittle the gravity of inter-Palestinian violence, but rather to place it in its proper perspective. Moreover, according to the Palestinian Central Bureau of Statistics, the total number of Palestinians injured by live ammunition, rubber bullets, gas and other weapons in the OPT between January 2000 and March 2008 amounted at 32,569.[27]

C. Somalia

Somalia has not experienced stability since the fall of the Siad Barre regime in 1991. Years of African, Arab, and UN efforts failed to lead to the creation of a single government capable of controlling the whole country, and in particular autonomous Somaliland in the northwest and Puntland in the northeast. When the current TFG was formed in 2004, it had to operate initially out of Baidoa in the centre of the country, and only succeeded in establishing itself in the capital with the assistance of Ethiopian troops. The numerous domestic parties to the violence that erupted with the fall of the Barre regime

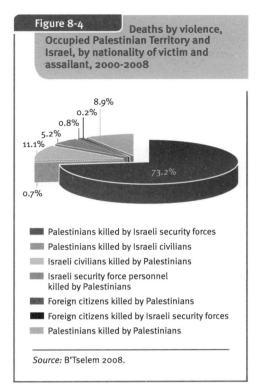

Figure 8-4 Deaths by violence, Occupied Palestinian Territory and Israel, by nationality of victim and assailant, 2000-2008

- Palestinians killed by Israeli security forces
- Palestinians killed by Israeli civilians
- Israeli civilians killed by Palestinians
- Israeli security force personnel killed by Palestinians
- Foreign citizens killed by Palestinians
- Foreign citizens killed by Israeli security forces
- Palestinians killed by Palestinians

Source: B'Tselem 2008.

There were 4,908 fatalities among Palestinians and 1,062 fatalities among Israelis between 2000 and 2008

The total number of Palestinians injured between January 2000 and March 2008 amounted to 32,569

Table 8-1	Fatal incidents in the Occupied Palestinian Territory and Israel, 2000-2008			
Type of Incident	**Occupied Palestinian Territory**			**Israel**
	Gaza Strip	**West Bank**	**Total**	
Palestinian minors killed by Israeli security forces	634	318	952	3
Israeli minors killed by Palestinians	4	35	39	84
Palestinians killed during the course of a targeted killing	279	107	386	
Palestinians who were the object of a targeted killing	151	82	233	
Palestinians killed by Palestinians for suspected collaboration with Israel	11	109	120	
Palestinians who took part in the hostilities and were killed by Israeli security forces	1,221	467	1,688	60
Palestinians who did not take part in the hostilities and were killed by Israeli security forces (not including the objects of targeted killings).	1,382	840	2,222	5
Palestinians killed by Israeli security forces whose role in hostilities is not known.	387	484	871	4

Source: B'Tselem 2008.

include the many militias formed by local leaders or "warlords," the Somali army and the ICU forces. The violent clashes in Somalia have pitted local militias against one another, the ICU against the militias and TFG forces, and, finally, Ethiopian forces, supported by US aerial assaults, against the ICU.

After the Ethiopian forces entered Mogadishu in December 2006 to support the TFG, the brutal conflict in Somalia escalated, which resulted in more devastation in the country and laid waste to the capital. The magnitude of the Somali crisis at the time of writing dwarfs what the country has endured during the last decade. According to Human Rights Watch, the bloodshed of the past two years has done what the previous 16 years of statelessness and strife could not—the parties fighting to drive one another from the capital have largely managed to destroy it, along with the lives of many who were living there.[28] Thousands of civilians have been killed. More than 2,200 casualties of the fighting were treated in Mogadishu's Medina and Keysaney hospitals between the beginning of 2008 and end-September that year. Tens of thousands more have felt compelled to leave.

Since early 2007, all sides to the conflict in Mogadishu have, almost daily, fired indiscriminately upon populated residential neighbourhoods. Mortars, "Katyusha"

The magnitude of the present Somali crisis dwarfs what the country has endured during the last decade

---

Box 8-4   ABDELQAWI A. YUSUF* – Somalia, a State under siege

In Somalia, a state is under siege. The entity, which was constructed on 1 July 1960 after the unification of the regions formerly under British and Italian administration, now risks being shattered by the storms assailing it. The transitional federal government (TFG) that emerged from the thirteenth national reconciliation conference held in 2004 is still struggling to bolster its authority and bring peace and stability to Mogadishu and the surrounding areas as it continues to wage battle with organised crime rings, anarchists, Islamist extremists, and separatists who oppose the restoration of the institutions of government in the country.

Under such conditions, Somalia is in danger of reverting to that primal state of nature, where, as the British philosopher, Thomas Hobbes, put it, the life of man is "solitary, poor, nasty, brutish and short". Indeed, some claim that Somalia has already succumbed to this state. How did the situation deteriorate so drastically? The primary responsibility for safeguarding human security in any country falls upon the state and its institutions and agencies of government. But if the state itself is unsafe and unstable, it is difficult to conceive how it can possibly undertake that role that is so vital to the lives of its people.

The state, indeed, shrank after the collapse in 1991 of Barre's military dictatorship. It was reduced to a miniature of its past, its authority barely extending beyond the capital Mogadishu. The brutal one-man rule that had lasted for more than two decades had ended by consigning the state and its institutions to the scrap heap of history. Worse yet, the insurgents who had taken over the city brought havoc with them, committing mass murders and executing civilians for their tribal affiliations. Corruption reigned amid the plundering of the state and private property. Banks, museums, national archives, and government buildings were ransacked while industries and state-owned enterprises were dismantled and sold abroad. Not even electricity cables and water pipes were spared this fate. Anything of value was stolen for the purposes of enriching the rival warlords in Mogadishu and financing their militias.

From that time forward, Somalia was torn into two zones. One became a region of anarchy and lawlessness whose centre was in Mogadishu, in which resided the organised crime rings and outlaw militia groups called, respectively, the *moryaan* (parasites) and Islamist extremists, who have all made it impossible to restore the institutions of state. The second zone consists of the self-governing areas in the northeast and northwest of the country, known respectively as Puntland and Somaliland. Puntland is an officially autonomous state that continues to claim it is part of Somalia. On the other hand, the popularly elected government of Somaliland declared its independence from Somalia in 1992 without securing international recognition.

While the secession of Somaliland represents a challenge to the TFG, it is the TFG's role in the zone of anarchy and lawlessness that poses the greater danger to the state establishment in Somalia and to neighbouring states and the international community. A host of diverse interests have intertwined and taken root in this zone of anarchy. Their ravages range from selling off the remains of foreign enterprises to importing food and medicines long past their sell-by dates, and from running terrorist military training camps to trafficking in drugs and appropriating public and private assets. Consequently, nothing is more feared or more likely to be resisted by this armed alliance between organised crime rings and Islamist extremists than the restoration of the institutions of the state.

Human security will remain a slippery mirage in Somalia until the TFG succeeds in restoring government and law and order to this zone of anarchy. This will require the concerted help of the African Union and the UN and successful negotiations with the two self-ruling entities, Puntland and Somaliland, with the objective of creating a Somali state on a non-centralised and democratic federal basis.

* Somali international legist.

rockets, and artillery have been used with such little precision that those firing them have no reasonable expectation of striking any military target or avoiding civilian casualties.[29]

According to the Report of the UN Secretary-General on children and armed conflict in Somalia, children have been the victims of armed violence in many regions in Somalia, particularly those living in Internally Displaced Person (IDP) settlements close to military or government buildings.[30] In the year between March 16, 2007 and March 15, 2008, violence between TFG and Ethiopian forces and anti-Government groups, including Al-Shabaab, remnants of ICU and Hawiya and other clan militias, led to high civilian casualties, particularly in Mogadishu. Over 1,850 people, including 217 children, wounded by weapons, were examined by one hospital in Mogadishu alone. More than 125 children were recorded by protection monitors as having been killed between 16 March 2007 and 15 March 2008—up from 82 reported in the preceding twelve months. The risks posed to children in Mogadishu by indiscriminate shelling, mortar attacks and gunfire increased during the first months of 2008. Thirty-three children, many under 10 years of age, were reported seriously wounded in the crossfire in just two districts of Mogadishu between February and mid-May 2008 alone. Child protection monitors have reported cases of children being injured or killed as a result of crossfire, mortar attacks, grenades or the rare targeted shooting, while in their homes, on the street, in the market, walking home from school or playing football.

The conduct of all parties has been questionable, in failing to warn civilians about potential fighting or to prevent looting, and in impeding relief efforts and mistreating dozens of people detained in mass arrest campaigns.[31]

II. Threats to liberty

A further threat to human security in the three cases under discussion is unlawful arbitrary detention, which violates the fundamental human right to liberty. Many of the acts of arrest, imprisonment, detention, and abduction have been indiscriminate. This is especially the case in Iraq and Somalia, where, again, government forces and the militias that are locked in combat have all committed these violations.

A. Iraq

The UN Assistance Mission for Iraq (UNAMI) reported that, according to the Ministry of Human Rights in Baghdad, by the end of June 2008, the total number of detainees, security internees and sentenced prisoners across Iraq stood at 50,595 with a peak at 56,320 at the end of March 2008. According to this report, out of this total, by the end of June 2008, 23,229 detainees were in the custody of the Multinational Forces; 17,152 detainees held by the Ministry of Justice; 613 detainees held by the Ministry of Labour and Social Affairs; 5,535 held by the Ministry of Interior and 1,060 by the Ministry of Defence.[32] Furthermore, according to Human Rights Watch (HRW), the Multinational Forces (MNF) in Iraq, were, as of May 12, 2008, holding 513 Iraqi children as "imperative threats to security," and have transferred an unknown number of other children to Iraqi custody. HRW also notes that children in Iraqi custody are at risk of physical abuse.[33]

According to HRW,[34] the swell in the total number of detainees across Iraq and those held by the MNF as reflected in Table 8-2, resulted from Iraq's broad counter-terrorism legislation, which has been the main legal basis for arrests and prosecutions stemming from the Baghdad

Children have been the victims of armed violence in many regions in Somalia

Table 8-2	Total number of detainees across Iraq and detainees held by the Multinational Forces, 1 January 2006 – 30 June 2008	
Time period	**Total number of detainees, security internees and sentenced prisoners across Iraq**	**Number of detainees held by the Multinational Forces (MNF-I)**
1 Jan – 28 Feb 2006	29,565	14,229
1 Mar – 30 Apr 2006	28,700	15,387
1 May – 30 Jun 2006	25,707	12,616
1 Jul – 31 Aug 2006	35,542	13,571
1 Sept – 31 Oct 2006	29,256	13,571
1 Nov – 31 Dec 2006	30,842	14,534
1 Jan – 31 Mar 2007	37,641	17,898
1 Apr – 30 Jun 2007	44,325	21,107
1 Jan – 30 Jun 2008	50,595	23,229

Source: UNAMI 2006, 2007, 2008. (See Statistical references)

Security Plan.[35] The security plan, launched in conjunction with the US troop surge of 2007, rapidly expanded detainee populations in Iraqi and MNF custody.

The cruelty of conditions of imprisonment and captivity in Iraq has become public knowledge. In June 2007, UNAMI expressed concern about the internment of suspects in MNF custody for prolonged periods without judicial review of their cases, and administrative review procedures that do not grant detainees due process in accordance with internationally recognized norms.[36] Some of the prisons operated by the Iraqi ministries had been secret establishments unearthed by the US forces which, in turn, sometimes practiced forms of torture that stirred international outrage when the media in the United States published reports and photographs of acts committed in Abu Ghraib prison. In February 2007, the Iraqi prime minister issued orders granting military leaders broad powers to detain individuals and restrict their freedoms of expression and assembly. The authority to arrest without warrant was only one of the powers granted to military leaders in the name of preventing further escalation of the conflict. Prison conditions and practices have been among factors adding to political tension in Iraq, which finally moved the foreign military authorities and the Iraq government, in late 2007, to begin to eliminate secret jails and clean up prison procedures.

Kidnapping is another violation of liberty. The UNAMI report of May-June 2006 notes that this has become one of the most widespread crimes in Iraq. Kidnappers normally request significant amounts of money from the victims' families, or, if the victims are foreigners, make political demands on their countries of origin. Many hostages are killed even after ransom is paid. Foreign hostages are killed if their country does not meet the kidnappers' demands, or to settle a score with the government of the country concerned. UNAMI has also received reports of sectarian connotations connected with some kidnappings, as well as alleged collusion between kidnappers and the police. [37]

B. The Occupied Palestinian Territory

Detention, imprisonment, and kidnapping are the second most serious human rights abuse in the Occupied Palestinian Territory. Amnesty International confirms that Israeli authorities have arrested many thousands of Palestinians since the turn of the century. Approximately 10,000 remain in custody in some thirty detention centers, according to Palestine's Ministry of Prisoners' Affairs.[38] Some have been deprived of their liberty for many years. The rulings were handed down by military courts whose procedures failed to meet international standards for fair trial. Fewer numbers—about 700 individuals detained in October 2006 according to Amnesty International estimates—are under administrative custody, which is to say, detained without being charged and without the intention of being brought to trial.

Israeli military command is the authority empowered to issue orders for administrative detention, the terms of which can last up to six months and are renewable without limit. While the Israeli government claims that this measure is founded on Article 78 of the fourth Geneva Convention on the protection of civilians in time of war, which allows an occupying power to inter persons for "imperative reasons of security," Amnesty International believes that Israel's treatment of administrative detainees is inconsistent, not only with international human rights standards, but also with the very convention it cites. Israel has exploited the provisions of Article 78 by turning what was intended as an exceptional precautionary measure into a routine instrument for punishing persons suspected by the military of working against Israeli interests.[39]

On the other hand, Amnesty International also points out that, in the OPT, the governments in the West Bank and Gaza have both abused the right to liberty of the Palestinians under their authority, especially following the armed clash between Fatah and Hamas in 2007. In the West Bank, there has been a marked deterioration in the human rights situation. Arbitrary detention of suspected Hamas supporters by Palestinian Authority security forces has become routine and detainees are often subject to torture or other ill-treatment. Similarly, in Gaza, arbitrary detentions and torture or other ill-treatment of detainees by Hamas forces are now widespread and the initial improvements in the security situation

Detention, imprisonment, and kidnapping are the second most serious human rights abuse in the OPT

Approximately 10,000 remain in custody in some thirty detention centers

that followed Hamas's takeover are fast being eroded.[40]

C. Somalia

As formidable as the threats to human security in Somalia remain, restricting the freedom of civilians has not necessarily taken the form of arrest and imprisonment. This is hardly an indication of the rule of law but rather of its opposite, a lawless situation where dysfunction characterizes even the workings of oppression, and where warring factions frequently resort to more violent forms of persecution. In most of the country, judicial systems are not well established, are not based on codified law, do not work, or simply do not exist. Against this background, information in the African press and from human rights organisations does not suggest a markedly high rate of arbitrary detention and imprisonment, although internment without trial and mistreatment of prisoners are practiced by all parties to the Somali conflict. In Mogadishu, dissidents have been imprisoned for opposing the government and on suspicion of conducting anti-Islamic activities. In Somaliland, the government has arrested journalists and harassed others. Public floggings of convicted or suspected offenders are a common occurrence. [41]

According to Human Rights Watch, TFG police personnel have frequently arrested residents of Mogadishu on suspicion of links to the insurgency.[42] Persons who are arrested as suspected insurgents often face abusive interrogation at the hands of TFG officers.

III. Threats to economic conditions and livelihoods

In all three cases examined here, occupation and military intervention and the different forms of violence they spark have been highly detrimental to economic conditions, as this section illustrates.

A. Iraq

Under conditions of insecurity, internal strife, and the impacts of the hasty economic transition that Iraq was launched on after 2003, the Iraqi economy cannot be expected to revive sufficiently in the short term. The former Baath regime had clearly wasted Iraq's resources and left behind an economy ruined by years of wars, sanctions, economic mismanagement, fitful development, infrastructural and institutional collapse, and meagre opportunities for private enterprise. (Salah Al-Nasrawi, in Arabic, background paper for the report)

Even so, bad as Iraq's economic legacy was, it does not compare to the economic breakdown that followed the US-led invasion of Iraq. The slight recovery that has occurred since mid-2007 has not had a tangible impact on general standards of living. World Bank figures indicate that Gross Domestic Product (GDP) in Iraq dropped at a rate of 11.4 per cent annually between 2000 and 2006. This deterioration was a consequence of a drop in industrial production by 17 per cent annually and a 3.6 per cent decline in agricultural production. Production in the manufacturing industries fell by 12.8 per cent annually.[43]

A study on Iraq by the Council on Foreign Relations in the United States describes the economy as hobbled by rampant unemployment, sluggish growth, and sub-par oil revenues.[44] Of the nearly $20 billion of US-appropriated funds to jump-start the private sector in Iraq, only $805 million had been spent by mid-2007. Meanwhile, GDP growth remains at about 4 per cent, although estimates vary. In part, this is due to the fact that Iraqi oil revenues, estimated at $3 billion per month, are considerably less than the potential of the country's enormous reserves.

According to the International Labour Organization (ILO), data from different sources covering the period from 2004 to the end of 2006 suggests that as many as 1.3 to 2 of the 7 million-strong labour force were unemployed.[45] Unemployment among the young (15-24 years), at around 30 per cent, has been nearly double the overall unemployment rate.

Oil market sources say that while Iraqi oil production has begun to climb again, as of March 2008 it had not yet reached this target. Oil production rose from 2.290 million barrels per day in January 2008 to 2.4 million barrels per day in February 2008 but then fell off to 2.37 million barrels per day in March 2008.[46] The study does note some positive trends in the Iraqi economy. It cites the claims

Internment without trial and mistreatment of prisoners are practiced by all parties to the Somali conflict

Gross Domestic Product in Iraq dropped at a rate of 11.4 per cent annually between 2000 and 2006

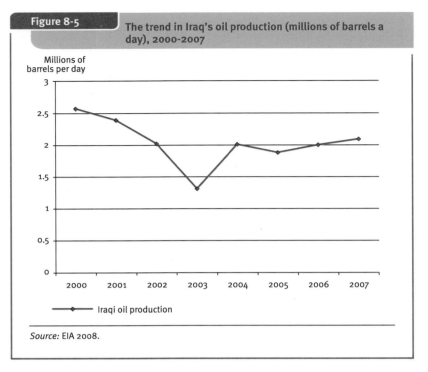

Figure 8-5 The trend in Iraq's oil production (millions of barrels a day), 2000-2007

Millions of barrels per day

Source: EIA 2008.

of some analysts that the actual growth rate is about 17 per cent, that salaries have doubled since 2003, that cheaper goods are now available in the market and that the numbers of mobile phone subscribers and internet users have skyrocketed. The study also notes that the economy of the Northern Kurdish zone is prospering. Nevertheless, it concludes that, on the whole, standards of living are still lower than they were before the invasion and that pre-war oil production peak levels were higher than in 2007, four years after the invasion.

The Council on Foreign Relations study attributes Iraq's poor economic performance to four factors, all connected with the military intervention:[47]

1. ***Lack of security:*** private investors continue to stay away because of the high-risk security situation and because the precautions it demands increase transport time, production costs and the costs of doing business in general.

2. ***Oil smuggling:*** lack of controls and smuggling contribute to sub-optimal oil production levels. A May 2007 report by the US Government Accountability Office estimates that oil valued at between $5 million and $15 million—or roughly between 100,000 and 300,000 barrels per day—has been siphoned off daily since 2003 as result of collusion between corrupt

officials, smugglers, and insurgents. Smugglers can earn as much as $5 million per week in parts of southern Iraq. Although about $7.4 billion has been spent to rebuild Iraq's electricity and oil sectors, output in both sectors remains below pre-war levels.

3. ***Bureaucratic inertia:*** given high levels of insecurity, rampant corruption and a fragmented society, government agencies cannot perform efficiently. The problem is further exacerbated by a high turnover of public employees, which began with the dismantling of the government by the Bremer administration, and the lack of skilled technocrats.

4. ***Brain drain:*** conditions generated by the military intervention have caused an estimated two million Iraqis to flee the country, many of them highly skilled professionals such as engineers and doctors. Some estimates indicate that 40 per cent of Iraq's professional class has fled the country. In addition, an aspect of the violence rooted in class divisions is the singling out of professionals by militias. Around two thousand Iraqi physicians have been killed since 2003, for example. Also, according to UNICEF, enrolment in Iraqi schools has dropped 45 per cent between 2005 and 2007 owing to "missing teachers."

Another study attributes the economic deterioration in Iraq directly to the actions of US forces.[48] The country's poor economic performance, it observes, is also due to the destruction of Iraqi infrastructure during the first Gulf War and the war on Iraq in 2003. The damages resulting from the Second Gulf War such as repeated attacks on power generators as well as other facilities have complicated the task of infrastructure reconstruction following the invasion in 2003.

An Iraqi researcher has detailed the effects of rampant corruption in Iraq. In his view, the corruption that took hold after the invasion of Iraq in 2003 drove the country to ruin (Salah Al-Nasrawi, in Arabic, background paper for the report).[49] Within weeks, corruption began to spread at an unprecedented rate such that, by 2008, Transparency International ranked Iraq second from the top of 180 nations in terms of public sector corruption.[50]

B. The Occupied Palestinian Territory

Forty one years of occupation, as well as the expansion of Israeli settlements, have prevented Palestinians from controlling their own affairs, and render illusory any notion of the economy as a means of meeting their most basic needs.

According to a report of the UN Secretary General to the United Nations General Assembly in May 2008, Israeli settlement construction in the West Bank has taken place under every Government since the 1967 Arab-Israeli war.[51] In 2007, there were more than 450,000 settlers living in 149 settlements in the West Bank, including East Jerusalem. According to United Nations sources, almost 40 per cent of the West Bank is now taken up by Israeli infrastructure associated with the settlements, including roads, barriers, buffer zones and military bases.[52]

In June 2002, Israel began construction of a wall on the line separating it from the West Bank. When complete, approximately 10.2 per cent of West Bank territory, including East Jerusalem, will be isolated by the wall and physically connected to Israel.[53] In 2004, the International Court of Justice issued an advisory ruling that the wall violated international law. Meanwhile, Israeli authorities continue to violate Palestinian Authority (PA) autonomy by controlling transportation networks, border crossings, the airport, and extensive portions of land. In addition, they restrict the Palestinians' freedom of movement by forcing them to pass through checkpoints. By September 2007, the West Bank had 607 such checkpoints[54] where Palestinians, regardless of the urgency of their needs, were forced to stand for long hours in inspection queues before being allowed to go on to their destinations.[55]

Other Israeli practices have impaired the Palestinians' ability to conduct their economic affairs in a stable and predictable way. This applies as much to wage earners as it does to business owners. Prominent among such practices is the policy of closures in the OPT, which paralyses the movement of people, goods and services at many levels. Another detrimental practice is the withholding of disbursals to the PA from tax revenues levied by Israel. There is also the total embargo that Israel imposed on Gaza following Hamas's electoral victory in January 2006, an embargo Israel tightened further in the wake of the fissure between Hamas and Fatah in 2007.

A 2008 World Bank study on the costs of the closures regime in the West Bank and Gaza explains that this policy imposes three types of restrictions on the movement of Palestinians: internal closures, which restrict free mobility inside the West Bank and Gaza; external closures, which restrict access from the West Bank and Gaza to Israel and Jerusalem; and external international closures, which restrict access from the West Bank to Jordan and from Gaza to Egypt.[56] To drive home the extent of the closures regime, the report notes that, in November 2005, there were more than 600 physical barriers (more than ten per square kilometre), consisting of 61 full-time and 6 partially staffed checkpoints, 102 roadblocks, 48 road gates, 374 earth mounds, 28 earth walls and 61 trenches.

Almost 40 per cent of the West Bank is now taken up by Israeli infrastructure

By September 2007, the West Bank had 607 checkpoints

Table 8-3	Number of damaged buildings in the Occupied Palestinian Territory between 2000-2007 by type of damage				
	Number of partly damaged buildings	Number of completely damaged buildings	Number of damaged public buildings	Number of damaged security buildings	Total
West Bank	42,752	2,855	155	83	45,845
Gaza Strip	26,578	5,248	88	...	31,914
Palestinian Territory	69,330	8,103	243	83	77,759

Source: PCBS 2008.

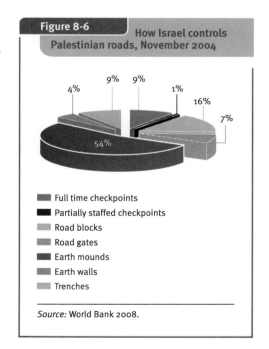

Figure 8-6 How Israel controls Palestinian roads, November 2004

- 4%
- 9%
- 9%
- 1%
- 16%
- 7%
- 54%

- ■ Full time checkpoints
- ■ Partially staffed checkpoints
- ■ Road blocks
- ■ Road gates
- ■ Earth mounds
- ■ Earth walls
- ■ Trenches

Source: World Bank 2008.

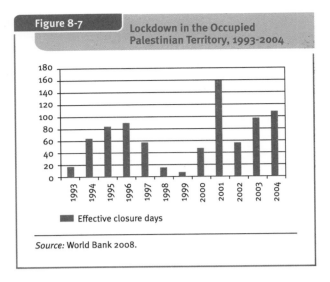

Figure 8-7

Lockdown in the Occupied Palestinian Territory, 1993-2004

■ Effective closure days

Source: World Bank 2008.

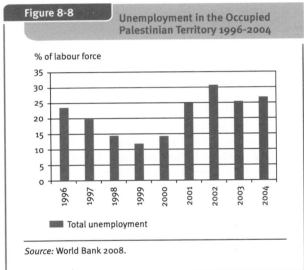

Figure 8-8

Unemployment in the Occupied Palestinian Territory 1996-2004

% of labour force

■ Total unemployment

Source: World Bank 2008.

A single full-day closure inflicts a $7 million dollar income-related loss in the West Bank and Gaza

Closures fragment the Palestinian economic space. Cut off by impediments to mobility, and unable to predict when closures will occur, Palestinian villages and towns struggle to survive on whatever resources they have. The frequent revocation of permits for West Bank and Gaza residents working in Israel diminishes their income, as does the reduction of working days for labourers unable to reach their jobs in Israel or in the West Bank. Closures also make it difficult for businesses to obtain the intermediate supplies they need to produce goods, and to market them in areas other than their own.

The World Bank study estimates that a single full-day closure inflicts a $7 million dollar income-related loss in the West Bank and Gaza. For 2001 to 2005, the total employment-related loss is estimated at $2.4 billion and the total closure-related loss is estimated at $928 million,

which comes to a total estimated loss of $3.3 billion for that period, or the equivalent of 58 per cent of the total foreign aid provided to the PA.

The economic costs of closures go beyond their impact on income. Production costs rise sharply when closures force goods to move via long detours, or when they block commerce altogether. According to the World Bank study, between 2000 and 2005, transportation costs from Ramallah to Bethlehem soared by 348 per cent; from Ramallah to Nablus by 105 per cent; and from Ramallah to Jenin by 167 per cent.[57] Such handicaps reduce the competitiveness of the Palestinian economy and deter investment.[58]

It is thus hardly surprising that poverty and unemployment are widespread among Palestinians. The Human Development Report 2007/2008 records that, from 1990 to 2005, the West Bank and Gaza registered a negative annual per capita GDP growth rate of -2.9 per cent. It further records that, between 1996 and 2005,[59] unemployment affected more than a quarter of the labour force (26.7 per cent) and that the ratio of unemployed women to men was 71 per cent.[60]

A 2003 World Bank report on the state of the Palestinian economy two years after the Al Aqsa intifada noted a sharp decline in all major economic indicators.[61] By the end of August 2002, per capita income had dropped to half its 2001 level, joblessness affected half of the labour force, and infrastructure had sustained $728 million worth of damage. Moreover, Palestinian exports were down by half, imports by a third, and the volume of investment, at $140 million, was then less than a tenth of its 1999 level, when it had reached $1.5 billion. The report added that the chief cause of the Palestinian crisis was Israel's blockade.

Another report, from the International Labour Organisation in 2008, observes that one in three people of working age (15 years and above) was employed full or part time in the OPT. Annual per capita GDP stabilised in 2007 at $1,178, which is some 27 per cent below its historic peak of 1999. In November 2007, extreme poverty affected 40 per cent of the population in Gaza and 19 per cent in the West Bank, lower than the levels of the previous year owing mostly to the resumption of wage payments to civil servants which Israel had cut off following the Hamas electoral victory.[62]

The Palestinians have paid a heavy price for exercising their democratic rights via the ballot box. After the peaceful January 2006 election which put Hamas in power, international financial aid stopped flowing. Although this aid has become available again to the Fatah government in the West Bank since the break with Hamas, there has been no radical improvement in economic conditions, primarily because of Israel's repeated incursions into these areas. What is new, however, is the punishment that Israel has inflicted on Gaza following the Hamas takeover in the strip. Such punishment has taken the form of a total blockade, obstructing all communication with the outside world for whatever purpose. The measure has induced the collapse of most industrial and agricultural activity in the area, disrupted essential infrastructure and services through frequent and long power shortages, and further damaged water quality. The Israeli assault on Gaza that began on December 27, 2008 created massive infrastructural damage and marked a new level of violence in the treatment of Palestinian civilians.

C. Somalia

The country collapsed in 1991 after the overthrow of Siad Barre, into a stateless existence, with Somaliland and Puntland as the two northern secessionist regions. This collapse outlasted US and international military intervention in the early 1990s. Over the past few years, an attempt at unification was made, with ideological underpinnings, led by the so-called Islamic Courts Union in an effort to extend central authority over most of Somalia. The efforts, however, were thwarted by an outright military intervention by Ethiopia in December 2006 to support the TFG. Despite such efforts at 'unification', the Somali state is a fragile construct that risks reverting to the kind of failed state it was known as in the preceding two decades.

The record of Somalia's central government since the 1960s and 1970s shows that, owing to a low resource base, the government either relied on foreign assistance (the Soviet Union at the time) or adopted highly inefficient economic policies (in the

| Box 8-5 | Piracy in Somalia |

Piracy off the coast of Somalia is growing at an alarming rate and threatens to drastically disrupt international trade. It provides funds that feed the vicious war in Somalia and could potentially become a weapon of international terrorism or a cause of environmental disaster. Up to 30 September 2008, 63 actual and attempted hijacks had been recorded by the International Chamber of Commerce (ICC) and the International Maritime Bureau (IMB). Since end-2007, piracy activity has shifted away from the Mogadishu port area and into the Gulf of Aden. Some 16,000 ships a year pass through the Gulf of Aden, carrying oil from the Middle East and goods from Asia to Europe and North America. So one of the most important trade routes in the world is now threatened by the chronic instability in Somalia.

Piracy has been a problem in Somali waters for at least ten years. However, the number of attempted and successful attacks has risen over the last three years. The only period during which piracy virtually vanished around Somalia was during the six months of rule by the Islamic Courts Union in the second half of 2006. This indicates that a functioning government in Somalia is capable of controlling piracy. After the removal of the courts, piracy re-emerged. With little functioning government, long, isolated, sandy beaches and a population that is both desperate and used to war, Somalia offers a perfect environment for piracy to thrive.

Puntland, the semi-autonomous region in the northeast of the country, appears to be the base for most pirates in Somalia. It is one of the poorest areas of Somalia, so the financial attraction of piracy is strong. Somalia's fishing industry has collapsed in the last fifteen years and its waters are being heavily fished by European, Asian and African ships. Some pirates have claimed that they are involved in protecting Somalia's natural resources and that ransom payments should be viewed as legitimate taxation. In a region where legitimate business is difficult, where drought means agriculture is nothing more than subsistence farming, and instability and violence make death a very real prospect, the dangers of engaging in piracy must be weighed against the potentially massive returns.

In late 2007, the danger of Somali waters forced the World Food Programme (WFP) to suspend food deliveries by sea (the route by which ninety per cent of all WFP food deliveries for Somalia is delivered since transport by land is just as risky and is impractical for conveying large quantities of food aid). In November 2007, through the implementation of a naval escort system, WFP was able to resume its food deliveries to Somalia. Since then, although no pirate attacks have been reported, naval escorts for ships carrying WFP food continue to be absolutely essential to ward off the ever-present threat of piracy. In a country without a functioning central government that is suffering from drought and war, and with over a million internally displaced people, imported food aid is essential.

While pirates themselves keep the majority of the funds they generate, a significant amount is passed on to important locals, some of whom are involved in the ongoing war. These regular injections of cash undoubtedly help to finance the war. Eradicating piracy will not stop the war, but it may reduce the money available for arms purchases. The lack of maritime security also allows a busy people- and arms-smuggling trade to flourish and encourages illegal fishing in Somali waters. Large oil tankers pass through the Gulf of Aden and the danger exists that a pirate attack could cause a major oil spill in what is a very sensitive and important ecosystem. As pirates become bolder and use ever more powerful weaponry, a tanker could be set on fire, sunk or forced ashore, any of which could result in an environmental catastrophe that would devastate marine and bird life for years to come.

Source: Middleton 2008.

post-socialist period starting from 1980). Public infrastructure, including electricity production, has been destroyed and, in the absence of a central government, key public institutions do not exist. On the other hand, the comparative stability of the breakaway state, Somaliland, has allowed the economy in the north to experience a relative revival.

According to the World Bank, in 2002,[63] in Somalia overall, the distribution of total unemployment rates amounts to 65.5 per cent (urban), 40.7 per cent (rural) and 47.4 per cent (national).[64] These figures are only indicative, as they do not take into account the extent of under-employment, seasonal unemployment, etc.

The proportion of population living in extreme poverty is estimated as 43.2 per cent for Somalia, for the year 2002. The extreme poverty in urban areas is 23.5 per cent and in rural and nomadic areas 53.4 per cent. In absolute terms, the population living in extreme poverty is estimated as 2.94 million, consisting of 0.54 million in urban and 2.4 million in rural and nomadic areas. General poverty estimates based on the number of people living on $2 per day are 73.4 per cent for Somalia, consisting of 60.7 per cent for urban and 79.9 per cent for rural and nomadic areas. According to this measure, 5 million people in Somalia live in poverty; 1.4 million in urban and 3.6 million in rural and nomadic areas.[65]

IV. Threats to people's access to food, health and education

With the violence, poverty, unemployment, and displacement of persons that accompany occupation and military intervention, people's opportunities to obtain sufficient food, appropriate health care, and adequate housing inevitably crumble.[66]

A. Iraq

In Iraq, the worsening food crisis, which had reached worrisome proportions under sanctions, and the failure of the oil-for-food programme, led to a sharp rise in starvation. Indeed, the extent of the situation required international agencies and organizations to respond with emergency food aid to the Iraqi people. Foremost among these were the World Food Programme (WFP)

and Oxfam. By the beginning of 2008, the WFP launched a 12-month emergency operation worth US$126 million to provide food assistance for up to 750,000 Internally Displaced Persons (IDPs).[67] Oxfam, which initiated a similar programme, estimated the number of people unable to obtain food in Iraq at four million.[68]

The invasion of Iraq came on top of twelve years of sanctions and, before then, the Iraq-Iran war, both of which damaged Iraq's ability to sustain and operate health care services. Before the invasion, the infant mortality rate was 102 per 1,000, the maternal mortality rate was 291 per 100,000, and the malnourishment rate had climbed to 19 per cent of the population. Five years later, the state of health in Iraq had worsened as a result of several factors (Samer Jabbour and Iman Nuwayhid, in Arabic, background paper for the report).

Firstly, the security breakdown in the immediate aftermath of the invasion unleashed a wave of pillaging and plundering that did not spare hospitals and medical centres. Secondly, the continuing violence and counter-violence gravely disrupted the health system while creating new pressures on hospitals, clinics and paramedical services. As mentioned earlier, estimates of mortalities from this violence between March 2003 and June 2006 range from about 47,000[69] to nearly 600,000[70] and the numbers of wounded were much greater than these figures. Thirdly, standards of living fell sharply: a survey conducted in Iraq in 2004 found that 54 per cent of the families polled had access only to non-potable water, 78 per cent suffered daily power blackouts, and 36 per cent did not have appropriate sanitary facilities in their homes.[71] Fourthly, according to a joint report by the World Health Organisation and its Middle East bureau[72], a total of 18,000 doctors—a quarter of the total number of Iraqi doctors—and unknown numbers of nurses, dentists, and pharmacists have left Iraq. (Samer Jabbour and Iman Nuwayhid, in Arabic, background paper for the report).

Damage, neglect and violence since 2003 have devastated Iraq's health sector. Public hospitals suffer from chronic systems failures: elevators, heating systems, air conditioning and sewage systems all frequently break down, decrepit kitchens and laundry rooms cannot keep up with

Public infrastructure has been destroyed and key public institutions do not exist

5 million people in Somalia live in poverty

mounting needs, and a lack of medicines, equipment and materials often brings emergency wards and operating theaters to a halt. These are common challenges in all health institutions in Iraq, even those formerly well equipped.[73] A report by the Committee of the International Red Cross (ICRC) states that Iraqi hospitals are overflowing with more caseloads than they can handle, swollen further by victims of street violence.[74] Many lack sufficient medicines and medical supplies. Half of those admitted to hospitals following outbreaks of violence die because specialized medical teams and blood are unavailable.

Primary health care centres are also clogged and under-supported by a centralized health system that has collapsed. Efforts are in progress to put the system back on its feet under extremely difficult circumstances. Child health has been markedly affected; however, conditions have also been harsh on adults. Widespread insecurity, combined with the inability to obtain adequate health services, has led to delays or gaps in treating non-communicable diseases. Not surprisingly, symptoms of trauma associated with violent circumstances are on the rise in Iraq. Anxiety and depression are common in most communities in Iraq, and mental illness will probably rise in the face of continued disruption of the social fabric and of the protection offered by the family and local community. It is noticeable—and regrettable—that most reports on the state of psychological health focus almost exclusively on the foreign forces (Samer Jabbour and Iman Nuwayhid, in Arabic, background paper for the report).

According to a report by Save the Children, 122,000 Iraqi children died in 2005 before reaching the age of five.[75] Medical reports have cautioned that such diseases as pneumonia, malaria, measles, and dysentery form the primary cause of children's deaths in Iraq.

Another growing phenomenon is the employment of minors, which conflicts with international conventions regarding the employment and use of children at work. Several international, regional, and Iraqi reports, including some by human rights and civil society organisations, affirm that underage employment in Iraq has spread considerably, even among children below ten, and in activities unsuited to their age and physical makeup. It has become a familiar sight to see children cleaning streets, especially now that the municipality of Baghdad and other municipalities have hired minors as "sanitation workers" for less than a dollar a day, which has lured innumerable children away from school.

A third grave development affecting children is the rise in truancy and school drop-out rates. Circumstances of material need and abject poverty are responsible, but these are aggravated by the dangerous security conditions. The rising levels of violence and terrorism, and especially ethnic and sectarian cleansing, have forced hundreds of thousands of families to leave their homes and take refuge in other areas which have no provisions for additional children.

Children are pressed into strenuous and dangerous activities, such as construction work, domestic services and, recently, as gangs of body guards, or in public or privately owned workshops and factories. The human rights office of the UNAMI has warned, in a special report, of a humanitarian catastrophe against the children of Iraq, who suffer from cruel social and health problems and from declining levels of education.[76] The report appealed for efforts to guarantee a suitable standard of living for children that will reflect positively on their life in general and the life of society as a whole. Other reports tell of addictions that have become widespread among minors, such as drugs, various intoxicants, and cigarettes. According to one, at the end of 2004, more than a million minors work in harsh circumstances and are exposed to sexual abuse and violence.

Scenes of violence and war daily overshadow growing children's lives. Ethnic and sectarian tensions, cleansing and evacuation operations, daily murders over identity, and unidentifiable headless bodies may not immediately endanger children but will certainly scar their psyches, affect their relations with others and leave them feeling more insecure in future.[77]

B. The Occupied Palestinian Territory

In the West Bank and Gaza, economic decline is clearly reflected in the food supply situation. According to the ILO, approximately half of all Palestinian households are dependent on food assistance

Damage, neglect and violence since 2003 have devastated Iraq's health sector

Symptoms of trauma associated with violent circumstances are on the rise in Iraq

provided by the international community. Some 33 per cent (or 0.7 million people)of what was formerly a middle-income society in the West Bank now relies on food aid. Worse still, the figure for Gaza stands at 80 per cent of households, or 1.3 million people.

Prevailing health conditions similarly reflect a slumping economy. The United Nations Relief and Works Agency (UNRWA) and the Israeli authorities were in charge of health conditions in the West Bank and Gaza until this responsibility was transferred to the PA in 1994. In spite of forty one years of occupation, Palestinians, in 2004, enjoyed reasonable levels of health: an average annual income of $1,026, a 91 per cent literacy rate, a life expectancy of 72, a low infant mortality rate (20.5 per 1,000 births)[78] and a low maternity mortality rate (11 deaths out of 100,000 live births). The reason for this is to be found in the Palestinian spirit of solidarity and the support given by civil society to health care centres and other medical institutions. However, these conditions began to deteriorate after 2003 with the outbreak of the Al-Aqsa intifada, the construction of the separation wall, and the blockade of Palestinian territories.

Together, the wall, along with the check points, road barriers, and blockades that stifle Palestinian towns and villages, have cut off access to 41 health care facilities and obstructed access to others, as well as to schools and places of work. Thirty six per cent of these health care facilities reported

> **80 per cent of households in Gaza rely on food aid**

> **From 2000 to 2005, 300 schools were closed down and eight universities bombed in the OPT**

that many of their patients can no longer reach them, 53 per cent reported receiving additional patients diverted to them by the blockade, 63 per cent encountered delays in providing emergency services, and 55 per cent of them had difficulty obtaining medicines for the treatment of chronic illnesses. When completed, the wall is expected to isolate a total of 71 clinics and will become a barrier even to Palestinian ambulances which are forbidden to enter in the area between the wall and the 1967 Green Line (Samer Jabbour and Iman Nuwayhid, in Arabic, background paper for the report).

In the Occupied Palestinian Territory, the absence of a budget in 2006 and the Western boycott of the Palestinian government caused an acute educational crisis. This was aggravated by the strike of employees in the education sector in protest against non-payment of wages, which deprived public school children of their right to education and forced some 2,000 higher education students to interrupt their studies for about two months.[79]

From 2000 to 2005, according to the Palestinian Ministry of Higher Education, 300 schools were closed down and eight universities bombed. In March 2004, the Palestinian Centre for Human Rights reported that seventy-three educational institutes, including occupational training institutes, were destroyed in Gaza. Also, according to these records, the University of Hebron and the Hebron Polytechnic were kept closed throughout 2003, to the detriment of 60,000 Palestinian students. In the same year, the University of Jerusalem was threatened by the construction of a wall that would have divided the university and appropriated a third of its land. Only after an international campaign against this violation was the wall relocated outside the university compound.[80]

Roadblocks and similar obstacles to freedom of movement have also had an impact on education in the Occupied Palestinian Territory. For example, between April 2001 and December 2003, the earth mound barrier on the Sarda road from Ramallah to Birzeit University in the West Bank caused such delays that commuting times for students and professors doubled; occasionally the Israeli authorities would prohibit passage altogether. Because of this, two-thirds of the second

Figure 8-9 Food aid dependence and extreme poverty, West Bank and Gaza, 2007

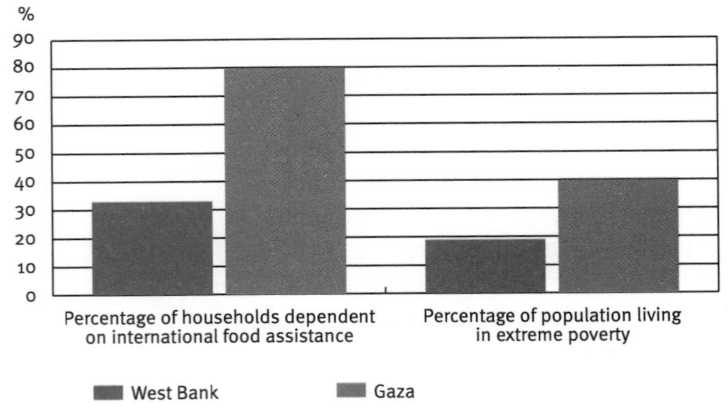

Source: ILO 2008.

2001/2002 academic term were lost, forcing a two-month extension at the expense of the summer term.[81] Birzeit was thus unable to fulfil its role as an institute open to all members of the same nation, because most of its students were unable to reach their university. From 2000 to 2005, Gazan enrolment at the university dropped from 400 to thirteen. In the 2004/2005 academic year, the enrolment rate of students from Jenin and Nablus in the northern West Bank dropped from 120 per year to zero.[82]

In addition, throughout the Territory, primary school enrolment has been eroded by frequent obstacles to pupils' access.

The real fear is that, with these reductions in attendance and enrolment, Palestinian schools and universities will become increasingly unable to contribute to the development of Palestinian society as a whole.[83]

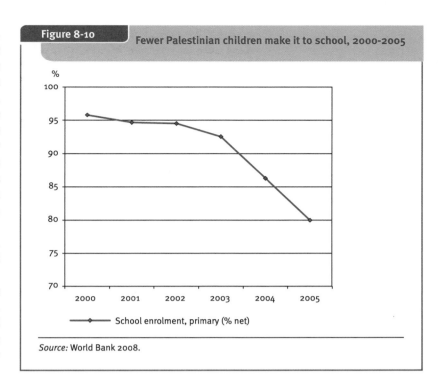

| Figure 8-10 | Fewer Palestinian children make it to school, 2000-2005 |

School enrolment, primary (% net)

Source: World Bank 2008.

C. Somalia

The ongoing civil conflicts in Somalia, coming on top of widespread poverty, weak infrastructure and poor health conditions, have gravely impacted health conditions. Mortality rates among infants, children under five and women during birth in Somalia are among the highest in the world: 90 infant deaths per 1,000 births in 2006, 145 deaths per 1,000 children below the age of five in 2006 and 1,400 women per 100,000 live births in 2005.[84] Dehydration from illnesses related to dysentery, pulmonary ailments, and malaria are among the chief causes of death for infants and young children, accounting for more than half of children's deaths. Inoculations against the major paediatric diseases covered only 20 per cent of children in 1998. Malnourishment and anaemia are also widespread.

In Somalia, average life expectancy at birth was under 47 in 2006.[85] The country has the world's highest rates of tuberculosis infection, at 374 cases per 100,000 inhabitants. In 2003, there were more than 30,000 cases of malaria. In addition, numerous cases of polio were discovered that year and, by 2006, it had become impossible to stem the spread of that disease. The country has always lacked resources and systems for providing primary health care. However, the situation is even worse at present, as there are

only four doctors, less than one dentist, less than one medical assistant, and nine nurses for every 100,000 persons. Somalia could well lose some of the health care workers who remain, for many must be eager to emigrate in search of a safer life and better income (Samer Jabbour and Iman Nuwayhid, in Arabic, background paper for the report).

World Food Programme statistics indicate that a large proportion of the population suffers undernourishment. More than a fifth of the undernourished are located in severe food insecurity areas such as the Juba Valley and the Gedo, Bakol, and Bay regions of the south. There are approximately 1.53 million recipients of food relief across Somalia.[86]

In education, primary school net enrolment dropped to 22 per cent of school-age children during 2000-2006[87], which lowered the adult literacy rate to 19.2 per cent.[88] According to a survey conducted in 2002 by UNDP and the World Bank, Somalia has one of the lowest school enrolment rates in Africa.[89] The primary school enrolment survey undertaken by UNICEF estimated the number of pupils enrolled in grades 1-8 as 286,808, consisting of 64 per cent boys and 36 per cent girls for 2002. These enrolment figures were used to estimate the primary school enrolment rates for boys and girls with the estimated population for the corresponding age

Mortality rates in Somalia are among the highest in the world

The country has the world's highest rates of tuberculosis infection

groups. The overall primary school enrolment rate is 16.9 per cent for Somalia, 20.8 per cent for boys and 12.7 per cent for girls. Moreover, thousands of orphaned and homeless children have been left to struggle alone against brutal conditions. Among the young, the recruitment of children by militias is widespread, a sad development that is recorded in UN reports and which is discussed in Chapter 4.

Somalia's overall adult literacy rate is one of the lowest in the world and varies from 34.9 per cent in urban areas to 10.9 per cent in rural and nomadic regions. The female adult literacy rate in the latter regions is as low as 6.7 per cent. This partly reflects the lack of educational opportunities after the civil war, particularly in remote areas, where a large proportion of the school-age population missed out on opportunities for basic education.

Somalia's overall literacy rate is one of the lowest in the world

V. Threat to the environment

As a form of warfare, occupation and military intervention can impact ecosystems in two key respects. The environment, itself, may be a source of the conflict in that it contains the resources over which competition may arise and intensify into armed conflict. At the same time, the environment itself can be damaged by warfare arising from this competition or other causes of conflict. For example, warfare harms the environment through the destruction of agriculture and infrastructure, which the state must rehabilitate after the cessation of hostilities at considerable cost. But even after the fighting ends, the environment is still at risk from the detritus of war, such as undetonated bombs, discarded weapons, collapsed buildings, sunken ships and crashed airplanes, not to mention landmines and toxic debris released into the water or air.

During the war in Iraq, water, air, and soil were all contaminated by various pollutants

A. Iraq

The 2003 war led to occasional uncontrolled dumping of municipal waste into the streets, owing to the failure of collection systems, looting or restrictions. In addition, the conflict generated large volumes of demolition waste from bomb-damaged buildings (potentially impacted by depleted uranium and asbestos) and military hardware (vehicles, unexploded ordnance, and depleted uranium).[90]

During the war in Iraq, water, air, and soil were all contaminated by various pollutants. In addition to the dumping of war debris into the Tigris, frequent power blackouts obstructed water supplies, forcing people to turn to unsafe water sources. An example of air pollution in wartime occurred on 20 March 2003 when Iraqi authorities set fire to the Al-Rumeila oilfield in order to cloud the sights of attacking aircraft. The smoke from the oilfields could be seen from Kuwait. Iraqi authorities employed this tactic in other locations. The heavy smoke contained noxious substances that affected the health of civilians and combatants alike. Trenches dug during the war exposed the soil, subterranean water resources, and drinking water to contamination.[91]

B. The Occupied Palestinian Territory

Israeli policies have negatively affected the environment in the territories. Among the gravest impacts is the enormous attrition of Palestinian water resources, which has undermined general water conditions. The annual water deficit in the West Bank and in Gaza is as high as 50 million cubic metres a year and water pollution rates are high. In 90 per cent of the water supplies, chloride concentrations range from 250 to 2,000 millilitres/litre (international standards stipulate that levels should not exceed 250 millilitres per litre) while nitrate concentrations also exceed the internationally acceptable level of 50 millilitres/litre.[92]

Israel's actions have also contributed to the deterioration of the Palestinian environment through its neglect of wastewater systems in the territories and its failure to meet international health standards in this regard. Settlements pour millions of cubic metres of wastewater into riverbeds and elsewhere on Palestinian land. In the West Bank alone, settlements inhabited by some 350,000 settlers pump out 40 million cubic metres of waste water a year, compared to 33.72 million cubic metres produced by the entire Palestinian population in the West Bank. In Gaza, wastewater flows into sandy areas or is removed by tanker trucks and pumped into Wadi al-Salqa, Wadi Gaza, and other riverbeds. However, a considerable portion of it flows into the Mediterranean or seeps into the ground, mixing with the water in subterranean reserves.[93]

The occupation authorities have constructed a wastewater collection station in Beit Lahya in the Northern Gaza Governorate. The facility is adjacent to large residential complexes. The Mizan Human Rights Centre reports that the station stands atop the largest and once highest quality aquifer in Gaza. The aquifer is now polluted, ruining prospects for agricultural development and cultivation.[94]

C. Somalia

The military intervention in Somalia came on top of, and further accelerated, a breakdown of legislative and traditional controls over the use of and access to natural resources. According to the World Conservation Union, group struggles, land grabs and pressures on resources have long ravaged Somalia and visibly degraded its environment.[95] The damage, which successive foreign interventions and conflicts have aggravated, is reflected in advancing deforestation near, but no longer limited to, populated areas; in the over-fishing of selectively targeted marine species by foreign fisheries operating illegally offshore; in desertification hastened by over-grazing and the mismanagement of land tenure in a chaotic and predatory political and military context; and in the rise of a rapacious charcoal trade, mainly to Gulf countries, that is responsible for accelerating deforestation and thus worsening annual flooding and soil erosion.

The charcoal trade in Somalia takes a heavy toll on the acacia forests of southern Somalia which provide ecological stability for pastoralists. Profiteering traders clear entire swaths of forest mostly for shipment abroad. Turning cut wood into charcoal is a dirty process that pollutes the local air. In 2000, total charcoal production was estimated to be 112,000 metric tons; by 2005, it was estimated at 150,000 metric tons of which approximately 80 per cent is destined for stoves in the Gulf States, while only 20 per cent is for domestic consumption.[96] Another cruel exploitation of Somalia's lawless situation has been the dumping in local waters of toxic waste from pesticides used in Europe.

Conclusion

This chapter has illustrated the exponential impacts of military intervention on human security in three Arab cases. In the Occupied Palestinian Territory, Iraq and Somalia, occupation and military intervention have exacted a heavy price in terms of lost lives and freedoms, with negative repercussions on income, employment, nutrition, health, education and the environment. They have sparked both legitimate resistance and a cycle of violence and counter-violence that engulfs occupied and occupier alike and that spills over into adjacent countries, disrupting human and national security across a wider front.

Prospects for settling the three major conflicts are very largely governed by the will of non-Arab parties. Yet Arab states have a role to play. Even when Arab governments have adopted unified positions on some of these questions, they have failed to abide by the commitments they have consequently undertaken, or to put their resolutions into effect.

The question posed by current conditions is, what action should be taken to end military intervention? It is useful to recall that, in all three cases, with all their different circumstances, the invading powers or occupying authorities have acknowledged that their presence or occupation is temporary. The government of Israel has not refuted the concept of two states, one Israeli, the other Palestinian, living side by side. The withdrawal of United States troops from Iraq is expected to become effective by the end of 2011,[97] and Addis Ababa announced that its mission was completed in December 2008.[98]

Nevertheless, serious efforts are required to translate elusive intentions into tangible plans, particularly in the case of the Israeli-Palestinian conflict where Israel's military dominance creates an imbalance in attempts to negotiate a settlement and where special diplomatic efforts are required to overcome suspicions, acts of provocation and hostilities on both sides. In the case of Iraq, the agreement between the US and the Government on the withdrawal of US troops points in the right direction. Similarly, Ethiopia's withdrawal from Somalia sets the stage for new diplomatic initiatives.

Settlements pour millions of cubic metres of wastewater on Palestinian land

Group struggles, land grabs and pressures on resources have visibly degraded Somalia's environment

But in all three cases, hard questions remain about the reconstruction of state institutions, society and the economy in the post-conflict phases in these countries. The Iraqi factions have yet to meet within the framework of a comprehensive political process, reconciliation efforts in Somalia are going around in circles, and the dispute between Fatah and Hamas has not been resolved. New attempts to build peace in the region should start with a fresh dialogue on the Israeli-Palestinian conflict and involve neighbouring countries such as Syria. Moreover, priority must be given to removing obstacles to the development process in the Occupied Palestinian Territory. As a New York Times editorial put it: "In the West Bank, that means freezing further settlement construction and expansion. It means lifting roadblocks between Palestinian cities and towns that are not needed for security. In East Jerusalem, it means stopping the humiliating eviction of Palestinians. And in Gaza, it means expanding exceptions to the blockade to allow the import of cement and reconstruction materials."[99]

The situation in the region throws into strong relief the responsibility the UN must bear with regard to the fate of the countries under occupation or subject to military intervention. Yet, on the questions of Iraq and the Occupied Palestinian Territory, the UN has been marginalized. On Somalia, it has once more resumed intensive efforts to restore stability and more humane conditions, which however requires the cooperation of all vested interests. The fact remains that the only impartial framework for realising human and national security in the three cases is that provided by the UN. The League of Arab States could acquire greater credibility and efficacy if it cooperates with the international organisation towards this end. However, for that to happen, global and regional powers must summon the will to leave the field open for the UN and the League of Arab States to remedy the extensive damage on the ground.

Endnotes

1 Galtung1964.
2 Israel withdrew from Sinai in 1982 as a result of the Peace Agreement with Egypt.
3 The Knesset ratified the Golan Heights Law in December 14, 1981, extending Israeli law to the area of the Golan Heights.
4 Government of the United States 2003.
5 Government of the United States 2004.
6 Government of the United States and the Republic of Iraq 2008.
7 Government of the United States 2009c.
8 Federal Democratic Republic of Ethiopia 2006.
9 Federal Democratic Republic of Ethiopia 2009.
10 Charter of the United Nations 1945.
11 Dale 2008.
12 Government of the United Kingdom 2008.
13 Elsea, Schwartz and Nakamura 2008.
14 Global Security Organization, online database 2008.
15 Geneva Academy of International Humanitarian Law and Human Rights, online database 2008.
16 Iraq Body Count 2003-2009, online database 2008.
17 Burnham et al. 2006.
18 Iraq Family Health Survey Study Group 2006.
19 Government of the United States 2009b.
20 Government of the United Kingdom 2008.
21 Fischer 2006.
22 Government of the United States 2009a. AHDR calculations for the period June 2003 - November 2006. [http://siadapp.dmdc.osd.mil/personnel/CASUALTY/OIF-Total-by-month.pdf].
23 Iraq Coalition Casualty Count, online database 2008.
24 Iraq Coalition Casualty Count, online database 2008.
25 UN-News and Media Division 2008; 2009a; 2009b.
26 Data for the period 2000-2008 based on B'Tselem 2009.
27 PCBS 2008.
28 HRW 2008a.
29 HRW 2008a.
30 UN Secretary-General Report, 2008a.
31 HRW 2008a.
32 UNAMI 2008.
33 HRW 2008 (in Arabic).
34 HRW 2008b.
35 Anti-Terrorism Law, no. 13 (2005). The anti-terrorism law broadly defines terrorism as "every criminal act committed by an individual or an organized group that targeted an individual or group of individuals or groups or official or unofficial institutions and caused damage to public or private properties, with the aim to disturb the peace, stability, and national unity or to bring about horror and fear among people and create chaos to achieve terrorist goals." As cited in the HRW report.
36 HRW 2008b.
37 HRW 2008b.
38 Ferwana 2006.
39 Amnesty International 2006.
40 Amnesty International 2007a.
41 Amnesty International 2007b.
42 HRW 2008b.
43 World Bank 2008b.
44 Beehner 2007.
45 ILO 2007.
46 Platts 2008.
47 Beehner 2007.
48 Arnove and Abounimah 2003.
49 It is difficult to supply precise statistics on institutionalized corruption in the new government agencies. However, Iraq's Commission on Public Integrity (CPI), created after the war, reports more than 2,500 corruption cases involving a total of $18 billion. Director-generals, deputy ministers, and ministers were implicated in forty-two of these cases, some of which involved various types of smuggling. Although Iraqi courts adjudicated in some cases involving senior officials and passed sentences against the defendants, in most instances guilty parties were not taken into custody. Some were even helped to flee the country before the government could recover embezzled funds. The most serious cases of profiteering and corruption were those that took place in the petroleum sector, where investigators at the CPI and other international bodies discovered massive oil smuggling in the years following the occupation. A report by the Inspector-

General of the Ministry of Petroleum, indicates that corruption in the energy sector has cost Iraq millions of dollars, as a consequence of incomplete production records, lack of effective internal control systems, and weak organisational structures and work teams, particularly in the auditing departments. Perhaps worse, yet, is that some militias and political forces allied with tribal leaders control petroleum installations, including oil fields, pipelines, and ports, which they administer as private fiefdoms, beyond supervision by the government, international bodies, or even the occupying forces. This phenomenon has hampered any real possibility of accurately gauging the actual volume of oil exports (Salah Al-Nasrawi, in Arabic, background paper for the report).

[50] Transparency International 2008.
[51] UN Report of the Secretary-General, 2008f.
[52] UN Report of the Secretary-General, 2008f.
[53] UN-OCHA 2007.
[54] UN-OCHA 2008a.
[55] Al-Tufakji 2003 (in Arabic).
[56] Akkaya, Fiess, Kaminski and Raballand 2008.
[57] Akkaya, Fiess, Kaminski and Raballand 2008.
[58] Akkaya, Fiess, Kaminski and Raballand 2008.
[59] Latest available data in the period.
[60] UNDP 2007.
[61] World Bank 2004.
[62] ILO 2008b.
[63] Latest data available on Somalia from international organizations are for the year 2002.
[64] UNDP and World Bank 2003.
[65] UNDP and World Bank 2003.
[66] The issue of displaced persons is discussed in chapter four, The Personal Insecurity of Vulnerable Groups.
[67] WFP 2009.
[68] Oxfam 2007.
[69] Iraq Body Count 2003-2009, online database 2008.
[70] Burnham et al. 2006.
[71] UNDP and Ministry of Planning and Development Cooperation 2005.
[72] Watts, Susan, Sameen Siddiqi, Alaa Shukrullah, Kabir Karim, and Hani Serag 2007.
[73] Al-Awqati 2008 (in Arabic).
[74] ICRC 2007.
[75] Save the Children 2007.
[76] UNAMI 2006.
[77] WHO 2006a.
[78] WHO 2005c..
[79] Independent Commission for Human Rights 2006.
[80] The Palestinian Centre for Human Rights 2005 (in Arabic).
[81] UNESCO 2005.
[82] Barghouti and Murray 2005.
[83] Barghouti and Murray 2005.
[84] UNICEF 2009b.
[85] UNICEF 2009b.
[86] FAO 2006.
[87] UNICEF 2009b. Latest available data in the period.
[88] UNDP and World Bank 2003.
[89] UNDP and World Bank 2003.
[90] UNEP 2007.
[91] UNEP 2007.
[92] Ministry of Environmental Affairs 2000 (in Arabic).
[93] Ministry of Environmental Affairs 2000 (in Arabic).
[94] The Applied Research Institute 2005 (in Arabic).
[95] IUCN 2006.
[96] Baxter 2007.
[97] Government of the United States and the Republic of Iraq 2008.
[98] Federal Democratic Republic of Ethiopia 2009.
[99] New York Times 2009.

Chapter 9

Concluding reflections

Human security protects human development during political, societal and economic downturns

This Report began by defining human security as "the liberation of human beings from those intense, extensive, prolonged, and comprehensive threats to which their lives and freedom are vulnerable". The first chapter proposed that this definition, and the concept from which it flows, have particular relevance to Arab countries at this juncture, and can help to prioritize components of their development strategies and plans. Human security protects human development during political, societal and economic downturns such as those the region has experienced in recent years and which continue to curtail its prospects. Human security is distinct from state security yet the one is not necessarily at odds with the other. Indeed, state security is necessary for individual human security. Contradictions are however incurred when the state pursues absolute notions of national security at the expense of citizens' basic rights and freedoms or when its practices flout the rule of law. At that point, the state ceases to be a principal means of ensuring human security, and becomes part of the problem.

Putting people's security first

Threats to human security are multidimensional and interdependent, with compound effects. They originate in a diverse array of sources, ranging from the natural world, to authoritarian states, to the ambitions of regional and international powers. They can be associated with local actors, such as state security forces or insurgents, as well as regional and international actors such as human trafficking networks or occupying military forces. And they can be aggravated by universal phenomena, such as globalisation, which has increased the cross-border transmission of risk factors affecting human security.

Some of the actors have been part of the problem, but could be part of the solution through shifts in course

Some of the actors identified in this Report have been part of the problem, but could be part of the solution through shifts in course. Others, including the emerging Arab civil society, as well as regional and international bodies, could do still more to contribute to solutions through continued and constructive engagement with the task of building human security. The preceding chapters have suggested various policy orientations that different actors could adopt within their respective spheres of action, outlining specific steps that can be taken to reduce threats across all dimensions of human security.

The Report's analysis has illustrated that the concept of human security provides a framework for re-centring the Arab social contract and development policy on those vital yet neglected priorities that most affect the wellbeing of Arab citizens.

While the state of human security is not uniform throughout the Arab countries, none can claim to be free from fear or free from want and many are affected by spillovers from insecurity in neighbouring countries. The Report has therefore underscored the central importance of:

• *Protecting the environment:* The preservation and enhancement of the land, water and air that sustain the Arab peoples' very existence under rising national, regional and global environmental, population and demographic pressures;

• *Strengthening the rule of law:* The guarantees of essential rights, freedoms and opportunities without discrimination that only a well-governed, accountable and responsive state ruled by just laws can provide; and the mitigation of identity conflicts rooted in competition for power and wealth that becomes possible when such a state wins the trust of all citizens;

• *Safeguarding the rights of the vulnerable:* The recognition by the state and society of the abuse and injustice that vulnerable groups, especially women,

---

Box 9-1   RAMI G. KHOURI – The year that was

The core weaknesses, distortions and dysfunctionalities of the Arab world all seemed to worsen during the past year. Here are the major trends that I believe define our region these days, and will persist for some years to come.

A strange combination of self-assertion and reliance on foreign actors is the major characteristic of the Arab world, reflecting the massive polarization of our societies into two opposing camps.

On the one hand, many in our region continue to look abroad for protection or salvation, in the form of countries, ethnic groups or political movements that rely on foreign patronage for their survival more than they do on their own people. We remain deeply mired in a colonial-era mentality in many respects. The massive attention paid to awaiting the new Middle East policies of the Obama administration in the United States is the most dramatic manifestation of this trend.

On the other hand, the single most important change in the Arab world in the past two decades has been the attempt by several hundred million people to break away from this "vassals-of-the-West" mentality, and to assert their own identity and interests. The various Islamist movements in the region have been the main vehicles for such self-assertion, but these movements have not been able to translate their proven credibility into coherent state-building momentum.

Islamists remain primarily defensive and reactionary movements—very effective at confronting Western powers, Israel, and some domestic forces, but lacking any proven capacity to address mass needs in sectors such as job creation, environmental protection and political modernization.

Formerly integrated and cohesive societies throughout the Middle East continue to fracture into four main components: state-run bureaucracies with a heavy security element; the private sector with a heavy, globalized consumer dimension; assertive traditional identities (mainly Islamism and tribalism); and assorted criminalized groups, including youth gangs, militias, illegal migrants, drugs networks, and structured theft networks that live off government resources. These four different sectors of society coexist relatively comfortably with one another, each occupying its own space in society and relying on its own resources.

The big loser in this trend has been the cohesion and integrity of the modern Arab state, which has broadly failed to develop a viable sense of citizenship among its nationals.

Political liberalization and democratization are dormant for the time being. These remain buried beneath the stultifying weight of corruption-riddled Arab security states, emotion- and fear-driven mass movements, and the debilitating impact of Israeli, American, and other foreign interventions.

Like nationalism, genuine politics and the peaceful electoral contesting of power in the Arab world are victims of our own excesses. As economic stress throughout the Middle East increases in the wake of the current global downturn, prospects for political democratization will further recede on the regional priority list.

As a consequence of these trends, major political issues of importance to the people of this region are increasingly inconsequential to most people and powers around the world.

The worst ramifications of the Middle East's dysfunctions—terrorism, illegal migration, ethnic strife, corruption, police states, and assorted atrocities perpetuated by both state and private actors—are only occasional irritants for the rest of the world, not pressing strategic threats. We have marginalized ourselves as serious players on the global political stage and now assume the role of nagging annoyances and miscreants.

The oldest and most powerful driver of discontent, disequilibrium, and radicalism in our region—the Arab-Israeli conflict—remains totally stalemated, more an object of insincere and unconvincing "peace process" rhetoric than any genuine sense of diplomatic urgency. It is also now more difficult to resolve than ever, given complicating new factors.

This is a depressing list of broad trends in the Arab world—but also a volatile one that the people and states of the region cannot withstand for many more years. The good news is that these trends are all the consequences of man-made decisions and policies that can all be corrected by more constructive and equitable policies in the future.

Source: Khouri 2009.

children, and refugees encounter each day across the region, and the resolve to improve their legal, economic, social and personal conditions;

- *Reorienting the economy:* The will to address the weak structural underpinnings of the Arab oil economy, reduce income poverty and move towards knowledge-based, equitable and diversified economies that will create the jobs and protect the livelihoods on which coming generations will depend in the post-oil era. The global financial and economic crisis that set in during the finalization of this Report only increases the urgency of this need;

- *Ending hunger:* Ending persisting hunger and malnutrition, which continue to erode human capabilities, cut short millions of lives and set back human development in all sub-regions, but especially the poorest. As the recent food crisis made clear, the economics of food security in the global economy may call for a new realism in defining food security in the region, which needs to focus less on attaining absolute food sovereignty and more on achieving sufficiency in essential commodities for all members of society.

- *Boosting health:* The promotion of health for all as a human right, a prerequisite for human security and an instrumental enabler across the gamut of human functioning. The significant progress that Arab countries have made in this field is being undercut by policy and institutional failures that produce disparities in access, affordability and quality, and by the growing health threats from serious diseases such as HIV/AIDS, malaria and tuberculosis.

- *Resolving and preventing conflicts:* Long-standing conflicts in the region, including those related to interventions by international and regional powers, have proven to be destructive to human security and human development. Such conflicts have inflicted enormous damage through the use of force against populations and the disregard for civilian lives. These hostilities have caused untold human suffering and chaos, stained the image of the powers implicated in them and undermined the fragile progress of political reform in the region by bolstering extremist forces and driving moderate voices out of the public arena. Progress in human security requires an end to these conflicts and the initiation of post-conflict recovery.

The environment: protecting tomorrow today

Population and demographic pressures increase demand for critical resources such as energy, water, and arable land, all of which are under mounting stress in the Arab region. Acute natural resource scarcity, in turn, can contribute to economic stagnation, increased migration, and competition among social groups and countries. The latter can spill over into social conflicts, especially when exploited for ideological ends. Unless patterns of development address the issue of sustainability, the region's future growth and human security could be undermined.

A marked youth bulge such as that found in the region presents an additional and special challenge. Youth represents the future of any people, the largest investment any nation can make in its own development, and a central issue for policy makers. Young people consume resources and require substantial investments, notably in education, before they become economically productive. And if youth remain unemployed for long periods, this unproductive stage of life can become fraught with frustration and personal insecurity, while also taxing family savings, the economy and the resource base. All Arab countries urgently require comprehensive population and development policies, aimed at capturing the demographic dynamism of its young population, a 'window of opportunity' that has so far eluded the region. The steady decline in fertility rates across the region must be maintained through social policies aimed at overcoming rigid gender roles and barriers to women's advancement, as well as development policies targeting productive job creation, and education policies for building human capital geared to contemporary job markets.

The marked youth bulge presents an additional and special challenge

Arab countries urgently require comprehensive population and development policies

Arab countries have not shown a level of environmental stewardship that is consistent with protecting environmental security. Indeed, only three Arab countries score among the top 100 countries on the Environmental Sustainability Index, a composite measure that ranks countries by their plans for managing environmental and natural resources and population and development. Significantly greater efforts are required to formulate and implement national sustainable development strategies and to monitor the state of the environment within and across countries. Arab governments have several means available to them to encourage the participation of key social forces and the private sector in environmental protection efforts. Such means include the taxation system, incentives to use environmentally friendly technology, campaigns to adopt non-polluting renewable energy sources, policies that encourage sustainable uses of energy sources, the encouragement of mass transport over private automobiles, and the implementation of strong measures to combat desertification and deforestation.

Water scarcity is one of the most acute environmental challenges facing the Arab region, which is the most water-scarce of all regions in the world. This challenge needs to be met by applying Integrated Water Resources Management (IWRM) principles to development policies, institutional frameworks and the regulation of water supply and demand. These principles call for the integrated management of land and water resources and other related natural resources in a coordinated approach that aims to maximize socio-economic welfare in an equitable manner without sacrificing the sustainability of ecological systems.[1]

Environmental issues are global in nature and initiatives to address them need to be global as well. The Arab countries have taken part in the global concern for environmental security and ratified most international environmental conventions. While the larger share of responsibility for some critical aspects of climate change lies with the highly industrialized countries, the Arab countries can make their contribution by implementing their commitments under these conventions and by developing strong national and regional authorities, early warning systems and action plans to address water scarcity,

desertification, air pollution and land degradation on a regional scale. It would be advisable for Arab countries to introduce various climate change adaptation and mitigation measures through the formulation of "disaster risk reduction strategies and risk management practices" as a critical element for adaptation.[2] Chapter Two of this report provided several programmatic recommendations in these areas.

In this context, the major recommendations of the October 2008 Annual Conference of the Arab Forum for Environment and Development, which convened to examine the findings of the report, *'Arab Environment: Future Challenges'*, are timely and relevant.[3] In addition to recommending specific national environmental plans and programmes, the Conference called for serious action on the following cross-sectoral challenges:

"a) *Environmental institutions:* environmental institutions must be strengthened financially and empowered with executive authority to plan, coordinate, and enforce legislative programmes for environmental protection as well as provide the long-term planning necessary to cope with global changes, such as changing economic growth patterns and the use of crops for the production of fuels and its effects on food availability, national oil incomes and development plans in general.

b) *Integration of environmental considerations into development planning:* the incorporation of market mechanisms, natural resources and ecological accounting principles and the various types of environmental assessment (strategic, cumulative, project) are urgent needs.

c) *Environmental legislation:* provisions should be included in Arab environmental legislation that commit to harnessing market forces and mechanisms for compliance with environmental law. Other provisions must be incorporated to professionalize environmental occupations and vocations in a manner that permits only those who are qualified to practice. Finally, environmental legislative mandates and laws must be made effective and any impediments to enforcement have to be removed.

d) *Education:* the revamping of academic curricula aimed at including environmental education at all levels, and at raising the level of environmental commitment in students, is a major priority.

e) *Scientific research:* allotting more funds for environmental research. Moreover, researchers and centers of research networks need to be created at the national and regional levels.

f) *Communications and media:* environmental training programmes for reporters and media experts should be developed. In addition, committing space and programmes in the print and audio-visual media is needed in order to raise public awareness about environmental degradation, the costs and benefits of environmental protection, and the rational use of natural resources."

The State: solution or problem?

Considerable hopes are pinned on the civil state—one which is ruled by laws that respect civil and political rights—as the overarching champion and guarantor of human security. However, the Report has emphasized that the expectations of citizens in Arab countries for the protection of their rights and freedoms are seldom fulfilled on the ground, even if the distance between hopes and reality is not the same in all Arab states. Arab leaders recognized clearly the importance of rule of law and political rights in the Declaration on Modernization and Reform, launched at the Tunis Summit in 2004.[4] Since that time, however, only slight improvements have been achieved. Accordingly, the recommendations of the Arab Human Development Report 2004, *Towards Freedom in the Arab World*, are still relevant today.[5]

All Arab countries need to widen and deepen democratic processes to enable citizens to participate in framing public policy on an equal footing. A political system controlled by elites, however decked out with democratic trappings, will not produce outcomes conducive to human security for all citizens, irrespective of class, creed, gender, and ethnic/tribal affiliation. It is therefore imperative to restructure the social contract and modes of political interaction on the basis of equal rights and opportunities in order to forge cohesive bonds of citizenship among individuals in society. These bonds must be regulated by the state as the institution that stands above societal groupings, transcending the tribe and its elders, the ethnic group and its leaders, and the sect and its preachers. This is the state for all its citizens, the protector of their personal and human security, and the guarantor of their individual and human rights.

Such a state would unambiguously affirm its commitment to the international understanding of human rights. It would not merely ratify international conventions, but also would reflect their provisions in national legislation, and remove regulatory and legal obstacles to their meaningful implementation. This state would also embody a clear separation of powers: the concentration of all authority in the executive would give way to public oversight and checks and balances provided by an independent judiciary and a genuinely representative and empowered legislature.

Considerable hopes are pinned on the civil state as the overarching champion and guarantor of human security

Box 9-2	Arab leaders commit to advance political reform in their countries

We, the Leaders of the Arab States, meeting at the Summit Conference of the Arab League Council in its 16th ordinary session held in Tunis, assert our firm determination:

- To materialize our common will to develop the system of joint Arab action, through the Tunis Summit resolution to amend the Arab League Charter and to modernize its work methods and its specialized institutions, based on the various Arab initiatives and ideas included in the proposals put forward by the Secretary General as well as on a consensual and coherent vision and on a gradual and balanced approach.
- To reaffirm our states' commitment to the humanitarian principles and the noble values of human rights in their comprehensive and interdependent dimensions, to the provisions of the various international conventions and charters, and to the Arab Human Rights Charter adopted by the Tunis Summit, as well as to the reinforcement of the freedom of expression, thought and belief and to the guarantee of the independence of the judiciary.
- Endeavour, based on the Declaration on the process of reform and modernization in the Arab world, to pursue reform and modernization in our countries, and to keep pace with the rapid world changes, by consolidating the democratic practice, by enlarging participation in political and public life, by fostering the role of all components of the civil society, including NGOs, in conceiving of the guidelines of the society of tomorrow, by widening women's participation in the political, economic, social, cultural and educational fields and reinforcing their rights and status in society, and by pursuing the promotion of the family and the protection of Arab youth.

Source: LAS 2004.

The security sector would be reformed along principles of professionalism and public service. And this state would also prize its independence in fashioning its policies, mediating external and internal social pressures and winning the approval and support of its own people. It would, in short, be a legitimate state, distinct from the various interests in its political space, and distinguished by its citizens' voluntary acceptance of the principles by which they are governed. In order to bring about such a state, progress will be needed in the following areas:

Citizenship: Citizenship in the Arab region must be made more equal and meaningful. Human beings are born into different circumstances, with varied access to options to expand their capabilities, but all are entitled to the same basic rights. The right of citizenship should be identical for all persons living in a given country, regardless of ethnic origin, religious belief, gender, health, culture, wealth or any other personal attribute. Part-and-parcel of such equality is also the recognition and acceptance of diversity, in all its components, which derives from the same basic human right. The implementation of these basic rights requires both the recognition of citizenship for all and measures to address the entire range of resources, services, protections and opportunities available to these citizens, and how these are distributed. Many studies have shown that discrimination and socioeconomic inequality are detrimental to human security and human development. Equality, by contrast, is an essential means of mobilizing and enhancing human capabilities and performance in all dimensions of development.

Independent judiciaries: Judicial independence is critical to improve human security in the Arab countries. First, protection of human rights depends on a robust, fair, and independent judiciary willing to hold all political and social actors accountable under legal and constitutional protections. Second, judicial independence facilitates political stability and fairness. Finally, judicial independence is vital for the development of healthy, sound, and inclusive economies. Judicial independence is not achieved through static institutions only; it also needs

continuous attention and development. If the pledges of Arab constitutions and international instruments are to be taken seriously, legislative bodies in the Arab countries must be willing and empowered to deal with the judiciaries directly and as a co-equal branch of government, rather than only through the mediation of the executive branch. Executive authorities throughout the region must make a similar commitment to treating the judiciary as a co-equal branch.

Empowered legislative branches: Despite the wide range of constitutional powers granted to the legislative bodies in the Arab countries, parliaments generally play a subordinate role. And where parliaments are able to establish a degree of independence from the executive, they are generally unable to use it as effectively to control the legislative process. Two areas should be considered in order to address the legal incapacitation of parliamentary bodies in Arab countries. First, the electoral process, which is often designed in such a way as to limit the possibilities for parliamentary independence—for elections, too, remain in the grip of the executive in Arab countries. Elections are generally overseen by the Ministry of Interior, which often leads to some mistrust because of the Ministry's traditional emphasis on issues of internal security. And election rules beyond the balloting itself are often tailored to favour specific results. Impartiality both in general electoral procedures and in balloting itself is important. But perhaps still more significant than the procedures themselves is the general political climate in which elections take place: pluralism has been the exception rather than the rule in the Arab region, so that voters in parliamentary elections often face a constricted set of choices. The process of regularly modifying electoral laws must end. The second aspect of parliamentary bodies in Arab countries that requires changing is their lack of ways and means to hold executive authorities truly accountable.

Reform of the security sector: In many cases, the State itself can be the source of violence, yet remains central to the ability to control violence. This is the case in many Arab countries. The dominant internal security thinking in the Arab

It is imperative to restructure the social contract and modes of political interaction on the basis of equal rights

The concentration of all authority in the executive should give way to public oversight

countries remains heavily influenced by the traditional approach to security, with the disadvantage that security is conceived in a very narrow sense and hence does not address major imbalances. As an instrument for regime stability, the security sector in the Arab countries is subject to tight political control of the government, which compromises the former's integrity and ability to guarantee the safety and security of all those living within the state's boundaries. Arab societies are also increasingly facing threats that are transnational and collective in nature, including arms and drug trafficking, international crime and the allocation of scarce natural resources such as water among countries. Such threats require a rethinking of overall security policy, as well as of roles and missions, procurement, training, and resource allocation. Security needs to be approached from the perspective of protecting individuals and communities of individuals from violence. Security decisions in the Arab countries have to be analyzed and weighed in relation to their impact on development and social cohesion.

The core objectives of security sector reform are the development of affordable security bodies capable of providing security, and effective oversight mechanisms consistent with democratic norms. The security sector must be subject to a system of checks and balances at state level. Civil management and oversight of these forces, as well as the disengagement of security agencies from politics and from other non-security roles, are required for the transparent and accountable management of the security sector. In post-conflict Arab countries, the reform of this sector has to tackle a third objective, namely to address the legacies of past conflicts including disarmament, demobilization and reintegration of former combatants, judicial reform in the form of transitional justice, the proliferation of small arms and light weapons, and anti-personnel landmines.[6]

Civil Society: Successful institutional reforms are characterized by demand for change across the board, not merely change instituted at the top. The role of civil society organizations in promoting institutional reform has been often addressed in Arab reform strategies, such as in the Tunis Declaration and the Alexandria Declaration.[7] However, non-state participation in reform goes beyond civil society organizations. It also embraces the private sector. Arab countries are facing a new reality where business sectors are being increasingly represented at several levels of the legislative and executive arenas and have become influential in the formulation of public policies, especially those relating to economic and social affairs. Experiences with democratization outside the Arab region have often been associated with the growing political weight of the business sector and its partnership with ruling elites in the management of society and politics. Although these alliances have sometimes simply involved the co-opting of business elites as junior partners of the state, in many cases they have pushed state authorities to consider public governance, rule of law, accountability, and transparency, as founding principles. The rise of the Arab private sector and its growing political influence will very likely stimulate the democratic transformation of social and political environments.[8]

Towards increased security for vulnerable groups

Violence against women is not a phenomenon particular to the Arab countries, although some forms of it, namely honour crimes and female genital mutilation (FGM), are more acute in some Arab countries than they are in other countries of the world. However it is the institutional and cultural vulnerability of women that does constitute an Arab specificity. More particularly, the family in the Arab region continues to be the first social institution that reproduces patriarchal relationships, values and pressures through gender discrimination. Arab states should provide women the means to ensure and guarantee their human rights and security. In line with the calls in previous *Arab Human Development Reports* for comprehensive, rights-based societal reforms, the rise of Arab women requires the total respect for the rights of citizenship of all Arab women, the protection of women's rights in the area of personal affairs and family relations, as well as guarantees of total respect for women's personal rights and freedoms—and in particular their lifelong

The core objective of security sector reform is the development of effective oversight mechanisms

Successful institutional reforms are characterized by demand for change across the board

protection from physical and mental abuse. The achievement of these rights requires extensive legal and institutional changes aimed at bringing national legislations in line with the Convention on the Elimination of All Forms of Discrimination against Women (CEDAW).

In addition to the legal framework, the social environment is a crucial factor in discrimination against women. Violence against women in the Arab countries should not only be dealt with in its legal dimension but should also be addressed in society at large through public education. As pointed out in previous reports,[9] the lack of clarity in cultural and social concepts about roles, functions and rights constitutes an obstacle to the rise of women. Education and the media have an obligation to work on changing misleading images through a societal programme for the rise of women. The cultural roots of discrimination against women extend to several levels, all of which require action simultaneously:

- *Family upbringing* discriminates between the male and female in matters of freedoms, responsibilities and rights. This environment shakes women's self-confidence and undermines their self-image. These processes of discrimination must be better understood, and brought to a halt.

- *In education*, efforts to promote equal treatment between the sexes would benefit from the introduction of modern pedagogy, methodologies and technologies as aids in revamping curricula, teaching and assessment methods.

- *In the media*, the problem is not only that programmes intended to strengthen the status of women and build respect for their role in society are sometimes deficient. It is also that a significant portion of media programming erodes serious efforts to promote the rise of women. The problem is compounded by the spread of illiteracy, which has made the broadcast media a primary source of popular culture. The strengthening of methods for monitoring and analyzing women's image in the Arab media is an important priority. The media should also play an active role in educating the public about CEDAW.

More generally, there is a crisis in the Arab countries in terms of vulnerable groups' alienation, and governments'

neglect of their basic rights as human beings. In many Arab countries, vulnerable groups are subjected not only to institutional discrimination but also to the prejudices of the population at large. Such vulnerability is not confined to women; it extends to other marginalized groups such as minorities, the elderly, youth, children, disabled persons, internally displaced persons (IDPs) and refugees. The neglect and marginalization of these vulnerable groups is a blemish on the human rights records of Arab countries, which must be removed without prevarication or delay.

In many Arab countries, refugees and IDPs suffer from institutional and societal discrimination and are treated as second-class residents. In accordance with human rights principles and in order to ensure the human rights of all asylum seekers on their territories, Arab states are strongly urged to:

- Ratify the Convention relating to the Status of Refugees. At the time of the preparation of this Report, Jordan, Lebanon and Syria had still not ratified this important treaty.

- Tackle root causes of war and conflict and support peace-building initiatives involving grass-roots actors, NGOs and governments in the region.

- Focus on integrated projects to incorporate both long and short-term residents of refugee settlements, which would help to alleviate some of the pressures on the resources and infrastructures of Arab cities that are being strained by arriving refugees.

- Implement the rehabilitation of refugee camps and their design as an urban space, not only with reference to their political and social status, but also to becoming an integrated part of the city. Urban master plans based on rehabilitation should take into account the physical, socio-economic, and cultural fabric of the concerned spaces. A bottom-up participatory approach should be used to outline the differentiated needs of the refugee population: women, men, children, people of different income levels, etc.

- Ensure that labour, social welfare, and justice ministries, as well as national human rights bodies, are fully engaged in monitoring and promoting the human rights of asylum seekers.

The achievement of women's rights requires extensive legal and institutional changes

The neglect and marginalization of vulnerable groups stains human rights records in the region

- Ensure that individuals are not returned to countries where their life or liberty would be put at risk, in accordance with the binding principle of *non-refoulement*.

Re-defining economic security

Arabs will have to look seriously at a future beyond the current pattern of the region's economy, and the type of society it sustains. Procrastination can only heighten the economic insecurities of the region.

A basic feature of the social contract in the Arab countries is that the citizen accepts limitations on public representation and state accountability in return for state-provided benefits. Such a contract is only possible when states have sources of revenue other than direct taxes, such as oil, to finance public expenditure. Although the extent to which this rentier model applies varies across Arab countries, it is known to have influenced patterns of development negatively throughout the region. These impacts include under-investment in other productive sectors, which leaves state income hostage to finite oil reserves and fluctuating world prices; a trend in some cases towards consumption that has not created productive jobs; and the undervaluation of knowledge in societies where advancement often comes from access to wealth, rather than through scholarship and intellectual pursuits. This type of social contract does not make for secure, self-reliant and competitive economies in the long run, and needs to be surpassed.

One silver lining in the expected decline in oil income and Official Development Assistance in coming years is that perhaps it will induce greater reliance on national sources of revenue and consequently strengthen the mutual accountability of state and citizen.

The economic experience of the Arab region, as of other regions around the world, including OECD countries, has called into question the advisability of relying on market forces alone to regulate economic affairs. Addressing the economic security challenges in the region therefore will require an alternate Arab development model standing on three pillars—diversified economic growth, employment generation and poverty reduction—resting on a foundation of regional integration. Embodying the lessons of recent global economic failures, its policy instruments would be heterodox: they would reflect a pragmatic middle position between laissez-faire market policies and heavy-handed state interventionism. Specifically, this *Report* made clear the need for priority action in the following three areas:

Economic diversification: The revival and diversification of the productive base of Arab economies is critical to addressing the forms of economic insecurity analyzed in this report. Re-orienting the region's current concentration on oil-led growth would largely take the shape of a steady increase in the share and productivity of the industrial sector, a sharp rise in agricultural productivity and a greater refocusing of the service sector. This, in turn, requires a revised macroeconomic framework that allows for higher public investment in infrastructure, which is key for the facilitation of export-led manufacturing growth. The revised framework would feature prominently a stronger financial sector and a robust and accessible credit environment that enables private firms to finance investment and growth.

One way to provide stable, long-term finance to strategic sectors is through the creation of development banks, whether public institutions as in Brazil, Korea, and Japan or privately-owned as in Germany. Countries late to industrialization have achieved significant successes by utilizing such development banks as the financial arm of their industrial policy strategy.

These two policy objectives, the improvement of infrastructure and the provision of stable and reliable credit are essential pillars for national and regional industrial strategies aimed at diversifying sources of growth. With respect to agricultural policy, attention is needed to policy issues including securing access to productive land and credit, targeted price support benefits, changing gender roles, and effective water resources management.

Globalization is a contemporary reality for Arab countries no less than it is for other nations around the world. Its forces must be harnessed and managed. Fast-

The rentier model is known to have influenced patterns of development negatively

Addressing economic security challenges will require an alternative Arab development model

Any pro-poor macroeconomic strategy needs to incorporate a renewed commitment to employment

moving technological change constantly raises the technological bar, requiring developing countries to increase their productivity and competitiveness in the global economy in order to find a fruitful role in the unfolding of globalization. Indeed, the most dynamic sectors in the integrated world economy are high-technology goods and services. In contrast, recent history shows that reliance on commodities and unskilled labour can lead to "immiserising growth", which leaves developing economies highly insecure. Accordingly, a key stage of the Arab region's path to economic security entails the expansion of local technological capacities, the development and mobilization of knowledge-based assets and a shift towards higher value-added goods and services. In this respect, the original recommendations of the *Arab Human Development Report 2003, Building a Knowledge Society*, are as relevant today as they were in 2003.

Employment generation: Any Arab pro-poor macroeconomic strategy would also need to incorporate a renewed commitment to employment and public investment

---

Box 9-3   **GEORGES CORM* – The Arabs in the post-oil era**

Among factors destabilising Arab societies, since the 1970s, has been the tyranny of oil over the course of Arab economies, petro- or not. Earnings from the oil sector do not only affect exporting countries; a portion of this income has diffused into all Arab economies through guest worker remittances to non-oil exporting countries, and through investments. Thus annual growth rates in the Arab world have become firmly linked to the ups and downs of oil prices, with the pace of growth hostage to global price fluctuations.

Oil, and the *rentier* economy that goes with it, has accustomed the Arab world to consuming a large number of imported commodities and services that do not increase its productivity, or level of exports outside the oil sector, to a degree that would finance these large imports. The focus for investment during the oil era has been on expanding energy production and exportation to enlarge revenues. Investment activity resulting from fiscal surpluses has been distributed among giant family financial consortiums on the one hand and the humble savings of the large number of Arab guest workers in the Gulf on the other. In both cases, investments have been chiefly directed to the property, housing, tourism, and foreign exchange sectors. Surpluses have not been deployed effectively to build local productive capacity so as to meet the challenges of globalisation and the post-oil era.

It is therefore essential to begin thinking seriously about modifying Arab development tracks to make the Arab economies productive in the fields that globalisation relies on, as once under-developed countries such as Ireland, Singapore, South Korea, Taiwan, and Malta have done. This requires coordinated planning to limit the Arab brain drain, because the workings of globalisation demand that all states develop their knowledge and innovation capacities. These capacities are, in the first degree, human qualifications. It is essential as well to improve organisation and to promote technological creativity in new fields such as electronics, information technology, medical and biological research, and food technology. Further, it is vital to develop competencies in the fields of pollution control and the production of alternative energy.

Arab countries have made great efforts in the educational arena. However, they have not ensured sufficient suitable job opportunities for the hordes of qualified Arabs who enter the labour market every year and are forced to migrate in the search of that respected and active professional life missing in their own countries. This situation is part of a vicious circle which produces a concentration of investments in the property, business, and foreign exchange sectors and in certain light industries that are not technologically intensive (with the exception of the petrochemical industry that is integral to the oil sector).

In addition to oil rents, Arab economies depend on *rentier* income from property, from foreign goods import agencies, and from financial and exchange operations; they have yet to enter the age of revenues derived from the technological capacity to produce modern goods and services based more on knowledge than on manual labour. Taxation systems and investment incentive packages must be adjusted so as to encourage diversification. This is what will encourage Arab economic trailblazers to engage in investment projects that require high-level human competencies and practical and technological know-how, and that generate profits from technological innovation.

There are many highly-qualified Arab professionals developing new methods and techniques to produce modern goods in demand worldwide, yet they cannot find anyone in their home countries to finance the protection of their innovations through international patents, or to develop and adapt them for use in modern industries and services. In this sphere, we can follow the example of other countries that were poorer than the Arab countries yet succeeded in completely changing the course of low-performing and fettered development by turning to knowledge and technology, by engaging with globalisation, and by taking advantage of it.

The Arab world, in its oil and other centres, has yet to modernize itself in line with the requirements of globalisation. Building skyscrapers and state-of-the-art airports and owning luxury cars are the external shell of economic modernity, not its beating heart, which lies in science, knowledge, and technological innovation.

* Lebanese international economic and financial consultant and former Minister of Finance.

as a core vehicle for rejuvenating growth. The current 'reform' agenda in the Arab region discards a state-led development model in favour of a market-driven one, emphasizing improvements in the investment climate and private capital. Such a model, however, is not a solution to the region's large and increasing unemployment since the essence of the problem, as the Report argues, lies in the nature of oil-led growth.

The region's oil-driven development model has led to volatile and job-less growth. In the Arab countries, this pattern has produced lower income inequality than found in other world regions, but has nonetheless left entrenched pockets of income poverty. Productive growth has to be linked to poverty reduction, which entails generating widespread employment at decent wages. Apart from its economic implications, unemployment is the most sensitive political and social challenge the region will face in the foreseeable future. The challenge is not only to create employment, but also to provide decent and productive jobs to all the working-age population. To that end, macroeconomic policies can have as much impact as targeted anti-poverty programmes. But the question is: what makes growth more pro-poor? The general answer given is that three conditions should be created: a concentration of growth in economic sectors that can directly benefit the poor; an enabling environment that promotes their employment, and real incomes; and the enhancement of their basic human capabilities.

This requires that macroeconomic policies be embedded in a broader development strategy that allows for investment not only in infrastructure, but also in specific employment generating activities such as public works, as well as human capabilities through investments in education and health.

Poverty reduction: Even concerted efforts for economic diversification and employment generation will inevitably still leave some men, women and children in dire circumstances of impoverishment. In order to bring these people out of the cycle of poverty, specific and targeted policies and programmes must be developed to bolster incomes and increase access to services within the context of national development strategies.

One important component that has not been fully utilized in Arab countries is the use of public works. These projects should try to target poor areas and should strive to create assets that are of value to poor communities. Where the non-poor groups are likely to be significant beneficiaries of such created assets, co-financing should be mandatory and should be ploughed back into the budgets of public works projects.

Also important is the provision and functioning of social safety nets, which are essential for mitigating the impact of economic downturns on vulnerable groups, yet which remain uneven across the country groups of the region. All Arab countries have an interlocking web of traditional social safety nets, and these have been complemented by formal, or state-run, social safety nets in a variety of ways across countries. The high income Arab countries have erected fairly wide and deep formal social safety nets that provide special support for widows, the divorced, the sick, the elderly, unmarried and unemployed young women, families of prisoners, and students. Middle income countries have pursued similar paths, but have fallen short when it comes to coverage, equality, level, and cost-effectiveness of programs. And low income countries have only recently begun to adopt formal social safety nets, which tend to suffer from the same shortcomings as those in the middle income countries, and to a greater degree.

In order to finance greater pro-poor and employment generating public investment, reliance primarily on domestic resource mobilization is recommended. Depending on Official Development Assistance or inflows of private capital to jump-start growth is considered ill advised. Some resources can be mobilized by tilting public expenditures more towards productive investment—in human capital as well as in physical and natural capital. Public policies can also create an environment more conducive to broad-based private investment, through either more favourable macroeconomic policies or more equitable redistribution of assets. With greater opportunities for investment, people save more and/or work more to expand their asset base. The potential for domestic resource mobilization in the region is high given its low tax rates.

Productive growth has to be linked to poverty reduction

Also important is the provision and functioning of social safety nets

Reducing food and health insecurity

Food insecurity, hunger and malnutrition still afflict too many Arabs. While some states are well ahead of others in meeting the hunger-reduction target of Goal One of the Millennium Development Goals (MDGs) the region as a whole is off track. This largely reflects the continuing prevalence of hunger in the least developed countries (LDCs) of the region.

This Report has interpreted food security not in terms of absolute sovereignty in food production, a goal impractical in light of regional water scarcities, but rather in terms of sufficiency for all members of society in essential commodities. That is, the Report has focused not on the state level, but rather on the human level. In this context, the region's low self sufficiency rate in staple foods is one of its most serious development gaps. Around the world, as well as in the region, unregulated market policies have led to an increasing concentration of prime land and water resources in fewer and fewer large commercial farms. This trend has forced small farmers to eke out an existence on increasingly marginal land. Prime land that once produced food for those who farmed it is increasingly devoted to crops that turn a high profit, catering to the consumption patterns of the rich or to the export market. At the same time, unequal power relations, particularly in rural areas, have given influential groups control over prime land and water at substantially lower cost than the social value of these resources.

Altogether, these policies have contributed to a situation in which the market has produced sub-optimal quantities of the basic foodstuffs that make up the bulk of the diet and food expenditure of the poor. In this context, food security could be bolstered in the Arab region through policy interventions in line with the following principles:

Promote access to land: Arab countries may need to introduce progressive land taxation by levying higher land tax-rates on productive lands as the size of land-ownership increases. This could induce large landowners to sell part of their land and use the proceeds to finance irrigation expansion. Land access, distribution

and tenure need to be addressed within the context of a set of pro-poor policy interventions. In this respect, the legal and institutional framework to guarantee women's command over resources is critical. Given women's large role in agriculture, it is essential to ensure that property rights systems are not biased against them. A change in statutory laws to strengthen women's entitlements and increase the enforceability of their claims over natural and physical assets will both create new incentives for production and remove a major cause of insecurity among rural women.

Extend credit and finance for rural development: Government intervention may also be necessary to ensure that credit and jobs are available to support pro-poor rural development. This means directed and concessional credits for rural and agricultural activities. Regulations requiring commercial banks to diversify their lending and extend their operations to rural areas, as adopted in India and Vietnam, would help to expand small-scale agricultural production and small agri-business. Financing for non-farm labour-intensive activities in rural areas through public works projects would create income stabilizers against sudden climatic shocks.

Invest in water: Large investments are required to improve water availability, yield, and distribution for all uses. According to some estimates, the total capital needed to increase the region's desalination capacity alone over the next three decades comes to around $73 billion or an annual average of $2.6 billion. In addition, without investment in irrigation, it will be difficult to increase food production, reduce the financial burden of agricultural imports, and increase food security. These investments should be combined with major reforms in water governance to guarantee equitable and sustainable access to water resources in rural areas.

Emphasize research and development: Knowledge is vital for agriculture and food production but it is an under-provided asset. Research is needed on problems of communities in risk-prone areas, including on the protection of local varieties

This Report interprets food security in terms of sufficiency for all members of society in essential commodities

The region's low self sufficiency rate in staple food is one of its most serious development gaps

from diseases and pests; greater variety in nutrients; the creation of niche markets; and plants that can grow in warmer and drier climates. Currently, the region's total research-and-development (R&D) budget in agriculture and food production is insignificant; the combined R&D budget in this sector for all Arab countries over the last 20 years equals a fraction of the annual R&D budget of a single multinational agro-food company.

Health is a central human goal and a vital enabler of human capabilities, which affects many other aspects of human security. It is therefore of concern that, while Arab countries have secured some appreciable gains in the general status of public health, they still lag behind the industrialized countries. True, increases in life expectancy and reductions in child mortality have been impressive, but other major health indicators in the region have stagnated for several years. There are evident disparities in public health care between countries and within them. Health systems often mismanage their data, making it difficult to form an accurate picture of public health. Moreover, certain practices rooted in culture continue to harm the health of many, chiefly women, and require attitudinal changes in society at large. Malnutrition and stunting rates among children need to be brought down and poor diets that account for both under-nutrition and obesity in all countries must be enriched by ensuring that balanced nutrients are affordable and available to families. This challenge implicates food as well as health policies, and calls for targeted food pricing mechanisms and the expansion of primary health centres and public health education.

Debate is needed about the priorities, scope, and tools for improving health. Arab countries have the material and human resources needed for change, as well as the public will. What is needed is a vision for the future that considers all complex issues, admits to no easy solutions, and proposes gradual and realizable steps. In order for this vision to be developed and realized, several key principles need to be considered:

Focus on people and prevention: In most Arab countries, the public health system needs to be made more proactive, preventive and people-centered.[10] The typical biomedical model found in the region, which is centered on hospital care, curative services and the treatment of diseases rather than people, is too narrow to meet real needs. The system as a whole must engage with non-health sectors in promoting and financing public health through appropriate inter-sectoral mechanisms.

Access for all: Other required changes include steps to reduce the cost of health care for ordinary citizens, whose out-of-pocket expenses on health are increasing. This may entail reprioritizing public spending, especially in the low and middle income countries where government expenditure on health is relatively low. The high-income countries, on the other hand, which spend heavily on health, need to transform these investments into gains by overcoming inefficiencies in their health systems and by increasing the focus on preventive care. Most Arab countries could also do more to legislate and maintain social health insurance schemes and to create incentives for private employers to provide adequate health benefits.

Increasing public knowledge and involvement: Public involvement is crucial in setting the right agenda and enacting it. Occupied with more immediate concerns and threats to human security (food, liberty and liberation), the average citizen of an Arab country rarely thinks of health as a priority. Increasing public knowledge of health issues and increasing awareness of the related rights and duties is essential. An enlightened and empowered

The food security challenge implicates food as well as health policies

Debate is needed about the priorities, scope, and tools for improving health

Box 9-4	Priorities for public health

- Reducing inequalities by putting emphasis on the most disadvantaged groups
- Population based prevention and essential care with proven cost effectiveness
- Strengthening primary health care and integrating fragmented health services
- Strengthening public health institutions
- Supporting community based and community-designed health improvement initiatives

Source: Jabbour 2007.

population and responsive governments can, with international support, develop a local agenda for health action.

A platform with broad representation, especially of citizens, is needed and must be given powers to implement consensus recommendations. For example, Arab countries could launch programmes for healthy cities, neighbourhoods, or villages based on public participation. Such programmes, in which the usual top down approach is replaced by partnerships between governments and citizens, offer instructive guides that can be replicated in other fields of development.

Regional and international coordination and cooperation: Regional coordination of both policies and programmes can promote health and development. Cooperation has contributed to improved health status in the rich Gulf countries, but continued poor health indicators in neighbouring countries are unacceptable and indicate the need for more cooperation. The resources and experiences of the people and non-governmental organizations should also be pooled, not just those of governments. International cooperation agencies also have a key role to play in this regard, in connecting national governments to knowledge and resources to bolster national health plans.

Responding to emerging health threats: Emerging health threats, including HIV/AIDS and chronic communicable diseases, demand to be taken seriously. Yet policy attention to such threats is deficient or absent in a culture of denial where high-risk groups remain neglected and under-served. Medical science has developed effective methods of antiretroviral treatment for those living with HIV/AIDS which, although available free of charge in most Arab countries, will not be effectively utilized without attitudinal shifts in society. Nor is prevention possible without new social and personal behaviours among those affected. Dispelling the climate of secrecy and stigma enveloping HIV/AIDS through compassionate public education programmes is thus an urgent priority that calls for leadership by example from eminent persons, religious leaders and other public figures. As for major communicable diseases, health infrastructure at the national and local level should incorporate protection, prevention and early warning as core functions.

Mitigating external threats and resolving conflicts

The Arab region continues to be labeled as volatile and still suffers occupation by outside forces and internal and cross-border conflicts that deprive people of their inalienable rights and impede human development in affected areas. The Report presented the institutional, structural and material violence inflicted on Arab countries by occupation and foreign military intervention, reviewing the different cases of Iraq, the Occupied Palestinian Territory and Somalia.

The international community has a primary responsibility to assist regional organisations, notably the League of Arab States and the African Union, in overcoming the acute threats to human security posed in such cases. The UN's first and foremost responsibility is to safeguard international peace and security, and it must not forfeit the major role it has to play in that respect in the region. It can make a significant contribution in Iraq in helping the country to make the transition to recovery and reconstruction in tandem with the US exit strategy. The UN also has an evident, if underutilized, capacity to help in negotiating an end to the Arab-Israeli conflict over the Occupied Palestinian Territory. In Somalia, the international community can facilitate the Arab-African joint forces under the UN umbrella as recommended by the National Reconciliation Conference led by Somali elders.

Whatever agenda is agreed on, action to prevent suffering and death caused by conflict must come first. The catastrophic situations in the Occupied Palestinian Territory, Sudan, and Somalia and the looming humanitarian crisis and collapse of infrastructure in Iraq, which follows two decades of senseless wars and sanctions, are priorities that cannot wait for attention. Although international aid is important, local and regional initiatives are indispensable as well in addressing emergencies and can contribute to developing the needed infrastructure.

Health infrastructure should incorporate protection, prevention and early warning as core functions

The international community has a primary responsibility to assist regional organisations in overcoming these acute threats to human security

The continuing destabilization of the region by such threats underlines that human security is closely connected with conventional security at the national, regional, and global levels. Foreign occupation, armed conflict, identity struggles and recourse to violence all undercut the safety and wellbeing of affected peoples in the region. The geopolitical environment often exploits the Arab countries' stress points, and they continue to depend on international powers to help resolve regional conflicts. Yet this reliance is itself a source of deep discontent among Arab populations, turning popular opinion against the powers that are perceived as threats to human security because of the occupation of Arab states' lands and the destruction of citizens' lives.

Diminishing popular resentment of foreign powers will take much more than a counter-campaign to win "hearts and minds". These reactions are the legacy of a historical relationship of power, in which Arab countries have often found themselves vulnerable to outside interference and double standards in matters of political and human rights. This experience remains painful in the collective memory and overcoming it will require demonstrated respect for Arab political, civil and religious rights, rather than mere palliative statements. Such demonstrated sincerity, the signs of which have recently appeared, will materially improve the climate for the effective participation of regional actors in negotiated settlements of conflicts that have long eroded human security in the region.

Conflicts in the Arab countries may not be fully resolved soon. Nevertheless, the level of conflicts and their repercussions can be reduced. The most significant challenge in the Middle East is the Arab-Israeli conflict and its core, the dispute between Israelis and Palestinians. It is a centre of gravity around which the political life of the region has revolved, and it remains of vast practical and symbolic significance. It was not until the early 1990s that the Palestinian problem was taken up. For decades, the conflict had been subsumed under other confrontations at both the global level, during the Cold War, and at the regional level. Without a more comprehensive approach to resolving this conflict and its linkages to other political

and economic issues, it is likely to remain a thorny issue.

Under international law, an occupation that turns into a long-term regime is illegal and unjustified. Occupation can only be admissible as an interim measure that maintains law and order in a territory following an armed conflict and pending a peace settlement. What, then, are the legal consequences of a regime of occupation that has continued for over 41 years? Certainly, none of the obligations of the occupying power as enjoined by international law are reduced as a result of such a prolonged imposition. Rather the reverse, which raises further questions. Can such a long-imposed occupation ever constitute a lawful regime in the OPT? What are the legal consequences for the occupied people and the occupying power?

From a human development perspective, only the end of Israel's occupation of the territories it occupied in 1967 and the restoration of the Palestinian rights, foremost among which is the right to self determination, will bring about that lasting peace the absence of which so far has

The most significant challenge is the Arab-Israeli conflict and its core, the dispute between Israelis and Palestinians

| Box 9-5 | United Nations Secretary General on the vital need for Palestinian statehood and for a just, lasting and comprehensive peace |

"The Middle East region is more complex, more fragile and more dangerous than it has been for a very long time. Deep mistrust continues to constrain Palestinians and Israelis from conducting a meaningful peace process... There are a number of growing causes of instability and uncertainty in this region. But for most in the Arab world, the wound that is still fresh, even after 40 years, is the continued occupation of Arab territory and the denial of legitimate Palestinian claims to statehood

The basis for a solution is clear: an end to the occupation that began in 1967, the creation of an independent and viable Palestinian State, alongside a secure and fully recognized State of Israel, and a just, lasting and comprehensive peace in the region, as called for in the resolutions of the United Nations Security Council."

Source: UN (United Nations) – News and Media Division 2007.

"If anything, the crisis in Gaza underscored the depth of the political failures of the past, and the urgent need to achieve a just, lasting and comprehensive peace for all peoples in the Middle East. Just as we need a unified Palestinian government committed to the peace process, we need an Israeli government that will uphold its commitments. Just as we need the Palestinians to address security issues—as the Palestinian Authority is doing so commendably in the West Bank—we need the Israelis to implement a genuine settlement freeze."

Source: Ban Ki-Moon 2009.

contributed to frustrating human development in the region.[11]

Somalia's seventeen-year-old crisis has become one of the world's worst humanitarian catastrophes. The country remains a challenge for the international community. Since 1991, Somalia has been the archetypal failed state. The deteriorating security situation there continues with an alarmingly high rate of civilian casualties, in particular women and children, who are bearing the brunt of the conflict. Several attempts to create a transitional set-up have failed, and the conflict has also aggravated grievances between different national groups. The scenario is constantly changing, making it difficult to give fully detailed and timely picture of political developments in the country.

The international community appears to be preoccupied with a symptom – the piracy phenomenon – instead of with the core of the crisis, the need for a political settlement. Hopefully, a more constructive

In Somalia, the international community appears to be preoccupied with the symptoms, not the core, of the crisis

approach will become possible now that Ethiopia has withdrawn its forces (as of January 2009) and a new government has taken office (as of February 2009), opening up a new window of opportunity to re-launch a credible political process.

In the last few decades Iraq saw its once burgeoning wealth and gleaming infrastructure crumble. The country's destructive legacies have seriously hindered the security of the Iraqi people, including the war with Iran (1980-1988), the Gulf war (1991), the sanctions regime (1990-2003) and brutal acts of violence under the former regime of Saddam Hussein as well as the US-led occupation of the country that began in 2003.

The cycle of violence that started in 2003 has had devastating humanitarian consequences on Iraqi society and has practically brought development in the country to a halt. The tensions and conflicts in Iraq stemming from military operations by armed groups, individual and organized crime, massive corruption and the violence inflicted by an array of actors have damaged Iraq's social fabric and infrastructure faster than it can be repaired. In addition, and perhaps even more critically, the combined effect of all these factors is the refugee crisis, which has displaced some four million Iraqis, including some two million who have fled the country entirely.

Many analysts and policy makers agree that an opening now exists for post-conflict reconstruction in Iraq, as a result of a number of factors occurring at the same time, these include: the relative improvement of security in Baghdad, the planned withdrawal of US troops, and the results of the local elections in January 2009, which have introduced some hope that the political system could contribute to a stabilization of the country as a whole. National elections at the end of 2009 will be even more important. They are a potential bellwether for nationwide political trends, including the role of religion, the endurance of ethnic and sectarian identities, and the deepening conflict over decentralization.

However, even with these relatively positive developments, the country's future remains uncertain. The national elections at the end of 2009 will be important in themselves, but they will also set the stage

---

Box 9-6	Arab Peace Initiative at the Arab Summit in Beirut, 2002

The Council of the League of Arab States:
1. Requests Israel to reconsider its policies and declare that a just peace is its strategic option as well.
2. Further calls upon Israel to affirm:
   a. Full Israeli withdrawal from all the territories occupied since 1967, including the Syrian Golan Heights to the lines of June 4, 1967 as well as the remaining occupied Lebanese territories in the south of Lebanon.
   b. Achievement of a just solution to the Palestinian Refugee problem to be agreed upon in accordance with UN General Assembly Resolution 194.
   c. The acceptance of the establishment of a Sovereign Independent Palestinian State on the Palestinian territories occupied since the 4th of June 1967 in the West Bank and Gaza strip, with East Jerusalem as its capital.
3. Consequently, the Arab Countries affirm they will:
   a. Consider the Arab-Israeli conflict ended, and enter into a peace agreement with Israel, and provide security for all the states of the region.
   b. Establish normal relations with Israel in the context of this comprehensive peace.
4. Assure the rejection of all forms of Palestinian repatriation which conflict with the special circumstances of the Arab host countries.
5. Call upon the Government of Israel and all Israelis to accept this initiative in order to safeguard the prospects for peace and stop the further shedding of blood, enabling the Arab countries and Israel to live in peace and good neighbourliness and provide future generations with security, stability, and prosperity.

Source: LAS 2002.

for Iraq's most pressing challenge: creating a new national compact that ensues stability beyond a U.S. withdrawal. In the absence of the overarching external power that has hitherto dominated the political process, the country's major political actors will be forced to decide how the workings of government should be organized and shared among them, how matters relating to disputed territories should be resolved, and how state revenues from oil and other sources should be allocated. These goals are all achievable in Iraq, but a successful outcome will depend on the consolidation of a political framework for national reconciliation and reconstruction. It will also be affected by factors beyond the control of Iraqi society, such as the manner in which the withdrawal of US troops is organized and the influence of regional powers.

In all societies emerging from conflict, reconciliation efforts are the glue that holds the post-conflict reconstruction process together. Reconciliation must

An opening now exists for post-conflict reconstruction in Iraq

---

Box 9-7 | **MOHAMED EL BARADEI* – The quest for peace in the Middle East**

The Arab-Israeli conflict, at its most basic level, comes down to two passionate peoples claiming the same piece of land. These claims are rooted in religious belief and differing views of history. The sense of entitlement is fervent on both sides. For the Jewish people, reclaiming their 'Promised Land' symbolizes a positive end to centuries of pogroms that culminated in the Holocaust. The Palestinians, on the other hand, cannot conceive why the 'Jewish Question' had to be settled at their expense, and why, after living there for one or two millennia, their land had to be divided into two states.

The state of insecurity

Israel lives with a constant sense of insecurity, in a neighbourhood in which it is largely boycotted and isolated. In less than 60 years, there have been four wars, two intifadas, and many smaller conflicts involving the loss of innocent lives. Only two countries—Egypt and Jordan—formally recognize and have peace agreements with Israel. The peace that has existed for most of that time has more or less been a 'Cold Peace'—a 'formal' peace only minimally supported by interaction between people. And the wisdom of that peace is often called into question by critical voices in the two countries, as well as in the Arab world at large, in the face of the continued Israeli occupation of the Palestinian Territories. Meanwhile, many of the Palestinian refugees have for decades lived in squalor—unable to own land, for example, or to obtain proper travel documents—conditions that have added to their humiliation.

Today, the Arabs continue to show little readiness to accept Israel as long as there is no resolution to the Palestinian issue. Israel, on the other hand, continues to consolidate its occupation in the face of its perceived existential threat and the absence of peace in the region.

If the recent history of the Middle East teaches us nothing else, it should teach us that these conflicts cannot be solved through military force. Every type of violence has been tried, from occupation by force and outright military confrontation, to oppression, terrorism and targeted assassination—without a single instance that brought either party closer to peace or security. Each act of violence in the region only begets more violence and added insecurity.

The solution will not lie in reconstructing history. And it will not lie in redressing all past injustice. If we are to solve the central conflict of the Middle East, we must begin by looking forward, not backward, by being ready to reconcile and recognize mutual rights, and above all by finding in our hearts the ability to forgive.

One thing is clear: the status quo is not acceptable. The threat of other regional states acquiring nuclear weapons or other weapons of mass destruction will continue to be a grave international concern. The rise of extremist groups originating in the Middle East—and the ease with which they recruit in the region—will continue to be high on the list of international insecurities. The dependency of many countries on Middle East oil and natural gas will continue to add a dimension of global economic risk to any conflict. And when events in the region give rise to perceived religious and cultural divisions between the Muslim world and the West, the repercussions will continue to be felt everywhere.

Reasons to hope

In spite of this rather gloomy state of affairs, I believe there is a glimmer of hope. Lost in the middle of all this conflict and violence are two major psychological breakthroughs.

The first is the readiness of the Arab countries, expressed at the level of the Arab Summits, to have full normal relations with Israel, provided that Israel would withdraw to the June 1967 borders, ensure a just solution for Palestinian refugees and recognize the establishment of a Palestinian State. This is a far cry from the Arab Summit decision of 1967 in Khartoum, which formulated its policy towards Israel as "no peace, no recognition and no negotiation".

The second is the recognition by Israel of the right of the Palestinians to have their own independent state. This is also a far cry from Israel's previous position, which for many years questioned the right of the Palestinians to independence or even their separate identity.

Achieving security in the Middle East will naturally require more than a solution to the Israeli–Palestinian issue. Building stability in Iraq and Lebanon, normalizing relations with Iran, and addressing pressing issues of development, governance and modernity throughout the region are only a few of the substantial challenges that must be dealt with.

* Director General of the International Atomic Energy Agency (IAEA)

Source: El-Baradei 2006.

be pursued not only at a national level but also on local levels. It must be both political and social at the same time, encompassing a process to resolve issues of collective memory and history, through an organized movement involving people and institutions of civil society. By consolidating a consensual national historiography, national reconciliation can prevent the use of partisan reinterpretations of past events to mobilize sects and groups for political purposes. Such healing initiatives should be encouraged in Somalia and Iraq, as well as in Sudan.

Distressingly, Arab regional organizations have been remarkably weak, showing themselves to be incapable of playing a decisive role in crisis management and conflict resolution. This incapacity is itself partially a product of the fragmentation and tensions that characterize the region. The League of Arab States, which is premised on Arab cultural unity, functions as an arena to establish or exhibit consensus among the Arab states; however, specific conflict management and dispute resolution efforts have been handled by individual actors outside the scope of the League. The establishment of effective regional mechanisms for dealing with crises is as much one of the challenges before Arab countries, as it is a necessary response to the manifold hot spots in the region. So long as that regional capacity, which states would be expected to develop in their own common interest, remains missing, the region's crises will continue to invite external intervention, whether unilateral or within a multilateral framework.

End note

With the enormous challenges facing Arab countries today, it is easy to lose sight of the possibility of change. Nevertheless, Arab countries must find a way to improve their lot. Debate is needed about the priorities, scope, and tools for improving and enhancing development. The objective of this report is to help identify priorities based on the challenges facing the peoples in Arab countries.

The concept of human security constitutes a valid contribution to a world citizenry free from fear and free from want. Approaching human development through the lens of human security has three advantages: it empowers people to make choices; it does not rely on military force and is not imposed on peoples; and it is not achieved for one party or nation at the expense of the human security of others.

For international actors, approaching development in the Arab countries from the perspective of human security, in its true sense, could underpin an important policy shift: it could lead those actors to respond to regional issues not from the narrow perspective of their own strategic concerns, an approach which has largely failed to ensure stable ties with Arab countries, but with the interests, rights and security of the peoples who live in those countries in mind. This new approach would offer an altogether more sustainable basis for productive partnership with the Arab region.

The authors of this Report believe that ending the foreign occupation of Arab lands, forging bonds of equal citizenship among all members of society, and establishing government by rule of law in Arab countries are prerequisites for addressing political, social and personal insecurity in the region. They also accord the greatest importance to Arab cooperation in all dimensions of human security. Such co-operation would rest on a realistic, incremental vision that takes into account the interests of each individual Arab country and that builds upon the interests these countries have in common, starting with the welfare of their peoples.

Projects emanating from this vision could contribute greatly to alleviating environmental stresses, unemployment and poverty, the lack of social protection networks, and food and health security crises. Effective co-operation is also needed to rebuild Arab solidarity within the larger international system where unity of purpose and greater integration could tip the scales in favour of the region's interests. The responsibility for devising realistic projects in these domains falls upon the supervisory institutions for collective Arab action, notably the League of Arab States, the Council for Arab Economic Unity, the Arab Organization for Agricultural Development, the Arab Office for Drug Affairs, the Arab Labour Organization, the Arab Organization for Human Rights, and other such entities.

The establishment of effective regional mechanisms for dealing with crises is necessary

Effective co-operation is needed to rebuild Arab solidarity within the larger international system

At the country level, this report urges a move away from development strategies that stress economic growth as their prime goal and towards pro-poor strategies that address economic growth, employment generation and poverty reduction as inter-related priorities. Such strategies would be consistent with a march toward achieving Millennium Development Goals, and would take as their primary intellectual source of inspiration the concept of human development in its richest definition, which includes the value of freedom.

Will the Arab states, on which many hopes remain pinned, rise to these aspirations? Will their emerging civil societies develop the capacity to play their part?

In most Arab countries, the public has become restive in the grip of authority fashioned in a bygone age, and the state's hold on power grows more fragile each year. At the same time, public confidence in the nascent institutions of civil society has not yet solidified into complete trust. Rather, the tendency of many Arabs is to place their trust in institutions rooted in primordial loyalties, notably kinship, clanism, and religion. As formidable as these additional challenges to the state and civil society are, overcoming them successfully is an essential condition for strengthening human security in the Arab countries.

Endnotes

[1] For details on the main challenges confronting the implementation of IWRM principles in Arab countries and on respective recommendations for addressing them, see: Arab Water Council 2008.

[2] For additional details see "The Arab Ministerial Declaration on Climate Change." LAS 2007.

[3] AFED 2008a.

[4] LAS 2004.

[5] "The Arab Human Development Report 2004: Towards Freedom in the Arab World", dealt with the issue of state performance on human rights and elaborated policy recommendations aiming at enhancing human freedom. The main recommendations essentially revolved around: Enhancing the legal and institutional foundations that underpin freedom, Adherence to international human rights law, Binding the ruling authority to the rule of law, Guaranteeing freedoms and rights at the heart of the constitution, Strengthening civil and political rights in law, Guaranteeing the independence of the judiciary, Abolishing the state of emergency, and Guaranteeing personal freedoms. UNDP 2005.

[6] Sayigh. 2007.

[7] Bibliotheca Alexandrina 2004.

[8] Hamzaoui 2009 (in Arabic).

[9] UNDP 2006a.

[10] Jabbour 2007.

[11] In relation to the Palestinian right to self-determination, the International Court of Justice, in its Advisory Opinion on the Legal Consequences of the Construction of a Wall in the Occupied Palestinian Territory, issued in The Hague on 9 July 2004, stated the following:

"The International Court of Justice finds that the construction of the (separation) wall severely impedes the exercise by the Palestinian people of its right to self-determination and is therefore a breach of Israel's obligation to respect that right.

The Court also notes that the principle of self-determination of peoples has been enshrined in the United Nations Charter and reaffirmed by the General Assembly in resolution 2625 (XXV), pursuant to which "Every State has the duty to refrain from any forcible action which deprives peoples referred to [in that resolution] . . . of their right to self-determination." Article 1 common to the International Covenant on Economic, Social and Cultural Rights and the International Covenant on Civil and Political Rights reaffirms the right of all peoples to self-determination, and lays upon the States parties the obligation to promote the realization of that right and to respect it, in conformity with the provisions of the United Nations Charter.

The Court would recall that, in 1971, it emphasized that current developments in "international law in regard to non-self-governing territories, as enshrined in the Charter of the United Nations, made the principle of self-determination applicable to all [such territories]". The Court went on to state that "These developments leave little doubt that the ultimate objective of the sacred trust" referred to in Article 22, paragraph 1, of the Covenant of the League of Nations "was the self-determination . . . of the peoples concerned". The Court has referred to this principle on a number of occasions in its jurisprudence. The Court indeed made it clear that the right of peoples to self-determination is today a right erga omnes."

Bibliography and references

List of background papers

In Arabic

Abdel-Fadil, Mahmoud. 2008. "Al-Masarat al-Badila lil Siyasat al-'Inma'iyya fi Buldan al-Khalij fi Haqabat "ma ba'd al-Naft" (Alternative Paths for Development Policies for the Gulf Countries in the "Post-Oil" Era).

Abdul Hadi, Lubna. 2008. "Intihak Amn al-Insan fi Filastin" (Human Security Violations in Palestine).

Alashaal, Abdallah. 2008. "Al-Irhab min Manthur Qanuni" (Terrorism from a Legal Perspective).

Al-Mashat, Abdul Monem. 2008. "Ab'ad al-Amn al-Insani fil-Watan al-'Arabi" (Dimensions of Human Security in the Arab World).

Al-Nasrawi, Salah. 2008. "Amn Al-Dawla wa Amn al-Insan: Halat al-Iltiqa', Halat al-'Iraq" (State Security and Human Security: Cases of Intersection, the Iraqi Case).

Bishara, Azmi. 2008. "Waqe' Al-Muwatinin al-'Arab fil-'Aradi al-Muhtalla 'Am 1948 / "Al-Filastiniyyun fi 'Isra'il" (The Situation of Arab Citizens in the 1948 Occupied Territories / "Palestinians in Israel").

Chekir, Hafidha. 2008. "Al-'Amn Al-Insani fi Tunis Bayn Moqtadayat al-Dawla wa Huquq al-Muwaten" (Human Security in Tunisia: Between State Requirements and Citizen Rights).

Eid, Mohammed Fathi. 2008. "Al-Amn al-Shakhsi" (Personal Security).

El-Ati, Jalila. 2008. "Aman al-Insan fil-Taharur min al-Ju' wa Naqs al-Ghitha'" (Human Safety in Liberation from Hunger and Food Shortages).

El-Nur, Ibrahim. 2008. "Al-Sudan: Min al-Hurub al-Tahina 'ila al-Salam al-Hash" (Sudan: From Grinding Wars to Fragile Peace).

El-Quosy, Dia El-Din. 2008. Al-Tahdidat al-Bi'iyya al-lati Yata'arad Laha Wadi al-Nil wa Tu'adi 'ila al-Tasahur" (Environmental Threats Facing the Nile Valley and Leading to Desertification).

El-Sabae, Lafteya. 2008. "Al-Mumarasat al-Thaqafiya al-Dara bi Sohat al-Mar'a fil-Watan al-'Arabi" (Cultural Practices Harmful to Women's Health in the Arab World).

Farahat, Mohamed Nour. 2008. "Hudud al-Himaya al-Qanuniyya lil-Fard fil-Nuthum al-'Arabiyya" (The Limits of the Individual's Legal Protection in the Arab Regimes).

Hanoun, Rasmia. 2008. "Al-Amn wal-Mukhadarat" (Security and Drugs).

Ismail, Saif el-Dien A. 2008. "Al-Amn Al-Insani: Ru'ya Islamiyya Bayn Takaful al-Madakhil wal-Bahth al-Muqarin" (Human Security: Islamic Perspective between Complementary Approaches and Comparative Analysis).

Khanfar, Ayed Radi. 2008. "Al-Tanawu' al-Bi'i fil-Watan al-'Arabi" (Biodiversity in the Arab World).

Lootah, Maryam Sultan. 2008. "Amn al-Mar'a al-'Arabiyya wa Huquqaha Bayn al-Khususiyya wal-Tadwil" (Arab Women's Security and Rights between Specificity and Internationalization).

Moalla, Khadija and Ihab El-Kharrat. 2008. "Al-AIDS fil-Bilad Al-'Arabiyya: Ab'ad al-Khatar al-Muhtamal wal Furas li-Tafadih" (AIDS in the Arab Countries: Dimensions of Potential Risk and Avoidance Opportunities).

Morcos, Samir. 2008. "Amn Al-Insan min Wejhat Nathar al-Masihiyya al-Sharqiyya" (Human Security from the Perspective of Eastern Christianity).

Mossaad, Nevine. 2008. "Tanawu' al-Hawiyat fil-Watan al-'Arabi" (Diversity of Identities in the Arab World).

Nufal, Ahmed Said. 2008. "Al-'Irhab Ab'adoh wa Tahadiyatoh 'ala al-'Arab" (Terrorism: Dimensions and Challenges for Arabs).

Shaban, Abd El-Hussein. 2008. "Al-'Iraq wa 'Ishkaliyat al-Dawla wal-Hawiyya wal-Muwatana (Iraq and Issues of State, Identity and Citizenship).

Wardam, Batir. 2008. "Al-Talawuth al-Bi'i wal-Amn al-Inasani fil-'Alam al-'Arabi" (Environmental Pollution and Human Security in the Arab World).

Zaidan, Thamer. 2008. "Athar Al-'Awlama 'ala Al-'Alam Al-'Arabi" (The Impact of Globalization on the Arab World).

In English and French

Awad, Ibrahim. 2008. "Migration and Human Security in the Arab Region."

El-Laithy, Heba. 2008. "Poverty in Arab Countries."

Ghazi, Ali. 2008. "Problématique de la Désertification et des Ressources en Eau dans les Pays du Maghreb."

Gomaa, Mohammed. 2008. "Humanitarian Intervention: Legality and Morality Defied."

Hanafi, Sari. 2008. "Refugees in the Arab Region."

Jabbour, Samer and Iman Nuwayhid. 2008. "Health and Human Security in the Arab World."

Salah, Idil. 2008. "Human Security in Somalia: Challenges and Opportunities."

Salem, Paul. 2008. "The Lebanese Formula: Strengths and Weaknesses."

Textual references

In English

Abdel Samad, Ziad and Diana Zeidan. 2007. "Social Security in the Arab Region: The Challenging Concept and the Hard Reality." Paper prepared for the Social Watch annual report 2007. [http://www.socialwatch.org/en/informesTematicos/113.html]. June 2008.

Abdel Samad, Ziad. 2004. "The Linkages Between International, National and Human Security." The Big Issues: Reports by commitment. Social Watch. [http://www.socialwatch.org/en/informesTematicos/76.html]. June 2008.

Abdullatif, Ahmed Ali. 2006. "Hospital care in WHO Eastern Mediterranean Region: an agenda for change." International Hospital Perspectives: Eastern Mediterranean. International Hospital Federation Reference Book 2005/2006. [http://www.ihf-fih.org/pdf/Abdullatif.pdf]. April 2008.

Abu Zayd, Karen. 2008. "Exile, Exclusion and Isolation: the Palestine Refugee Experience." Speech, To Mark World Refugee Day. UNRWA (United Nations Relief and Works Agency for Palestine Refugees in the Near East), 20 June 2008, Gaza. [http://domino.un.org/unispal.nsf/2ee9468747556b2d85256cf60060d2a6/9ab8f1cef06addeb8525746e00469db8!OpenDocument]. June 2008.

AFED (Arab Forum for Environment and Development). 2008a. "Conference Recommendations." Arab Forum for Environment and Development First Annual Conference. 26-27 October 2008, Manama. [http://www.afedonline.org/en/inner.aspx?contentID=348]. December 2008.

———. 2008b. *Arab Environment: Future Challenges.* (Tolba, Mostafa, and Najib W. Saab eds.). Chemaly & Chemaly, Beirut. [http://www.afedonline.org/afedreport/Full%20English%20Report.pdf]. June 2008.

Ahmed, W. et al. 1981. "Female Infant in Egypt: Mortality and Child Care." *Population Sciences*, 1981, (2):25-39.

Amnesty International. 2006. "Israel and the Occupied Territories: Road to Nowhere." 1 December 2006. [http://www.amnesty.org/ar/library/asset/MDE15/093/2006/d2608334-a4ad-11dc-bac9-0158df32ab50/mde150932006ar.pdf]. January 2008.

———. 2007a. "Hundreds Killed in Gaza Strip Violence", 24 October, 2007. [www.amnesty.org/en/news-and-updates/reports/hundreds-killed-gaza-strip-violence]. January 2008.

———. 2007b. "Somalia: Prisoners of Conscience/incommunicado detention/fear of ill-treatment." 19 February 2007. [http://asiapacific.amnesty.org/library/index/ENGAFR520032007]. January 2008.

Akkaya, Sebnem, Norbert Fiess, Bartlomiej Kaminski, and Gael Raballand. 2008. "Economics of Policy-Induced Fragmentation: The Costs of Closure Regime to West Bank and Gaza." Working Paper Series No.50. January 2008. The World Bank, Middle East and North Africa.

Al-Haq. 2005. "Palestinian Education under Israeli Occupation." Paper presented at the Conference on International Law in the Shadow of Israeli Occupation. 12 April 2005. Stockholm, Sweden.

Ali Abdel-Gadir, Ali and Khalid Abu-Ismail. 2009. *Development Challenges for the Arab Region: A Human Development Approach.* UNDP (United Nations Development Programme) and LAS (League of Arab States).

Ali Abdel-Gadir, Ali. 2008. "Rural Poverty in the Arab Countries: A Selective Review." Unpublished Manuscript. Kuwait.

Al-Jawadi, Asma, and Abdul-Rahman Shatha. 2007. "Prevalence of childhood and early adolescence mental disorders among children attending Primary Health Care centers in Mosul, Iraq." A cross-sectional study. BMC Public Health.

Al-Khalidi, Ashraf, Sophia Hoffmann and Victor Tanner. 2007. "Refugees in the Syrian Arab Republic: A Field Based Snapshot." Occasional Paper. June 2007. The Brookings Institution-University of Bern project on Internal Displacement.

Al-Khatib, Isam and Rula Abu Safia. 2003. "Solid Waste Management in Emergency: A Case Study from Ramallah and Al-Bireh Municipalities." Institute for Community and Public Health, 5 January 2003. Birzeit University, Palestine.

Annan, Kofi. 2000. "UN Secretary-General Kofi Annan Offers 21st Century Action Plan, Urges Nations to Make Globalization Work for People." *We the peoples: Press Releases.* DPI/2106 -March 2000. [http://www.un.org/millennium/sg/report/press1.htm]. May 2008.

Arab Water Council. 2008. "Messages for the Ministerial Process." MENA/Arab Region Contribution to the Political Process of the 5th World Water Forum. [http://www.arabwatercouncil.org/administrator/Modules/SpotLights/MessagesfortheMinisterialProcess.pdf]. May 2008.

Arnove, Anthony and Ali Abounimah. 2003. "Iraq under Seige: The Deadly Impact of Sanctions and War". *South End Press.* Cambridge, Massachusetts.

Bajpai, Kanti. 2000. "Human Security: Concept and Measurement." Occasional Paper 19. Kroc Institute.

Barghouti, Riham and Helen Murray. 2005. "The Struggle for Academic Freedom in Palestine." Paper presented at the Academic Freedom Conference – Problems and Challenges in Arab and African Countries, 10-11 September 2005. Alexandria, Egypt. [http://right2edu.birzeit.edu/downloads/pdfs/AcademicFreedomPaper.pdf]. June 2008.

Baxter, Zach. 2007. "Inventory of Conflict and Environment (ICE)." Case Studies No. 201. Somalia's Coal Industry, May 2007.

Bayat, Asef. 2003. "The "Street" and the Politics of Dissent in the Arab World" *Middle East Report*, No.226. Spring 2003.

———. 2005. *Making Islam Democratic: Social Movements and the Post-Islamist Turn.* Stanford University Press, Stanford.

BBC News. 2007a. US soldier sentenced to 110 years: A US soldier has been sentenced to 110 years in prison for his role in the rape and murder of a 14-year-old Iraqi girl and the killing of her family. 5 August 2007.

———. 2007b. US soldier jailed for Iraq murder: A US soldier has been sentenced to 100 years in prison for the gang rape of a 14-year-old Iraqi girl and the killing of her and her family. 23 February 2007.

———. 2008. US inquiries into Iraqi deaths: The US military has been conducting a number of investigations into incidents of alleged unlawful killings by US forces in Iraq. 5 June 2008.

Beehner, Lionel. 2007. "Economic Doldrums in Iraq." *Council on Foreign Relations.* 20 June 2007.

Beydoun, Azza Charara. 2008. *Femicide in the Lebanese Courts.* KAFA Organization, Beirut.

Bibliotheca Alexandrina. 2004. "Issues of Reform in the Arab World." Final Statement of Arab Reform Issues: Vision and Implementation, 12 -14 March 2004. Alexandria Statement. [http://www.bibalex.org/arf/en/Files/Document.pdf]. June 2008.

Bienen, Henry. 1978. "Military and Society in East Africa: Thinking Again about Praetorianism" *Analyzing the Third World: Essays from Comparative Politics.* (Norman Provizer ed.). Cambridge, Massachusetts.

Braine, Theresa. 2006. "Reaching Mexico's poorest." *Bulletin of the World Health Organization* 84 (8). Mexico. [http://www.who.int/bulletin/volumes/84/8/news10806/en/index.html]. April 2009.

Brown, Nathan, Amr Hamzawy, and Marina Ottaway. 2006. "Islamist Movements and the Democratic Process in the Arab World: Exploring Gray Zones." *Carnegie Endowment for International Peace.* Washington, DC.

B'Tselem The Israeli Information Center for Human Rights in the Occupied Territories. 2008. Online database. Jerusalem. [http://www.btselem.org/English/Statistics/Index.asp]. Accessed December 2008.

———. 2009. Statistics – Fatalities. Jerusalem. Online database. [http://www.btselem.org/English/Statistics/Casualties.asp]. April 2009.

Burnham, Gilbert et al. 2006. *The Human Cost of the War in Iraq: A Mortality Study 2002-2006.* Bloomberg School of Public Health Johns Hopkins University. Baltimore, Maryland. [http://web.mit.edu/cis/human-cost-war-101106.pdf]. April 2008.

Chan, Margaret. 2008. "Global Health Diplomacy: Negotiating Health in the 21st Century." Speech addressed at the Second High-level Symposium on Global Health Diplomacy, 21 October 2008. Geneva, Switzerland.

Clapham, Christopher. 1985. *Third World Politics: An Introduction.* Croom Helm. London and Sydney.

Coalition to Stop the Use of Child Soldiers. 2004. *Child Soldiers: Global Report.* United Kingdom.

———. 2008. *Child Soldiers: Global Report.* United Kingdom.

Dale, Catherine. 2008. "Operation Iraqi Freedom: Strategies, Approaches, Results and Issues for Congress." Congressional

Research Service (CRS), Washington, DC. [http://fas.org/sgp/crs/natsec/RL34387.pdf]. December 2008.

El-Baradei, Mohamed. 2006. "Human Security and the Quest for Peace in the Middle East." Speech to the Eighth Annual Sadat Lecture for Peace, 24 October 2006. University of Maryland, New York. [http://sadat.umd.edu/lecture/lecture/ElBaradei.htm]. January 2008.

El-Laithy, Heba, and Alastair McAuley. 2006. "Integrated Social Policies in Arab Countries," Integration and Enlargement of The European Union: Lessons for the Arab Countries. El Ahwany, N. (ed.). Center for European Studies Cairo University and Conrad Edenhawar.

Elsea, Jennifer, Moshe Schwartz and Kennon H. Nakamura. 2008. "Private Security Contractors in Iraq: Background, Legal Status and Other Issues." Congressional Research Service (CRS), Washington, DC. [http://www.fas.org/sgp/crs/natsec/RL32419.pdf]. August 2008.

FAO (Food and Agriculture Organization of the United Nations). 1999. *The State of Food Insecurity in the World 2000.* Rome, Italy. [ftp://ftp.fao.org/docrep/fao/x8200e/x8200e00.pdf]. April 2009.

———. 2006. *The State of Food Insecurity in the World 2006: Eradicating world hunger – taking stock ten years after the World Food Summit.* Rome, Italy. [ftp://ftp.fao.org/docrep/fao/009/a0750e/a0750e00.pdf]. April 2008.

———. 2009. *Crop Prospects and Food Situation.* [www.fao.org/docrep/010/ah881e/ah881e02.htm]. Accessed April 2009.

Federal Democratic Republic of Ethiopia. 2006. "Ethiopia Does Not Have Any Agenda in Somalia But Avert the Threat Posed to Its Sovereignty by the Extremist Leadership of Union of Islamic Courts." Press Statement, 29 December 2006. Ministry of Foreign Affairs, Addis Ababa. [http://www.mfa.gov.et/Press_Section/publication.php?Main_Page_Number=3305]. February 2008.

———. 2009. "Mission Accomplished: Ethiopian National Defence Forces Start to Pull out of Somalia." Press Statement, 4 January 2009. Ministry of Foreign Affairs, Addis Ababa. [http://www.mfa.gov.et/Press_Section/Press_Statement_3_January_2009.htm]. January 2009.

Ferwana, Abdul-Naser. 2006. "Palestinian Ministry of Prisoners' Affairs." Statistical Report. Al- Zaytouna Centre for Studies and Consultations, 21 November 2006, Beirut. [http://www.alzaytouna.net/data/attachments/2007/report_Palestinian_Prisoners%20Israel.pdf]. February 2009.

Fidler, David. 2003. "Public Health and National Security in the Global Age; Infectious Diseases, Bioterrorism and Realpolitik." *George Washington International Law Review.*

Fischer, Hannah. 2006. "Iraqi Police and Security Forces Casualty Estimates." Congressional Research Service (CRS), Washington, DC. [http://fpc.state.gov/documents/organization/77707.pdf]. December 2008.

Foreign Policy Magazine. 2008. "The Failed States Index 2008." *Foreign Policy.* July/August 2008.

Galtung, Johan. 1964. "Structural Theory of Aggression." *Journal of Peace Research* 1:95-119, 8 (2). Oslo.

Geneva Academy of International Humanitarian Law and Human Rights. Iraq: Non-State armed group, Rule of Law in Armed Conflicts Project. [http://www.adh-geneva.ch/RULAC/non-state_armed_groups.php?id_state=110]. Accessed February 2008.

Global Security Organization. Iraqi Insurgency Groups. [http://www.globalsecurity.org/military/ops/iraq_insurgency.htm]. Accessed February 2008.

Government of the United Kingdom. 2008. Defence Factsheet, Operations in Iraq: Facts and Figures. [http://www.mod.uk/DefenceInternet/FactSheets/OperationsFactsheets/OperationsInIraqFactsandFigures.htm]. Accessed January 2009.

Government of the United States and the Republic of Iraq. 2008. "Withdrawal of United States Forces from Iraq and the Organization of their Activities During their Temporary Presence in Iraq." Agreement, signed on 17 November 2008, Baghdad. [http://www.mnf-iraq.com/images/CGs_Messages/security_agreement.pdf].

Government of the United States. 2003. "President Says Saddam Hussein Must Leave Iraq Within 48 Hours." Speech by President George W. Bush. Office of the Press Secretary, the White House, 17 March 2003. United States Capitol, Washington, DC.

———. 2004. "US Intelligence Community's Prewar Intelligence Assessment on Iraq." Report of the Select Committee on Intelligence. United States Senate. 7 July 2004. Washington, DC. [http://www.gpoaccess.gov/serialset/creports/iraq.html]. June 2008.

———. 2009a. "Global War on Terrorism – Operation Iraqi Freedom." US Department of Defense. [http://siadapp.dmdc.osd.mil/personnel/CASUALTY/OIF-Total-by-month.pdf]. January 2009.

———. 2009b. "Operation Iraqi Freedom Military Deaths, March 19, 2003 through January 3, 2009." US Department of Defense. [http://siadapp.dmdc.osd.mil/personnel/CASUALTY/oif-deaths-total.pdf]. January 2009.

———. 2009c. "Responsibly Ending the War in Iraq." Remarks of the President Obama, Camp Lejeune, North Carolina. Office of the Press Secretary, the White House, 27 February 2009. United States Capitol, Washington, DC. [http://www.whitehouse.gov/the_press_office/Remarks-of-President-Barack-Obama-Responsibly-Ending-the-War-in-Iraq/].

Gutlove, Paula. 2002. "Consultation on Health and Human Security." Summary Report. Cairo Consultation on Health and Human Security, Cairo, 15 – 17 April 2002. Institute for Resource and Security Studies, Cambridge, Massachusetts. [http://www.irss-usa.org/pages/documents/CairoReport02.pdf]. May 2008.

Hafez, Mohamed M. 2003. "Why Muslims Rebel: Repression and Resistance in the Islamic World." *Lynne Reinner Press*, Boulder.

Hamdan, Fouad. 2007. "Arab States Ignore Climate Change." *Executive Magazine.* April 2007. [http://www.klima-der-gerechtigkeit.de/wp-content/fouad-hamdan-arab-states-ignoreclimate-change-english.pdf]. May 2008.

Heydemann, Steven (ed.). 2004. *Networks of Privilege in the Middle East: The Politics of Economic Reform Revisited.* Houndmilles Palgrave Macmillan, Basingstoke and New York.

Hoyek, Danielle, Rafif Rida, Sidawi and Amir Abou Mrad. 2005. *Murders of Women in Lebanon: Crimes of Honour between Reality and the Law,* in *"Honour: Crimes, Paradigms, and Violence Against Women".* (Welchman, Lynn and Sara Hossain, eds.). ZedBooks Ltd.

HRW (Human Rights Watch). 2007. *Darfur 2007: Chaos by Design – Peacekeeping Challenges for AMIS and UNAMID.* Vol.19, No.15(A). 19 September 2007. [http://www.hrw.org/sites/default/files/reports/sudan0907webwcover.pdf]. June 2008.

———. 2008a. *So Much to Fear - War Crimes and the Devastation of Somalia.* December 2008. Geneva.

———. 2008b. *The Quality of Justice Failings of Iraq's Central Criminal Court.* United States of America. [http://www.hrw.org/sites/default/files/reports/iraq1208webwcover.pdf]. June 2008.

———. 2008c. Five Years On: No Justice for Sexual Violence in Darfur. Summary & Conclusion, April 2008. [http://www.hrw.org/en/node/62269/section/2]. January 2009.

Human Security Report Project. 2008. Iraq conflict has killed a million Iraqis: survey. [http://www.humansecuritygateway.info/showRecord.php?RecordId=27096]. April 2009.

ICG (International Court of Justice). 2004. "Advisory Opinion on the Legal Consequences of the Construction of a Wall in the Occupied Palestinian Territory." 9 July 2004. The Hague.

ICRC (International Committee of the Red Cross). 2007. *Annual Report 2007.* Middle East and North Africa.

ILO (International Labour Organization). 2007. *Jobs for Iraq: An Employment and Decent Work Strategy.* (Amjad, Rashid and Julian Havers, eds.) Regional Office for the Arab States. International Labour Office. Beirut. [http://www.ilo.org/public/english/employment/crisis/download/iraqjobs.pdf]. June 2008.

———. 2008a. "Fighting Human Trafficking: The Forced Labour Dimensions." Background Paper prepared for the Vienna Forum on Human Trafficking. Vienna. [http://www.ilo.org/sapfl/Events/ILOevents/lang--en/WCMS_090236/index.htm]. February 2008.

———. 2008b. "Report of the Director General...The Situation of Workers of the Occupied Arab Territories." International Labour Conference, 97th Session 2008. June 2008. Geneva.

Independent Commission for Human Rights. 2006. "Status of Palestinian Citizens' Rights during 2006." Twelfth Annual Report. Independent Commission for Human Rights.

Inglehart, Ronald et al. 2008. *World Values Surveys, 1981-1984, 1990-1993 and 1995-1997.* European Values Survey group and World Values Survey group. [http://www.icpsr.umich.edu/DDI/samples/02790.pdf]. April 2008.

Internal Displacement Monitoring Centre. 2008. *Internal Displacement – Global Overview of Trends and Developments in 2007.* Norwegian

Refugee Council, Imprimerie Lenzi, Geneva. [http://www.internal-displacement.org/8025708F004BE3B1/(httpInfoFiles)/BD8316FAB5984142C125742E0033180B/$file/IDMC_Internal_Displacement_Global_Overview_2007.pdf]. April 2008.

International Knowledge Network of Women in Politics. 2008. "King announced withdrawal of reservations on CEDAW," submitted by *i know politics*. 11 December 2008. [http://www.iknowpolitics.org/en/node/8141]. January 2009.

Iqbal, Zaryab. 2006. "Health and Human Security: The Public Health Impact of Violent Conflict." *International Studies Quarterly*, 50 (3). September 2006.

Iraq Body Count 2003-2009. Online Database. [http://www.iraqbodycount.org/]. Accessed June 2008.

Iraq Coalition Casualty Count. Online Database. [www.icasualties.org]. Accessed 24 March 2008.

Iraq Family Health Survey Study Group. 2006. "Violence-Related Mortality in Iraq from 2002 to 2006" in *The New England Journal of Medicine*. [http://content.nejm.org/cgi/reprint/358/5/484.pdf]. January 2008.

Islam, Yan and Anis Chowdhury. 2006. *Macroeconomic developments, labour market performance and poverty reduction: the case of the Arab states in the Middle East and North Africa*. UNDP (United Nations Development Programme), New York.

IUCN (International Union for Conservation of Nature). 2006. "Country Environmental Profile for Somalia." Prepared for the European Commission.

Jabbour, Samer. 2007. "Health and Development in the Arab World: Which Way Forward?" *British Medical Journal*, 25 June 2007.

Jha, Prabhat and Frank Chaloupka (eds.). 2000. *Tobacco Control in Developing Countries*. Oxford University Press, Oxford.

Jolly, Richard and Deepayan Basu Ray. 2006. "The Human Security Framework and National Human Development Reports: A Review of Experiences and Current Debates." Occasional Paper 5. UNDP (United Nations Development Programme), National Human Development Report Unit, May 2006. Institute of Development Studies, Sussex. [http://hdr.undp.org/en/media/human_security_gn.pdf]. May 2008.

Kabbani, Nader and Yassin Wehelie. 2004. "Measuring Hunger and Food Insecurity in Yemen." Working Paper Series. Economic Research Forum, Cairo.

Karyabwite, Diana Rizzolio. 2000. *Water Sharing in the Nile River Valley*. Project GNV011: Using GIS/Remote Sensing for the Sustainable use of Natural Resources, UNEP/DEWA/GRID, January-March 1999, January-June 2000. Geneva. [http://www.grid.unep.ch/activities/sustainable/nile/nilereport.pdf]. December 2008.

Kawthar. 2008. "Nujood Ali wins "Woman of the Year" award," *Mideast Youth*, 12 November 2008. [http://www.mideastyouth.com/2008/11/12/nujood-ali-wins-woman-of-the-year-award/]. January 2009.

Kelle, Alexander. 2007. "The Securitization of International Public Health, Implications for Global Health Governance and the Biological Weapons Prohibition Regime." Global Governance: A Review of Multilateralism and International Organizations, Vol. 13.

Khouri, Rami. 2009. "Arabia's troubling trends," in *International Herald Tribune*, 1 January 2009. [http://www.iht.com/bin/printfriendly.php?id=19029348]. January 2009.

Korany, Bahgat. 2005a. "Human Security: From a Respectable Slogan to Comparative World Application." Paper prepared for the 1st United Nations International Study Group on Human Security. Johannesburg, July 2005.

———. 2005b. "Measuring Human Security: Is a Global Index Possible?" Paper prepared for the 2nd UN International Study Group on Human Security. New York, November 2005.

LAS (League of Arab States). 2002. Arab Peace Initiative Adopted at the Annual Arab League Summit, Beirut.

———. 2004. "Tunis Declaration." Summit Conference of the Arab League Council in its 16th ordinary session. May 22-23, 2004. Tunisia.

———. 2007. "The Arab Ministerial Declaration on Climate Change." 19th session of the Council of Arab Ministers Responsible for the Environment at the Headquarters of the League of Arab States, December 5 and 6, 2007, Cairo.

Marshall, Thomas. 1977. *Class, Citizenship and Social Development*. University of Chicago Press. Chicago.

Maxwell, Kenneth. 2002. "Brazil: Lula's Prospect." *New York Review of Books* 49 (19). [http://www.nybooks.com/articles/article-preview?article_id=15876]. April 2009.

McManimon, Shannon. 1999. "Use of Children as Soldiers." *Foreign Policy in Focus*, 4 (27). November 1999.

Middleton, Roger. 2008. Piracy in Somalia, Threatening Global Trade, Feeding Local Wars, Chatham House. Briefing Paper, Africa Programme. October 2008.

Nasr, Salim. 2001. "Issues of Social Protection in the Arab Region – A Four-Country Overview." *Cooperation South*, No. 2. [tcdc1.undp.org/CoopSouth/2001_2/31-48.pdf]. November 2008.

New York Times. 2009. "Fresh Start in the Middle East." Editorial, 5 March 2009. [http://www.nytimes.com/2009/03/06/opinion/06fri2.html].

OHCHR (United Nations Office of the High Commissioner for Human Rights). 2008. "UN Expert on the Situation of Human Rights in the Sudan Concludes Visit." Media centre. 10 July 2008. [http://www.unhchr.ch/huricane/huricane.nsf/0/DBBEAE5C1553065AC1257483002C88F4?opendocument]. August 2008.

Oxfam. 2007. "Rising to the Humanitarian Challenge in Iraq." Briefing Paper. July 2007.[http://www.oxfam.org.uk/resources/policy/conflict_disasters/downloads/bp105_iraq.pdf]. May 2008.

PCBS (Palestinian Central Bureau of Statistics). 2001. Distribution of Dumping Sites by Estimation of Solid Waste Quantity Coming Daily to the Dumping Site and Governorate in the Palestinian Territory, 2001.[http://www.pcbs.gov.ps/Portals/_pcbs/Environment/statist_tab10.aspx]. Accessed July 2008.

———. 2008. Injured Palestinians in Al-Aqsa Uprising (Intifada), by Year and Tool of Injury, 29 September 2000-31 March 2008. [https://www.pcbs.gov.ps/Portals/_pcbs/intifada/98dd344c-21be-4672-a252-c6890e201d58.htm]. Accessed July 2008.

Platts. *OPEC Guide*. [www.platts.com]. Accessed 11 June 2008.

Rouidi-Fahimi, Farzaneh and Mary Mederios Kent. 2007. "Challenges and Opportunities – the Population of the Middle East and North Africa" *Population Reference Bureau*, Population Bulletin 62(2). [http://www.prb.org/pdf07/62.2MENA.pdf]. January 2009.

Sager, Abdulaziz. 2007. "The Private Sector in the Arab World – Road Map towards Reform" in *Arab Reform Initiative*, 10 December 2007. [http://arab-reform.net/IMG/pdf/ARB19_Gulf_Sager_ENG.pdf]. April 2009.

Saiman, Magida. 2003. The Arab Woman: A Threatening Body, a Captive Being. London.

Save the Children. 2007. *State of the World's Mothers 2007: Saving Lives of Children Under Five*. Save The Children, May 2007. [http://www.savethechildren.org/publications/mothers/2007/SOWM-2007-final.pdf]. February 2008.

Sayigh, Yezid. 2007. "Security Sector Reform in the Arab Region, Challenges to Developing an Indigenous Agenda." *Arab Reform Initiative*. Thematic Papers n° 2. December 2007. [http://www.arab-reform.net/IMG/pdf/Thematic_Study_SSR_Yezid_Sayigh.pdf]. April 2009.

Schweidler, Jillian. 2003. "More than a Mob: The Dynamics of Political Demonstrations in Jordan." *Middle East Report, No.226*. Spring 2003.

Sester, Brad and Rachel Ziemba. 2009. "GCC Sovereign Funds, Reversal of Fortune." Council on Foreign Relations, Working Paper. New York. [http://www.cfr.org/content/publications/attachments/CGS_WorkingPaper_5.pdf]. January 2009.

SEDAC (Socioeconomic Data and Applications Centre). 2005. Environmental Sustainability Index. [http://sedac.ciesin.columbia.edu]. Accessed June 2008.

Sibai, Armenian and Alam. 1991. "Wartime determinants of arterio graphically confirmed coronary artery disease in Beirut." *American Journal of Epidemiology*. 15 January 1991.

Sobal, J. and Stunkard, A.J. 1989. Socioeconomic status and obesity: a review of the literature. *Psychological Bulletin*, American Psychological Association.

Stern, Nicholas. 2006. "The Economics of Climate Change." *The Stern Review*. Cambridge University Press, Cambridge and New York. [http://www.hm-treasury.gov.uk/stern_review_report.htm]. December 2008.

Tabutin and Schoumaker. 2005. "The demography of the Arab world and the Middle East from the 1950s to the 2000s - A survey of changes and a statistical assessment." *Population* 60, 2005/5-6.

The Emirates Centre for Strategic Studies and Research. 2004. *Islamic Movements: Impact on Political Stability in the Arab World.* I.B. Tauris, London.

The Human Security Center. 2005. *The Human Security Report: War and Peace in the 21st Century- Part II.* University of British Colombia, Canada.

The Pew Global Project Attitudes. 2007. *47-Nation Pew Global Attitudes Survey.* Pew Research Centre. 4 October 2007. Washington, DC. [http://pewglobal.org/reports/pdf/258.pdf]. June 2008.

Transparency International. 2008. The Most and Least Corrupt Nations. [http://www.infoplease.com/world/statistics/2008-transparency-international-corruption-perceptions.html]. Accessed March 2009.

UN (United Nations). 1945. *Charter of the United Nations.* Chapter 1, article 2, provision 4. [http://www.un.org/aboutun/charter/chapter1.shtml]. May 2008.

———. **1994a.** *Convention to Combat Desertification in Those Countries Experiencing Serious Drought and/or Desertification, Particularly in Africa,* Part I, Introduction, Article 1(a). [http://www.unccd.int/convention/text/convention.php?annexNo=-1#art1].

———. **1994.** "Declaration on the Elimination of Violence against Women." A/RES/48/104. UN General Assembly, Forty-eighth session, Agenda item 11. 23 February 1994. [http://www.achpr.org/english/Special%20Mechanisms/Women/UN%20Decl_violence%20against%20women.pdf]. January 2008.

———. **2005.** "Report of the International Commission of Inquiry on Darfur to the United Nations Secretary-General". Pursuant to Security Council Resolution 1564 of 18 September 2004. 25 January 2005. Geneva. [http://www.un.org/news/dh/sudan/com_inq_darfur.pdf]. January 2009.

———. **2006.** "Violence against Women, its Causes and Consequences: Communications to and from Governments." Report of the Special Rapporteur , Yakin Ertürk. E/CN.4/2006/61/Add.1. Human Rights Council, Sixty-second session. Item 12 (a) of the provisional agenda. 27 March 2006. [http://www2.ohchr.org/english/bodies/chr/docs/62chr/ecn4-2006-61-Add1.doc]. May 2008.

———. **2007a.** "Children and armed conflict in Somalia." Report of the Secretary-General. S/2007/259. Security Council Resolution. 7 May 2007. [http://www.mineaction.org/downloads/1/s2007259.pdf]. January 2009.

———. **2007b.** "Children and Armed Conflict in Sudan." Report of the Secretary-General. S/2007/520. Security Council Resolution. 29 August 2007. [http://daccessdds.un.org/doc/UNDOC/GEN/N07/492/69/PDF/N0749269.pdf?OpenElement]. January 2009.

———. **2007c.** "Deployment of the African Union-United Nations Hybrid Operation in Darfur." Report of the Secretary-General. S/2007/517. 30 August 2007. [http://daccessdds.un.org/doc/UNDOC/GEN/N07/493/10/PDF/N0749310.pdf?OpenElement]. January 2009.

———. **2007d.** "Final report on the situation of human rights in Darfur prepared by the group of experts mandated by the Human Rights Council in its resolution 4/8, presided by the Special Rapporteur on the situation of human rights in the Sudan and composed of the Special Rapporteur on extrajudicial, summary or arbitrary executions, the Special Representative of the Secretary-General for children and armed conflict, the Special Rapporteur on violence against women, its causes and consequences, the Special Representative of the Secretary-General on the situation of human rights defenders, the Representative of the Secretary-General on the human rights of internally displaced persons and the Special Rapporteur on the question of torture and other cruel, inhuman or degrading treatment or punishment." A/HRC/6/19. Human Rights Council, Sixth session. Agenda item 4. 28 November 2007. [http://www.unhcr.org/refworld/pdfid/475d1d352.pdf]. January 2009.

———. **2008a.** "Children and armed conflict in Somalia." Report of the Secretary-General. S/2008/352. Security Council. 30 May 2008. [http://www.un.org/Docs/sc/sgrep08.htm]. January 2009.

———. **2008b.** "Deployment of the African Union-United Nations Hybrid Operation in Darfur." Report of the Secretary-General. S/2008/558. 18 August 2008. [http://daccessdds.un.org/doc/UNDOC/GEN/N08/463/80/PDF/N0846380.pdf?OpenElement]. December 2008.

———. **2008c.** "Economic and social repercussions of the Israeli occupation on the living conditions of the Palestinian people in the occupied Palestinian territory, including East Jerusalem, and of the Arab population in the occupied Syrian Golan." A/63/74; E/2008/13. General Assembly Sixty-third session. Item 41 of the preliminary list. 6 May 2008. [http://domino.un.org/UNISPAL.NSF/5ba47a5c6cef541b802563e000493b8c/c7ed9f55068f00ee852574 64004a5679!OpenDocument]. January 2009.

———. **2008d.** "Gaza: Silence is not an option". Press release. 9 December 2008. Geneva. [http://www.unhchr.ch/huricane/huricane.nsf/0/183ED1610B2BCB80C125751A002B06B2?opendocument]. February 2009.

———. **2008e.** "Human Rights Situations that require the Council's Attention." Secretary General Resolution. A/HRC/9/NGO/50. Written statement submitted by Amnesty International to the Secretary-General. Ninth session, agenda item 4. 4 September 2008. [http://www.cmi.no/sudan/doc/?id=1206]. December 2008.

———. **2008f.** "Israeli Practices Affecting the Human Rights of the Palestinian People and Other Arabs of the Occupied Territories. Israeli settlements in the Occupied Palestinian Territory, including Jerusalem, and the occupied Syrian Golan." Report of the Secretary-General. A/63/519. Sixty-third session. 5 November 2008.

———. **2008g.** "Security Council Resolution 1820." S/RES/1820 (2008). Adopted by the Security Council at its 5916th meeting, on 19 June 2008. [http://daccessdds.un.org/doc/UNDOC/GEN/N08/391/44/PDF/N0839144.pdf?OpenElement]. December 2008.

———. **2008h.** "Situation of human rights in the Sudan." Resolution 9/17. A/HRC/RES/9/17. 18 September 2008. [http://ap.ohchr.org/documents/E/HRC/resolutions/A_HRC_RES_9_17.pdf]. January 2009.

———. **2008i.** "The situation in Somalia." Report of the Secretary-General. S/2008/466. Security Council Resolution. 16 July 2008.

———. **2008j.** "The situation in Sudan." Report of the Secretary-General. S/2008/266. Security Council resolution. 20 October 2008.

———. **2008k.** "The situation of human rights in the Sudan on the status of implementation of the recommendations compiled by the Group of Experts mandated by the Human Rights Council in resolution 4/8 to the Government of the Sudan for the implementation of Human Rights Council resolution 4/8 pursuant to Human Rights Council resolution 6/34." Report prepared by the Special Rapporteur. A/HRC/9/13/Add.1. Human Rights Council, Ninth Session. Agenda item 4. 2 September 2008. [http://daccessdds.un.org/doc/UNDOC/GEN/G08/154/14/PDF/G0815414.pdf?OpenElement]. January 2009.

———. **2008l.** "The situation of human rights in the Sudan." Report prepared by the Special Rapporteur, Sima Samar. A/HRC/9/13. Human Rights Council, Ninth Session. Agenda item 4. 2 September 2008. [http://daccessdds.un.org/doc/UNDOC/GEN/G08/153/54/PDF/G0815354.pdf?OpenElement]. January 2009.

———. **2008m.** "Violence against Women, its Causes and Consequences: Indicators on Violence against Women and State Response." Report of the Special Rapporteur. A/HRC/7/6. Human Rights Council, Seventh session, Agenda item 3. 29 January 2008.

———. **2008n.** "Violence against women, its causes and consequences, Addendum Communications to and from Governments." Report of the United Nations Special Rapporteur. Promotion and Protection of all Human Rights, Civil, Political, Economic, Social and Cultural, including the Right to Development. A/HRC/7/6/Add.2. 13 February 2008.

———. **2009.** *World Economic Situation and Prospects.* New York. [http://www.un.org/esa/policy/wess/wesp2009files/wesp2009.pdf.] February 2009.

———. **2009a.** *"Reconstructing Gaza and the Peace Process"* by Ban Ki-Moon. New York. [http://www.un.org/sg/articlefull.asp?TID=948Type=Op-Ed]. 2 March 2009.

UN (United Nations)-Department of Economic and Social Affairs (DESA). 2007a. *World Population Prospects: The 2006 Revision Population Database.* Online Database. [http://esa.un.org/unpp]. Accessed December 2008.

———. **2007b.** *World Urbanization Prospects: The 2007 Revision Population Database.* Online Database. [http://esa.un.org/unpp]. Accessed December 2008.

UN (United Nations) – News and Media Division. 2007. "Secretary-General, citing growing causes of Middle East Instability in address to Arab League Summit, Pinpoints vital need for Palestinian Statehood." Secretary General (SG/SM/10926) 28 March 2007. [http:www.un.org/News/Press/docs/2007/sgsm10926.doc.html].

———. **2008.** "Demanding Immediate Ceasefire in Gaza, Secretary-General Urges Avoidance of Civilian Casualties, End to 'Inflammatory Rhetoric'." 29 December 2008. Geneva. [http://www.un.org/News/Press/docs/2008/sgsm12027.doc.htm]. February 2009.

———. **2009a.** "Gaza Humanitarian Situation." 15 January 2009. Press Conference. Geneva. [http://domino.un.org/unispal.nsf/3822b5e3 9951876a85256b6e0058a478/b974aca8e8fe201d85257540004ffe dc!OpenDocument]. January 2009.

———. **2009b.** Regular Press Briefing by the Press Service. 6 January 2009. Geneva. [http://domino.un.org/unispal.nsf/1ce874ab1832a 53e852570bb006dfaf6/0864af6b9ec82e03852575360069b6e6!O penDocument]. February 2009.

UNAIDS (United Nations Program on HIV/AIDS) and WHO (World Health Organization). 2005a. Middle East and North Africa, HIV and AIDS Statistics and Features in 2003 and 2005. December 2005. [http://www.unaids.org/epi/2005/doc/EPlupdate2005_html_en/epi05_11_en.htm]. Accessed February 2009.

———. **2005b.** *HIV and AIDS Statistics and Features, in 2003 and 2005.* AIDS Epidemic Update: Middle East and North Africa. [http://www.unaids.org/epi/2005/doc/EPlupdate2005_html_en/epi05_11_en.htm]. Accessed June 2008.

———. **2006a.** *AIDS Epidemic Update.* Geneva.

———. **2006b.** "Keeping the Promise: An Agenda for Action on Women." The Global Coalition on Women and AIDS. Geneva. [http://data.unaids.org/pub/Booklet/2006/20060530_FS_Keeping_Promise_en.pdf]. June 2008.

———. **2006c.** Progress in Scaling Up Access to HIV Treatment in Low and Middle-Income Countries. June 2006. [http://www.who.int/hiv/toronto2006/FS_Treatment_en.pdf]. January 2009.

———. **2008.** *Report on the Global Aids Epidemic.* Geneva. [http://data.unaids.org/pub/GlobalReport/2008/20080820_gr08_annex1_table_en.xls]. Accessed January 2009.

UNAIDS (United Nations Programme on HIV/AIDS). 2006. Global Facts and Figures. [http://data.unaids.org/pub/GlobalReport/2006/200605-FS_globalfactsfigures_en.pdf]. Accessed January 2009.

UNAMI (United Nations Assistance Mission for Iraq). 2006. *Human Rights in Iraq, No.5 for May and June 2006.* UNAMI, 26 July 2006.

———. **2007.** *Human Rights Report, 1 April - 30 June 2007.* October 2007. [http://www.uniraq.org/documents/UNAMI_Human_Rights_Report_January_June_2008_EN.pdf]. December 2008.

———. **2008.** *Human Rights Report, 1 January - 30 June 2008.* [http://www.uniraq.org/documents/UNAMI_Human_Rights_Report_January_June_2008_EN.pdf]. December 2008.

UN Comtrade database (United Nations Commodity Trade Statistics Database). 2008. Online database. [http://www.comtrade.un.org/db/default.aspx]. Accessed December 2008.

UNCTAD (United Nations Conference on Trade and Development). 2008. Online Statistical Databases, 2006 and 2007. [http://www.unctad.org/Templates/Page.asp?intItemID=1888&lang=1]. Accessed December 2008.

UNDP (United Nations Development Programme) and Article 19 Global Campaign for Free Expression. 2007. *Free Speech in Iraq: Recent Developments.* London, August 2007. [http://www.article19.org/pdfs/publications/iraq-free-speech.pdf]. June 2008.

UNDP (United Nations Development Programme) and Ministry of Planning and Development Cooperation. 2005. Iraq Living Conditions Survey 2004. Volume III: Socio-economic Atlas of Iraq. Baghdad, Iraq. [http://www.fafo.no/ais/middeast/iraq/imira/Tabulation%20reports/english%20atlas.pdf]. April 2009.

UNDP (United Nations Development Programme) and World Bank. 2003. "Socio Economic Survey 2002." Somalia Watching Brief, Report no.1. World Bank, New York.

UNDP (United Nations Development Programme). 1994. *Human Development Report 1994. New Dimensions of Human Security.* Oxford University Press, New York.

———. **2002.** *Arab Human Development Report 2002. Creating Opportunities for Future Generations.* New York.

———. **2005.** *Arab Human Development Report 2004. Towards Freedom in the Arab World.* New York.

———. **2006a.** *Arab Human Development Report 2005: Towards the Rise of Women in the Arab World.* New York.

———. **2006b.** *Human Development Report 2006. Beyond scarcity: power, poverty and the global water crisis.* Palgrave Macmillan, New York.

———. **2007.** *Human Development Report 2007/2008. Fighting Climate Change: Human Solidarity in a Divided World.* Palgrave Macmillan, New York.

UNDP/SURF-AS (United Nations Development Programme / Sub-Regional Resource Facility for Arab States). 2006. *Macroeconomic Policies for Growth, Employment and Poverty Reduction in Yemen.* Beirut.

UNEP (United Nations Environment Programme). 2007. *UNEP in Iraq: Post Conflict Assessment, Clean-up and Reconstruction.*December 2007. Nairobi, Kenya. [http://postconflict.unep.ch/publications/Iraq.pdf]. June 2008.

UNESCO (United Nations Educational, Scientific and Cultural Organization). 2005. "Academic Freedom Conference, Problems and Challenges in Arab and African Countries." UNESCO Forum. 10-11 September 2005. Alexandria, Egypt.

———. **2006.** Water: A Shared Responsibility. The United Nations World Water Development Report 2. February 2006. Barcelona. [http://unesdoc.unesco.org/images/0014/001454/145405E.pdf]. April 2009.

UN-ESCWA (Economic and Social Commission for Western Asia). 2005a. "Integrated Water Resources Management." Executive Summary of ESCWA Briefing Paper No. 12. New York. [http://www.escwa.un.org/divisions/sdpd/wssd/pdf/12.pdf]. June 2008.

———. **2005b.** "Towards Integrated Social Policies in Arab Countries, Framework and Comparative Analysis." 10 November 2008, New York. [http://www.escwa.un.org/sp-readings/Final%20Towards%20Integrated%20Social%20Policy%20in%20Arab%20Region-En.pdf]. June 2008.

———. **2005c.** *The Environment in the Transboundary Context in the ESCWA Region: Situation and Recommendations.* New York. [http://www.escwa.un.org/information/publications/edit/upload/sdpd-05-5.pdf]. June 2008.

———. **2007a.** *The Millennium Development Goals in the Arab Region 2007: A Youth Lens, an Overview.* June 2007. Beirut. [http://www.escwa.un.org/divisions/div_editor/Download.asp?table_name=other&field_name=ID&FileID=951]. December 2008.

———. **2007b.** *Water Development Report 2, State of Water Resources in the ESCWA Region.* 4 December 2007. United Nations, New York. [http://www.escwa.un.org/information/publications/edit/upload/sdpd-07-6-e.pdf]. January 2008.

———. **2008.** "Situation Analysis of Population Ageing in the Arab Countries: The Way Forward Towards Implementation of MIPAA." Technical Paper 2. 6 June 2008. United Nations, New York. [http://www.globalaging.org/elderrights/world/2008/situation.pdf]. June 2008.

UNFPA (United Nations Population Fund). 2009. Arab States Overview. [http://unfpa.org/arabstates/overview.cfm]. Accessed March 2009.

UNHCR (United Nations High Commissioner for Refugees). 2008. "Statistical Online Population Database". Geneva. [http://www.unhcr.org/statistics/45c063a82.html]. Accessed December 2008.

UNHCR (United Nations High Commissioner for Refugees). 2009. *Global Appeal 2008-2009.* [http://www.unhcr.org/home/PUBL/474ac8cbo.pdf].

UNICEF (United Nations Children's Fund) and Innocenti Research Center. 2000. Domestic Violence against Women and Girls. *Innocenti Digest, No. 6.* June 2000. Italy. [http://www.unicef-irc.org/publications/pdf/digest6e.pdf]. June 2008.

UNICEF (United Nations Children's Fund). 2002. *The State of the Arab Child.* UNICEF Regional Office for the Middle East and North Africa. November 2002. [http://www.amr-group.com/documents/Amr-SOAC.pdf]. June 2008.

———. **2007.** "Progress for Children: A World Fit for Children." Statistical review, number 6, December 2007. [http://www.childinfo.org/files/progress_for_children_2007.pdf]. June 2008.

———. **2009a.** *Child Protection from Violence, Exploitation and Abuse.* [http://www.unicef.org/protection/index_genitalmutilation.html]. Accessed January 2009.

———. **2009b.** Statistics –Somalia.Online database. [http://www.unicef.org/infobycountry/somalia_statistics.html]. Accessed March 2009.

UNIFEM (United Nations Development Fund for Women). 2003. *Not a Minute More: Ending Violence against Women.* New York.

UNIFEM – Stop Violence Against Women. 2008. "Morocco's King Lifts Reservations to CEDAW," a compilation. 16 December 2008. [http://www.stopvaw.org/Morocco_s_King_Formally_Bans_Gender_Discrimination.html]. January 2009.

UN-OCHA (United Nations Office for the Coordination of Humanitarian Affairs). 2007. The Humanitarian Impact on Palestinians of Israeli Settlements and Other Infrastructure in the West Bank. July 2007.

———. **2008a.** "Israel-OPT: UN says number of West Bank checkpoints on the rise." IRIN humanitarian news and analysis. 28 May 2008. [http://www.irinnews.org/report.aspx?ReportID=78455]. June 2008.

———. **2008b.** *Somalia: Humanitarian Overview,* January 2008. [http://ochaonline.un.org/OchaLinkClick.aspx?link=ocha&docId=1086443]. Accessed **17 June 2008.**

UNODC (United Nations Office on Drugs and Crime). 2005. *Why Fighting Crime Can Assist Development in Africa: Rule of Law and Protection of the Most Vulnerable.* [http://www.iss.co.za/cjm/analysis/unodcmay05.pdf]. May 2005.

UNRWA (United Nations Works and Reliefs Agency). 2008. "Statistics". [http://www.un.org/unrwa/publications/index.html]. Accessed December 2008.

Van Hensbroek, Pieter Boele. 2007. "The Concept of Citizenship in Political Theory - Reflections on Globalised Applications of the Idea." Paper presented at the conference: *Citizen in East Asia,* 14 December 2007. University of Groningen. [http://www.rug.nl/cds/asianNetworks/PaperBoele.pdf]. June 2008.

Verma, Sonia. 2008. "The children who could be seeking divorce" *Times Online.* 30 October 2008. [http://women.timesonline.co.uk/tol/life_and_style/women/article5040749.ece]. January 2009.

Villatoro Saavedra, Pablo. 2007. "Las Transferencias Condicionales en America Latina: Luces y Sombras." Intervención en el Seminario Internacional Evolución y Desafíos de los Programas de Transferencia Condicionadas. UN Economic Commission for Latin America and the Caribbean (ECLAC). 21 November 2007. Brasilia. [http://www.eclac.cl/dds/noticias/paginas/1/30291/CEPAL_PabloVillatoro.ppt.pdf]. February 2009.

Watts, Susan, Sameen Siddiqi, Alaa Shukrullah, Kabir Karim, and Hani Serag. 2007. Social Determinants of Health in Countries in Conflict: The Eastern Mediterranean Perspective. WHO/EMRO. June 2007. [http://www.who.int/social_determinants/links/events/conflicts_and_sdh_emro_revison_06_2007.pdf]. April 2009.

WFP (World Food Programme). 2008a. "The World Food Programme today hailed the French navy for protecting WFP food ships from pirate attacks in Somalia, and thanked Denmark for taking over the operation to ensure critical escorts continue for the next two months." Press Release. 2 February 2008. [http://www.wfp.org/english/?ModuleID=137&Key=2755]. March 2008.

———. **2008b.** *Fighting hunger worldwide.* [http://www.wfp.org/hunger]. Accessed April 2008.

———. **2009.** *Iraq Overview.* [http://www.wfp.org/country_brief/indexcountry.asp?country=368#Overview]. Accessed January 2009.

WHO (World Health Organization). 1997. "Violence against Women In Situations of Armed Conflict and Displacement." July 1997. [www.who.int/gender/violence/v7.pdf]. May 2008.

———. **2002.** Epidemic and Pandemic Alert and Response (EPR), Hepatitis C. [http://www.who.int/csr/disease/hepatitis/Hepc.pdf]. December 2008.

———. **2003.** "Investing in Health of the Poor: Regional Strategy for Sustainable Health Development and Poverty Reduction." Strategy Paper, Fiftieth Session, Agenda item 9. Regional Committee for the Eastern Mediterranean Region. (EM/RC50/INF.DOC.6). 28 July 2003. [http://www.who.int/macrohealth/documents/en/strategypaper_final_july28.pdf]. June 2008.

———. **2004.** "Health systems priorities in the Eastern Mediterranean Region: challenges and strategic directions." Technical Paper, Fifty-first Session, Agenda item 6(b). (EM/RC51/5). Regional Committee for the Eastern Mediterranean Region. September 2004. [http://gis.emro.who.int/HealthSystemObservatory/PDF/TechnicalandDiscussionPapers/Health%20systems%20priorities%20in%20the%20Eastern%20Mediterranean%20Region%20challenges%20and%20strategic%20directions.pdf]. June 2008.

———. **2005a.** "Water pipe tobacco smoking: Health effects, research needs and recommended actions by regulators." Study Group on Tobacco Product Regulation. Geneva.

———. **2005b.** *Towards a National Health Insurance System in Yemen.* November 2005. Sana'a.

———. **2005c.** Health Systems Profiles – Palestine. Regional Office for the Eastern Mediterranean, Regional Health System Observatory website. [http://gis.emro.who.int/HealthSystemObservatory/PDF/Palestine/Health%20status%20and%20demographics.pdf]. March 2009.

———. **2006a.** "Healing Minds: Mental Health." Progress Report 2004-2006. Iraq.

———. **2006b.** The Role of Medical Devices and Equipment in Contemporary Health Care Systems and Services. Regional Office for the Eastern Mediterranean. June 2006, Cairo.

———. **2007.** *World Health Statistics 2007.* France. [http://www.who.int/whosis/whostat2007.pdf]. January 2009.

———. **2008a.** Female genital mutilation: an interagency statement. Geneva, Switzerland. [http://www.unfpa.org/webdav/site/global/shared/documents/publications/2008/eliminating_fgm.pdf]. December 2008.

———. **2008b.** Regional Office for the Eastern Mediterranean, Regional Health System Observatory website. [http://gis.emro.who.int/healthsystemobservatory/main/Forms/main.aspx].

Wolfe, Alan. 1977. *The Crisis of Legitimacy: Political Contradictions of Contemporary Capitalism.* The Free Press & Collier Macmillan Publishers, New York and London.

World Bank. 2004. Four Years - Intifada, Closures and Palestinian Economic Crisis – An Assessment. October 2004. Washington, DC. [http://siteresources.worldbank.org/INTWESTBANKGAZA/Resources/wbgaza-4yrassessment.pdf]. April 2008.

———. **2006.** "Economic Developments and Prospects 2006: Financial Markets in a New Age of Oil." Main Report. Middle East and North Africa Region, Office of the Chief Economist. Washington DC. [http://siteresources.worldbank.org/INTMENA/Resources/MainReport.pdf]. June 2008.

———. **2007a.** Economic Developments and Prospects, Job Creation in an Era of High Growth. Washington, DC. [http://topics.developmentgateway.org/arab/rc/filedownload.do~itemId=1123820]. December 2008.

———. **2007b.** *World Development Indicators.* Washington, DC.

———. **2008a.** Social safety nets [www.worldbank.org/safetynets]. Accessed December 2008.

———. **2008b.** *World Development Indicators.* CD-ROM. Washington, DC.

———. **2009.** "Crisis Hitting Poor Hard in Developing World, World Bank says." Press Release No: 2009/220/EXC. 12 February 2009. Washington, DC. [http://web.worldbank.org/WBSITE/EXTERNAL/NEWS/0,,contentMDK:22067892~pagePK:64257043~piPK:437376~theSitePK:4607,00.html]. February 2009.

In Arabic

African Commission on Human and Peoples' Rights. 2008. *Al-Mithaq al-Ifriqi li-Huquq al-Insan wal-Shu'ub (African (Banjul) Charter on Human and Peoples' Rights).* Adopted 27 June 1981. CAB/LEG/67/3 rev. 5, 21 I.L.M. 58 (1982), entered into force Oct. 21, 1986. [http://www.arablegalportal.org/associations/Images/Convention/G1.pdf]. June 2008.

ALO (Arab Labour Organization). 2008. Online Database. [http://www.alolabor.org/nArabLabor/images/stories/Statistics/socan%20tashghel%202006.xls]. April 2009.

Al-Tufakji, Khalil. 2003. "Al-Jidar al-Fasil Yadumm 20% min al-Diffa al-Gharbiya" (The Separation Wall Annexes 20 Per Cent of the West Bank). *Al-Shaab.* 28 October 2003. Cairo.

AMF (Arab Monetary Fund), AFESD (Arab Fund for Economic and Social Development), LAS (League of Arab States) and OAPEC (Organization of Arab Petroleum Exporting Countries). 2001. "Al-Taqrir al-Arabi al-Iqtisadi al-Muwahad 2001 (Joint Arab Economic Report 2001). Cairo. [http://www.amf.org.ae/amf/website/pages/page.aspx?Type=8&ID=455&forceLanguage=ar]. June 2008.

———. **2006.** *Al-Taqrir al-'Arabi al-Iqtisadi al-Muwahad 2006 (Joint Arab Economic Report 2006).* Cairo. [http://www.amf.org.ae/amf/

website/pages/page.aspx?Type=8&ID=549&forceLanguage=ar].
June 2008.

AOAD (Arab Organization for Agricultural Development). 2003. *Dirassa Hawl Mo'asheerat Rased al-Tasahor fil-Watan al-'Arabi (Study of Desertification Monitoring Indicators in the Arab region).* League of Arab States (LAS), Khartoum, January 2003. [http://www.aoad.org/ftp/desertification.pdf]. June 2008.

AOHR (Arab Organization for Human Rights). 2008. *Huquq al-Insan fil-Watan al-'Arabi (The Status of Human Rights in the Arab World).* Cairo. [http://www.aohr.net/arabic/data/Annual/2008/02.pdf]. March 2008.

Commission on Human Security. 2003. *Amn al-Insan al-'An. (Human Security Now.)* New York. [http://www.humansecurity-chs.org/finalreport/Arabic/arabic_report.pdf]. February 2008.

Fu'ad, Muhammad and Samer Jabbour. 2004. "Mafahim Jadida fil-Fikr al-Suhhi Tata'arad ma'a Masalih al-Kahanut al-Tubbi" (New concepts in thinking about health clash with the interests of the medical establishment). *Al-Nahar Newspaper.* 13 June 2004, Beirut.

Hamzaoui, Amr. 2009. "Dawr Rijal al-A'mal fi Sina'at al-Siyasa fil-'Alam al-'Arabi" (The Role of Businessmen in Policy Making in the Arab World). *Al-Hayat,* 12 February 2009. [http://www.daralhayat.com/opinion/02-2009/Item-20090211-664f6726-c0a8-10ed-0095-ef17f5b65e16/story.html]. February 2009.

HRW (Human Rights Watch). 2008. "Al-Wilayat al-Muttahida: Yanbaghi Ihtiram Huquq al-Atfal al-Muhtajazin fil-'Iraq." (Us: respect Rights of Child Detainees in Iraq – Children in US Custody Held Without Due Process). News Release. 19 May 2008. [http://www.hrw.org/en/news/2008/05/19]. June 2008.

KUNA (Kuwait News Agency). 2009. "Lijnat Huquq al-Insan al-'Arabia Ta'qidu Awwal 'Ijtima' bi Maqarr Jami'at al-Duwal al-'Arabia bil Qahira" (Arab Commission on Human Rights Holds its First Meeting at the Arab League Headquarters in Cairo). 04 May 2009. [http://www.kuna.net.kw/NewsAgenciesPublicSite/ArticleDetails.aspx?id=1995533&language=ar]. 27 May 2009.

LAS (League of Arab States) – The Council of Arab Ministers Responsible for the Environment (CAMRE), The Arab Center for the Studies of Arid Zones and Dry Lands (ACSAD) and UNEP (United Nations Environment Programme). 2004. *Halat al-Tasahhur fil-Watan al-'Arabi: Dirasa Mustahdatha (State of Desertification in the Arab World: updated study)* Damascus. [http://www.unep.org.bh/Publications/Natural%20Resources%20Final/State_of_Desertification_in_the_Arab_World_ar.pdf]. May 2008.

LAS (League of Arab States). 2004. *"Tahdeeth Al-Mithaq al-'Arabi li Huquq al-'Insan" (The Arab Charter of Human Rights).* March 2004. [http://www.arableagueonline.org/las/picture_gallery/covenant4mar2004_.pdf]. April 2008.

———. 2007. "Majliss Jami'at al-Duwal al-'Arabia 'ala Mustawa al-Qumma Qararat al-Dawra al-'adiyya (19)". (Decisions of the 19th Session of the Council of the League of Arab States' meeting at the summit level). 28-29 March 2007. Riyadh – Saudi Arabia. [http://www.arableagueonline.org/las/picture_gallery/decision18-3-2007.pdf]. April 2008.

Ministry of Environmental Affairs. 2000. "Al-Intihakat al-Isra'iliya lil-Bi'a al-Filastiniya." (Israeli Abuses of the Palestinian Environment.) September, 2000.

Moghaizel, Fadi and Abd el Sater. 1996. *Jara'im al-Sharaf fi Lubnan – Dirassa Qanuniya (Honour Killings in Lebanon – A Legal Study).* Joseph and Laure Moghaizel Foundation for Democracy and Human Rights, 1999. Beirut.

The Applied Research Institute. 2005. Al-Bi'a al-Filastinniya fi Yawm al-Bi'a al-'Alamiyya (The Palestinian Environment on World Environment Day). June 2005.

The Arab Republic of Egypt. 2008. *Qanun Raqam 126 li Sanat 2008* (Law number 126 for the year 2008). Amendment to Article IV, article 242, in the official journal, No. 24, 15 June 2008.

The Palestinian Centre for Human Rights. 2005. "Al-Ta'lim al-'Ali fi Filastin: al-Waqi' wa Subul Taghyirih." (Higher Education in Palestine: the Reality and Ways to Change It). Study Series 38. March 2005. Gaza.

UNEP (United Nations Environment Programme) – DEWA (Division of Early Warning and Assessment). 2007. *Al-Kitab al-Sanawi li Tawaqu'at al-Bi'a al-Alamia (Global Environment Outlook Yearbook 2007. An Overview of Our Changing Environment).* Nairobi. [http://

www.unep.org/geo/yearbook/yb2007/PDF/GYB2007_Arabic_Full.pdf]. May 2008.

UN-ESCWA (Economic and Social Commission for Western Asia). 2005. "Nahwa Siyasat 'Ijtima'iya Mutakamila fil-Duwal al-'Arabiyya, Itar wa Tahlil Muqarin" (Towards Integrated Social Policies in Arab Countries, Framework and Comparative Analysis). United Nations, New York. [http://www.escwa.un.org/information/publications/edit/upload/SDD-2005-4-a.pdf]. June 2008.

WHO (World Health Organization). 2000. *Al-Taqrir al-Khass bil Soha fil-'Alam 2000 – Tahsin 'Ada' al-Nothom al-Sohia (Health Systems: Improving Performance – World Health Report 2000).* Geneva. [http://www.who.int/whr/2000/en/whr00_ar.pdf]. December 2008.

———. 2005. "Al-Lawa'eh al-Sohia al-Duwaliya" (International Health Regulations 2005). 2nd Edition, Switzerland. [http://www.who.int/csr/ihr/IHR_2005_ar.pdf]. April 2008.

World Bank. 2008. "Irtifa' As'ar al-Mawad al-Ghitha'ia – Haqiqa Jadida Qasiya" (High Food Prices – A Harsh New Reality). [http://econ.worldbank.org/WBSITE/EXTERNAL/EXTDEC/0,,contentMDK:21665883~pagePK:64165401~piPK:64165026~theSitePK:469372,00.html]. Accessed 12 April 2008.

Kawakibi, Salam. 2004. "Al-'Islah fi-Qita' al-'Amn fil-Duwal al-'Arabiyya" (Reform of the Security Sector in the Arab States). Summary Report. Cairo Meeting on 3-4 March 2004.

Naira Al-Awqati. 2008. "Al-'Iraq 7000 Sana min al-Hadara" (Iraq 7000 Years of Civilization). Background paper prepared for the National Human Development Report 2008. UNDP (United Nations Development Programme) and The Ministry of Planning and Development Cooperation, Iraq.

Statistical references

Figures

Chapter 2: The environment, resource pressures and human security in the Arab countries

Figure	Source
Figure 2-1a: Average annual population growth rates have declined for most Arab countries since the 1980s	**United Nations Population Division. 2008.** World Population Prospects: The 2008 Revision Population Database. Online Database. [http://esa.un.org/unpp]. Accessed March 2009.
Figure 2-1b: But the population build-up continues	**United Nations Population Division. 2008.** World Population Prospects: The 2008 Revision Population Database. Online Database. [http://esa.un.org/unpp]. Accessed March 2009.
Figure 2-2: Average annual urban population growth rates (%) by country, 2000-2005*	**United Nations Population Division. 2006.** World Population Prospects: The 2006 Revision Population Database. Online Database. [http://esa.un.org/unpp]. Accessed March 2009. **United Nations Population Division. 2007.** World Urbanization Prospects: The 2007 Revision Population Database. Online Database. [http://esa.un.org/unup]. Accessed March 2009. *UNDP/AHDR calculations for aggregate figure.
Figure 2-3: Projected Arab population aged 15-24 up to 2050	**United Nations Population Division. 2008.** World Population Prospects: The 2008 Revision Population Database. Online Database. [http://esa.un.org/unpp]. Accessed December 2008.
Figure 2-4: Arab internal freshwater resources are often below scarcity levels and the world average, 2005	**World Bank. 2008.** World Development Indicators 2008. CD-ROM. Washington, DC.
Figure 2-5: Use of withdrawn water in Arab countries (%) by sector, 1999-2006*	**FAO (Food and Agriculture Organization). 2009.** AQUASTAT Database. [http://www.fao.org/nr/water/aquastat/data/query/index.html]. Accessed February 2009. *UNDP/AHDR calculations.
Figure 2-6: Extent of desertification in 9 affected Arab countries (%), 1996	**LAS (League of Arab States) – The Council of Arab Ministers Responsible for the Environment (CAMRE), The Arab Center for the Studies of Arid Zones and Dry Lands (ACSAD) and UNEP (United Nations Environment Programme). 2004.** *Halat al-Tasahhur fil-Watan al-'Arabi: Dirasa Mustahdatha* (State of Desertification in the Arab World: updated study). Damascus. [http://www.unep.org.bh/Publications/Natural%20 Resources%20Final/State_of_Desertification_in_the_Arab_World_ar.pdf]. May 2008.
Box 2-6: Proportion of population with access to improved drinking water sources in urban and rural areas, 1990 and 2004(%)	**UN-ESCWA (Economic and Social Commission for Western Asia). 2007.** The Millennium Development Goals in the Arab Region 2007: A Youth Lens, an Overview. Beirut. [http://www.escwa.un.org/rcg/documentation/12sep08/MDGsArab2007.pdf]. December 2008.
Box 2-6: Arab countries will miss the 2015 target for access to safe drinking water by 27 years	**UNDP (United Nations Development Programme). 2006.** Human Development Report 2006. Beyond scarcity: power, poverty and the global water crisis. Palgrave Macmillan, New York.
Figure 2-7: Percentage of population without access to safe water and sanitation services, 15 Arab countries, 2007	**UNDP (United Nations Development Programme). 2007.** Human Development Report 2007/2008. Fighting Climate Change: Human Solidarity in a Divided World. Palgrave Macmillan, New York.
Figure 2-8: Rising carbon dioxide emissions in Arab countries, 1990 and 2003	**World Bank. 2007.** World Development Indicators 2007. CD-ROM. Washington, DC.
Box 2-7: Number of vehicles per 1000 inhabitants (2002-2004), 16 Arab countries	**AFED (Arab Forum for Environment and Development). 2008.** Arab Environment: Future Challenges. Beirut. [http://www.afedonline.org/afedreport/]. June 2008.

Chapter 3: The Arab State and human security – performance and prospects

Figure	Source
Figure 3-1: Homicide rates (per 100,000 of the population), world regions, 2002	**UNODC (United Nations Office on Drugs and Crime). 2005.** Crime and Development in Africa. [http://www.unodc.org/pdf/African_report.pdf]. May 2005.
Figure 3-2: The Rule of law - the Arab countries compared to other regions, 1998 and 2007	**World Bank. 2008.** World Governance Indicators 2008. Washington, DC. [http://info. worldbank.org/governance/wgi/index.asp].

Chapter 4: The personal insecurity of vulnerable groups

Figure	Source
Figure 4-1: Proportion of women aged 20-24 married by 18 years: 15 Arab countries, 1987-2006	**UNICEF (United Nations Children's Fund). 2007.** The State of the World's Children 2008. New York. [http://www.unicef.org/sowc08/docs/sowc08.pdf]. January 2009.
Figure 4-2 :Location of UNRWA - registered Palestinian refugees in thousands, 2008	**UNRWA (United Nations Reliefs and Works Agency). 2008.** UNRWA in Figures. 2008. [http://www.un.org/unrwa/publications/pdf/uif-june08.pdf]. January 2009.

Chapter 5: Challenges to economic security

Figure	Source
Figure 5-1: Riding a rollercoaster: regional GDP growth based on constant 1990 prices, and growth in nominal oil prices, 1976-2007	**UNSD (United Nations Statistics Division). 2008.** "National Accounts Main Aggregates 2008". New York. [http://unstats.un.org/unsd/snaama/Introduction.asp]. Accessed December 2008. **BP (British Petroleum). 2008.** "Statistical Review of World Energy 2008". London. [http://www.bp.com/productlanding.do?categoryId=6929&contentId=7044622]. Accessed January 2009.
Figure 5-2 a: Distribution of regional GDP: by country group, 2007	**IMF (International Monetary Fund). 2008.** World Economic and Financial Surveys: Regional Economic Outlook: Middle East and Central Asia. October 2008. Washington DC. **World Bank. 2008.** World Development Indicators 2008. Washington, DC. [http://info.worldbank.org/governance/wgi/index.asp].
Figure 5-2 b: Distribution of regional population: by country group, 2007	**IMF (International Monetary Fund). 2008.** World Economic and Financial Surveys: Regional Economic Outlook: Middle East and Central Asia. October 2008. Washington DC. **World Bank. 2008.** World Development Indicators 2008. Washington, DC. [http://info.worldbank.org/governance/wgi/index.asp].
Figure 5-3: Arab countries' exports and GDP growth (average annual change (%) in constant 1990 US$)	**UNSD (United Nations Statistics Division). 2008.** "National Accounts Main Aggregates 2008". New York. [http://unstats.un.org/unsd/snaama/Introduction.asp]. Accessed December 2008.
Figure 5-4: Structure of GDP, by economic sector (A) and type of expenditure (B), 1970-2007 for the region, HICs, MICs, and LICs, respectively	**UNSD (United Nations Statistics Division). 2008.** "National Accounts Main Aggregates 2008". New York. [http://unstats.un.org/unsd/snaama/Introduction.asp]. Accessed December 2008.
Figure 5-5: (A) Change in share of manufacturing to GDP(%), 1970 to 2007, by country; (B) Share of manufacturing in GDP(%), 2007, by country; (C) Share of manufacturing in GDP(%), 1970-2007, by country group; and (D) Share of non-oil productive sectors in GDP(%), 1970, 1990 and 2007, by country group	**UNSD (United Nations Statistics Division). 2008.** "National Accounts Main Aggregates 2008". New York. [http://unstats.un.org/unsd/snaama/Introduction.asp]. Accessed December 2008.
Figure 5-6: (A) Unemployment rate among Arab youth and (B) share of Arab youth in total unemployment (%), in the year 2005/2006	**ALO (Arab Labor Organization). 2008.** Online database (in Arabic). [http://www.alolabor.org/nArabLabor/images/stories/Statistics/tashghel%20statistic%202006.xls]. Accessed December 2008.
Figure 5-7: Percentage of workers in the informal sector (% in non-agricultural employment) by sex, in 5 Arab countries, 1994-2003	**UNDP (United Nations Development Programme). 2007.** Human Development Report 2007/2008. Fighting Climate Change: Human Solidarity in a Divided World. Palgrave Macmillan, New York.
Figure 5-8: The incidence of human poverty in 2006 and its decline, by country (%), since 1996	**UNDP (United Nations Development Programme). 1996.** *Human Development Report 1996.* Economic growth and human development. Oxford University Press, New York. **UNDP (United Nations Development Programme). 1998.** Human Development Report 1998. Consumption for Human Development. Oxford University Press, New York. **UNDP (United Nations Development Programme). 2007.** Human Development Report 2007/2008. Fighting Climate Change: Human Solidarity in a Divided World. Palgrave Macmillan, New York.

Chapter 6: Hunger, nutrition and human security

Figure	Source
Box 6-1: Proportion of population below the minimum level of dietary energy consumption (%)	**UN-ESCWA (Economic and Social Commission for Western Asia). 2007.** The Millennium Development Goals in the Arab Region 2007: A Youth Lens, an Overview. Beirut. [http://www.escwa.un.org/rcg/documentation/12sep08/MDGsArab2007.pdf]. December 2008.
Figure 6-1: Counting the hungry: world regions compared over three periods	**FAO (Food and Agriculture Organization). 2008.** FAOSTAT Database. [http://www.fao.org/faostat/foodsecurity/index_en.htm]. Accessed February 2009.
Figure 6-2: Counting the hungry in 15 Arab countries, 1990-1992 and 2002-2004	**FAO (Food and Agriculture Organization). 2008.** FAOSTAT Database. [http://www.fao.org/faostat/foodsecurity/index_en.htm]. Accessed February 2009.
Figure 6-3: Changes in the prevalence of under-nourishment, 1990-2004	**FAO (Food and Agriculture Organization). 2008.** FAOSTAT Database. [http://www.fao.org/faostat/foodsecurity/index_en.htm]. Accessed February 2009.
Figure 6-4: Prevalence of obesity in Arab countries, Nauru and Japan, by gender and age group 15+, 2005	**WHO (World Health Organization). 2005.** Global Comparable Estimates. Geneva. [http://www.who.int/infobase/comparestart.aspx]. Accessed January 2009.
Figure 6-5: Average daily caloric intake per capita in 11 Arab countries, 1990-1992 and 2002-2004	**FAO (Food and Agriculture Organization). 2008.** FAOSTAT Database. [http://www.fao.org/faostat/foodsecurity/index_en.htm]. Accessed February 2009.
Figure 6-6: Daily per capita gram consumption from different nutrient sources, 1990 and 2004, 11 Arab countries and Greece	**FAO (Food and Agriculture Organization). 2008.** FAOSTAT Database. [http://www.fao.org/faostat/foodsecurity/index_en.htm]. Accessed February 2009.
Figure 6-7: Daily caloric intake and its division by major nutrient groups, 11 Arab countries, 1990-1992 and 2002-2004	**FAO (Food and Agriculture Organization). 2008.** FAOSTAT Database. [http://www.fao.org/faostat/foodsecurity/index_en.htm]. Accessed February 2009.
Figure 6-8: Cereal production, 21 Arab countries, 1990 and 2005	**World Bank. 2008.** World Development Indicators 2008. CD-ROM. Washington, DC.
Figure 6-9: Regional self-sufficiency ratios (SSRs) in major food commodities (%), by type, 1990-2004*	**Arab Organization for Agricultural Development. 2008.** Arab Agricultural Statistics Database. Khartoum. [http://www.aoad.org/aas2/index.htm]. Accessed December 2008. *UNDP/AHDR calculations.
Figure 6-10: Reliance on food imports, 15 Arab countries, 2005	**World Bank. 2008.** World Development Indicators 2008. CD-ROM. Washington, DC.
Figure 6-11: The association of poverty and hunger	**UNDP (United Nations Development Programme). 2007.** Human Development Report 2007/2008. Fighting Climate Change: Human Solidarity in a Divided World. Palgrave Macmillan, New York.
Figure 6-12: Declining value added of agriculture in economic output, 12 Arab countries, 1990 and 2005	**World Bank. 2008.** World Development Indicators 2008. CD-ROM. Washington, DC.

Chapter 7: Approaching health through human security – a road not taken

Figure	Source
Figure 7-1: The regional trend in life expectancy (years), 1960- 2005	**World Bank. 2008.** World Development Indicators 2008. CD-ROM. Washington, DC. *UNDP/AHDR calculations.
Figure 7-2: The regional trend in infant mortality rates (per 1000 live births), 1960-2005	**World Bank. 2008.** World Development Indicators 2008. CD-ROM. Washington, DC. *UNDP/AHDR calculations.
Figure 7-3: Life expectancy at birth, 22 Arab countries, 2005	**UNDP (United Nations Development Programme). 2007.** Human Development Report 2007/2008. Fighting Climate Change: Human Solidarity in a Divided World. Palgrave Macmillan, New York.
Figure 7-4: Maternal mortality ratio (deaths per 100 thousand live births), 21 Arab countries, 2005	**UNDP (United Nations Development Programme). 2007.** Human Development Report 2007/2008. Fighting Climate Change: Human Solidarity in a Divided World. Palgrave Macmillan, New York.
Box 7-2: Maternal mortality ratio, Arab countries (per 100,000 live births)	**UN-ESCWA (Economic and Social Commission for Western Asia). 2007.** The Millennium Development Goals in the Arab Region 2007: A Youth Lens, an Overview. Beirut. [http://www.escwa.un.org/rcg/documentation/12sep08/MDGsArab2007.pdf]. December 2008.
Figure 7-5: Infant mortality rates per 1,000 live births, 19 Arab countries, 2005	**UNDP (United Nations Development Programme). 2007.** Human Development Report 2007/2008. Fighting Climate Change: Human Solidarity in a Divided World. Palgrave Macmillan, New York.
Figure 7-6: Mortality rates of children under five per 1,000 live births, 19 Arab countries, 2005	**UNDP (United Nations Development Programme). 2007.** Human Development Report 2007/2008. Fighting Climate Change: Human Solidarity in a Divided World. Palgrave Macmillan, New York.

Box 7-3: Tuberculosis prevalence rate (per 100,000)	**UN-ESCWA (Economic and Social Commission for Western Asia). 2007.** The Millennium Development Goals in the Arab Region 2007: A Youth Lens, an Overview. Beirut. [http://www.escwa.un.org/rcg/documentation/12sep08/MDGsArab2007.pdf]. December 2008.
Figure 7-7: Health disparities in Arab countries, infant and under-5 mortality rates (per 1,000 births), 2005	**World Bank. 2008.** World Development Indicators 2008. CD-ROM. Washington, DC. *UNDP/AHDR weighted average calculations.
Figure 7-8: Health disparities in the Arab countries, maternal mortality rates (per 100,000 live births), 2005	**World Bank. 2008.** World Development Indicators 2008. CD-ROM. Washington, DC. *UNDP/AHDR weighted average calculations.
Figure 7-9: Burden of communicable, and non-communicable disease and injuries, 21 Arab countries, 2002	**WHO (World Health Organization). 2008.** Statistical Information System Database. Geneva. [http://www.who.int/whosis/en/]. Accessed December 2008.
Figure 7-10: Disparities in health expenditures in Arab countries, 2004	**UNDP (United Nations Development Programme). 2007.** Human Development Report 2007/2008. Fighting Climate Change: Human Solidarity in a Divided World. Palgrave Macmillan, New York.
Figure 7-11: Share of public health expenditure in total government spending (%), 20 Arab countries, 2005	**World Bank. 2008.** World Development Indicators 2008. CD-ROM. Washington, DC.
Figure 7-12: Out-of-pocket health expenditure as share in private health expenditure (%) in 20 Arab countries, 2005	**World Bank. 2008.** World Development Indicators 2008. CD-ROM. Washington, DC.

Chapter 8: Occupation, military intervention and human insecurity

Figure	Source
Figure 8-1: Number of deaths by violence in Iraq per day, 2003-2006, according to three sources	**The New England Journal of Medicine. 2006.** "Violence-Related Mortality in Iraq from 2002 to 2006 - Iraq Family Health Survey Study Group." [http://content.nejm.org/cgi/reprint/358/5/484.pdf]. January 2008.
Figure 8-2: Estimated mortality rates (per 1000) from all causes according to age group and gender, before and after invasion, 2002-2006	**The New England Journal of Medicine. 2006.** "Violence-Related Mortality in Iraq from 2002 to 2006 - Iraq Family Health Survey Study Group." [http://content.nejm.org/cgi/reprint/358/5/484.pdf]. January 2008.
Figure 8-3: Estimated mortality rates from violence in Iraq (per 1,000) – two field surveys, 2003-2006	**The New England Journal of Medicine. 2006.** "Violence-Related Mortality in Iraq from 2002 to 2006 - Iraq Family Health Survey Study Group." [http://content.nejm.org/cgi/reprint/358/5/484.pdf]. January 2008.
Box 8-3: Number of Palestinian children killed in Gaza 1 – 15 Jan 2009 (MoH figures)	**UN-OCHA (United Nations Office for the Coordination of Humanitarian Affairs). 2009.** Protection of Civilians Weekly Report. 9-15 January 2009. [http://www.ochaopt.org/documents/ocha_opt_protection_of_civilians_weekly_2009_01_16_english.pdf].
Box 8-3: Number of Palestinians in Gaza UNRWA shelters 2 Jan – 14 Jan 2009	**UN-OCHA (United Nations Office for the Coordination of Humanitarian Affairs). 2009.** Protection of Civilians Weekly Report. 9-15 January 2009. [http://www.ochaopt.org/documents/ocha_opt_protection_of_civilians_weekly_2009_01_16_english.pdf].
Figure 8-4: Deaths by violence, Occupied Palestinian Territory and Israel, by nationality of victim and assailant, 2000-2008	**B'Tselem The Israeli Information Center for Human Rights in the Occupied Territories. 2008.** Online Database. Jerusalem. [http://www.btselem.org/English/Statistics/Index.asp]. Accessed December 2008.
Figure 8-5: The trend in Iraq's oil production (millions of barrels a day), 2000-2007	**EIA (Energy Information Administration). 2008.** "Official Energy Statistics from the U.S. Government". Washington, DC. [http://www.eia.doe.gov/emeu/cabs/Iraq/Oil.html]. Accessed December 2008.
Figure 8-6: How Israel controls Palestinian roads, November 2004	**World Bank. 2008.** The Economics of Policy-Induced Fragmentation: The Costs of Closure Regime to West Bank and Gaza. Washington, DC. [http://siteresources.worldbank.org/INTMENA/Resources/WP50.pdf].
Figure 8-7: Lockdown in the Occupied Palestinian Territory, 1993-2004	**World Bank. 2008.** The Economics of Policy-Induced Fragmentation: The Costs of Closure Regime to West Bank and Gaza. Washington, DC. [http://siteresources.worldbank.org/INTMENA/Resources/WP50.pdf].
Figure 8-8: Unemployment in the Occupied Palestinian Territory, 1996-2004	**World Bank. 2008.** World Development Indicators 2008. CD-ROM. Washington, DC.
Figure 8-9: Food aid dependence and extreme poverty, West Bank and Gaza, 2007	**ILO (International Labor Organization). 2008.** The Situation of Workers of the Occupied Arab Territories. Geneva. [http://www.ilo.org/wcmsp5/groups/public/---ed_norm/---relconf/documents/meetingdocument/wcms_092729.pdf].
Figure 8-10: Fewer Palestinian children make it to school, 2000-2005	**World Bank. 2008.** edstats Data Query. Washington, D.C. [http://ddp-ext.worldbank.org/ext/DDPQQ/member.do?method=getMembers&userid=1&queryId=189]. Accessed December 2008.

Tables

Chapter 1: Applying the concept of human security in the Arab countries

Table	Source
Table: 1-1: State security versus human security	The Report team.

Chapter 2: The environment, resource pressures and human security in the Arab countries

Table	Source
Table 2-1: Levels of water stress in thirteen Arab countries, 2006	**UN-ESCWA (Economic and Social Commission for Western Asia). 2007.** Water Development Report 2, State of Water Resources in the ESCWA Region. 4 December 2007. United Nations, New York. [http://www.escwa.un.org/information/publications/edit/upload/sdpd-07-6-e.pdf]. January 2008.
Table 2-2: Precipitation in the Arab countries, long term annual average	**UNSD (United Nations Statistics Division). 2008.** Environmental Indicators. Water resources: long term annual average. Last updated April 2007. [http://unstats.un.org/unsd/ENVIRONMENT/waterresources.htm]. Accessed January 2009. *UNDP/AHDR calculations.
Table 2-3: Water pollution levels from organic pollutants in 15 Arab countries and 2 industrialised countries, 1990 and 2003, (in descending order based on 1990 pollution levels)	**World Bank. 2007.** *World Development Indicators 2007.* Washington, D.C.
Table 2-4: Climate change future scenarios – water and agriculture	**UNDP (United Nations Development Programme). 2006.** Human Development Report 2006. Beyond scarcity: power, poverty and the global water crisis. Palgrave Macmillan, New York. **Stern, Nicholas. 2006.** "The Economics of Climate Change." *The Stern Review.* Cambridge University Press, Cambridge and New York. [http://www.hm-treasury.gov.uk/stern_review_report.htm]. December 2008.

Chapter 3: The Arab State and human security – performance and prospects

Table	Source
Table 3-1: Arab countries under a declared state of emergency in 2008	**AOHR (Arab Organization for Human Rights). 2008.** *Huquq al-Insan Fil-watan al-'Arabi* (The Status of Human Rights in the Arab World). Cairo. [http://www.aohr.net/arabic/data/Annual/2008/02.pdf]. March 2008.
Table 3-2: Political prisoners in 5 Arab states, 2005 and 2007	**AOHR (Arab Organization for Human Rights). 2008.** *Huquq al-Insan Fil-watan al-'Arabi* (The Status of Human Rights in the Arab World). Cairo. [http://www.aohr.net/arabic/data/Annual/2008/02.pdf]. March 2008.
Table 3-3: Electoral turnout in eighteen Arab states between 2003 and 2008	**UNDP/RBAS-Programme on Governance in the Arab Region (POGAR). 2008.** Online Database. [http://www.pogar.org/countries/]. **IPU (Inter-Parliamentary Union). 2008.** Governmental Sources. Online Database. [http://www.ipu.org/english/home.htm]. **Egypt State Information Service (SIS). 2008.** Online Database. [http://www.sis.gov.eg/En/]. Algeria: [http://www.ipu.org/parline-e/reports/2003_E.htm]; and [http://www.pogar.org/countries/theme.asp?cid=1&th=3#sub3]. Bahrain: [http://www.ipu.org/parline-e/reports/2371_E.htm]; and [http://www.pogar.org/countries/theme.asp?cid=2&th=3#sub5]. Djibouti: [http://www.ipu.org/parline-e/reports/2089_E.htm]. Egypt: [http://www.ipu.org/parline-e/reports/2097_E.htm]; and [http://www.ipu.org/parline-e/reports/2374_E.htm]; and [http://www.sis.gov.eg/Ar/Politics/PSystem/Election/statistics/040201100000000001.htm]. Iraq: [http://www.ipu.org/parline-e/reports/2151_E.htm]. Jordan: [http://www.ipu.org/parline-e/reports/2163_E.htm]; and [http://jcsr-jordan.org/Registrationforms/633246675648146428.PDF]. Kuwait: [http://www.ipu.org/parline-e/reports/2171_E.htm]; and [http://www.pogar.org/countries/theme.asp?cid=8&th=3#sub4]. Lebanon: [http://www.ipu.org/parline-e/reports/2179_E.htm] Mauritania: [http://www.ipu.org/parline-e/reports/2207_E.htm]; [http://www.ipu.org/parline-e/reports/2208_E.htm]; [http://www.eueommauritania.org/mauritania/MOE%20UE%20Mauritanie_07_rapport%20final_Version_Arabe.pdf]; and [http://www.eueommauritania.org/mauritania/MOE%20UE%20Mauritanie_07_rapport%20final_Version_Arabe.pdf]. Morocco: [http://www.ipu.org/parline-e/reports/2221_E.htm]. Oman: [http://www.ipu.org/parline-e/reports/2378_E.htm].

	Palestine: [http://www.elections.ps/template.aspx?id=288]; and [http://www.elections.ps/atemplate.aspx?id=23]. Syria: [http://www.ipu.org/parline-e/reports/2307_E.htm]; and [http://www.sana.org ; http://www.sana.org/ara/148/2007/08/29/136544.htm]. Tunisia: [http://www.ipu.org/parline-e/reports/2321_E.htm]; and [http://www.alkhadra.com/elections2004/nouvelles/251004-6.htm]; and [http://www.alkhadra.com/municipales2005/n_1_10.html]. Yemen: [http://www.ipu.org/parline-e/reports/2353_E.htm]; and [http://www.carnegieendowment.org/files/Yemen_APS.doc].

Chapter 4: The personal insecurity of vulnerable groups

Table	Source
Table 4-1: Estimated prevalence of female genital mutilation (FGM), 6 Arab countries	**WHO (World Health Organization). 2008.** Interagency statement on Eliminating Female Genital Mutilation. Geneva. [www.unfpa.org/webdav/site/global/shared/documents/publications/2008/eliminating_fgm.pdf]. December 2008.
Table 4-2: Estimated prevalence of assaults on women (Physical violence), 7 Arab countries	**UN-ESCWA (Economic and Social Commission for Western Asia). 2007.** Violence Against Women. Beirut. [http://www.escwa.un.org/divisions/ecw_editor/Download.asp?table_name=other%20&field_name=id%20&FileID=%2061]. **UNFPA (United Nations Population Fund) and Yemeni High Council for Women. 2007.** Wade' al-Mar'a fil Yaman (Situation of Women in Yemen). Yemen. [http://www.yemen-women.org/reports/wmenreport.pdf]. **United Nations. 2008.** Report of the Special Rapporteur on violence against women, its causes and consequences, Yakin Ertürk – Indicators on violence against women and State response. New York. [http://www.unhcr.org/refworld/publisher,UNHRC,,DZA,47ce626c2,0.html]. **UNIFEM (United Nations Development Fund for Women). 2005.** Violence against Women –Study. Syria [http://www.unifem.org/attachments/stories/currents_200606_SyriaVAWstudyKeyFindings.pdf]. **UNFPA (United Nations Population Fund). 2005.** Government, NGOs Cooperate on Issue of Gender Violence. IRIN humanitarian news and analysis. 5 December 2005. [http://www.irinnews.org/report.aspx?reportid=25772] **WHO (World Health Organization); Iraqi Ministry of Planning, Development Cooperation; and the Iraqi Ministry of Health. 2007.** Iraq family Health Survey Report 2006/2007. Iraq. [http://www.emro.who.int/iraq/pdf/ifhs_report_en.pdf]. **UNICEF (United Nations Children's Fund). 2000.** "Domestic violence against women and girls", in *Innocenti Digest* No. 6, June 2000. Innocenti Research Center, Florence, Italy.
Table 4-3: Convention on the Elimination of All Forms of Discrimination against Women (CEDAW) - overview of Arab countries' ratifications, 2009	**United Nations Division for the Advancement of Women.** Convention on the Elimination of all Forms of Discrimination against Women (CEDAW). [http://www.un.org/womenwatch/daw/cedaw/states.htm]. Accessed January 2009.
Table 4-4: Reported honour killings, 5 Arab countries	Jordan: **UN-ESCWA (Economic and Social Commission for Western Asia). 2007.** Violence Against Women. Beirut. [http://www.escwa.un.org/divisions/ecw_editor/Download.asp?table_name=other%20&field_name=id%20&FileID=%2061]. OPT and Lebanon: **Save the Children. 2007.** Gender- Based Sexual violence Against teenage Girls in the Middle East. Beirut. [http://www.scsmena.org/Gender%20Viol%20ag%20Girls%20MENA%20study%202007.pdf]. Iraq: **UNAMI (United Nations Assistance Mission for Iraq). 2007.** Human Rights Report. 1 April – 30 June 2007. [http://www.uniraq.org/FileLib/misc/HR%20Report%20Apr%20Jun%202007%20EN.pdf]. Egypt: **United Nations Division for the Advancement of Women and UNODC (United Nations Office for Drugs and Crime). 2005.** Honour Killings in Egypt. Vienna. [http://www.un.org/womenwatch/daw/egm/vaw-gp-2005/docs/experts/khafagy.honorcrimes.pdf].
Table 4-5: Incidence of reporting trafficking in persons according to the UN Office on Drugs and Crime (UNODC) citation index (alphabetical order)	**UNODC (United Nations Office for Drugs and Crime). 2006.** Trafficking in Persons: Global Patterns. [http://www.unodc.org/pdf/traffickinginpersons_report_2006ver2.pdf]
Table 4-6 : Total UNHCR and UNRWA refugees, by country of origin and residence, 2007	**UNHCR (United Nations High Commissioner for Refugees). 2008.** "Statistical Online Population Database". Geneva. [http://www.unhcr.org/statistics/45c063a82.html]. Accessed December 2008. **UNRWA (United Nations Works and Reliefs Agency). 2008.** "Statistics". [http://www.un.org/unrwa/publications/index.html]. Accessed December 2008.

Table	Source
Table 4-7 : Estimated numbers of internally displaced persons in Arab countries, 2007	**UNHCR (United Nations High Commissioner for Refugees). 2008.** Statistical Online Population Database. Geneva. [http://www.unhcr.org/statistics/45c063a82.html]. Accessed December 2008. **IDMC (Internal Displacement Monitoring Centre). 2008.** Global Statistics. Geneva. [http://www.internal-displacement.org/8025708F004CE90B/(httpPages)/22FB1D4E2B 196DAA802570BB005E787C?OpenDocument&count=1000]. Accessed January 2009.

Chapter 5: Challenges to economic security

Table	Source
Table 5-1: Volatile real GDP growth per capita in the Arab countries, 1961-2006 (coefficient of variation)	**World Bank. 2008.** World Development Indicators 2008. CD-ROM. Washington, DC.
Table 5-2: Value of petroleum exports of oil-producing countries, 2003 and 2006 (US$ million in current prices)	**OPEC (Organization of the Petroleum Exporting Countries). 2007.** Annual Statistical Bulletin. Vienna. [http://www.opec.org/library/Annual%20Statistical%20Bulletin/ interactive/FileZ/Main.htm]. Accessed December 2008.
Table 5-3: Military expenditure in four Arab countries (millions of dollars in constant 2005 prices)	**SIPRI (Stockholm International Peace Research Institute). 2008.** The SIPRI Military Expenditure Database. Stockholm. [http://milexdata.sipri.org/]. Accessed January 2009.
Table 5-4: Incidence of income poverty – world regions compared, 1981-2005 (percentage living below two dollars a day)	**Chen, Shaohua, and Martin Ravallion. 2007.** Absolute poverty measures for the developing world 1981-2004. World Bank. Washington, DC.
Table 5-5: The incidence of (extreme) poverty based on national lower poverty lines (1991-1999 and 1999-2006)	Morocco, Mauritania, Algeria, Tunisia, and Jordan: **World Bank. 2008.** World Development Indicators 2008. CD-ROM. Washington, DC. Egypt: **World Bank. 2007.** A Poverty Assessment Update. Cairo. Lebanon: **UNDP (United Nations Development Programme). 2008.** Poverty, Growth and Income Distribution in Lebanon. Beirut. [http://www.undp-povertycentre.org/pub/ IPCCountryStudy13.pdf]. Syria: **UNDP (United Nations Development Programme). 2005.** Poverty in Syria: 1996 – 2004 - Diagnosis and Pro-Poor Policy Consideration. Damascus. [http://www.arab-hdr.org/ publications/other/undp/hdr/2005/syria-poverty-05e.pdf]. Yemen: **UNDP (United Nations Development Programme). 2007.** Poverty, Growth, Employment, and Income Distribution in Yemen 1998 – 2006. Sana'a. * UNDP/AHDR calculations.
Table 5-6: The incidence of poverty at the national upper poverty line, 9 Arab countries 2000 -2006	**World Bank. 2008.** PovcalNet. Online poverty analysis tool. [http://go.worldbank.org/ YMRH2NT5V0]. Accesed April 2009.
Table 5-7: The rural population in the Arab countries, 2007	**UNDP (United Nations Development Programme). 2007.** Human Development Report 2007/2008. Fighting Climate Change: Human Solidarity in a Divided World. Palgrave Macmillan, New York. *UNDP/AHDR calculations.
Table 5-8: Incidence of human poverty in 18 Arab countries in 2006	**UNDP (United Nations Development Programme). 2007.** Human Development Report 2007/2008. Fighting Climate Change: Human Solidarity in a Divided World. Palgrave Macmillan, New York.

Chapter 6: Hunger, nutrition and human security

Table	Source
Table 6-1: Food relief to conflict zones in the Arab countries, 2000-2008	**WFP (Word Food Programme). 2008.** Online data. Iraq. [http://www.wfp.org/ node/3488]. Accessed December 2009. **WFP (Word Food Programme). 2008.** Online data. Occupied Palestinian Territory. [http://www.wfp.org/countries/occupied-palestinian-territory]. Accessed December 2009. **WFP (Word Food Programme). 2008.** Online data. Somalia. [http://www.wfp.org/ countries/somalia]. Accessed December 2009. **WFP (Word Food Programme). 2008.** Online data. Sudan. [http://www.wfp.org/ countries/sudan]. Accessed December 2009.

| Table 6-2: The effects of hunger on children – Arab countries compared with other regions and country groups | **World Bank. 2007.** *World Development Indicators 2007*. Washington, DC. |
| Box 6-5: Virtual water content of selected products, 2003 | **UNESCO 2006.** Water: A Shared Responsibility. The United Nations World Water Development Report 2. February 2006. Barcelona. [http://unesdoc.unesco.org/images/0014/001454/145405E.pdf]. April 2009. |

Chapter 7: Approaching health through human security – a road not taken

Table	Source
Table 7-1: Estimated number of people living with HIV, 12 Arab countries, 2007	**UNAIDS. 2008.** Report on the global AIDS epidemic. Geneva. [http://data.unaids.org/pub/GlobalReport/2008/20080820_gr08_annex1_table_en.xls]. Accessed January 2009.
Table 7-2: Comparative rates of access to HIV/AIDS treatment in low and middle-income countries, December 2003-June 2006	**UNAIDS (United Nations Program on HIV/AIDS) and WHO (World Health Organization).** Progress in Scaling Up Access to HIV Treatment in Low and Middle-Income Countries. June 2006. [http://www.who.int/hiv/toronto2006/FS_Treatment_en.pdf]. January 2009.

Chapter 8: Occupation, military intervention and human insecurity

Table	Source
Table 8-1: Fatal incidents in the Occupied Palestinian Territory and Israel, 2000-2008	**B'Tselem The Israeli Information Center for Human Rights in the Occupied Territories. 2008.** Online Database. Jerusalem. [http://www.btselem.org/English/Statistics/Index.asp]. Accessed December 2008.
Table 8-2: Total number of detainees across Iraq and detainees held by Multinational Forces, 1 January 2006 - 30 June 2008	**UNAMI (United Nations Assistance Mission for Iraq).** Human Rights Report. • 1 Jan– 28 Feb 2006. [http://www.uniraq.org/documents/HR%20Report%20Jan%20Feb%2006%20EN.PDF]. • 1 Mar –30 Apr 2006. [http://www.uniraq.org/documents/HR%20Report%20Mar%20Apr%2006%20EN.PDF]. • 1 May – 30 Jun 2006. [http://www.uniraq.org/documents/HR%20Report%20May%20Jun%202006%20EN.pdf]. • 1 Jul – 31 Aug 2006. [http://www.uniraq.org/documents/HR%20Report%20July%20August%202006%20EN.pdf]. • 1 Sept – 31 Oct 2006.[http://www.uniraq.org/documents/HR%20Report%20Sep%20Oct%202006%20EN.pdf]. • 1 Nov – 31 Dec 2006. [http://www.uniraq.org/FileLib/misc/HR%20Report%20Nov%20Dec%202006%20EN.pdf]. • 1 Jan – 31Mar 2007. [http://www.uniraq.org/FileLib/misc/HR%20Report%20Jan%20Mar%202007%20EN.pdf]. • 1 Apr – 30 Jun 2007. [http://www.uniraq.org/FileLib/misc/HR%20Report%20Apr%20Jun%202007%20EN.pdf]. • 1 Jan – 30 Jun 2008. [http://www.uniraq.org/documents/UNAMI_Human_Rights_Report_January_June_2008_EN.pdf].
Table 8-3: Number of damaged buildings in the Occupied Palestinian Territory between 2000-2007 by type of damage	**PCBS (Palestinian Central Bureau of Statistics). 2008.** Online database. [http://www.pcbs.gov.ps/Portals/_pcbs/intifada/damage.htm]. Accessed May 2009.

Annex I: Human development indicators in the Arab countries[1]

Monitoring human development: enlarging people's choices...

   1   Human development index
   2   Human development index trends
   3   Human and income poverty: developing countries

. . . to lead a long and healthy life...

   4   Demographic trends
   5   Commitment to health: resources, access and services
   6   Water, sanitation and nutritional status
   7   Inequalities in maternal and child health
   8   Leading global health crises and risks
   9   Survival: progress and setbacks

. . . to acquire knowledge...

  10   Commitment to education: public spending
  11   Literacy and enrolment
  12   Technology: diffusion and creation

. . . to have access to the resources needed for a decent standard of living ...

  13   Economic performance
  14   Inequality in income or expenditure
  15   Structure of trade
  16   Flows of aid, private capital and debt
  17   Priorities in public spending
  18   Unemployment and informal sector work in non-OECD countries

. . . while preserving the environment for future generations...

  19   Energy and the environment
  20   Energy sources
  21   Carbon dioxide emissions and stocks
  22   Status of major international environmental treaties

. . . protecting personal security ...

  23   Refugees and armaments
  24   Crime and justice

. . . and achieving equality for all women and men

  25   Gender-related development index
  26   Gender empowerment measure
  27   Gender inequality in education
  28   Gender inequality in economic activity
  29   Women's political participation

Human and labour rights instruments

  30   Status of major international human rights instruments
  31   Status of fundamental labour rights conventions

Symbols used in the tables
..   Data not available
(.) Greater (or less) than zero but small enough to be rounded off to zero at the displayed number of decimal points
<   Less than
-   Not applicable
T   Total

---

1   For technical details and clarifications, please refer to the Human Development Report 2007/2008.

Acronyms and abbreviations

CIS	Commonwealth of Independent States
CO2	Carbon dioxide
DOTS	Directly Observed Treatment Short courses (method of detection and treatment of tuberculosis)
GDI	Gender-related development index
GDP	Gross domestic product
GEM	Gender empowerment measure
HDI	Human development index
HDR	Human Development Report
HIV/AIDS	Human Immunodeficiency Virus/Acquired Immune Deficiency Syndrome
HPI-1	Human poverty index (for developing countries)
MDG	Millennium Development Goals
Mt	Megatonne (one million tonnes)
ODA	Official development assistance
OECD	Organization for Economic Co-operation and Development
PPP	Purchasing power parity
R&D	Research and development
TPES	Total primary energy supply

Table **01**

Human development index

HDI Rank	Human development index (HDI) value 2005	Life expectancy at birth (years) 2005	Adult literacy rate (% aged 15 and older) 1995-2005	Combined gross enrolment ratio for primary, secondary and tertiary education (%) 2005	GDP per capita (PPP US$) 2005	Life expectancy index	Education index	GDP index	GDP per capita (PPP US$) rank minus HDI rank
HIGH HUMAN DEVELOPMENT									
33 Kuwait	0.891	77.3	93.3	74.9	26,321	0.871	0.871	0.930	-8
35 Qatar	0.875	75.0	89.0	77.7	27,664	0.834	0.852	0.938	-12
39 United Arab Emirates	0.868	78.3	88.7	59.9	25,514	0.889	0.791	0.925	-12
41 Bahrain	0.866	75.2	86.5	86.1	21,482	0.837	0.864	0.896	-8
56 Libyan Arab Jamahiriya	0.818	73.4	84.2	94.1	10,335	0.806	0.875	0.774	4
58 Oman	0.814	75.0	81.4	67.1	15,602	0.833	0.766	0.843	-15
61 Saudi Arabia	0.812	72.2	82.9	76.0	15,711	0.787	0.806	0.844	-19
MEDIUM HUMAN DEVELOPMENT									
86 Jordan	0.773	71.9	91.1	78.1	5,530	0.782	0.868	0.670	11
88 Lebanon	0.772	71.5	..	84.6	5,584	0.775	0.871	0.671	8
91 Tunisia	0.766	73.5	74.3	76.3	8,371	0.808	0.750	0.739	-23
104 Algeria	0.733	71.7	69.9	73.7	7,062	0.778	0.711	0.711	-22
106 Occupied Palestinian Territories	0.731	72.9	92.4	82.4	..	0.799	0.891	0.505	33
108 Syrian Arab Republic	0.724	73.6	80.8	64.8	3,808	0.811	0.755	0.607	7
112 Egypt	0.708	70.7	71.4	76.9	4,337	0.761	0.732	0.629	-1
126 Morocco	0.646	70.4	52.3	58.5	4,555	0.757	0.544	0.637	-18
134 Comoros	0.561	64.1	..	46.4	1,993	0.651	0.533	0.499	10
137 Mauritania	0.550	63.2	51.2	45.6	2,234	0.637	0.493	0.519	-5
147 Sudan	0.526	57.4	60.9	37.3	2,083	0.540	0.531	0.507	-10
149 Djibouti	0.516	53.9	..	25.3	2,178	0.482	0.553	0.514	-15
153 Yemen	0.508	61.5	54.1	55.2	930	0.608	0.545	0.372	16
WITHOUT HDI RANK									
Iraq	..	57.7	74.1	59.6	..	0.545	0.692	..	..
Somalia	..	47.1	..	..	..	0.368	..	..	..
All developing countries	0.691	66.1	76.7	64.1	5,282	0.685	0.725	0.662	..
Least developed countries	0.488	54.5	53.9	48.0	1,499	0.492	0.519	0.452	..
Arab States	0.699	67.5	70.3	65.5	6,716	0.708	0.687	0.702	..
East Asia and the Pacific	0.771	71.7	90.7	69.4	6,604	0.779	0.836	0.699	..
Latin America and the Caribbean	0.803	72.8	90.3	81.2	8,417	0.797	0.873	0.740	..
South Asia	0.611	63.8	59.5	60.3	3,416	0.646	0.598	0.589	..
Sub-Saharan Africa	0.493	49.6	60.3	50.6	1,998	0.410	0.571	0.500	..
Central and Eastern Europe and the CIS	0.808	68.6	99.0	83.5	9,527	0.726	0.938	0.761	..
OECD	0.916	78.3	..	88.6	29,197	0.888	0.912	0.947	..
High-income OECD	0.947	79.4	..	93.5	33,831	0.906	0.961	0.972	..
High human development	0.897	76.2	..	88.4	23,986	0.854	0.922	0.915	..
Medium human development	0.698	67.5	78.0	65.3	4,876	0.709	0.738	0.649	..
Low human development	0.436	48.5	54.4	45.8	1,112	0.391	0.516	0.402	..
High income	0.936	79.2	..	92.3	33,082	0.903	0.937	0.968	..
Middle income	0.776	70.9	89.9	73.3	7,416	0.764	0.843	0.719	..
Low income	0.570	60.0	60.2	56.3	2,531	0.583	0.589	0.539	..
World	0.743	68.1	78.6	67.8	9,543	0.718	0.750	0.761	..

Source: UNDP, HDR 2007/2008, Table 1: 229-232.

* Data for Iraq and Somalia are from the HDRO online database at [http://hdr.undp.org/en/statistics/data].

Human development index trends

HDI Rank		1975	1980	1985	1990	1995	2000	2005
HIGH HUMAN DEVELOPMENT								
33	Kuwait	0.771	0.789	0.794	..	0.826	0.855	0.891
35	Qatar	..	..	..	..	..	..	0.875
39	United Arab Emirates	0.734	0.769	0.790	0.816	0.825	0.837	0.868
41	Bahrain	..	0.747	0.783	0.808	0.834	0.846	0.866
56	Libyan Arab Jamahiriya	..	..	..	..	..	..	0.818
58	Oman	0.487	0.547	0.641	0.697	0.741	0.779	0.814
61	Saudi Arabia	0.611	0.666	0.684	0.717	0.748	0.788	0.812
MEDIUM HUMAN DEVELOPMENT								
86	Jordan	..	0.647	0.669	0.684	0.710	0.751	0.773
88	Lebanon	..	..	..	0.692	0.730	0.748	0.772
91	Tunisia	0.519	0.575	0.626	0.662	0.702	0.741	0.766
104	Algeria	0.511	0.562	0.613	0.652	0.672	0.702	0.733
106	Occupied Palestinian Territories	..	..	..	..	..	..	0.731
108	Syrian Arab Republic	0.547	0.593	0.628	0.646	0.676	0.690	0.724
112	Egypt	0.434	0.482	0.532	0.575	0.613	0.659	0.708
126	Morocco	0.435	0.483	0.519	0.551	0.581	0.613	0.646
134	Comoros	..	0.483	0.500	0.506	0.521	0.540	0.561
137	Mauritania	0.383	0.410	0.435	0.455	0.487	0.509	0.550
147	Sudan	0.354	0.381	0.400	0.429	0.463	0.491	0.526
149	Djibouti	..	..	..	0.476	0.485	0.490	0.516
153	Yemen	..	..	..	0.402	0.439	0.473	0.508
WITHOUT HDI RANK								
	Iraq	..	..	..	..	..	..	0.556
	Somalia	..	..	..	..	..	..	..

Source: UNDP, HDR 2007/2008, Table 2: 234-237.

* Data for Iraq and Somalia are from the HDRO online database at [http://hdr.undp.org/en/statistics/data].

Table **03**

Human and income poverty: developing countries

HDI Rank		Human poverty index (HPI-1)		Probability at birth of not surviving to age 40 (% of cohort) 2000-05	Adult illiteracy rate (% aged 15 and older) 1995-2005	Population not using an improved water source (%) 2004	MDG Children under weight for age (% under age 5) 1996-2005	MDG Population below income poverty line (%)			HPI-1 rank minus income poverty rank
		Rank	Value (%)					$1 a day 1990-2005	$2 a day 1990-2005	National poverty line 1990-2004	
HIGH HUMAN DEVELOPMENT											
33	Kuwait	..	..	2.7	6.7	..	10	..	..	..	..
35	Qatar	13	7.8	3.7	11.0	0	6	..	..	..	..
39	United Arab Emirates	17	8.4	2.1	11.3	0	14	..	..	..	..
41	Bahrain	..	..	3.4	13.5	..	9	..	..	..	..
56	Libyan Arab Jamahiriya	..	..	4.6	15.8	..	5	..	..	..	..
58	Oman	..	..	3.7	18.6	..	18	..	..	..	..
61	Saudi Arabia	..	..	5.7	17.1	..	14	..	..	..	..
MEDIUM HUMAN DEVELOPMENT											
86	Jordan	11	6.9	6.4	8.9	3	4	<2	7.0	14.2	5
88	Lebanon	18	8.5	6.3	..	0	4	..	..	..	..
91	Tunisia	45	17.9	4.6	25.7	7	4	<2	6.6	7.6	27
104	Algeria	51	21.5	7.7	30.1	15	10	<2	15.1	22.6	31
106	Occupied Palestinian Territories	9	6.6	5.2	7.6	8	5	..	..	..	..
108	Syrian Arab Republic	31	13.6	4.6	19.2	7	7	..	..	..	..
112	Egypt	48	20.0	7.5	28.6	2	6	3.1	43.9	16.7	18
126	Morocco	68	33.4	8.2	47.7	19	10	<2	14.3	19	41
134	Comoros	61	31.3	15.3	..	14	25	..	..	..	..
137	Mauritania	87	39.2	14.6	48.8	47	32	25.9	63.1	46.3	12
147	Sudan	69	34.4	26.1	39.1	30	41	..	..	..	..
149	Djibouti	59	28.5	28.6	..	27	27	..	..	..	..
153	Yemen	82	38.0	18.6	45.9	33	46	15.7	45.2	41.8	21
WITHOUT HDI RANK											
	Iraq	..	..	23.8	25.9	19	12	..	..	..	..
	Somalia	..	..	38.9	..	71	26	..	..	..	..

Source: UNDP, HDR 2007/2008, Table 3: 238-240.

* Data for Iraq and Somalia are from the HDRO online database at [http://hdr.undp.org/en/statistics/data].

Demographic trends

HDI Rank	Total population (millions)			Annual population growth rate (%)		Urban population (% of total)			Population under age 15 (% of total)		Population aged 65 and older (% of total)		Total fertility rate (births per woman)	
	1975	2005	2015	1975-2005	2005-2015	1975	2005	2015	2005	2015	2005	2015	1970-1975	2000-2005
HIGH HUMAN DEVELOPMENT														
33 Kuwait	1.0	2.7	3.4	3.3	2.2	89.4	98.3	98.5	23.8	22.5	1.8	3.1	6.9	2.3
35 Qatar	0.2	0.8	1.0	5.1	1.9	88.9	95.4	96.2	21.7	20.6	1.3	2.1	6.8	2.9
39 United Arab Emirates	0.5	4.1	5.3	6.8	2.5	83.6	76.7	77.4	19.8	19.7	1.1	1.6	6.4	2.5
41 Bahrain	0.3	0.7	0.9	3.3	1.7	85.0	96.5	98.2	26.3	22.2	3.1	4.2	5.9	2.5
56 Libyan Arab Jamahiriya	2.5	5.9	7.1	2.9	1.9	57.3	84.8	87.4	30.3	29.4	3.8	4.9	7.6	3
58 Oman	0.9	2.5	3.1	3.4	2.0	34.1	71.5	72.3	33.8	28.6	2.6	3.6	7.2	3.7
61 Saudi Arabia	7.3	23.6	29.3	3.9	2.1	58.3	81.0	83.2	34.5	30.7	2.8	3.3	7.3	3.8
MEDIUM HUMAN DEVELOPMENT														
86 Jordan	1.9	5.5	6.9	3.5	2.2	57.7	82.3	85.3	37.2	32.2	3.2	3.9	7.8	3.5
88 Lebanon	2.7	4.0	4.4	1.3	1.0	67.0	86.6	87.9	28.6	24.6	7.2	7.6	4.8	2.3
91 Tunisia	5.7	10.1	11.2	1.9	1.0	49.9	65.3	69.1	26.0	22.5	6.3	6.7	6.2	2.0
104 Algeria	16.0	32.9	38.1	2.4	1.5	40.3	63.3	69.3	29.6	26.7	4.5	5.0	7.4	2.5
106 Occupied Palestinian Territories	1.3	3.8	5.1	3.7	3.0	59.6	71.6	72.9	45.9	41.9	3.1	3.0	7.7	5.6
108 Syrian Arab Republic	7.5	18.9	23.5	3.1	2.2	45.1	50.6	53.4	36.6	33.0	3.2	3.6	7.5	3.5
112 Egypt	39.2	72.8	86.2	2.1	1.7	43.5	42.8	45.4	33.3	30.7	4.8	5.6	5.9	3.2
126 Morocco	17.3	30.5	34.3	1.9	1.2	37.8	58.7	65.0	30.3	26.8	5.2	5.9	6.9	2.5
134 Comoros	0.3	0.8	1.0	3.1	2.3	21.2	37.0	44.0	42.0	38.5	2.7	3.1	7.1	4.9
137 Mauritania	1.3	3.0	3.8	2.7	2.4	20.6	40.4	43.1	40.3	36.9	3.6	3.6	6.6	4.8
147 Sudan	16.8	36.9	45.6	2.6	2.1	18.9	40.8	49.4	40.7	36.4	3.5	4.1	6.6	4.8
149 Djibouti	0.2	0.8	1.0	4.3	1.7	67.1	86.1	89.6	38.5	33.5	3.0	3.7	7.2	4.5
153 Yemen	7.1	21.1	28.3	3.6	2.9	14.8	27.3	31.9	45.9	42.4	2.3	2.5	8.7	6.0
WITHOUT HDI RANK														
Iraq	12.0	28	34.9	2.8	2.2	61.4	66.9	66.9	41.5	36.6	2.8	3.1	7.2	4.9
Somalia	4.1	8.2	10.9	2.3	2.8	25.5	35.2	40.1	44.1	42.9	2.6	2.7	7.3	6.4
All developing countries	2,972.0 T	5,215.0 T	5,956.6 T	1.9	1.3	26.5	42.7	47.9	30.9	28.0	5.5	6.4	5.4	2.9
Least developed countries	357.6 T	765.7 T	965.2 T	2.5	2.3	14.8	26.7	31.6	41.5	39.3	3.3	3.5	6.6	4.9
Arab States	144.4 T	313.9 T	380.4 T	2.6	1.9	41.8	55.1	58.8	35.2	32.1	3.9	4.4	6.7	3.6
East Asia and the Pacific	1,312.3 T	1,960.6 T	2,111.2 T	1.3	0.7	20.5	42.8	51.1	23.8	20.6	7.1	8.8	5.0	1.9
Latin America and the Caribbean	323.9 T	556.6 T	626.5 T	1.8	1.2	61.1	77.3	80.6	29.8	26.3	6.3	7.7	5.0	2.5
South Asia	835.4 T	1,587.4 T	1,842.2 T	2.1	1.5	21.2	30.2	33.8	33.6	29.5	4.7	5.4	5.5	3.2
Sub-Saharan Africa	314.1 T	722.7 T	913.2 T	2.8	2.3	21.2	34.9	39.6	43.6	41.7	3.1	3.2	6.8	5.5
Central and Eastern Europe and the CIS	366.6 T	405.2 T	398.6 T	0.3	-0.2	57.7	63.2	63.9	18.1	17.4	12.8	12.9	2.5	1.5
OECD	928.0 T	1,172.6 T	1,237.3 T	0.8	0.5	66.9	75.6	78.2	19.4	17.8	13.8	16.1	2.6	1.7
High-income OECD	766.8 T	931.5 T	976.6 T	0.6	0.5	69.3	77.0	79.4	17.6	16.5	15.3	18.0	2.2	1.7
High human development	1,280.6 T	1,658.7 T	1,751.1 T	0.9	0.5	66.4	76.8	79.4	20.2	18.8	12.7	14.5	2.7	1.8
Medium human development	2,514.9 T	4,239.6 T	4,759.8 T	1.7	1.2	23.8	39.3	44.9	29.3	26.0	5.8	6.8	5.3	2.6
Low human development	218.5 T	508.7 T	653.0 T	2.8	2.5	18.6	33.2	38.6	44.9	43.0	2.9	3.0	6.9	6.0
High income	793.3 T	991.5 T	1,047.2 T	0.7	0.5	69.4	77.6	80.0	18.1	17.0	14.8	17.3	2.3	1.7
Middle income	2,054.2 T	3,084.7 T	3,339.7 T	1.4	0.8	34.7	53.9	60.3	25.1	22.5	7.3	8.6	4.6	2.1
Low income	1,218.0 T	2,425.5 T	2,894.7 T	2.3	1.8	20.5	30.0	34.2	36.6	33.3	4.2	4.7	5.9	3.8
World	4,076.1 T	6,514.8 T	7,295.1 T	1.6	1.1	37.2	48.6	52.8	28.3	26.0	7.3	8.3	4.5	2.6

Source: UNDP, HDR 2007/2008, Table 5: 243-246.

* Data for Iraq and Somalia are from the HDRO online database at [http://hdr.undp.org/en/statistics/data].

Table  05

Commitment to health: resources, access and services

| HDI Rank | | Health expenditure | | | One-year-olds fully immunized | | Children with diarrhoea receiving oral rehydration and continued feeding (% under age 5) 1998-2005 | MDG Contraceptive prevalence rate (% of married women aged 15-49) 1997-2005 | MDG Births attended by skilled health personnel (%) 1997-2005 | Physicians (per 100,000 people) 2000-04 |
		Public (% of GDP) 2004	Private (% of GDP) 2004	Per capita (PPP US$) 2004	MDG Against tuberculosis (%) 2005	Against measles (%) 2005				
HIGH HUMAN DEVELOPMENT										
33	Kuwait	2.2	0.6	538	..	99	..	50	98	153
35	Qatar	1.8	0.6	688	99	99	..	43	99	222
39	United Arab Emirates	2.0	0.9	503	98	92	..	28	99	202
41	Bahrain	2.7	1.3	871	70	99	..	62	98	109
56	Libyan Arab Jamahiriya	2.8	1.0	328	99	97	..	45	94	129
58	Oman	2.4	0.6	419	98	98	..	32	95	132
61	Saudi Arabia	2.5	0.8	601	96	96	..	32	91	137
MEDIUM HUMAN DEVELOPMENT										
86	Jordan	4.7	5.1	502	89	95	44	56	100	203
88	Lebanon	3.2	8.4	817	..	96	..	58	89	325
91	Tunisia	2.8	2.8	502	97	96	..	66	90	134
104	Algeria	2.6	1.0	167	98	83	..	57	96	113
106	Occupied Palestinian Territories	7.8	5.2	..	99	99	..	51	97	..
108	Syrian Arab Republic	2.2	2.5	109	99	98	..	48	77	140
112	Egypt	2.2	3.7	258	98	98	29	59	74	54
126	Morocco	1.7	3.4	234	95	97	46	63	63	51
134	Comoros	1.6	1.2	25	90	80	31	26	62	15
137	Mauritania	2.0	0.9	43	87	61	28	8	57	11
147	Sudan	1.5	2.6	54	57	60	38	7	87	22
149	Djibouti	4.4	1.9	87	52	65	..	9	61	18
153	Yemen	1.9	3.1	82	66	76	23	23	27	33
WITHOUT HDI RANK										
	Iraq	4.2	1.1	135	93	90	54	44	72	66
	Somalia	1.2	1.4	..	50	35	..	..	25	4
All developing countries		..	..	..	83	74	..	..	60	..
Least developed countries		..	..	..	82	72	..	..	35	..
Arab States		..	..	..	86	86	..	..	74	..
East Asia and the Pacific		..	..	..	87	84	..	..	87	..
Latin America and the Caribbean		..	..	..	96	92	..	..	87	..
South Asia		..	..	..	79	65	..	..	39	..
Sub-Saharan Africa		..	..	..	76	65	..	..	43	..
Central and Eastern Europe and the CIS		..	..	..	95	97	..	..	97	..
OECD		..	..	..	92	93	..	..	95	..
High-income OECD		..	..	..	86	92	..	..	99	..
High human development		..	..	..	96	95	..	..	97	..
Medium human development		..	..	..	84	75	..	..	63	..
Low human development		..	..	..	71	61	..	..	38	..
High income		..	..	..	87	93	..	..	99	..
Middle income		..	..	..	90	87	..	..	88	..
Low income		..	..	..	77	65	..	..	41	..
World		..	..	..	83	77	..	..	63	..

Source: UNDP, HDR 2007/2008, Table 6: 247-250.

* Data for Iraq and Somalia are from the HDRO online database at [http://hdr.undp.org/en/statistics/data].

Table 06

Water, sanitation and nutritional status

HDI Rank		MDG Population using improved sanitation (%)		MDG Population using an improved water source (%)		MDG Population undernourished (% of total population)		MDG Children under weight for age (% of children under age 5)	Children under height for age (% of children under age 5)	Infants with low birthweight (%)
		1990	2004	1990	2004	1990/92	2002/04	1996-2005	1996-2005	1998-2005
HIGH HUMAN DEVELOPMENT										
33	Kuwait	..	..	..	..	24	5	10	7	7
35	Qatar	100	100	100	100	..	..	6	..	10
39	United Arab Emirates	97	98	100	100	4	<2.5	14	..	15
41	Bahrain	..	..	..	..	..	..	9	..	8
56	Libyan Arab Jamahiriya	97	97	71	..	<2.5	<2.5	5	..	7
58	Oman	83	..	80	..	..	..	18	16	8
61	Saudi Arabia	..	..	90	..	4	4	14	..	11
MEDIUM HUMAN DEVELOPMENT										
86	Jordan	93	93	97	97	4	6	4	12	12
88	Lebanon	..	98	100	100	<2.5	3	4	6	6
91	Tunisia	75	85	81	93	<2.5	<2.5	4	16	7
104	Algeria	88	92	94	85	5	4	10	22	7
106	Occupied Palestinian Territories	..	73	..	92	..	16	5	..	9
108	Syrian Arab Republic	73	90	80	93	5	4	7	24	6
112	Egypt	54	70	94	98	4	4	6	24	12
126	Morocco	56	73	75	81	6	6	10	23	15
134	Comoros	32	33	93	86	47	60	25	47	25
137	Mauritania	31	34	38	53	15	10	32	40	..
147	Sudan	33	34	64	70	31	26	41	48	31
149	Djibouti	79	82	72	73	53	24	27	29	16
153	Yemen	32	43	71	67	34	38	46	60	32
WITHOUT HDI RANK										
	Iraq	81	79	83	81	..	..	12	28	15
	Somalia	..	26	..	29	..	..	26	29	..
All developing countries		33	49	71	79	21	17	..	..	..
Least developed countries		22	37	51	59	38	35	..	..	..
Arab States		61	71	84	86	..	..	..	..	..
East Asia and the Pacific		30	50	72	79	17	12	..	..	..
Latin America and the Caribbean		67	77	83	91	14	10	..	..	..
South Asia		18	37	72	85	25	21	..	..	..
Sub-Saharan Africa		32	37	48	55	36	32	..	..	..
Central and Eastern Europe and the CIS		..	..	93	94	..	..	..	..	..
OECD		94	96	97	99	..	..	..	..	..
High-income OECD		100	100	100	100	..	..	..	..	..
High human development		90	92	96	98	..	..	..	..	..
Medium human development		30	48	73	82	20	16	..	..	..
Low human development		26	34	43	49	36	34	..	..	..
High income		..	..	100	100	..	..	..	..	..
Middle income		46	61	78	84	14	11	..	..	..
Low income		21	38	64	76	28	24	..	..	..
World		49	59	78	83	20	17	..	..	..

Source: UNDP, HDR 2007/2008, Table 7: 251-254.

* Data for Iraq and Somalia are from the HDRO online database at [http://hdr.undp.org/en/statistics/data].

Table 07

Inequalities in maternal and child health

HDI Rank		Survey year	Births attended by skilled health personnel, (%)		One-year-olds fully immunized, (%)		Children under height for age, (% under age 5)		Infant mortality rate (per 1,000 live births)		Under-five mortality rate (per 1,000 live births)	
			Poorest 20%	Richest 20%	Poorest 20%	Richest 20%	Poorest 20%	Richest 20%	Poorest 20%	Richest 20%	Poorest 20%	Richest 20%
HIGH HUMAN DEVELOPMENT												
33	Kuwait	..	..	..	..	..	..	..	..	..	..	..
35	Qatar	..	..	..	..	..	..	..	..	..	..	..
39	United Arab Emirates	..	..	..	..	..	..	..	..	..	..	..
41	Bahrain	..	..	..	..	..	..	..	..	..	..	..
56	Libyan Arab Jamahiriya	..	..	..	..	..	..	..	..	..	..	..
58	Oman	..	..	..	..	..	..	..	..	..	..	..
61	Saudi Arabia	..	..	..	..	..	..	..	..	..	..	..
MEDIUM HUMAN DEVELOPMENT												
86	Jordan	1997	91	99	21	17	14	5	35	23	42	25
88	Lebanon	..	..	..	..	..	..	..	..	..	..	..
91	Tunisia	..	..	..	..	..	..	..	..	..	..	..
104	Algeria	..	..	..	..	..	..	..	..	..	..	..
106	Occupied Palestinian Territories	..	..	..	..	..	..	..	..	..	..	..
108	Syrian Arab Republic	..	..	..	..	..	..	..	..	..	..	..
112	Egypt	2005	51	96	85	91	24	14	59	23	75	25
126	Morocco	2003-04	30	95	81	97	29	10	62	24	78	26
134	Comoros	1996	26	85	40	82	45	23	87	65	129	87
137	Mauritania	2000-01	15	93	16	45	39	23	61	62	98	79
147	Sudan	..	..	..	..	..	..	..	..	..	..	..
149	Djibouti	..	..	..	..	..	..	..	..	..	..	..
153	Yemen	1997	7	50	8	56	58	35	109	60	163	73
WITHOUT HDI RANK												
	Iraq	..	..	..	..	..	..	..	..	..	..	..
	Somalia	..	..	..	..	..	..	..	..	..	..	..

Source: UNDP, HDR 2007/2008, Table 8: 255-256.

* Data for Iraq and Somalia are from the HDRO online database at [http://hdr.undp.org/en/statistics/data].

Leading global health crises and risks

HDI Rank		HIV prevalence (% aged 15-49) 2005	MDG Condom use at last high-risk sex (% aged 15-24)		MDG Antimalarial measures Use of insecticide treated bednets	MDG Fevers treated with antimalarial drugs	MDG Prevalence (per 100,000 people)	MDG Tuberculosis cases Detected under DOTS	MDG Cured under DOTS	Prevalence of smoking (% of adults)	
			Women 1999-2005	Men 1999-2005	(% of children under five) 1999-2005	1999-2005	2005	(%) 2005	(%) 2004	Women 2002-04	Men 2002-04
HIGH HUMAN DEVELOPMENT											
33	Kuwait	[<0.2]	..	..	..	..	28	66	63	..	..
35	Qatar	[<0.2]	..	..	..	..	65	47	78	..	..
39	United Arab Emirates	[<0.2]	..	..	..	..	24	19	70	1	17
41	Bahrain	[<0.2]	..	..	..	..	43	77	82	3	15
56	Libyan Arab Jamahiriya	[<0.2]	..	..	..	..	18	178	64	..	..
58	Oman	[<0.2]	..	..	..	..	11	108	90	..	..
61	Saudi Arabia	[<0.2]	..	..	..	..	58	38	82	8	19
MEDIUM HUMAN DEVELOPMENT											
86	Jordan	[<0.2]	..	..	..	..	6	63	85	8	51
88	Lebanon	0.1 [0.1–0.5]	..	..	..	..	12	74	90	31	42
91	Tunisia	0.1 [0.1–0.3]	..	..	..	..	28	82	90	2	50
104	Algeria	0.1 [<0.2]	..	..	..	..	55	106	91	(.)	32
106	Occupied Palestinian Territories	..	..	..	..	..	36	1	80	..	..
108	Syrian Arab Republic	[<0.2]	..	..	..	..	46	42	86	..	..
112	Egypt	<0.1 [<0.2]	..	..	..	..	32	63	70	18	40
126	Morocco	0.1 [0.1–0.4]	..	..	..	..	73	101	87	(.)	29
134	Comoros	<0.1 [<0.2]	..	..	9	63	89	49	94	..	..
137	Mauritania	0.7 [0.4–2.8]	..	..	2	33	590	28	22	..	..
147	Sudan	1.6 [0.8–2.7]	..	..	0	50	400	35	77	..	..
149	Djibouti	3.1 [0.8–6.9]	..	..	..	..	1,161	42	80	..	..
153	Yemen	[<0.2]	..	..	..	..	136	41	82	..	..
WITHOUT HDI RANK											
	Iraq	[<0.2]	..	..	0	1	76	43	85	..	..
	Somalia	0.9 [0.5–1.6]	..	19	0	..	286	86	91	..	..

Source: UNDP, HDR 2007/2008, Table 9: 257-260.

* Data for Iraq and Somalia are from the HDRO online database at [http://hdr.undp.org/en/statistics/data].

Table 09

Survival: progress and setbacks

HDI Rank		Life expectancy at birth (years)		MDG Infant mortality rate (per 1,000 live births)		MDG Under-five mortality rate (per 1,000 live births)		Probability at birth of surviving to age 65 (% of cohort)		MDG Maternal mortality ratio (per 100,000 live births)	
								Female	Male	Reported	Adjusted
		1970-75	2000-05	1970	2005	1970	2005	2000-05	2000-05	1990-2005	2005
HIGH HUMAN DEVELOPMENT											
33	Kuwait	67.7	76.9	49	9	59	11	88.9	83.8	5	4
35	Qatar	62.1	74.3	45	18	65	21	80.1	78.7	10	12
39	United Arab Emirates	62.2	77.8	63	8	84	9	90.2	85.3	3	37
41	Bahrain	63.3	74.8	55	9	82	11	85.9	80.2	46	32
56	Libyan Arab Jamahiriya	52.8	72.7	105	18	160	19	82.1	72.2	77	97
58	Oman	52.1	74.2	126	10	200	12	84.9	79.5	23	64
61	Saudi Arabia	53.9	71.6	118	21	185	26	82.0	73.7	..	18
MEDIUM HUMAN DEVELOPMENT											
86	Jordan	56.5	71.3	77	22	107	26	78.2	70.9	41	62
88	Lebanon	65.4	71.0	45	27	54	30	80.6	72.1	100	150
91	Tunisia	55.6	73.0	135	20	201	24	85.3	76.5	69	100
104	Algeria	54.5	71.0	143	34	220	39	78.9	75.9	120	180
106	Occupied Palestinian Territories	56.5	72.4	..	21	..	23	81.8	75.5	..	..
108	Syrian Arab Republic	57.3	73.1	90	14	123	15	83.6	76.4	65	130
112	Egypt	51.1	69.8	157	28	235	33	80.2	70.4	84	130
126	Morocco	52.9	69.6	119	36	184	40	79.4	71.2	230	240
134	Comoros	48.9	63.0	159	53	215	71	66.9	58.3	380	400
137	Mauritania	48.4	62.2	151	78	250	125	69.4	60.4	750	820
147	Sudan	45.1	56.4	104	62	172	90	55.3	49.7	550	450
149	Djibouti	44.4	53.4	..	88	..	133	50.4	43.7	74	650
153	Yemen	39.8	60.3	202	76	303	102	61.7	55.0	370	430
WITHOUT HDI RANK											
	Iraq	57	57	90	102	127	125	59.6	50	290	300
	Somalia	41	45.9	..	133	..	225	41.1	36.6	..	1,400
All developing countries		55.8	65.5	109	57	167	83	70.3	62.6	..	..
Least developed countries		44.6	52.7	152	97	245	153	49.9	44.3	..	..
Arab States		51.9	66.7	129	46	196	58	73.5	66.4	..	..
East Asia and the Pacific		60.6	71.1	84	25	123	31	79.6	71.8	..	..
Latin America and the Caribbean		61.2	72.2	86	26	123	31	80.8	69.3	..	..
South Asia		50.3	62.9	130	60	206	80	66.0	58.4	..	..
Sub-Saharan Africa		46.0	49.1	144	102	244	172	43.3	37.8	..	..
Central and Eastern Europe and the CIS		68.7	68.2	39	22	48	27	79.5	54.9	..	..
OECD		70.3	77.8	41	9	54	11	89.2	80.5	..	..
High-income OECD		71.7	78.9	22	5	28	6	90.3	82.4	..	..
High human development		69.4	75.7	43	13	59	15	86.6	74.8	..	..
Medium human development		56.6	66.9	106	45	162	59	72.6	64.5	..	..
Low human development		43.7	47.9	155	108	264	184	42.6	37.4	..	..
High income		71.5	78.7	24	6	32	7	90.2	82.2	..	..
Middle income		61.8	70.3	87	28	127	35	78.9	68.4	..	..
Low income		49.1	59.2	130	75	209	113	60.0	53.2	..	..
World		58.3	66.0	96	52	148	76	72.0	63.1	..	..

Source: UNDP, HDR 2007/2008, Table 10: 261-264.

* Data for Iraq and Somalia are from the HDRO online database at [http://hdr.undp.org/en/statistics/data].

Commitment to education: public spending

HDI Rank		Public expenditure on education				Current public expenditure on education by level (% of total current public expenditure on education)					
		As a % of GDP		As a % of total government expenditure		Pre-primary and primary		Secondary and post-secondary non-tertiary		Tertiary	
		1991	2002-05	1991	2002-05	1991	2002-05	1991	2002-05	1991	2002-05
HIGH HUMAN DEVELOPMENT											
33	Kuwait	4.8	5.1	3.4	12.7	..	31	..	38	..	30
35	Qatar	3.5	1.6	..	..	..	..	..	..	..	..
39	United Arab Emirates	2.0	1.3	15.0	27.4	..	..	..	..	..	..
41	Bahrain	3.9	..	12.8	..	..	..	..	..	..	..
56	Libyan Arab Jamahiriya	..	2.7	..	..	..	12	..	19	..	69
58	Oman	3.0	3.6	15.8	24.2	52	50	40	41	7	8
61	Saudi Arabia	5.8	6.8	17.8	27.6	..	..	..	..	..	..
MEDIUM HUMAN DEVELOPMENT											
86	Jordan	8.0	4.9	19.1	20.6	..	..	..	..	..	..
88	Lebanon	..	2.6	..	11.0	..	33	..	30	..	31
91	Tunisia	6.0	7.3	14.3	20.8	..	35	..	43	..	22
104	Algeria	5.1	..	22.0	..	95	..	..	..	..	..
106	Occupied Palestinian Territories	..	..	..	..	..	..	..	..	..	..
108	Syrian Arab Republic	3.9	..	14.2	..	..	..	..	..	..	..
112	Egypt	3.9	..	..	..	..	..	..	..	..	..
126	Morocco	5.0	6.7	26.3	27.2	35	45	49	38	16	16
134	Comoros	..	3.9	..	24.1	..	..	..	..	..	..
137	Mauritania	4.6	2.3	13.9	8.3	..	62	..	33	..	5
147	Sudan	6.0	..	2.8	..	..	..	..	..	..	..
149	Djibouti	3.5	7.9	11.1	27.3	53	44	21	42	14	15
153	Yemen	..	9.6	..	32.8	..	..	..	..	..	..
WITHOUT HDI RANK											
	Iraq	..	..	..	..	..	..	..	..	..	..
	Somalia	..	..	..	..	..	..	..	..	..	..

Source: UNDP, HDR 2007/2008, Table 11: 265-268.

* Data for Iraq and Somalia are from the HDRO online database at [http://hdr.undp.org/en/statistics/data].

Literacy and enrolment

HDI Rank		Adult literacy rate (% aged 15 and older)		MDG Youth literacy rate (% aged 15-24)		MDG Net primary enrolment rate (%)		Net secondary enrolment rate (%)		MDG Children reaching grade 5 (% of grade 1 students)		Tertiary students in science, engineering, manufacturing and construction (% of tertiary students)
		1985-1995	1995-2005	1985-1995	1995-2005	1991	2005	1991	2005	1991	2004	1999-2005
HIGH HUMAN DEVELOPMENT												
33	Kuwait	74.5	93.3	87.5	99.7	49	87	..	78	..	..	..
35	Qatar	75.6	89.0	89.5	95.9	89	96	70	90	64	..	19
39	United Arab Emirates	79.5	88.7	93.6	97.0	99	71	60	57	80	97	..
41	Bahrain	84.0	86.5	96.9	97.0	99	97	85	90	89	99	17
56	Libyan Arab Jamahiriya	74.7	84.2	94.9	98.0	96	..	..	..	..	..	31
58	Oman	..	81.4	..	97.3	69	76	..	75	97	98	20
61	Saudi Arabia	70.8	82.9	87.9	95.8	59	78	31	66	83	96	17
MEDIUM HUMAN DEVELOPMENT												
86	Jordan	..	91.1	..	99.0	94	89	..	79	..	96	22
88	Lebanon	..	..	..	..	73	92	..	..	..	93	24
91	Tunisia	..	74.3	..	94.3	94	97	..	65	86	97	31
104	Algeria	49.6	69.9	74.3	90.1	89	97	53	66	95	96	18
106	Occupied Palestinian Territories	..	92.4	..	99.0	..	80	..	95	..	..	18
108	Syrian Arab Republic	..	80.8	..	92.5	91	95	43	62	96	92	..
112	Egypt	44.4	71.4	63.3	84.9	84	94	..	82	..	94	..
126	Morocco	41.6	52.3	58.4	70.5	56	86	..	35	75	79	21
134	Comoros	..	..	..	..	57	55	..	..	..	80	11
137	Mauritania	..	51.2	..	61.3	35	72	..	15	75	53	6
147	Sudan	..	60.9	..	77.2	40	43	..	..	94	79	..
149	Djibouti	..	..	..	..	29	33	..	23	87	77	9
153	Yemen	37.1	54.1	60.2	75.2	51	75	..	..	..	73	..
WITHOUT HDI RANK												
	Iraq	..	74.1	..	84.8	94	88	..	38	..	81	24
	Somalia	..	..	..	..	9	..	..	..	..	..	..
All developing countries		68.2	77.1	80.2	85.6	80	85	..	53	..	..	..
Least developed countries		47.4	53.4	56.3	65.5	47	77	..	27	..	..	..
Arab States		58.2	70.3	74.8	85.2	71	83	..	59	..	..	..
East Asia and the Pacific		..	90.7	..	97.8	..	93	..	69	..	..	..
Latin America and the Caribbean		87.6	89.9	93.7	96.6	86	95	..	68	..	..	..
South Asia		47.6	59.7	60.7	74.7	..	87	..	..	..	..	..
Sub-Saharan Africa		54.2	59.3	64.4	71.2	52	72	..	26	..	..	..
Central and Eastern Europe and the CIS		97.5	99.1	..	99.6	90	91	..	84	..	..	..
OECD		..	..	..	..	97	96	..	87	..	..	..
High-income OECD		98.9	99.1	99.4	..	97	96	..	92	..	..	..
High human development		..	94.1	..	98.1	93	95	..	..	..	..	..
Medium human development		..	78.3	..	87.3	..	87	..	..	..	..	..
Low human development		43.5	54.1	55.9	66.4	45	69	..	..	..	..	..
High income		98.4	98.6	99.0	..	96	95	..	91	..	..	..
Middle income		82.3	90.1	93.1	96.8	92	93	..	70	..	..	..
Low income		51.5	60.8	63.0	73.4	..	81	..	40	..	..	..
World		76.4	82.4	83.5	86.5	83	87	..	59	..	..	..

Source: UNDP, HDR 2007/2008, Table 12: 269-272.

* Data for Iraq and Somalia are from the HDRO online database at [http://hdr.undp.org/en/statistics/data].

Technology: diffusion and creation

HDI Rank	MDG Telephone mainlines (per 1,000 people)		MDG Cellular subscribers (per 1,000 people)		MDG Internet users (per 1,000 people)		Patents granted to residents (per million people) 2000-05	Receipts of royalties and licence fees (US$ per person) 2005	Research and development (R&D) expenditure (% of GDP) 2000-05	Researchers in R&D (per million people) 1990-2005
	1990	2005	1990	2005	1990	2005				
HIGH HUMAN DEVELOPMENT										
33 Kuwait	156	201	10	939	0	276	..	0.0	0.2	..
35 Qatar	197	253	8	882	0	269	..	..	..	..
39 United Arab Emirates	224	273	19	1,000	0	308	..	..	..	..
41 Bahrain	191	270	10	1,030	0	213	..	..	..	..
56 Libyan Arab Jamahiriya	51	133	0	41	0	36	..	0.0	..	361
58 Oman	57	103	1	519	0	111	..	..	..	..
61 Saudi Arabia	75	164	1	575	0	70	(.)	0.0	..	..
MEDIUM HUMAN DEVELOPMENT										
86 Jordan	78	119	(.)	304	0	118	..	..	..	1,927
88 Lebanon	144	277	0	277	0	196	..	0.0	..	..
91 Tunisia	37	125	(.)	566	0	95	..	1.4	0.6	1,013
104 Algeria	32	78	(.)	416	0	58	1	..	..	..
106 Occupied Palestinian Territories	..	96	0	302	0	67	..	..	..	..
108 Syrian Arab Republic	39	152	0	155	0	58	2	..	..	29
112 Egypt	29	140	(.)	184	0	68	1	1.9	0.2	493
126 Morocco	17	44	(.)	411	0	152	1	0.4	0.6	..
134 Comoros	8	28	0	27	0	33	..	..	..	..
137 Mauritania	3	13	0	243	0	7	..	..	..	..
147 Sudan	2	18	0	50	0	77	..	0.0	0.3	..
149 Djibouti	10	14	0	56	0	13	..	..	..	..
153 Yemen	10	39	0	95	0	9	..	..	..	..
WITHOUT HDI RANK										
Iraq	38	37	0	20	0	1	..	..	..	..
Somalia	2	12	0	61	0	11	..	..	..	..
All developing countries	21	132	(.)	229	(.)	86	..	..	1.0	..
Least developed countries	3	9	0	48	0	12	..	0.2	..	..
Arab States	34	106	(.)	284	0	88	..	0.9	..	..
East Asia and the Pacific	18	223	(.)	301	(.)	106	..	1.7	1.6	722
Latin America and the Caribbean	61	..	(.)	439	0	156	..	1.1	0.6	256
South Asia	7	51	(.)	81	0	52	..	(.)	0.7	119
Sub-Saharan Africa	10	17	(.)	130	0	26	..	0.3	..	..
Central and Eastern Europe and the CIS	125	277	(.)	629	0	185	73	4.1	1.0	2,423
OECD	390	441	10	785	3	445	239	104.2	2.4	3,096
High-income OECD	462	..	12	828	3	524	299	130.4	2.4	3,807
High human development	308	394	7	743	2	365	189	75.8	2.4	3,035
Medium human development	16	135	(.)	209	0	73	..	0.3	0.8	..
Low human development	3	7	0	74	0	17	..	0.2	..	..
High income	450	500	12	831	3	525	286	125.3	2.4	3,781
Middle income	40	211	(.)	379	0	115	..	1.0	0.8	725
Low income	6	37	(.)	77	0	45	..	(.)	0.7	..
World	98	180	2	341	1	136	..	21.6	2.3	..

Source: UNDP, HDR 2007/2008, Table 13: 273-276.

* Data for Iraq and Somalia are from the HDRO online database at [http://hdr.undp.org/en/statistics/data].

... to have access to the resources needed for a decent standard of living ...

Table **13**

Economic performance

HDI Rank	GDP US$ billions 2005	GDP PPP US$ billions 2005	GDP per capita US$ 2005	GDP per capita 2005 PPP US$ 2005	Annual growth rate (%) 1975-2005	Annual growth rate (%) 1990-2005	Highest value during 1975-2005 2005 PPP US$	Year of highest value	Average annual change in consumer price index (%) 1990-2005	Average annual change in consumer price index (%) 2004-05
HIGH HUMAN DEVELOPMENT										
33 Kuwait	80.8	66.7	31,861	26,321	-0.5	0.6	34,680	1979	1.8	4.1
35 Qatar	42.5	..	52,240	..	..	..	..	..	2.7	8.8
39 United Arab Emirates	129.7	115.7	28,612	25,514	-2.6	-0.9	50,405	1981	..	..
41 Bahrain	12.9	15.6	17,773	21,482	1.5	2.3	21,482	2005	0.5	2.6
56 Libyan Arab Jamahiriya	38.8	..	6,621	..	2.5	..	..	..	1.9	..
58 Oman	24.3	38.4	9,584	15,602	2.4	1.8	15,602	2004	0.1	1.2
61 Saudi Arabia	309.8	363.2	13,399	15,711	-2.0	0.1	27,686	1977	0.4	0.7
MEDIUM HUMAN DEVELOPMENT										
86 Jordan	12.7	30.3	2,323	5,530	0.5	1.6	5,613	1986	2.8	3.5
88 Lebanon	21.9	20.0	6,135	5,584	3.2	2.8	5,586	2004	..	..
91 Tunisia	28.7	84.0	2,860	8,371	2.3	3.3	8,371	2005	3.6	2.0
104 Algeria	102.3	232.0	3,112	7,062	0.1	1.1	7,062	2005	10.7	1.6
106 Occupied Palestinian Territories	4.0	..	1,107	..	..	-2.9	..	..	..	..
108 Syrian Arab Republic	26.3	72.5	1,382	3,808	0.9	1.4	3,808	2005	4.9	..
112 Egypt	89.4	321.1	1,207	4,337	2.8	2.4	4,337	2005	6.6	4.9
126 Morocco	51.6	137.4	1,711	4,555	1.4	1.5	4,555	2005	2.8	1.0
134 Comoros	0.4	1.2	645	1,993	-0.6	-0.4	2,272	1984	..	..
137 Mauritania	1.9	6.9	603	2,234	-0.1	0.3	2,338	1976	5.8	12.1
147 Sudan	27.5	75.5	760	2,083	1.3	3.5	2,083	2005	41.8	8.5
149 Djibouti	0.7	1.7	894	2,178	-2.7	-2.7	3,200	1990	..	..
153 Yemen	15.1	19.5	718	930	1.5	1.5	943	2002	20.8	..
WITHOUT HDI RANK										
Iraq	12.6	..	..	..	..	..	..	..	..	..
Somalia	..	..	..	..	-0.4	..	..	..	..	..
All developing countries	9,812.5 T	26,732.3 T	1,939	5,282	2.5	3.1	..	..	..	..
Least developed countries	306.2 T	1,081.8 T	424	1,499	0.9	1.8	..	..	..	..
Arab States	1,043.4 T	1,915.2 T	3,659	6,716	0.7	2.3	..	..	..	..
East Asia and the Pacific	4,122.5 T	12,846.6 T	2,119	6,604	6.1	5.8	..	..	..	..
Latin America and the Caribbean	2,469.5 T	4,639.2 T	4,480	8,417	0.7	1.2	..	..	..	..
South Asia	1,206.1 T	5,152.2 T	800	3,416	2.6	3.4	..	..	..	..
Sub-Saharan Africa	589.9 T	1,395.6 T	845	1,998	-0.5	0.5	..	..	..	..
Central and Eastern Europe and the CIS	1,873.0 T	3,827.2 T	4,662	9,527	1.4	1.4	..	..	..	..
OECD	34,851.2 T	34,076.8 T	29,860	29,197	2.0	1.8	..	..	..	..
High-income OECD	32,404.5 T	30,711.7 T	35,696	33,831	2.1	1.8	..	..	..	..
High human development	37,978.4 T	39,633.4 T	22,984	23,986	1.9	1.8	..	..	..	..
Medium human development	5,881.2 T	20,312.6 T	1,412	4,876	3.2	4.0	..	..	..	..
Low human development	236.4 T	544.2 T	483	1,112	-0.7	0.6	..	..	..	..
High income	34,338.1 T	32,680.7 T	34,759	33,082	2.1	1.8	..	..	..	..
Middle income	8,552.0 T	22,586.3 T	2,808	7,416	2.1	3.0	..	..	..	..
Low income	1,416.2 T	5,879.1 T	610	2,531	2.2	2.9	..	..	..	..
World	44,155.7 T	60,597.3 T	6,954	9,543	1.4	1.5	..	..	..	..

Source: UNDP, HDR 2007/2008, Table 14: 277-280.

* Data for Iraq and Somalia are from the HDRO online database at [http://hdr.undp.org/en/statistics/data].

... to have access to the resources needed for a decent standard of living ...

Table 14

Inequality in income or expenditure

			MDG Share of income or expenditure (%)				Inequality measures		
HDI Rank		Survey Year	Poorest 10%	Poorest 20%	Richest 20%	Richest 10%	Richest 10% to poorest 10%	Richest 20% to poorest 20%	Gini index
HIGH HUMAN DEVELOPMENT									
33	Kuwait	..	..	..	..	..	..	..	..
35	Qatar	..	..	..	..	..	..	..	..
39	United Arab Emirates	..	..	..	..	`	..	..	..
41	Bahrain	..	..	..	..	..	..	..	..
56	Libyan Arab Jamahiriya	..	..	..	..	..	..	..	..
58	Oman	..	..	..	..	..	..	..	..
61	Saudi Arabia	..	..	..	..	..	..	..	..
MEDIUM HUMAN DEVELOPMENT									
86	Jordan	2002-03	2.7	6.7	46.3	30.6	11.3	6.9	38.8
88	Lebanon	..	..	..	..	..	..	..	..
91	Tunisia	2000	2.3	6.0	47.3	31.5	13.4	7.9	39.8
104	Algeria	1995	2.8	7.0	42.6	26.8	9.6	6.1	35.3
106	Occupied Palestinian Territories	..	..	..	..	..	..	..	..
108	Syrian Arab Republic	..	..	..	..	..	..	..	..
112	Egypt	1999-00	3.7	8.6	43.6	29.5	8.0	5.1	34.4
126	Morocco	1998-99	2.6	6.5	46.6	30.9	11.7	7.2	39.5
134	Comoros	..	..	..	..	..	..	..	..
137	Mauritania	2000	2.5	6.2	45.7	29.5	12.0	7.4	39.0
147	Sudan	..	..	..	..	..	..	..	..
149	Djibouti	..	..	..	..	..	..	..	..
153	Yemen	1998	3.0	7.4	41.2	25.9	8.6	5.6	33.4
WITHOUT HDI RANK									
	Iraq	..	..	..	..	..	..	..	..
	Somalia	..	..	..	..	..	..	..	..

Source: UNDP, HDR 2007/2008, Table 15: 281-284.

* Data for Iraq and Somalia are from the HDRO online database at [http://hdr.undp.org/en/statistics/data].

... to have access to the resources needed for a decent standard of living . . .

Table 15

Structure of trade

HDI Rank	Imports of goods and services (% of GDP)		Exports of goods and services (% of GDP)		Primary exports (% of merchandise exports)		Manufactured exports (% of merchandise exports)		High-technology exports (% of manufactured exports)		Terms of trade (2000=100)
	1990	2005	1990	2005	1990	2005	1990	2005	1990	2005	2004-2005
HIGH HUMAN DEVELOPMENT											
33 Kuwait	58	30	45	68	94	93	6	7	3.5	1.0	..
35 Qatar	..	33	..	68	82	84	18	7	0.4	1.2	..
39 United Arab Emirates	41	76	66	94	88	76	12	24	(.)	10.2	..
41 Bahrain	95	64	116	82	54	93	45	7	..	2.0	..
56 Libyan Arab Jamahiriya	31	36	40	48	96	..	4	..	..	..	186
58 Oman	28	43	47	57	94	89	5	6	2.1	2.2	..
61 Saudi Arabia	32	26	41	61	92	90	8	9	0.7	1.3	..
MEDIUM HUMAN DEVELOPMENT											
86 Jordan	93	93	62	52	44	28	56	72	6.8	5.2	88
88 Lebanon	100	44	18	19	..	29	..	70	..	2.4	..
91 Tunisia	51	51	44	48	31	22	69	78	2.1	4.9	99
104 Algeria	25	23	23	48	97	98	3	2	1.3	1.0	126
106 Occupied Palestinian Territories	..	68	..	14	..	..	..	..	..	..	..
108 Syrian Arab Republic	28	40	28	37	64	87	36	11	..	1.0	..
112 Egypt	33	33	20	30	57	64	42	31	..	0.6	107
126 Morocco	32	43	26	36	48	35	52	65	..	10.1	100
134 Comoros	37	35	14	12	..	89	..	8	..	0.5	58
137 Mauritania	61	95	46	36	..	..	..	..	..	..	95
147 Sudan	..	28	..	18	98	99	2	(.)	..	(.)	121
149 Djibouti	78	54	54	37	44	..	8	..	..	..	..
153 Yemen	20	38	14	46	85	96	15	4	..	5.3	..
WITHOUT HDI RANK											
Iraq	..	..	..	..	..	..	..	..	..	..	..
Somalia	38	..	10	..	..	..	..	..	..	..	..
All developing countries	24	40	25	44	40	28	59	71	10.4	28.3	..
Least developed countries	22	34	13	24	..	..	31	..	..	..	..
Arab States	38	38	38	54	87	..	14	..	1.2	2.0	..
East Asia and the Pacific	32	59	34	66	25	13	73	86	15.3	36.4	..
Latin America and the Caribbean	15	23	17	26	63	46	36	54	6.6	14.5	..
South Asia	13	25	10	23	28	47	71	51	2.0	3.8	..
Sub-Saharan Africa	26	35	27	33	..	66	..	34	..	4.0	..
Central and Eastern Europe and the CIS	28	43	29	45	..	36	..	54	..	8.3	..
OECD	18	23	17	22	21	18	77	79	18.1	18.2	..
High-income OECD	18	22	17	21	19	17	79	79	18.5	18.8	..
High human development	19	25	19	25	24	20	74	76	18.1	20.3	..
Medium human development	21	34	20	35	42	30	55	69	7.2	24.3	..
Low human development	28	36	28	38	98	93	1	7	..	3.1	..
High income	19	24	18	24	21	18	77	78	18.3	20.9	..
Middle income	21	33	22	36	48	33	50	65	..	21.5	..
Low income	16	29	13	25	50	49	49	50	..	3.8	..
World	19	26	19	26	26	21	72	75	17.5	21.0	..

Source: UNDP, HDR 2007/2008, Table 16: 285-288.

* Data for Iraq and Somalia are from the HDRO online database at [http://hdr.undp.org/en/statistics/data].

... to have access to the resources needed for a decent standard of living ...

Table 16

Flows of aid, private capital and debt

		Official development assistance (ODA) received (net disbursements)			Net foreign direct investment inflows (% of GDP)		Other private flows (% of GDP)		MDG Total debt service			
		Total (US$ millions)	Per capita (US$)	As % of GDP					As % of GDP		As % of exports of goods, services and net income from abroad	
HDI Rank		2005	2005	1990	2005	1990	2005	1990	2005	1990	2005	1990	2005
HIGH HUMAN DEVELOPMENT													
33	Kuwait	..	..	(.)	..	0.0	0.3	..	..	..	..	..	..
35	Qatar	..	..	(.)	..	..	..	..	..	..	..	..	..
39	United Arab Emirates	..	..	(.)	..	..	..	..	..	..	..	..	..
41	Bahrain	..	..	3.2	..	..	..	..	..	..	..	..	..
56	Libyan Arab Jamahiriya	24.4	..	(.)	0.1	..	..	..	..	..	..	..	..
58	Oman	30.7	12.0	0.5	..	1.2	0.8	0.0	-0.1	..	4.1	..	7.5
61	Saudi Arabia	26.3	1.1	(.)	(.)	..	..	..	..	..	..	..	..
MEDIUM HUMAN DEVELOPMENT													
86	Jordan	622.0	114.9	22.0	4.9	0.9	12.1	5.3	1.6	15.6	4.8	20.4	6.5
88	Lebanon	243.0	67.9	8.9	1.1	0.2	11.7	0.2	11.3	3.5	16.1	..	17.7
91	Tunisia	376.5	37.6	3.2	1.3	0.6	2.5	-1.6	-0.4	11.6	7.2	24.5	13.0
104	Algeria	370.6	11.3	0.2	0.4	(.)	1.1	-0.7	-0.8	14.2	5.8	63.4	..
106	Occupied Palestinian Territories	1,101.6	303.8	..	27.4	..	..	..	..	..	..	..	..
108	Syrian Arab Republic	77.9	4.1	5.5	0.3	0.6	1.6	-0.1	(.)	9.7	0.8	21.8	1.9
112	Egypt	925.9	12.5	12.6	1.0	1.7	6.0	-0.2	5.8	7.1	2.8	20.4	6.8
126	Morocco	651.8	21.6	4.1	1.3	0.6	3.0	1.2	0.3	6.9	5.3	21.5	11.3
134	Comoros	25.2	42.0	17.9	6.5	0.2	0.3	0.0	0.0	0.4	1.0	2.3	..
137	Mauritania	190.4	62.0	23.2	10.3	0.7	6.2	-0.1	0.8	14.3	3.6	29.8	..
147	Sudan	1,828.6	50.5	6.2	6.6	-0.2	8.4	0.0	0.2	0.4	1.4	8.7	6.5
149	Djibouti	78.6	99.1	42.8	11.1	..	3.2	-0.1	0.0	3.3	2.6	..	..
153	Yemen	335.9	16.0	8.3	2.2	-2.7	-1.8	3.3	0.2	3.5	1.4	5.6	2.6
WITHOUT HDI RANK													
	Iraq	21,653.50	..	..	..	..	..	..	..	..	..	..	..
	Somalia	236.4	28.7	53.6	..	0.6	..	0	..	1.2	..	..	..
All developing countries		86,043.0 T	16.5	1.4	0.9	0.9	2.7	0.5	1.5	4.4	4.6	..	13.0
Least developed countries		25,979.5 T	33.9	11.8	9.3	0.3	2.6	0.5	0.8	3.0	2.3	16.9	7.0
Arab States		29,612.0 T	94.3	2.9	3.0	..	..	..	1.8	..	..	..	..
East Asia and the Pacific		9,541.6 T	4.9	0.8	0.2	..	..	..	..	..	..	..	..
Latin America and the Caribbean		6,249.5 T	11.3	0.5	0.3	0.8	2.9	0.5	1.2	4.0	6.6	23.7	22.9
South Asia		9,937.5 T	6.3	1.2	0.8	(.)	0.8	0.3	1.2	2.3	2.6	..	15.4
Sub-Saharan Africa		30,167.7 T	41.7	5.7	5.1	0.4	2.4	0.3	1.7	..	..	..	..
Central and Eastern Europe and the CIS		5,299.4 T	13.1	(.)	0.3	..	..	(.)	4.4	..	..	..	..
OECD		759.4 T	..	..	(.)	1.0	1.6	..	..	..	..	..	..
High-income OECD		0.0 T	0.0	..	0.0	1.0	1.6	..	..	..	..	..	..
High human development		2,633.0 T	1.6	..	(.)	1.0	1.7	..	..	..	..	..	..
Medium human development		40,160.4 T	9.4	1.8	0.7	0.7	2.8	0.6	1.9	4.8	3.7	22.2	10.3
Low human development		21,150.9 T	42.0	9.7	9.0	0.7	1.5	0.4	0.6	6.4	5.6	22.0	12.2
High income		.. T	..	..	..	1.0	1.6	..	..	..	..	..	..
Middle income		42,242.2 T	13.7	0.7	1.3	0.9	3.1	0.4	2.2	4.5	5.5	20.3	14.3
Low income		44,123.0 T	18.2	4.1	3.2	0.4	1.4	0.3	1.0	3.7	3.1	27.1	13.7
World		106,372.9 T	16.3	0.3	0.2	1.0	1.9	..	2.0	..	5.1	..	..

Source: UNDP, HDR 2007/2008, Table 18: 290-293.

* Data for Iraq and Somalia are from the HDRO online database at [http://hdr.undp.org/en/statistics/data].

Table **17**

Priorities in public spending

HDI Rank		Public expenditure on health (% of GDP) 2004	Public expenditure on education (% of GDP)		Military expenditure (% of GDP)		Total debt service (% of GDP)	
			1991	2002-05	1990	2005	1990	2005
HIGH HUMAN DEVELOPMENT								
33	Kuwait	2.2	4.8	5.1	48.5	4.8	..	..
35	Qatar	1.8	3.5	1.6	..	..	..	..
39	United Arab Emirates	2.0	2.0	1.3	6.2	2.0	..	..
41	Bahrain	2.7	3.9	..	5.1	3.6	..	..
56	Libyan Arab Jamahiriya	2.8	..	2.7	..	2.0	..	..
58	Oman	2.4	3.0	3.6	16.5	11.9	..	4.1
61	Saudi Arabia	2.5	5.8	6.8	14.0	8.2	..	..
MEDIUM HUMAN DEVELOPMENT								
86	Jordan	4.7	8.0	4.9	6.9	5.3	15.6	4.8
88	Lebanon	3.2	..	2.6	7.6	4.5	3.5	16.1
91	Tunisia	2.8	6.0	7.3	2.0	1.6	11.6	7.2
104	Algeria	2.6	5.1	..	1.5	2.9	14.2	5.8
106	Occupied Palestinian Territories	7.8	..	..	..	..	..	..
108	Syrian Arab Republic	2.2	3.9	..	6.0	5.1	9.7	0.8
112	Egypt	2.2	3.9	..	4.7	2.8	7.1	2.8
126	Morocco	1.7	5.0	6.7	5.0	4.5	6.9	5.3
134	Comoros	1.6	..	3.9	..	..	0.4	1.0
137	Mauritania	2.0	4.6	2.3	3.8	3.6	14.3	3.6
147	Sudan	1.5	6.0	..	3.5	2.3	0.4	1.4
149	Djibouti	4.4	3.5	7.9	5.9	4.2	3.3	2.6
153	Yemen	1.9	..	9.6	7.9	7.0	3.5	1.4
WITHOUT HDI RANK								
	Iraq	4.2	..	..	..	..	..	..
	Somalia	1.2	..	..	..	..	1.2	..

Source: UNDP, HDR 2007/2008, Table 19: 294-297.

* Data for Iraq and Somalia are from the HDRO online database at [http://hdr.undp.org/en/statistics/data].

... to have access to the resources needed for a decent standard of living ...

Table 18

Unemployment and informal sector work in non-OECD countries

HDI Rank		Unemployment rate			Employment by economic activity				Employment in informal sector as a % of non-agricultural employment			
		Unemployed people (thousands) 1996-2005	Total (% of labour force) 1996-2005	Female (% of male rate) 1996-2005	Total (thousands) 1996-2005	Agriculture (%) 1996-2005	Industry (%) 1996-2005	Services (%) 1996-2005	Survey year 1990-2004	Both sexes (%) 1990-2004	Female (%) 1990-2004	Male (%) 1990-2004
HIGH HUMAN DEVELOPMENT												
33	Kuwait	15	1.1	173	..	..	..	..	..	..	..	..
35	Qatar	13	3.9	548	438	3	41	56	..	..	..	..
39	United Arab Emirates	41	2.3	118	1,779	8	33	59	..	..	..	..
41	Bahrain	16	..	..	..	..	..	..	..	..	..	..
56	Libyan Arab Jamahiriya	..	..	..	..	..	..	..	..	..	..	..
58	Oman	53	..	..	282	6	11	82	..	..	..	..
61	Saudi Arabia	327	5.2	274	5,913	5	21	74	..	..	..	..
MEDIUM HUMAN DEVELOPMENT												
86	Jordan	..	..	..	43	4	22	74	..	..	..	..
88	Lebanon	116	..	..	..	..	..	..	..	..	..	..
91	Tunisia	486	14.2	132	..	..	..	..	1994-95	50	39	53
104	Algeria	1,475	15.3	103	7,798	21	26	53	1997	43	41	43
106	Occupied Palestinian Territories	212	26.7	71	578	16	25	58	..	..	..	..
108	Syrian Arab Republic	638	11.7	290	4,822	30	27	43	2003	22	7	24
112	Egypt	2,241	11.0	311	18,119	30	20	50	2003	45	59	42
126	Morocco	1,226	11.0	106	9,603	44	20	36	1995	45	47	44
134	Comoros	..	..	..	..	..	..	..	..	..	..	..
137	Mauritania	..	..	..	..	..	..	..	..	..	..	..
147	Sudan	..	..	..	..	..	..	..	..	..	..	..
149	Djibouti	..	..	..	77	2	8	80	..	..	..	..
153	Yemen	469	11.5	66	3,622	54	11	35	..	..	..	..
WITHOUT HDI RANK												
	Iraq	..	26.8	51	..	..	..	..	..	..	..	..
	Somalia	..	..	..	..	..	..	..	..	..	..	..

Source: UNDP, HDR 2007/2008, Table 21: 299-301.

* Data for Iraq and Somalia are from the HDRO online database at [http://hdr.undp.org/en/statistics/data].

Energy and the environment

HDI Rank	Electricity consumption per capita (kilowatt-hours) 2004	(% change) 1990-2004	Electrification rate (%) 2000-05	Population without electricity (millions) 2005	GDP per unit of energy use (2000 PPP US$ per kg of oil equivalent) 2004	(% change) 1990-2004	Forest area: % total land (%) 2005	Total (thousand sq km) 2005	Total change (thousand sq km) 1990-2005	Average annual change (%) 1990-2005
HIGH HUMAN DEVELOPMENT										
33 Kuwait	15,423	75.0	100	0.0	1.9	63.1	0.3	0.1	(.)	6.7
35 Qatar	19,840	101.8	71	0.2	..	..	(.)	..	..	..
39 United Arab Emirates	12,000	41.5	92	0.4	2.2	15.7	3.7	3.1	0.7	1.8
41 Bahrain	11,932	52.3	99	0.0	1.8	21.5	0.6	..	..	..
56 Libyan Arab Jamahiriya	3,147	-22.2	97	0.2	..	..	0.1	2.2	0.0	0.0
58 Oman	5,079	83.2	96	0.1	3.0	-29.9	(.)	(.)	0.0	0.0
61 Saudi Arabia	6,902	57.9	97	0.8	2.0	-28.2	1.3	27.3	0.0	0.0
MEDIUM HUMAN DEVELOPMENT										
86 Jordan	1,738	53.4	100	0.0	3.6	4.3	0.9	0.8	0.0	0.0
88 Lebanon	2,691	374.6	100	0.0	3.5	29.9	13.3	1.4	0.2	0.8
91 Tunisia	1,313	93.7	99	0.1	8.2	22.2	6.8	10.6	4.1	4.3
104 Algeria	889	40.7	98	0.6	6.0	4.5	1.0	22.8	4.9	1.8
106 Occupied Palestinian Territories	513	..	..	..	..	..	1.5	0.1	0.0	0.0
108 Syrian Arab Republic	1,784	88.4	90	1.9	3.4	19.9	2.5	4.6	0.9	1.6
112 Egypt	1,465	93.0	98	1.5	4.9	-2.2	0.1	0.7	0.2	3.5
126 Morocco	652	84.7	85	4.5	10.3	-13.9	9.8	43.6	0.8	0.1
134 Comoros	31	3.3	..	..	..	..	2.9	0.1	-0.1	-3.9
137 Mauritania	112	60.0	..	..	..	..	0.3	2.7	-1.5	-2.4
147 Sudan	116	123.1	30	25.4	3.7	33.2	28.4	675.5	-88.4	-0.8
149 Djibouti	260	-46.8	..	..	..	..	0.2	0.1	..	..
153 Yemen	208	34.2	36	13.2	2.8	-6.0	1.0	5.5	0.0	0.0
WITHOUT HDI RANK										
Iraq	1,280	-20	15	22	..	..	1.9	8.2	0.2	0.1
Somalia	36	-10	..	..	..	..	11.4	71.3	-11.5	-0.9
All developing countries	1,221	..	68	1569.0	4.6	..	27.9	21,147.80	-1381.7	-0.4
Least developed countries	119	..	..	..	..	..	27.5	5,541.60	-583.6	-0.6
Arab States	1,841	..	..	..	3.4	..	7.2	877.7	-88.0	-0.6
East Asia and the Pacific	1,599	..	..	..	..	..	28.6	4,579.30	-75.5	0.1
Latin America and the Caribbean	2,043	..	90	45.0	6.2	..	45.9	9,159.00	-686.3	-0.5
South Asia	628	..	..	..	5.1	..	14.2	911.8	12.5	0.1
Sub-Saharan Africa	478	..	26	547.0	..	..	26.8	5,516.40	-549.6	-0.6
Central and Eastern Europe and the CIS	4,539	..	..	..	2.6	..	38.3	8,856.50	22.7	(.)
OECD	8,795	..	100	..	5.3	..	30.9	10,382.40	67.9	0.1
High-income OECD	10,360	..	100	..	5.3	..	31.2	9,480.80	105.6	0.1
High human development	7,518	..	99	..	5.0	..	36.2	24,327.10	-366.8	-0.1
Medium human development	1,146	..	72	..	4.5	..	23.3	10,799.60	-462.4	-0.2
Low human development	134	..	25	..	..	..	29.8	4,076.50	-379.5	-0.5
High income	10,210	..	100	..	5.2	..	29.2	9,548.40	107.1	0.1
Middle income	2,039	..	90	..	4.2	..	33.8	23,132.30	-683.1	-0.2
Low income	449	..	45	..	..	..	23.9	6,745.60	-676.2	-0.6
World	2,701	..	76	1577.0	4.8	..	30.3	39,520.30	-1252.7	-0.2

Source: UNDP, HDR 2007/2008, Table 22: 302-305.

* Data for Iraq and Somalia are from the HDRO online database at [http://hdr.undp.org/en/statistics/data].

Energy sources

HDI Rank	Total primary energy supply (Mt of oil equivalent)		Fossil fuels Coal (%)		Oil (%)		Natural Gas (%)		Renewable energy Hydro, solar, wind and geothermal (%)		Biomass and waste (%)		Other Nuclear (%)	
	1990	2005	1990	2005	1990	2005	1990	2005	1990	2005	1990	2005	1990	2005
HIGH HUMAN DEVELOPMENT														
33 Kuwait	8.5	28.1	0.0	0.0	40.1	66.5	59.8	33.5	0.0	0.0	0.1	0.0	0.0	0.0
35 Qatar	6.3	15.8	0.0	0.0	12.1	15.7	87.8	84.3	0.0	0.0	0.1	(.)	0.0	0.0
39 United Arab Emirates	22.5	46.9	0.0	0.0	39.9	27.9	60.1	72.1	0.0	0.0	0.0	(.)	0.0	0.0
41 Bahrain	4.8	8.1	0.0	0.0	26.5	23.2	73.5	76.8	0.0	0.0	0.0	0.0	0.0	0.0
56 Libyan Arab Jamahiriya	11.5	19.0	0.0	0.0	63.8	72.2	35.1	27.0	0.0	0.0	1.1	0.8	0.0	0.0
58 Oman	4.6	14.0	0.0	0.0	46.6	33.3	53.4	66.7	0.0	0.0	0.0	0.0	0.0	0.0
61 Saudi Arabia	61.3	140.3	0.0	0.0	64.7	63.6	35.3	36.4	0.0	0.0	(.)	(.)	0.0	0.0
MEDIUM HUMAN DEVELOPMENT														
86 Jordan	3.5	7.1	0.0	0.0	95.3	78.5	2.9	19.5	1.7	1.0	0.1	(.)	0.0	0.0
88 Lebanon	2.3	5.6	0.0	2.4	93.7	92.9	0.0	0.0	1.9	1.8	4.4	2.3	0.0	0.0
91 Tunisia	5.5	8.5	1.4	0.0	57.5	50.0	22.3	36.6	0.1	0.2	18.7	13.3	0.0	0.0
104 Algeria	23.9	34.8	2.6	2.0	40.6	31.7	56.7	66.0	(.)	0.1	0.1	0.2	0.0	0.0
106 Occupied Palestinian Territories	..	..	..	..	..	..	..	..	..	..	..	..	..	..
108 Syrian Arab Republic	11.7	17.9	0.0	(.)	86.3	65.3	11.7	33.0	2.0	1.7	(.)	(.)	0.0	0.0
112 Egypt	31.9	61.3	2.4	1.5	70.5	49.2	21.1	45.3	2.7	1.9	3.3	2.3	0.0	0.0
126 Morocco	6.7	13.8	16.8	32.3	76.1	60.2	0.6	2.8	1.6	1.0	4.7	3.3	0.0	0.0
134 Comoros	..	..	..	..	..	..	..	..	..	..	..	..	..	..
137 Mauritania	..	..	..	..	..	..	..	..	..	..	..	..	..	..
147 Sudan	10.6	18.4	0.0	0.0	17.5	19.9	0.0	0.0	0.8	0.6	81.7	79.5	0.0	0.0
149 Djibouti	..	..	..	..	..	..	..	..	..	..	..	..	..	..
153 Yemen	2.6	6.7	0.0	0.0	97.0	98.8	0.0	0.0	0.0	0.0	3.0	1.2	0.0	0.0
WITHOUT HDI RANK														
Iraq	19.1	30.8	0.0	0.0	90.2	92.3	8.5	7.0	1.2	0.1	0.1	0.1	0.0	0.0
Somalia	..	..	..	..	..	..	..	..	..	..	..	..	..	..
All developing countries	.. T	.. T	30.3	32.5	30.5	31.0	9.4	14.1	2.7	2.9	26.3	18.0	0.8	1.4
Least developed countries	.. T	.. T	..	..	..	17.4	..	..	..	..	..	..	..	..
Arab States	237.4 T	477.1 T	1.1	1.3	59.5	54.2	33.9	40.2	0.7	0.4	4.8	3.8	0.0	0.0
East Asia and the Pacific	.. T	.. T	..	..	..	25.1	..	..	..	..	..	..	..	..
Latin America and the Caribbean	.. T	.. T	4.5	4.8	51.9	48.7	16.8	21.7	7.9	9.0	17.7	14.3	0.7	1.1
South Asia	456.2 T	818.9 T	23.9	26.1	27.7	28.3	9.0	17.9	1.9	1.7	37.1	25.3	0.4	0.6
Sub-Saharan Africa	.. T	.. T	..	..	..	13.6	..	..	..	..	..	..	..	..
Central and Eastern Europe and the CIS	1,751.5 T	1,266.3 T	27.6	22.6	29.8	20.5	36.1	46.0	1.4	2.2	1.2	2.1	4.0	7.0
OECD	4,525.5 T	5,547.6 T	23.5	20.4	42.0	40.5	18.6	21.8	2.9	2.7	3.1	3.5	9.9	11.0
High-income OECD	4,149.4 T	5,101.1 T	22.2	19.9	42.3	40.6	19.0	21.7	2.9	2.6	3.0	3.4	10.6	11.6
High human development	5,950.8 T	6,981.2 T	21.7	18.3	40.9	39.3	22.8	26.0	2.8	2.9	3.4	3.9	8.3	9.5
Medium human development	.. T	3,816.7 T	36.8	40.7	24.7	25.1	12.9	13.8	2.0	2.5	22.7	16.8	1.0	1.2
Low human development	.. T	.. T	..	..	..	13.1	..	..	..	..	..	..	..	..
High income	4,300.4 T	5,423.2 T	21.7	19.0	42.9	41.5	19.5	22.7	2.8	2.5	2.9	3.2	10.2	11.0
Middle income	3,556.4 T	4,594.4 T	31.6	34.3	31.0	28.3	21.7	21.7	2.3	3.1	11.4	10.1	2.1	2.4
Low income	.. T	.. T	..	23.4	..	20.6	..	11.6	..	2.3	..	41.6	..	0.5
World	8,757.7 T	11,433.9 T	25.3	25.3	36.8	35.0	19.1	20.7	2.5	2.6	10.3	10.0	6.0	6.3

Source: UNDP, HDR 2007/2008, Table 23: 306-309.

* Data for Iraq and Somalia are from the HDRO online database at [http://hdr.undp.org/en/statistics/data].

Carbon dioxide emissions and stocks

		Carbon dioxide emissions											Carbon dioxide emissions from forests biomass (Mt CO2 per year)	Carbon stocks in forests biomass (Mt Carbon)
		Total (Mt CO2)		Annual change (%)	Share of world total (%)		Per capita (t CO2)		Carbon intensity of energy CO2 emissions per unit of energy use (kt of CO2 per kt of oil equivalent)		Carbon intensity of growth CO2 emissions per unit of GDP (kt of CO2 per million 2000 PPP US$)			
HDI Rank		1990	2004	1990-2004	1990	2004	1990	2004	1990	2004	1990	2004	1990-2005	2005
HIGH HUMAN DEVELOPMENT														
33	Kuwait	43.4	99.3	9.2	0.2	0.3	20.3	37.1	5.13	3.95	..	1.81	..	..
35	Qatar	12.2	52.9	23.9	0.1	0.2	24.9	79.3	1.76	2.93	..	..	..	..
39	United Arab Emirates	54.7	149.1	12.3	0.2	0.5	27.2	34.1	2.43	3.40	1.19	1.57	-0.7	16.6
41	Bahrain	11.7	16.9	3.2	0.1	0.1	24.2	23.9	2.43	2.26	1.92	1.30	..	..
56	Libyan Arab Jamahiriya	37.8	59.9	4.2	0.2	0.2	9.1	9.3	3.27	3.29	..	..	0.0	6.4
58	Oman	10.3	30.9	14.3	(.)	0.1	6.3	13.6	2.25	2.61	0.52	0.88	..	..
61	Saudi Arabia	254.8	308.2	1.5	1.1	1.1	15.9	13.6	3.78	2.19	1.18	1.02	0.0	17.5
MEDIUM HUMAN DEVELOPMENT														
86	Jordan	10.2	16.5	4.4	(.)	0.1	3.1	2.9	2.91	2.52	0.84	0.66	0.0	2.3
88	Lebanon	9.1	16.3	5.6	(.)	0.1	3.3	4.2	3.94	3.01	1.24	0.92	..	1.8
91	Tunisia	13.3	22.9	5.2	0.1	0.1	1.6	2.3	2.40	2.63	0.35	0.32	-0.9	9.8
104	Algeria	77.0	193.9	10.8	0.3	0.7	3.0	5.5	3.23	5.89	0.56	0.99	-6.0	114.0
106	Occupied Palestinian Territories	..	0.6	..	..	(.)	..	0.2	..	..	..	..	..	..
108	Syrian Arab Republic	35.9	68.4	6.5	0.2	0.2	3.0	3.8	3.08	3.71	1.11	1.11	..	..
112	Egypt	75.4	158.1	7.8	0.3	0.5	1.5	2.3	2.37	2.78	0.48	0.58	-0.6	7.1
126	Morocco	23.5	41.1	5.4	0.1	0.1	1.0	1.4	3.49	3.59	0.29	0.34	-9.5	240.0
134	Comoros	0.1	0.1	2.4	(.)	(.)	0.1	0.1	..	..	0..08	0.09	0.2	0.8
137	Mauritania	2.6	2.6	-0.2	(.)	(.)	1.3	0.8	..	..	0.70	0.44	0.9	6.6
147	Sudan	5.4	10.4	6.6	(.)	(.)	0.2	0.3	0.51	0.59	0.19	0.17	48.9	1530.7
149	Djibouti	0.4	0.4	0.3	(.)	(.)	1.0	0.5	..	..	0.22	0.25	..	0.4
153	Yemen	10.1	21.1	8.3	(.)	0.1	0.9	1.0	3.25	3.31	1.15	1.25	0.0	5.1
WITHOUT HDI RANK														
	Iraq	48.5	81.6	4.9	0.2	0.3	2.8	3.0	2.55	2.74	..	..	..	..
	Somalia	(.)	..	..	(.)	..	..	..	..	..	..	..	15.2	386.6
All developing countries		6,831.1 T	12,303.3 T	5.7	30.1	42.5	1.7	2.4	2.34	2.59	0.64	0.56	5,091.5	190,359.7
Least developed countries		74.1 T	146.3 T	7.0	0.3	0.5	0.2	0.2	..	..	0.14	0.17	1,097.8	50,811.2
Arab States		733.6 T	1,348.4 T	6.0	3.2	4.7	3.4	4.5	3.02	2.94	0.75	0.86	44.4	2,393.3
East Asia and the Pacific		3,413.5 T	6,682.0 T	6.8	15.0	23.1	2.1	3.5	..	..	0.90	0.63	2,293.8	27,222.9
Latin America and the Caribbean		1,087.7 T	1,422.6 T	2.2	4.8	4.9	2.5	2.6	2.25	2.19	0.40	0.36	1,667.0	97,557.2
South Asia		990.7 T	1,954.6 T	7.0	4.4	6.7	0.8	1.3	1.94	2.34	0.49	0.46	-49.3	3,843.5
Sub-Saharan Africa		454.8 T	663.1 T	3.3	2.0	2.3	1.0	1.0	..	..	0.55	0.57	1,153.6	58,523.2
Central and Eastern Europe and the CIS		4,182.0 T	3,168.0 T	-2.0	18.4	10.9	10.3	7.9	2.71	2.51	1.49	0.97	-165.9	37,592.0
OECD		11,205.2 T	13,318.6 T	1.3	49.4	46.0	10.8	11.5	2.47	2.42	0.54	0.45	-999.7	59,956.6
High-income OECD		10,055.4 T	12,137.5 T	1.5	44.3	41.9	12.0	13.2	2.42	2.39	0.52	0.45	-979.6	45,488.9
High human development		14,495.5 T	16,615.8 T	1.0	63.9	57.3	9.8	10.1	2.45	2.40	0.60	0.48	89.8	152,467.3
Medium human development		5,944.4 T	10,215.2 T	5.1	26.2	35.2	1.8	2.5	2.39	2.76	0.83	0.61	3,026.5	86,534.2
Low human development		77.6 T	161.7 T	7.7	0.3	0.6	0.3	0.3	..	..	0.24	0.36	858.0	41,254.0
High income		10,572.1 T	12,975.1 T	1.6	46.6	44.8	12.1	13.3	2.44	2.40	0.53	0.46	-937.4	54,215.3
Middle income		8,971.5 T	12,162.9 T	2.5	39.5	42.0	3.4	4.0	2.57	2.76	0.95	0.65	3,693.1	170,735.6
Low income		1,323.4 T	2,083.9 T	4.1	5.8	7.2	0.8	0.9	..	..	0.47	0.43	1,275.1	56,686.1
World		22,702.5 T	28,982.7 T	2.0	100.0	100.0	4.3	4.5	2.64	2.63	0.68	0.55	4,038.1	282,650.1

Source: UNDP, HDR 2007/2008, Table 24: 310-313.

* Data for Iraq and Somalia are from the HDRO online database at [http://hdr.undp.org/en/statistics/data].

Status of major international environmental treaties

HDI Rank		Cartagena Protocol on Biosafety 2000	Framework Convention on Climate Change 1992	Kyoto Protocol to the Framework Convention on Climate Change 1997	Convention on Biological Diversity 1992	Vienna Convention for the protection of the Ozone Layer 1988	Montreal Protocol on Substances that deplete the Ozone Layer 1989	Stockholm Convention on Persistent Organic Pollutants 2001	Convention of the Law of the Sea 1982	Convention to Combat Desertification 1994
HIGH HUMAN DEVELOPMENT										
33	Kuwait	..	1994	2005	2002	1992	1992	2006	1986	1997
35	Qatar	2007	1996	2005	1996	1996	1996	2004	2002	1999
39	United Arab Emirates	..	1995	2005	2000	1989	1989	2002	**1982**	1998
41	Bahrain	..	1994	2006	1996	1990	1990	2006	1985	1997
56	Libyan Arab Jamahiriya	2005	1999	2006	2001	1990	1990	2005	**1984**	1996
58	Oman	2003	1995	2005	1995	1999	1999	2005	1989	1996
61	Saudi Arabia	..	1994	2005	2001	1993	1993	**2002**	1996	1997
MEDIUM HUMAN DEVELOPMENT										
86	Jordan	2003	1993	2003	1993	1989	1989	2004	1995	1996
88	Lebanon	..	1994	2006	1994	1993	1993	2003	1995	1996
91	Tunisia	2003	1993	2003	1993	1989	1989	2004	1985	1995
104	Algeria	2004	1993	2005	1995	1992	1992	2006	1996	1996
106	Occupied Palestinian Territories	..	..	..	..	..	..	..	..	..
108	Syrian Arab Republic	2004	1996	2006	1996	1989	1989	2005	..	1997
112	Egypt	2003	1994	2005	1994	1988	1988	2003	1983	1995
126	Morocco	2000	1995	2002	1995	1995	1995	2004	2007	1996
134	Comoros	..	1994	..	1994	1994	1994	2007	1994	1998
137	Mauritania	2005	1994	2005	1996	1994	1994	2005	1996	1996
147	Sudan	2005	1993	2004	1995	1993	1993	2006	1985	1995
149	Djibouti	2002	1995	2002	1994	1999	1999	2004	1991	1997
153	Yemen	2005	1996	2004	1996	1996	1996	2004	1987	1997
WITHOUT HDI RANK										
	Iraq	..	..	..	..	..	..	..	1985	..
	Somalia	..	..	..	..	2001	2001	..	1989	2002

Data refer to year of ratification, accession approval or succession. All these stages have the same legal effects. **Bold** signifies signature not yet followed by ratification.

Source: UNDP, HDR 2007/2008, Table 25: 314-317.

* Data for Iraq and Somalia are from the HDRO online database at [http://hdr.undp.org/en/statistics/data].

Table 23

Refugees and armaments

HDI Rank	Internally displaced people (thousands) 2006	Refugees By country of asylum (thousands) 2006	Refugees By country of origin (thousands) 2006	Conventional arms transfers (1990 prices) Imports (US$ millions) 1996	Imports (US$ millions) 2006	Exports US$ millions 2006	Exports Share (%) 2002-2006	Total armed forces Thousands 2007	Total armed forces Index (1985=100) 2007
HIGH HUMAN DEVELOPMENT									
33 Kuwait	..	(.)	1	1,161	107	0	(.)	16	133
35 Qatar	..	(.)	(.)	201	0	0	(.)	12	200
39 United Arab Emirates	..	(.)	(.)	474	2,439	7	(.)	51	119
41 Bahrain	..	..	(.)	181	60	0	(.)	11	393
56 Libyan Arab Jamahiriya	..	3	2	0	5	24	(.)	76	..
58 Oman	..	(.)	(.)	284	406	0	(.)	42	144
61 Saudi Arabia	..	241	1	1,725	148	0	(.)	225	360
MEDIUM HUMAN DEVELOPMENT									
86 Jordan	..	500	2	76	117	13	(.)	101	144
88 Lebanon	216-800	20	12	20	0	0	(.)	72	414
91 Tunisia	..	(.)	3	56	16	..	..	35	100
104 Algeria	1,000	94	8	87	173	..	..	138	81
106 Occupied Palestinian Territories	25-57	..	334	9	0	..	..	..	..
108 Syrian Arab Republic	305	702	12	21	9	3	(.)	308	77
112 Egypt	..	88	8	986	526	0	(.)	469	105
126 Morocco	..	1	5	86	49	..	..	201	135
134 Comoros	..	..	(.)	..	..	..	..	..	..
137 Mauritania	..	1	33	2	0	..	..	16	188
147 Sudan	5,355	202	686	29	48	..	..	105	186
149 Djibouti	..	9	(.)	0	0	..	..	11	367
153 Yemen	..	96	1	0	0	..	..	67	105
WITHOUT HDI RANK									
Iraq	1,884	44	1,451	0	195	..	..	227	23
Somalia	400	1	464	0	0	..	..	..	..
All developing countries	..	7,084 T	..	..	..	..	..	13,950 T	90
Least developed countries	..	2,177 T	..	..	..	..	..	1,781 T	152
Arab States	..	2,001 T	..	..	..	..	..	2,167 T	80
East Asia and the Pacific	..	..	..	..	..	..	..	5,952 T	80
Latin America and the Caribbean	..	..	..	..	..	..	..	1,327 T	99
South Asia	..	2,326 T	..	..	..	..	..	2,877 T	113
Sub-Saharan Africa	..	2,227 T	..	..	..	..	..	1,102 T	130
Central and Eastern Europe and the CIS	..	168 T	..	..	..	..	..	2,050 T	..
OECD	..	2,556 T	..	..	..	..	..	4,995 T	69
High-income OECD	..	2,533 T	..	..	..	..	..	4,028 T	69
High human development	..	2,885 T	..	..	..	25,830 T	..	7,101 T	52
Medium human development	..	5,389 T	..	..	..	..	..	10,143 T	91
Low human development	..	1,453 T	..	..	..	..	..	835 T	146
High income	..	..	..	..	..	..	..	4,611 T	74
Middle income	..	3,267 T	..	..	..	..	..	9,440 T	..
Low income	..	3,741 T	..	..	..	..	..	5,413 T	110
World	23,700 T	9,894 T	9,894 T	22,115 T	26,130 T	26,742 T	..	19,801 T	73

Source: UNDP, HDR 2007/2008, Table 26: 318-321.

* Data for Iraq and Somalia are from the HDRO online database at [http://hdr.undp.org/en/statistics/data].

Table **24**

Crime and justice

HDI Rank		Intentional homicides (per 100,000 people) 2000-2004	Prison population			Year in which countries have partially or completely abolished the death penalty
			Total 2007	(per 100,000 people) 2007	Female (% of total) 2007	
HIGH HUMAN DEVELOPMENT						
33	Kuwait	1.0	3,500	130	15	..
35	Qatar	0.8	465	55	1	..
39	United Arab Emirates	0.6	8,927	288	11	..
41	Bahrain	1.0	701	95	..	..
56	Libyan Arab Jamahiriya	..	11,790	207	3	..
58	Oman	0.6	2,020	81	5	..
61	Saudi Arabia	0.9	28,612	132	6	..
MEDIUM HUMAN DEVELOPMENT						
86	Jordan	0.9	5,589	104	2	..
88	Lebanon	5.7	5,971	168	4	..
91	Tunisia	1.2	26,000	263	..	1991
104	Algeria	1.4	42,000	127	1	1993
106	Occupied Palestinian Territories	4.0	..	..	..	..
108	Syrian Arab Republic	1.1	10,599	58	7	..
112	Egypt	0.4	61,845	87	4	..
126	Morocco	0.5	54,542	175	2	1993
134	Comoros	..	200	30	..	..
137	Mauritania	..	815	26	3	1987
147	Sudan	0.3	12,000	36	2	..
149	Djibouti	..	384	61	..	1995
153	Yemen	4.0	14,000	83	..	..
WITHOUT HDI RANK						
	Iraq	6.3	15,000	60	3	..
	Somalia	..	..	..	..	..

Source: UNDP, HDR 2007/2008, Table 27: 322-325.

* Data for Iraq and Somalia are from the HDRO online database at [http://hdr.undp.org/en/statistics/data].

Gender-related development index

HDI Rank		Gender-related development index (GDI)		Life expectancy at birth (years) 2005		Adult literacy rate (% aged 15 and older) 1995-2005		Combined gross enrolment ratio for primary, secondary and tertiary education (%) 2005		Estimated earned income (PPP US$) 2005		HDI rank minus GDI rank
		Rank	Value	Female	Male	Female	Male	Female	Male	Female	Male	
HIGH HUMAN DEVELOPMENT												
33	Kuwait	32	0.884	79.6	75.7	91.0	94.4	79	71	12,623	36,403	0
35	Qatar	37	0.863	75.8	74.6	88.6	89.1	85	71	9,211	37,774	-3
39	United Arab Emirates	43	0.855	81.0	76.8	87.8	89.0	68	54	8,329	33,555	-5
41	Bahrain	42	0.857	77.0	73.9	83.6	88.6	90	82	10,496	29,796	-2
56	Libyan Arab Jamahiriya	62	0.797	76.3	71.1	74.8	92.8	97	91	4,054	13,460	-9
58	Oman	67	0.788	76.7	73.6	73.5	86.9	67	67	4,516	23,880	-13
61	Saudi Arabia	70	0.783	74.6	70.3	76.3	87.5	76	76	4,031	25,678	-13
MEDIUM HUMAN DEVELOPMENT												
86	Jordan	80	0.760	73.8	70.3	87.0	95.2	79	77	2,566	8,270	-2
88	Lebanon	81	0.759	73.7	69.4	93.6	93.6	86	83	2,701	8,585	-1
91	Tunisia	83	0.750	75.6	71.5	65.3	83.4	79	74	3,748	12,924	-1
104	Algeria	95	0.720	73.0	70.4	60.1	79.6	74	73	3,546	10,515	-2
106	Occupied Palestinian Territories	..	..	74.4	71.3	88.0	96.7	84	81	..	..	..
108	Syrian Arab Republic	96	0.710	75.5	71.8	73.6	87.8	63	67	1,907	5,684	0
112	Egypt	..	..	73.0	68.5	59.4	83.0	..	..	1,635	7,024	..
126	Morocco	112	0.621	72.7	68.3	39.6	65.7	55	62	1,846	7,297	-1
134	Comoros	116	0.554	66.3	62.0	63.9	63.9	42	50	1,337	2,643	0
137	Mauritania	118	0.543	65.0	61.5	43.4	59.5	45	47	1,489	2,996	1
147	Sudan	131	0.502	58.9	56.0	51.8	71.1	35	39	832	3,317	-3
149	Djibouti	129	0.507	55.2	52.6	79.9	79.9	22	29	1,422	2,935	1
153	Yemen	136	0.472	63.1	60.0	34.7	73.1	43	67	424	1,422	-3
WITHOUT HDI RANK												
	Iraq	..	..	59.9	55.7	64.2	84.1	51	67	374	1,925	..
	Somalia	..	..	48.2	45.9	..	..	..	..	477	1,000	..

Source: UNDP, HDR 2007/2008, Table 28: 326-329.

* Data for Iraq and Somalia are from the HDRO online database at [http://hdr.undp.org/en/statistics/data].

Table **26**

Gender empowerment measure

HDI Rank		Gender empowerment measure (GEM)		MDG Seats in parliament held by women (% of total)	Female legislators, senior officials and managers (% of total)	Female professional and technical workers (% of total)	Ratio of estimated female to male earned income
		Rank	Value				
HIGH HUMAN DEVELOPMENT							
33	Kuwait	..	..	3.1	..	..	0.35
35	Qatar	84	0.374	0.0	8	24	0.24
39	United Arab Emirates	29	0.652	22.5	8	25	0.25
41	Bahrain	..	..	13.8	..	..	0.35
56	Libyan Arab Jamahiriya	..	..	7.7	..	..	0.30
58	Oman	80	0.391	7.8	9	33	0.19
61	Saudi Arabia	92	0.254	0.0	31	6	0.16
MEDIUM HUMAN DEVELOPMENT							
86	Jordan	..	..	7.9	..	..	0.31
88	Lebanon	..	..	4.7	..	..	0.31
91	Tunisia	..	..	19.3	..	..	0.29
104	Algeria	..	..	6.2	..	32	0.34
106	Occupied Palestinian Territories	..	..	..	11	35	..
108	Syrian Arab Republic	..	..	12.0	..	40	0.34
112	Egypt	91	0.263	3.8	9	30	0.23
126	Morocco	88	0.325	6.4	12	35	0.25
134	Comoros	..	..	3.0	..	..	0.51
137	Mauritania	..	..	17.6	..	..	0.50
147	Sudan	..	..	16.4	..	..	0.25
149	Djibouti	..	..	10.8	..	..	0.48
153	Yemen	93	0.129	0.7	4	15	0.30
WITHOUT HDI RANK							
	Iraq	..	..	25.5	..	..	0.19
	Somalia	..	..	8.2	..	..	0.48

Source: UNDP, HDR 2007/2008, Table 29: 330-333.

* Data for Iraq and Somalia are from the HDRO online database at [http://hdr.undp.org/en/statistics/data].

Table **27**

Gender inequality in education

HDI Rank	Adult literacy Female rate (% aged 15 and older) 1995-2005	Adult literacy Ratio of female rate to male rate 1995-2005	MDG Youth literacy Female rate (% aged 15-24) 1995-2005	MDG Youth literacy Ratio of female rate to male rate 1995-2005	Net primary enrolment Female rate (%) 2005	Net primary enrolment Ratio of female rate to male rate 2005	MDG Gross primary enrolment Female ratio (%) 2005	MDG Gross primary enrolment Ratio of female rate to male rate 2005	MDG Gross secondary enrolment Female ratio (%) 2005	MDG Gross secondary enrolment Ratio of female rate to male rate 2005	MDG Gross tertiary enrolment Female ratio (%) 2005	MDG Gross tertiary enrolment Ratio of female rate to male rate 2005
HIGH HUMAN DEVELOPMENT												
33 Kuwait	91.0	0.96	99.8	1.00	86	0.99	97	0.98	98	1.06	29	2.66
35 Qatar	88.6	0.99	97.5	1.03	96	1.00	106	0.99	99	0.98	33	3.45
39 United Arab Emirates	87.8	0.99	95.5	0.98	70	0.97	82	0.97	66	1.05	39	3.24
41 Bahrain	83.6	0.94	97.3	1.00	97	1.00	104	0.99	102	1.06	50	2.23
56 Libyan Arab Jamahiriya	74.8	0.81	96.5	0.97	..	..	106	0.98	107	1.19	59	1.09
58 Oman	73.5	0.85	96.7	0.99	76	1.01	85	1.00	85	0.96	19	1.09
61 Saudi Arabia	76.3	0.87	94.7	0.98	79	1.03	91	1.00	86	0.96	34	1.47
MEDIUM HUMAN DEVELOPMENT												
86 Jordan	87.0	0.91	99.0	1.00	90	1.02	96	1.01	88	1.02	40	1.06
88 Lebanon	..	..	..	..	92	0.99	105	0.97	93	1.10	54	1.15
91 Tunisia	65.3	0.78	92.2	0.96	97	1.01	108	0.97	88	1.09	35	1.40
104 Algeria	60.1	0.76	86.1	0.92	95	0.98	107	0.93	86	1.07	24	1.37
106 Occupied Palestinian Territories	88.0	0.91	98.8	1.00	80	0.99	88	0.99	102	1.07	39	1.04
108 Syrian Arab Republic	73.6	0.84	90.2	0.95	..	..	121	0.95	65	0.94	..	..
112 Egypt	59.4	0.71	78.9	0.88	91	0.95	97	0.94	82	0.92	..	..
126 Morocco	39.6	0.60	60.5	0.75	83	0.94	99	0.89	46	0.85	10	0.85
134 Comoros	..	..	..	..	..	..	80	0.88	30	0.76	2	0.77
137 Mauritania	43.4	0.73	55.5	0.82	72	1.00	94	1.01	19	0.85	2	0.33
147 Sudan	51.8	0.73	71.4	0.84	..	..	56	0.87	33	0.94	..	..
149 Djibouti	..	..	..	..	30	0.81	36	0.82	19	0.66	2	0.73
153 Yemen	34.7	0.47	58.9	0.65	63	0.73	75	0.74	31	0.49	5	0.37
WITHOUT HDI RANK												
Iraq	64.2	0.76	80.5	0.91	81	0.86	89	0.83	35	0.66	11	0.59
Somalia	..	..	..	..	..	..	..	..	..	..	..	..
All developing countries	69.9	0.91	81.4	0.91	83	0.95	104	0.94	58	0.93	16	0.91
Least developed countries	44.3	0.80	58.0	0.80	70	0.92	90	0.89	28	0.81	3	0.63
Arab States	59.4	0.88	79.5	0.88	77	0.92	88	0.90	65	0.92	21	1.01
East Asia and the Pacific	86.7	0.99	97.5	0.99	93	0.99	110	0.98	72	1.00	21	0.93
Latin America and the Caribbean	89.7	1.01	97.0	1.01	95	1.00	115	0.96	91	1.08	32	1.17
South Asia	47.4	0.81	66.6	0.81	82	0.92	109	0.93	48	0.83	9	0.74
Sub-Saharan Africa	51.2	0.84	65.1	0.84	68	0.93	92	0.89	28	0.79	4	0.62
Central and Eastern Europe and the CIS	98.7	1.00	99.6	1.00	91	1.00	107	0.99	90	0.98	63	1.30
OECD	..	..	..	..	96	1.00	101	0.99	98	1.00	65	1.17
High-income OECD	..	..	..	..	96	1.01	102	0.99	103	1.00	76	1.20
High human development	93.6	1.01	98.4	1.01	..	..	..	..	..	..	..	..
Medium human development	71.2	0.92	83.2	0.92	..	..	..	..	..	..	..	..
Low human development	43.8	0.80	58.9	0.80	..	..	..	..	..	..	..	..
High income	..	..	..	..	95	1.01	101	0.99	102	1.00	73	1.21
Middle income	86.5	0.99	96.2	0.99	92	0.99	110	0.97	78	1.01	28	1.09
Low income	48.8	0.82	65.8	0.82	76	0.92	99	0.91	41	0.82	7	0.68
World	72.7	0.92	82.5	0.92	85	0.96	104	0.95	64	0.94	25	1.05

Source: UNDP, HDR 2007/2008, Table 30: 334-337.

* Data for Iraq and Somalia are from the HDRO online database at [http://hdr.undp.org/en/ statistics/data].

Gender inequality in economic activity

HDI rank		Female economic activity (aged 15 and older)			Employment by economic activity (%)						Contributing family workers (%)	
					Agriculture		Industry		Services			
		Rate (%) 2005	Index (1990=100) 2005	As % of male rate 2005	Women 1995-2005	Men 1995-2005	Women 1995-2005	Men 1995-2005	Women 1995-2005	Men 1995-2005	Women 1995-2005	Men 1995-2005
HIGH HUMAN DEVELOPMENT												
33	Kuwait	49.0	141	58	..	..	..	..	..	..	..	..
35	Qatar	36.3	123	41	(.)	3	3	48	97	49	..	..
39	United Arab Emirates	38.2	152	42	(.)	9	14	36	86	55	..	..
41	Bahrain	29.3	103	33	..	..	..	..	..	..	..	..
56	Libyan Arab Jamahiriya	32.1	168	40	..	..	..	..	..	..	..	..
58	Oman	22.7	149	28	5	7	14	11	80	82	..	..
61	Saudi Arabia	17.6	118	22	1	5	1	24	98	71	..	..
MEDIUM HUMAN DEVELOPMENT												
86	Jordan	27.5	155	36	2	4	13	23	83	73	..	..
88	Lebanon	32.4	102	41	..	..	..	..	..	..	..	..
91	Tunisia	28.6	138	38	..	..	..	..	..	..	..	..
104	Algeria	35.7	158	45	22	20	28	26	49	54	..	..
106	Occupied Palestinian Territories	10.3	111	15	34	12	8	28	56	59	..	..
108	Syrian Arab Republic	38.6	135	44	58	24	7	31	35	45	..	..
112	Egypt	20.1	76	27	39	28	6	23	55	49	..	..
126	Morocco	26.8	110	33	57	39	19	21	25	40	..	..
134	Comoros	57.9	92	67	..	..	..	..	..	..	..	..
137	Mauritania	54.4	98	65	..	..	..	..	..	..	..	..
147	Sudan	23.7	86	33	..	..	..	..	..	..	..	..
149	Djibouti	52.9	94	64	(.)	3	1	11	88	78	..	..
153	Yemen	29.7	108	39	88	43	3	14	9	43	..	..
Developing countries		52.4	101	64	..	..	..	..	..	..	..	..
Least developed countries		61.8	95	72	..	..	..	..	..	..	..	..
Arab States		26.7	110	34	..	..	..	..	..	..	..	..
East Asia and the Pacific		65.2	96	79	..	..	..	..	..	..	..	..
Latin America and the Caribbean		51.9	127	65	..	..	..	..	..	..	..	..
South Asia		36.2	99	44	..	..	..	..	..	..	..	..
Sub-Saharan Africa		62.6	96	73	..	..	..	..	..	..	..	..
Central and Eastern Europe and the CIS		52.4	89	79	..	..	..	..	..	..	..	..
OECD		50.3	105	72	..	..	..	..	..	..	..	..
High-income OECD		52.8	107	76	..	..	..	..	..	..	..	..
High human development		51.6	107	73	..	..	..	..	..	..	..	..
Medium human development		52.2	98	64	..	..	..	..	..	..	..	..
Low human development		63.4	97	72	..	..	..	..	..	..	..	..
High income		52.1	107	75	..	..	..	..	..	..	..	..
Middle income		57.0	101	72	..	..	..	..	..	..	..	..
Low income		45.7	96	55	..	..	..	..	..	..	..	..
World		52.5	101	67	..	..	..	..	..	..	..	..

Source: UNDP, HDR 2007/2008, Table 31: 338-341.

Women's political participation

HDI rank		Year women received right		Year first woman elected (E) or appointed (A) to parliament	Women in government at ministerial level (% of total) 2005	MDG Seats in parliament held by women (% of total)		Upper house or senate 2007
		To vote	To stand for election			Lower or single house		
						1990	2007	
HIGH HUMAN DEVELOPMENT								
33	Kuwait	2005	2005	2005 A	0.0	..	3.1	—
35	Qatar	2003	..	..	7.7	..	0.0	—
39	United Arab Emirates	—	—	—	5.6	0.0	22.5	—
41	Bahrain	1973, 2002	1973, 2002	2002 A	8.7	..	2.5	25.0
56	Libyan Arab Jamahiriya	1964	1964	..	..	..	7.7	—
58	Oman	1994, 2003	1994, 2003	..	10.0	..	2.4	15.5
61	Saudi Arabia	—	—	—	0.0	..	0.0	—
MEDIUM HUMAN DEVELOPMENT								
86	Jordan	1974	1974	1989 A	10.7	0.0	5.5	12.7
88	Lebanon	1952	1952	1991 A	6.9	0.0	4.7	—
91	Tunisia	1959	1959	1959 E	7.1	4.3	22.8	13.4
104	Algeria	1962	1962	1962 A	10.5	2.4	7.2	3.1
106	Occupied Palestinian Territories	..	..	..	..	..	..	..
108	Syrian Arab Republic	1949, 1953	1953	1973 E	6.3	9.2	12.0	—
112	Egypt	1956	1956	1957 E	5.9	3.9	2.0	6.8
126	Morocco	1963	1963	1993 E	5.9	0.0	10.8	1.1
134	Comoros	1956	1956	1993 E	..	0.0	3.0	—
137	Mauritania	1961	1961	1975 E	9.1	..	17.9	17.0
147	Sudan	1964	1964	1964 E	2.6	..	17.8	4.0
149	Djibouti	1946	1986	2003 E	5.3	0.0	10.8	—
153	Yemen	1967, 1970	1967, 1970	1990 E	2.9	4.1	0.3	1.8
WITHOUT HDI RANK								
	Iraq	1980	1980	1980 E	18.8	10.8	25.5	—
	Somalia	1956	1956	1979 E	..	4.0	8.2	—

Source: UNDP, HDR 2007/2008, Table 33: 343-346.

* Data for Iraq and Somalia are from the HDRO online database at [http://hdr.undp.org/en/statistics/data].

Table 30

Status of major international human rights instruments

HDI rank		International Convention on the Prevention and Punishment of the Crime of Genocide 1948	International Convention on the Elimination of All Forms of Racial Discrimination 1965	International Covenant on Civil and Political Rights 1966	International Covenant on Economic, Social and Cultural Rights 1966	Convention on the Elimination of All Forms of Discrimination against Women 1979	Convention against Torture and Other Cruel, Inhuman or Degrading Treatment or Punishment 1984	Convention on the Rights of the Child 1989
HIGH HUMAN DEVELOPMENT								
33	Kuwait	1995	1968	1996	1996	1994	1996	1991
35	Qatar	..	1976	..	..	..	2000	1995
39	United Arab Emirates	2005	1974	..	..	2004	..	1997
41	Bahrain	1990	1990	2006	..	2002	1998	1992
56	Libyan Arab Jamahiriya	1989	1968	1970	1970	1989	1989	1993
58	Oman	..	2003	..	..	2006	..	1996
61	Saudi Arabia	1950	1997	..	..	2000	1997	1996
MEDIUM HUMAN DEVELOPMENT								
86	Jordan	1950	1974	1975	1975	1992	1991	1991
88	Lebanon	1953	1971	1972	1972	1997	2000	1991
91	Tunisia	1956	1967	1969	1969	1985	1988	1992
104	Algeria	1963	1972	1989	1989	1996	1989	1993
106	Occupied Palestinian Territories	..	..	..	..	..	..	.. ..
108	Syrian Arab Republic	1955	1969	1969	1969	2003	2004	1993
112	Egypt	1952	1967	1982	1982	1981	1986	1990
126	Morocco	1958	1970	1979	1979	1993	1993	1993
134	Comoros	2004	2004	..	..	1994	**2000**	1993
137	Mauritania	..	1988	2004	2004	2001	2004	1991
147	Sudan	2003	1977	1986	1986	..	**1986**	1990
149	Djibouti	..	**2006**	2002	2002	1998	2002	1990
153	Yemen	1987	1972	1987	1987	1984	1991	1991
WITHOUT HDI RANK								
	Iraq	1959	1970	1971	1971	1986	..	1994
	Somalia	..	1975	1990	1990	..	1990	**2002**

Data refer to year of ratification, accession or succession. All these stages have the same legal effects. **Bold** signifies signature not yet followed by ratification.

Source: UNDP, HDR 2007/2008, Table 34: 347-350.

* Data for Iraq and Somalia are from the HDRO online database at [http://hdr.undp.org/en/statistics/data].

Table **31**

Status of fundamental labour rights conventions

HDI rank		Freedom of association and collective bargaining		Elimination of forced and compulsory labour		Elimination of discrimination in respect of employment and occupation		Abolition of child labour	
		Convention 87	Convention 98	Convention 29	Convention 105	Convention 100	Convention 111	Convention 138	Convention 182
HIGH HUMAN DEVELOPMENT									
33	Kuwait	1961	..	1968	1961	..	1966	1999	2000
35	Qatar	..	..	1998	2007	..	1976	2006	2000
39	United Arab Emirates	..	..	1982	1997	1997	2001	1998	2001
41	Bahrain	..	..	1981	1998	..	2000	..	2001
56	Libyan Arab Jamahiriya	2000	1962	1961	1961	1962	1961	1975	2000
58	Oman	..	..	1998	2005	..	..	2005	2001
61	Saudi Arabia	...	...	1978	1978	1978	1978	...	2001
MEDIUM HUMAN DEVELOPMENT									
86	Jordan	..	1968	1966	1958	1966	1963	1998	2000
88	Lebanon	..	1977	1977	1977	1977	1977	2003	2001
91	Tunisia	1957	1957	1962	1959	1968	1959	1995	2000
104	Algeria	1962	1962	1962	1969	1962	1969	1984	2001
108	Syrian Arab Republic	1960	1957	1960	1958	1957	1960	2001	2003
112	Egypt	1957	1954	1955	1958	1960	1960	1999	2002
126	Morocco	..	1957	1957	1966	1979	1963	2000	2001
134	Comoros	1978	1978	1978	1978	1978	2004	2004	2004
137	Mauritania	1961	2001	1961	1997	2001	1963	2001	2001
147	Sudan	..	1957	1957	1970	1970	1970	2002	2003
149	Djibouti	1978	1978	1978	1978	1978	2005	2005	2005
153	Yemen	1976	1969	1969	1969	1976	1969	2000	2000
WITHOUT HDI RANK									
	Iraq	..	1962	1962	1959	1963	1959	1985	2001
	Somalia	..	..	1960	1961	..	1961	..	..

Years indicate the date of ratification.

Source: UNDP, HDR 2007/2008, Table 35: 351-354.

* Data for Iraq and Somalia are from the HDRO online database at [http://hdr.undp.org/en/statistics/data].

Annex II: Indicators of governance in the Arab countries

Table 1: Institutional quality in the Arab countries in 1996

	Voice and accountability	Political stability	Government effectiveness	Regulatory quality	Rule of law	Control of corruption	Average institutional quality
LOW INCOME	**-1.59**	**-1.97**	**-1.17**	**-1.53**	**-1.50**	**-0.90**	**-1.44**
Comoros	-0.04	1.05	-0.71	-0.82	..	..	-0.13
Mauritania	-0.95	0.56	0.20	-0.86	-0.88	..	-0.39
Somalia	-1.91	-2.30	-1.77	-2.91	-2.10	-1.74	-2.12
Sudan	-1.95	-2.58	-1.49	-1.88	-1.63	-1.13	-1.78
Yemen	-0.94	-1.15	-0.55	-0.44	-1.15	-0.29	-0.75
LOWER MIDDLE INCOME	**-1.17**	**-1.33**	**-0.26**	**-0.47**	**-0.41**	**-0.27**	**-0.65**
Algeria	-1.36	-2.44	-0.39	-0.94	-1.21	-0.37	-1.12
Djibouti	-0.72	0.21	-0.98	0.17	-0.24	..	-0.31
Egypt	-1.04	-1.07	-0.03	0.24	0.08	0.06	-0.29
Iraq	-1.96	-2.90	-1.49	-2.95	-1.61	-1.39	-2.05
Jordan	-0.37	0.17	0.23	0.29	0.44	-0.15	0.10
Morocco	-0.63	-0.61	-0.05	0.15	0.12	0.22	-0.13
Syria	-1.61	-0.82	-0.15	-0.91	-0.49	-0.79	-0.80
Tunisia	-0.85	0.16	0.51	0.56	-0.20	-0.10	0.01
OPT	-0.70	..	..	..	..	..	-0.70
UPPER MIDDLE INCOME	**-1.18**	**-0.88**	**-0.22**	**-0.94**	**-0.49**	**-0.51**	**-0.70**
Lebanon	-0.39	-0.52	0.21	0.02	-0.22	-0.23	-0.19
Libya	-1.82	-1.76	-1.02	-2.10	-1.29	-0.97	-1.49
Oman	-1.02	0.47	0.86	0.10	0.87	0.06	0.22
HIGH INCOME	**-1.44**	**-0.34**	**-0.17**	**-0.22**	**0.50**	**-0.27**	**-0.33**
Bahrain	-1.19	-0.82	0.43	0.51	0.17	0.02	-0.15
Kuwait	-0.47	0.01	0.35	-0.04	0.74	0.61	0.20
Qatar	-0.94	0.33	0.49	0.34	0.10	-0.12	0.03
Saudi Arabia	-1.62	-0.52	-0.34	-0.38	0.45	-0.42	-0.47
UAE	-1.02	0.74	0.42	0.53	0.84	0.13	0.27
OVERALL AVERAGE	**-1.28**	**-1.35**	**-0.44**	**-0.69**	**-0.56**	**-0.41**	**-0.80**

Source: Kauffman, World Bank Governance Indicators, 2008.
Note: Estimates between -2.5 and 2.5; higher is better.

Table 2: Institutional quality in the Arab countries in 2007

	Voice and accountability	Political stability	Government effectiveness	Regulatory quality	Rule of law	Control of corruption	Average institutional quality
LOW INCOME	**-1.49**	**-2.03**	**-1.25**	**-1.22**	**-1.40**	**-1.10**	**-1.42**
Comoros	-0.45	-0.40	-1.80	-1.43	-0.93	-0.69	-0.95
Mauritania	-0.75	-0.33	-0.68	-0.36	-0.60	-0.50	-0.54
Somalia	-1.89	-3.01	-2.35	-2.72	-2.64	-1.87	-2.41
Sudan	-1.73	-2.30	-1.18	-1.25	-1.46	-1.25	-1.53
Yemen	-1.06	-1.48	-1.02	-0.71	-0.94	-0.62	-0.97
LOWER MIDDLE INCOME	**-1.15**	**-1.00**	**-0.54**	**-0.53**	**-0.46**	**-0.58**	**-0.71**
Algeria	-1.01	-1.18	-0.52	-0.66	-0.72	-0.47	-0.76
Djibouti	-1.06	-0.05	-0.98	-0.80	-0.51	-0.48	-0.65
Egypt	-1.24	-0.77	-0.44	-0.31	-0.13	-0.58	-0.58
Iraq	-1.29	-2.82	-1.68	-1.35	-1.89	-1.39	-1.74
Jordan	-0.64	-0.29	0.27	0.35	0.51	0.32	0.09
Morocco	-0.62	-0.52	-0.07	-0.11	-0.15	-0.24	-0.29
Syria	-1.77	-0.61	-0.88	-1.22	-0.55	-0.88	-0.99
Tunisia	-1.22	0.10	0.46	0.15	0.32	0.08	-0.02
OPT	-1.28	-2.07	-1.24	-1.38	-0.84	-0.77	-1.26
UPPER MIDDLE INCOME	**-1.28**	**-0.29**	**-0.63**	**-0.41**	**-0.36**	**-0.48**	**-0.58**
Lebanon	-0.45	-2.09	-0.61	-0.21	-0.66	-0.65	-0.78
Libya	-1.94	0.47	-1.07	-0.98	-0.62	-0.83	-0.83
Oman	-1.03	0.76	0.38	0.63	0.73	0.62	0.35
HIGH INCOME	**-1.36**	**-0.29**	**0.01**	**0.08**	**0.38**	**0.14**	**-0.17**
Bahrain	-0.82	-0.28	0.41	0.89	0.66	0.60	0.24
Kuwait	-0.46	0.40	0.20	0.29	0.69	0.49	0.27
Qatar	-0.64	0.81	0.06	0.55	0.89	1.00	0.45
Saudi Arabia	-1.59	-0.59	-0.18	-0.10	0.27	-0.10	-0.38
UAE	-0.89	0.76	0.86	0.70	0.66	1.00	0.52
OVERALL AVERAGE	**-1.25**	**-1.13**	**-0.65**	**-0.62**	**-0.58**	**-0.62**	**-0.81**

Source: Kauffman, World Bank Governance Indicators, 2008.

Note: Estimates between -2.5 and 2.5; higher is better.

Table 3: Direction of institutional reforms in Arab countries: change in governance indicators between 1996 and 2007

	Voice and accountability	Political stability	Government effectiveness	Regulatory quality	Rule of law	Control of corruption	Average institutional quality
LOW INCOME	**0.09**	**-0.09**	**-0.09**	**0.29**	**0.10**	**-0.18**	**0.02**
Comoros	-0.41	-1.45	-1.09	-0.61	..	..	-0.89
Mauritania	0.20	-0.89	-0.88	0.50	0.28	..	-0.16
Somalia	0.02	-0.71	-0.58	0.19	-0.54	-0.13	-0.29
Sudan	0.22	0.28	0.31	0.63	0.17	-0.12	0.25
Yemen	-0.12	-0.33	-0.47	-0.27	0.21	-0.33	-0.22
LOWER MIDDLE INCOME	**0.01**	**0.34**	**-0.27**	**-0.05**	**-0.05**	**-0.31**	**0.00**
Algeria	0.35	1.26	-0.13	0.28	0.49	-0.10	0.36
Djibouti	-0.34	-0.26	0.00	-0.97	-0.27	..	-0.37
Egypt	-0.20	0.30	-0.41	-0.55	-0.21	-0.64	-0.29
Iraq	0.67	0.08	-0.19	1.60	-0.28	0.00	0.31
Jordan	-0.27	-0.46	0.04	0.06	0.07	0.47	-0.02
Morocco	0.01	0.09	-0.02	-0.26	-0.27	-0.46	-0.15
Syria	-0.16	0.21	-0.73	-0.31	-0.06	-0.09	-0.19
Tunisia	-0.37	-0.06	-0.05	-0.41	0.52	0.18	-0.03
OPT	-0.58	..	..	..	..	..	-0.58
UPPER MIDDLE INCOME	**-0.08**	**0.62**	**-0.38**	**0.57**	**0.15**	**0.04**	**0.15**
Lebanon	-0.06	-1.57	-0.82	-0.23	-0.44	-0.42	-0.59
Libya	-0.12	2.23	-0.05	1.12	0.67	0.14	0.67
Oman	-0.01	0.29	-0.48	0.53	-0.14	0.56	0.13
HIGH INCOME	**0.06**	**0.01**	**0.15**	**0.27**	**-0.13**	**0.38**	**0.12**
Bahrain	0.37	0.54	-0.02	0.38	0.49	0.58	0.39
Kuwait	0.01	0.39	-0.15	0.33	-0.05	-0.12	0.07
Qatar	0.30	0.48	-0.43	0.21	0.79	1.12	0.41
Saudi Arabia	0.03	-0.07	0.16	0.28	-0.18	0.32	0.09
UAE	0.13	0.02	0.44	0.17	-0.18	0.87	0.24
OVERALL AVERAGE	**0.03**	**0.22**	**-0.19**	**0.08**	**-0.02**	**-0.19**	**-0.02**

Source: UNDP/AHDR calculations based on World Bank Governance Indicators, 2008.

Note: Positive differences indicate improvements in the governance dimension while negative differences indicate a deterioration. As the average institutional change for the Arab countries is -0.02, there is no evidence of any overall improvements in governance. Indeed, the period 1996-2007 saw a deterioration. On the sub-regional level, the following conclusions may be drawn from Table 3: 1) For low income countries, the institutional reform challenge resides in Government Effectiveness, Political Stability and Control of Corruption where a deterioration is recorded in the 11 years under consideration. 2) For the lower middle income countries a small improvement in political stability is noticeable; however the obvious explanation for this is that each of these populous countries, namely Algeria, Egypt and Iraq, started in 1996 with very low achievements in this dimension. On the other dimensions of governance, they record a deterioration. 3) The upper middle income countries recorded improvements on 4 of the 6 governance indicators. 4) The high income countries recorded improvements on all fronts, with the exception of the rule of law indicator. However, despite these achievements, the high income countries score below average on "Voice and Accountability", which remains a significant priority for their reform efforts.

Annex III: The human security survey

A. Survey implementation team

- Alfa International for Research Polling and Informatics/Ramallah, West Bank.
- Société d'Etudes de Realisation de Consultants (SEREC)/Casablanca, Morocco.
- Statistics Lebanon Ltd./Beirut, Lebanon.
- The Nielsen Company – ACNielsen/Kuwait.

B. Note on survey questionnaire

The concept of human security: This included five questions on how satisfied the individual feels with his or her life in general and how secure s/he feels. Respondents were asked to specify the three most important sources of threat in relation to themselves personally, and to state what made them feel secure. The questionnaire then asked them to consider twenty-two potential threats to human security, and to say whether each was related to human security. In this way, an attempt was made to explore the various dimensions of the concept as understood by Arab citizens.

Environmental security: This section presented a number of negative environmental phenomena and asked if they were problematic in the respondents' countries and, if so, whether the problem was becoming worse over time; to what extent respondents were aware of efforts to deal with the problem; by what party those efforts were being made; and whether they were proving successful. Finally, respondents were asked how able they felt personally to help confront or alleviate the problem in question.

Security in its political and international dimensions: The question here was which states presented the greatest threat to the country's security and which states did the most to enhance it. The individual was asked to state his/her attitude toward foreign military bases, peace-keeping forces, and the role played by regional and international institutions in enhancing Arab human security.

Social security (relations among groups): Questions related to how aware citizens were of ethnic, religious, sectarian, class, or political differences among citizens of their country, whether these differences caused problems, and whether such problems were getting worse or better. Respondents were asked what efforts were being made to deal with such problems, what parties were making these efforts, how effective they were proving, and how far individuals felt able to contribute to solutions themselves. Other questions concerned how far society was predisposed against particular groups, how this prejudice was manifested, whether external forces had intervened on behalf of such groups; who those forces were; and whether such interventions had benefitted the affected groups and the country in general. Still other questions probed the degree to which the respondent's society favoured certain social groups, and how much confidence people had in those groups, public institutions and opportunities for political participation. Respondents were also asked if they thought the state supported fundamental rights, such as the freedoms of opinion, expression and association, and justice.

Economic security: This section enquired if income was adequate to cover basic human needs, to what degree the state contributed in that connection through subsidies and social security, to what extent groups often subject to prejudice—such as women, the poor, and young people—enjoyed access to employment, and how respondents' viewed globalization.

Nutritional security: Questions related to the ability to obtain necessary and sufficient nutrition and how varied and safe food supplies were.

Health security: This section contained questions relating to health care and psychological health. They dealt with the availability of health care and psychological health services and, where these were unavailable, the reasons for this. Respondents were asked about the efficiency of health insurance systems and emergency medical services, and how far they were aware of health issues such as HIV/AIDS and other major health threats.

Personal safety: Individuals were asked how safe they thought they and their families were and whether state organs (the police, the judiciary) provided effective personal and family protection. They were asked about particular sources of threats to personal security in their countries, trends in that respect, whether efforts were being made to confront these threats, how successful such efforts were, and whether individuals felt able to help alleviate such threats. They were also asked to name the greatest threats to personal security in their countries, how they individually dealt with those threats, and which institutions were most supportive of human security.